ESSENTIAL
CRIMINOLOGY

ESSENTIAL CRIMINOLOGY

THIRD EDITION

MARK M. LANIER
University of Central Florida

STUART HENRY
San Diego State University

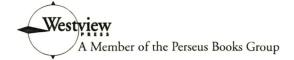

Westview
PRESS
A Member of the Perseus Books Group

Mark dedicates this book to
Laura and Wanda
for walking to the beat
of their own drummer

Stuart to Lee
for her uncompromising integrity

Published by Westview Press,
A Member of the Perseus Books Group

Find us on the World Wide Web at www.westviewpress.com.

Westview Press books are available at special discounts for bulk purchases in the United States by corporations, institutions, and other organizations. For more information, please contact the Special Markets Department at the Perseus Books Group, 2300 Chestnut Street, Suite 200, Philadelphia, PA 19103, or call (800) 810-4145, ext. 5000, or e-mail special.markets@perseusbooks.com.

Designed by Pauline Brown

Library of Congress Cataloging-in-Publication Data

Lanier, Mark.
  Essential criminology / Mark M. Lanier, Stuart Henry. — 3rd ed.
     p.   cm.
  Includes bibliographical references and index.
  ISBN 978-0-8133-4416-4 (paperback : alk. paper) 1. Criminology. I. Henry, Stuart, 1949- II. Title.
  HV6025.L25 2010
  364—dc22

                                                           2009019214

                   10 9 8 7 6 5 4 3 2 1

Contents

Tables and Figures

Tables

Figures

Preface and Acknowledgments

The idea that "the only constant is change" has been around at least since the time of Heracleitus in 500 BC. Since we first wrote this book in 1997 and the second edition in 2003, the world has certainly changed. It has become increasingly globalized, and we appear more interconnected with others. That change also includes the nature of crime: environmental and financial harms from multinational corporations and investment bankers, global political terrorism, and violence at home, work, and school, all of which have become more significant, in terms of the seriousness and extent of harm caused, than the threat from strangers on the street. The threat of terrorism affects everyone, everywhere. New vulnerabilities have appeared. For example, the means we use to communicate, interact, and converse have changed and opened up opportunities for new types of white-collar fraud, sexual predatory practices, and identity theft. The business community has been wracked by one scandal after another, eroding confidence in our economic and political systems. The nature of war has also changed. Rather than nation to nation, wars have become endless and ongoing conflicts between ethnic and sectarian groups. These changes, coupled with the many suggestions we received from readers and users of the first and second editions, led us to revise and update this third edition of *Essential Criminology*. In particular, we revised the book in the spirit of social philosopher Eric Hoffer (1902–1983), who said, "In times of profound change, the learners inherit the earth, while the learned find themselves beautifully equipped to deal with a world that no longer exists."

On the surface, this is still a book about crime and criminality. It is about how we study crime, how we explain crime, how we determine who is—and is not—a criminal, and how we reduce the harm caused by crime. It is also a book about difference. Crime is something we know all about—or do we? You may see crime differently from the way it is seen by your parents or even by your peers. You may see your own behavior as relatively acceptable, apart from a few minor rule violations here and there. But real crime? That's what others do—criminals, right? You may change how you view crime and criminals after reading this text.

As authors, we also reflect difference: Stuart was raised in working-class South London, England. Mark was a "military brat" living in England, California, Florida, and Alabama during his formative years. Stuart was educated via traditional, long-tested, yet very narrow British standards, Mark in a unique multidisciplinary U.S.

doctoral program. Stuart seriously questions the utility of scientific methods (positivism); Mark relies on them daily. Stuart rarely does anything outdoors, except watch an occasional rock concert. Mark builds and rides custom motorcycles, and is an active wakeboarder and surfer who loves outdoor life. Yet, despite these differences, we found common ground for our analysis of crime and criminality. Our differences provide for a balanced analysis of crime.

We see crime as complex, political, and harmful to victims and perpetrators, as well as to the institutions and fabric of society. We also acknowledge and celebrate the differences among people, cultures, and regions. Thus, we embrace conflict as not only inevitable but a positive force. Conflict promotes contemplation and understanding of others, including their cultures, educational backgrounds, experiences, and worldviews. Conflict also prompts change and thus provides the opportunity for improving our social world. It presents the opportunity to confront our dissatisfactions and search for better solutions and alternative interpretations of the world in which we live.

Most people throughout the world are concerned about the way criminal justice systems handle crime and criminals. This dissatisfaction raises questions not only about what constitutes effective justice but about what crime is and what causes it. As Timothy Akers and Joseph Whittaker ask in Chapter 4, does crime exist *"because of economics? Family dynamics? Social interactions? Behavioral or other biologically linked dysfunction that remains unaddressed or unrecognized? Did criminals receive an adequate education? Was it something they ate? Did they bang their heads too many times growing up? Or were they born with a 'predisposition' toward criminal behavior?"*

We also must question how to deal with crime. Should crime be handled by the criminal justice system? By social policy? By public health officials (did you know that the Centers for Disease Control and Prevention tracks homicides)? By you and other citizens through "take back the streets" and "neighborhood partnership" programs, which have become a significant part of community crime control? Conflict over these issues and the need for a good (relatively) short criminology text contributed to our original desire to write this book.

At first we decided to write *Essential Criminology* as a concise introductory text, aimed at examining the nature and extent of crime and surveying the main theoretical perspectives on crime causation and their criminal justice policy implications. We believe, and several of our students tell us, that the book is written in a clear and straightforward style, uses great examples, yet also progressively builds students' criminological knowledge. Much to our surprise, we found that programs adopting the text ranged from the Ivy League graduate level to freshman courses at community colleges. Thus, in this third edition we have tried to broaden the scope and increase the depth. We are delighted that the first and second editions had such broad appeal, and we have tried to build on that. To that end we edited a companion book, *The Essential Criminology Reader*, published by Westview in 2006, containing original articles by key theorists representing each of the different theories in this main textbook. These theorists address the reasoning behind their theories and consider criticism and empirical support; they also correct us on occassion. We believe that together the two books make for engaging reading.

Many users of the text have suggested that we begin by framing the theoretical chapters in the context of globalization. We followed their advice and used it to guide the writing and examples used in each chapter. Following a discussion of the scope of the subject, *Essential Criminology* guides students through the diverse definitions of crime. It then turns to the major theoretical explanations for crime, from individual-level classical and rational choice through biological, psychological, social learning, social control, and interactionist perspectives. It explains the more sociocultural theories, beginning with social ecology, and moves on to strain and subcultural theory and conflict and radical approaches. We reorganized the final chapters to better reflect feminist contributions and the exciting new changes in left realism, postmodernism, restorative justice, and integrative theories. Brief background information is provided on major theorists, demonstrating that they are real people who share the experiences life offers us all. We have also tried to cover the theories completely, accurately, and evenhandedly, and have made some attempt to show how each is related to, or builds on, the others. But concerns about length mean that the student wishing to explore these connections in depth should consult the several more comprehensive theory texts available and review the original articles in *The Essential Criminology Reader*.

Essential Criminology has several unique student-friendly features. We begin each chapter with examples of specific crimes to illustrate the theory. The book includes an integrated "prismatic" definition of crime. This prism provides a comprehensive, multidimensional way of conceptualizing crime in terms of seriousness of harm, degree of consensus about social outrage, and societal reaction through the institutions of justice. Our "crime prism" integrates virtually all of the major disparate definitions of crime. Throughout the text, we provide "equal time" examples from both white-collar ("suite") and conventional ("street") crimes with the objective of drawing students into the realities of concrete cases. We make a conscious effort to include crimes that are less often detected, prosecuted, and punished. These white-collar, corporate, occupational, and state crimes have serious consequences but are often neglected in introductory texts. We present chapter-by-chapter discussions of each perspective's policy implications, indicating the practical applications that the theory implies. Finally, summary concept charts conclude each theory. These charts provide a simple yet comprehensive analytical summary of the theories, revealing their basic assumptions on a range of comparable criteria, such as their respective views on human nature, social order, crime, law, crime causation, and criminal justice policy.

Our book is primarily intended for students interested in the study of crime. This includes such diverse fields as social work, psychology, sociology, political science, and history. We expect the book to be mainly used in criminology and criminal justice courses, but students studying any topic related to crime, such as juvenile delinquency or deviant behavior, will also find the book useful. Interdisciplinary programs will find the book particularly helpful because of the multiple disciplines represented and the way they are integrated to explain crime.

Words of Thanks

Rarely is any book the product of only one or two individuals. We drew on the talents, motivation, and knowledge of many others. Thus, several people have earned our thanks and respect. In keeping with our title, however, we mention only key helpers. We would particularly like to thank our graduate research assistants: Katy Hancock and Jacqueline Brown. Gregg Barak has always been at the forefront of recent theoretical movements, and we are each indebted to him for his thought-provoking prose and friendship. Mark Lanier owes a special debt of gratitude to Robert "Bob" Langworthy for his leadership by example. He also specifically thanks the teachers who first interested him in theory, William Osterhoff, Peter K. Manning, Frank Horvath, Brent Smith, and John Sloan and the teachers, family, and friends who provided additional insight: Larry, Tae and Laura, Samantha, Karen, and Jim Amato, Terry Miller, Rob Pack, John Smykla, Karol Lucken, Barbie Shold, Gene Paoline and of course mostly Stuart. A brief visit to the University of Pretoria in South Africa greatly expanded his appreciation of globalization—thanks to his hosts and new friends there: Antoinette, Christiaan, Thozama, Terry, Vanitha, Rob, Sulina, and Isobel. We jointly would also like to thank all the teachers outside the classroom: friends, students, deviants (bikers, surfers, and professors mostly), criminals, and police officers who broadened our view of crime. We would like to commend the formal and informal reviewers of this and the previous editions: Laura and Larry Myers, Lisa Briggs, Mark Stafford, and especially Martha A. Myers, who provided a thoroughly constructive commentary that made this book far better than what we could have written without her valuable input. Our editor, Alex Masulis, was patient, encouraging, and supportive throughout the whole revision process. Laura Stine kept the whole project moving along at breakneck speed compared with the old days when books took a couple of years "in production" until print. Laura has this down to six months! In thanking our copy editor, Annette Wenda, we are both agreed that her outstanding copyediting added greatly to the book's clarity; she is, quite simply, the best we've ever had. Finally, we would like to thank Rene van Swaaningen, Dragan Milovanovic, and several anonymous reviewers for helpful suggestions for the book's third revision.

—Mark Lanier and Stuart Henry

1

What Is Criminology?

The Study of Crime, Criminals, and Victims in a Global Context

The horrendous events of September 11, 2001, in which the World Trade Center in New York was totally destroyed, and the Pentagon in Washington substantially damaged, by hijacked commercial airliners that were flown into them, killing 2,982 people, have proved to be the defining point of this decade. The United States was horrified, unified, motivated, and eager to apply its superior military might immediately and unequivocally against the aggressors. However, unlike the Japanese attack on Pearl Harbor on December 7, 1941, this time it was not clear who to strike or what effect a strike would have. For the first time in its history the United States did not have a well-defined nation-state enemy. Clearly, the nature of war, the American way of life, what counts as "crime," and how a society responds to harms, internal or external, changed on that day. This act of terrorism was undoubtedly aimed at the American people. The terrorist organization al-Qaeda claimed responsibility. From a geopolitical perspective, the major consequence of 9/11 was that an explicitly hostile Islamic state, Iraq, was soon invaded/liberated/occupied on the rationale that it was storing weapons of mass destruction that could be targeted at Western interests. (We purposefully say "invaded/liberated/occupied," as one's worldview, political beliefs, and context determine which word is most appropriate.) The logic was that a preemptive attack was necessary to prevent a catastrophe worse than 9/11 (a concept known as the Bush Doctrine). Yet the 9/11 attackers were predominantly from Saudi Arabia, and al-Qaeda was substantially based in Afghanistan; seven years later the 2008 presidential debate was dominated by discussions about whether Iraq or Afghanistan was the best place to fight against those who perpetrated this and other acts of terrorism. The purpose of this introductory chapter is to show how the changing geopolitical landscape and other factors shape our renewed discussion of crime and its causes, as well as possible policy responses.

Six fundamental changes can be identified that demonstrate the changed nature of our world. These changes all move toward increasing interconnection and interdependence. They are: (1) globalization; (2) the communications revolution, particularly the Internet; (3) privatization and individualization; (4) the global spread of disease; (5) changing perceptions of conflict and national security; and (6) the internationalization of terrorism.

Globalization

Globalization is the process whereby people react to issues in terms of reference points that transcend their own locality, society, or region. These reference points include material, political, social, and cultural concerns that affect the planet, such as environmental challenges (e.g., global warming or overpopulation) and commercial matters (e.g., fast food, in particular so-called McDonaldization, which describes the spread of McDonald's restaurants throughout the world's economies). Globalization is a process of unification in which differences in economic, technological, political, and social institutions are transformed from a local or national network into a single system. Globalization also relates to an international universalism, whereby events happening in one part of the world affect those in another, none more dramatic than the collapse of world financial markets (Stiglitz 2002, 2006), which went global in September 2008. Indeed, the emergence of worldwide financial markets and under- or unregulated foreign exchange and speculative markets resulted in the vulnerability of national economies. In short, "'Globalization' refers to all those processes by which peoples of the world are incorporated into a single world society, global society" (Albrow 1990, 9). Conversely, while globalization relates to the way people in different societies identify with values that cut across nations and cultures, it also relates to the recognition of different cultures' diversity of experience and the formation of new identities. As globalization integrates us, these new identities and our sense of belonging to differentiated cultures are also driving many of us apart (Croucher 2004, 3).

The greatest effect of the global society is the global economy as it relates to the increasing multinationalization of corporations that produce on the "global assembly line" (Ehrenreich and Fuentes 1994). The result is that "economic goods, services, and personnel flow back and forth across national, hemispheric and continental boundaries" such that "economic, social, political and environmental events in one part of the world have significant impacts in other parts of the world . . . beyond the ability of any one society to control" (Soroka and Bryjak 1999, 176). Indeed, both advocates and critics of globalization agree that it has resulted in the circumvention of both national boundaries and state controls over economic trade and production processes. Further, ethnic identities and religious affiliations transcend both political and geographic boundaries. As Frank Schmalleger says:

On a global scale, there appears to be a shared agreement that society is experiencing a period of unprecedented change. Both the substance and the pace of change are fundamentally different from what has occurred in past decades and centuries. No longer are sequences of events occurring in relative isolation over longer patterns of time. No longer are discrete groups of people affected by each change; rather, there is a greater simultaneity of occurrence, swifter interpenetration, and increased feedback of one set of changes upon another. ([1999] 2002, 480)

A classic example of the interconnection and inability of individual societies to influence and control the crime and harm created by globalization is the case of one of the worst industrial accidents in the world: In 1984, in Bhopal, India, Union Carbide's insecticide plant leaked toxic gas, resulting in between 4,000 and 15,000 deaths and injuries to as many as 600,000 people (Beirne and Messerschmidt 2000, 494–495).

What is most frightening about Bhopal is . . . the way people are routinely treated by corporations. . . . Cancer-causing pesticides banned in the West are freely sold to farmers in Latin America, Eastern Europe and Asia. Native American Nations are bribed to accept nuclear waste. . . . Malaysian hill people are killed or run off their land so Japanese companies can cut down their forests to make chopsticks. Leaded gasoline, banned in the West because of its devastating health effects on children, is sold to Thailand, Mexico and India. This kind of corporate violence is repeated in every corner of the Earth. (Cohen 1998, 3, cited in Beirne and Messerschmidt 2000, 494–495)

Some critics of globalization, known as the antiglobalization movement, such as Nikos Passas (2000), have argued that the process of globalization, including the spread of capital, labor, management, news, and information across national borders, is itself "criminogenic," because it provides motivation and opportunities for corporate deviance at the same time that it leads to less effective control systems (M. Robinson 2004). Other critics, such as Noam Chomsky, argue that it is not so much the existence of global integration they oppose but the way in which it occurs, in that it benefits the rich nations at the expense of the poor and polarizes and accentuates inequality within societies.

The Globalization of Communications

Prior to 1985 global communication was largely restricted to the affluent. The advent of the personal computer and the development of the Internet transformed the way we communicate. Now people connect daily with others all over the world at little or no expense. They exchange ideas, performances, propaganda, ideologies, and technical information; through Internet search engines they can draw on knowledge from any part of the globe. Members of any society can read newspapers and opinions, engage in chat-room discussions, and take university courses via the Internet.

They can also share the most intimate details of their daily lives through Web blogs and social-networking sites such as YouTube, Facebook, and MySpace, communication mechanisms that have become global. No longer are people limited to what their own government's or society's ideology and culture feed them, which paradoxically can lead to expanded knowledge and perspectives or reinforcement for any idea or view, however strange or outrageous it may seem. This means that we are increasingly interconnected with the world in both positive and negative ways. What affects people in one part of the globe can affect others in another.

At the same time, the development in global communications has led to a massive shift of jobs from manufacturing into service, communications, and information (called the postindustrial society), and because the latter jobs require higher education and training, increasing numbers of people the world over are underemployed or unemployed. The result has been to increase worker anxiety and job stress among those who have "not yet been 'bumped,' 'deselected,' 'surplussed,' 'vocationally relocated,' 'de-hired,' 'decruited' or otherwise done away with" (Soroka and Bryjak 1999, 180). Work-related stress leads to increased competition, "backstabbing," isolation, detachment, and alienation as well as increased family and workplace violence.

Increased global communication has also brought a rush of new crimes that are perpetrated on and via the Internet, such as fraud and identity theft, drug smuggling, and bomb making. The growing dependence on global communications has also made national infrastructures and governments vulnerable to Internet terrorism through hacking and computer viruses.

Privatization and Individualization

Related to globalization and global unemployment are two trends that, in spite of our being connected to ever-greater numbers of people, have produced a reduction in our concern for others. We have already mentioned the increased competition in the workplace, the attitude of everyone looking out for themselves. This is in contrast to the shared movement around trades and professions that culminated in unionization and collective action during the middle of the twentieth century, when people banded together for strength and solidarity.

More and more we are seeing the "death of society," that is, the decline in collective action and social policy requiring some to give up part of their wealth to help the less fortunate or to increase the public good. Instead, partly because of government fiscal crises and partly because of conservative ideology, the twenty-first century has witnessed a growing privatization of government, particularly in the areas of welfare and social programs. Privatization reinforces the individualization of human actions, as well as allowing major policy decisions to be made not in terms of a society's public or social interests but in terms of what maximizes profit for corporate shareholders. Thus, the 1980s and 1990s saw massive deregulation and privatization, from transportation, communications, and energy to finance, welfare, and even law enforcement.

We have also seen the increasing tendency for family members to stay at home, not as families but as appendages to technology, such as televisions, computers, and video games. The result is an impersonal society, one where we are living in isolation from other real people, "bowling alone" (Putnam 1995), where media images and game characters become interspersed with real people who are seen as superficial, objectlike caricatures.

Moreover, because of the impact of globalization on the economic structures of societies, there has been a polarization of rich and poor, with numerous groups excluded from opportunities (J. Young 1999). In their relatively impoverished state, they are vulnerable to violence, both in their homes and in their neighborhoods.

Globalization of Disease

Although the black death, or plague, smallpox, and polio have demonstrated that throughout human history, disease can be a global phenomenon, the systemic use of hygienic practices, including clean water and effective sanitation and sewerage, and the discovery and use of antibiotics, vaccines, and other drugs meant that for much of the twentieth century the global spread of disease was seen as a thing of the past, or at least occurring only in underdeveloped countries. But by the end of the twentieth century, through the advent of increased global travel, the terror of disease on a global scale was given new meaning, first with HIV/AIDS, then with mad cow disease, West Nile virus, SARS (severe acute respiratory syndrome), and resistant strains of tuberculosis. Worse was the fact that, unlike times past, groups could potentially introduce disease, such as smallpox or anthrax, on a global scale as part of a terrorist operation against individuals or governments. Like the previous developments, the dual effect was, on the one hand, to render people increasingly fearful of contact, especially intimate contact with strangers, tending to undermine interpersonal relations, while, on the other, demonstrating just how interconnected we have become.

This area of change has led to the development of an emerging semiparadigm in criminology. Timothy Akers and Mark Lanier (2009) founded the Virtual Center for Epidemiological Criminology (VCEC) to address the correlates and causes of crime and health issues. Public health and criminal justice issues are closely related and often inseparable. Many diverse entities are now acknowledging the connections between crime and health variables. For example, recent data sets released by the Centers for Disease Control and Prevention (CDC) include crime statistics. On January 8, 2008, the CDC made the following announcement: "The CDC Behavioral Surveillance Branch (BSB) is pleased to announce the release of a county-level data set [that] will allow users to compare health behaviors with . . . core health outcomes and risk factors such as cardiovascular disease (CVD), diabetes, asthma, physical activity, obesity, and smoking. . . . These variables include health care delivery information, health and vital statistics indicators, environmental measures, *crime statistics*, business indicators, and poverty/income figures" (emphasis added).

Moving beyond what the CDC and others have accomplished, VCEC seeks to theoretically and empirically link and examine the two disciplines of crime and public health. VCEC's primary function is to research specific strategies that integrate long-tested public health and criminological theories to produce practical interventions that will improve the well-being of communities. The objective is to isolate interventions that simultaneously impact the co-occurrence of crime and public health problems. VCEC and the related online journal *Epidemiological Criminology* clearly suggest the linkages between the issues.

The Changing Nature of Global Conflict

During the twentieth century, until the end of the cold war, each generation faced a significant war or warlike threats to its survival. Examples include the two world wars, Korean War, Vietnam War, and cold war. In these twentieth-century global conflicts it was possible to clearly identify the enemy posing the threat, and to come together as nations to wage war to defeat that threat. In contrast, in the twenty-first century it is becoming ever more apparent that for many nations, "the enemy" is multiple, diffuse, and interwoven into the very fabric of society.

Globalization is not simply an economic process but, rather, the term for the technological movement away from the dyadic analysis of "independent events" toward complex, interdependent "systems analysis." The most fundamental questions for peace researchers at the present time include: "What is the general quality of peace and is it improving, stagnating, or deteriorating?" "Where, and under what conditions,

FIGURE 1.1   Global Trends in Armed Conflict

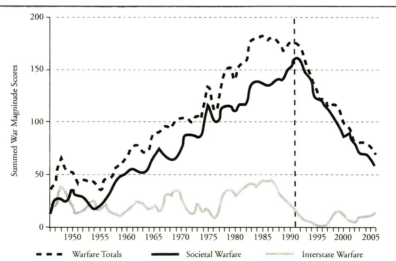

SOURCE: Center for Systemic Peace. http://www.systemicpeace.org.

is organized violence most likely to occur?" "How do we understand the quality of peace in its many systemic variations, both successes and failures?" (CSP 2009).

Nations in the continent of Africa, for example, face very serious threats on several fronts, including starvation, the spread of HIV/AIDS, and numerous civil wars. For example, civil wars in Sierra Leone, Rwanda, Ethiopia, and Mozambique have resulted in the deaths of millions of innocent people over the past two decades. But as the Center for Systemic Peace (CSP) indicates, although "the level of societal warfare increased dramatically and continuously through the Cold War period," it was a result of "the protractedness of societal wars during this period and not from a substantial increase in the numbers of new wars" (ibid.). In the twentieth century former colonial powers would step in during such times of civil conflict, while multinational peacekeeping forces, such as the United Nations, NATO, and the "Coalition of the Willing," appeared, at least on the surface, to provide both clarity and stability. Since the 1990s, however, these bodies seem reluctant to intervene everywhere that violence occurs. Part of the explanation may be that the "international community is increasingly reluctant to provide peacekeeping forces for difficult, expensive and politically unrewarding operations" (Brayton 2002, 304).

Another part of the explanation is the changing nature of war and conflict. The two superpowers of the cold war, the United States and the Soviet Union, no longer square off since the latter's breakup in 1991, and so far Russia has presented a limited challenge to America. The United States has emerged as the world's dominant military power, and as a result, "America has reduced the military role of its European allies in NATO to that of its strategic reserve, to be used where the job is relatively easy, requires less capable forces, and where such tasks require long-term commitment of troops and peace building rather than fighting duties" (Cilliers 2003, 112). The role of allies and multinational organizations, such as NATO and the United Nations, is changing. Consequently, the nature of war is also changing. Today, "to an extent unprecedented in modern times, entities other than nation-states wage war across multiple physical and ideological boundaries. The Cold War's clear dichotomies and array of proxy wars have devolved into myriad intrastate conflicts and cross-border wars of uncertain and shifting ideological foundation" (Brayton 2002, 305).

The incidence of both societal and interstate warfare has declined dramatically since the 1990s, and this trend continues in the early 2000s, falling more than 60 percent from its peak level. For example, there were twenty-five major armed conflicts (societal warfare) in 2000, yet only two were between nation-states (interstate warfare), according to a 2001 report by the Stockholm International Peace Research Institute (cited in Brayton 2002). If nation-states are not waging war with each other, and if major powers are not intervening in conflict resolution or conflict promotion (except, of course, when oil is involved), how are the conflicts that do occur resolved, and why are their numbers declining? Part of the answer is the withdrawal of superpowers supporting civil unrest, particularly since the end of the cold war.

In the poorest of countries and regions, conflicts do continue, albeit at a lesser rate. According to the CSP:

In late 2007, there are 24 states directly affected by ongoing wars (28 wars total, up from 26 at the end of 2006). Of these 24 states, half (12) are affected by protracted wars, that is, armed conflicts persisting for more than ten years. These protracted societal conflicts include Afghanistan (30 years), Colombia (24), D. R. Congo (16), India (56), Iraq (28), Israel (43), Myanmar (60), Nigeria (11), Philippines (36), Somalia (20), Sri Lanka (25), Sudan (25), Turkey (24), and Uganda (37). These wars continue to defy concerted efforts to gain settlement or resolution. (CSP 2009)

Moreover, the end of the cold war saw the rise of numerous ethnic wars: "Ethnic wars, which had previously paralleled the trend of revolutionary war, continue to rise through the late 1980s and early 1990s as separatists and other political entrepreneurs attempt to take advantage of the vast changes in political arrangements that accompanied the transformation of the post–Cold War world system" (ibid.).

One way the conflicts that do occur are being resolved is through the use of armies for hire, that is, mercenaries who fight for pay. Increasingly, small countries, and some large ones, are finding themselves unable to "protect the political, military, economic social and cultural life of their citizens" (Brayton 2002, 303). Papua New Guinea provides an illustrative example. In 1997, the Bougainville Revolutionary Army was seriously threatening the regime of Prime Minister Julius Chan. As a result of this conflict the Panguan copper mine was closed—the source of 30 percent of the country's export income. Chan hired the mercenary force Sandline International for $36 million. Sandline recognized the economic advantages of opening and protecting the mine, and Chan was able to obtain the military assistance he needed.

FIGURE 1.2   Trends by Armed Conflict Type

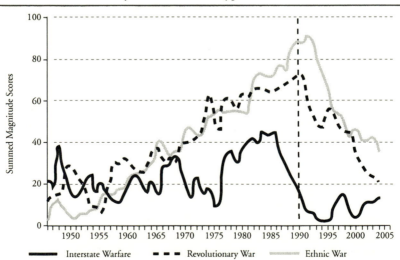

SOURCE: Center for Systemic Peace. http://www.systemicpeace.org.

What's wrong with using private security firms? Some argue that "in proffering security to collapsing, mineral-rich states . . . multinational corporations accentuate the international exploitation and marginalization of the states in question" (ibid., 310). The proliferation of these large, well-organized private armies also alarms the United Nations, which views them as a threat to "sovereign equality, political independence and territorial integrity" (ibid., 304). There are dozens of these huge corporate armies for hire around the world. Their "peacekeeping" role is based solely on profit and armed conflict.

Large, well-funded nation-states, such as the United States, are also increasingly using mercenaries. In fact, the best-known example of a private army served primarily at the discretion of the second Bush administration. Founded in 1997, Blackwater Worldwide is an American company that provides military private-sector solutions to both government and nongovernment clients. A former Navy Seal, Erik Prince, started the company as a basic-training operation to help support the needs of local and regional law enforcement. Its main headquarters is in Moyock, North Carolina, where its 7,000-acre training facility is the largest private training center in the United States. The company claims to be the world's most successful security-service corporation, having designed and manufactured remotely piloted airships, IED safe-armored personnel carriers, and training support systems. It operates in nine countries, delivering critical assistance to clients focused on postconflict and postdisaster stabilization efforts (Blackwater, USA 2008).

Through its contract with the U.S. Defense Department, Blackwater Worldwide and two other security companies had an estimated 137,000 employees working in Iraq as of 2007. The U.S. government pays these private firms to supply armed guards to protect people and buildings and furnish transportation in hostile areas. The security contractors also provide protective services for diplomats and for companies working on reconstruction projects, including escorting people to and from meetings and job sites.

On September 16, 2007, Blackwater employees were on a mission to evacuate senior American officials after a nearby explosion. (Some question the need for the evacuation because the officials were already in a secure compound.) After the explosion at 11:50 A.M., the diplomats were escorted via a Blackwater convoy to a Green (safe) Zone. To get to the Green Zone they had to go through Nisour Square, in Baghdad. Another convoy went to Nisour first to block off traffic so the convoy could get through without delay. At least four SUVs blocked lanes entering the square, and some guards got out of their vehicles and took positions on the street. At 12:08 P.M. at least one guard began to fire in the direction of a car, killing its driver. The same guard walked toward the car, firing more shots, killing a woman and an infant.

There are several different versions explaining how the shooting began. The Blackwater guards said they believed they were fired upon first. An Iraqi preliminary investigation concluded that there was no enemy fire, but some Iraqi witnesses said that Iraqi commandos in nearby guard towers could have been shooting. Ultimately, eight civilians were killed and fourteen others injured.

Whereas national conflicts have become decentralized, global conflicts have become dispersed. Rather than nations facing off, we now have terrorist tactics, once limited to anarchists and fringe radical groups, becoming a method of war for a variety of causes, from antiabortionists to Muslim extremists.

Global Terrorism

The single most feared event, and according to surveys of public opinion the "crime" considered most serious, is a terrorist attack. Events such as the September 11, 2001, suicide airliner bombings and the Mumbai hotel takeover in December 2008 illustrate that the threat of terrorism on a global scale has become part of the daily fear of populations around the world, not least because of the ways these events are instantly communicated to everyone, everywhere, as they happen. No longer restricted to the tactics of a few extreme radical or fringe groups in certain nations, terrorism has become the method of war for any ethnic or religious group that does not have the power to succeed politically. It has been facilitated by developments in communication, transportation, and technology that have enabled explosives and other weapons to become smaller and more lethal. Whether there is an interconnected web of terrorism around fundamentalist Muslim religious extremism (such as that claimed by followers of Osama Bin Laden and al-Qaeda), an Arab-led terrorist movement opposed to Western culture, more specific actions such as those in Northern Ireland by the IRA and splinter groups against Protestants and the British government, or in Indonesia or Bali against supporters of the West, it is clear that terrorism has become a global threat. Data assembled by the Center for Systemic Peace show that since 2001, both the number and the severity of terrorist incidents have increased.

What is significant about the way terrorist tactics are used is that they exploit the very systems of interconnection that globalization has spawned, whether these are via transportation, communication, energy, or immigration and democracy. Theories based on particular assumptions of biology, or psychology, or those based on the sociology of particular societies are inadequate to deal with the global dimensions of twenty-first-century crime.

So how do societies reconfigure their vision of crime to deal with its global dimensions? Should acts of terrorism and acts of war be considered crimes? What about the actions of states that abuse human rights? Are there new criminologies that are able to confront these more integrated global-level forms of harm creation?

In part due to these changes, in the early twenty-first century we have witnessed some surprising and shocking changes in the study of crime. Theoretically, the most significant change is the increased attention given to defining crime (which we address in the next chapter), not least because global terrorism has caused us to question the connection among politics, harm creation, and what kinds of actions should count as crime. There is also greater attention being focused on crimes of the powerful, from governments to corporations, more generally known as white-collar crime.

FIGURE 1.3   Annual Number of International Terrorist Attacks

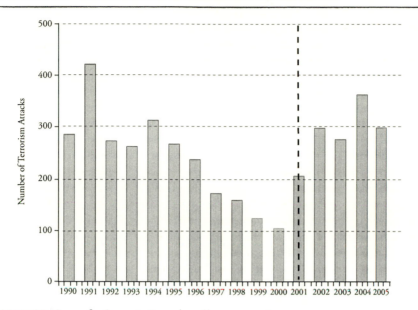

SOURCE: Center for Systemic Peace. http://www.systemicpeace.org.

FIGURE 1.4   Annual Number of Deaths from International Terrorism

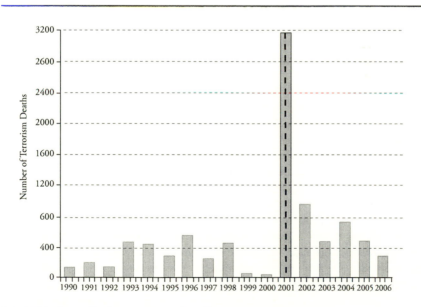

SOURCE: Center for Systemic Peace. http://www.systemicpeace.org.

In practical terms the increase in severity and frequency of terrorism has altered our belief in the amount of freedom that individuals are prepared to sacrifice to the government in exchange for state protection. Instead of security in the home to protect our private property, we are now more interested in "homeland security," to protect our energy resources, health network, water supply, communications system, and mass transportation facilities, including ports, airports, and trains. We are also strengthening public safety services: police, firefighting, emergency medical services, and the National Guard. We are moving from decentralized and fragmented protective services to an integrated national system of security designed to protect "the homeland" of America. Fear in the minds of Western populations has shifted from burglars in the night to low-flying aircraft and bombs at movie theaters and sporting events. The perceived vulnerability of Western civilizations stemming from the combination of openness and large concentrations of population has reached a national crisis.

As a result of these changes, criminology is itself undergoing major changes. What historically has been a discipline focused on explaining individual criminal motivations in relation to domestic institutions and social processes has become a multifaceted examination that links genetic disposition to political and global forces. What is this discipline, this study of crime? To contemporary criminologists, the scope of crime is much broader than media portrayals of inner-city gang violence, child abductions, carjackings, drive-by shootings, serial murders, workplace homicides, and drug wars. Crime also includes a variety of misdeeds by governments, political corruption, corporate fraud, employee theft, and offenses committed by "ordinary" Americans.

Ever since the watershed of Watergate in the early 1970s when it was reluctantly realized that even a president could be a "crook," there has been accelerating media coverage of crimes by those in positions of power. Former president Bill Clinton reinforced this realization. The incredibly bad intelligence—or, worse, outright lies—that led to the hunt for weapons of mass destruction in Iraq provides yet another presidential example of abuse of power. Also consider the harm caused by U.S. government radiation experiments on unknowing citizens who subsequently developed cancer. Consider also the 1930s syphilis experiments that were conducted on African American men in Tuskegee, Alabama. These infected men were diagnosed with syphilis but deliberately not treated, even when penicillin was discovered as a cure, in order for government doctors to study the long-term effects of syphilis. False advertising and price-fixing by corporate giants like the Archer Daniels Midland Company (forcing consumers to pay more than the market price by undermining competition) are just some of the crimes committed by corporations. Other crimes of the powerful involve corporate executives deceiving investors, as in the Enron, WorldCom, and Arthur Andersen scandals; even Martha Stewart has made *insider trading* a household phrase. Corporate crime can also include manufacturers and hazardous-waste companies that pollute the environment; the knowing manufacture of defective products, as in the case of the Ford Pinto gas tank that exploded on low-speed rear-end impact or the use of dangerous Firestone tires on Ford Motor Company automobiles, particularly its SUVs; and unsafe food-handling practices by meat-processing companies resulting in E. coli contamination.

Also falling within the scope of criminology are the unsafe production practices that result in death and injury in the workplace, such as the case of the Imperial chicken plant in Hamlet, North Carolina, where twenty-five deaths occurred when the factory caught fire. Imperial's owners had padlocked the plant's fire exits to stop petty pilfering of chicken; each of the owners received a ten-year prison sentence for nonnegligent manslaughter. Contemporary criminologists also study employees who steal from their bosses, bosses who employ workers "off the books" to evade taxes, and professionals such as doctors who defraud the government and rob the public purse through Medicare and Medicaid fraud.

Finally, and most glaring, the United States has become the target of terrorist groups, as evidenced by the 9/11 suicide hijackings and the attacks on American interests abroad, including the USS *Cole* and the U.S. Embassy in Nairobi. What light can criminology shed on the political movements that lead humans to commit suicide bombings in furtherance of their cause? What global forces congeal to produce such widespread human suffering, and what can we learn about the forces that prevent these devastating consequences?

Criminologists study not only the nature of this harmful behavior but also its causes and the systemic practices that produce patterns of harms in a variety of social contexts. Take something as seemingly innocent as a recreational activity like surfing. This may seem to be a crime-free activity, and generally it is. But in September 1995 at Laguna Beach, California, two surfers were videotaped beating another surfer who had ventured into their designated contest area. The two surfers were arrested and charged with felony assault. In court on December 20, 1995, the two surfers had their charges reduced through a plea bargain, and each was released on three years' probation. The videotape played a vital role in the case. Media coverage was vast, and the case was featured on *Court TV*. Since we first provided this example, there has been a flurry of similar cases involving surfers and violence. A September 2, 2002, *People* article on the problem may have further influenced the prosecution of these territorial violent surfers, or it may have increased the violence. Indeed, the media play a significant role in shaping our conception of what crime is, especially through such infamous cases as the police beating in Inglewood, California, of a young teen, the Clarence Thomas–Anita Hill sexual harassment hearings, and the murder and kidnapping trials of O. J. Simpson and Michael Skakel (Barak 1994, 1996). The movie *Point Break* (1991) with Keanu Reeves even focused on territorially violent surfers.

What do these various crimes have in common? What kinds of cases grab media attention? Which do people consider more criminal? Which elicit the most concern? How does the social context affect the kind of crime and the harms suffered by its victims? How are technology and the media changing the face of crime? What do these events have to do with criminology? After reading this book, you should have a better understanding of these issues, if not clear answers.

BOX 1.1 Crime, Risk, and the Changing World Order.
Christiaan Bezuidenhout, University of Pretoria

As perceived risks increase, spurred on by the global spread of crime, particularly terrorism, many countries around the world are having to pay excessive prices for freedom, liberty, and equality. The global terrorist attacks on innocent people to convey a specific message in an attempt to achieve political and ideological objectives illustrate the extent of the problem. Following the 9/11 attacks on the United States, the United Kingdom and Spain were also targeted. The attacks in Spain (2004) and in the UK (2005) highlighted the change in global risk and challenged our conception of crime. India has also been the target of several terrorist attacks on hotels in which many innocent people were killed, most recently in December 2008. These criminal attacks have impacted the global community on several levels. For the members of any specific country, death, destruction, financial loss, as well as psychological and physical suffering are some of the direct, blatant aftereffects of such an attack. However, the impact on confidence and security in the global community is more indirect but perhaps more pervasive in its long-term implications. Consider how global air travel has changed in the past few years. Travelers face security delays and invasive screening, are required to remove shoes and clothing at the security and customs areas at airports, and are not allowed to carry any liquids or knives on board the airplane. The risks and resultant security measures have become very apparent and present challenges for newly formed, struggling democracies.

Consider South Africa as an example. The changes within the "new" South Africa as well as the adoption of a Bill of Human Rights and Constitution have resulted in drastic changes being made to the way in which accused offenders are being processed and treated in this country. More restorative justice programs and less incarceration are being utilized. In addition, the freedoms that have come with South African democracy have been accompanied by extraordinarily high crime and homicide rates. Serious crimes in any country cause fear and insecurity, and dramatic increases in crime rates intensify the perceived personal risk of victimization. Risk is part of any society and does not discriminate with regard to social class, level of development, or the size of law enforcement or defense budgets. Risk is real and very relevant to the study of criminology. In this context it could be assumed that many governments have lost their monopoly on crime control, and this predicament has forced them to adapt to the changing landscape of crime, order, and control. Increasingly, law enforcement is being contracted out to private security organizations.

Taking this argument to the next level, some criminologists (e.g., Garland 2001) have proposed that because crime and risk have become part of everyday life, and because governments in general have lost their ability to control crime over the past thirty years, societal adjustments, particularly in the manner of governance, have become obligatory for survival. The new global hum in governance is "risk," "actuarial thinking," and "early intervention"—also known as proactive prevention. The logic of risk is inherently political, stimulates action, and triggers communication (Loader and Sparks 2002). The term *risk society* is used to describe a society that is organized in

CONTINUES

response to risk. According to sociologist Anthony Giddens, a risk society is "a society increasingly preoccupied with the future (and also with safety), which generates the notion of risk" (1999, 3). Risk here can be defined as a systematic way of dealing with hazards and insecurities induced and introduced by modernization itself. Risk becomes a way of thinking in all spheres of day-to-day life. We live in a world of manufactured uncertainty (crime, terrorist attacks, school and hotel shootings) and external risks (hurricanes, tsunamis, earthquakes). Risk management—in other words, how to identify and manage risk—has become the focus of the new actuarial criminology (Beck 1992; Giddens 1999).

Garland refers to the changing landscape of the global crime canvas in his theory on social control and governance through crime as the "new predicament" (2001, 110). In his view, the government's capacity to deliver security is being questioned. Globally, police and criminal justice officials are finding it more and more difficult to control crime. A managerial or value-for-money approach in crime prevention is becoming increasingly evident in a global context. Local-level crime-prevention partnerships between the police and the citizens are being formed, and citizens are increasingly expected to take responsibility for their own safety. They should install safety mechanisms such as alarms in their homes and electric fences around their properties, or consider moving to a gated community. In addition, policing and security have become commodities for the so-called haves. The middle and upper classes can afford private security, armed-response protection, and closed-circuit television monitoring. Security companies categorize citizens as high or low risk and adapt their policies and payouts based on age, gender, and level of risk. This commodity (security) and the false belief in safety do not take the lower classes and the poorest of the poor into consideration (e.g., the majority of citizens in South Africa). Think too of a country like Zimbabwe, where daily survival is a huge challenge. It is probably the country with the poorest citizens in the world; food is its most valuable commodity. Thus, the safety commodity is of little value to them (although they really are in need of safety and protection), as they have to struggle on a daily basis to get food to see the next day.

The changing world order and the crime phenomenon have changed significantly in the new millennium. Criminology as a science is therefore challenged in many new ways to provide answers to these changes. It is becoming apparent that criminology not only offers theoretical insights but also serves a practical function in society.

Christiaan Bezuidenhout is Associate Professor in the Department of Social Work and Criminology at the University of Pretoria in Pretoria, South Africa.

References

Beck, Ulrick. 1992. *Risk Society: Towards a New Modernity.* London: Sage.
Garland, David. 2001. *The Culture of Control: Crime and Social Order in Contemporary Society.* Oxford: Oxford University Press.

CONTINUES

BOX 1.1 (CONTINUED)

Giddens, Anthony. 1999. "Risk and Responsibility." *Modern Law Review* 62, no. 1: 1–10.

Loader, Ian, and Richard Sparks. 2002. "Contemporary Landscapes of Crime, Order, and Control: Governance, Risk, and Globalization." In *The Oxford Handbook of Criminology,* edited by M. Maguire, R. Morgan, and R. Reiner, 83–111. 3d ed. Oxford: Oxford University Press.

What Is Criminology?

At its simplest, criminology can be defined as the systematic study of the nature, extent, cause, and control of lawbreaking behavior. Criminology is an applied social science in which criminologists work to establish knowledge about crime and its control based on empirical research. This research forms the basis for understanding, explanation, prediction, prevention, and criminal justice policy.

Ever since the term *criminology* was coined in 1885 by Raffaele Garofalo (1914), the content and scope of the field have been controversial. Critics and commentators have raised several questions about its academic standing. Some of the more common questions include the following: Is criminology truly a science? Does its applied approach, driven predominantly by the desire to control crime, inherently undermine the value-neutral stance generally considered essential for scientific inquiry? Is criminology an autonomous discipline, or does it rely on the insights, theory, and research of other natural and social science disciplines, and increasingly the media and public opinion? Which of the several theories of criminology offers the best explanation for crime? Answers to these questions are complex, and they are further complicated by criminology's multidisciplinary nature, its relative failure to recommend policy that reduces crime, and its heavy reliance on government funding for research. The complexity of these issues has been further compounded by increasing globalization, which has spawned crimes across national boundaries, and the failure of national enforcement agencies to prevent crime's global effects.

Criminology's subject matter is elastic. Unquestionable core components include: (1) the definition and nature of crime as harm-causing behavior; (2) different types of criminal activity, ranging from individual spontaneous offending to collective organized criminal enterprises; (3) profiles of typical offenders and victims, including organizational and corporate law violators; (4) statistical analysis of the extent, incidence, patterning, and cost of crimes, including estimates of the "dark figure" of hidden or unreported crime, based on surveys of victims and self-report studies of offenders; and (5) analysis of crime causation. Less agreement exists about whether the scope of criminology should be broadened to include society's response to crime, the formulation of criminal laws, the role of victims in these processes, and the extent to which criminology needs to adopt a comparative global perspective.

In the United States, the inclusive term *criminal justice* generally refers to crime-control practices, philosophies, and policies used by the police, courts, and system of corrections (in Europe it is called penology). Those who study such matters are as likely to identify themselves, or be identified by others, as criminologists, however, as are those who study criminal behavior and its causes. Criminology, by contrast, concerns itself with the theoretical and empirical study of the causes of crime. The two areas are obviously closely related, but a distinction is necessary.

Is Criminology Scientific?

Criminology requires that criminologists strictly adhere to the scientific method. What distinguishes science from nonscience is the insistence on testable hypotheses whose support or refutation through empirical research forms the basis of what is accepted among scientific criminologists as valid knowledge. Science, then, requires criminologists to build criminological knowledge from logically interrelated, theoretically grounded, and empirically tested hypotheses that are subject to retesting. These theoretical statements hold true as long as they are not falsified by further research (Popper 1959).

Theory testing can be done using either qualitative or quantitative methods. Qualitative methods (Berg [1989] 2000) may involve systematic ethnographic techniques, such as participant observation and in-depth interviews. These methods are designed to enable the researcher to understand the meaning of criminal activity to the participants. In participant observation, the researcher takes a role in the crime scene or in the justice system and describes what goes on between the participants. Criminologists using this technique study crime and its social context as an anthropologist would study a nonindustrial society. These methods have produced some of criminology's richest studies, such as Laud Humphries's study of homosexuality in public restrooms, *Tearoom Trade* (1970), and Howard Becker's study of jazz musicians and marijuana smoking in his book *Outsiders* ([1963] 1973).

Quantitative methods involve numbers, counts, and measures that are arrived at via a variety of research techniques. These include survey research based on representative random samples and the analysis of secondary data gathered for other purposes, such as homicide rates or corporate convictions for health and safety violations. Criminologists using quantitative techniques make up the mainstream of academic criminology. Perhaps one of the most illustrative examples of quantitative research is the series of longitudinal studies of a cohort of 10,000 boys born in Philadelphia in 1945 and followed through age eighteen with respect to their arrests for criminal offenses (Wolfgang, Figlio, and Sellin 1972) and a second cohort of 27,000 boys and girls born in 1958 (Tracy, Wolfgang, and Figlio 1990). Each study seemed to indicate that a small proportion of offenders (6 percent), called "chronic offenders," accounted for more than half of all offenses. Other quantitative research methods include the use of historical records, comparative analysis, and experimental research. Unfortunately, most quantitative research is not theory driven; in other words, it does not involve theory testing. A survey conducted in 1992 revealed that only 27 percent of the articles published over a period of twenty-eight years in the journal *Criminology* tested theory (Stitt and Giacopassi 1992). Thus, apparently, theoretically grounded research is lacking. This begs the question: Is criminology scientific?

Disciplinary Diversity

Although strongly influenced by sociology, criminology also has roots in a number of other disciplines, including anthropology, biology, economics, geography, history, philosophy, political science, psychiatry, psychology, and sociology (Einstadter and Henry 2006). Each of these disciplines contributes its own assumptions about human nature and society, its own definitions of crime and the role of law, its own preference of methods for the study of crime, and its own analysis of crime causation with differing policy implications. This diversity presents a major challenge to criminology's disciplinary integrity. Do these diverse theoretical perspectives, taken together when applied to crime, constitute an independent academic discipline? Are these contributing fields of knowledge merely subfields, or special applications of established disciplines? Alternatively, is criminology interdisciplinary? If criminology is to be considered interdisciplinary, what does that mean? Is interdisciplinarity understood as the integration of knowledge into a distinct whole? If so, then criminology is not yet interdisciplinary. Only a few criminologists have attempted such integration (see Messner, Krohn, and Liska 1989; Barak 1998; and M. Robinson 2004). There is sufficient independence of the subject from its constituent disciplines and an acceptance of their diversity, however, to prevent criminology from being subsumed under any one of them. For this reason, criminology is best defined as multidisciplinary. Put simply, crime can be viewed though many lenses. This is well illustrated through an overview of its component theories, discussions of which form the bases of subsequent chapters. There is, however, a caveat that suggests a question: Because globalization makes us interdependent, is integrated theory more necessary in the future to capture this complexity?

Comparative and Global Criminology

Comparative criminology has been defined as the systematic study of crime, law, and social control of two or more cultures (Beirne and Hill 1991). As Winslow has argued, "The global approach to the study of crimes recognizes its growing international nature and, in time, may become the primary focus of criminology in a world rapidly being unified by technological improvements in transportation and communication" (1998, 6). Winslow and Zhang's *Criminology: A Global Perspective* (2007) includes a Web site that provides a window on global crime (http://www-rohan.sdsu .edu/faculty/rwinslow/index.html). Beirne and Messerschmidt have argued that comparative analysis of crime enables criminologists to overcome their ethnocentric tendencies and sharpen their understanding of key questions: "Indeed, one reason why the United States has experienced such relatively high crime rates is that policy makers have relied on limited parochial theories regarding the causes of crime" (2000, 478). They show the value of looking at cross-national data on crime and victimization and countries and cities with low crime rates. Increasingly important also is the ability of corporations to evade the regulatory policies of one country by moving their operations to other countries. Clearly, this applies to regulatory attempts to control environmental pollution. However, it also applies to the ways that deliberately contaminated food, such as the Chinese production of milk products containing melamine that injured many babies, can be distributed globally.

What Is Victimology?

The scientific study of victimology is a relatively recent field, founded by Hans von Hentig (1948) and Benjamin Mendelsohn (1963), who claims to have coined the term in 1947. It is almost the mirror image or "reverse of criminology" (Schafer 1977, 35). Criminology is concerned mainly with criminals and criminal acts and the criminal justice system's response to them. Victimology is the study of who becomes a victim, how victims are victimized, how much harm they suffer, and their role in the criminal act. It also looks at victims' rights and their role in the criminal justice system.

Victimology has been defined as "the scientific study of the physical, emotional, and financial harm people suffer because of criminal activities" (Karmen 2001, 9). This interrelationship has a long history. Prior to the development of formal social control mechanisms, society relied on individualized informal justice. Individuals, families, and clans sought justice for harms caused by others. Endless feuding and persistent physical confrontation led to what has been called the "Golden Age" (Karmen 2001), when restitution became the focus of crime control (see Chapter 5). With the advent of the social contract, individuals gave up the right to retaliation, and crimes became crimes against the state—not the individual. The classicist social contract, simply put, says that individuals must give up some personal liberties in exchange for a greater social good. Thus, individuals forfeited the right to individualized justice, revenge, and vigilantism. This creed is still practiced today. For that reason, O. J. Simpson's first criminal trial for murder was *The State of California v. Orenthal J. Simpson*, not *Goldman and Brown-Simpson v. Orenthal J. Simpson*, which was the realm of the civil trial. Advanced societies relying on systems of justice based on the social contract increasingly, though inadvertently, neglected the victims of crime. In the United States, "Public prosecutors . . . took over powers and responsibilities formerly assumed by victims. . . . Attorneys decided whether or not to press charges, what indictments to file, and what sanctions to ask judges to invoke. . . . When the overwhelming majority of cases came to be resolved through confessions of guilt elicited in negotiated settlements, most victims lost their last opportunity to actively participate" (Karmen 1990, 17).

Since the founding of victimology, there has been controversy between the broad view (Mendelsohn 1963) that victimology should be the study of all victims and the narrow view that it should include only crime victims. Clearly, if a broad definition is taken of crime as a violation of human rights (Schwendinger and Schwendinger 1970; S. Cohen 1993; Tifft and Sullivan 2001), this is more consistent with the broad view of victimology.

It is only since the early 1970s that victimization has been included in mainstream criminology. This followed studies by Stephen Schafer (1968, 1977) and a flurry of victimization studies culminating in the U.S. Department of Justice's annual National Crime Victimization Survey, begun in 1972. There are numerous texts on the field (see Elias 1986; Walklate 1989; and Karmen [2001] 2006).

Victimology has also been criticized for the missionary zeal of its reform policy (Fattah 1992; Weed 1995) and for its focus on victims of individual crimes rather than socially harmful crimes, although there are rare exceptions to this in French victimology studies (Joutsen 1994). The more recent comprehensive approach considers the victim in the total societal context of crime in the life domains of family, work, and leisure as these realms are shaped by the media, lawmakers, and interest groups (Sacco and Kennedy 1996).

Summary

We began this chapter by showing how the "world" has changed and how criminology has had to change with it. We looked at six major changes that have impacted the ways that we see crime and the way that we think about its causes: (1) globalization and its impact on economic, social, and political institutions; (2) the globalization of communications, particularly the advent of the Internet; (3) privatization and individualization and the decline of group and class solidarity; (4) the global spread of disease and the development of epidemiological criminology; (5) changing perceptions of conflict and national security since the end of the cold war; and (6) the internationalization of terrorism. Criminology has evolved and will continue to expand to provide improved methods of study and more comprehensive explanatory theories for understanding crime. The current direction is moving toward a more inclusive and expansive criminology that considers crime as deprivation and harm—regardless of legislated law. It also is beginning, through comparative and global criminology, to move toward recognizing the interconnectedness of people across countries and cultures, and so needs to be both integrated and comparative in its approach.

We have also seen that criminology has a much broader scope than simply studying criminals. If nothing else, the reader should have developed a sense that there are few definitive "truths" in the study of crime. Controversy and diverse views abound. This is not without good reason. Criminology is perhaps the most widely examined (by the public, media, and policy makers) of the social sciences. As a result of the nightly news, talk shows, newsmagazine programs, and popular television dramas, such as *Law and Order*, *CSI*, and *Criminal Minds*, crime and its control are topics in which everyone's interest is engaged and everyone has an opinion.

Criminology is clearly also policy oriented. The criminal justice system that implements the law and policy of governments itself is a significant source of employment and expenditure. Considering only corrections, twenty years ago the combined states spent $10.6 billion from their general funds on corrections. In 2007, they spent more than $49 billion—a 362 percent increase. By comparison, inflation-adjusted prison spending increased 127 percent, while the budget for higher education increased only 21 percent nationwide (Pew Charitable Trusts 2008). In 2008 the states spent a record $51.7 billion on corrections, 6.7 percent of state budgets, which rises to $68 billion when local, federal, and other funding is included. Moreover, in 2008, 7.3 million, or 1 in 31, Americans were under some supervision by the U.S. corrections system, including people on probation and parole (Pew Charitable Trusts 2009). The long-term implications of this decreased emphasis on education and increased focus on punishment and incarceration are disturbing and the subject of much debate. Several states have taken steps to reduce prison expenses. California has taken the lead, reducing its prison population by 4,068 in 2007 (Pew Charitable Trusts 2008). However, thirty-six states and the Federal Bureau of Prisons experienced increases in 2007. Similar debate was lacking, however, following the terrorist attacks against the United States. Government powers were increased dramatically following the events of September 11, 2001, with little or no debate.

Regardless of one's theoretical inclinations, preferred research tools, or policy preferences, dissension demands a clear articulation of one's position. Such articulation requires considerable thought in order to make convincing arguments and the insight to appreciate other positions. The end result is that criminology as a whole is strengthened.

In the next chapter, we turn to the first building block of the criminological enterprise and examine how crime is defined. We look at how what counts as crime varies depending on who defines it, where it is defined, and when. We see how the definition is shaped by our personal experiences (whether we are victimized or victimizer), our social standing (whether we stand to benefit or lose from crime), and many other factors, such as the media, family, and friends as well as those who are in a position to influence the way laws are created.

2

What Is Crime?
Defining the Problem

Calvin Johnson was the second overall pick in the 2007 National Football League draft, signing a six-year multimillion-dollar contract with the Detroit Lions. While in college at Georgia Tech, All-American wide receiver Johnson was the school's all-time leader in touchdown receptions, receiving yards, and touchdown catches for a season. His high school career at Sandy Creek High was equally impressive. However, when the six-foot-five, 235-pound Johnson faced Douglas County High School in Georgia, a small, overachieving defensive back named Genarlow Wilson limited the superstar to just four catches in two games. Who was this diminutive, hardworking defensive player? He was bright, having a 3.2 grade point average. Wilson was popular, elected homecoming king by his classmates. The Ivy League football coach at Brown University said to Wilson, "You have been recommended to me as one of the top scholar-athletes in your area" (Thompson 2008). Genarlow was friendly and popular and had a bright future in both athletics and academics.

In 2005 Genarlow Wilson and several teammates and students rented a room at the Days Inn just off I-20 in Georgia. As at many teenage parties, alcohol and marijuana were consumed. At some point during the evening a fifteen-year-old female classmate provided oral sex to one of Wilson's friends. She then performed oral sex on seventeen-year-old Wilson as well. One of the partygoers videotaped the incident. Later even the girl's mother testified that her daughter had instigated the sex act, not Wilson (ibid.).

Unfortunately for Wilson, the videotape ended up in the hands of Douglas County district attorney David McDade. A week later the police went to the high school and arrested Wilson and several of his friends, removing them from class in handcuffs. McDade originally charged Genarlow with four felonies—including rape. For the next eight months McDade tried to get the young men to accept plea bargains. To his credit, Wilson refused. For one thing, had he accepted McDade's offer he would have served two years in state prison and been labeled a child molester (meaning he could not live with his much loved younger sister again). Another football player accepted the "deal" and got five years. By the time the case came to trial, the only suspect willing to exercise his constitutional "right" to a jury trial was Wilson. (We discuss plea bargains later in the text, but need to point out the abusive and pervasive nature of that practice here. Justice is rarely served by plea bargains, and Americans may lose constitutional guarantees by accepting them.)

Wilson went to trial before a jury. The jury found him innocent of rape but guilty of aggravated child molestation. The jury forewoman was crying when she read the verdict. When the judge imposed the mandatory ten-year *minimum* sentence, several jury members were outraged. Genarlow Wilson, his little sister, and their mother cried.

According to ESPN writer Wright Thompson,

> Every story needs a villain, and in this one, the villain's hat has been placed squarely on the head of Barker, the prosecutor and a former college baseball player. Barker doesn't write the laws in the books to the left of his desk. He simply punishes those who break them. "We didn't want him to get the 10 years," he says. "We understand there's an element out there scratching their heads, saying, 'How does a kid get 10 years under these facts?'" In Barker's eyes, Wilson should have taken the same plea agreement as the others. Maintaining innocence in the face of the crushing wheels of justice is the ultimate act of vanity, he believes. "I understand what he's saying," Barker says. "I think he's making a bad decision in the long run. Being branded a sex offender is not good; but at the same time, if it made the difference between spending 10 years as opposed to two? Is it worth sitting in prison for eight more years, and you're still gonna be a sex offender when you get out?" Barker is quick to point out that he offered Wilson a plea after he'd been found guilty—the first time he has ever done that. Of course, the plea was the same five years he'd offered before the trial—not taking into account the rape acquittal. Barker thinks five years is fair for receiving oral sex from a schoolmate. None of the other defendants insisted on a jury trial. Wilson did. He rolled the dice, and he lost. The others, he says, "took their medicine." (ibid.)

The case was appealed to the Georgia Supreme Court, and Wilson lost, by a vote of four to three, with all four white justices voting against him. After the composition of the Georgia Supreme Court changed in 2007, it found Wilson's sentence to be "cruel and unusual"—with all three white judges still voting against the ruling. After more than two years and legislative intervention (they changed the law but did not apply it retroactively to Wilson), he was finally released from prison (CNN.com 2007). He hopes to attend college and study sociology. Football is no longer in his plans.

What was the crime here? Who was the criminal? Who was the victim? What was the harm committed? Does the public agree that harm occurred, and does society's reaction, reflected in the sentence given, reflect the indignity of the public against the harm committed? These are precisely the kinds of questions that we need to ask when considering whether an act is a crime. This chapter is intended to help answer these questions.

Most people have a sense of what is criminal, but deciding precisely what is—or is not—criminal is not as obvious as it may seem. What for one person is deviance, or shrewd business practice, may for others be crime. What is morally reprehensible to one group may be a lifestyle preference to another. For example, prostitution is condemned by the "moral Right" yet celebrated by sex-worker organizations for prostitutes such as COYOTE (Cast Off Your Old Tired Ethics), BAYSWAN (the Bay Area Sex Worker Advocacy Network), and SWOP USA (Sex Workers Outreach Project—USA) who argue for sex workers' rights. Like deviance, crime is a concept with elusive, varied, and diverse meanings.

Nor is establishing whether someone was harmed an obvious answer to the "What is crime?" question. As we argued previously (Henry and Lanier 2001), if the definition of crime is too narrow, harms that might otherwise be included are ignored. This was the case for years with domestic violence, racial hatred, and much of what now counts as corporate and white-collar crime. Conversely, if the definition is too broad, then almost every deviation becomes a crime. This was the case with the old concept of sin, where anything that deviated from the sexual mandates (i.e., the missionary position for procreation purposes only) could be prosecuted by the church, and state, as an offense against God. But even when harm looks obvious, is it a crime? For example, in the aftermath of the 9/11 attacks in 2001 the annual crime figures reported to the FBI for New York City excluded the thousands of victims who died. These were victims of a terrorist attack, and people and a society were killed and injured. So why was this not seen as a crime? Should it have been?

Is the obvious solution to the question "What is a crime?" to find out what the law says is criminal? Again, this is more complicated than it seems, and "going to the law" as a solution leaves many unanswered questions. In fact, since we wrote the first two editions of this text there have been significant changes in the way both criminologists and the "law" look at what counts as "crime." In the United States we gathered scholars together who had been debating different views about the issue to consider what they thought were the essential elements that make a behavior or action "criminal," how crime should be defined, and how it was defined in law enforcement practice. This resulted in an edited volume titled *What Is Crime?* (Henry and Lanier 2001). In 2002, the Law Commission of Canada, a body that serves the Canadian Parliament, launched a project with a similar title called "What Is a Crime?" in which they hosted a series of meetings and conferences in Ottawa and Vancouver to reconsider the various issues of defining crime (Canadian Law Commission 2003). Indeed, it even sponsored a nationwide student essay competition on the topic. Clearly, "What is crime?" is a hotly debated topic at all levels of international society.

An important consideration when defining crime is the observation that crime is *contextual.* Criminal harm takes different forms depending on the historical period, specific context, social setting, location, or situation in which it occurs. The written law might seem to provide an answer, but laws are open to interpretation. In this chapter, we look at the various definitions of crime, ranging from the legal definition to definitions that take into account crime's changing meaning as social harm.

The definitions of crime arrived at by law, government agencies, and criminologists are used by others to measure the extent of crime. Put simply, if crime is the problem, then how big is it? How much of it exists? Is there more of it in one part of the country than another, more in cities than in rural settings? Do different societies have different rates of the activities we have defined as crime? The reason that the definition and measurement of crime are necessary is that several policy decisions concerning social control are made based on a particular definition of crime. These include the selection of priorities in policing and what to police, budget allocations for measures such as crime prevention programs, how to "handle" offenders, and what a "crime-free" neighborhood actually looks like. For example, is a crime-free neighborhood one where there are low rates of crimes known to the police, or one where there is a low incidence of serious harm? Is a crime-free neighborhood one where the public streets are safe but fraud in businesses is rampant? What is the real level of crime when the incidence of serious crime, such as homicide, burglary, rape, and aggravated assault, is low but the level of crimes that disturb the public, such as prostitution, vandalism, public drunkenness, and panhandling, is high? Should the public or community define crime, or should this be a matter for legislators or the police? Does a "crime-free" neighborhood allow freedom of expression and personal liberty, or does it desire uniformity? This chapter addresses these issues first, in particular looking at how different entities see crime from their perspective. In considering these different "takes" on crime it is worth considering that not only have criminologists and others been arguing about this topic for much of the past century, but as one commentator observed at the century's end, "An appropriate definition of crime . . . remains one of the most critical unresolved issues in criminal justice today" (Bohm and Haley 1999, 24).

Legal Definition

Since the eighteenth century, the legal definition of crime has referred to acts prohibited, prosecuted, and punished by criminal law (Henry and Lanier 2001, 6). Most commentators have agreed with Michael and Adler that "criminal law gives behavior its quality of criminality" (1933, 5). In other words, criminal law specifies the acts or omissions that constitute crime. Tappan's classic definition is illustrative. He defined crime as "an intentional act or omission in violation of criminal law (statutory and case law), committed without defense or justification, and sanctioned by the state as a felony or misdemeanor" (1947, 100). Tappan believed that the study of criminals should be restricted to those convicted by the courts. In fact, "most criminologists have traditionally relied on the legal conception, which defines crime as behavior in violation of criminal law and liable for sanctioning by the criminal justice system" (R. Kramer 1982, 34). And "most criminologists today act as if the debate is settled in favor of a 'legal' definition" (Bohm 1993, 3).

Other criminologists, however, argue that the legal definition is too limited in scope. First, it takes no account of harms that are covered by administrative law and are considered regulative violations. This is not a new debate. Fifty years ago, Edwin

Sutherland (1949a) first argued that a strict legal definition excluded "white-collar crime." Suffering salmonella poisoning as a result of eating spoiled or contaminated food in a restaurant that systematically violates FDA regulations governing hygienic food preparation is no less criminal, according to Sutherland, than being robbed in the street. Both injure human life in the interest of profit. Sutherland argued for extending the legal definition of crime to include all offenses that are socially injurious or socially harmful. He also maintained that repeat white-collar offenders deserve the label "habitual white-collar criminals." How do the systematic deceptive practices of subprime mortgage lenders compare to the systematic check forger? The law defines the check forger as a criminal but not the banker or mortgage broker.

A second problem with a strict legal definition of crime is that it ignores the cultural and historical context of law. What is defined as crime by the legal code varies from location to location and changes over time. For example, prostitution is generally illegal in the United States but is legal in some states, such as Nevada and Rhode Island. Gambling is often illegal, yet an ever-increasing number of states now conduct lotteries to increase their revenue, and today many cities have legal casinos. Tappan (1947) acknowledged the cultural and historical variability of crime in society's norms but said this is why the law's precision makes it the only certain guide. Others have claimed that the law offers only a false certainty, for what the law defines as crime "is somewhat arbitrary, and represents a highly selective process" (Barak 1998, 21). Indeed, Barak notes with regard to crime, "There are no purely objective definitions; all definitions are value laden and biased to some degree" (ibid.).

Consider, for example, the criminalization of substance abuse. During Prohibition, the production and distribution of alcoholic beverages in the United States were illegal. Today, the same acts are generally legal, although some counties still prohibit the sale of alcohol, and some states regulate its sale more than others. In colonial Virginia, smoking tobacco was encouraged for medicinal purposes. In much of the twentieth century, smoking was celebrated as an aid to relaxation and social enjoyment. Yet today it is illegal to smoke in an increasing number of public places, and some states, such as Illinois, impose fines for violators. In the 1920s, cocaine was promoted as a pick-me-up and was even included in the original formula for Coca-Cola. Today, such activity would result in a long prison sentence for drug dealing. Clearly, what counts as a crime at one point in time or in one culture may not be considered criminal at another time or in another culture. Nettler summed up the relativity problems with a strict legal definition: "Because there are so many possible wrongs and because 'crime' denotes only a select sample of all disapproved acts, the definition of crime varies from time to time and from place to place and there is continuing controversy about what should or should not be called 'crime'" (1984, 1).

Who Defines Crime?

A related issue is who defines the kinds of behavior labeled crime. Crimes are not produced by legislation alone. Judicial interpretation also determines what is or is not crime. Judicial decisions can also be appealed, overturned, and revised. The Georgia Supreme Court on two occasions reviewed the oral sex case of Genarlow Wilson and interestingly was split each time along racial lines. Consider also *Roe v. Wade*, the 1973 Supreme Court case that legalized abortion during the first three months of pregnancy (Fiero 1996, 684), and the more recent limitations that recriminalize certain aspects of abortion. Even where legislators make law, a significant problem is whose views they represent, as illustrated by the example of Genarlow Wilson.

Some critical criminologists argue that criminal actions by corporations often go unrecognized because those who hold economic power in society are, in effect, those who make the law. Legislators are influenced through lobbyists and through receiving donations from political action committees set up by owners of corporations and financial institutions (Simon and Eitzen 1982). Their influence minimizes the criminalization of corporate behavior. This was at the heart of Edwin Sutherland's original concern (1949a) to incorporate crimes defined by administrative regulations into the criminological realm.

In short, relying on a strict legal definition for crime may be appropriate study for police cadets but is sorely inadequate for students of criminology or the thinking criminal justice professional. The contextual aspects of crime and crime control require serious reflective study. A more comprehensive approach to accommodate the range of definitions is to divide them into one of two types depending on whether they reflect consensus or conflict in society.

In this chapter we try to show the complexities of identifying crime. Crime is contextual. Gary Yourofsky is perhaps the leading advocate for animal rights. The following summarizes his view of human treatment of animals. As you read it, ask yourself, "What is the crime? Who is the criminal?"

BOX 2.1 Abolition, Liberation, Freedom.
GARY YOUROFSKY

Isaac Bashevis Singer, the compassionate Jewish humanitarian who escaped Nazi-occupied Poland, once condemned every meat eater by stating, "What do they know—all these scholars, all these philosophers, all the leaders of the world? They have convinced themselves that man, the worst transgressor of all the species, is the crown of creation. All other creatures were created merely to provide him with food, pelts, to be tormented, exterminated. In relation to them [animals], all people are Nazis; for the animals it is an eternal Treblinka."

Singer's indictment is probably the most damning statement ever about humankind. It establishes the fact that violence is violence and murder is murder even if the victims have beaks, horns, gills, feathers, or fur.

CONTINUES

BOX 2.1 (CONTINUED)

Worldwide, 45–50 billion land animals (10 billion in the United States) and 85 billion marine animals (18 billion in the United States) are killed and eaten every year in a monumental Holocaust born of ignorance, arrogance, and racism. The human race versus animal race brand of racism permits humans to enslave and kill any other species with impunity. Singer calls speciesism the "purest form of racism" because it kills more innocent beings that any form of human-to-human racism. Each carnivore is responsible for the death and dismemberment of more than 3,000 land animals and thousands of marine animals throughout his lifetime.

To understand the compassionate movement of animal rights, empathy must be used to examine the issue from the animals' (victim's) point of view. This isn't a radical concept, either. Abolitionists looked at slavery through the eyes of subjugated blacks, just as the Allied forces looked at Nazism through the eyes of Jews and other non-Aryans whom Hitler labeled unworthy and expendable. Empathy allows people to understand the injustice without overanalyzing the issue, especially when those in power deem the victims unworthy and expendable, something Hitler, slave owners, and meat eaters have all done to their respective victims.

When I became vegan on July 24, 1996, and finally understood that animals had an inherent right to be free and live completely unfettered by human domination, I wondered why it took more than twenty-five years to attain this nonviolent awakening. I began to ask, "Who taught me that animals were put on this earth for food? Who taught me to disrespect animals and view them as mere commodities? Who stole my compassion, my empathy, and my conscience? Who instilled this vicious mind-set of human-to-animal exploitation as standard operating procedure?"

Nowadays, as I travel the country giving around 250 lectures each year in scores of college classrooms, I ask thousands of meat eaters similar questions. "Who told you to eat the corpses of dismembered animals and reduce your body to a walking graveyard? Who stole your compassion, your empathy, and your conscience? Why do you embrace such meaningless violence and then make inane rationalizations about the suffering of innocent creatures?"

In the book *Dominion* (2004), Matthew Scully explains that people can be either radically kind or radically cruel. This illuminates the hypocrisy of the meat-eating animal welfare movement that seeks to regulate the enslavement and killing of billions of animals via "humane slaughter" laws. By definition alone, slaughter is radically cruel and can never be humane. What else can happen in a slaughterhouse besides the psychological and physical abuse, harm, and murder of animals? Candle making? Band practice? Taking an animal's life for profit or preference is the crime. And if anyone believes animals can be humanely slaughtered, I wonder if they also irrationally believe that women can be humanely raped, or children humanely molested? Is a humane Holocaust possible? Humane slavery?

Reduction and abolition are the only options to ending a massacre. Welfare regulations are a stamp of approval to let the carnage continue unabated because compassionate ways of enslaving and killing billions of animals do not exist.

CONTINUES

BOX 2.1 (CONTINUED)

Will the Violence Against
Animals Ever End?

The 9/11 incidents temporarily restored my faith in humanity because I witnessed such an outpouring of love, empathy, compassion, and community. The world was condemning evil and the taking of innocent lives. Would the terror that humans inflict upon animals for food, clothing, sport, entertainment, and research end or at least abate? Would the camouflaged hunters lurking on American soil, skulking in the distance with guns and bows, waiting to terrorize and kill more than 200 million innocent animals annually, throw their weapons to the ground? Would the animal researchers who terrorize tens of millions of dogs, cats, primates, and mice annually in medieval-minded vivisection procedures have a revelation? The March of Dimes experimenters who sew shut the eyes of kittens and ferrets to see if blindness affects their brains would surely stop their barbaric acts of terrorism. The UCLA vivisectionists who drill holes in the heads of primates in order to attach metal devices to their brains so they can monitor "waves" surely were going to be arrested and charged with terrorism.

Would terrorist fur farmers and trappers be sent to prison for breaking the necks of mink, anally electrocuting foxes, genitally electrocuting chinchillas, and catching wild animals in steel-jaw leghold traps? Would humankind realize that animals do not want to be our food, clothing, entertainment, and research specimens? Would we finally understand the words of British bishop William Inge when he said that if animals ever formulated an organized religion, the devil would be depicted in human form? Would Gandhi's immortal words of peace, "The life of a lamb is no less precious than that of a human," be recited at every school across America and beyond?

Sadly, not a damn thing changed. The routine violence of human customs was swept even further under the rug. The repetitive talk of people revolting against evil sickened me because it was clearly hypocritical and deceitful. It seems that the hatred that human animals have toward nonhuman animals is so vicious, bitter, and entrenched that a thousand peaceful gods and goddesses couldn't eradicate it.

For that brief moment, though, I saw a glimmer of hope. Reporters, civilians, and government officials kept saying, "We will destroy the evil." Unfortunately, they were referring only to the evil people who disrupt the rest of society from performing its own evil deeds. Each year—after living in concentration camps and being stolen from their family members—billions of chickens, cows, pigs, and turkeys are sent to killing houses where knife-wielding terrorists slit their throats, drain their blood, and dismember their bodies, all too often while the animals are fully conscious.

If people truly want to end violence, then they should discard animal flesh from refrigerators, toss bows and bullets into the trash, insist that universities close down their vivisection laboratories, demand that department stores close their fur salons, make circuses shift to only human performers, abolish the rodeo once and for all, and support the courageous Animal Liberation Front (ALF) humanitarians who liberate animals from places of terror. People who yearn for a compassionate world should

CONTINUES

BOX 2.1 (CONTINUED)

have nothing but praise for these amazing altruists. Otherwise, any talk of peace, civilization, and justice will remain the most hypocritical rhetoric that has ever existed.

Remember, just because an act might be classified as illegal does not make it morally wrong. And just because an act is legal does not make it the best avenue for facilitating substantive change. Laws have always been broken by freethinking, radical individuals who realize that it is impossible to make progressive changes within a corrupt, discriminatory system. Nelson Mandela, Rosa Parks, Martin Luther King Jr., Mohandas Gandhi, Henry David Thoreau, and Jesus, to name a few, were routine, radical lawbreakers who went to jail many times for disobeying unjust laws. We see them as heroes today, but in their time they were considered by many to be lawbreakers, villains, and radicals.

Radical has a negative connotation in society today. However, it is simply the Latin word meaning *root*. What radicals do is bypass pseudosolutions and get to the root of a problem. Everyone should realize that all social justice activists were considered radical in their time. It is only after social justice activists die and society begins to evolve and comprehend their actions that the "radical" is placed on a pedestal and embraced. Without question, ALF liberators are akin to Harriet Tubman and the Underground Railroad that assisted in the liberation of blacks from white slave owners. In fact, a wise ALF adage states, "If we are trespassing, then so were the American soldiers who broke down the gates of Hitler's death camps. If we are thieves, then so were the members of the Underground Railroad who freed the slaves from the South. And if we are vandals, then so were those who destroyed forever the gas chambers of Buchenwald and Auschwitz."

It is fantasy to believe that those directly involved in torturing and murdering animals, and profiting handsomely from it, will listen to reason, common sense, and moral truth. Contrary to the sound bites from revisionist historians, love does NOT conquer hate. Reason does NOT conquer ignorance or stupidity. And passing out a leaflet does NOT eradicate institutionalized violence. "By any means necessary" has its role right alongside pacifism and education.

ALF activists are not terrorists; those who abuse animals for a living are! ALF activists are not criminals; those who enslave, torture, mutilate, dismember, and murder animals for a living are! Activists who liberate animals should not go to prison; animal exploiters should! It should never be viewed as a crime to try to forcibly stop hatred and discrimination and terrorism; it is an act of compassion and courage.

All animals are simply disenfranchised nations in search of the one thing that every sentient being demands: FREEDOM! They are not property. They are not objects. And they are not commodities. The earth and its inhabitants do not belong to humans, under any circumstance.

Gary Yourofsky is the founder of Animals Deserve Absolute Protection Today and Tomorrow (ADAPTT). He is a full-time animal rights activist, author, and revolutionary who resides in Michigan—while not on the road promoting animal rights and veganism.

CONTINUES

BOX 2.1 (CONTINUED)

References

Scully, Matthew. 2004. *Dominion: The Power of Man, the Suffering of Animals, and the Call to Mercy.* New York: St. Martin's.

Consensus and Conflict Approaches

Consensus refers to definitions of crime that reflect the ideas of the society as a whole. It assumes that all agree on what should be considered crime, such as homicide and rape. Consensus definitions constitute a set of universal values. Conflict refers to definitions of crime based on the belief that society is composed of different interest groups. These various groups are in competition with one another, and the competition is most pronounced between the powerful and powerless.

Consensus Approaches

Consensus theorists try to get around the problem of variations in the law by linking the definition of crime to what was once called "social morality." They draw on the seminal ideas of nineteenth-century French sociologist Émile Durkheim ([1893] 1984), who believed that in the kind of integrated community that preceded industrialization, people were held together by common religious beliefs, traditions, and similar worldviews. The similarity between people acted as a "social glue" that bonded them to each other in a shared morality. Thus, the consensus position states that crimes are acts that shock the common conscience, or collective morality, producing intense moral outrage in people. Thus, for Ernest Burgess, "A lack of public outrage, stigma, and official punishment, attached to social action indicates that such action is not a violation of society's rules, independent of whether it is legally punishable" (1950, quoted in Green 1990, 9). Current supporters of this position claim there is a "consensus," or agreement, between most people of all economic, social, and political positions about what behaviors are unacceptable and what should be labeled criminal. Indeed, echoing Durkheim, some commentators, such as Roshier, define crime "as only identifiable by the discouraging response it evokes" (1989, 76). Even this definition has problems, however. What at first appears as an obvious example of universally agreed-upon crime—the malicious, intentional taking of human life—may appear less malicious, or even justified, when we take into account the social or situational context. Closer inspection reveals that killing others is not universally condemned. Whether it is condemned depends on the social context and the definition of human life. For example, killing humans is regrettable yet acceptable in war. It is even honored. Humans identified as "the enemy" (as in the Iraq war) are redefined as "collateral," and their deaths are described as "collateral damage." Those governments that employ massive violent force to overthrow other governments that they define as "oppressive" consider themselves "liberators." The deaths are not described as murder, even though intended. Instead, the killed are described as "regrettable" but "legitimate" targets. Soldiers have followed "illegal" orders, taken lives, and avoided punishment and the stigma associated with crime.

War is not the only area of debate. Consider also prolife advocates in the abortion debate who define life as beginning with conception. They believe abortion of a fetus is murder. Extreme prochoice advocates, by contrast, do not believe life begins until birth, so abortion of a fetus is seen as an expression of a woman's right to choose—no more, no less. Others define life as starting at some other arbitrary point. Similarly, questions and controversy arise around the idea of self-defense. Some states allow terminal force to protect one's self and property, whereas other states criminalize the same defensive act.

Another major problem with the consensus view is the question of whose morality is important in defining the common morality. If the harm affects a minority, will the majority be outraged? Is the conduct any less harmful if they are not outraged? Examples abound. Sexual harassment in the workplace, which was not previously defined as a crime, was no less harmful to those forced to engage in sexual relations, or received sexual pressure, under the threat of losing their job. Because men were the predominant employers and managers, women's needs were not addressed and their complaints were not heard. The 1990s sexual harassment cases in the military and the Anita Hill case provide vivid illustrations of this problem. Finally, although empirical research in the 1970s claimed "there is widespread consensus both within and across cultures concerning the relative gravity of various criminal acts" and that "the ubiquitous agreement on seriousness rankings is often cited in support of a consensus as opposed to a conflict model of criminal law," commentators have since argued that this may be more a reflection of the methods used to measure consensus than evidence of an underlying normative agreement on the seriousness of crime (Cullen et al. 1985, 99–100; see also Miethe 1982, 1984; and Stylianou 2003).

Social Context

Clearly, understanding the social context is the first step toward defining crime. Consider sexual behavior as an example. Sexual intercourse with a minor, or statutory rape, is in the United States universally agreed to be a crime—that is, until we consider the social context. On closer inspection, legally defined rape is not universally condemned. For example, sexually active boys and girls under the age of legal consent often do not consider themselves raped. In previous historical eras, adolescents of the same age were often married and shared the rights of adults. In this same historical era, husbands could not "rape" their spouses, though they could force themselves on unwilling wives. Under old German law, an act of sexual intercourse with a woman would be considered "as rape only if it was committed against a respectable women, but not a 'vagrant woman'" (Hinckeldey 1981, 107). Whether the physical act is condemned depends on the social and historical context and on the definition of rape. For example, if parents give permission to marry, two sexually active teens are no longer committing "rape," though their physical actions (intercourse) and circumstances (age) are the same. Rape laws have historically had a gender bias as well. Young girls have traditionally been treated much more harshly "by the law" than are young boys (Edwards 1990). The social reaction to sexual activity and prowess continues to reflect gender bias. However, this gender bias can also harm males, as Genarlow Wilson found.

Furthermore, whether an issue becomes a public harm depends on a group's ability to turn private concerns into public issues (Mills 1959) or their skills at moral entrepreneurship (H. Becker [1963] 1973). This is the ability to whip up moral consensus around an issue that affects some individuals or a minority and to recruit support from the majority by convincing them it is in their interest to support the issue, too. Creating a public harm often involves identifying and signifying offensive behavior and then attempting to influence legislators to ban it officially. Becker argued that behavior that is unacceptable in society depends on what people first label unacceptable and whether they can successfully apply the label to those designated "offenders." For example, prior to the 1930s smoking marijuana in the United States was generally acceptable. Intensive government agency efforts, particularly by the Federal Bureau of Narcotics, culminated in the passage of the Marihuana Tax Act of 1937. This type of smoking was labeled unacceptable and illegal, and those who engaged in it were stigmatized as "outsiders." Even obesity is now being viewed as criminal by some. In this tradition, Pavarini (1994) points out that what becomes defined as crime depends on the power to define and the power to resist definitions. This in turn depends on who has access to the media and how skilled moral entrepreneurs are at using such access to their advantage (Barak 1994; Pfhul and Henry 1993). As the following discussion illustrates, for these and other reasons the consensus position is too simplistic.

Conflict Approaches

Conflict theory is based on the idea that rather than being similar, people are different and struggle over their differences. According to this theory, society is made up of groups that compete with one another over scarce resources. The conflict over different interests produces differing definitions of crime. These definitions are determined by the group in power and are used to further its needs and consolidate its power. Powerless groups are generally the victims of oppressive laws. For example, prison sentences for using crack cocaine, the form of the drug generally preferred by African Americans, are ten to fifteen years longer than sentences for using powder cocaine, favored mainly by the white middle and upper classes (DeKeseredy and Schwartz 1996, 61; Tonry 1995). Orlando, Florida, passed a law banning sitting in downtown areas. Violation of the controversial ordinance results in a fine of five hundred dollars and sixty days in jail (Harris and Mathers 2002). Presumably, businesspersons will not be subjected to this law, but many homeless people will.

In addition to being based on wealth and power, groups in society form around culture, prestige, status, morality, ethics, religion, ethnicity, gender, race, ideology, human rights, the right to own guns, and so on. Each group may fight to dominate others on issues. Approaches to defining crime that take account of these multiple dimensions are known as pluralist conflict theories. Ethnic or cultural conflict is a good example. From the perspective of cultural conflict, different cultures, ethnic groups, or subcultures compete for dominance. According to Sellin's classic cultural conflict theory (1938), criminology should not merely focus on crime but also include violations of "culture norms," that is, behaviors that are considered standard for a specific cultural group, such as Arab Americans or Asian Americans. Sellin describes two forms of conflict. The first, *primary conflict,* occurs when a person raised in one culture is transposed into a different one. As an immigrant, the person may follow traditional cultural norms, such as the assumption by those of the Islamic faith that women revealing bare skin are sexually promiscuous and can be propositioned for sex. But acting on such assumptions may violate the norms of the host country. Where these norms are expressed in law, criminal violations occur. *Secondary conflict* occurs between groups of people who live in the same geographic area but create their own distinct value systems. Where these clash, conflict and norm violation occur. An example of secondary cultural conflict as crime is when the behavior of subgroups of society are targeted by laws. For example, some places specifically ban skateboarding and in-line skating that others consider harmless recreational activities (Orlando City Council 2006, Sec. 18A.09). Of course, some police reactions to skateboarders should be considered criminal, as one Baltimore police officer showed us (see http://youtube.com/watch?v=1hxOr3q7nrk&feature=related). In other places, skateboarders are permitted and even encouraged.

When power is determined by wealth, the conflict is considered class based. Analysis of this type of conflict is founded on principles outlined by nineteenth-century social philosopher Karl Marx. In Marxist conflict theory, the definition of crime focuses on conflicts that arise in capitalist society. Crime is rooted in the vast differences of wealth and power associated with class divisions. Groups that acquire power through political or economic manipulation and exploitation place legal constraints on those without power. A definition of crime based on economic interests emphasizes that "crime and deviance are the inevitable consequences of fundamental contradictions within society's economic infrastructure" (Farrell and Swigert 1988, 3). Crime is defined as the activities of those who threaten the powerful. Such a view explains why the crimes of street offenders are considered serious, whereas those of corporate or white-collar "suite" offenders are considered less serious, even though the financial losses from such white-collar crimes amount to at least ten times the cost incurred from street crimes (Timmer and Eitzen 1989; Friedrichs 1996). Richard Quinney has expressed this position: "Crime is a definition of human conduct created by authorized agents in a politically organized society. . . . [It describes] behaviors that conflict with the interests of the segments of society that have the power to shape public policy" (1970, 15–16). In other words, the definition of crime is a political tool used to protect power, wealth, and position in a society. Not surprising, this power-and-wealth version of conflict theory has been termed *critical criminology* (I. Taylor, Walton, and Young 1975). This is because it criticizes the overall kind of society in which we live and suggests we replace it with a socialist system.

Critical criminologists also suggest that the harm of crime should become the main reason for law. Following Edwin Sutherland's ideas, they assert that the definition of crime should be expanded to include the socially injurious activities of powerful groups against the powerless as well as behavior that violates or intrudes upon others' human rights (Schwendinger and Schwendinger 1970; see also S. Cohen 1993, 98–101; Lea and Young 1984, 55; Michalowski 1985; Reiman [1979] 2007; and Von Hirsch and Jareborg 1991). Thus, they argue that criminal harm can come not just from individuals but also from the social contexts of conditions such as imperialism, racism, sexism, and poverty.

The idea of crime as a violation of human rights has become a major theme of critical humanist criminologists. As Quinney and Wildeman note, "The notion of crime as social injury, social harm, or a violation of human rights is, in effect, basic to those who strive to improve the human condition, for it provides the intellectual and practical tools for the reconstruction of society" (1991, 5; see also S. Cohen 1993). Yet other criminologists want to extend these rights to animals, arguing that harm to animals is a crime (Beirne 1994). This movement is gaining popularity among animal interest groups as well (e.g., PETA). Gary Yourofsky, the founder of ADAPTT (Animals Deserve Absolute Protection Today and Tomorrow), has been arrested thirteen times in an effort to draw attention to animal rights (see Box 2.1).

Marxist conflict theorists are furthest away from the view that law should define the content of crime. Instead, they argue that any behavior that causes harm is a crime (Reiman [1979] 2007). Expanding Sutherland's definition (1949a), Michalowski (1985) used the term *analogous social injury*, which includes harm caused by acts or conditions that are legal but produce similar consequences to those produced by illegal acts. For example, promoting and selling alcoholic beverages and cigarettes (described as "drug delivery systems"), though legal, still produce considerable social, health, and psychological problems. Other substances that are illegal, such as marijuana, may produce less negative consequences. The insidious injuries produced by the Johns-Manville asbestos company's knowing exposure of millions to deadly asbestos dust, in spite of the company's own research evidence that showed asbestos has carcinogenic effects (Calhoun and Hiller 1986), would be a good example of producing "analogous social injury."

Beyond Consensus and Conflict

Going beyond consensus, pluralist conflict, and critical Marxist theorists, other criminologists have begun to redefine crime more broadly. One such approach has pluralist leanings, but instead of seeing established groups as significant, it sees the situational context and its constituent players as important. Crime is defined as a social event, involving many players, actors, and agencies. Thus, crimes "involve not only the actions of individual offenders, but the actions of other persons as well. In particular, they involve the actions of such persons as victims, bystanders and witnesses, law enforcement officers, and members of political society at large. A crime, in other words, is a particular set of interactions among offender(s), crime target(s), agent(s) of social control and society" (Gould, Kleck, and Gertz 1992, 4; see also 2001). This broader view of crime highlights the complexities associated with defining crime by recognizing its socially constructed nature.

Another recent reassessment of the definition of crime that takes into account the total context of powerful relations and the situational context comes from postmodernist-influenced constitutive criminologists (Henry and Milovanovic 1996, 2001; Arrigo and Young 1996). Postmodernism is a perspective that rejects claims that any body of knowledge is true or can be true. Instead, its advocates believe that "claims to know" are simply power plays by some to dominate others. These theorists advocate an anarchy of knowledge giving the oppressed, marginalized, and excluded their own voice to define what harms them rather than having others claim to know how to protect them. For example, consistent with the important place given to power, Henry and Milovanovic see constitutive criminology as "the framework for reconnecting crime and its control with the society from which it is conceptually and institutionally constructed by human agents. . . . Crime is both in and of society" (1991, 307). They define crime as an agency's ability to make a negative difference to others (1996, 104). Thus, they assert, "Crimes are nothing less than moments in the expression of power such that those who are subjected to these expressions are denied their own contribution to the encounter and often to future encounters. Crime then is the power to deny others . . . in which those subject to the power of another suffer the pain of being denied their own humanity, the power to make a difference" (1994, 119).

Perhaps the most dramatic call to expand the definition of crime comes from Larry Tifft and Dennis Sullivan (2001), who argue that the hierarchical structure and social arrangements of society produce harm that evades the legal definition and that these harms must be brought back in. They recognize that doing so will render many contemporary legal modes of production and distribution criminal, as will many of our criminal justice system's responses to crime, based on the harms that they produce. They call for a "needs-based" system of justice that focuses on the concept of equality of well-being as the objective.

It is clear that criminological approaches to crime have come a long way from the simplistic idea that crime is behavior defined by law. Recent ideas suggest that far more is involved than law. These ideas resurrect the central role of harm, the victim, and the context. Importantly, they even suggest that law itself can create crime, not merely by definition but by its use of power over others. Together, these definitions express the increasingly broad range of conceptions of crime that criminologists now share. Even though the division between consensus and conflict theory is helpful to gain an overall sense of different definitions, it does not present an integrated approach. But there is one attempt to define crime that, with modification, helps us overcome many of the difficulties so far identified.

Hagan's Pyramid of Crime

From the previous discussion, it is clear that there is little agreement among criminologists about what constitutes crime. One very useful conception of crime was provided by Canadian criminologist John Hagan in his notion of crime and deviance as "a continuous variable" (1977, 1985). Explaining this concept, Hagan notes that rule breaking ranges from minor deviance from accepted standards of behavior, such as public drunkenness or dress-code violations, to highly offensive acts that involve serious harm, such as urban terrorism or mass murder. He defines crime as "a kind of deviance, which in turn consists of variation from a social norm that is proscribed by criminal law" (1985, 49). His definition includes three measures of seriousness, each ranging from low and weak to high and strong.

First is the degree of consensus or agreement, the degree to which people accept an act as being right or wrong. Most Americans believe that hijacking a plane and crashing it into a building is very wrong. In contrast, few people consider a sixteen-year-old skipping school seriously wrong (see table 2.1). All crimes can be ranked on a scale of seriousness between these extremes. Hagan offers as the first measure of seriousness the degree of consensus or agreement about the wrongfulness of an act, which "can range from confusion and apathy, through levels of disagreement to conditions of general agreement" (1985, 49).

FIGURE 2.1   Hagan's Pyramid of Crime

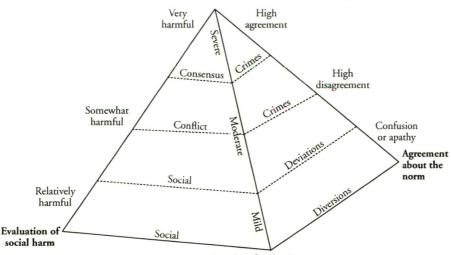

SOURCE: Hagan 1977, p. 14.

TABLE 2.1 The Seriousness of Crimes

Conventional Crimes
Severity Score and Offense

72.1	Planting a bomb in a public building that explodes, killing twenty people.	15.5	Breaking into a bank at night and stealing $100,000.
52.8	A man forcibly rapes a women who dies from her injuries.	12.2	Paying a witness to give false testimony in a criminal trial.
43.2	Robbery at gunpoint during which the victim is shot to death.	12.0	Intentionally injuring a victim resulting in hospitalization.
39.2	A man stabs his wife who dies from the injuries.	10.5	Smuggling marijuana into the country for resale.
35.7	Stabbing a victim to death.	10.4	Intentionally hitting a victim with a lead pipe resulting in hospitalization.
33.8	Running a narcotics ring.		
27.9	A woman stabs her husband and he dies from the injuries.	10.3	Illegally selling barbiturates, such as sleeping pills, to others for resale.
26.3	An armed person hijacks a plane and demands to be flown to another country.	10.3	Operating a store that knowingly sells stolen property.
25.9	A man forcibly rapes a woman.	9.7	Breaking into a school and stealing equipment worth $1,000.
24.9	Intentionally setting fire to a building, causing $100,000 of damage.	9.7	Walking into a museum and stealing a painting worth $1,000.
22.9	A parent beats his young child with his fists and the child requires hospitalization.	9.6	Breaking into a home and stealing $1,000.
		9.4	Robbing a victim of $10 at gunpoint without physical harm resulting.
21.2	Kidnapping a victim.		
20.7	Selling heroin to others for resale.	9.3	Threatening to seriously injure a victim.
19.5	Smuggling heroin into the country.	8.5	Selling marijuana to others for resale.
19.5	Killing a victim by reckless driving.	7.9	A teenage boy beats his father with his fists resulting in hospitalization.
17.9	Robbing a victim of $10 at gunpoint, resulting in the victim being wounded.	7.5	Robbing a victim armed with a lead pipe without injury resulting.
16.9	A man drags a woman into an alley and tears her clothes but flees before causing further harm.	7.3	Threatening a victim with a weapon, receiving $10 with no harm to the victim.
16.4	Attempting to kill a victim with a gun, which misfires and the victim escapes.	7.3	Breaking into a department store and stealing $1,000 worth of merchandise.
15.9	A teenage boy beats his mother with his fists and she requires hospitalization.	7.2	Signing someone else's name on a check and cashing it.

(continues)

TABLE 2.1 *(continued)*

Conventional Crimes
Severity Score and Offense

6.9	Stealing property worth $1,000 from outside a building.	2.1	A woman engages in prostitution.
6.5	Using heroin.	1.9	Making an obscene phone call.
6.4	Getting customers for a prostitute.	1.8	A minor being drunk in public.
6.3	Failure to appear at court while on bail for a serious offense.	1.8	Being a knowing customer in a place holding illegal gambling.
5.4	Possessing heroin for personal use.	1.7	Stealing $10 worth of property from outside a building.
5.1	A man runs his hands over the body of a female victim, then runs away.	1.6	Being a customer in a brothel.
		1.6	A male over 16 has sexual relations with a willing female under age 16.
5.1	Using force to rob a victim of $10 but without causing injury.	1.6	Taking barbiturates without a prescription.
4.9	Snatching a handbag containing $10.	1.5	Intentional shoving or pushing without resulting injury.
4.8	A man exposes himself in public.	1.4	Smoking marijuana.
4.6	Carrying a gun illegally.	1.3	A consensual homosexual act.
4.4	Picking a victim's pocket of $100.	1.1	Disturbing a neighbor with noisy behavior.
4.2	Attempting to break into a home but leaving when disturbed by police.	1.1	Taking bets on numbers.
		1.1	Loitering after being told to move on by police.
3.8	Turning in a false fire alarm.	0.9	Teenager under 16 runs away from home.
3.6	Knowingly passing a bad check.	0.8	Being drunk in public.
3.6	Stealing property worth $100 from outside a building.	0.7	Teenager under 16 breaks curfew laws.
3.5	Running illegal gambling premises.	0.6	Trespassing in the backyard of a home.
2.5	Knowingly carrying an illegal knife.	0.3	Being a vagrant.
2.2	Stealing $10 worth of merchandise from a department store.	0.2	Youth under 16 plays hooky from school.

White-Collar Crimes
Severity Score and Offense

14.1	A doctor cheats on claims to a federal health insurance plan for patient service.	13.0	A factory knowingly gets rid of its waste in a way that pollutes a city water supply.
13.9	A legislator takes a bribe from a company to vote for a law favoring the company.	12.0	A police officer takes a bribe not to interfere with an illegal gambling operation.

(continues)

TABLE 2.1   *(continued)*

White-Collar Crimes
Severity Score and Offense

10.0	A government official intentionally hinders the investigation of a criminal offense.	6.5	An employer refuses to hire a qualified person because of the person's race.
9.6	A police officer knowingly makes a false arrest.	6.3	An employee embezzles $1,000 from the employer.
9.5	A public official takes $1,000 of public money for personal use.	5.4	A real estate agent refuses to sell a house to a person because of the person's race.
9.2	Several large companies illegally fix the retail prices of their products.	5.3	Loaning money at an illegally high interest rate.
8.6	Performing an illegal abortion.	4.5	Cheating on federal income tax.
8.2	Knowing that a shipment of cooking oil is bad, a store owner decides to sell it anyway, resulting in one person being sick and treated by a doctor.	3.7	A labor union official illegally threatens to organize a strike if an employer hires nonunion workers.
7.7	Knowing that a shipment of cooking oil is bad, a store owner decides to sell it anyway.	3.2	An employer illegally threatens to fire employees if they join a labor union.
7.4	Illegally getting monthly welfare checks.	1.9	A store owner intentionally puts "large" eggs in containers marked "extra large."

SOURCE: Adapted from Bureau of Justice Statistics 1983.

A second dimension of Hagan's approach is the severity of society's response in law. This may range from social avoidance or an official warning, through fines and imprisonment, to expulsion from society or ultimately the death penalty. Hagan argues, "The more severe the penalty prescribed, and the more extensive the support for this sanction, the more serious is the societal evaluation of the act" (ibid.). Clearly, the sentencing to death of a convicted child murderer in Utah and the state's execution of the offender by firing squad would rank higher on the scale of social response than imprisonment of a small businessperson for tax evasion.

Hagan's third dimension is the relative seriousness of crime based on the harm it has caused. He argues that some acts, like drug use, gambling, and prostitution, are victimless crimes that harm only the participants. Victimless crimes, or crimes without victims, are consensual crimes involving lawbreaking that does not harm anyone other than perhaps the perpetrator (Schur 1965).[1] Many crimes, such as domestic violence, harm others, and some crimes harm more than one person at a time, as in the Beechnut Corporation's export of sugar water as 100 percent apple juice for babies or the export of infant formula that denied third world babies necessary nutrients, exacerbating their malnourishment (Ermann and Clements 1984).

Hagan illustrates the integration of these three dimensions in his "pyramid of crime" (see figure 2.1). On the consensus dimension is the degree of agreement among people about the wrongfulness of an act. On the societal response dimension is the severity of penalties elicited in response to the act. Finally, on the harm dimension is social evaluation of the harm an act inflicts on others. This can range from crimes of violence such as murder or terrorism at the peak down to victimless crimes at the base. Hagan claims:

> The three measures of seriousness are closely associated . . . the more serious acts of deviance, which are most likely to be called "criminal," are likely to involve (1) broad agreement about the wrongfulness of such acts, (2) a severe social response, and (3) an evaluation of being very harmful. However, the correlation between these three dimensions certainly is not perfect, and . . . in regard to many acts that are defined as crimes, there is disagreement as to their wrongfulness, an equivocal social response, and uncertainty in perceptions of their harmfulness. (1985, 50)

Although Hagan goes further than most criminologists in attempting an integrated definition of crime, we believe that his analysis can be improved by adding three more dimensions and by configuring the pyramid display into a "crime prism."

From Hagan's Pyramid to the Prism of Crime

We suggest that Hagan's pyramid is incomplete because it neglects public awareness of crime—that is, the realization that one has been a victim. Crime takes many forms, all of which involve harm, but not all of those harmed necessarily realize they have been victimized. We have already seen that participants in victimless crimes may claim that the criminal label is wrong. In the case of victims of government and corporate crimes, it is often a long time before the victims become aware that they have been harmed, and many never realize it! For example, the effects of environmental crimes may be so slow and diffused that no one notices any harm or change in the environment. Yet over a period of years a particular area may become uninhabitable due to environmental crimes, as happened in the case of New York's infamous Love Canal near Niagara Falls, in which the Hooker Chemical Corporation dumped fifty-five-gallon drums of toxic waste. When the area was subsequently developed by an unwitting school board and settled as a residential area, children and residents were, over several decades, exposed to noxious fumes and surfacing chemicals resulting in birth defects, liver disease, and emotional disorders (Mokhiber 1988). More recently, in Orlando several elementary schools and neighborhoods were built on top of former military bombing ranges. Large piles of unexploded bombs, hand grenades, missiles, and other ordinance have been found on school grounds and in surrounding neighborhoods. Who knows what long-term health consequences may result? Not surprisingly, house values have plummeted, forcing families to incur considerable losses. Such crimes can result in insidious injuries when the links between the causes and the effects are obscure, take a long time to appear, affect only a segment of the population, result in increased risk of injury or disease, and are widely dispersed through the population (Calhoun and Hiller 1986). Thus, we argue that crime can range from being "obvious" or "readily apparent" to "relatively hidden" and, finally, so "obscure" that it is accepted by many as normal, even though it harms its victims (e.g., environmental crimes, racism, and patriarchy). Hagan acknowledges this but does not include the measure of obscurity as one of his dimensions.

A second missing, though implied, part of the pyramid of crime is the number of victims. If only one person is affected by a crime, this is certainly tragic and serious, as in the example of a person shot to death. But this crime is qualitatively different from, say, the Japanese religious cult that murdered many people by intentionally releasing poisonous fumes in the subway system or the deliberate terrorist act of Islamic fundamentalists on 9/11. These two additional dimensions, visibility and numbers harmed, are implied in surveys that depict the perceived seriousness of various acts. Note the difference in seriousness rating for different types of terrorism in table 1.1. Absolute numbers of victims influence a society's perception as to the seriousness of crime.

A third limitation of Hagan's pyramid relates to his dimension of seriousness of response. This dimension fails to capture the probability or likelihood that a convicted offender will receive a serious response even when the law sets such a penalty. Crimes of the powerless are far more likely to receive the full weight of the law than are crimes of the powerful. For example, the average prison term given for those convicted in the savings and loan scandal of the 1980s was 2.4 years, whereas the average bank robber gets 7.8 years. Further, more than 75 percent of the cases against those corporate executives were dropped. Rarely are charges against bank robbers dropped (Pizzo and Muolo 1993, 26; Calavita and Pontell 1993). Another limitation of Hagan's analysis is its visual structure. The way that it is laid out does not allow other elements (such as the ones we have noted) to be included. The pyramid suggests that crimes for which conflict exists about their criminality are only somewhat harmful. Some crimes may be extremely harmful yet still not be seen as harms by society, perhaps because the media present them in a way that favors the perpetrators. Until recently, this was the case with crimes of gender, such as sexual harassment and date rape, in which the male offender was shown as having poor judgment but not intending harm. It is clear to us that there is not always consensus about the seriousness of such actions as corporate crimes (such as pollution from toxic waste, deaths from avoidable faulty product manufacture, and deliberate violations of health and safety regulations). We should be perfectly clear that corporate crimes can be extremely harmful. This is in spite of the moderate societal response to such acts and the conflict between interest groups in society over the need for health and safety regulations and the like and whether their violation constitutes a crime. For example, corporations historically oppose health and safety regulations if they slow down production or add to cost, depicting consumer and environmental protections as government interference in industry. Consumer protection groups such as Ralph Nader's Common Cause earn a living from disputing this point.

Crime Prism

To solve the problems with Hagan's pyramid, we have redesigned the visual structure of this depiction of crime by making it a double pyramid, or what we call the "crime prism" (see figure 2.2). A further refinement of this concept appears in Henry and Lanier (1998). In our schema, we place an inverted pyramid beneath the first pyramid. The top pyramid represents the highly visible crimes that are typically crimes of the powerless committed in public. These include crimes such as robbery, theft, auto theft, burglary, assault, murder, stranger rape, and arson. The bottom, inverted, pyramid represents relatively invisible crimes. These include a variety of crimes of the powerful, such as offenses by government officials, corporations, and organizations, as well as crimes by people committed through their occupations, such as fraud and embezzlement, and even some crimes such as date rape, sexual harassment, domestic violence, sexism, racism, ageism, and crimes of hate. These are crimes typically conducted in private contexts, such as organizations and workplaces, that involve violations of trusted relationships. Together, crimes of the powerless and crimes of the powerful constitute the visible and invisible halves of our prism of crime.

FIGURE 2.2   The Crime Prism

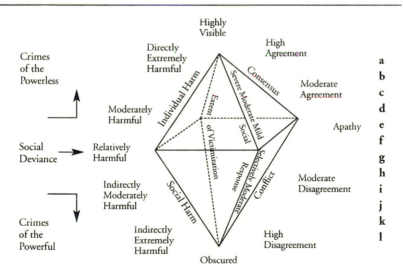

We use the term *prism* not only because of the visual appearance of the figure. Just as a prism is used to analyze a continuous spectrum, in our case the crime prism can be used to analyze the spectrum of important dimensions that make up crime. We provide new variables: social agreement, probable social response, individual and social harm, and extent of victimization. Each of these varies by degrees, and depending on the particular crime in question. The prism, like a lens, also means that two people may view the same act quite differently. For example, a person's life experiences may cause him or her to have a different worldview. A crime victim may view an act more seriously than a nonvictim would. Our prior exposure to events enables us to filter and view them differently from one another.

Integrating the Dimensions

Now that we have briefly illustrated the dimensions of the crime prism, let us discuss the spatial location of a few examples. Take the earlier example of terrorism. Here, crime is obvious, highly visible, extremely harmful, and noncontroversial with regard to the measure of consensus and conflict. Smith and Orvis (1993) indicate that this kind of crime can be horrifying to the sensibilities of virtually all people, though directly harming relatively few (e.g., the Oklahoma City bombing). Societal response and outrage to this type of crime are immediate and pointed. Law enforcement agencies devote all available resources and form special task forces to deal with these crimes. Punishment is severe and can include the death penalty. As a result, such crimes would be placed on the top or very near the apex of the prism, at point *a*. The more people harmed, the greater the government and social response (e.g., the September 11 tragedies). If fewer were harmed, and if the act is less visible, then the rank of the crime on the extent of victimization scale moves down.

Toward the middle of the prism, but still in its upper half, are violent acts of individual crime. These are also readily apparent as being criminal. They were traditionally called *mala in se*, meaning "acts bad in themselves," or inherently evil; they are universally recognized as being crimes. Crimes of this type would include homicide, rape, incest, and so on. Relatively few people are hurt by each act, yet societal reaction is severe and involves little controversy. Law enforcement considers these crimes its top priority. Sanctions are very severe, ranging from lengthy penal confinement to death. Beneath these come acts of robbery, burglary, larceny, and vandalism, perhaps at location *b* or *c*.

At the very center is where social deviations and social diversions would fall. Deviance, the higher placed of the two, includes acts such as public drunkenness and juvenile-status offenses (acts that if committed by an adult would be legal). It should be noted, however, that these are small-scale or low-value violations. Beneath the social deviations are what Hagan calls social diversions of unconventional lifestyles or sexual practices and so on. These offenses are relatively harmless and are met with confusion or apathy, a lack of consensus about their criminal status, and little formal law enforcement response. Examples would be certain "Goth" practices and skateboarding in public places (our earlier skateboarding police reaction notwithstanding). These will be located at *f* on the prism.

As we move into the lower section of the prism, the obscurity of the crime increases. Its harm becomes less direct. Conflict over its criminal definition increases, and the seriousness of society's response becomes more selective. Acts that have been called *mala prohibita* are positioned here. *Mala prohibita* crimes are those that have been created by legislative action (i.e., they are bad because they have been created or legislated as being bad). *Mala prohibita* definitions of crime necessarily involve a social, ecological, and temporal context. As we have seen, these acts may be criminal in one society but not criminal in another. Likewise, an act that is criminal in one county or state may be legal in another (e.g., prostitution). Such crimes also change over time. Crimes that do not reflect a consensus in society move toward the lower inverted part of the prism. Often, fines and "second chances" are given to violators of these laws. For example, on February 2, 2008, the manager of an Abercrombie and Fitch store was cited for displaying a corporate poster showing a scantily clad, but not nude, young couple. He was not arrested but cited on a misdemeanor obscenity charge: "The Class One misdemeanor was issued to the manager because there is no legal way to issue a summons to a corporate entity in such circumstances. The manager was not arrested but faces a fine of up to $2,000 and as much as a year in jail, if convicted" (Stone 2008).

At a lower level, crime is unapparent (hidden) and indirect yet hurts many people over an extended time period. For example, in 1987 and 1988, 11,319 savings and loan cases were referred to the Justice Department for possible criminal prosecution. It has been estimated that criminal activity was involved in 70 to 80 percent of the thrift institution failures (Calavita and Pontell 1993). Yet the impact of this type of crime is diffused and societal reactions diluted. Law enforcement is rarely equipped to handle it. As we mentioned earlier, more than three-quarters of the cases were dropped. Prison sentences are rarely given in these type of crimes; the more common sanctions are fines, restitution settlements, censure, and signs of disapproval. Regulatory agencies rather than conventional police agencies are responsible for law enforcement. Unless the offense is made public, corporations and their trade associations often handle these problems through their own disciplinary mechanisms. These offenses will be located at point *i* on the prism.

At the final level, crimes are so hidden that many may deny their existence and others may argue as to whether they are in fact crimes. Sexism, for example, is an institutionalized type of crime. It is patriarchal, subdued, and so ingrained into the fabric of a society as to often go unnoticed, yet the impact is very influential. Former mayor of Detroit Kwame Kilpatrick, a onetime rising star and Detroit's youngest elected leader, was charged with perjury after sending and later lying about sending sexually explicit text messages to a top aide. In 2008 he agreed to a plea bargain that involved his resigning from office. An ethics "reformer" and antiprostitution governor of New York, Eliot Spitzer resigned from his office after being linked in news reports to a prostitution ring. Gary Condit lost his U.S. Senate seat due to an affair with murdered intern Chandra Levy, although someone else was later charged with her murder, and Bob Packwood was forced to resign his U.S. Senate seat as a result of sexual improprieties. Yet no criminal charges were filed in these cases. The law enforcement community generally scoffs at consideration of these harms as criminal. These acts are rarely, if ever, punished as crimes. Those sanctions that occur generally involve social disapproval (some organized groups will even voice approval) and verbal admonishment, although occasionally symbolically severe sentences are given.

It is clear that a vast range of different crimes can be located on the crime prism. To better understand the prism, attempt to identify some different types of crimes and consider where they would be positioned. In the next section we consider how the prism of crime concept would apply to school violence, a crime that covers a wide range of levels and locations on the crime prism.

Application of the Prism to the Problem of School Violence

In analyzing school violence, the tradition has been to focus on interpersonal violence: students versus students, students toward their teachers, or aggressors against both students and teachers. In terms of our prism, a focus on the visible harms of violence between students would be located in the top half of the prism but fail to recognize the broader dimensions of the crime that extend into the lower levels of the prism. We argue that the complexity of crimes like school violence defies such a simplistic framing. It fails to address the wider context of school violence, the wider forms of violence in schools, and the important interactive and causal effects arising from the confluence of these forces. What is demanded is an integrated, multilevel definition of the problem that will lead to a multilevel causal analysis and a comprehensive policy response that takes account of the full range of constitutive elements (Henry 2009). It is our view that the prism provides us with a conceptual framework to define the full dimensional scope of the problem.

The Paucity of the School Violence Concept

Public analysis of social problems tends to be framed very narrowly. Violence is visible and manifest among school students, so it is assumed that they constitute the scope of the problem. Yet any analysis of school violence that looks at simply one factor, such as human fallibility, gun availability, or cultural toxicity, is in grave danger of missing the wider constitutive elements.

Violence is generally defined as the use of force toward another that results in harm. Simplistic versions limit the concept to "extreme physical force" (Champion 1997, 128; Rush [1994] 2000, 54), which may include intimidation by the threat of force (Bureau of Justice Statistics 1998). Omitted here are several critical elements of harm: (1) emotional and psychological pain that results from domination of some over others; (2) harms by institutions or agencies to individuals; (3) the violence of social processes that produces a systemic social injury, such as that perpetuated through institutionalized racism and sexism; and (4) the "symbolic violence" of domination (Bourdieu 1977) that brings coercion through the power exercised in hierarchical relationships.

In the school context, studies of violence typically refer to student-on-student and student-on-teacher acts of physical harm or interpersonal violence: "Violence refers to the threat or use of physical force with the intention of causing physical injury, damage, or intimidation of another person" (Elliott, Hamburg, and Williams 1998, 13–14). This definition clearly refers to acts located in the upper half of our prism. However, considering the lower half of the prism is suggestive because it draws our attention to other hidden dimensions of the problem that we have described as the hidden crimes of the structurally powerful in society (Henry and Lanier 1998). It also sensitizes us to the symbolic social harms that deny humanity through violating human rights. In the school context these harms, located in the lower half of the prism, include harms committed by teachers on students and by school administrators on both students and teachers. They also include the organization of schooling when it creates harm to both student creativity and the educational process. Conventional definitions of school violence, located in the upper half of the prism, neglect harmful institutionalized social and educational practices. These include acts and processes of institutionalized racism and sexism, discrimination, labeling, and tracking (Yogan 2000); authoritarian discipline (Adams 2000); militaristic approaches to school security (Thompkins 2000; Pepinsky 2000); sexual harassment; and predation, all of which would be located in the lower half of the prism.

For example, gender discrimination has been shown to create harmful effects on female students' learning experience. When teachers favor male students over females, because of their seemingly extroverted classroom participation, they disadvantage females and oppress their potential development, which can lead to feelings of inadequacy, anger, and long-term depression. Such practices are not defined as violence, but they are symbolically violent with long-term harmful consequences.

Consider, as further examples, a school administration that exercises arbitrary, authoritarian discipline or teachers who "get by" without their best effort and lack commitment to their students' education or the message conveyed to students about "trust" and "freedom" of educational thought when we deploy metal detectors, video cameras, identity tags, drug-sniffing dogs, and guards to "secure" that freedom (Adams 2000; Thompkins 2000). This "hidden curriculum" can have a significant negative impact on students' moral and social development (Yogan and Henry 2000). Yet these strategies are at the forefront of recent discussions of the many school massacres.

At a broader level, consider the harm of inequitable school funding, such that one school will receive better funding due to its location in a wealthy area compared to a school located in a poverty-stricken urban setting. Finally, consider the harm created by celebrating competitive success while condemning academic failure; is it any wonder that "children who do poorly in school, lack educational motivation, and feel alienated are the most likely to engage in criminal acts"? (Siegel 1998, 197–198). And this analysis does not even begin to address how competitive success corrupts the morality of the successful, driving them to win at all costs, regardless of the harm they cause to others in the process (Nicholson 2000; Staples 2000).

Toward an Expansive Integrated Concept of School Violence

Since we first wrote this text in 1998, the term *school violence* has taken on a whole new meaning. The list of shocking tragedies now referred to as "rampage school shootings" (K. Newman et al. 2004) involving what the media describe as "crazed" killers who turn on their teachers, classmates, and others continues to grow: Columbine, Beslan, North Ossetia in Russia, Virginia Tech, Northern Illinois University—and other tragedies will likely follow. Each of these tragedies arouses shock and outrage. As we argued above, a critical issue in understanding crime is the role of the media in framing it and communicating it. News events are now displayed, sometimes in "real time" as they happen, everywhere at once. The media have also contributed to the proliferation of "copycat" crimes. Communications, coupled with globalization, make instant "celebrities" out of the disturbed shooters. Other misguided and troubled youth may identify with the killers. Closely related, some Web sites have made martyrs and celebrities out of those individuals who shoot up our schools and universities. In addition, we have become somewhat desensitized to these actions due to their frequency. We are no longer as shocked by a school shooting as we were when Columbine occurred in 1999. Interestingly, analysis of the media coverage of school shootings in the period 1997–2001 has shown that its framing was initially "an issue of concern primarily to the present-tense concerns of the communities in which they occurred, but over time, the shootings were increasingly discussed in terms of their societal impact, both present and future." However, toward the end of this period, "the societal frame again decreased, while community-level discussions appeared to increase" (Muschert and Carr 2006, 760).

Because of the omission of these broader dimensions of school violence, we are also missing much of the content and causes of violence in schools. We are blind to the part played by this wider context of violence in shaping the more visible forms of interpersonal physical violence manifested by some students. A more inclusive integrated concept of school violence is necessary. With regard to the perpetrators of harm, the concept of "offender," used for those who exercise the power to harm others, is limiting because it assumes that only individuals offend. Yet harms can operate at many levels, from individual, organization, and corporation to community, society, and nation-state. Further, the exercise of the power to harm, as mentioned earlier, can also be accomplished by social processes—such as sexism, ageism, and racism—that go beyond the individual acts of people. The exercise of power to harm others by some agency or process also takes place in a spatial social context. Even though the term *school violence* implies that the spatial location is the "school building, on the school grounds or on a school bus" (Bureau of Justice Statistics 1998), such a limited definition denies the interconnections between the school context and the wider society of which it is apart. It ignores the ways in which these acts of violence permeate social and geographical space.

In short, existing fragmented approaches to school violence fail to recognize that what may appear as an outburst in the school is merely one manifestation of more systemic societal problems. These may begin in, or be significantly impacted by, activities in other spatial locations such as households, public streets, local neighborhoods, communities, private corporations, public organizations, national political arenas, the global marketplace, or the wider political economy. As such, the social and institutional space of the school is merely one forum for the appearance of a more general systemic problem of societal violence.

The Pyramidal Analysis of Dimensions of School Violence

In this section we will relate school violence to the dimensions of the prism. How does the acknowledgment of multiple dimensions of defining school violence affect our analysis? First is the dimension of the relative seriousness of the crime based on the harm it has caused. Some acts, like alcohol use and truancy, are victimless crimes in that they harm only the participants; others, such as the high-profile shootings in schools, harm more than one person at a time, and that pain can extend to the victims' relatives, friends, and even their community (see Nicholson 2000). Second is the degree of moral consensus or agreement as to whether an act is right or wrong that "can range from confusion and apathy, through levels of disagreement, to conditions of general agreement" (J. Hagan 1985, 49). Thus, although there is consensus that drugs should not be in schools, the consensus is much greater against heroin and cocaine than marijuana and against all three compared to alcohol and cigarettes (see Venturelli 2000). The third dimension is the severity of society's formal response. Severity may range from social ostracism by school peers toward their fellow students to informal reprimands by teachers, official warnings, expulsion and exclusion from school, prosecution, imprisonment, and ultimately to the death penalty.

As we have seen, school violence takes many forms, all of which involve harm, but not all of those harmed necessarily realize they have been victimized. This relates then to the visibility dimension of the crime prism. For example, it is difficult to see the negative effects of tracking, yet the "track system" has been shown to reinforce class and racial segregation; over time this practice operates as a crime of repression, limiting the intellectual, social, and moral development of those subject to it (Yogan 2000). The harmful effects of this practice are obscure and may take a long time to appear (in lowered expectations for self, poor self-esteem, and so on). The visibility of some aspects of school violence is an important dimension because it is partly a reflection of the force of existing legal definitions, themselves shaped by powerful economic, political, and class interests. These interests, in turn, partly reflect the commercial interests of the mass media, which limit their framing of the crime. In part, they reflect the popular culture's trivialization and sensationalization of direct

FIGURE 2.3   Why People Fail to Report Crimes to the Police

Crime	Most frequent reasons for not reporting to the police
Violent Crime	
Rape	Private or personal matter,* 18% Police inefficient, ineffective, or biased,* 13% Offender unsuccessful,* 13%
Robbery	Object recovered, offender unsuccessful, 19% Lack of proof, 13% Police would not want to be bothered, 11%
Aggravated assault	Private or personal matter, 22% Offender unsuccessful, 16% Lack of proof, 9%
Simple assault	Private or personal matter, 26% Offender unsuccessful, 19% Reported to another official, 13%
Theft	
Personal larceny with contact	Object recovered, offender unsuccessful, 25% Lack of proof, 22% Police would not want to be bothered, 11%
Personal larceny without contact	Object recovered, offender unsuccessful, 28% Reported to another official, 18% Lack of proof, 11%
Household Crime	
Burglary	Object recovered, offender unsuccessful, 24% Lack of proof, 11% Not aware crime occurred until later, 11%
Household larceny	Object recovered, offender unsuccessful, 31% Police would not want to be bothered, 12% Lack of proof, 11%
Motor vehicle theft	Object recovered, offender unsuccessful, 36% Police would not want to be bothered, 10% Lack of proof, 7%

‹ The most common reasons for not reporting violent crimes to the police are that the crime was a personal or private matter and that the offender was not successful.

‹ The most common reasons for not reporting thefts are that the object was recovered or the offender was unsuccessful, the theft was reported to another official, and lack of proof.

‹ The most common reasons that victims of household crimes did not report to the police are because the object was recovered or the offender was unsuccessful, the police would not want to be bothered, and lack of proof.

*Estimate is based on about 10 or fewer sample cases.

SOURCE: Bureau of Justice Statistics 1993, p. 33.

interpersonal "true crimes" in preference to complex, diffuse social harms and injuries that have become institutionalized, compartmentalized, privatized, and justified via the legitimate goals of the organization.

In light of the pyramid discussion and analysis, an expansive integrated definition and reconception of school violence allow us to reframe our analysis of types of school violence. Types of school violence can be distinguished by the level of their perpetrators within the social structure, and these in turn reflect their positioning at different levels within the prism. Five levels of violence are identified, though the accuracy of the distinction between levels is less important than that the range of levels be addressed:

Level 1: Student-on-student; student-on-teacher; student-on-school.
Level 2: Teacher-on-student; administrator-on-student; administrator-on-teacher; teacher/administrator-on-parents; parent-on-teacher/administrator.
Level 3: School board–on-school/parent; school district–on-school/parent; community-on-school/parent; local political decisions–on-school/parent.
Level 4: State and national educational policy–on-school; state and national juvenile justice policy–on-student; media and popular culture–on-student/ administrator; corporate exploitation–on-student; national and state policies on guns and drugs.
Level 5: Harmful social processes and practices that pervade each of the above levels. Here social processes are the patterns of interaction that over time take on the appearance of a natural order or social reality existing above the individuals whose actions constitute that structure. (Henry 2000)

Discussion of school violence tends to be restricted to level 1 and some aspects of level 4. Even within level 1, some important distinctions can be made. In contrast to the excessive discussion of level 1 and some of level 4, there has been virtually no discussion of levels 2, 3, and 5, which, given the interrelations among these types, represents a glaring deficiency.

Causal Implications of the Prismatic Analysis of School Violence

This expansive integrated approach to defining school violence allows us to better identify different types of school violence. But it also raises the question of whether the different levels of violence manifested in the school setting are interrelated. In other words, are the different levels of violence in school causally interrelated, such that invisible institutional violence at the level of, say, administrators and teachers is generative of visible violence among school students? There is growing evidence that lethal school violence is the result of multiple causes. In his book *Lost Boys*, Garabino says, "The origins of lethal violence lie in a complex set of influences. . . . No single factor . . . can provide the answer to the question of why kids kill" (1999, 13). Similarly, as Katherine S. Newman and colleagues state in *Rampage: The Social Roots of School Shootings*: "Any particular episode arises from multiple causes interacting with one another. . . . This approach is useful because . . . it combines elements at the individual, community and national levels, providing a more realistic understanding of how each one contributes to these explosions of rage. Take away any one of these elements, and the shootings . . . would not have happened" (2004, 229). Most recently, Muschert maintains, "School shooting incidents need to be understood as resulting from a constellation of contributing causes, none of which is sufficient in itself to explain a shooting" (2007, 68).

Therefore, if we are going to examine school violence comprehensively, or any one form of it, such as school shootings, we need an expansive, not a restrictive, definition; we need to see school violence as the outcome of several processes, and we need to look beneath the obvious "factors" to see them as points on a continuum. Although in some senses it is valuable to distinguish between types of school violence, such as the rampage school shootings perpetrated by white male teenagers in suburban and rural communities that target the school as a symbol of the community and the inner-city urban violence that escalates through interpersonal and gang-related disputes over time (K. Newman et al. 2004), it is also important to recognize that these may be different manifestations of a similar confluence of violent and subviolent themes that permeate our society. In his examination *Violence and Nonviolence: Pathways to Understanding*, Gregg Barak has argued that in spite of clear evidence that violence is cumulatively interrelated across a range of societal levels, most analyses of it are "un-reflexive":

> Since violence takes many forms—individual, interpersonal, family, groups, mass, collective, organizational, bureaucratic, institutional, regional, national, international and structural—it makes sense to study the interrelations and interactions between these. Most analyses of violence, however, tend to focus on one particular form of violence, without much, if any, reflection on the other forms. In turn, these fragmented and isolated analyses seek to explain the workings of a given form of violence without trying to understand the common threads or roots that may link various forms of violence together. (2003, 39)

Although individuals contribute to these interrelated social processes, and analysis of cases of school violence has demonstrated that key factors involve depression and suicidal thoughts, the majority of such offenses have also involved the offender suffering marginalization and bullying over time (K. Newman et al. 2004). Indeed, it is the collective and cumulative repetition of actions by different people that creates harm to others. In the context of school violence, these harm-producing processes comprise not only individual and group actions by other students but also the practices and policies of the school, or what Welsh calls the "school climate" (2000). They can include the policies and practices of school boards and their detrimental effects on school districts and the local politics of communities. At a broader level, the collective actors can operate on the state and national level to include educational policy. An example would be the decision to expand prison-building programs at the expense of school building (as California has done, as we show in the next chapter), to hire corrections officers rather than schoolteachers, and even to submit to the apparent "economy of scale" that leads to building large schools over small ones when all the evidence suggests that they are more alienating and more crimino-genic. Although these collective and policy decisions may seem distant from the day-to-day activities of the school, their shadow and effects reach long into the class-room and constitute part of the formative context for violence that is played out there. For example, Ronald Kramer (2000) distinguishes between three types of stu-dent violence: (1) predatory economic crimes, which involve the pursuit of material goals by any means, including violence; (2) drug-industry crimes, which involve vio-lent gang turf wars; and (3) social relationship violence from powerless, angry youths who use acts of violence to resolve issues of humiliation (see also Staples 2000; Cin-tron 2000; and K. Newman et al. 2004). This third type may be a manifestation of the deeper social processes of harm in the lower level of our prism. In addition, it has been argued that not all school students respond in the same way to the conditions that generate violence, even within level 1, and this has much to do with the influ-ence of class, race, and gender (Yogan and Henry 2000).

Thus, the prismatic definitional framework outlined above suggests that we need to take a much broader approach to examining the causes of school violence. Rather than operating simply on the individual analytic level that looks to psychological and situational explanations for why students act violently, we need to address the con-text of students' lives—their families, race, ethnicity, gender, and social class. We need to explore how these dimensions interconnect through social processes to shape and structure human thinking, moral development, and individual choices. We need to examine how these social forces shape school curricula, teaching practices, and ed-ucational policies. Thus, at a deeper level we should be concerned with identifying the ways parents and schools themselves harm the lives of students, and the ways they shape the content of young people's lives. Finally, at the wider level we need to examine the ways the culture and the economic, social, and political structure of American society are both reproduced and reproduce harmful processes. Although it may seem that this level has been addressed through the discussions, analysis, and attempt to legislate against "toxic culture," this is an inadequate approach to macro-level analysis. Discussion of cultural causes of school violence has focused on the role of violence in the media—in movies, in video games, and on the Internet—and on gun culture. The argument is that cultural violence amplifies young male aggressive tendencies. It devalues humans into symbolic object images of hate or derision, trains youth to use violent skills, celebrates death and destruction as positive values, and provides exciting and colorful role models who use violence as the solution to problems, glorifying the most powerful and destructive performances via news me-dia infotainment. Although these points may be true, it is not enough to simply blame toxic culture for poisoning kids' minds without also looking at the ways in which corporate America invests in the exploitation of violence for profit that feeds this cultural industry. A macroanalysis of "culture," therefore, has to connect that culture to the political economy of the society in which it is generated.

Policy Implications of the Prismatic Analysis of School Violence

The use of the prismatic analytical framework to defining crime may allow us to identify the multiple interrelated causes of such violence, but this also has implications for policy and practice. Indeed, it affects the societal response dimension of the prism. Such an analysis is likely to provide for a more comprehensive approach to policy that reaches deeper into the roots of systemic violence than superficial quick-fix responses. It allows us to see the interconnections between different types or levels of school violence and develop integrated policies designed to respond to them. An adequate policy response must be comprehensive, dealing simultaneously with each of the causes identified at each of the levels of definition. It must penetrate the built-in protections of systems that conceal their own practice from analysis and change. It must be reflexive enough to recognize that policy itself can be part of the problem rather than the solution; policy should be self-critical and self-correcting. Although this chapter does not allow us to expand on the immensity of the policy question called for by such an analysis, the question of "dispute resolution" can be indicative in illustrating how a restrictive versus an expansive definition of school violence would operate (see Adams 2000; Pepinsky 2000; Caulfield 2000; and Nicholson 2000).

FIGURE 2.4 Percentage of Crimes Reported to the Police, 2005

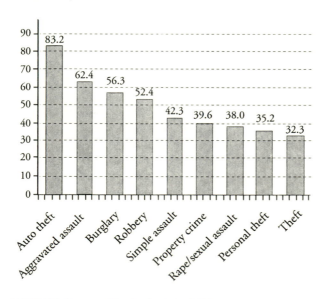

SOURCE: Bureau of Justice Statistics 2005.

Dispute Resolution

A narrow approach to school violence prevention policy would begin by assuming a level 1 definition of the problem. For example, kids are violent in schools because they are taught to use violence to solve their problems or, at best, are not taught non-violent ways of dealing with conflict. The simplistic restrictive policy response would suggest that dispute resolution training in techniques of nonviolent problem solving would be appropriate.

In contrast, an expansive definition and an integrated causal analysis would tie the use of violence by students to the use of symbolic and other forms of violence by adults, whether these are parents, teachers, administrators, or politicians. Instead of just implementing such training for students, it would argue for all school personnel, at every level, to undergo and practice nonviolent problem solving. Further, the school organization, curricula, and educational processes would be subject to the same "violence-cleansing" scrutiny to be replaced by what Pepinsky calls "educating for peace" rather than "educating about peace" (2000).

In short, viewed through the prism of crime the issue of school violence is not just about kids in schools; it is about the total coproduction of harm in our society by each of its constituent elements. To approach school violence another way is not merely shortsighted; it is to do more violence to those who have already suffered so much pain.

Other Implications

Considering the location of crimes on the prism makes three things apparent. First, the positioning varies over time as society becomes more or less aware of the crime and recognizes it as more or less serious. For example, consider the changing position of domestic violence and sexual harassment, both of which have recently begun to move from the lower half to the upper half of the prism. In contrast, other acts that were once in the upper half have become so common as to be hidden, are relatively harmless, and evoke neither public outcry nor societal response. For example, Edwin H. Sutherland and Donald R. Cressey (1966) pointed out that at different times it has been a crime to print a book professing the medical doctrine of blood circulation, to drive with reins, to sell coins to a foreigner, to keep gold in the house, or to write a check for less than a dollar.

Second, as our application of the crime prism to school violence has shown, harm created at different levels within an organization and across society is not isolated and unrelated. Rather, it has interrelated and cumulative effects. This means in any analysis of crime we need to be aware of the reciprocal effects of harm production in society and critical of attempts that treat them as isolated instances.

Third, the upper half of the prism (Hagan's pyramid) contains predominantly conventional crimes, or "street crimes," whereas the lower half of the prism contains the greater preponderance of white-collar crimes, or "suite crimes." Some have suggested that the characteristic of offenders committing the majority of the former crimes is that they are relatively powerless in society, whereas those committing the majority of the latter hold structural positions of power (Balkan, Berger, and Schmidt 1980; Box 1983). A central question is, What does being powerful affect? Is it the type of crime that is committed or the ability to escape the effects of the law? Perhaps more interestingly, how does the perpetration of crimes by the powerful affect the production of crimes by the powerless? Let us conclude our examination of definitions of crime by looking a little more closely at these two broad spheres of crime and what the criminological research about them reveals.

Crimes of the Powerless

Power can be considered in several dimensions, including class, gender, race, and ethnicity (Barak, Leighton, and Flavin 2006). Consider social class as an illustration as captured in Reiman's book *The Rich Get Richer and the Poor Get Prison* (1979). The original conception of crimes of the powerless was based on the accumulated evidence from data gathered by the criminal justice system. This showed that those predominantly arrested for conventional criminal activities were from lower- or working-class backgrounds. It seemed clear that these street crimes of theft and personal violence, such as homicide, rape, aggravated assault, robbery, burglary, larceny, and auto theft, were committed by people holding relatively weak legitimate economic and political positions in society. For example, Balkan, Berger, and Schmidt argued that street crime, "conventionally considered the most serious form of crime, is committed primarily by working-class persons" (1980, 340).

But the findings from numerous self-report surveys in which people are asked to anonymously report to researchers the kinds of crimes they actually commit rather than those they are arrested for suggest that this view is inaccurate. Except for the most serious crimes, it was found that the proportions of street crimes committed by middle-class and lower-class youths are similar (E. Currie 1985; Elliott and Huizinga 1983). However, it was further found that the lower-class offender is more likely to be arrested, charged, and convicted by the criminal justice system (Liska and Chamlin 1984; Sampson 1986). Other dimensions of power, such as race or gender, are interlocked with the class dimension and can be subject to a similar analysis. Take race as an illustration. Self-report surveys found that African American and white offense rates were similar except for serious offenses, but African American arrest and conviction rates were higher (Elliott and Ageton 1980; Huizinga and Elliott 1987; Reiman [1979] 2007). Thus, poor African Americans are more likely to be arrested than wealthy whites.

These findings show the importance of criminological research in shaping our thinking about crime. They suggest that we need to revise our conception of crimes of the powerless. Taking account of these data, the phrase "crimes of the powerless" refers to crimes for which those in relatively weak economic and political positions in society are predominantly arrested. In other words, powerlessness reflects qualities affecting not so much the commission of crimes but the ability to resist arrest, prosecution, and conviction.

FIGURE 2.5   Likelihood of Victimization by Age, Race, and Sex

Black male teens have the highest violent victimization rates

Personal theft rates are highest for teenagers and young adults

Victimization rate per 1,000 persons

Victimization rate per 1,000 persons

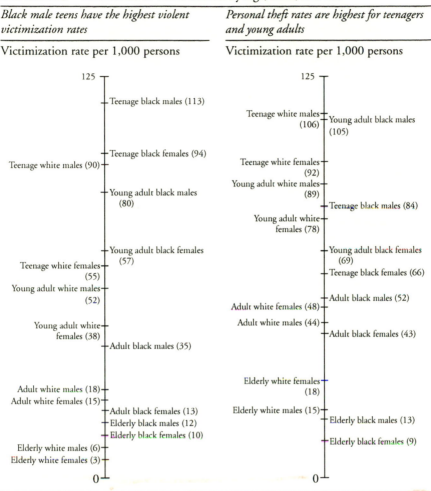

NOTE: Teenage = age 12–19
       Young adult = age 20–24
       Adult = 35–64
       Elderly = age 65 and over

SOURCE: Bureau of Justice Statistics 1993, p. 20.

Crimes of the Powerful

Crimes of the powerful are those crimes committed by people who are in relatively strong legitimate economic and political positions in society (D. Simon 2002; Reiman [1979] 2007). Again, let us illustrate the argument on the social class dimension of power. Such crimes include offenses by those in powerful occupational or political positions, such as business executives, professionals, lawyers, doctors, accountants, and politicians. Here, we see crimes such as insider trading, tax evasion, bribery and corruption, Medicare fraud, price-fixing, pollution, occupational hazards, dangerous consumer products, and so on. Crimes of the powerful include much of what are called white-collar crimes (E. Sutherland 1949a) because of the occupational position of those who carry them out. They are also called "suite crimes" because of where they occur—typically in offices, corridors of power, and corporate boardrooms.

As with crimes of the powerless, it helps to understand the range of crimes committed. These are offenses not only by individuals but also by corporations, organizations, and agencies of government (Ermann and Lundman [1992] 1996; Schlegel and Weisburd 1994) and government policies (Barak 1991). Thus, we need to include the following: (1) corporate crimes, such as faulty product manufacture, dangerous work conditions, price-fixing, and consumer fraud; (2) government agency crimes, such as systemic police corruption, subversion of regulatory enforcement, and violence (e.g., the case of more than one hundred agents of the Bureau of Alcohol, Tobacco, and Firearms in Waco, Texas, in 1993 in which senior agents altered written plans and tried to cover up the "facts" after eighty-two Branch Davidians burned to death); and (3) state crimes resulting from government policy such as violations of privacy rights, involuntary medical experimentation (e.g., radiation tests on unwitting subjects and the Tuskegee syphilis study), state monopolies and government subsidies, and crimes against other states.

It is also important to note, as with crimes of the powerless, that power shapes not only the opportunity to commit crime but also the ability to resist arrest, prosecution, and conviction: "Crimes committed by the powerful are responsible for even greater social harms than those committed by the powerless. The former have escaped public attention precisely because, given the individualistic political-legal framework of capitalist society, it is difficult to identify and prosecute the persons who are responsible for crimes that take place within organizations" (Balkan, Berger, and Schmidt 1980, 145).

Considering our crime prism, the power of some to influence the government, the law, and the media, to obscure their harms, to resist arrest and prosecution, and to minimize sentences is why such crimes are located in the bottom segment. They are very harmful but obscured, and they harm their victims indirectly and diffusely, often without the victims realizing who the offender is or perhaps even that they have been victimized. The victims of these crimes are blamed for being stupid, careless, or unfortunate (as in the savings and loan fraud, injury and death in the workplace, and pollution and food poisoning). Only in recent years has social reaction begun to respond to these offenses and then only feebly, through selective regulatory control rather than criminalization. Until victims are clearly identified, crimes of the powerful are brought to public awareness, and governments are more democratically representative of the people rather than industry lobbyists, the location of these crimes on the crime prism will be low.

Summary

We began this chapter by showing the difficulties that exist when trying to define crime. Clearly, one's definition is ideologically based. In this chapter, we have seen that although harms against others can be quantified, this alone does not enable us to draw conclusions without considerable caution.

We then continued discussing the legal definition of crime and its limitations in accounting for the variability of crime across time and cultures. We looked at how consensus theorists had tied crime to societal agreement about universal morality. We went on to discuss the criticisms of this approach by those who saw division and conflict in society. We saw how conflict theorists disagreed in their ideas about the basis of division in society and how their differences produced definitions of crime highlighting different issues, not least of which is the nature of harm itself.

After exploring some social constructionist and postmodernist alternatives, we explained Hagan's crime pyramid and then offered a modified version through our prism of crime. The prism aimed at integrating the range of different approaches previously discussed. This was followed by showing how the crime prism can be applied to school violence. We demonstrated through this application that such an approach allows us to see the interrelatedness of several levels of harm that can each cumulatively build over time to more serious crime.

We concluded by briefly outlining crimes of the powerful and crimes of the powerless and noted how these too can be interrelated. We noted that empirical research suggests that power shapes not only the opportunity to commit crime but also a person's likelihood of getting arrested and convicted for one kind of crime rather than another.

Notes

1. Unfortunately, when examples are given of so-called consensual crimes, such as personal drug use, prostitution, and gambling, the role of power in the structural context in which the offender-victim eventually "chooses" the behavior is ignored.

3

Classical, Neoclassical, and Rational Choice Theories

Classical theory was prevalent prior to "modern" criminology's search for the causes of crime, which did not begin until the nineteenth century. Classical theory did not seek to explain why people commit crime; rather, it was a strategy for administering justice according to rational principles (D. Garland 1985). It was based on assumptions about how people living in seventeenth-century Europe, during the Enlightenment, began to reject the traditional idea that people were born into social types (e.g., landed nobility and serfs) with vastly different rights and privileges. Classical thinkers replaced this bedrock of the feudal caste system with the then-radical notion that people are individuals having equal rights.

Prior to the Enlightenment, during a period of absolute monarchies, justice was arbitrary, barbarous, and harsh. Rulers used torture to coerce confessions, and corporal punishments such as whipping, flogging, and pillorying were common. The death penalty had also been expanded to apply to numerous offenses, including petty theft, deception, and poaching. However, even by 1520 reformers began to recognize that not all who violated society's norms should be subject to harsh and arbitrary punishments. Although the poor and unemployed who stole to survive were still treated harshly by today's standards, in England and Belgium, for example, a distinction was made between the deserving and undeserving poor. Though both were to be punished for wrongdoing, the deserving poor, who were "poor through no fault of their own" and included vagrants, discharged soldiers, women, and children, were sent to workhouses. The first "house of correction," London's Bridewell, was established in 1556 and was designed to train the poor to work through discipline. "Bridewells," eventually numbering some two hundred in England, would subsequently form the basis of what would become a cornerstone of the American system of corrections.

By the seventeenth century a major change was taking place. Utilitarian philosophers recognized the gross injustices of the legal and political system and saw much of the problem as resulting from the enormity of church and state power. Their solution was legal and judicial reform, which was consistent with emerging ideas about human rights and individual freedom. They sought philosophical justification for reform in the changing conception of humans as freethinking individuals. People were reinvented as rational and reasoning beings whose previously scorned individuality was now declared superior. These ideas about the "new person" built on the naturalist and rationalist philosophy of Enlightenment scholars such as Hutcheson, Hume, Montesquieu, Voltaire, Locke, and Rousseau. Classical theory was originally a radical rather than a conservative concept because it opposed traditional ways, challenged the power of the state, was heretical to the orthodoxies of the Catholic Church, and glorified the common people (F. Williams and McShane 1988). However, it was in some ways also conservative in that it sought to expand the scope of disciplinary punishment (not its severity), having it apply to everyone, while ignoring the social conditions of the crime problem (Beirne and Messerschmidt 2000, 72; D. Garland 1997).

The original concepts and ideals presented by the social philosophers Cesare Beccaria and Jeremy Bentham included such now-familiar principles as innocent until proven guilty, equality before the law, due process procedure, rules of evidence and testimony, curbs on judges' discretionary power, the right to be judged by a jury of one's peers, individual deterrence, and equal punishment for equal crimes. These ideas were incorporated into the U.S. Declaration of Independence and the U.S. Constitution. They laid the basis of the modern U.S. legal system, shaping the practices of law enforcement and the operation of the courts. Thus, anyone working in the criminal justice system needs to understand the origin of these principles and why they were deemed necessary.

In this chapter, we outline the central theoretical ideas of classical theory and illustrate how classicism applies to contemporary crime and justice. Later in the chapter, we discuss theoretical extensions of classicism. These include early-nineteenth-century French neoclassicism, which revised the original ideals to take into account pragmatic difficulties, and the late-twentieth-century postclassical developments of the justice model, together with criminology's theories of rational choice, situational choice, and routine activities. Finally, we consider the empirical support for classical and rational choice assumptions—in other words, does research indicate that classical ideas are effective in practice? In our evaluation of this perspective, we examine the empirical support for three key areas: (1) research on the deterrent effect of legal punishments, including the death penalty; (2) the extent to which offenders make rational choice decisions prior to committing crimes; and (3) the extent to which rational choice precautions by potential victims reduce the probability of subsequent victimization.

The Preclassical Era

To fully appreciate classical thought, it is necessary to understand the historical context in which it developed and, in particular, how humans viewed each other before the onset of classical thought. By the sixteenth century, several European societies had undergone considerable transformation since the feudal era. Political power was consolidated in states whose monarchical rulers aspired to complete domination. Many rulers claimed to have special relations with the Deity, and they conducted their affairs with limited interference from representatives of the people (L. Smith 1967). People were born into positions of wealth and power, positions that they claimed as their natural right. The law was the will of the powerful applied to the lower members of society. The administration of justice was based on inflicting pain, humiliation, and disgrace to those accused of offenses. This occurred in spite of a growth in scientific knowledge throughout Europe and was validated by the church.

Although the political and religious order of life in pre-seventeenth-century Europe sounds fundamentally different from today's U.S. society, some similarities were beginning to emerge. If still a class-based society, post-Renaissance Europe had broken from the rigid feudal order of the "ancient regime," in which a person's birth determined his or her place in life. By 1650, many governments adopted the new mercantile system of trade, especially colonial trade monopolies, and this paved the way for upward (and downward) mobility. Humans (meaning men) were now seen as capable of making a difference in their lives and situations through acts of will. The concept of "the individual" was thus born, with the highly revered qualities of rationality and intelligence.

In sixteenth-century England, for example, the middle classes enjoyed considerable economic and social advancement. The state had divested feudal families of their land, and middle-class land speculators were rewarded with land for their loyalty to the monarchy. As a result, the emerging middle class, or bourgeoisie (meaning those beneath the aristocracy), of merchants and traders rose to form a new power elite. This was at the expense of farmers, artisans, laborers, and the poor, many of whom became beggars and thieves. This polarization between riches and poverty was caused by a combination of events, including government-decreed fixed wages for the lower classes at a time of massive price inflation; the decline of arable farming and the shift to animal husbandry, particularly sheep farming; and the enclosure of common lands, which converted cropland to pasture, enabling quicker profits. "Acts of Enclosure" deprived common people of their traditional right to use the land and declared such use to be the crimes of poaching and theft. At the same time, urbanization was accelerating and cities were growing but also becoming crowded with the dispossessed poor. Several families were often forced to share single-room houses.

Those newly urban dwellers who could not survive the lack of work, hunger, and insecurity roamed from town to town as homeless vagabonds; others were forced, by sickness or misfortune, into an impoverished life of debauchery, begging, and theft. So grew a population that the rising merchant class and gentry referred to as "savages," "beasts," and "incorrigibles" in need of harsh discipline. This attitude contrasted to, and indeed conflicted with, the nonpunitive relief policies of the medieval monasteries (Jansson 2001, 32–33).

The problem of vagabondage as a constant feature of social life all over England had significantly existed since 1520, but was especially rampant in the towns (Salgado 1972, 10). During this time the "idle and dangerous classes" swarmed into the towns in search of food and shelter. Hospitals and houses giving relief to the poor were seen as breeding grounds for those who became beggars, thieves, and drunkards. Thieve rookeries in the slums threatened to envelop the metropolis in vice and crime: "Citizens found themselves besieged in their streets by the leper with his bell, the cripple with his deformities and the rogue with his fraudulent scheme" (O'Donoghue 1923, 137).

The growth in street crime was not slowed by the pervasive corruption in the criminal justice system. Officials whose job was to control common crime actually encouraged it by accepting bribes. The absence of effective organized law enforcement at a time when informal social and kinship network ties had been broken was another factor facilitating the growing crime problem. The lackadaisical manner in which laws were enforced compounded the problems associated with the existing laws. "Justice" was questionable, as the judicial system operated arbitrarily and unpredictably. Juries could be corrupted, and witnesses would sell their evidence. Indeed, the term *straw man* referred to "witnesses" who wore a piece of straw in their shoe buckles, indicating that they could be bought (Hibbert [1963] 1966). Secret accusations and private trials were not uncommon. Justice was anything but blind, and the economically and socially disadvantaged were held accountable to different standards, since the legal system reflected the interests of the wealthy.

Concern for the poor soon became mixed with fear of a threat to public order. "Respectable" citizens—and especially the new merchant classes—wanted "to protect themselves from the unscrupulous activities of this vast army of wandering parasites" (Salgado 1972, 10) and demanded that something be done to make city streets safe for the conduct of business. In response to the rising fear of crime, European parliaments passed more and harsher penalties against law violators. In England alone, during the sixteenth century, more than two hundred crimes warranted the death penalty, and many persons died during the torture used by governments to extract their confessions. Yet there were already stirrings of change. By the middle of the sixteenth century English reformers were calling for a clear distinction between the respectable, deserving poor and the unrespectable, undeserving poor.

The *respectable poor* included those suffering from sickness and contagious diseases, wounded soldiers, curable cripples, the blind, fatherless and pauper children, and the aged poor. They were seen as the responsibility of the more fortunate and would be segregated by their class and condition and given immediate assistance, including shelter, treatment, adequate maintenance, and, in the case of the children, education and training, in a variety of houses and hospitals around the country. Such "respectable" citizens, who had fallen on hard times through no moral fault of their own, by reason of failure in business, ill health, or other misfortunes, were to be given weekly pensions and might be employed in doing such tasks as clearing the church porches of beggars.

In contrast, the *unrespectable poor*, which included vagabonds, tramps, rogues, and dissolute women, were described as worthless, and were to be punished with imprisonment and whipping before being trained for honest work (O'Donoghue 1923, 139–140). A prison was proposed for this group, the Bridewell, which should also be a house of work, with opportunities for the amendment of character. The premises would also be used to train poor and resistant children in various trades. Most vilified was the "robust beggar," whose presence among beggary was seen as a choice for a soft and easy life. The "stubborn and foul" would be set to make nails and to do blacksmiths' work; the weaker, the sick, and the crippled might make beds and bedding. Bridewell was intended "to deal with the poverty and idleness of the streets, not by statute, but by labor. The rogue and the idle vagrant would be sent to the treadmill to grind corn, but the respectable poor—whether young, not very strong, or even crippled—would be taught profitable trades, or useful occupations" (ibid., 151–152). The justification was that enforced labor would permanently cure begging and thievery where statutes of law had failed. By the middle of the eighteenth century, the target of reform was the law and justice itself.

The Classical Reaction

The combination of a rising propertied middle class and a rising crime rate led the philosophical leaders of the classical movement to demand double security for their newfound wealth. They needed protection against the threat from below, the "dangerous" classes, symbolized by the growing crime rates. They also wanted protection against threats from above, the aristocracy that still held the reins of government power and legal repression. The middle classes saw a solution to their dilemma in a reformed legal system that "would defend their interests and protect their 'rights and liberties' against the arbitrary power hitherto wielded exclusively by the landed classes and the Crown" (J. Young 1981, 253). Indeed, to be free to move up the class hierarchy, reformers needed a new legal concept of humans that would limit the power of the old aristocratically run state and liberate the freedom, safety, and security of the individual to create and keep wealth. This emerged in the concept of universal rights to liberty and freedom that would apply equally to all people (though many classes beneath the middle classes were excluded). Universal rights demanded predictability and calculatedness, neither of which was present in the existing system of arbitrary justice.

Thus, the primary focus of utilitarian philosophers was to transform arbitrary justice into a fair, equal, and humanitarian system. They sought to do this by aligning the law and its enforcement and administration with logical and rational principles. These principles were consistent with the emerging concept of humans as individuals and were most eloquently expressed by the philosophers Cesare Beccaria and Jeremy Bentham, although several others contributed.

Cesare Beccaria

Perhaps the most influential protest writer and philosopher of the period was the Italian marquis Cesare Bonesana, Marchese di Beccaria (1738–1794), or as he is more popularly known, Cesare Beccaria. Beccaria's ideas were molded by his friends the Milanese political activist brothers Pietro and Alessandro Verri. These intellectuals formed a radical group called the "Academy of Fists," which was "dedicated to waging relentless war against economic disorder, bureaucratic petty tyranny, religious narrow-mindedness, and intellectual pedantry" (Paolucci 1963, xii). With considerable prodding and much editorial help from Pietro Verri, in 1764, at age twenty-six, Beccaria published a small book on penology translated into English as *On Crimes and Punishment*. It gained much notoriety after the pope banned it for what he alleged to be highly dangerous, heretical, and extreme rationalism (Beirne 1991). Anticipating just such a reaction, Beccaria had originally published the book anonymously. His modest work became highly influential, first in Paris and then worldwide. By 1800, it had appeared in twenty-three Italian editions, fourteen French editions, and eleven English editions. The book justified massive and sweeping changes to European justice systems. The founding fathers of the United States relied on it. Thomas Jefferson used it as "his principal modern authority for revising the laws of Virginia" (Wills 1978, 94). The writers of the U.S. Constitution and the Bill of Rights utilized it as a primary source. In addition, its impact remains very clear in contemporary U.S. judicial and correctional policy.

What was it that caused so much reaction to just one small book? Certainly, Beccaria's motivation for writing the book was rooted in the resentment he felt toward the authoritarian aristocracy into which he was born. Unquestionably, it was fueled by his friends' radical ideas about the state of Italian society and particularly the abuse and torture of prisoners. Arguably, the book drew together, in a readable, poetic way, all the main intellectual ideas of the era, providing an exemplar for change. Expressed alone, these ideas had little force. Expressed together, as part of a logical framework, they were revolutionary.

Beccaria challenged the prevailing idea that humans are predestined to fill certain social statuses. Instead, he claimed, they are born as free, equal, and rational individuals having both natural rights, including the right to privately own property, and natural qualities, such as the freedom to reason and the ability to choose actions that are in their own best interests. Drawing on the ideas of Hobbes's and Rousseau's "social contract" and Locke's belief in humans' inalienable rights, Beccaria believed that government was not the automatic right of the rich. Rather, it was created through a social contract in which free, rational individuals sacrificed part of their freedom to the state to maintain peace and security on behalf of the common good. The government would use this power to protect individuals against those who would choose to put their own interests above others'. As a contemporary example, we give up the right to drive where and whenever we want at whatever speed we want and submit to government traffic laws designed to promote rapid and safe transportation. Some individuals are tempted to disregard these laws. When they do so, the government, through its agents of enforcement, punishes or removes these individuals so that we may all travel with relative predictability and peacefulness. Indeed, part of the government's role in maintaining individual rights is to ensure that governing itself does not become excessively powerful and that citizens' voices are always represented.

Taken together, these assumptions led to the principle of individual sovereignty (Packer 1968). This means that individual rights have priority over society's or the state's interests. This was especially important in the exercise of law to protect individuals. Thus, Beccaria was opposed to the practice of judges making laws through interpreting their intent. Instead, he insisted that lawmaking and resolving legal ambiguities should be the exclusive domain of elected legislators who represented the people. He believed that the wisest laws "naturally promote the universal distribution of advantages while they resist the force that tends to concentrate them in the hands of the few." He argued that laws should always be designed, like government itself, to ensure "the greatest happiness shared by the greatest number" ([1764] 1963, 8).

Beccaria also shifted the focus of what counted as crime. Rather than crimes being offenses against the powerful, he saw them as offenses against fellow humans and thus against society itself. He believed crimes offended society because they broke the social contract, resulting in an encroachment on others' freedom.

It was in the administration of justice that Beccaria saw individual sovereignty most at risk, so he sought reforms that would guarantee justice. He argued that the law, the courts, and especially judges have a responsibility to protect the innocent from conviction and to convict the guilty, but to do so without regard to their status, wealth, or power. The only basis for conviction was the facts of the case. This led to the principle of the presumption of innocence (Packer 1968), designed to protect individual rights against excessive state power or corrupt officials. Several procedural elements were necessary for a system of justice to ensure this protection, including procedural restraint over arbitrary power, protection of the accused defendant against abuses and error, and minimizing discretion or arbitrariness by rules that limit police power and govern what constitutes acceptable evidence.

Beccaria also believed that individuals would be best protected through an adversarial trial in which the accused had the right to be represented and was ensured equality of inquiry and equality before the law. Moreover, this trial should be judged not by the government but by a jury of the accused's peers (but he also believed that half the jury should be of the victim's peers), and the procedures should provide the accused the right to appeal to an independent body.

When it came to the issue of crime prevention, Beccaria did not believe that the best way to reduce crime was to increase laws or increase the severity of punishment, since doing so would merely create new crimes and "[embolden] men to commit the very wrongs it is supposed to prevent" ([1764] 1963, 43). Instead, he argued, laws and punishments should be only as restrictive as necessary to just deter those who would break them by calculating that it would not be in their interests to do so.

To maximize the possibility of justice and deterrence, Beccaria believed that punishments should fit the crime, that is, be proportionate to the harm caused. Thus, the severity of the harm determines the level of punishment. Punishment should not affect others or influence their future offending. *General deterrence*, which means using the punishment of one individual to discourage others from committing crime, should, according to Beccaria, be replaced by individual or *specific deterrence*, which encourages each individual to calculate the costs of committing the crime. The level of punishment would be assessed by relating punishment to what an offense warranted. This is the principle of "just deserts," which means that convicted offenders deserve punishment commensurate with the seriousness of the harm they caused. This punishment is for the specific offense they committed and not for any other reason, such as to teach others a lesson or because they had committed other crimes in the past and so might be more likely to in the future.

In order for deterrence to work, three things must occur: certainty, severity, and celerity. If punishments are to be an effective deterrent in individual calculations, they must be certain, argued Beccaria, since "the certainty of punishment, even if moderate, will always make a stronger impression than the fear of another which is more terrible but combined with the hope of impunity" (ibid., 58). *Certainty* means a high chance of apprehension and punishment. Beccaria believed that it was more important that potential offenders know certain punishment would follow a crime than that they merely associate crime with severe sanctions. If the severity of punishment is high but the likelihood of apprehension and punishment low, then people are still likely to commit the act. This was dramatically illustrated at the public executions of pickpockets in London, which attracted large crowds of spectators—whose pockets were picked by the clearly undeterred pickpockets among them.

Severity of punishment means that the level of punishment must be appropriate. In other words, the severity of the punishment should just outweigh the benefit derived from the crime. If the punishment is too severe (e.g., death for minor offenses), it is counterproductive and results in a lack of respect for the law. If the punishment is too lenient, it will not serve as a deterrent. The optimum punishment is a combination of sufficient certainty that people calculate they are more likely than not to get caught and sufficient severity that the punishment seems just rather than excessive.

Finally, for punishment to appear as a deterrent to potential offenders in relation to the offense committed, then it must also occur swiftly after apprehension, that is, with *celerity*. As Beccaria wrote, "The more promptly and the more closely punishment follows upon the commission of a crime, the more just and useful will it be" (ibid., 55).

Jeremy Bentham

An influential social philosopher and a supporter of Beccaria's ideas was the Englishman Jeremy Bentham (1748–1832). Bentham expanded on Beccaria's initial contribution by offering the notion of the "hedonistic, or felicity, calculus" as an explanation for people's actions. This calculus states that people act to increase positive results through their pursuit of pleasure and to reduce negative outcomes through the avoidance of pain. Bentham's conception of pain and pleasure was complex, involving not just physical sensations but also political, moral, and religious dimensions, each of which varied in intensity, duration, certainty, and proximity ([1765] 1970; Einstadter and Henry 2006, 51). Bentham believed that people broke the law because they desired to gain money, sex, excitement, or revenge. Like Beccaria, Bentham saw law's purpose as increasing the total happiness of the community by excluding "mischief" and promoting pleasure and security. For individuals to be able to rationally calculate, he believed, laws should ban harmful behavior, provided there is a victim involved. Crimes without victims, consensual crimes, and acts of self-defense should not be subject to criminal law, because they produce more good than evil. Laws should set specific punishments (pain) for specific crimes in order to motivate people to act one way rather than another. But since punishments are themselves evil mischief, the utility principle (the idea that the greatest good should be sought for the greatest number) justifies their use only to exclude a greater evil, and then only in sufficient measure to outweigh the profit of crime and to bring the offender into conformity with the law ([1765] 1970). Bentham argued that punishments should be scaled so that an offender rationally calculating whether to commit a crime would choose the lesser offense. For example, if rape and homicide were both punished by execution, the rapist might be more inclined to kill the victim. Doing so would reduce the risk of identification and execution. But if harsher punishment resulted from murder than rape, the offender would be more likely to refrain from the more harmful crime.

In contrast to Beccaria, Bentham believed that in the case of the repeat offender it might be necessary to increase the punishment to outweigh the profit from offenses likely to be committed. Also, Bentham introduced the notion that different kinds of offenses required different types of punishment, ranging from confinement for failure to conform to the law, such as nonpayment of taxes, to enforced labor in a penal institution for those guilty of theft. Like Beccaria, he rejected the death penalty because it brought more harm than good and therefore violated his utility principle. Instead, Bentham preferred fines and prison. Judges could equalize fines and stage them in progressive severity. Similarly, prison allowed judges to vary the time served and set terms at different levels for different offenses. Indeed, Bentham was responsible for designing the ultimate disciplinary prison, known as the Panopticon (meaning "all seeing"), designed "to control not only the freedom of movement of those confined but their minds as well" (Shover and Einstadter 1988, 202; see also Foucault 1977). Bentham's prison was a circular structure organized so that a guard in the center could see into each cell without being seen by the prisoner, with the result that prisoners would believe they were under constant surveillance. Pennsylvania and Illinois constructed Panopticon-type prisons, but England did not. Bentham believed that this disciplinary system should also extend to factories, hospitals, and schools.

Limitations of Classical Theory

Although radical and influential for their times, the ideas discussed here were not without certain contradictions. First and foremost was the assumption that people were equal. What could this really mean? Were all people equal? Did equality include people of different intellectual ability? What about children? What about the insane? Did equal mean to the classicists that men and women were equal? Second, how could a system designed to allow some people to create more wealth than others, and therefore to become materially unequal, maintain that in law all persons were formally equal? How could there be equal punishments for equal crimes without taking into account differences in wealth? Third, why do some people commit more crimes than others, if they are all equally endowed with reason? It soon became necessary to revise classical ideas to fit emerging realities.

Neoclassical Revisions

The first significant legislation based on classical concepts was the famous French Code of 1791. Following the successful French Revolution of 1789, the victors focused on equality and justice. In seeking fairness and the elimination of discriminatory misuses of justice, the French Code of 1791 treated all offenders equally—regardless of individual circumstances. But the French soon recognized that justice required some discretion and latitude. Pure classicism took no account of individual differences. Yet differences were obvious. For example, should children receive the same penalties as adults? What should happen to those with limited mental faculties? What about women who had long been denied equal status to men?

In 1819, the French revised the code to permit judges some discretion. This neoclassical position recognized "age, mental condition and extenuating circumstances" (Vold and Bernard 1986, 26). Despite these changes, the basic underlying assumptions—that humans are rational, calculating, and hedonistic—remained the cornerstone of criminal justice policy.

Thus, fifty-five years after Beccaria first presented his original thesis, an actual justice system incorporated the new revisions. These changes have remained virtually the same since. But the growth of scientific criminology in the nineteenth and early twentieth centuries led to a considerable slippage, since the focus of criminal justice shifted away from the criminal act and how equal individuals chose it toward what kinds of individuals would choose such acts and why other kinds would not. We shall discuss the rise of scientific criminology in the next chapter, but it is important here to recognize certain parallel histories that led to the resurrection of a version of neoclassicism, or postclassicism, that has become known as contemporary rational choice theory. Crucial in this history is the emergence of modernism, science, and progress during the nineteenth and twentieth centuries. This is the notion that scientific laws, the development of rational thought, and empirical research could help society progress to a better world. Harnessing the forces of science and incorporation of its discourse into government policies served to legitimate government domination and control. The application of scientific methods to all fields, including criminal justice, combined with a political climate in which government grew in its responsibility to serve the public, soon translated into more power for the state and more discretion for its institutions and agencies. There was a growing observation that modern (i.e., scientific) solutions, while producing massive changes in technological development, also brought human suffering and increased rather than reduced social problems, resulting in a questioning of faith in science. Nowhere was this more apparent than in the failure of scientific principles applied to the problems of crime and justice. They had brought a considerable abandonment of the principles of equality of the individual before the law, as increased discretion was used in courts and by judges to adjust sentences to fit the particular circumstances of individual offenders.

It was against this background, then, that by the 1970s a familiar call was being heard from those challenging the power and growing discretion of the state in matters of justice. These postclassicists were calling for a return to equality standards, protesting that discretion based on the dubious claims of science and social science had gone too far. Two developments in this regard were particularly important. The first is justice theory and related developments toward a conservative "law-and-order" approach to crime control, and the second is rational choice theory and its extension, routine activities theory.

Criminal Justice Implications: The Move to "Justice" Theory

By the 1960s, classical theory had become little more than a footnote to scientific and sociological theories of crime. In the decades following 1859, Darwinist evolutionary ideas, science, and technology promised to liberate humankind from the philosophical speculations of the Enlightenment era. The scientific search for the causes of crime (which we discuss in detail later) displaced the armchair philosophers of rationality and reason. The new scientific method relied on the manipulation of variables, observation, and measurement and employed specific rules that had to be followed. It changed criminal justice policy to take into account individual and social differences, especially in sentencing practices. In attempting to address individual differences, criminal justice returned to discretionary sentencing, which some saw as similar to the policies existing prior to the classical movement. But instead of arbitrary justice, scientific evidence justified disparate sentences based on offender "needs." Offenders were diagnosed as having specific problems and were deemed to need sentences (treatment) based on their diagnosed problems. Thus, because of a reliance on the scientific method, diagnosis, and rehabilitation, the emphasis shifted from deterrence to treatment under what was termed *rehabilitative justice*.

The outcome, however, was the same as before. Convicted offenders received different sentences for similar crimes and different treatments depending on the diagnosis of cause. For example, one juvenile offender might get sent to a detention center, another to probation, and a third to boot camp, all for the same offense, because a social worker's or probation officer's presentence report claimed that each individual offender had different needs.

By the 1970s, critics raised two central problems. First, for all the effort at reha-bilitation, did it work, that is, did it prevent recidivism, or reoffending? The answer from the rehabilitation skeptics was "Nothing works." Martinson concluded that with few and isolated exceptions, "rehabilitative efforts . . . have had no effect on re-cidivism" (1974, 25).

The second charge against rehabilitative justice was that it was unfair. In the con-text of the slide from classical principles, some called for the "rehabilitation of pun-ishment." Bottomley argued that rehabilitative justice "culminated in the entire notion of the indeterminate sentence coming under attack for its therapeutic preten-sions in a situation where not only was hard evidence of therapeutic effectiveness lacking . . . but where indeterminacy created unacceptable tensions for prisoners and their families, providing further scope for discretionary decision-making by the exec-utive and instruments of control within penal institutions" (1979, 127).

Justice theorists pointed to a tendency for rehabilitation and treatment to drift to-ward discretion and inconsistency. They claimed that in spite of its advocates' em-phasis on understanding and concern, rehabilitation often inflicted more cruelty than the punitive approach. They despised the "discriminatory use of penal sanc-tions" and the "wide margins of discretionary power in the hands of police, district attorneys, judges, correctional administrators, parole boards, and parole agents" (American Friends Service Committee 1971, 124). This position has a similar ring to Beccaria's earlier criticisms about preclassical punishment. These new critics ar-gued that allowing prosecutors and judges the flexibility to plea-bargain, grant con-cessions, or pass harsh sentences based on individual circumstances resulted in "a system of wide disparities in charging and sentencing similarly situated individuals, a system that has lost sight of its goals in its eagerness to dispose of cases" (Heumann and Loftin 1979, 393).

In response to these problems, a move back toward policies based on classical principles developed. From the ashes of rehabilitation skepticism rose the justice, or "just deserts," model (Fogel 1975). This model was a reflection of many of the origi-nal principles presented by Beccaria and Bentham. The justice model contained four key elements: (1) limited discretion at all procedural stages of the criminal justice system, (2) greater openness and accountability, (3) punishment justified by the last crime or series of crimes (neither deterrence goals nor offender characteristics justify punishment), and (4) punishment commensurate with the seriousness of the crime, based on actual harm done and the offender's culpability. The move back to justice gave priority to punishment "as a desirable value and goal in its own right"; this was different from the traditional justification of penal goals, such as deterrence or reha-bilitation (Bottomley 1979, 139).

An application of these revised classical principles was a renewed emphasis on equal punishment for equal crimes. This required replacing the broad range of sen-tences available for particular classes of felonies with a "tariff system" of determinate sentences. Each punishment was a fixed sentence with only a narrow range of adjust-ments allowed for seriousness or mitigating circumstances (Fogel 1975, 254). Per-haps the best example of a tariff system is the parking fine or speeding ticket for which each offender, regardless of circumstances, receives the same penalty and the penalties increase by fixed amounts for offenses of increasing seriousness.

The Conservative Law-and-Order Turn

Instead of the neoclassical school's influence waning, as many predicted, it continues to exist today, and as one commentator says, its "demise is greatly exaggerated" (Schmalleger [1999] 2002, 163). Combined with a conservative or "law-and-order approach" to crime control, the prevailing just deserts model holds that crime is freely chosen and rewarding, and, therefore, it demands both deterrent and retributive responses. This is not only because of the harm done but also because the offender knew the consequences before committing the crime. Although this position fudges the original classical principles (see Einstadter and Henry 2006, 47, for a discussion of the differences between classical theory and conservative theory), it is popular with politicians and, as Schmalleger points out, "is now in its ascendency" ([1999] 2002, 163). When combined with other law-and-order elements such as "boot camp" for juvenile offenders, "incapacitation" (the idea of removing an offender's ability to commit further offenses), mandatory sentencing (which fixes the minimum sentence for various crimes), truth in sentencing (requiring judges to state the actual sentence that will be served), three-strikes-and-you're-out laws (requiring three-time felons to serve long sentences, typically life without the possibility of parole), and the death penalty as a general deterrent, the conservative distortion of neoclassical thought provides a formidable and popular election platform. However, the reality of criminal justice is often different from the rhetoric and the result of failed conservative policies, and the accumulated evidence on the ineffectiveness of some of the key elements is beginning to lead to a rethinking during the first decade of the twenty-first century. Below we look at four of these elements: determinate sentencing, incapacitation, three-strikes laws, and the death penalty.

Determinate or Mandatory Sentencing

Determinate sentences are designed to make justice "fair" and to make potential offenders aware of what sentences they can expect for committing specific crimes. Several questions remain, however. Does determinate sentencing reduce the sentencing disparity between those sentenced for similar types of crimes? Does it increase levels of incarceration? Does any increase in incarceration from determinate sentencing result in early release of more serious offenders? Does determinate sentencing undermine the role of judges and juries? Finally, does determinate sentencing increase the tendency for alternative systemic discretion, such as plea bargaining?

Evidence from research on state-level sentencing reform shows that the policy of determinate sentencing both reduces sentencing disparity (Blumstein et al. 1983; Tonry 1988) and increases prison populations at both state (Kramer and Lubitz 1985; Goodstein and Hepburn 1986; Hepburn and Goodstein 1986; Bogan 1990; Pew Charitable Trusts 2008) and federal institutions (Mays 1989; Pew Charitable

Trusts 2008). One exception seems to be in Minnesota. The effects of Minnesota's determinate sentencing reform show overwhelmingly that the policy of sentencing guidelines has reduced sentencing disparity without producing increased prison populations (Blumstein et al. 1983; Miethe and Moore 1985). When judges are concerned about prison overcrowding, however, they are motivated to circumvent the guidelines. In doing so, they shift the burden of incarcerating offenders to the local level, resulting in increases in jail incarceration rates (D'Alessio and Stolzenberg 1995; Miethe and Moore 1989).

BOX 3.1   Michigan Abandons Mandatory Sentencing for Drug Offenses After
a Twenty-three-Year Experiment

On Christmas Day 2002, in one of his last acts before leaving office, Governor John Engler signed a bill that brought an end to Michigan's inflexible mandatory minimum sentencing laws for drug convictions.

During the 1970s, following New York's lead, several states, including Michigan, enacted tough laws that mandated a minimum sentence for people convicted of major drug offenses. A 1978 law mandated minimum sentences of twenty years to life without parole, even for a first offense, for possession of 650 grams (23 ounces) of certain "hard" drugs such as cocaine and heroin. The laws were passed during a time when there was much concern about crack cocaine epidemics in the nation's cities and fear that well-organized, armed, and violent gangs, such as Detroit's Young Boys, Inc., were overtaking the streets. The tough mandatory sentencing laws were seen as a way of removing "drug kingpins." The effects of the law were to incarcerate lower-level young offenders. The prisons became overcrowded, and there seemed to be little effect on the drug problem.

In response, the judicial system began to look for ways around the sentencing laws. "'Many prosecutors now reduce charges through plea-bargaining to avoid what they see as excessively harsh penalties,' said Michigan Department of Corrections spokesperson Russ Marlan. Judges also use an option that permits them to depart from mandatory-minimum sentences if they can find compelling reasons to do so" (Heinlein 2002, A9).

By 1998 Michigan's lawmakers slightly relaxed the mandatory minimums for nondrug offenses, but by December 2002 the Michigan legislature repealed the mandatory drug sentencing laws completely, allowing judges full discretion. Under the new law tough sentences are possible, but judges will be able to use their discretion to not only order shorter sentences but also give alternatives to punishment, such as drug treatment. The Michigan legislation leads the nation in reforming drug laws, placing the sentences for drug offenses back in the indeterminate sentencing guideline structure.

Source: Adapted from Gary Heinlein, "Michigan Eases Drug Sentences: Judges' Discretion Replaces Mandatory Terms for Offenders." *Detroit News and Free Press*, December 29, 2002, A1, A9.

At the federal level, Lanier and Miller (1995) found several other problems with determinate sentencing. Most of them have to do with plea bargaining, which results in more than 90 percent of criminal defendants pleading guilty to lesser charges in exchange for having the more serious charge (and therefore sentence) reduced. Any plea bargaining necessarily circumvents the principles of classical theory and the intentions of determinate sentencing guidelines. A major question therefore becomes, Does determinate sentencing increase the use of plea bargains? Several commentators predicted that when judges could no longer select from a wide variety of sanctions, prosecutors' discretion would increase (Sarat 1978; D. Horowitz 1977). Research has confirmed that in spite of formal compliance with mandatory laws, when both judges and prosecutors consider the required penalties to be too harsh they circumvent the guidelines. Thus, they can avoid mandatory minimum sentences by dismissing charges or acquitting defendants (J. Cohen and Tonry 1983). The logical solution seems to be to eliminate plea bargains, which would also prevent any tendency for police to "overcharge" on the assumption that a plea bargain will occur. The recommendation has a long history (National Advisory Commission 1971), but so far only one state (Alaska) and a few county jurisdictions have implemented it.

Simply put, policies that mandate justice and equity do not guarantee equal justice unless the realities of the system as a whole are taken into account. These total system effects are further complicated by the fact that sentence length is also affected by other considerations such as probation officers' presentence reports (see Lanier and Miller 1995).

In conclusion, it seems that the introduction of mandatory sentencing, although theoretically consistent with the ideals of classical theory, is ultimately faced with the realities of a system that has its own inertia. The U.S. justice system is so vast and so encumbered with the institutional practices associated with other correctional ideologies that changes to any part of it that do not take into account the whole are unlikely to succeed. Moreover, in spite of reformers' intentions to improve justice and equity, they are more likely to produce unintended effects that may even counter those objectives. Thus, the existence of judicial discretion, whether through plea bargains, reduced sentences for circumstances, or early release from parole, seriously undermines neoclassical principles, but so too does the selection of some dimensions of the classical principles, such as certainty of punishment and deterrence, without also incorporating the others, such as minimal and proportionate punishment. Nowhere is this more evident than in the politically popular extension of the mandatory prison sentence idea known as the "three-strikes law."

Three-Strikes Laws

It might seem strange that a nation as complex and sophisticated as the United States would formulate a corner of its criminal justice policy on a baseball analogy, but that is precisely what three-strikes-and-you're-out laws offered. As another attempt to embody the classical principle of "certainty of punishment," three-strikes laws (also known as habitual-offender laws) were introduced in the early 1990s largely in response to the drug problem. A year after Washington State passed its Initiative 593 in 1993, California passed its Proposition 184 "Three Strikes and You're Out" law, with 72 percent voting in favor of the measure to incarcerate felony offenders on convictions for their third offense, with no parole. More consistent with Bentham's idea that repeat offenders should receive higher sentences to outweigh the profit from offenses likely to be committed, this concept resulted in long and harsh sentences for persons convicted of three felonies, even if the crimes were nonviolent drug offenses and even if the third offense was less serious than the previous two (even purse snatching and shoplifting count as strikes). These laws, a variation of the mandatory minimum sentence laws, imposed stiff penalties for the third conviction, such as twenty-five years to life, under the 1994 California law. Moreover, the California law doesn't even require the third offense to be a felony if the previous two were serious. In 1995 thirteen states had three-strikes laws, and Georgia even had a two-strikes law that resulted in a life sentence without parole (Rush [1994] 2000, 321). By 2007, twenty-six states had three-strikes laws (J. Walsh 2007).

Here again we see the distortion of classical principles, which exaggerates one element (higher punishment for repeaters) at the expense of the others (such as proportionate punishment for the crime related to the harm committed). The objective again was deterrence; the reality was, again, different. Consider the case of Jona Rottenberg, arrested for possession of less than 1 gram of cocaine, who under California law faced twenty-five years to life (Pape 1999), or the case of Leandro Andrade, who shoplifted $153 worth of children's videos from Kmart, imprisoned until 2046, or the theft of three golf clubs worth $400 that convicted Gary Ewing for life. Critics argued that not only is three-strikes punishment excessive and unnecessary, but it also contributes to the problem of clogged courts and prison overcrowding, as well as increasing the determination of third-time offenders to avoid being caught (Schmalleger [1999] 2002, 138–139). The likely effect is quite the reverse of the classical principle that offenders choose the lesser offense; rather, the existence of three-strikes laws means they will likely calculate that it is in their interests to choose additional and more serious offenses to avoid apprehension and conviction, increasing the risk to police officers, although so far evidence does not support this effect (Moody, Marvell, and Kaminski 2002). Moreover, the policy was seriously questioned by the empirical evidence on its effectiveness at incapacitating the most serious offenders (Campaign for Effective Crime Policy 1998). Indeed, whereas advocates claim that crime in some states, such as California, has gone down 40 percent since the three-strikes laws were first implemented in 1993, critics, such as the Sentencing Project, argue that other states and cities have shown a similar crime reduction but do not have three-strikes laws, such as New York (41 percent), Massachusetts (33 percent), and Washington, D.C. (31 percent), questioning the contribution of the laws (Kasindorf 2002).

In 2000 a California amendment to the three-strikes law, supported by voters (Proposition 36), allowed drug offenders to be given drug treatment rather than prison sentences. Then in 2002 the Supreme Court considered the case of a court of appeals ruling that California's three-strikes law was unconstitutional due to its violation of the Eighth Amendment ban on cruel and unusual punishment, which ruled, consistent with original classical principles, that "the punishment for a third-strike crime cannot be grossly disproportionate to the offense committed" (ibid.). However, by a five-to-four majority, in 2003 the Court ruled that three-strikes sentences do not violate the "cruel and unusual punishment" ban of the Eighth Amendment. A subsequent attempt to amend the California law to make the third conviction a felony (Proposition 66) also failed in 2004. Similarly, Georgia's two-strikes law remains in effect, and in the United Kingdom a two-strikes law first introduced in 1997 was further strengthened in 2003 by limiting judicial discretion because judges had been using their discretion of "unjust" punishment and not imposing harsh life sentences for a second serious offense. By 2008 the original position granting judicial discretion had been restored by statute as a result of increasing concerns about prison overcrowding.

One of the main justifications for three-strikes laws is their incapacitation effects: Criminals who are locked away for twenty-five years are not going to victimize their communities. Indeed, writing for the majority of the Supreme Court justices in the case of *Ewing v. California*, Sandra Day O'Connor stated, "To be sure, Ewing's sentence is a long one. But it reflects a rational legislative judgment, entitled to deference, that offenders who have committed serious or violent felonies and who continue to commit felonies must be incapacitated" (538 U.S. 11 [2003]). Let us examine this element in the conservative distortion of classical thought.

Incapacitation

Incapacitation, or "containment," as it is also called, is the penal policy of taking the offender "out of circulation" through a variety of means, the most common of which is the use of confinement in prison, which is designed "to deny offenders the opportunity to commit additional offenses and further victimize society for the duration of their incarceration" (Hussey 1997, 120). Incapacitation policy related to penal confinement asserts that by putting adjudicated offenders "in prison" they are stopped from practicing criminal behaviors, and the "outside world" is correspondingly safer, albeit temporarily. It is based on a set of questionable empirically derived assumptions, such as the finding that 50 percent of all crimes are committed by 6 percent of the population of some cities (Wolfgang, Figlio, and Sellin 1972), and that a five-year sentence for any felony would reduce the rate of crime by 15 percent (Greenwood 1983; Murray 1997). Some critics see this "actuarial" approach as a "new penology" that is less interested in the lives of offenders than in risk management and case processing—in short, with "techniques of identifying, classifying and managing groups sorted by levels of dangerousness" (Carrabine 2001, 147; see also Feeley and Simon 1992). For others, incapacitation is an illusion for its claim of removing offenders from the rest of the population, since, as Arrigo and Milovanovic (2009) point out, there are not only the costs of prison that affect everyone but also the impact of imprisonment on the family lives of the convicted, their communities, and race relations, as a disproportionate number of those convicted are African

American. They point out that we pay the economic cost of the massively expanded prison programs, 2 million incarcerated in our state and federal prisons and jails in 2002, and 2.3 million by 2006, compared to fewer that 200,000 in the 1970s. And this is for a relatively small reduction in the actual crime rate of 5 percent, which itself is only questionably attributable to the policy of incapacitation (E. Currie 1998). According to *The Pew Report*, "For the first time in history more than one in every 100 adults in America are in jail or prison—a fact that significantly impacts state budgets without delivering a clear return on public safety" (Pew Charitable Trusts 2008). Moreover, Arrigo and Milovanovic (2008) argue that the "new penology" of incapacitation has accentuated the issue of race in American society, since one in three African American males aged twenty to twenty-nine are in prison, on probation, or on parole (Mauer 1997). This permeates the minority mind-set of those African Americans outside of prison who withdraw sentiment for the society's formal institutions, especially government and law enforcement.

Deterrence and the Death Penalty

From the criminal justice policy perspective, unless offenders think rationally before committing their crimes, there is little point to the deterrence argument. A second related issue is that unless we know the meaning of the gain or satisfactions to the offender, there is no precise way to design punishments that will counter the potential gain. A third issue in deterrence theory is the extent to which potential offenders using rational thought processes perceive the same risks and severity in punishments set by the legal system and how well they know its penalties (Geerken and Gove 1975). Indeed, this is a pillar of classical theory, for if people's perceptions of sanctions are more different than they are similar, the issue becomes one of scientific criminology (i.e., to determine how and why they are different). A related issue is what makes perceptions of sanctions different. If it has to do with differences between people rather than differences in information, then the focus again should be on what causes individual differences. Not surprisingly, classical theories (and rational choice theories that we look at later) assume that individual differences are "relatively much less significant in accounting for variations in criminal action between different individuals, different groups and over different time-periods than are variations in the control exercised by perceived incentives and disincentives" (Roshier 1989, 74).

Illustrating the idea of deterrence is the contemporary example of capital punishment. In spite of the link between classical theory and deterrence, it is important to remember that classical theorists, as we saw earlier, were actually opposed to the death penalty (Beccaria did support it in the extreme case of persons attempting to overthrow the state). Furthermore, although U.S. public opinion consistently supports the use of the death penalty—the 1990s showed the highest numbers since the 1950s, at 79 percent in favor of death for convicted murderers (Bureau of Justice Statistics 1996, 181; Bohm 1991)—most of the empirical research evidence shows that execution does not have a deterrent effect on crime or murder, and more recent evidence supporting the relationship of homicide reduction to capital punishment has been shown to be methodologically flawed (Weisberg 2005; Donohue and Wolfers 2006; Fagan 2005).

The original research by economist Isaac Ehrlich (1975) linked an offender's decision to commit a crime to his or her perception of the risk of being executed; Ehrlich claimed that every additional execution would save seven or eight victims from murder. A replication study by Bowers and Pierce (1975) refuted Ehrlich's findings, however, and went on to show that executions actually increase the homicide rate (Bowers and Pierce 1980). They found that over a period of fifty-seven years the homicide rate in New York State went up by two for each additional execution. This is known as the "brutalization" thesis, first put forward by Beccaria and empirically documented by Dann (1935) and Forst (1983). The argument is that the more violence people see by legitimate government, the more numbed they become to its pain, and the more acceptable it becomes to commit violent acts, including murder. The brutalization effects of capital punishment are supported by global research showing a decline in homicide rates in countries around the world following the abolition of the death penalty. Bailey and Peterson (1989) found that executions do not deter criminal homicides. However, Cochran and Chamlin (2000) in a more sophisticated analysis divided homicide into two types: nonstranger felony murders (murder between intimates and acquaintances) and argument-based homicides between strangers. They found that state executions were positively related to the brutalization hypothesis (homicides may actually increase), yet deterrence was effective at reducing nonstranger murders.

Some of the best studies on the deterrence effect of punishment have been conducted by Ray Paternoster. Paternoster and his colleagues (Paternoster et al. 1983, 1985) have shown that the perceived risk of certainty of arrest is not constant but declines with experience in committing offenses. Indeed, a study on recidivist property offenders shows that although they may use the rational thought process, their perception of sanctions did not deter them because they thought that they would not get caught, that any prison sentences would be relatively short, and that prison was nonthreatening (Tunnell 1992).

Paternoster (1989), in researching the effects of certainty and severity on high school children's decision to offend, found that certainty of punishment had more impact than severity of punishment (which had no significant impact on the delinquency decision). Moreover, he determined that the greatest effect came from the perceived certainty of informal sanctions from peers or parents rather than any sanctions from the legal system, a finding supported by others (Hollinger and Clark 1983; Grasmick and Bursik 1990; Williams and Hawkins 1989). Pogarsky (2002) found severity to have more effect than certainty with "deterrable" university students. As Ronald Akers (1994, 57) pointed out, traditionally conceived deterrence from legal sanctions, even if they are a catalyst to informal social sanctions, is undermined by such evidence. Indeed, in a review of the overall evidence, Akers concluded: "Studies of both objective and perceptual deterrence often do find negative correlations between certainty of criminal penalties and the rate or frequency of criminal behavior, but the correlations tend to be low. Severity of punishment has an even weaker effect on crime. Neither the existence of capital punishment nor the certainty of the death penalty has ever had a significant effect on the rate of homicide. . . . The empirical validity of deterrence theory is limited" (ibid., 54).

Although this matter seemed settled, an article by Hashem Dezhbakhsh, Paul Rubin, and Joanna Shepherd (2003), supported by Posner (2006), reignited the controversy with its claim that new evidence shows each execution saves eighteen lives. However, Donohue and Wolfers argued that these estimates have no credibility since Dezhbakhsh, Rubin, and Shepherd's regression analysis, if they ran it correctly, would show the opposite result: more lives lost per execution. Indeed, Donahue and Wolfers stated: "Our reading of these results suggests (weakly) that the preponderance of the evidence supports the view that increases in executions are associated with *increases* in lives lost," and "the view that the death penalty deters is still the product of a belief not evidence." They concluded, "In light of this evidence, is it wise to spend millions on a process with no demonstrated value that creates at least some risk of executing innocents when other proven crime-fighting measures exist?" (2006, 5–6).

Not only is the deterrence effect of capital punishment highly questioned, and its brutalization effect agreed upon, but, like incapacitation, capital punishment disproportionately impacts races, with 50 percent of those on death row being from minority groups; 40 percent of those executed are African American, when they account for only 12 percent of the U.S. population. Finally, as Donahue and Wolfers pointed out, serious questions have been raised since the late 1990s about how many innocents have been executed, as DNA evidence was found to exonerate numerous convicted death-row inmates, resulting in a moratorium on the death penalty by then-governor of Illinois George Ryan. Most of this research has been conducted by the Innocence Project rather than the criminal justice system or government. Barry Scheck and Peter J. Neufeld founded the Innocence Project in 1992 at Yeshiva University to assist inmates with having DNA tests conducted—often facing opposition from criminal justice officials. So far, 233 inmates have been exonerated by DNA testing, including 17 who were on death row. The Innocence Project found that "use of DNA technology to free innocent people has provided irrefutable proof that wrongful convictions are not isolated or rare events but instead arise from systemic defects" (2009). Some of these defects include eyewitness misidentification, unreliable or limited science, false confessions, forensic science fraud, government misconduct, or bad lawyering.

Critics of deterrence theory argue that it is founded on a narrow view of humans and the reasoning behind their actions. They believe "we need to develop a considerably more sophisticated theory of human behavior which explores the internal and external checks on why people do or do not engage in criminal activity. This theory must also recognize that there are a bewildering number of motivational states, rational and irrational, that lead to the commission of criminal acts" (McLaughlin 2001, 88). Some criminologists believe they have begun to do just that.

Redefining Rational Choice:
Situational Factors and Routine Activities Theory

The political and philosophical backlash against the rehabilitation models of the 1960s created a second development that had less to do with the administration of justice and more to do with how offenders decided to commit crime. This was a renewed and more refined interest in classical economic ideas of rational choice. A principal advocate of this renewed idea was Ronald Clarke, who at the time was head of the British government's crime research unit. Clarke and his colleague Derek Cornish (Clarke and Cornish 1983; Cornish and Clarke 1986, 2006) developed a more sophisticated understanding of how people make rational choices about whether to act—and about whether to commit crimes. They spawned a whole new direction in postclassical contemporary criminological research that looked at the situational factors that influence offenders to choose to commit crimes. In the United States, Marcus Felson and Lawrence Cohen (Cohen and Felson 1979; Felson 1986) were working on similar ideas, although they were looking at how the regular daily patterns of citizens' behavior create or inhibit the opportunities for offenders to commit crimes. Clarke and Felson would eventually collaborate at Rutgers University, where Clarke became the dean of criminal justice. Let us explore these ideas in more detail.

Rational choice theories explain how some people consciously and rationally choose to commit criminal acts. Consider the example of burglary. Beyond the monetary motive as a factor that leads to burglary, research shows that burglars decide to commit their offenses through a variety of rational decisions (D. Walsh 1980; T. Bennett and Wright 1984). These are based on situational circumstances, including their mood (Nee and Taylor 1988). Consider the questions a burglar might ask: Which area offers the best burglary targets—middle-class suburban housing or wealthy residential areas? Does it matter if the occupant is at home? Is burglary likely to be more successful during the day when people are out on short trips, when they are away on vacation, or at night when they are home? Do neighbors watch each other's houses? Will the method of entry to the property attract undue attention, and is there a system of surveillance? Once entrance to the residence has been gained, what kinds of goods will be taken—jewelry, antiques, electronics, or strictly cash? Are there two entrances so that one can serve as an escape route? What means are available to dispose of the goods? These are just some of the questions a burglar might ask in his or her rational choice approach to the crime. Some "professional" burglars specialize in certain property types and plan their entry into a target house over a period of time, whereas others are occasional opportunists. One study found that the most important environmental factor in target choice was the existence of two escape routes, one at the front and another at the rear of the building, especially where the rear exit has vegetation obscuring visibility. Dogs and alarms are only conditionally a deterrent. Occupancy in the day is checked, typically by knocking on the front or rear door and if someone answers making up an excuse about needing directions. But some burglars actually prefer the residents at home and asleep because then usually more cash, jewelry, and checkbooks are available (ibid.).

According to rational choice theorists, then, potential offenders consider the net benefits gained from committing crimes. Offenders, as in the burglar example, use free will and weigh the perceived costs against the potential benefits. This weighing is called choice structuring. Offenders choose to engage in criminal acts if their rough calculations suggest the actions might result in net gains. As we can see, circumstances, situation, and opportunities affect their decision, since these are factors to be considered when calculating the cost-benefit estimations of risk.

Contemporary rational choice theory differs from classical ideas in the degree of rationality attributed to offenders. Both rational or situational choice theory (Clarke and Cornish 1983, 1985) and routine activities theory (L. Cohen and Felson 1979; L. Cohen and Machalek 1988) emphasize the limits of rational thought in the decision to commit crime. They claim that criminal decisions are neither fully rational nor thoroughly considered. A variety of individual and environmental factors affect the choices made. Instead of pure rational calculation, offenders exercise "limited rationality" (Clarke and Cornish 1983, 49–50). Offenders, like everyone else, vary in their perceptions, motives, skills, and abilities to analyze a situation and structure choices toward desirable outcomes (Cornish and Clarke 1987, see figure 4.1). Cornish and Clarke assume the "purposive" rather than the "senseless" actor, who is goal directed toward "excitement, fun, prestige, sexual gratification and defiance or domination of others." They argue that even where clinical delusions or pathological compulsions might seem to be powerful explanations, "rationality is not completely absent" (2006, 20). The concept of a limited or "bounded" rationality is developed. Under this model, then, the offender "seeks to achieve an acceptable decision, a best-they-can at the time decision, rather than an optimal or maximal outcome, not least because the offender rarely has all the information, makes rushed decisions, and does so for the short rather than long term, using general models of past success" (Einstadter and Henry 2006, 57). Thus, Cornish and Clarke argue, "criminal choice cannot properly be studied in the abstract" but only "for specific categories of crime," which means context specific, as in automobile joyriding compared to systematic auto theft for resale (2006, 21). Moreover, they argue that the criminal is in a variable state of being such that "offenders' readiness to commit particular crimes varies according to their current needs and desires, and they constantly reassess their involvement in criminal activity. This assessment is deeply affected by their experience of committing particular acts and what they learn from the consequences" (ibid., 25).

Policy Implications of Rational Choice and Routine Activities Theories

Rational choice theorists suggest there are differences in the circumstances or the situations in which offenders select their crimes. As we have seen, these different situations can affect the criminal's choice of target (Clarke and Cornish 1983, 49). In short, these theories emphasize crime as the outcome of "choices and decisions made within a context of situational constraints and opportunities" (ibid., 8). Thus, a central policy issue is identifying the environmental triggers that facilitate the choice of criminal action.

A major element in the preventive policy of rational choice is to manipulate the opportunity structure in a particular environment to reduce the likelihood that offenders will choose to commit crimes. These theorists believe that "a way is opened to influence such decisions by seeking to make criminal behavior less rewarding, more risky and more difficult" (Cornish and Clarke 2006, 27). In the case of our burglar, more than one car in the driveway and several lights on in the house might indicate more than one person is at home and not asleep. Nosy neighbors might also act as a deterrent. Moriarty and Williams (1996) found that the absence of home owners between six and eleven at night made the residences most likely to be victimized. Manipulation of the environment, then, is designed to make the choice of crime more difficult and costly (Clarke and Cornish 1983, 48; Cornish and Clarke 1987). This leads to a variety of situational crime prevention strategies. The practice, known as "target hardening," decreases the chance that someone or something will be a victim of crime. Target hardening requires the potential victim to be more active in the process of crime control. Target hardening has been particularly prominent in the related theory of routine activities (L. Cohen and Felson 1979, 589).

We have seen that routine activities theory considers how everyday life brings together at a particular place and moment potential offenders, crime targets, and vulnerability. As is clear from the burglary example, the presence of guardians is a key factor affecting vulnerability (Felson 1987, 911; L. Cohen and Felson 1979; Felson and Cohen 1981; Felson 1986). Therefore, increasing the presence of capable, caring, intimate guardians (such as friends, relatives, and neighbors) of potential victims reduces the probability of victimization. Walking with another person to a parking lot at night offers more protection against a solitary robber than walking alone. Another strategy is for potential victims to change or vary their routine activities, behavior, and lifestyle. This makes them less vulnerable to personal crimes. Rational choice theorists suggest that crime prevention has brought major successes, "including the virtual elimination of airline hijackings in the 1970s by baggage screening, the elimination of robberies of bus drivers in American cities in the 1970s by the introduction of exact fare systems, and the virtual elimination in the 1990s of graffiti on New York City subway cars by systematic and prompt graffiti removal" (Cornish and Clarke 2006, 27).

Conceptual and Empirical Limitations: What the Research Shows

Both the rational or situational choice and the routine activities theories make some dubious assumptions. They claim the benefits of one type of crime are not equally available from another or from the same crime in another place. Criminologists call this the problem of "crime displacement." Consider, for example, whether a

FIGURE 3.1   Cornish and Clarke's Reasoning Criminal

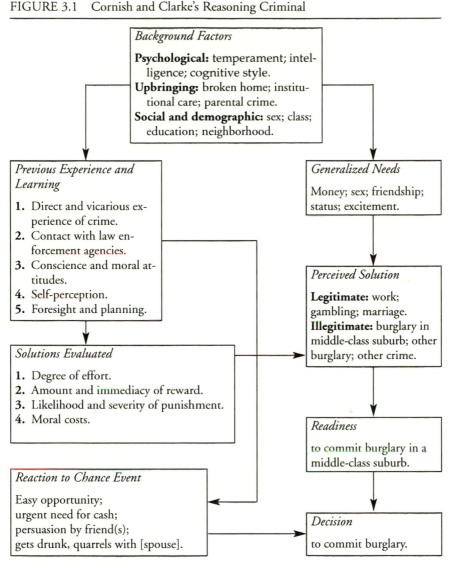

SOURCE: Cornish and Clarke 1986, p. 3.

shoplifter is likely to become a robber if he or she reasons that this will reduce the chance of success. Similarly, would a shoplifter at a high-security store switch to a low-security store? Indeed, Cornish and Clarke admit that the readiness to substitute one offense for another depends on whether "alternative offenses share characteristics which the offender considers salient to his or her goals and abilities" (1987, 935). As many people living in areas surrounding former drug neighborhoods have learned, however, one neighborhood's cleanup can become another's crime problem. As we shall see later, there are other problems with rational choice theories, as evidenced by empirical research.

We can evaluate the contribution of classical and rational choice theories to criminology on several levels. Space precludes an extensive review and critique (for these, see R. Akers 1990, 1994). It is necessary, however, to briefly summarize the evidence in relation to rational choice in the motivation to commit crime and the extent to which rational choice precautions by potential victims affect the probability of subsequent victimization.

Evidence on the Rational Choice Decision-Making Process

The central issue in rational choice theory is whether potential offenders use a rational thought process in their decision to commit crime. We have already argued that rational choice, even as proclaimed by its advocates (Cornish and Clarke 1986), involves a limited notion of rationality ("partial rationality" or "soft rationality") and that any theory assuming "pure" rationality "has virtually no empirical validity" (R. Akers 1994, 58). Studies focusing on part of the process in committing a crime, such as target selection by burglars (Maguire and Bennett 1982; T. Bennett and Wright 1984; Rengert and Wasilchick 1985), "provide considerable empirical support for a 'limited rationality' view of decision making by lawbreakers" (Gibbons 1994, 124). For example, Nee and Taylor's interviews with fifty convicted residential burglars (1988) support the view of the offender as a "rational" agent, making decisions under a variety of prevailing circumstances. Similarly, Trevor Bennett's study of rational choice by opiate users (1986) challenges the arguments about crime displacement, because he shows that their original motivation is the particular opiate drug culture and that in its absence alternative subcultures may not be as appealing. Finally, Vaughan's study of rational choice decision making by corporate organizations in the case of NASA's fatal decision to launch *Challenger* (1998) leads her to conclude that the rationality of corporate officials is a complex process, affected by a corporate organizational bias toward making risky decisions, and differing little from the rationality of robbers and burglars in its "bounded" nature.

As Akers (1990; 1994, 60) has pointed out, however, when other factors that constrain rationality are factored into the decision-making process (such as effective ties to parents, moral beliefs, and peer influences), it is questionable whether what is being supported is rational choice or the other theories that assume nonrational factors, such as social learning theory (Chapter 7) or social bonding theory (Chapter 8).

Evidence on Routine Activities and Crime

In addition to rational thought processes and the deterrent effects of sanctions, a third factor in the equation of the criminal event is the coincidence of them in time and place. According to routine activities theory, the presence of motivated offenders and suitable targets in the absence of capable guardians is more likely to lead to crime. Leaving aside the question of what makes a motivated offender, empirical research has focused on targets and guardians. The main findings suggest that certain areas, known as "hot spots," account for most victimizations and that people who go out to these places, such as bars, dances, parties, shopping centers, and so on, at night are more vulnerable to being victimized than those who stay home (Messner and Blau 1987; L. Kennedy and Forde 1990a, 1990b). In the case of property crimes such as burglary, however, victims' absence may seem more conducive to crime than their presence. For example, the more people are absent from home, as happens when both parents are working, the more likely they are to be victimized. O'Shea found that "ten of eleven predictors of burglary victimization reflected the efficacy of security measures" (2000, 162). Matthew B. Robinson (2000) found further support for altering physical and social environments to reduce the risk of victimization. Some studies, however, have been criticized for relying too much on stereotyped conceptions of crime and of the different kinds of offender (Nee and Taylor 1988) and ignoring hidden crime and gender issues. Indeed, because of the link between intimates and violence, those who stay at home may be more likely to be victimized (Messner and Tardiff 1985; Maxfield 1987). In particular, DeKeseredy and Schwartz (1996) point out that women actually suffer a greater likelihood of personal victimization in the home from husbands and partners than from going out. Furthermore, they argue for a feminist routine activities theory that explains why college campuses are dangerous places for women whose susceptibility to sexual attack is increased by alcohol and socializing with sexually predatory men in the absence of capable guardians. Again, the explanation of why men are sexually predatory has more to do with nonrational choice theory, since it relies on notions of socialization into peer subcultures supportive of sexual exploitation and on the social construction of masculinity (see Chapter 11).

Indeed, in spite of the claims of this perspective, policy success has not been universal. Farrington and Welsh (2002) conducted a meta-analysis on the effects of street lighting and found mixed results in the United States. However, when research from Britain was included, improved street lighting led to reductions in crime.

One major study (Weisburd 1997) suggests that many additional environmental manipulations show how a school may reduce its vulnerability to crime, including access control, offender deflection, facilitator control, entry and exit screening, formal surveillance, employee surveillance, natural surveillance, and rule setting. Although each practice involves empirical research on why an offender chooses to refrain from crime rather than commit it, it is clear that since the 1990s in the case of schools, the increase in serious violence has led many schools to adopt such environmental measures under "safe school" programs. The critical question is whether, through such environmental manipulations, we have transformed schools into institutions more like prisons (Crews and Tipton 2002) and in the process undermined the very purpose that the institution was designed to serve such that the controls are more destructive than the original problem (Hinkle and Henry 2000).

It is this kind of response to the fear of crime that has created some considerable controversy. Critics, particularly feminists, argue that routine activities theory blames the victim. This is especially true for rape victims. In effect, potential male rapists are forcing women to change behavior, lifestyle, and even appearance. The policy approach of this theory appeals to those favoring cost cutting and simplistic technical solutions to crime. The perspective may lead to a siege mentality, however, as society increasingly orients itself "to ever-increasing oversight and surveillance, fortification of homes, restrictions on freedom of movement, and the proliferation of guns for alleged self-defense" (Einstadter and Henry 2006, 71).

TABLE 3.1 Characteristics of Security in American Educational Institutions and the Penal System

American Public School	*American Correctional System*
Metal Detectors	Metal Detectors
Identification Badges	Identification Badges
Uniforms or Clothing Standard	Uniforms
Surveillance Cameras	Surveillance Cameras
Searches (Personal Property, Lockers, etc.)	Searches (Personal Property, Housing Units)
Teachers Use of 2-Way Radios	Correctional Personnel Use 2-Way Radios
Panic Button in Classrooms	Correctional Officer Panic Button
American Public School	*American Correctional System*
Locked Perimeter Doors	Locked Perimeter Doors
School Resource Officers	Correctional Officers
Controlled Movements	Controlled Movements
In-School Suspension/ Detention	Solitary Confinement/ Protective Custody

SOURCE: Crews and Tipton 2002.

In spite of its theoretical and empirical limitations, the idea that criminals choose to commit crime reflects the U.S. public's psyche. The consequential strategy of denying an offender the opportunity to engage in crime by manipulating the physical environment through target hardening, environmental design, and other measures gives people a sense of control over their fear of crime. Regardless of its effectiveness, rational choice theory is valuable on these grounds alone. A fundamental question remains, however: Should crimes by the powerful also be subject to rational choice analysis and environmental manipulation?

BOX 3.2 The Challenge of Rational Choice Policy and Crimes of the Powerful
The Case of Surveillance?
STUART HENRY

Clearly, the implications for policy from rational choice and routine activities theory, as we have seen, are an increase in a variety of crime prevention measures designed to prevent crime by creating barriers and frustrating the opportunities for offending. Situational crime prevention has grown to include a variety of technologies designed to monitor our movements, from closed-circuit television (CCTV) and sensor tracking to GPS tracking and a variety of policing activities, including wiretapping of cell phone conversations and monitoring of personal computers. The effectiveness and indeed ethical problems associated with the use of these technologies can be illustrated by the case of CCTV. What are the ethical issues involved in the technology of surveillance? Does surveillance work? Is the technology up to the job, and is it being deploying in the right way?

Surveillance cameras are increasingly prying into our public spaces and our private lives. Advocates of CCTV believe that security cameras deter crime and help fight the war on terrorism. If people know they are being watched, they will change their behavior. That's the rationale that's turning the United States into the kind of "surveillance nation" that the United Kingdom has already become.

In addition to mass transit systems, video surveillance is deployed at banks, stores, shopping malls, ports, harbors, airports, military installations, public parks, construction sites, industrial plants, school and university campuses, toll booths, freeways, town centers, and public streets. But cameras are also creeping into our homes, the latest example being "virtual proctors" designed to spy on students taking online classes so that they don't cheat.

Public opinion surveys find that few people mind that they are being watched. Seventy percent of the public support CCTV (Ditton 1998; Harris Poll 2006). That's because most people think they are doing nothing wrong: "nothing to hide; nothing to fear." Never mind privacy issues—these can be sacrificed for security. In fact, security

CONTINUES

BOX **3.2** (CONTINUED)

industry analysts emphasize that it is not Big Brother but "safety and security" that are the key to further expansion. The question is whether surveillance produces a false sense of security and whether we are actually watching the right people. Are we deluding ourselves that cameras protect us when the majority of evidence shows that they make very little difference to the incidence of crime?

In 2007 a German transit authority study on the Berlin subway system tested whether twenty-four-hour surveillance of subway stations would reduce crimes such as assault and vandalism and found that the number of crimes slightly increased. Nor did the cameras contribute to a higher detection rate because the quality of the recordings was poor and offenders took their crimes off camera.

In Britain, the leading "surveillance nation," where there are 4.2 million CCTV cameras, one for every fourteen people, government studies have consistently shown that cameras make very little difference to most street-crime rates (2.5 percent), with the exception of auto theft from parking structures (28 percent reduction) (Welsh and Farrington 2002). Nor is detection improved since the quality of the image is often poor, and there are not the resources to review the many hours of footage shot. Ironically, to improve the quality it would be necessary to have multiple cameras at each incident site, each taking different-angled shots, and that would mean even more footage to review.

And then there is the cost-effectiveness of deploying this technology in public places and whether the money could be better spent elsewhere, such as on community policing, neighborhood amenities, and building social capital. The concern in Britain, a country where microcontrol is typically exercised by anyone with a position of authority, is that this mass surveillance would increasingly focus on minor deviance. The result is a widening net catching minor offenders. Examples abound, such as the report in 2007 of a man in Bristol facing the equivalent of a $2,000 fine after his dog was videotaped allegedly defecating on the sidewalk. Even here, the quality of the picture was so poor the man said, "It didn't show any poo" (Kelland 2008). Things have gone to the extreme. In some towns "guardians" of morality are watching the streets for deviance, littering, or jaywalking and use megaphones to command the public to correct their unacceptable behavior. Drunks regularly perform on the street in front of the CCTV cameras whose monitors are captive audiences.

Those in favor of surveillance believe that the problems can be overcome by combining intelligence software with wireless cameras. The technical trend is to move away from analog-based CCTV using fixed-wired cameras to wireless cameras that can transmit images to computer screens forty miles away. Smart software can now be used to filter images to only those showing threatening or suspicious behavior. Other technological advances include image stabilization and greater image range. Although this might improve quality and reduce the resources needed to operate the system, the question remains whether surveillance cameras are deployed in the most effective locations. Is the public our biggest crime problem?

CONTINUES

BOX 3.2 (CONTINUED)

References

Ditton, Jason. 2006. "Public Support for Town Centre CCTV Scheme: Myth or Reality?" In *Surveillance, Closed Circuit Television, and Social Control,* edited by Clive Norris, Jade Morgan, and Gary Armstrong. Aldershot, UK: Ashgate.

Harris Poll. 2006. "Large Majorities of Public Support Surveillance of Suspected Terrorists." In *The Harris Poll*, no. 63. August 17. http://www.harrisinteractive.com/harris _poll/index.asp?PID=690 (accessed March 25, 2009).

Kelland, Kate. 2008. "Stop Using Laws to Spy on Public, UK Councils Told." Reuters North American News Service. http://www.blnz.com/news/2008/06/23/Stop_using _laws_public_councils_9351.html (accessed March 18, 2009).

Welsh, Brandon, and David Farrington. 2002. *Crime Prevention Effects of CCTV: A Systematic View.* Home Office Research Study 252. London: Home Office.

Is the crime problem in America in the streets or in the suites? If more harm is committed to Americans by white-collar offenders, corporate fraud, environmental pollution, faulty product manufacture, and government corruption than by street crime, then why aren't we putting surveillance cameras in the corporate boardrooms, finance houses, and government offices and on golf courses? Cost-benefit calculations about "sharp practice" and "screwing the client" are much more likely to be curbed by the very rational executives who run these entities. Modifying their behavior to reduce costs is certainly more predictable than speculating about whether the emotive drunk, drugged, or rash, opportunistic, risk-taking offender is likely to care about the future consequences of apprehension for a crime. After all, President Nixon's ultimate demise came as a result of revealing tapes. Would we have had the Enron scandal if there had been cameras in the company's executive offices? Would the current housing crisis have wrought its effects if wireless cameras viewed by inspectors at the Securities and Exchange Commission had monitored the day-to-day operations of subprime lenders and the banks hyping worthless securities?

Although privacy issues around technology use are important, perhaps more important is the nature of the deployment of the technology we use. In reality, it is not the harms that we most fear that are the most destructive but the harms produced by the people and institutions we most trust.

So should we place surveillance cameras in corporate boardrooms and corridors of power? A further argument for this is that it is not just individuals who use rational thought processes to satisfy their goals without regard for the harm caused to others but also corporations that do this, with often deadly results. That is, there is no question that rational choice decision making affects the decisions in cases of corporate crime, but rational choice theory is rarely focused on this issue.

An excellent illustration of the priority of rational cost-benefit calculation in corporate fraud is found in the case of the Ford Pinto. In the 1970s, the Ford Motor

Company, under then-president Lee Iacocca, was trying to reclaim some of its lost car market from foreign competition. Both Volkswagen and the makers of the growing Japanese imports had been particularly successful selling subcompact cars at relatively low prices. To compete, Ford designed and developed the Pinto as its under-$2,000 car ($10,570 adjusted for inflation to 2007). From its introduction in 1970, the Pinto soon became the fastest-selling domestic subcompact. Preproduction crash tests showed the vehicle's fuel tank was easily ruptured during rear-end collisions at speeds greater than twenty-five miles per hour, however.

But even as fatal fiery crashes began to occur involving the Pinto's inadequate gas tank, Ford made the rationally based decision not to replace it. A contemporary investigative news report supports rational choice assumptions about the decision-making process (Dowie [1977] 1979). It showed that the cost of making each car safe would be $11 ($58.14 at 2007 prices). But when multiplied by the number of cars, the sum was more costly than the expected liability from injury suits: "Although the company calculated that eleven dollars per car would make the car safe, it decided that this was too costly. They reasoned that 180 burn deaths and 180 serious burn injuries and 2,100 burned vehicles would cost $49.5 million dollars (each death was figured at $200,000 dollars) but that recall of all the Pintos and the eleven-dollar repair would amount to $137 million" (D. Simon and Eitzen 1982, 99). (Translating this to 2007 prices, the cost of burn deaths and injuries and burned vehicles was estimated at $261.6 million, based on a cost of each death at $1.6 million, whereas the cost of safety repairs at $58 per car would have been $724 million.) Moreover, evidence obtained from a Ford memorandum titled "Fatalities Associated with Crash-Induced Fuel Leakage and Fires" laid out these rational calculations. As one commentator noted, "This cold calculation demonstrated Ford's lack of concern for anything but profit" (Green 1990, 129).

Deaths from dangerous gas tanks in the Pinto (and the Mercury Bobcat) were estimated by 1977 to number between five hundred and nine hundred (Dowie [1977] 1979; Box 1983, 24). In 1978, Ford was indicted by a grand jury in Indiana on three counts of reckless homicide for the deaths of three teenage girls in a fiery rear-end collision, but the company was acquitted of this criminal charge in 1980 (Cullen, Maakestad, and Cavender 1987). The Elkhart, Indiana, county prosecutor, Michael Consentino, believed corporations, like individuals, should be held accountable for their actions (P. Becker, Jipson, and Bruce 2002). Also in 1978, the U.S. Department of Transportation ordered a recall of all 1971–1976 Pintos. Only then, after months of vehement denials of the problem, did Ford comply. As Green states:

> Occupational violations (unlike rape, assault or drug use) are most often the result of calculated risks that seek to increase financial benefits. The vast majority of persons who commit occupational crimes seem to do so after considering the certainty, celerity, and severity of formal and nonformal consequences. . . . Almost all persons who plan to commit an occupational crime . . . are potentially deterrable. . . . Occupa-

tional criminals should receive a greater severity of punishment for their offenses than do street criminals because occupational offenders usually have more investment in the social order (job, respectability, education, career) and therefore perceive that they have more to lose if caught. ([1990] 1997, 68–69)

If rational choice theory has a place in criminology, it certainly needs to be applied to all forms of criminal harm. Policies that emerge from the theory need to go beyond the individual to include organizational and even state levels of rational choice decision making (Henry 1991; Barak 1991). Consumers and clients need to develop ways to avoid their routine vulnerability, such as avoidance of relying on expert knowledge of professionals, developing cynicism over commercial and industrial processes (such as food production and waste disposal), and avoiding relations with corporate and government systems that use and abuse power. Fortunately, some criminologists are aware of this and have begun applying both rational choice and routine activities theories to corporate and white-collar crime (Paternoster and Simpson 1993, 1996; Shover and Wright 2001; Vaughan 1998).

Finally, it is worth considering in the wider sense of this perspective from classical theory to rational choice and routine activities that criminal justice practices deriving from manipulating the environmental conditions can ultimately undermine the original principles, especially when the threat is perceived as external. The fact that any nation's criminal justice system is set in a wider global context can and does affect its operations. Einstadter and Henry (2006, 71–73) describe how the effects of being in global conflict, in particular the fear of global terrorism, have forced the U.S. criminal justice system to become more repressive, removed many of the individual protections granted through its classically rooted constitutional principles, and even allowed the return of torture:

> Major challenges usually arise when the nation is in perceived peril. The most recent example of a reversion to reactionary legal constructs is the Patriot Act of 2001. Its passage, rationalized by the terrorist attack of September 11, 2001, allows invasions of privacy and nullifies certain due process guarantees. For example, under its provisions it becomes possible for the federal government to secretly inspect an individual's library, bank, and medical records with minimal judicial review. Police are also given powers that are antagonistic to due process rights all in the name of sifting out potential terrorists. World War II brought massive violations of civil liberties with the wholesale forced movement of Japanese American citizens to relocation centers. The point to be made is that while the basic structure of the legal system remains static, societal events may trigger repressive measures rationalized on the basis of security of the nation, seriously compromising the civil and due process protections that were the basis of the early classical school of criminology. (ibid., 71)

Clearly, the classical and rational choice explanations for crime and the policy implications that they have for criminal justice do not transcend the demands of the global context in which they are set.

Summary and Conclusion

Classical theory has been credited with enhancing democracy and with reforming harsh, arbitrary, and brutal techniques of crime control, including the elimination of torture (Einstadter and Henry 2006). But its limits were soon recognized. It is overly idealistic. It proved almost as unjust to treat people the same who were clearly different as to treat people differently arbitrarily and capriciously, as had pre-Enlightenment justice. A society that celebrates individual achievement produces disparities of wealth, status, and social standing. Any attempt to provide equal punishments that ignores this reality simply provides those who can afford punitive fines or an adequate legal defense with a license to commit crime. The result of such a system is that it proves to be "more just" for some than it is for others: "Whereas the rich offender may be cushioned by his or her wealth, the poor offender, with the same sentence but little to fall back on, is punished in fact disproportionately" (J. Young 1981, 266). Jeffrey Reiman also aptly proclaimed this in his book *The Rich Get Richer and the Poor Get Prison* ([1979] 2007).

Policy implications based on rational choice premises have both positive and negative effects on an individual's or a group's calculation. The U.S. system of criminal justice employs these principles in the due process model, but criminal justice deals with the issue very narrowly. Originally, classicists assumed that if punishment was certain, swift, and sufficiently severe, the potential offender would be less likely to commit the crime. Contemporary versions of classical ideas have reintroduced several of these ideas. Mandatory sentences and limited discretion are logical extensions of the tradition. These determinate sentencing policies deny consideration of individual circumstances and any need for rehabilitative corrections, however. Advocates also do not apply the same principles to offenders who are convicted of more than one offense. Selecting some aspects of the classical model (deterrence and certainty) while ignoring others (proportionality) can lead to law-and-order distortions of the classical position that produce outrageous injustices (life in prison without parole for small-scale property offenses).

Should corporations that have acted criminally be subject to mandatory sentences and limited discretion? Alternatively, are corporations sufficiently different that these differences must be recognized when dispensing justice? And what about corporate rehabilitation?

Rational choice and routine activities theorists focus on the design, security, and surveillance measures that potential victims may take to frustrate potential offenders. The goal is to increase the difficulty, risk of apprehension, and time involved in committing crime. These same theorists, however, rarely consider applying such environmental disincentives to crimes of the powerful. Should they do so? One ramification of adopting such practices is that potential criminals may seek other less vulnerable targets.

A further criticism of classical justice is that setting punishments equally, or even proportionately, takes no account of differences in offenders' motivation, in their ability to reason, or in their perception of the meaning and importance of punishment. It also fails to consider irrational behavior, spontaneous crimes (e.g., violent crimes committed in "the heat of the moment"), or the role of peer groups and their different effects on rationally calculating individuals. As soon as these differences are acknowledged, we are no longer dealing with a classical rational choice model. Indeed, recognition of these deficiencies coupled with scientific advances (in research methods, biophysiology, psychology, sociology, and so forth) led criminologists to focus on a variety of "causes" of criminal behavior. The following chapters explore these scientific criminologies in more detail.

Summary Chart: Classical, Rational Choice, and Routine Activities Theories

Basic Idea: Essentially an economic theory of crime captured in the idea that people are free to choose crime as one of a range of behavioral options.

Human Nature: Assumes that humans are freethinking, rational decision makers who choose their own self-interests by weighing pleasure against pain and choosing the former. Their choice is goal directed and aimed at maximizing their sense of well-being, or utility. Utility depends on wealth, and life is evaluated primarily in monetary terms and can include the value and use of time. Rational choice and routine activities theorists acknowledge a limited or conditional rationality.

Criminals: Rational, hedonistic, free actors no different from noncriminals except that they broke the law. Lawbreakers are those who choose to limit others' freedom as defined by law.

Social Order and Law: A consensus around a highly stratified hierarchy based on a social contract assumed between free individuals who choose to sacrifice a part of their freedom to the state so that they may enjoy the rest in security. Some economists, however, see order as a situation of conflict over interests. Law preserves individuals' freedom to choose. Crime is defined by the legal code such that there is no crime without law. There is a preference for statutory law.

Causal Logic: Free choice, lack of fear of punishment, an ineffective criminal justice system, available unguarded targets, and opportunistic situations. Crime is the outcome of rational calculation. Offenders act on their perception, rather than the reality, that the benefits of crime outweigh the costs. Recent theorists recognize this, arguing that a low perception of the probability of both apprehension and punishment together with the belief that punishment will be of uncertain, negotiable, or low severity combined with a relatively low expectation of gains from legitimate work and high expected gains from illegitimate work, in a context where moral reservations are absent, will lead to criminal activity.

Criminal Justice Policy: The social function of policy is to administer justice fairly, based on equal treatment before the law, so that individuals will accept responsibility for their offending and choose not to offend. Increased efficiency of criminal justice is desired, especially enforcement, making it visible, certain, and swift. Later policy also includes reducing the opportunities for crime to occur.

The due process model: (1) sovereignty of the individual, (2) presumption of innocence, (3) equality before the law and between parties in dispute, (4) restraint of arbitrary power, (5) protection of the defendant against abuses and error, (6) no discretion or arbitrariness but a rule-based system (rules limiting police procedure and power and governing what is acceptable evidence), (7) adversarial trial (ensuring equality of inquiry), (8) right to be represented, (9) efficiency and fairness in protecting the rights of individuals, (10) certainty of detection and more efficient police preferred to simple presence of police, (11) trial by peers, and (12) right to appeal to an independent body. The policy involves retribution, just deserts, individual deterrence, and prevention. Penalties to be only so severe as to just deter. Equal punishments for equal crimes, preferably by determinate or mandatory sentences. Punishment based only on the crime committed. Proportionality of punishment, so that potential offenders choose lesser crime. Increase security, reduce opportunity, and harden targets. Ensure legitimate wages, job creation, and job training. Raise perceptions of the value of gains from legitimate system and devalue those from illegitimate system.

Criminal Justice Practice: Fines because they can be equalized and staged in progressive severity, prison because time served can be adjusted and staged at different levels for different offenses, death penalty only as the ultimate sanction for serious offenders, and environmental manipulation and adjustments of routine activities of potential victims to avoid crime.

Evaluation: Explains the decision making involved in white-collar and corporate crime and some street crime. Any crime with a pecuniary or even instrumental motive is explainable, such as some theft and burglary. Ignores inequality of structure and assumes formal equality is perceived the same way irrespective of social class; difficult to achieve in pure form; fails to account for irrational behavior or spontaneous crimes; fails to consider the role of peer groups and their different effects on the rational calculus; allows those who can afford punishment to buy license to crime. Policies are applied only to crimes of the powerless, not to those of the powerful or the state. Can reverse sovereignty of the individual and replace with supremacy of the state in times of perceived external threat such as terrorism.

4

"Born to Be Bad"

Biological, Physiological, and Biosocial Theories of Crime

The idea that crime is "in the blood," that certain criminal behaviors are inherited, is the hallmark of the biological approach to criminological explanation. Contemporary bioethicists argue that with biotechnology we have the ability to manage high-risk populations. The term *biogovernance* (using biotechnology to manage potential deviants) is used through the Human Genome Project and in reproductive technologies, cloning, genetically engineered foods, hybrid animals, gene therapy, DNA profiling, and data banking (Gerlach 2001). Science and criminal justice are linked as never before with DNA and data banks containing considerable information, including fingerprints, palm prints, facial recognition, as well as voice, signature, keystroke, and gait recognition. "Biometrics," as this field is called, is increasingly being used "by governments and business organisations in their bid to fight fraud, organised crime and terrorism, as well as to combat illegal immigration. Biometrics technology using advanced computer techniques is now widely adopted as a front-line security measure for both identity verification and crime detection, and also offers an effective crime deterrent" (Motorola 2006, 3). Proponents argue that "developments in biotechnology and knowledge have opened up discussion and debate about biology, crime and social control in an unprecedented way. People have always linked criminality to heredity to some extent, but we are much closer to scientifically legitimating that link and developing strategies for doing something about it" (Gerlach 2001, 113). We are now seeing technology employed not only in detecting crime but also in examining the physical functioning of the brain through functional magnetic resonance imaging to establish the biological blood-flow patterns that occur when the brain processes deceptive thoughts (Haddock 2006; Willing 2006).

What if we could predict violent thought in advance of its practice? Consider the case of twenty-five-year-old Charles J. Whitman, who in 1966 killed his mother and wife and the next day shot sixteen people to death and wounded another thirty from a 307-foot tower on the campus of the University of Texas at Austin. Going up into the tower he also killed a receptionist by hitting her in the back of the head. After Whitman was killed by police sharpshooters, an autopsy revealed a walnut-size malignant tumor in the hypothalamus region of Whitman's brain. This type of tumor is known to cause irrational outbursts of violent behavior, which Whitman had himself reported experiencing in the months prior to the mass murders. According to thirty-two medical experts and scientists, the tumor "was the probable cause of his criminal actions" and the primary precipitating factor in the mass murder (Holman and Quinn 1992, 66–67). The note Whitman left next to his wife's body contained chilling insight into his medical abnormality. Parts of it read: "I have been a victim of many unusual and irrational thoughts . . . overwhelming violent impulses. . . . After my death I wish that an autopsy would be performed on me to see if there is any visible physical disorder. I have had some tremendous headaches. . . . I decided to kill my wife. . . . I cannot rationally pinpoint any specific reason" (http://www.pop culture.com/pop/bioproject/charleswhitman.html, December 5, 2002). Could this murder spree have been prevented using "modern" biotechnology or biometrics? Is it true that "a systematic predetection . . . to prevent risky individuals and groups from becoming manifestly dangerous" is now a reality (Gerlach 2001, 97)? If violence is the result of genetic inheritance, tumors, or changes in body chemistry, can the subject be held responsible?

Biological explanations of crime have appeared since the sixteenth-century "human physiognomy" (the study of facial features) of J. Baptiste della Porte (1535–1615), who studied the cadavers of criminals to determine the relationship between the human body and crime (Schafer 1976, 38). In the 1760s, Johann Kaspar Lavater (1741–1801) claimed to have identified a relationship between behavior and facial structure (Lilly, Cullen, and Ball [1989] 1995), and in 1810 Franz Joseph Gall (1758–1828) developed a six-volume treatise on "craniology," or "phrenology." According to Gall, crime was one of the behaviors organically governed by a certain section of the brain. Thus, criminality could be ascertained by measuring bumps on the head (Savitz, Turner, and Dickman 1977). The biological explanation for crime did not become fully established, however, until the late 1800s.

Following the 1930s there was a historical aversion to biological explanations among many criminologists (R. Wright and Miller 1998). This changed with the publication of E. O. Wilson's *Sociobiology: The New Synthesis* (1975). In the past twenty-five years there has been a huge increase in the numbers of studies dealing with genetics, personality traits, and behavior (Garland 2001) and even criminology textbooks taking a prosociobiological evolutionary perspective (Ellis and Walsh 2000). By the early 2000s there had been significant advances in the search for biological causes due to more sophisticated diagnostic procedures. We now know, for example, that "various kinds of brain injuries and cerebrospinal disorders can be related to severe personality changes and emotional problems, which, in their turn, can be paired with maladaptive behavior. . . . Also viral infections such as the Borna disease virus are often linked to neurobehavioral and 'emotional' disturbances" (Martens 2002, 172). In the recent work the biological contribution to explaining crime is seen as interrelated with the environmental causes such that "biology is not destiny" (Niehoff 1999, 30). Indeed, "The environment cannot be disconnected from the body any more than brain function can be understood out of context. And the belief that social factors, divorced from their biological impact, are the 'cause' of violence is just as misguided as the belief that violent behavior is written into the genes" (ibid., 258).

In this chapter, we present the basic premises of the search for the causes of crime, outline the historical context under which it evolved, provide illustrative examples of the early and contemporary studies, review some of the latest developments, evaluate findings and assumptions, and provide policy implications.

Biological and Positivistic Assumptions

To understand biological theories, it is necessary to grasp the underlying assumptions about humans that biological criminologists make. The major emphasis of this applied science of criminology is that humans have unique characteristics, or predispositions, that, under certain conditions, lead some to commit criminal acts. In other words, something within the individual strongly influences his or her behavior, but this factor will come out only in certain environmental conditions. For example, some people seem to behave perfectly normally most of the time, but when they get behind the wheel of a car the slightest inconvenience sends them into an angry rage (James and Nahl 2000). Without the automotive environment, they do not manifest anger. According to biological theory, the same can be true for other offenders. For some, perhaps actress Winona Ryder, who on November 6, 2002, was convicted of shoplifting more than $5,500 worth of merchandise, department stores and the consumer culture provide an environment that when combined with their personal predispositions results in shoplifting. The setting and act together provide a thrill that, according to biological theorists, might satisfy an abnormal need for excitement. For others, the environmental trigger to crime might be alcohol, drugs, or being subjected to authority.

For early biological criminologists, the classical philosophers and jurists' view of crime was unscientific speculation. Any serious examination of criminal behavior cannot assume humans are essentially all the same (rational thinkers). Rather, they argued, looking at individuals' unique characteristics and differences would reveal the underlying causes of criminal tendencies. The key to understanding crime, the early biological criminologists believed, was to study the criminal actor, not the criminal act. Criminologists should study the nature of criminals as "kinds of people" who would commit such acts (A. Cohen 1966).

Of central importance to these founding biological criminologists was how to study the criminal. Accurate study of human features demands rigorous methods and careful observation. The approach these pioneers of scientific criminology adopted is called the positivist method. It is defined as the "application of the scientific method to the study of the biological, psychological, and social characteristics of the criminal" (Vold and Bernard 1986, 45). Its detailed direct observation, experimentation, and use of controlled samples allowed criminologists to identify individuals with a predisposition for crime. This method of research is still very prevalent today and, indeed, forms the basis of most contemporary criminological theory, regardless of its disciplinary roots. As Rafter (1992, 1998) points out, however, unlike contemporary positivists, early positivists also accepted folk wisdom, anecdotes, and analogies to lower forms of life as part of their empirical data.

Those first interested in this approach were criminal anthropologists. They believed that criminals could be explained by physical laws that denied any free will (ibid.). They claimed it was possible to distinguish types of criminals by their physical appearance. The physical features most often studied were body type, shape of the head, genes, eyes, and physiological imbalances. Although their methods were crude and later shown to be flawed, an understanding of these founding ideas is instructive.

The Social Context of Criminal Anthropology

Evolutionary biology heralded a different way of looking at human development. In 1859, Englishman Charles Darwin (1809–1882) presented his theory of evolution, *On the Origin of Species* ([1859] 1968), in which he argued that the development of any species proceeds through natural variations among offspring. The weakest strains fail to adapt to their environment and die off or fail to reproduce, whereas the strong survive, flourish, and come to dominate the species at a more advanced state. Cesare Lombroso (1836–1909), a professor of forensic medicine, psychiatry, and later criminal anthropology, and his students Enrico Ferri and Raffaele Garofalo applied these ideas to the study of crime. This "holy three of criminology" became known as the Italian School (Schafer 1976, 41). Their position was radically opposed to Italian classicists such as Beccaria, whom they saw as overemphasizing free choice at the expense of determinism (Ferri's dissertation was on the problem of free will). Rather than seeing humans as self-interested, rational individuals possessing similar abilities to reason, the Italian School criminologists believed humans differ and that some are more crime-prone than others. As Jock Young has pointed out, their approach was the mirror image of classicism: "Free-will disappears under determinacy, equality bows before natural differences and expert knowledge, and human laws that are created become scientific laws that are discovered" (1981, 267). If classicism was the language of logical deduction, traditional opinion, and abstract reasoning, then, wrote Ferri, "We speak two different languages" (1901, 244).

The new scientific criminology, founded on positivist assumptions, valued the "experimental method" as the key to knowledge based on empirically discovered facts and their examination. This knowledge was to be achieved carefully, over years of systematic observation and scientific analysis. The task of the criminologist was to apply the appropriate scientific apparatuses, the calipers, dynamometer, and aesthesiometer, to measure and chart the offender's deformities (Rafter 1992). Only then would we discover the explanation for crime and for what would become known as the "born criminal."

The Born Criminal

To appreciate the revolutionary nature of these early biological and physiological theories, it is necessary to recall that in the late nineteenth century, science was viewed as a sort of "new religion," a source of knowledge and a solution to problems such as disease, starvation, unemployment, and—of interest to us—crime. Lombroso is widely recognized as the most influential founding scholar to rely on the scientific method to study crime and is often called the "father of modern criminology." With Ferri and Garofalo, and later his daughter Gina Lombroso-Ferraro, he explored the differences between ordinary "noncriminal" people and those who committed criminal offenses; therein, he argued, would be found the secret to the causes of crime.

Lombroso's theory of atavism, explained in his 1876 book *The Criminal Man*, was founded on Darwinian ideas about humanity's "worst dispositions," which were "reversions to a savage state" (Darwin 1871, 137). Atavism (meaning "derived from ancestor") is the reappearance of a characteristic in an organism or in families after it has been absent for several generations. According to this theory, criminals were hereditary throwbacks to less developed evolutionary forms. Since criminals were less developed, Lombroso believed they could be identified by physical stigmata, or visible physical abnormalities, which he called atavistic features: "For Lombroso, these anomalies resembled the traits of primitive peoples, animals and even plants, 'proving' that the most dangerous criminals were atavistic throwbacks on the evolutionary scale" (Gibson and Rafter 2006, 1). These anomalies or signs included such characteristics as asymmetry of the face; supernumerary nipples, toes, or fingers; enormous jaws; handle-shaped or sensile ears; insensitivity to pain; acute sight; and so on. Possessing five of the eighteen stigmata indicated atavism and could explain "the irresistible craving for evil for its own sake, the desire not only to extinguish life in the victim, but to mutilate the corpse, tear its flesh and drink its blood" (Lombroso 1911, xiv). Because these anomalies could be examined, counted, and classified, Lombroso "promised to turn the study of criminality into an empirical science . . . called . . . 'criminal anthropology,' reflecting his desire to reorient legal thinking from philosophical debate about the nature of crime to an analysis of the characteristics of the criminal" (Gibson and Rafter 2006, 1). As he says in the first 1876 edition of his classic work, "Most criminals really do lack free will" (quoted in ibid., 43).

Not all criminals, however, fell into the atavistic category. By the fifth edition of his book, Lombroso recognized four main classes of criminals. The first group, referred to as "born criminals," was atavistic, responsible for the most serious offenses, and recidivist. This group made up about a third of the criminal population and was considered by Lombroso to be the most dangerous and incorrigible. The second class, criminals by passion, commits crime to correct the emotional pain of an injustice.

Third was the insane criminal, who could be an imbecile or have an affected brain and is unable to distinguish right from wrong. Fourth, the occasional criminal included four subtypes: (a) the "criminaloid," who is of weak nature and easily swayed by others; (b) the "epileptoid," who suffers from epilepsy; (c) the habitual criminal, whose occupation is crime; and (d) the pseudocriminal, who commits crime by accident (Martin, Mutchnick, and Austin 1990, 29–32).

Eventually, Lombroso conceded that socioenvironmental factors, such as religion, gender, marriage, criminal law, climate, rainfall, taxation, banking, and even the price of grain, influence crime. By the time his last book, *Crime: Its Causes and Remedies* ([1912] 1968), was published in 1896, he had shifted from being a biological theorist to being an environmental theorist, but not without forcefully establishing the idea that criminals were different from ordinary people and especially from the powerful. Even though his main ideas were disproved and his research found to be methodologically unsound, the search for the biological cause of crime was inspired by his work (Goring [1913] 1972).

It is important to point out, however, that until recently, Lombroso's progression of work, though having serious flaws, has also been seriously distorted by translators, not least his daughter Gina Lombroso-Ferraro, whose popular *Criminal Man* has been shown to considerably simplify the complexity of his original ideas. One example is his biological determinism, which always recognized "multiple causes," and eventually included social causes, which allowed him to "continue denying free will by conceptualizing environmental and biological forces as equally determinate" (Gibson and Rafter 2006, 12). Often neglected, too, is that he proposed humanitarian reforms as alternatives to incarceration to prevent crimes by "occasional criminals," especially children, whose occasional criminality was a temporary phase, advocated institutions for the criminally insane, and urged that the severity of punishment match the dangerousness of the criminal (ibid., 2). Indeed, Gibson argues that Lombroso's work inspired liberal as well as conservative policy shifts in the Italian criminal justice system (2002). However, Lombroso did advocate the death penalty, abolished in Italy in 1889, for his category of the born criminal, arguing in the Darwinian fashion of the time that "progress in the animal world, and therefore the human world, is based on a struggle for existence that involves hideous massacres." Society need have no pity for born criminals who were "programmed to do harm" and are "atavistic reproductions not only of savage men but also the most ferocious carnivores and rodents." Capital punishment in this view would simply accelerate natural selection, ridding society of the unfit (Gibson and Rafter 2006, 15).

Lombroso's student at the University of Turin, Enrico Ferri (1856–1928), was even more receptive to environmental and social influences that cause crime, but he still relied on biological factors, and in fact coined the term *criminal man*, later used by Lombroso, and the term *criminal sociology*. Ferri studied statistics at the University of Bologna, and later, in Paris, he was influenced by the ideas of French lawyer and statistician A. M. Guerry (1802–1866) and Belgian mathematician and astronomer Lambert Adolphe Jacques Quételet (1796–1874). Ferri used his statistical training to analyze crime in France from 1826 to 1878. Ferri's studies (1901) suggested that the causes of crime were physical (race, climate, geographic location, and so forth), anthropological (age, gender, psychology, and so on), and social (population density, religion, customs, economic conditions, and others). This view was much more encompassing than Lombroso's original ideas, was accepted by Lombroso as furthering his theory, and is not dissimilar from modern theorists' ideas about multiple causality.

However, Ferri's anticlassicist ideas, and his Marxist leanings, cost him his university position. They also affected his views on criminal justice and policy, which he was invited to implement in Mussolini's fascist regime (and which were eventually rejected for being too radical). He reasoned that because causes needed scientific discovery, juries of laypeople were irrelevant and should, he believed, be replaced by panels of scientific experts, including doctors and psychiatrists. Not surprisingly, since he rejected the idea that crime was a free choice, Ferri also believed it was pointless to retributively punish offenders, preferring instead the idea of prevention through alternatives (which he called substitutions). His idea was to remove or minimize the causes of crime while protecting the state. He advocated "hygienic measures" such as social and environmental changes and, consistent with his socialist politics, favored the state provision of human services. He also advocated "therapeutic remedies" that were designed to be both reparative and repressive and "surgical operations," including death, to eliminate the cause of the problem (Schafer 1976, 45). Ferri's primary contribution was to offer a more balanced, complete picture of crime relying on scientific methods.

Raffaele Garofalo (1852–1934), also a student of Lombroso, trained in the law and was of Spanish noble ancestry, although he was born in Naples. He saw crime as rooted in an organic flaw that results in a failure to develop both altruistic sensibilities and a moral sentiment for others. Garofalo presented a principle called adaptation, which was based on Darwin's work. He argued that criminals who were unable to adapt to society, and who thereby felt morally free to offend, should be eliminated, consistent with nature's evolutionary process. This should be accomplished through one of three methods: death, long-term or life imprisonment, or "enforced reparation" (Vold and Bernard 1986, 44). Indeed, echoing Lombroso's Darwinist thinking on the state-administered death penalty, he stated: "In this way, the social power will effect an artificial selection similar to that which nature effects by death of individuals unassimilable to the particular conditions of the environment in which they are born or to which they have been removed. Herein the state will be simply following nature" (1914, 219–220, cited in Morrison 1995, 126).

These three theories have been relegated to the status of historical artifacts, and subject to some distortion, although each contains some resonance of truth. The research methods employed were simplistic or flawed, revealed a racist bias, and have not stood up to empirical verification. But the theories are important because they chart the course of later theories and also point out the importance of using scientific principles. Many of the research methods associated with the perspective of the Italian School persist into the twentieth century.

Early U.S. Family-Type
and Body-Type Theories

Shortly after the conclusion of the Civil War in 1865, it was widely believed that there were basic differences between individuals and between ethnic groups and that certain families could be mentally degenerate and "socially bankrupt." This notion has to be understood in historical context. U.S. society was undergoing rapid transformation with the abolition of slavery and massive immigration of Europeans of various ethnic groups, who, like the freed slaves, were largely poor and unskilled. These immigrants moved into the rapidly urbanizing cities, where, living in crowded conditions, they presented a threat of poverty and disease to established Americans. Indeed, since the 1870s some Americans had been calling for eugenics measures, according to which a nation could save its stock from degeneration by rejecting the unfit, preventing their reproduction, and encouraging the fit to procreate (McKim 1900; Rafter 1992).

Richard Louis Dugdale's work, which fascinated Lombroso, was consistent with these views. In his book *The Jukes: A Study in Crime, Pauperism, Disease, and Heredity* ([1877] 1895), Dugdale found that the Juke family (from the name of the family of illegitimate girls that a Dutch immigrant's sons had married) had criminals in it for six generations. Dugdale concluded that "the burden of crime" is found in illegitimate (nonmarried) family lines, that the eldest child has a tendency to be criminal, and that males are more likely than females to be criminal. Obviously, his conclusions are subject to varying interpretations.

Following Dugdale's degenerative theory, European criminal anthropology became available in the United States through a variety of works (e.g., MacDonald 1893; Boies 1893; Henderson 1893; Drahms [1900] 1971; and Lydston 1904; see Rafter 1998 for an overview). These authors were the first U.S. criminal anthropologists to claim that their approach was a new science studying the criminal rather than the crime, just as medicine studies disease. Rafter (1998) states that the central assumption of this new science was that the physical body mirrors moral capacity, and criminals were, as Boies argued, "the imperfect, knotty, knurly, worm-eaten, half-rotten fruit of the human race" (1893, 265–266).

After the turn of the nineteenth century, science was still viewed as being the solution to most human problems. Social science research became more rigorous, and improved research methods, such as larger sample sizes and control groups, became important. For example, in 1939 E. A. Hooton, a Harvard anthropologist, published *The American Criminal: An Anthropological Study* based on his research comparing 14,000 prisoners to 3,000 noncriminals. His results indicated that "criminals were organically inferior" and that this inferiority is probably due to inherited features, including physical differences such as low foreheads, compressed faces, and so on.

Hooton's methods have been criticized on several grounds. First, his control or comparison group included a large percentage of firefighters and police officers who were selected for their jobs based on their large physical size. Second, the differences he found were very small, and furthermore there was more variation between prisoners than between prisoners and civilians. Finally, his methods have been called tautological, meaning that they involved circular reasoning. For example, some people are violent so there must be something wrong with them; find out how they are different, and this explains their violent behavior.

Ten years later, in spite of a general decline in the idea of a correspondence between the human body and moral behavior, physician William Sheldon and his colleagues sought to explain the relationship between the shape of the human body and temperament. The most complete statement on this typology and crime was *Varieties of Delinquent Youth* (Sheldon, Hastl, and McDermott 1949). Using somatyping (classifying human bodies), Sheldon observed three distinct human body types. The first, endomorphs, were of medium height with round, soft bodies and thick necks. Mesomorphs were muscular, strong-boned people with wide shoulders and a tapering trunk. The final group, ectomorphs, had thin bodies and were fragile, with large brains and developed nervous systems. Sheldon recognized that no "pure" type existed and that each person shares some of all the features. Each type had a different personality and favored a different kind of criminal activity. Endomorphs, motivated by their gut, were tolerant, extroverted, sociable, and inclined to delinquency and occasional fraud. Ectomorphs had sensitive dispositions and were tense, thoughtful, and inhibited. They could become occasional thieves. Mesomorphs lacked sensitivity and were assertive, aggressive, and prone to habitual violence, robbery, and even homicide. Some of these results were confirmed in the 1950s studies on delinquency by Sheldon Glueck and Elinor Glueck (1956), whose study of 500 incarcerated persistently delinquent boys compared with 500 nondelinquent boys found that although only 31 percent of the noncriminal comparison group were mesomorphs, 60 percent of the delinquents had a mesomorphic body type. When other factors were considered, however, such as parenting practices, Glueck and Glueck found that body type was only one of several factors contributing to delinquency. Other controlled studies claim stronger correlations, one finding that 57 percent of delinquents were mesomorphic compared to 19 percent of nondelinquent controls (Cortes and Gatti 1972).

Fishbein points out that "early 'biological criminology' was eventually discredited for being unscientific, simplistic and monocausal" (1998, 92). The early studies suffered serious methodological weaknesses, including poor sample selection, inadequate measurement criteria, and the failure to control for factors, including unreported delinquency, social class, and criminal justice agency bias. In addition, one cannot avoid the observation that they tend to reinforce class, gender, and especially racial stereotypes. For these reasons a conference funded by the National Institutes of Health called "Genetic Factors and Crime" was canceled in 1992. Even though some data now suggest that higher violent crime rates among blacks could have a genetic basis (Rushton and Whitney 2002; Taylor and Whitney 1999), researchers feel the topic cannot be rationally considered because "the disparity between public sensibilities and empirical data in the United States has become so extreme that certain topics cannot be investigated without bringing down cries of 'racism'" (Taylor and Whitney 1999, 485).

By excluding hidden crime, crimes by women, occupational crimes, and crimes of the powerful, and by often relying on samples of convicted offenders, body-type theories tell us more about who is likely to be processed through criminal justice agencies than about what causes crime. These theories were sufficiently tantalizing, however, to inspire a new generation of inquiry into the nature of what was inheritable. This new era of biosocial criminological theory is more sophisticated and deserves serious consideration, not least because it is built on new knowledge about the human brain and the multidisciplinary insights gained from "genetics, biochemistry, endocrinology, neuroscience, immunology and psychophysiology" (Fishbein 1998, 92).

Contemporary Biological Perspectives

In spite of its earlier methodological shortcomings, biological theory and the use of scientific methods remain popular in criminology in the twenty-first century. Indeed, "a growing literature base has served to substantiate that genetic factors are as important to the development of some forms of criminal activity as are environmental factors" (Ishikawa and Raine 2002, 81). Rather than determining crime, "multiple genes—acting in combination—result in varying degrees of genetic disposition to criminal behavior . . . through heritable physiological processes such as neurotransmitter and autonomic nervous system functioning, which, in turn, predispose some individuals toward crime" (ibid., 82). Improved technology, computerization, and software design and advanced statistical techniques have allowed more precise measurement and improved data collection, especially with regard to detailing the genetic process and mapping genes.

Genes, called the "atoms of heredity," were discovered by Gregor Mendel in 1865 and reinvigorated again in the 1920s as essential elements in chromosomes. The 1952 discovery of the chemical constitution of genes as an explanation of how "like begets like" fueled the new genetic era of biology. By 1959, genes were being used to explain every aspect of individuals, every variation of their personality, yet, as Fishbein points out, although "numerous studies have attempted to estimate the genetic contribution to the development of criminality, delinquency, aggression and antisocial behavior . . . it is difficult to isolate genetic factors from developmental events, cultural influences and housing conditions" (1998, 95). First among the contemporary approaches were twin and adoption studies.

Twin Studies and Adoption Studies

A major boost to the genetic theory of crime came with evidence from twin studies and adoption studies. Put simply, if crime is the outcome of some genetically conveyed heritable factor (e.g., impulsivity, low arousal to pain, sensation seeking, or minimal brain dysfunction), then we would expect to find more crime in the twin partners of identical twins—where one twin is criminal—than in fraternal twins or between siblings. This is because monozygotic (MZ) twins are identical, with 100 percent of their genes in common, because they result from fertilization of a single egg. In contrast, fraternal, or dizygotic (DZ), twins occur when two separate eggs are fertilized at the same time and as a result share around 50 percent of the same genes. Genetically, they are no different from two separate eggs being fertilized at different times, as with other siblings. This explains why MZ twins are always of the same gender, whereas DZ twins may be a male and a female. Researchers have compared twins of each type and claim to find that there are greater similarities in criminal convictions between identical (MZ) twins than between fraternal (DZ) twins, which lends support to the genetic basis for crime. Fourteen of the analyses based on ten major studies conducted between 1929 and 1987 of the relation between twins and crime claim a greater concordance rate, an average 44 percent for criminality in MZ twins as opposed to 21.6 percent concordance rate in DZ twins, which suggests crime has some inheritability (Ishikawa and Raine 2002, 84).

The most comprehensive study of this type was conducted by Karl Christiansen (1977; Mednick and Christiansen 1977), who studied 3,568 pairs of Danish twins born between 1881 and 1910. He found that 52 percent of the identical twins (MZ) had the same degree of officially recorded criminal activity, whereas only 22 percent of the fraternal twins (DZ) had similar degrees of criminality. These findings persisted even among twins who were separated at birth and raised in different social environments. Moreover, in an overview of all previous twin studies Mednick and Volavka (1980) found the same basic relationship, with identical twin pairs being two and a half times more likely to have similar criminal records when one of the pair is criminal than are fraternal twin pairs. Similar results for aggression have since been found by others (Rowe 1986; Ghodsian-Carpey and Baker 1987).

This apparently consistent finding has been criticized for its methodological inadequacy. Factors criticized include dependence on official crime statistics, especially conviction records; unreliable processes for classifying twins; errors resulting from the pooling of small samples; failure to take into account the similar environmental upbringing of identical twins compared with fraternal twins; and the inability of genetics to explain "why the majority of twin partners of criminal twins are not themselves criminal" (Einstadter and Henry 2006, 97). However, an Ohio study based on self-reports rather than official crime statistics found both greater criminality and greater criminal association among identical twins where one twin admitted delinquency compared with fraternal twins (Rowe 1986). Yet several others, including Christiansen himself, argue that the higher-quality twin studies are less clear about the genetic contribution (Hurwitz and Christiansen 1983; Walters 1992). Indeed, controlling for the mutual behavioral influence of twins on each other (Carey 1992) and for other environmental effects has been found to render the differences between the two types of twins insignificant (Dalgard and Kringlen 1976).

Adoption studies seem to offer a way out of some of the environmental confusion plaguing twin studies. Adoption studies look at whether children adopted at birth carry their parents' criminality with them. If some biologically heritable predispositional factor is involved in criminality, we would expect that the biological children of convicted criminals would have criminal records more consistent with those of their natural fathers than with their adoptive fathers. Fifteen major adoption studies support the hypothesis that there is some genetic predisposition toward crime (Ishikawa and Raine 2002, 90). Barry Hutchings and Sarnoff Mednick (1975) studied adoptees born between 1927 and 1941. They found that if boys had adoptive parents with a criminal record but their natural parents had no criminal record, then 11.5 percent of the adoptive sons were also criminal. This was little different from cases where neither natural nor adoptive parents had a criminal record (10.5 percent). But where boys had noncriminal adoptive parents but criminal natural parents, 22 percent of the adoptive sons were found to be criminal. Moreover, these effects seem additive, such that where both fathers were criminal, 36 percent of adoptive sons were found to be criminal. Reporting more recent studies with larger samples and looking at both parents, the authors found similar though less pronounced results, with 15 percent of boys having criminal records when their adoptive parents also had criminal records and their natural parents did not, compared to 20 percent when the biological parents had criminal records but their adoptive parents did not (Mednick, Gabrielli, and Hutchings 1987, 79). This finding was confirmed between adoptive girls and their mothers (Baker et al. 1989) and has been supported by other studies (Crowe 1975; Cadoret 1978), in particular those examining the effect of a biological parent having alcohol and antisocial tendencies on the likelihood that their adopted offspring would also have these problems, relative to the adopted offspring of noncriminal biological parents (Cadoret et al. 1995). Mednick, Gabrielli, and Hutchings (1987) conclude that these data force them to accept the strong likelihood that genetic factors influence criminal behavior. More recently, Martens found that adoption and twin studies show that genetics and environmental factors have a measurable impact on antisocial personality disorder (1997, 2000). Martens thinks the justice system should rely more on science, arguing that "unfortunately the administration of justice often shows only minimal consideration for the neurobiological correlates and/or genetic determination of immorality and crime" (2002, 178).

In spite of proponents' claims, critics have raised several questions about adoption studies. A major problem is "selective placement," whereby the adoption agency may match the adoptive home with the natural home in terms of social class and physical characteristics (Kamin 1985; Walters and White 1989; Walters 1992; Rydenour 2000). Another problem is whether the effects being measured reflect prenatal or perinatal factors. Deborah Denno (1985, 1989) has questioned whether something happens to the mother during pregnancy, such as malnutrition or drug or alcohol abuse, that changes the fetus and results in later developmental problems, especially problems related to intellect. In addition, since up to 40 percent of children spend

TABLE 4.1   Some Claimed Biological Causes of Crime

Predisposing Cause	Basic Idea
XYY chromosomes	Having an extra male chromosome produces super-males who are more crime prone and more represented in prisons.
Defective genes	Some patterns of genes carry forward qualities, such as low emotional arousal and impulsivity, that affect the brain and conditionability, so that under certain environmental conditions criminal behavior is more likely.
Biochemical, endocrinal, and hormonal imbalances	Certain glands in the body produce hormones that affect the brain and the temperament. In men, high levels of testosterone are associated with aggression; in women, premenstrual syndrome (PMS): Changes in women's hormone levels prior to menstruation produce emotional disturbances, irritability, and violent rages.
Low intelligence or IQ, learning disabilities, attention deficit disorder	Low IQ and hyperactivity are seen as heritable qualities that affect children's ability to learn conventional morality.
Brain chemistry disorders, low arousal of autonomic nervous system, neurotransmitter imbalance	Those with low arousal of the autonomic nervous system need greater stimuli from the environment and can achieve this through crime, drug taking, and other risk-producing, highly stimulating activities. Those with low levels of the neurotransmitter serotonin are more likely to become violent.

time with their biological parents, with foster parents, and in institutions before adoption, the effects of early parenting need to be controlled for (Walters 1992). For one thing, children who spend more time in institutions show higher evidence of criminality in later life. Denno also points out that the adoption relationship, surprisingly, affects property crime but not violent crime, yet most violent offenders are also property offenders. She argues that the supposed genetic effect could be an artifact of the way we collect data, especially when we fail to take into account hidden crime, occupational crime, and corporate crime.

Overall, then, what at first seemed to offer solid and consistent scientific evidence of a heritable genetic predisposition to crime turns out to raise more questions than it answers. This has not stopped various processes from being identified as causal candidates for explaining crime.

Biosocial Criminology:
A Developmental Explanation of Crime

Since the 1950s, researchers have received media attention for various "discoveries" that they claim may explain the biological causes of crime (Nelkin 1993; Nelkin and Tancredi 1994). The April 21, 1997, cover of *U.S. News and World Report* carried a similar title to that of this chapter—"Born Bad?"—and dealt with the biological causes of crime.

Before examining illustrative examples of these processes, it is important to understand the logic used by the biosocial criminologists to explain crime. Biosocial criminology was founded on the ideas of E. O. Wilson (1975), whose book *Sociobiology* marked a resurrection of the role of biological thinking in social science. The basic idea is that the genetic makeup of humans controls their direction in life such that their "selfish genes" strive to reproduce themselves through whatever means is necessary, including crime, if committing crime will expand their ability to procreate and expand their gene pool. As Ellis and Walsh express it, "All versions of this gene-based theory of evolution have converged on a simple but powerful idea: To the degree that a particular characteristic is prevalent in a population, it is likely to have contributed to the reproductive success of the ancestors of the individuals currently living. Increasingly this fundamental principle has been applied to the study of behavior . . . including criminal behavior" (1997, 232). Thus, human development, through family, social, and organizational environments, interacts with the human gene machine and is adapted, even co-opted, to enhance the human organism's ability to dominate others. These environmental contexts together with each human organism's unique biology shape their subsequent behavioral patterns.

In short, all the serious advocates of genetic explanations for crime agree that they are not claiming that genes alone determine behavior or that there is a "crime gene" (ibid.; Ishikawa and Raine 2002, 82). Rather, criminal behavior is believed to result from the combination of hereditary factors interacting with environmental ones. Together, these factors affect the brain and cognitive processes that in turn control behavior (Jeffery 1994; Ellis 1988; Ellis and Walsh 1997; Fishbein and Thatcher 1986; Raine 2002; Wilson and Herrnstein 1985; Hurwitz and Christiansen 1983; Ishikawa and Raine 2002, 98–99). As Fishbein explains, "Behavior (criminal or otherwise) is not inherited; what is inherited is the way in which an individual responds to the environment. Inheritance provides an orientation, predisposition, or tendency to behave in a certain fashion" (1998, 94). For this reason, some researchers prefer the term *maladaptivity* over *criminality*, since it is more inclusive of a wider range of problem-causing behaviors stemming from a combination of predispositions and environment (Fishbein 1998).

In addition to the interaction between genetic predispositions and environment, contemporary biological theorists do not abandon the notion of free will, as their forerunners did. Instead, they prefer the concept of conditional free will. In this approach, various factors restrict and channel an individual's decision to act, and each "collaborates internally (physically) and externally (environmentally) to produce a final action: The principle of conditional free will postulates that individuals choose a course of action within a preset, yet changeable, range of possibilities and that, assuming the conditions are suitable for rational thought, we are accountable for our actions. . . . This theory . . . predicts that if one or more conditions to which the individual is exposed are disturbed or irregular, the individual is more likely to choose a disturbed or irregular course of action. Thus, the risk of such a response increases as a function of the number of deleterious conditions" (ibid., 104–105).

Unlike earlier deterministic biological theory, biosocial criminology proposes an interactive gene-based developmental theory of crime over the life course that integrates rather than opposes these classic notions of free will versus determinism. Yet even this advance in the age-old debate may be moot if Rose is correct in stating that "traditional dichotomies of sociological thought—free will versus determinism, society versus biology—are not very helpful in understanding the relationships of power, knowledge, ethics and subjectification that are taking shape within these new practices of control" (2000, 25).

The research on biosocial criminology and behavior has empirical support. For example, Raine conducted a review and semi-meta-analysis of thirty-nine studies and concluded, "When biological and social factors are grouping variables and when antisocial behavior is the outcome, then the presence of both risk factors exponentially increases the rates of antisocial and violent behavior" (2002, 311).

Chromosomes, Nervous System, Attention Deficit Disorder, Hormones, and the Brain

The list of causal candidates for the predispositional side of this interactive equation is long, and growing. None have captured the imagination more than those based on aspects of genetic theory. For example, in the 1960s a chromosomal theory of crime attributed violent male criminality to an extra Y chromosome. This extra chromosome created what was termed a "supermale," one who was excessively violent. This theory was initially supported by the finding that 1 to 3 percent of male inmates had an extra Y chromosome compared to less than 1 percent of the general population of males (P. Jacobs et al. 1965; Telfer, Baker, and Clark 1968). Further research revealed, however, that incarcerated inmates with an extra Y chromosome were less likely to be serving a sentence for a violent crime. Moreover, the XYY chromosome pattern was more prevalent among prison officers than prisoners (Sarbin and Miller 1970; R. Fox 1971). Consequently, the XYY theory has now largely been discarded, except for a few stalwart supporters (Ellis and Walsh 2000).

Another candidate used to explain the intergenerational transmission of criminality is the autonomic nervous system, which controls emotions. The argument here is that people who are not easily emotionally aroused are less responsive to conditioning, whether punishment or rewards. Consequently, they resist socialization processes and are more likely to break the law without fearing the consequences (Mednick 1977; Eysenck [1964] 1977). Lykken (1995) found that antisocial individuals had an inborn central nervous system defect. Other evidence for this is inconclusive.

Attention deficit disorder (ADD) and attention deficit hyperactivity disorder (ADHD) have also been targeted as possibly heritable factors in criminality (Moffitt and Silva 1988; S. Young and Gudjonsson 2008). Rose predicted we would begin to see "genetic screening of disruptive schoolchildren, with pre-emptive treatment a condition of continuing schooling" (2000, 23). ADD is already a relatively common diagnosis for children having difficulty in school, with up to 12 percent of U.S. schoolboys in 1996 diagnosed with ADD. This condition is said to contribute to crime by reducing the ability of ADD children to do well in conventional activities, especially schooling. It is found that children with ADD are more likely to be involved with the criminal justice system. ADD causes them to be less successful and less accepted in the mainstream school environment, and they seek notoriety in more criminal ways. Their lack of success in school also results in a lack of marketable job skills and decreased employment opportunities. But critics argue that ADD is no more than a device to legitimate the medical control of unruly children and to help teachers maintain order in the classroom (Box 1977). In a thirty-year longitudinal study, Brassett-Grundy and Butler (2004) found 7.4 percent of U.S. schoolboys to have ADHD by age ten and that those with ADHD had higher levels of criminal activity. Susan Young and H. Gisli Gudjonsson (2006) found an association with poor socialization, anxiety, and antisocial behavior. By adulthood, childhood ADHD is linked with antisocial personality disorders and crime.

Children with ADHD are less capable of dealing with stress and strain, which is correlated to an increased risk of criminal behavior (M. Johnson and Kercher 2007). Matsumoto and Imamura (2007) found support for this observation when they showed an association between childhood ADHD and adult crime—at least with male inmates. The strain has been empirically examined by Johnson and Kercher (2007). They studied ADHD, strain, and criminal behavior and concluded that people with ADHD are less able to cope with strain in legitimate ways. According to recent research, "Post-traumatic stress disorder caused by child abuse produces symptoms similar to ADHD symptoms, and . . . these disorders frequently coexist and overlap" (Matsumoto and Imamura 2007). Weinstein, Staffelbach, and Biaggio supported this observation in the case of victims of child sexual abuse (2000).

Hormones have also been claimed as causative agents in criminality. Hormones are biochemical substances produced by human cells that are transported via the blood to other cells, which they stimulate by chemical action. Higher than normal levels of testosterone in men have been linked to aggression and violence (Rushton [1995] 1999; Booth and Osgood 1993; Olweus 1987; Rubin 1987; Rada, Laws, and Kellner 1976). Raine found that testosterone-based aggression led to dominance and antisocial behavior (2002). Dabbs, Riad, and Chance (2001) found testosterone to be related to "familiarity and intent for homicide" but not other violent crimes such as assault, robbery, and sex offenses. Zuckerman found that sensation seeking was linked to "low levels of monoamine oxidase, cortisol and high concentrations of gonadal hormones" (1994, 175). In some women, a reduction in the hormone progesterone that precedes menstruation, and arguably produces premenstrual syndrome, has been said to cause sufficient stress and irritability that, under certain circumstances, make them irresponsible and prone to violent actions (Dalton 1961; Taylor and Dalton 1983). But reviews of the evidence suggest that neither of the hormonal explanations has adequate research support, and some have even argued that hormonal changes "may be the product rather than the cause of aggression" (Curran and Renzetti 1994, 73; see also Janet Katz and Chambliss 1991; and Horney 1978). Indeed, one journalist posed the key dilemma of assuming testosterone causes increased aggression:

> How much of this difference in aggression and dominance is related to environment? Are trial lawyers naturally more testosteroned, and does that lead them into their profession? Or does the experience of the courtroom raise their levels? Do working women have naturally higher T levels, or does the prestige of work and power elevate their testosterone? Because of the limits of researching such a question, it is hard to tell beyond a reasonable doubt. . . . Studies have shown that inner-city youths, often exposed to danger in high-crime neighborhoods, may generate higher testosterone levels than unthreatened, secluded suburbanites. And so high T levels may not merely be responses to a violent environment; they may subsequently add to it in what becomes an increasingly violent, sexualized cycle. (Sullivan 2000)

As we are increasingly seeing, the relationship between biology and crime is not simple, and probably not linear but more likely reciprocal, with both biological and environmental factors feeding into and enhancing each other.

The Importance of Neurotransmitters in Relation to Depression and Aggression

The role of neurochemical processes, particularly neurotransmitters, is increasingly seen as important. These are chemicals, such as serotonin and dopamine, released by electrical signals given off by nerves that transmit information to receptors in the brain. The brain then instructs the body to adjust various behaviors, including aggression, in relation to the human organism's environment. Serotonin in humans or animals inhibits aggression, and having relatively low levels of this substance released by neurotransmitters results in a failure to inhibit violent and impulsive behavior (Virkkunen et al. 1987, 1989; Fishbein 1990, 1998; Coccaro and Kavoussi 1996). A review of studies (meta-analysis) found that overall, the low-serotonin relationship to antisocial behavior is significant (Moore, Scarpa, and Raine 2002). This same relationship also holds for monkeys and apes, studies of which show that serotonin is associated with various kinds of aggression (Rubin 1987) and that low levels of serotonin are linked to impulsive aggression. In contrast, dopamine is an excitatory transmitter that offsets the effects of low serotonin. As Fishbein says, dopamine "operates as the 'fuel' while serotonin provides the 'brakes' for behavioral responses" (1998, 99). Moreover, the effects of dopamine go a long way toward explaining the "high" experienced by cocaine users. Ingested cocaine (and freebasing "crack" cocaine is a rapid way to do this) has the effect of attaching itself to dopamine that has been released from neurotransmitters in the brain on its way to the brain's dopamine receptors. The modified dopamine is prevented from returning to the transmitter with the result that more dopamine is released by the transmitters to correct the apparent deficit. It is this excessive production of dopamine that gives cocaine users their "high." Importantly, it is not the cocaine that makes for the excitement but its ability to trick the brain's own drug-production system. Unfortunately, since dopamine is only half of the equation, when the other half, serotonin, kicks in, the situation of "tolerance" occurs. Over time, in response to the higher levels of released dopamine, the brain produces higher levels of serotonin, which depresses the effect of dopamine. Once this occurs the experience is of normality, rather than a high, and more cocaine is needed to reach a high than previously. However, now serotonin is being produced when dopamine is not, with the effect that without taking cocaine, the drug user experiences intense "lows" and needs cocaine just to reach a normal balanced mood.

As with hormones, however, it is uncertain whether changes in serotonin and dopamine are the outcome of changes in environment or the reverse (W. Gibbs 1995). For example, some primate research indicates that dominant males do not have low serotonin levels before they move to the top of their social organizational hierarchy, but the level drops after they achieve their dominant position. Similarly, Klaus Miczek (Van Erp and Miczek 1996) found that aggression in rats can precede a drop in their serotonin levels, which can remain at normal levels at the start and for the duration of an aggressive attack, falling to lower levels only after the conflict. This seems to indicate that the low level of serotonin did not cause the violence. However, Miczek also showed that "an increase in serotonin can occur at the time of aggression and can continue to increase throughout a potential attack demonstrating that an environment or situation or social context can trigger appropriate serotonin production to help deal with it" (Einstadter and Henry 2006, 89). Indeed, as Miczek said, "Instead of only looking at biology as the cause of behavior, we also need to consider the reverse—that being the aggressor or victim of aggression is the event that sets the neurobiological processes in motion" (cited in Niehoff 1999, 116). Put simply, recent analyses of the relationship between the human brain, its environment, and behavior challenge notions of predisposition and suggest, rather, that the relationship might be reciprocal; that is, not only might biological factors result from behavioral and environmental ones, but the biological factors are not immutable and can be altered by changes in behavior and environment.

Recent Directions in Biosocial Criminology

Related to these new developments is a biocriminological theory that is increasingly seen as tying together many of the earlier findings. Lee Ellis (1987, 1990, 1995, 2005) has become one of the leading advocates in this field and has contributed significantly to its development following his early Wilsonian-influenced diatribe (1977) predicting the death of sociology (which he compared to astrology) and its replacement with biosocial theory (which he compared to astronomy). Although Ellis's prediction has not come true, his biocriminology has grown to command a significant place in criminological thinking. Ellis has several dimensions to his theory (Ellis and Hoffman 1990; Ellis and Walsh 1997; Ellis 2000, 2005). In his sensation-seeking and arousal theory, Ellis has argued that under normal environmental conditions as a result of low levels of dopamine, and dopamine-like neurotransmitters called endorphins, some people have lower than average emotional arousal (this is similar to the production of cocaine tolerance discussed above, but Ellis is arguing that for some, the "low" is a result of a predisposition). Whereas most people are excited by a wide range of stimuli found in their daily environment, dopamine-depressed people are easily bored. To raise their level of arousal and to bring back normal or even create accentuated levels of arousal, such individuals engage in superchallenging or intensely stimulating activities. Some of them surf in hurricanes, others street race, and yet others turn to crime. Indeed, such sensation seeking is "strongly linked to other antisocial traits such as impulsiveness, recklessness, irresponsibility, and criminality" (Martens 2002, 174). Criminal behavior provides this "on the edge" stimulation for such "sensation seekers" (Ellis 1995; Zuckerman 1979). Ellis argues that we can expect a higher level of criminality from sensation seekers than from those with normal sensitivities to stimulation. Evidence has accumulated supporting the idea that sensation seeking, risk taking, and impulsivity are biologically determined (Knoblich and King 1992; Magnusson, Klinteberg, and Stattin 1992), and studies of convicted offenders reveal that a key motivational factor is a neurophysiological "high" experienced in the course of committing an offense (Wood, Gove, and Cochran 1994; Gove and Wilmoth 1990). This high is similar to the intrinsic pleasure experienced from drugs and alcohol; it results from a similar external stimulation of internal opiates known as endorphins (Wood et al. 1995; Fishbein 1990; Fishbein and Pease 1988). As Barak (1998) observes, Ellis's theory of arousal may also explain corporate and white-collar crime. Indeed, corporations have been shown to seek precisely the kind of executive motivated to maximize sensations through risk taking, and it is just such a profile that is associated with corporate crime (Gross 1978; Box 1983).

More controversial, however, is Ellis's cluster of biocriminological theories based on the principle of the reproductive drives of the selfish (male) gene that he uses to explain behavior ranging from rape, spousal assault, and child abuse to male sexual promiscuity, cheating male spouses, and even theft (Ellis and Walsh 1997). The common theme underlying such explanations is the idea that it is in men's reproductive interest to behave these ways. For example, r/K theory assumes that rates of reproduction vary along an evolutionary continuum from *r* to *K*. Persons at the *r* end reproduce prolifically and, therefore, do not need to care much for their offspring, as there will be many and some will survive. In contrast, those at the *K* end produce a small number of offspring in which they invest much time and energy to ensure their survival, and are generally more caring and nurturing. Criminals and psychopaths are expected to be at the *r* end, to come from large families, begin sexual activity early, and themselves produce many offspring. Ellis acknowledges the racist inferences that could be drawn from such an idea and states, "Whichever racial/ethnic groups or social strata exhibit r-related traits to the greatest degree will also exhibit high rates of crime and psychopathy" (ibid., 257).

Ellis's most recent version is called evolutionary neuroandrogenic theory (ENA) and is used to explain the higher rates of violent crimes committed by males. According to Ellis, two primary propositions form the basis for ENA theory. The first addresses evolutionary issues, "by asserting that aggressive and acquisitive criminal behaviour evolved as an aspect of human reproduction, especially among males. The second proposition is concerned with identifying the neurochemistry responsible for increasing the probability of aggressive and acquisitive criminal behaviour among males" (2005, 288). He argues that male sex hormones affect the functioning of the human brain in ways that increase the likelihood of competitive or victimizing behavior. Competitive or victimizing behavior, according to Ellis, spans a continuum, "with 'crude' (criminal) forms at one end and 'sophisticated' (commercial) forms at the other." Those individuals endowed with the greatest capacities for learning new behavior and planning ahead will, after adolescence, move rapidly toward the noncriminal end of the continuum. As a result, he says, "serious criminality will be concentrated in adolescent and young adult males of low social status" (ibid., 287).

Related to these ideas, "cheater theory" argues that some men are sexually aggressive, seeking to dominate as many women as possible and to employ deception to appear like the high-investing males that women desire. They may use illegal and violent means to acquire the resources for multiple sexual access to females. Yet others, who find women resistant to their cautious mating behavior, will use force, including rape, which Ellis and Walsh refer to as "forceful copulatory tactics" (1997, 255), to overcome the tension between the sexes. These authors recount a similar line for spousal assault that is seen as "associated with maintaining exclusive copulatory access," and they predict that "spousal assaults should be most common in populations in which infidelity is most common" (Ellis 1997, 256). In short, male sex hormones and other neurochemical processes increase competitive or victimizing behavior or both, which in turn reciprocates with the chemical processes (Ellis 2005).

One might be forgiven for seeing these biological explanations as showing not only that "evolutionary theories of criminal and antisocial behavior have in fact reemerged during the past two decades" (Ellis and Walsh 1997, 260), but also that the racism and sexism that they embody resonate with the discredited history of

nineteenth-century biological criminology. One can only hope that the genuine contribution that biosocial knowledge can make to our understanding of crime is not
swept away by the broom of reaction to these applications of its insights. Indeed,
such controversy is already stirring. In general, Platt and Takagi (1979) called the
trend toward biological criminology "scientific racism." Their claim has some merit
based on past government practices, as we illustrate below.

Biosocial Theory and the Racism Controversy

Perhaps the most controversial theory links biology, race, and crime. At the forefront of this movement is the work of J. Phillippe Rushton ([1995] 1999; Rushton
and Jensen 2005). Rushton argues that races with lower intelligence are more
crime-prone. For example, African Americans constitute 12 percent of the population in the United States but account for around half of all violent crimes and 67
percent of robberies; three-quarters of the women arrested for homicide are black.
Meanwhile, Asians are dramatically underrepresented in crime statistics. In a 2002
article Rushton and Whitney expanded the study to an international level and also
examined r/K theory and income by comparing national crime-level data. They
found that "violent crime is lowest in East Asian countries, intermediate in European countries, and highest in African and Black Caribbean countries" (501).
Their study also considered wealth differentials and found that wealthier African
and black Caribbean countries had the highest rates of violence and so excluded
income as an explanatory variable. The basis for this study was apparently partially
a rebuttal to Lynch (2000). Lynch countered that Rushton can prove his claim of
an association between race and crime only by selectively focusing on street crime,
which excludes corporate and white-collar crime more likely to be committed by
whites.

Finally, races are influenced by human evolution and adaptation over a long
period of time. From this biological and evolutionary standpoint, whites and Hispanics are virtually identical, yet Hispanics are five times more likely to commit
street crimes. Since Rushton discounts cultural explanations, this finding cannot be
explained by the race and crime hypothesis (see Lynch 2000 for a more complete critique; Dickens and Flynn 2006 provide another more recent critique).

Crime is not the only characteristic of interest. Some people contend that in a
hundred years or so, there will not be distinct racial and ethnic groups due to cross-
fertilization. Some support for this argument comes from, surprisingly, hair research!
For example, (natural) redheads are becoming increasingly scarce. In fact, "as the rate
of migration, inter-marriage and mixing increases we will see them all but disappear," according to hair-cell biologists (Leake 2003). Rees, a professor of dermatol-
ogy at Edinburgh University, argues that "blondness appears to follow similar
patterns of inheritance" and will be the next extinct group (cited in ibid.).

BOX 4.1 Epidemiological Criminology
A Case for Sociobiological Determinism
TIMOTHY A. AKERS, M.S., PH.D., AND JOSEPH WHITTAKER, PH.D.

The very essence of this essay is best reflected in a recent question asked by my (Timothy's) daughter, Aubrey, who is twelve years old and already expressing her desire to be a criminologist, not because of her father but because of her favorite TV show, "Bones," which portrays a brilliant female forensic anthropologist working closely with the FBI to resolve challenging cases. While out for dinner, she asked, "Daddy, why is there crime?" As I thought about the question, I realized that I could not, in all honesty, provide a clear and definitive answer. Is it because of economics? Family dynamics? Social interactions? Behavioral or other biologically linked dysfunction that remains unaddressed or unrecognized? Did criminals receive an adequate education? Was it something they ate? Did they bang their heads too many times growing up? Or were they born with a "predisposition" toward criminal behavior? These questions, among many others, have guided the work of research scientists, educators, policy makers, criminologists, and dilettantes for centuries. Today, these questions are yet to be resolved and remain enigmatic and challenging, awaiting definitive answers based on solid evidence.

The scientific world, as we know it, comprises a vast number of disciplines and subdisciplines, spanning the sociobehavioral to the computational and biological, and everything in between these domains. As we advance technologically, and as our environments as well as world economies continue to undergo radical transformations, human behavior and associated social dynamics will, without a doubt, become significantly altered. Included among the outcomes of such complex dynamics are apparent erosions in the fundamental mores, folkways, and norms that help to keep us grounded and disciplined in response to socioeconomic, environmental, and other stressors. Starting with the most basic question, "Which came first, the crime or the criminal?" how do we determine the underlying causes of crime? Is there any one or multiple explanations? Can any single discipline explain crime, or is it such a complex phenomena that it cannot be explained without an interdisciplinary examination of the interactive effects of many possible causes, relative to each individual? Or can we aggregate and make reasonable, rational conclusions?

Now, let's try to set forth a scenario that tracks our future biological or surrogate mother or father, then move through the process where the baby is born and eventually commits a crime, as compared to a baby that does not commit a crime. From there, maybe we will come closer in terms of beginning to address Aubrey's question: "*Daddy, why is there crime?*"

Through an emerging paradigm titled "epidemiological criminology," new criminological tools, methods, models, processes, hypotheses, and theories can be proposed and developed (Akers and Lanier 2009; Lanier, Lucken, and Akers 2010). This notion is not unreasonable, given that almost fifty years ago, in 1960, noted criminologist and sociologist Donald Cressey advocated for the inclusion of epidemiology in crimi-

CONTINUES

BOX 4.1 (CONTINUED)

nological theory and research, as espoused in his 1960 article titled "Epidemiology and Individual Conduct: A Case from Criminology." As we begin to think more creatively and advance new interdisciplinary-based conceptual theories, the study of epidemiological criminology can serve as a case study for sociobiological determinists. In effect, we can begin to ask broad but basic and rudimentary questions such as, What are the sociobiological factors that will likely affect our understanding of crime and criminal behavior?

Many criminologists started out their original training as sociologists. As students of crime, many in the social and behavioral sciences often hold themselves out to also be considered as criminologists. More than any other, they subscribe to the concept of social determinism. In effect, when asking what causes crime and criminal behavior, they turn to issues around interpersonal interaction, education, racism, and injustice, among others. However, the scope of their arguments is often constrained when asked to consider other factors, causes, or explanations. Unfortunately, this results in paralysis through analysis—leading to generally limited and relatively myopic perspectives on very complex issues.

On the other hand, when crime is examined from a more biological deterministic perspective, we begin to head down a path fraught with risk, uncertainty, and professional liability. It is considered professional suicide to even postulate such a hypothesis, as it appears to some to be a rebirth or a resurgence of the old eugenics movement that occurred during the first half of the twentieth century, when it was assumed that a person's physical characteristics could help to determine the likelihood of criminal behavior. In reality, it has been the focus on genetic and environmental factors that has led biological determinists to appreciate the depth and breadth of both factors.

However, what happens when you take sociologists, psychologists, and biologists, among others, outside of their comfort zone—removing them from their comfort zone or away from their subject area of interest? Then what happens when you seek out their critique of how biological determinism has stepped forward to challenge other explanations of crime? That is, where does genetics play into this milieu, or does it? Or does only a part of it have an effect? Therefore, when we prematurely discount potential factors that may help to explain criminal behavior, we do so at our own scientific peril; in effect, we show our scientific ignorance, or what we may also call scientific fraud, by intentionally neglecting to consider other explanations of criminal behavior using interdisciplinary approaches.

When trying to merge a small fraction of sociobiological determinism in order to help explain aberrant behavior, we can see other examples that have more of an environmental influence, such as when biology and genetics play a role in understanding how toxic environmental contaminants may impact fetal development or early childhood development. The U.S. Centers for Disease Control and Prevention reports that roughly one in six children is diagnosed with a developmental disability—leading many to speculate that physical environments where one lives, works, and plays directly impact fetal and early childhood development. The more exposed the child is to

CONTINUES

BOX 4.I (CONTINUED)

a dangerous and toxic environment, the more likely the child will experience behavioral and maladaptive problems. In essence, the best way to help determine such impact is through the use of large-scale epidemiological studies, in which social, behavioral, biological, and environmental characteristics may directly impact or help predict an offspring's likelihood of committing a criminal act. A child falls or injures her head often and is neglected by not being taken to the emergency room. Brain lesions begin forming. Behavior starts to change, and, before we know it, the once innocent child has now stepped over the line into criminal behavior.

Therefore, when trying to explain "*Why is there crime?*" we are also left to ask ourselves if we have the right type of data to help scientifically predict a probability of committing a violent or nonviolent criminal act. Large-scale epidemiological studies have also revealed that biological and chemical agents present potential threats to the unborn, infant, and child; lead products, methylmercury, arsenic, toluene, and polychlorinated biphenyls are but a few examples of the type of environmental toxins that are known to cause birth defects, leading to neurobehavioral deficits. From an epidemiological criminology perspective, environmental exposures to such toxins can clearly serve as a bridging framework that can help to address the sociobiological deterministic divide, and therefore to provide one small piece to the question, "*Why is there crime?*"

Timothy A. Akers is currently Professor and Interim Associate Dean for Graduate Studies and Research in the School of Computer, Mathematical, and Natural Sciences at Morgan State University in Baltimore.

Joseph Whittaker is currently Professor and Dean of the School of Computer, Mathematical, and Natural Sciences at Morgan State University.

References

Akers, Timothy, and Mark Lanier. 2009. "'Epidemiological Criminology': Coming Full Circle." *American Journal of Public Health* 99, no. 3: 1–6.
Cressey, D. R. 1960. "Epidemiology and Individual Conduct: A Case from Criminology." *Pacific Sociological Review* 3: 47–58.
Lanier, Mark M., Karol Lucken, and Timothy Akers. 2010. "Correctional Opportunities: Epidemiological Criminology." In *Key Correctional Issues*, edited by Roslyn Muraskin. 2d ed. Englewood Cliffs, NJ: Prentice-Hall.

In summary, it is clear from this brief survey of the range of contemporary biological theories that these biological causes have so far proved difficult to assess in terms of the certainty of their contribution to criminal behavior. For some critics, the relevance of biology to criminology has more to do with crime control and is more related to genetic discrimination in insurance, employment, genetic risk management, and quasi-consensual treatment of offenders (Rose 2000). As the list of biological factors grows, so does the refutation from accumulated studies. Researchers have so far found some support for connections between aggression and physiology, brain chemistry, and hormones, although sensation-seeking and arousal theory may show more promise. Indeed, there are several conceptual and empirical limitations for this approach that we briefly explore next.

Conceptual and Empirical Limitations

We have already discussed several of the limitations in the research methodology with regard to the early biological theories. Even though contemporary genetic studies use far more sophisticated methodology, they too are fraught with numerous difficulties. One problem stems from the nature of criminal behavior itself being a legal rather than a behavioral category and a category that comprises different behavioral types. For example, just because rape is defined as a violent criminal offense, does this mean all rapists are similarly motivated? Some are motivated by sexual desire, others by opportunity (e.g., date rape), and others by power; yet others are rapists due to the age of their "willing" partner. If biological theory is to explain rape or violence—or whatever—researchers should disaggregate "behaviors that are reflective of actual acts that can be consistently and accurately measured and examined." Accordingly, "Genetic studies that focus on criminal behavior per se may be inherently flawed; as criminal behavior is heterogeneous, genetic effects may be more directly associated with particular traits that place individuals at risk for criminal labeling" (Fishbein 1998, 98). A second and related problem is that researchers rarely distinguish between those with an occasional criminal behavior pattern whose actions might be the result of situational factors and those whose criminal offending is more long term and repetitive whose actions may be more explainable by inherent predispositions (ibid.). Even if behavior is disaggregated, since no single gene has been associated with most behavior, research on antisocial behavior suggests multiple combined effects that are difficult to isolate, not only from each other but especially from developmental events, cultural influences, early experiences, and housing conditions (ibid., 94).

In spite of these limitations, the new multidisciplinary direction in biosocial research focused on the relative interaction between biological, psychological, and social factors seems to offer the best hope for the future. Meanwhile, contemporary theorists continue to suggest—if with caution—criminal justice policy implications based on their limited evidence. As we shall see in the next section, this approach has a poor and dangerous track record.

Criminal Justice Policy Implications

At its simplest, the policy of biological theory is the medical model, which involves identification, prevention, and treatment. Under this model, if inheritable predispositions, such as genes, chromosomes, hormones, or imbalances in brain chemistry, are the causes or at least the predisposers of crime, then preventive policy should involve identifying those individuals potentially predisposed prior to their creating harm. To be fair, though, biosocial criminologists also argue that "environmental manipulations can be successful in reducing the incidence of crime by preventing full expression of genetic predispositional factors" (Ishikawa and Raine 2002, 83). However, this has not always been the obvious policy conclusion. The policy legacy of biological theory is that it has been associated with interventions designed to prevent the proliferation of criminals by stopping their procreation, or, more accurately, through eugenics. The first cousin of Darwin, Francis Galton coined the term *eugenics* in 1883. He used the term to mean "purely born" and saw the betterment of the human species by planned breeding (Garland 2001).

As well as limiting the ability of the "undesirable" to reproduce, the logical policy from the biological perspective is to cure the "sickness," which in this analysis is equated to crime, and this is seen as more appropriate than punishment. From this perspective, sentences should be designed to address, as in "treat," whatever is diagnosed as the "cause," and expert science, rather than judicial analysis, should decide this. Thus, indeterminate sentences are designed for each individual offender, based on his or her needs, with treatment length dependent on the time taken to cure or remove the cause.

We have discussed how early anthropological biocriminologists proposed invasive criminal justice policy and practice to deal with offenders. Suggested measures ranged from drug treatment and surgery to segregation and elimination through negative eugenics (forced sterilization) and even death for those who could not be "cured." For example, in the early part of the twentieth century Henry H. Goddard found that prisoners and convicted juvenile delinquents had low IQ scores, with the assumption that their "feeblemindedness" was an inherited trait accounting for their criminal behavior. Goddard, among other eugenicists, "reasoned that if they could prevent feebleminded people from having children, they would be able to rid the country of feeblemindedness and crime in a few generations" (Rafter 2007). This led to the development of custodial institutions for the feebleminded where the mentally defective could be held for life for the purpose of segregating them and preventing them from reproducing, a policy that in its extreme led to calls for forced sterilization, as in the 1930s in the Weimer Republic (Wetzell 2000). This eugenics line of thought formed the basis of the U.S. Bureau for Social Hygiene, which was founded in 1913 and operated through the 1930s. The bureau, funded by John D. Rockefeller Jr., who was interested in promoting cutting-edge science, particularly biology, to control populations, combined the biological ideas of Goddard and contemporary social Darwinists in a search for the causes of crime and proposed eugenics policies to eliminate them. Indeed, the eugenics movement spread nationwide. As Tony Platt has pointed out, "Under the banner of 'national regeneration,' tens of thousands, mostly poor women, were subjected to involuntary sterilization in the United States between 1907 and 1940. And untold thousands of women were sterilized without their informed consent after World War II. Under California's 1909 sterilization law, at least 20,000 Californians in state hospitals and prisons had been involuntarily sterilized by 1964" (2003). In the United States as a whole the government involuntarily sterilized more than 60,000 institutionalized people prior to the 1960s (Garland 2001).

These ideas have raised fears because of their racist and sexist connotations, and because of politicians' inclinations for simple technological fixes based on apparently objective science to absolve them from dealing with more complex issues (Nelkin 1993; Nelkin and Tancredi 1994; Sagarin and Sanchez 1988). Civil rights and invasion of privacy issues involved in enacting policy on the basis of questionable evidence that affects some groups in society more than others have created considerable opposition that has resulted in canceled conferences and withheld federal research funds (J. Williams 1994). Nor have these fears been quelled by the support of some contemporary biocriminologists who have suggested screening clinics, early diagnosis, and preventive treatment as part of policy solutions. C. Ray Jeffery, for example, suggested, "Crime prevention programs including pre- and postnatal care, early help for under-weight infants, well baby clinics, nutritional programs, neurological examinations for brain injuries, examinations for lead contamination in children, examinations for learning disabilities and hyperactivity, and other public health projects would be of great value to the black community" (1993, 8).

In his book *Born to Crime: The Genetic Causes of Criminal Behavior*, Lawrence Taylor not only suggested genetic screening but also offered justifications for several "prophylactic" policies designed to protect society against a three-year-old diagnosed as a future criminal or others genetically diagnosed as potentially dangerous but who never committed a crime. These measures include execution; preventive isolation based on future risk, "before he or she commits the statistically probable crime"; medical treatment with chemical or hormonal therapy; prefrontal lobotomies, that is, "destruction of the amygdala or prefrontal lobes"; genetic splicing for violent conduct—"no reason why a 'bit of cut-and-sew work' could not be employed"; and for the general population, routinely administering some substance to the water supply to counter criminal tendencies (1984, 147–154). Taylor goes so far as to support abortion "if the fetus is found to have 'bad' genes" and raises again the possibility of sterilization "for any person genetically capable of transmitting aberrant genes to offspring" (ibid., 157–158).

Interestingly, and contrary to critics' expectations, not all biocriminologists have summoned such a totalitarian specter. Indeed, some of the leading contributors suggest that not only would invasive treatments be illegal and against due process rights, but they are not even the most appropriate. Instead, the gene-environment interaction thesis suggests that the environment of potential offenders can be manipulated to prevent their manifesting crime, including improving prenatal and perinatal care and, in the case of sensation seekers, providing alternatives that are less harmful but still exciting and challenging (Mednick 1985; Fishbein and Thatcher 1986). Indeed, as Wood, Gove, and Cochran note, "An effective crime control system would create conditions which minimize the likelihood that persons would commit crimes. . . . The key to preventing some crime may depend on finding alternative activities that both produce a neurophysiological 'high' and which are symbolically meaningful to the persons performing the crimes" (1994, 75–76). This might include competitive sports and Outward Bound programs as well as activities such as skydiving, bungee jumping, surfing, rock climbing, wakeboarding, and similar kinds of risky, thrilling, and nonharmful activities. On this basis, we might speculate that states such as North Dakota and Montana have low crime rates because of the large proportion of their male population who are hunters!

Summary and Conclusion

The early biological hereditary theories have been discredited since their findings have not been confirmed by later studies; however, they laid the foundations for current developments. Despite the reliance on observation and the scientific method, these early studies had serious methodological problems—including the failure to adequately define crime, reliance on official crime statistics, and failure to control for environmental factors—that rendered the results suspect. The early theorists stimulated research into the biological and environmental causes of crime, however, and they also promoted use of the scientific method. This was an improvement over the "armchair" classical philosophers who used logic and reason to develop their theories of crime.

Contemporary biological theories also have mixed validity. The search for causes of crime has become more sophisticated, in part due to improved technology. Particularly important has been the research with genetics. Furthermore, modern biological theories do not state that biological defects alone produce criminal acts; rather, biological factors in conjunction with certain environmental or social factors limit choices that result in criminality. But the modern studies still have questionable validity due to the research methods employed. At best, biological factors are viewed as indirect causes. The most recent neurophysiological studies (explaining the relationship between brain processes and behavior) seem to offer the best hope for the future of this perspective. However, to date their studies have not ruled out the possibility that physical and chemical changes in the brain are the result rather than the cause of criminal behavior.

One interesting unexplored avenue of research suggested by our changing world would be as follows: If, as biology suggests, redheads become increasingly rare, can the same be said for certain behaviors? What, then, is the dominant trait: deviant or conservative? Can traits such as hair color be related to behavior? Over time, with globalization and the intermingling of peoples, which characteristics will eventually dominate? Epidemiological criminology provides one tool for examining this issue. Nikolas Rose argues, "We are seeing the emergence of new conceptions of the individual's 'genetically at risk' of offending, and the development of crime prevention strategies based upon a rationale of public health. This is not a new eugenics, but a control strategy that aims to identify, treat and control individuals predisposed to impulsive or aggressive conduct" (2000, 5).

Such policy implications affiliated with biological positivism are troublesome. One objective is to identify potential criminals before they commit a crime. But trying to "cure" someone who has not committed a crime is unethical. Even after a crime is committed, the interventionist treatment policies associated with biological positivism raise ethical dilemmas, as is illustrated in the discussion of voluntary chemical castration. The less invasive alternatives involving environmental manipulation may seem preferable, but these theorists seem naive about society's willingness to accept policies that provide better options to those identified as potential criminals than to those predicted to be noncriminals.

The best role for the biological contribution to our understanding of crime seems to be as a contributing part of some overall integrated theory (Fishbein 1998; Barak 1998). So far, the theories most conducive to such a mix are the psychological, social learning, and social environmental theories that we explore in the next three chapters.

Summary Chart: Biological Theory

Basic Idea: Captured in the phrase that some are "born criminal" with a predisposition to crime. Theorists believe that human behavior is determined by biological forces that in some manifest as crime under certain environmental conditions.

Human Nature: Humans inherit biological and genetically determined attributes that make people different. Attributes are randomly distributed; genetic variation makes each person unique. Most people possess a similar normal range of attributes and capabilities. Extremes of this distribution include those who are exceptional, either positively or negatively. Human behavior is an outcome of the mix of the biologically inherited qualities and their environment.

Society and the Social Order: A consensus is implied. Law is a reflection of the consensus of society. Crime is a deviation from normal behavior that is prohibited by law. Science can measure what is normal and therefore aid in law creation, crime detection, and crime treatment.

Criminals: Break laws naturally and will break norms and laws in any society. Criminals are different from noncriminals in being defective. The predisposition to crime emerges under certain conditions.

Causal Explanation: Defective biological attributes make some people predisposed or prone to deviate, under certain environmental conditions. This is because they (1) are impelled to anger; (2) are impulsive; (3) have impaired learning ability, limiting their capacity for socialization; (4) are unable to control their behavior; and/or (5) are sensation seekers suffering from low arousal of the autonomic nervous system due to low production of dopamine or excessive production of serotonin, each of which might also result from environmental factors, including substance abuse. Early theorists believed that defects were reflected in physical appearance (physical stigmata, or body types), with somatypes such as mesomorphs being more crime-prone, and that science could discover the cause of crime by examining the appearance of criminals compared to "normals." Recent work has concentrated on genetic theory and the evidence from twin and adoption studies that shows a consistent relationship suggesting hereditary factors. Specific inheritable defects have included physical inferiority; XYY chromosome pattern; brain disorders or dysfunction; mental deficiency; feeblemindedness; low IQ; learning disabilities, especially hyperactivity; hormonal imbalance; low or high levels of serotonin; low levels of dopamine; defective genes resulting in a slow autonomous nervous system; blood chemistry disorders; and ecological stimuli or deficiencies such as excessive sugar consumption, allergens, or vitamin and mineral deficiencies.

Criminal Justice Policy: Treat the defect and protect society from the untreatable. This is achieved through the medical model of criminal justice, which involves (1) information collection, (2) individualized diagnosis, (3) discretion, (4) experts as decision makers, (5) prediction, (6) treatment presumption, (7) treatment selection, and (8) indeterminate sentencing.

Criminal Justice Practice: Treatments include surgery or drugs, incapacitation, eugenics for those who are untreatable, genetic counseling, environmental manipulation, and alternative environmental sources of stimulation.

Evaluation: May be useful for explaining some forms of crime resulting from insanity or delinquency resulting from attention deficit disorder, some aggressive offenses, and some addiction. Contradictory support for twin study and adoption data. The theory does not consider the majority not caught for offenses. Genetic defects are found in only a small proportion of the offenders. Tendency to medicalize political issues and potential for being used by governments as a harsh form of social control.

5

Criminal Minds
Psychiatric and Psychological Explanations for Crime

Some seventy years before Brian Harris and Dylan Klebold went on a shooting rampage at Columbine High School on April 20, 1999, America's worst case of school violence occurred in Bath, Michigan. On May 18, 1927, fifty-five-year-old elected school board member and anti–school tax campaigner Andrew Kehoe first killed his wife by bashing in her skull, blew up their farm, and then proceeded to blow up the village school using 1,000 pounds of dynamite that he'd secretly planted and wired while conducting his job as a school maintenance worker: "Maniac Blows Up School and Kills 42, Mostly Children," ran the headline in the *New York Times* of May 19, 1927 (Gado 2002; Ellsworth 1927). In fact, thirty-eight children and seven teachers were killed that day, in addition to Kehoe's wife and numerous horses and other animals that were tied up and burned alive on Kehoe's farm when he blew it up. Not insignificantly, also killed outside the school when Kehoe fired at more dynamite he'd loaded in his truck was school board president Emory Huyck, with whom Kehoe had been feuding for years, the village postmaster who'd been with Huyck, and Kehoe himself, whose body parts were later found in a nearby garden. Interestingly, found wired to a fence at Kehoe's demolished farm was a sign that read, "Criminals Are Made Not Born." Was Kehoe insane, as the newspapers suggested, or was he rational, focused, and determined? He certainly exhibited much rationally planned behavior, such as purchasing and testing explosives on his farm (he was known locally as the "dynamite farmer"), laying out and concealing the wiring for the explosions over a considerable period of time, earning respect as a handyman, and exhibiting a well-articulated debate against raising taxes for schools. Yet his mass homicide that day drew attention to the extremes of his traumatic past: as an abused stepchild of fourteen who watched his stepmother burn to death from a malfunctioning stove (some speculate he caused her death), who suffered a traumatic head injury from a fall at age twenty-nine, who was impatient and intolerant of criticism, whose antitax stance resulted in his refusing to pay his mortgage, and whose strange, compulsive behavior had him changing clothes many times a day in order to always appear neat and clean. Was Kehoe a biological defective, or was there a process in his development that led to this tragic outcome? Had Kehoe lived, could he have invoked the insanity defense?

In 1982, John Hinckley successfully used an insanity defense to avoid prosecution for attempting to assassinate then-president Ronald Reagan. In 1994, Lorena Bobbitt argued that an "irresistible impulse" caused her to slice off her husband's penis with a kitchen knife while he slept. She was found not guilty by reason of "temporary insanity," based on her state of mind following an alleged sexual assault by her husband. On Monday, December 8, 1980, John Lennon was fatally shot in front of the Dakota Hotel in New York City. His killer, Mark David Chapman, "suffered delusional paranoid schizophrenia. He had attempted suicide twice, and during 1979 became increasingly fixated on both Holden Caulfield (the fictional hero of J. D. Salinger's *The Catcher in the Rye*) and John Lennon. In the end, Chapman believed he was living a life that mirrored that of Holden Caulfield and mirrored the unreal superstar life of John Lennon. Chapman was confused and paranoid about who he really was, and perhaps in [the] killing of John Lennon, he was trying to kill himself" (http://www.lennon-chapman.com). Chapman pleaded guilty to murder, against the strenuous objections of his attorneys. They, and nine psychiatrists, felt that Chapman would be found not guilty by reason of insanity. He was examined and found to have an IQ of 121, well above average. These four exceptional, but widely publicized, cases illustrate the importance of psychiatry and psychology as a criminal defense and as an explanation for aberrant behavior that is accepted by the courts.

Criminal law requires two things for a crime to be proven: criminal intent, or *mens rea*—"a guilty mind"—and *actus reus*, the voluntary participation in overt willful behavior (Severance, Goodman, and Loftus 1992). The U.S. Supreme Court ruled in *In re Winship* (1970) that these mental and behavioral elements must each be proven beyond a reasonable doubt. Thus, if defense attorneys can establish that their client is, or was at the time of the offense, mentally ill, criminal responsibility, and therefore culpability based on mens rea, cannot apply.[1]

But even in the most heinous crimes, juries are reluctant to accept the insanity defense. Attorneys for Jeffrey Dahmer, the serial killer who drugged young gay men before strangling them, having sex with their corpses, eating their bodies, while preserving their severed heads and penises, were unable to convince the jury that their client was insane. Dahmer was found sane and convicted of fifteen counts of murder and sentenced to 957 years in prison before he was murdered by a fellow prisoner in 1994. John Salvi, who in 1996 argued the insanity defense for murdering abortion clinic personnel, was also found guilty; he committed suicide in prison. These cases show the typical outcome: Juries more often choose to reject criminal defenses relying on insanity or temporary insanity (Maedor 1985). Promoted by disproportionate media attention to certain kinds of lurid or bizarre crimes, a popular misconception prevails, however, that many criminals are "crazy" or "sick"—that something in their mind motivated their crime (Holman and Quinn 1992, 83; Pallone and Hennessy 1992). Moreover, as Szasz says, "Although no one can define insanity, everyone believes he can 'recognize it when he sees it.'" He continues: "The problem is that whenever a person factually guilty of committing a serious crime pleads insanity, the jury is asked to answer an intrinsically nonsensical question, namely, what 'caused' the defendant to commit his wrongful act: his self or his mental illness? If the former, then he is a guilty victimizer. If the latter, then he is an innocent victim [of insanity]" (2000, 31).

In addition to the popular imagery and the legal dimension, there are other reasons psychiatry and psychology are important components of criminological knowledge. There has been an enormous growth of interest in forensic psychology during the 1990s (Arrigo and Shipley 2004; Bartol and Bartol 2006). Psychological principles are applied in several criminal justice settings. For example, the apprehension of serial killers and rapists relies on psychological and offender profiling. Profiling techniques are developed by the Behavioral Science Unit of the FBI located at its training center in Quantico, Virginia. Psychology has led to the development of many screening, diagnostic, and analytical measures used in profiling (the television series *Criminal Minds* was based in this work). Profiles are composite characteristics of the personalities and behavioral attributes of the typical offender for different types of crimes, and involve building specific profiles based on the early crime-scene evidence in cases being investigated by the police. They are psychological identities parallel to the police-artist impressions of an offender. Psychological profiles are used not only to apprehend offenders but also to predict future strikes by an offender and preventatively to protect victims. Yet in the case of the "Unabomber" crimes, a suspect, Theodore Kaczynski, a former math professor, was eventually caught after seventeen years due to his brother's recognition of his writing style. Kaczynski had little in common with the profile created; in fact, he was the opposite of the profile in most respects. Likewise, the two African Americans arrested for the sniper killings in the Maryland area were far from the single white intelligent male in a white van profiled by the FBI. Despite these failures, criminal profiling holds great interest to many professionals and students. Movies like *The Silence of the Lambs* fuel this interest. Profiling does have a legitimate scientific base, as we show in this chapter, yet as psychologist Curt Bartol states, "Profiling is at least 95 percent an art based on speculation and only 5 percent science" (1999, 5). Not surprisingly, it seems to have been restricted to profiling "street" rather than "suite" offenders. As can be seen from table 5.1, "Profile of a Corporate Criminal," some indication of the psychological profile of a corporate offender can be seen and matches those such as the Enron executives, yet this profile is rarely discussed in media coverage.

Offenders and victims have also been diagnosed as having post-traumatic stress disorder (Riggs, Rothman, and Foa 1995), which can result in violence when their mind returns to the prior situation of stress. Traumatic head injuries are often associated with personality changes. Criminal offenders have been diagnosed as having a wide range of mental disturbances. Both victims and offenders can require diagnosis

TABLE 5.1   Profile of a Corporate Criminal

1. Caucasian male
2. Fights to the top of an organization against tough competition
3. Strong desire to secure career advancement
4. Pushiness designed to measure personal cleverness
5. Loyalty to the organization
6. Organizationally based social life
7. Shrewd
8. Opportunistic

SOURCE: Adapted from Stotland 1977, Gross 1978, and Box 1983.

and treatment based on psychological concepts. For these reasons, students of criminology need to understand the underlying assumptions of the psychological perspective, together with its study methods and policy implications and the limitations of this approach to criminal behavior. In this chapter, we outline the search for the psychological factors in crime causation, present the basic premises, describe some illustrative contemporary studies, and critique the findings and assumptions.

From Sick Minds to Abnormal Behavior

The human mind has long been considered a source of abnormal behavior, and this connection is sustained by the media's linking mental illness to incidents of violence (Monahan 1992). Indeed a 2005 study on media coverage of mental illness found that "thirty-nine percent of all stories focused on dangerousness and violence; these stories most often ended up in the front section" (Corrigan et al. 2005, 551). Since crime is seen as abnormal behavior, it has been subject to psychiatric and psychological analyses. English psychiatrist James Pritchard (1786–1848) used the term *moral insanity* to explain criminal behavior in 1835, and another psychiatrist, Henry Maudsley (1835–1918), argued that crime was a release for pathological minds that prevented them from going insane. Like Maudsley, Isaac Ray (1807–1881) believed that pathological urges drove some to commit crime. These early psychiatric explanations were founded on the assumptions that psychoses are biologically based and are, therefore, variations of the biological theories discussed in the previous chapter. More important, as Barak points out, "Like the theories of a 'born criminal' the theories of a 'sick criminal' are just as fallacious," in that those diagnosed as mentally ill are no more likely to commit crimes than those seen as mentally healthy (1998, 127). Indeed, more than sixty years ago Reckless observed, "It cannot be shown that the general run of adult offenders are alarmingly more psychotic than the non-delinquent population" (1940, 104). Extensive review of the evidence confirms that "offenders with mental disorders were no more criminally prone or violent than offenders without mental disorders" and, moreover, were found to be "less likely to recidivate than nondisordered offenders" (Bartol 1999, 141; see also Bonta, Law, and Hanson 1998). Studies conducted on extensive Swedish data from 1988 to 2000 have demonstrated that only one in twenty violent offenses are committed by people with serious mental illness—which means that nineteen out of twenty violent offenses are committed by those without mental illness. Moreover, 18 percent of murders and attempted murders are committed by the seriously mentally ill (Fazel and Martin 2006). Of course, the extent of white-collar and corporate crimes committed by mentally ill offenders is not documented.

There is one caveat to this general rule that crime is only marginally related to mental illness: the subtype of mental disorder known as *antisocial personality disorder*, also known as *psychopaths* and *sociopaths* (as discussed below). A useful way to think about the mind is to distinguish between differential psychology and process psychology: "Differential psychology takes as its province the illumination of differences between people that result in variant behavior between different behaviors. . . . Process psychology . . . focuses on the process by which criminal behavior is emitted, construing that process as a dynamic interchange between the person and environment—between intraperson propensities . . . and situational cues and variables which . . . seem to invite, permit, or tolerate certain ways of behaving" (Pallone and Hennessy 1992, 4–6).

Thus, from the process perspective, it is not so much that sick minds cause crime but that certain psychological processes in any mind may produce criminal behavior. The science of psychology is a way to examine these processes. Psychological theories of crime explain abnormal behavior as the result of mind and thought processes that form during human development, particularly during the early years. There are several different approaches taken by psychologists examining the mind, and most of them share certain common assumptions.

Shared Psychological Assumptions

Psychological explanations for crime, like biological theories, look for differences that might explain some people's predisposition toward crime. They look for either differences between individuals (differential psychology) or differences in the situation and emergent environment (process psychology). The view commonly held by those adopting psychological explanations is that humans are formed through socialization and developmental processes rather than being biologically predetermined. It is widely accepted that humans develop through a series of necessary mental, moral, and sexual stages. When this development is abnormal (usually beginning in early childhood) or subject to traumatic events, personality disorders and psychological disturbances may become part of the individual's personality characteristics, or may be constructed as an appropriate behavioral response under a particular set of emerging circumstances. These disorders and disturbances reside within the mind of the individual, but may be latent. Many psychologists agree that social or environmental factors may trigger erratic or criminal behavior in those psychologically predisposed.

Dysfunctional processing or traumatic experiences may also produce antisocial personality tendencies. This implies differences in mental functioning that may cause those affected to commit crimes. In this context, crimes are only one form of "aggressive or anti-social behavior" that "violates certain social norms" that may also be a violation of legal norms (Shoham and Seis 1993, 5; see also Fishbein 1998).

Psychologists, especially those taking a differential approach, rely heavily on scales, inventories, and questionnaires to identify and classify the differences between individuals who suffer from psychological disturbances and those who do not. Measurement is thus a very critical component, since what is "normal" must be differentiated from what is "pathological." Hoge (1999) and others (Zhang, Welte, and Wieczorek 2002) have outlined many of the scales and their application. These scales include measures of personality: the Basic Personality Inventory, Jesness Inventory, Millon Adolescent Personality Inventory, and Minnesota Multiphasic Personality Inventory (MMPI). Behavioral measures include the Revised Behavior Problem Checklist, Behavior Assessment System for Children, and Child Behavior Checklist. There are also scales that measure antisocial behavior: the Self-reported Delinquency Scale, Psychopathic States Inventory, and Drug Use Screening Inventory. And finally there are attitudinal measures, measures of environmental factors, risk-classification measures, and interview schedules. The Rorschach (inkblot) test is often used to assess aggressive and psychopathic personalities (Gacono and Meloy 1994).

Because criminal behaviors are said to stem from abnormal developmental processes affecting the mind, some form of psychological treatment intervention is necessary to correct or counteract those with criminal predispositions or change the process whereby these personalities are formed. Beyond these similarities, psychological approaches have important differences. We consider several different theoretical approaches that are evident in the literature and briefly describe each.

The development of psychological theory in relation to crime can be seen as a movement. It began with the idea of uncovering hidden unconscious forces within the individual's mind. It progressed to an increased recognition of the role of family influences on learning and led to a growing acknowledgment that the human learning process is not simply passive-reactive but involves complex, creative interpretation and analysis of information and that this is itself interrelated with the psychophysiology of the brain's function. It reached the stage where cognition is shaped by interaction of the mind with the wider social environment. We begin our analysis of this movement by looking at the pioneering work of Sigmund Freud and the various subtheories that emerged from his approach.

The Psychoanalytic Approach

Viennese psychiatrist Sigmund Freud (1856–1939) is most responsible for establishing the role of the unconscious mind in shaping behavior. Although Freud himself wrote little on crime, his theory has been applied by others of the Freudian psychoanalytic school (Aichhorn 1935; Healy and Bronner 1926, 1936; Alexander and

Healy 1935; Bowlby 1946; Abrahamsen 1944, 1960; Friedlander 1947; Redl and Wineman 1951, 1952; Redl and Toch 1979). The psychoanalytic approach is a relatively complicated theory of behavior based on several unproven, and arguably unprovable, assumptions about how human minds develop and function. The basic argument is that crime is an expression of buried internal conflicts that result from traumas and deprivations during childhood. Traumatic events that occur during childhood affect the unconscious component of the human mind.

Freud assumed that the mind was composed of conscious and unconscious components. The conscious personality he termed the ego. The ego is concerned with reality and attempts to rationally mediate between the conflicting demands of unconscious desires. The unconscious is divided into two parts. The id is the source of basic biological and psychological drives present from birth, including the libido, or sexual energy; Eros, the "life instinct"; and Thanatos, the destructive "death instinct." The id follows the pleasure principle—"If it feels good, do it." Opposing the id is the superego, the "moral police," or conscience, internalized from socialization into the norms of a society and containing moral and ethical restraints on behavior. The superego reflects each person's social experiences and becomes a source of self-criticism based on the production of guilt. The id and superego compete with one another to control behavior. The ego serves to balance the desires of the id and superego.

A basic conflict for individuals involves guilt: "The individual experiences all sorts of drives and urges coming from the id, and feels guilty about them because of the prohibitions of the superego" (Vold and Bernard 1986, 112). Freud identified two primary ways people handle this situation of guilt. First, in *sublimation* the desires and drives of the id are diverted to actions that meet the approval of the superego (e.g., aggression may be directed toward athletic events). A second reaction is *repression*, which occurs when the drives of the id are denied. This results in various abnormal reactions. Reaction formation is one manifestation of repression. In this case, a person with repressed sexual drives would be very prudish about sex. Another reaction to repression is projection, whereby people see their own desires and urges in others.

These basic conflicts occur in different stages of an individual's life. Freud said that during childhood, basic drives are oriented around oral, anal, phallic, latent, and genital drives that seek to be satisfied. These sequential stages of development cause problems when a person remains "fixated," or stuck at one stage, because satisfaction has been denied or as a result of experiencing a trauma. Freud argued that if the guilt associated with the various stages was not satisfactorily handled by the ego, then the personality of the individual would be negatively affected later in life. For example, Abrahamsen argues:

> Murder emerges from the intensity of death wishes that co-exist with our life saving emotions. . . . Homicide . . . is released by the intensity of inner conflicts. . . . Murderers were intensely tormented. Deep down, they felt beset, trapped in an intense conflict growing out of a struggle between their sexual and self-preserving feelings on

TABLE 5.2   Psychological Theories Compared

Theory	Basic concept	Key Theorists
Psychoanalytical • Attachment Theory • Frustration-Aggression Theory	Dysfunctional mind formed by inadequate childhood development processes, producing buried conflicts	Sigmund Freud, August Aichhorn, Kate Friedlander
	Failure to form attachment with mother produces insecurity and lack of empathy for others	John Bowlby
	Aggression as an adaptive mechanism to relieve stress	John Dollard, William Healy and Augusta Bronner, Seymour Halleck
Trait-Based • Personality Type • Self-control	Differences in personality traits/drives produce different behavioral responses; low self-control produces crime-prone behavior	Hervey Cleckley Hans Eysenck
Behavioral Learning Theory	Behavior depends on the rewards and punishments it receives	Pavlov B. F. Skinner
Social Learning and Modeling Theory	Learning to behave by imitating and modeling the behavior of others, from groups or in media images	Gabriel Tarde Albert Bandura Ronald Akers
Cognitive Theory	The mind is made up of patterns of thinking that develop through interactive experiences and can be underdeveloped and/or destructive	Jean Piaget, Lawrence Kohlberg, Aaron Beck, Stanton Samenow
Constructivist and Ecological Theory	People construct the meaning of their world from experiences with the broad social environment, particularly their community	George Kelly
Evolutionary	Mind is an epiphenomenon of evolutionary desire for genetic proliferation; selfish gene	William Rushton Lee Ellis

the one hand and their surroundings on the other. . . . The conflict I refer to is due to serious traumatic situations, primarily experienced in earliest childhood, before the child is one or two years old. (1973, 9–10)

Freud (1915, 1950) further argued that one outcome of the unconscious guilt complex is crime. This can occur in several ways. It can result from a fear of authority and an overdeveloped superego. Lawbreaking can allow persons feeling guilt to draw punishment on themselves and thereby temporarily relieve their guilt. This has been used to explain burglars who leave obvious clues to their identity and shoplifters who take few precautions to cover their acts. But guilt can also result in crime: "Freud discovered that such guilt can lead highly moral people to actually commit immoral deeds out of a need to punish themselves for their evil thoughts. Guilt in this case is not the result of an immoral act, but its cause" (Wallwork 1994, 235).

Blaming the Mother: Attachment Theory

For other post-Freudians, if the parental upbringing was important in forming a healthy personality, then the role of the mother (who at that time was seen as spending most of her time nurturing children) was crucial. As Aichhorn (1935) argued, for some children inadequate or faulty upbringing may result in a weak or underdeveloped ego and superego, in which state the child either is unable to control his or her riotous id or suppresses these instinctual desires, resulting in "latent delinquency" (Friedlander 1947). This failed developmental process is also found in Abrahamsen's concept of the damaged superego (1944, 1960), Bowlby's notion of the "affectionless character" (1946), and Friedlander's "anti-social character" (1947), each of which pointed to "maternal deprivation" or maternal mishandling of the child.

One of the enduring theories from this approach has become known as *attachment theory*, which emphasizes the importance of forming a secure emotional base for subsequent personality development. John Bowlby (1951, 1988) argued that infants form attachments to caregivers if they are sensitive and responsive. Time is less important than the quality of the interaction. The infant's biological mother is a key player in this relationship, but anyone who provides consistent quality interactional care can perform this role. Psychologists have criticized Bowlby, yet in spite of this, attachment theory has become the dominant approach to understanding how children develop in relation to their parents or other attachment figures from whom the caregiver bond emanates. Bowlby argued that children who have frequent breaks in relations with their mother or the significant quality caregiver in their early years up to the age of eight, or who have factors that mitigate against secure maternal bonding, (such as child abandonment, foster care, or child abuse), develop anxiety and have difficulty forming relationships with others. Part of that difficulty may be a maladaption that prevents them from getting involved with others in order to avoid the emotional pain of being hurt. In particular, these affectionless children lack the ability to empathize with others and, as a result, do not see or feel the pain that harm may cause them. Serious deficits in parenting may result in "reactive attachment disorder."

Maladaptive Coping Strategies: Frustration-Aggression Theory

For Healy and Bronner (1936), thwarted desires and deprivations cause frustration. When this frustration is combined with the failure of parenting to provide nondelinquent channels for compensatory gratification, affective ties to conventional adults fail to form, and the result is a weak superego that is unable to protect against delinquency. John Dollard and his colleagues (1939) argued that frustration emerges as a natural course of living but that most people are able to find socially acceptable outlets, such as sports, listening to rock or rap music or playing video games. For some, however, the frustration may be displaced onto other people who have nothing to do with the cause of the frustration, but this still serves as a release.

Indeed, there are similarities here to Alfred Adler's idea of the inferiority complex (1931): Those whose style of life fails to provide them a sense of superiority or status may compensate through abnormal forms of compensatory behavior. As both Adler (1931) and most recently Halleck (1971) have argued, those who feel the world is against them may turn to crime as a means of satisfying their creativity and autonomy. Halleck's theory of displaced aggression, enabling one to survive frustration with dignity, is echoed in the voices of delinquents who see murder as "righteous slaughter" (Jack Katz 1988). Thus, the ego develops defense mechanisms in the form of excuses and justifications to rationalize one's actions. This kind of psychoanalytical approach may explain theft from the workplace, which is found to be committed by those who express intense job dissatisfaction and frustration with their employers (Hollinger and Clark 1983) and may even explain the loner who commits violence against an employer (Fox and Levin 1994).

Limitations and Policy Implications of Psychoanalytical Theory

Most contemporary criminologists have largely discredited the psychoanalytic approach. One frequent criticism is that it is tautological. This means that the theory implies in its premise what is then made explicit in the conclusion, making it repetitious rather than explanatory. For example, Akers notes, "It is only the interpretation of the therapist that determines when the independent variables of unconscious urges and impulses are present. Psychoanalytic interpretations, therefore, tend to be after the fact, tautological, and untestable" (1994, 85). The lack of testability stems from the fact that rather than being a formal theory, the psychoanalytic approach is more a set of interrelated concepts that in combination provide a plausible explanation for human behavior, but one that defies empirical measurement (Vold and Bernard 1986; Martin, Mutchnick, and Austin 1990). Indeed, since these key concepts are located in the individual's unconscious, it is impossible to confirm or deny their existence. Moreover, psychoanalysts are frequently in disagreement about the diagnosis of a problem. Another difficulty with evaluating this approach is that most research has focused on a small number of subjects in a clinical setting. Thus, controlled comparisons with a larger healthy population have not been conducted. Finally, psychoanalysis is gender biased, assuming women are inherently abnormal (Klein [1973] 1980; Naffine 1987). Yet other aspects, such as the parental deprivation thesis (not specifically maternal) in the work of post-Freudians, have been supported by empirical findings (Cernkovich and Giordino 1987; Farrington and West 1993).

In spite of its limitations, there are several policy implications of psychoanalytical theory. According to this approach, a criminal offender is not necessarily responsible for his or her actions. Rather, the offender is sick and in need of a cure. (Punishment may actually make the illness worse, since it could tend to heighten feelings of guilt.) Because the sickness is located in the subconscious, treatment must address underlying emotional disturbances. Treatment involves evaluation and analysis to help the offender uncover the childhood root causes. Because repression is the root cause of so many dysfunctional reactions, it is important for repressed experiences and desires to be recognized and handled. To explore the subconscious, Freud developed the therapeutic technique of psychoanalysis, in which patients are asked to relax and talk about whatever comes to mind. Connections, or associations, are then made, and the patients can recognize and understand the unconscious and gain a degree of control over their actions.

Freud also relied on a technique called transference. This treatment is based on the assumption that past relationships (for example, with one's mother) influence current relationships. As the therapist becomes increasingly important to the patient, the patient will replay the earlier relationship with the therapist (the therapist assuming the role of the earlier problem-generating person). Treatment, then, consists of the therapist straightening out the current relationship between him- or herself and the client, which simultaneously resolves the earlier problem relationship.

The ultimate value of psychoanalytic therapy should be in helping individuals overcome their "problems." But it has been shown that patients who receive these treatments do no better than those who receive no treatment (Schwitzgebel 1974). Perhaps the best that can be stated is that the theory has a heuristic or sensitizing value (Shoham and Seis 1993), highlighting the importance of mental processes in producing behavioral outcomes. Indeed, in spite of its limitations, it also established psychology as a scientific academic discipline.

Since Freud, psychology has taken divergent directions. One direction, the *trait-based perspectives* founded on the work of Gordon Allport (1937, 1961), sees human development leading to distinctive personality types based on learned traits. Another direction, *behavioral and situational learning theories*, based on both Ivan Pavlov's ([1906] 1967) and B. F. Skinner's (1953) theories of operant conditioning, sees a person's current behavior as the result of accumulations of responses resulting from past learning. These two approaches have been combined in several applications to criminology, including Eysenck's criminal personality theory ([1964] 1977; Eysenck and Gudjonsson 1989), examining the role of extroversion and neuroticism as factors in criminal and psychopathic personalities. Eysenck combined trait theory and conditioned learning theory. Zuckerman's theory of criminal personality (1989) incorporated the traits of impulsivity, aggressiveness, and irresponsibility. Wilson and Herrnstein's "eclectic" integrated theory, incorporating "both genetic predispositions and social learning," is "built on modern behavioral psychology" (1985, 44). Let us first look in more detail at trait-based theory.

Trait-Based Personality Theories

Trait-based personality theories differ from the psychoanalytic approach in that abnormal behavior is said to stem from abnormal or criminal personality traits, which may develop from a variety of causes (environment, brain injury, illness, drug abuse, and so forth) rather than unconscious causes. Moreover, in some cases these traits are said to stem from biological causes, which provides a link between biological and psychological theories. Traits "represent consistent characteristics of individuals that are relevant to a wide variety of behavioral domains" (Caspi et al. 1994, 165). Allport defined personality as the dynamic organization of an individual's psychophysical systems of predispositions in response to certain environmental triggers (1937, 48). One task of trait-based theory, then, is to measure these various frequently occurring traits to see how they are assembled differently in different people and with what effects.

Several varieties of trait-based personality theory are applied to criminality. All share the view that criminal behavior is a manifestation of an underlying trait-based problem. Generally, criminological applications of trait theory look at personality characteristics such as impulsiveness, aggressiveness, extroversion, neuroticism, psychoticism, thrill seeking, hostility, and emotionality. As we saw in the previous chapter, these have also been tied to biological and neurological processes.

One of the first theorists to adopt a trait-based personality approach to crime was psychiatrist Hervey Cleckley in his book *Mask of Insanity* (1941). Cleckley laid the foundation for what would be an enduring composite description of what he called a psychopath, or what others call a sociopath and what most recently has become known as someone possessing an "antisocial personality disorder." Not only has the core of Cleckley's original observations found its way into the psychologists' bible, the *DSM (Diagnostic and Statistical Manual of Mental Disorders)*, but it is also found in the World Health Organization's Classification of Mental Disorders. The composite set of traits from all these sources describes someone with a self-obsessed personality who is disconnected from others and finds him- or herself in conflict with the social world (see table 5.3). The extreme version of this aberrant personality, the psychopath, "is an asocial, aggressive, highly impulsive person, who feels little or no guilt and is unable to form lasting bonds of affection with other human beings" (McCord and McCord 1964, 3). Psychopathy is also linked to an inability to delay gratification and to learn from experience, sensation seeking, and superficial charm (Zhang, Welte, and Wieczorek 2002). They are also found to be callous and unemotional (Caputo, Frick, and Brodsky 1999). The term *antisocial personality* (Lykken

1995) has largely replaced the term *psychopath*, though psychologists disagree about whether these are the same thing. According to the *DSM IV*, the essential feature of an antisocial personality "is a pervasive pattern of disregard for, and violation of, the rights of others that begins in childhood or early adolescence and continues into adulthood" (American Psychiatric Association 1994, 645–650). The disagreement comes because diagnosis for antisocial personality disorder is based on classifications of behavior, whereas diagnosis of psychopathy is based on affective and personality traits. The fundamental question that remains is whether these traits simply are a description of someone who repeatedly commits offenses or actually explain why a person possesses the traits and why he or she commits crimes.

One of the first to attempt to explain personality traits of offenders was Hans Eysenck ([1964] 1977), who, like Cleckley, tried to establish a criminal, or psychotic, personality. Drawing on Carl Jung's ideas of introversion and extroversion and Pavlov's learning theory, Eysenck claimed to show that human personalities are made up of clusters of traits. One cluster produces a sensitive, inhibited temperament that he called introversion. A second cluster produces an outward-focused, cheerful, expressive temperament that he called extroversion. A third dimension of personality, which forms emotional stability or instability, he labeled neuroticism; to this schema

TABLE 5.3 Core Traits of an Antisocial Personality (Sociopath or Psychopath)

Self   Intelligent
         Self-centered/egotistical/selfish/arrogant
         Shameless
         Guiltless
         Impulsive
         No life plan
         Intolerant   *Relations to society*
                                               Disregard for norms/
Relations with others   rules/obligations
         Superficial
         Disconnected
         Impersonal
         Unreliable
         Disloyal
         Deceptive/liar
         Lack of empathy toward/unable to love
         Unresponsive to interpersonal relations
         Unable to sustain enduring relations
         Blames others for problems

he subsequently added psychoticism, which is a predisposition to psychotic break-down. Normal human personalities are emotionally stable, neither highly introverted nor extroverted. In contrast, those who are highly neurotic, highly extroverted, and score high on a psychoticism scale have a greater predisposition toward crime, form-ing in the extreme the psychopathic personality. Eysenck explained that such person-alities (sensation seekers) are less sensitive to excitation by stimuli, requiring more stimulation than normals, which they can achieve through crime, violence, and drug taking. These people are impulsive, being emotionally unstable. They are also less easy to condition and have a higher threshold or tolerance to pain. Low IQ can affect the ability of such personalities to learn rules, perceive punishment, or experience pain, as in biological theory. The legacy of Eysenck's work, as Nicole Hahn Rafter points out, is that he was one of the first to identify the extroverted "sensation seeker." Indeed, she says, the 1964 publication of *Crime and Personality* "marked a turning point, the moment when biological theories began to regain a toehold in the criminological arena. Eysenck made the first thoroughgoing effort of the 20th cen-tury to formulate a biologically based theory of crime, setting in motion a return to biocriminology that continues into the present and promises to play an increasingly large role in the criminological future" (2006, 50).

BOX 5.1 Mental Illness and Cracks in the System
MARK LANIER

There are many people suffering from mental illness in the United States. Some are depressed and lethargic; others have more extreme problems such as schizophrenia and hallucinations. Recent research shows that between 25 and 29 percent of all Americans (*excluding* the homeless) suffer from some form of mental illness or sub-stance abuse (http://www.webmd.com/mental-health/news/20030507/us-lags-in-mental-illness-treatment, accessed January 9, 2009). Fourteen percent suffer from moderate to severe forms of mental illness. Some seek and find mental health counsel-ing (http://www.foxnews.com/story/0,2933,158742,00.html, accessed January 9, 2009). However, many are neglected, with the most wealthy being the ones to receive care in the United States. "Part of the problem stems from the evolution of how pub-lic mental health came into play in the U.S. It came into existence at the deepest end, with institutionalization of those most needing treatment," says Teri Odom, who continues, "Because we started at the deepest end, we don't have a balance between early intervention, immediate care, and more extreme mental illness, and people are not encouraged to seek treatment earlier. And even when they do and identify early warning times, the resources are not there to meet their need" (http://www.webmd .com/mental-health/news/20030507/us-lags-in-mental-illness-treatment). Increasing numbers find themselves homeless, and many of them end up in prisons and jails. Some, however, suffer even more tragic consequences. As shown below, Mark Rohlman was one of the many who fell through the cracks in the American mental health system,

CONTINUES

BOX 5.1 (CONTINUED)

I spent my childhood years at 302 Plymouth Avenue in Fort Walton Beach, Florida. Just down the street the Rohlman family had several boys my age. We played together on a regular basis. I moved to another state in the eighth grade, never to return. Years later, in July 2008, I was teaching a course for the Florida Department of Law Enforcement in Tallahassee when two officers were called out of the class to respond to an emergency situation. A strange premonition overcame me, even though I had no idea what the emergency was. I was shortly to learn the tragic story of what led to my premonition.

The following story by Andrew Gant was printed in the July 23 edition of the *Daily News*, a regional newspaper serving the panhandle of Florida:

Brothers Wonder What Else Could Have Been Done to Save Mark Rohlman and the Deputy He Killed

FORT WALTON BEACH—Mark Rohlman fell through the cracks—and took a good man down with him, Rohlman's grieving brothers said Wednesday. All they're left with is sorrow and doubt. "I tried to do something good for my brother," said Adam Rohlman, who filed the ex parte order Monday to have Mark taken in for treatment. "Instead, he's dead and an officer's dead." Adam and Erik Rohlman, both all too familiar with Mark's escalating paranoia and threats of violence, spoke quietly Wednesday after meeting with state investigators. They remembered their brother as a troubled man who used to be happy. "He's a normal guy like you and I, except instead of catching the flu, he had a chemical imbalance," Erik said. "Damn, it shouldn't have cost him his life."

Adam was not far down the street Tuesday morning as Okaloosa County sheriff's deputies tried to communicate with his brother inside 331 Plymouth Avenue—the now-vacant house where the Rohlmans grew up. Adam said no one told him the Special Response Team was going in with guns drawn. He would have liked to try coaxing out his brother before they did. Erik said deputies suspected Mark was in the attic as they went bedroom-to-bedroom. Instead, they found Mark Rohlman in one of those rooms—where he shot and killed Deputy Anthony Forgione. Deputies returned fire, wounding Mark twice before he fell into a closet and killed himself, too, Erik said.

It was not the resolution anyone wanted. "The sun was coming up in 30 minutes," said Erik, who wished someone could have used the sunlight to wait, "illuminate the house," and make visual contact with Mark inside. There was no furniture to hide him. Deputies say they used a throw phone and a bullhorn to no avail. Erik wishes they could have used a snaking camera to investigate the house.

In the ex parte order, Mark Rohlman is listed as armed, but not necessarily dangerous. "He is scared," Adam wrote on the form. In the past, Mark had threatened to shoot lawmen who came near his vehicle. He was paranoid ever since a land deal went bad in Santa Rosa County two years ago, paranoid that county commissioners "were going to have him taken out by authorities to

CONTINUES

BOX 5.1 (CONTINUED)

evade lawsuit," his brothers said. Mark was so paranoid that he carried a shotgun in his Ford Excursion at all times. Tragically, he used it.

Now the Rohlmans say they hurt the most for Forgione's two daughters, who will grow up without their father. All five brothers—Adam, Erik, Karl, Paul and Dana—say they've pooled $5,000 and donated it to Forgione's memorial fund. They stress that they don't blame deputies for following orders. They do question the orders, to some extent, because they don't believe lawmen exhausted every option.

At the Sheriff's Office, Chief Deputy Mike Coup said the family's questions deserved answers after a state investigation. Most vehemently, however, the Rohlmans question why Mark was able to leave Fort Walton Beach Medical Center twice. He should have been held there, they say. "That's the only reason (he died)," Erik said. "They didn't contain him." Evelyn Ross, director of risk management at the hospital, said Wednesday that the Baker Act does not give doctors the authority to hold a patient against his or her will. A particularly dangerous patient is the responsibility of law enforcement, said Ross. "You don't restrain people just because they've been Baker Acted," Ross said. "We're not a prison. We don't lock people up when they come in." Ross called the shooting "a tragic situation" and said the Rohlmans had "very legitimate feelings."

As the investigation unfolds, the Rohlmans say they feel partially responsible for both deaths—and pained that for many, Mark Rohlman will be remembered as a killer. "Mark shot a cop—how do you explain that to an 11-year-old little girl?" Erik said of the rest of the Rohlman family. "He fell through the cracks and he's dead. It's hard for me to say that."

Many of the psychological theories covered in this chapter may apply. However, trait-based (biological) psychology seems to make the best explanation. Had Mark Rohlman been on medication, it is probable that his delusions would have been controlled. Had the mental health and criminal justice systems functioned better, two lives would have been saved and the tragic consequences averted.

A major contribution made by the trait-based personality theorists is their reliance on relatively sophisticated diagnostic devices. For example, Starke Hathaway (1939) developed the Minnesota Multiphasic Personality Inventory (MMPI) to detect deviant personality patterns. The MMPI uses several scales to measure personality traits such as depression, hysteria, psychopathy, and compulsiveness. Five hundred and fifty true-or-false statements aid with the diagnosis. These statements are grouped into ten separate scales measuring different personality traits (e.g., depression, hysteria, and so on). The MMPI has "received considerable attention in the determination of criminal offender personality typology" (Carmin et al. 1989, 486). For example, using this scale Glaser, Calhoun, and Petrocelli (2002) were able to classify personality by type of offense committed by a group of juvenile offenders. Another common personality measure is the California Psychological Inventory (CPI). The CPI is used to determine if a person has traits such as dominance, tolerance, and sociability. Recent research using yet another scale, the Multidimensional Personality Questionnaire, correlates personality and delinquency, finding that "male and female delinquents exhibited convergent personality profiles characterized by impulsivity, danger seeking, a rejection of traditional values, aggressive attitudes, feelings of alienation and an adversarial interpersonal attitude" (Caspi et al. 1994, 176–177). Caspi et al. argued that crime proneness is correlated to multiple psychological components, particularly negative emotionality, such as experiencing states of anger, anxiety, and irritability, and by weak or low constraint, meaning a difficulty in controlling impulses, making these individuals "quick on the draw."

Others seeking to measure personality traits associated with crime have focused on specific offender types. Caputo, Frick, and Brodsky (1999) examined juvenile sex offenders and found them to have high levels of callous and unemotional traits. In another example, Myers et al. set out to study the diagnostic, behavioral, and offense factors in juvenile homicide and to identify profile characteristics of homicidal juveniles. They found:

> The juvenile murderer is typically a disruptive behavior-disordered youth with family and school problems who has been raised in a violent environment and abused by one or more caretakers. He has prior evidence of difficulty controlling aggressive urges toward others and has been arrested for earlier offense[s]. . . . In spite of diagnosable psychiatric disorders in 96% of these youths, only a few (14%) had ever received any mental health care. . . . The high frequency of neuropsychiatric vulnerabilities in this sample, primarily a history of psychotic symptoms (71%) and serious past head trauma, is not an unusual finding in juvenile murderers. Such vulnerabilities are postulated to be contributory factors in the etiology of violence. (1995, 1487)

Sutherland and Shepherd (2002) examined 13,650 English youth and found that lack of self-control and low self-esteem predict violence. In an even more comprehensive study, Miller and Lynam (2001) conducted a meta-analysis of personality traits and antisocial behavior. They found strong empirical support and were able to distinguish personality traits of antisocial individuals (hostile, self-centered, spiteful, jealous, and indifferent). They also provided a comprehensive description of various personality theories and relationships to crime. Given that such traits can be found in child and adolescent murderers, the critical question becomes, What is the causal relation of these traits to the crime, and what are the policy implications of these types of causal analysis? If we are born with certain traits, they are based on generation-to-generation transmission. This process may go back millions of years and involves evolution.

The Limitations and Policy Implications
of Trait-Based Psychology

A major limitation of trait-based personality theories is that, like psychoanalytical approaches, they are tautological (relying on circular reasoning). By definition, law-breakers have defective personalities, and this is used to classify them: Stealing may be taken as an indicator of impulsiveness and impulsiveness given as the reason for stealing. Similarly, committing offenses against others is seen as evidence of a lack of empathy, yet lack of empathy is seen as a trait to explain offending. Thus, a recurrent criticism of trait-based theories is that they represent correlational rather than causal connections. In other words, do the traits develop in advance of criminal behavior or as a result of it or its implications? Moreover, Akers has noted, "The concept of the psychopathic personality, for instance, is so broad that it could apply to virtually anyone who violates the law" (1994, 87).

In addition to these theoretical and methodological flaws, results of research into the effects of personality traits have been mixed. One of the first comprehensive reviews reported that most previous studies did not find significant differences between delinquents and nondelinquents (Schuessler and Cressey 1950). A review of the more sophisticated studies did find significant differences, however (Waldo and Dinitz 1967). The empirical research on Eysenck's theory provides a good illustration. Studies report that there is little relationship between crime and the major dimension of extroversion, although some support was found for the dimensions of psychoticism and neuroticism (Cochrane 1974; P. Burgess 1972; Passingham 1972; Feldman 1977). But Eysenck's theory is empirically and methodologically so flawed as to be discounted even by some sympathetic psychologists (Bartol 1999).

TABLE 5.4 Antisocial Personality Disorder

Repeated failure to conform to laws and social norms

Repeated deceitfulness and lying, for personal reward

Impulsivity or failure to plan ahead

Irritability and aggressiveness

Reckless disregard for own or others' safety

Consistent irresponsibility

Lack of remorse for suffering of others

SOURCE: Derived from American Psychiatric Association 1994.

The implication of trait-based personality theory for policy is that if traits exist, then they may be measured and used to predict and prevent future delinquency and crime. Thus, if traits can be identified in potential offenders at an early age, treatment should begin then, even before antisocial behavior has emerged. The traits may be counteracted through various therapeutic programs designed to compensate for them. Eysenck sees psychiatry as a practical intervention aimed at the "elimination of antisocial conduct" ([1964] 1977, 213). Similarly, one of the objectives of Myers et al.'s study (1995) was to identify profiles fitting juveniles who may be homicidal that might help to identify other juveniles who also murder. There are obviously serious moral questions about screening children for personality traits, defining them as "at risk," and giving them "preventive" treatment.

Overall, the trait-based approach is limited by its narrow focus, which excludes cognitive and social learning factors. Both cognitive and social learning theory grew out of disenchantment with the limits of behaviorism.

Behavioral, Situational, and Social Learning and Modeling Theories

Early learning theories assumed a passive model of individuals whose past experiences and associations led to their present actions. These theories evolved to a more active view of humans as making various judgments about current actions based on their interpretations of past and present experiences.

Behavioral Learning Theory

The passive behavioral version of learning theory, rooted in the work of Pavlov and Skinner, saw crime as the outcome of learning that under certain circumstances, certain behavior will be rewarded. Pavlov ([1906] 1967) discovered what has become known as classical conditioning. He argued that stimuli would consistently produce a given effect. In his classic example, a dog will always salivate when presented with meat. This is a passive learning approach, since the person learns what to expect from the environment. Skinner (1953, 1971) developed a slightly more active version with his notion of operant conditioning. In this case, behavior is controlled through manipulation of the consequences of previous behavior. This model of learning is more active because the individual learns how to get what she or he wants from the environment rather than passively waiting for it to materialize. A central idea of operant conditioning is reinforcement, which involves strengthening a tendency to act in a certain way. Such strengthening can be in the form of positive reinforcement, whereby past crimes are rewarded. An example would be a corporation that wins competitive bids by consistently undercutting the competition's costs through the manufacture of defective products. Negative reinforcement occurs where an unpleasant experience is avoided by committing crime (e.g., taking illegal drugs to avoid painful low self-esteem). A manufacturer's violation of health and safety laws would be an example of negative reinforcement if such action reduced productivity. It is important to note that in spite of popular misunderstanding, punishment itself is not negative reinforcement, because it is designed to weaken rather than strengthen a tendency to do something. But taking action to avoid anticipated punishment reflects the consequences of negative reinforcement.

Social Learning and Modeling Theory

A yet more complex and active approach called social learning theory gets close to the active learning of cognitive theory (see later discussion). Originating in the work of Gabriel Tarde (1843–1904) on imitation and developed by Albert Bandura (1969, 1973, 1977; Bandura and Walters 1963), social learning is initially based not on reward and punishment but on the idea that individuals are complex beings who do not simply respond mechanically but observe and analyze situations before they decide to act. Part of the learning process involves role modeling based on identification with others, either real or represented, such as persons or images portrayed in the media, on television, in the movies, or in video games. In social learning, we watch others and decide which patterns of behavior to imitate. These may be real-life heroes, celebrities, such as recording artist Marilyn Manson, or fictional or even cartoon characters such as Beavis and Butthead, or the children of the television series *South Park*. No specific reinforcement is necessary for this modeling to occur. However, Bandura says that once modeled, such patterned responses may be triggered by events or adverse situations in a person's life. Once acquired, however, the prospect or practice of the learned behavior may be goal directed toward a rewarding outcome, which then may become reinforced by its outcome if this is met by the desired result. The enactment of learned patterns thus can become self-rewarding, and thereby reinforced.

A particularly good example of role modeling from video games is seen in the arguments of former military officer Dave Grossman, who has coined the term *killology* for his Web site (http://www.killology.com/) and is explored in his book, *Stop Teaching Our Kids to Kill: A Call to Action Against TV, Movie, and Video Game Violence* (Grossman and DeGaetano 1999). Grossman argues that video games incorporate the very same elements that the military uses to train soldiers to kill the enemy, and provide the rationalizations and practice mechanisms to train teenagers to engage in school and other violence:

> In the military, you are immediately confronted with a role model: your drill sergeant. He personifies violence and aggression. Along with military heroes, these violent role models have always been used to influence young, impressionable minds. . . . Today the media are providing our children with role models. We get copycat, cluster murders that work their way across America like a virus spread by the six o'clock news. No matter what someone has done, if you put his picture on TV, you have made him a

celebrity, and someone, somewhere, will emulate him. . . . When the images of the young killers are broadcast on television, they become role models. The average pre-schooler in America watches 27 hours of television a week. The average child gets more one-on-one communication from TV than from all her parents and teachers combined. The ultimate achievement for our children is to get their picture on TV. (Grossman 1998, http://www.killology.com/art_trained_video.htm)

In short, social learning theory says that the observation and experience of poor role models produce imitation and instigation of socially undesirable behaviors. In this way, violent behaviors can be seen as acceptable behavioral options, as in the case of spousal abuse modeled on the way the abuser's parents interacted when dealing with conflict. Several criminologists have incorporated these different versions of learning into their theories, most notably Ronald L. Akers ([1977] 1985, 1998), and we shall examine these more fully in the next chapter, on learning criminal behavior.

Limitations and Policy Implications of Learning Theory

There are several limitations to learning theory, central to which is why only some of those exposed to negative learning patterns, role models, and reinforcement actually adopt them, whereas most know the difference between fiction and reality. Clearly, some people are more open to influence than others. As the more sophisticated of these arguments suggest, most people are endowed with, or also learn, "protective factors," such as believing in other values that serve as intervening variables limiting the enactment of the negative patterns. Social learning theory is also unable to easily explain gender, age, or racial differences in behavior, unless it incorporates a notion of identification with specific role models having significant meaning to the social learner. However, as soon as this is conceded, the theory moves beyond simple model-ing into cognitive theory, which we discuss below.

The policy implication of behavioral and learning models is to reward conven-tional and positive behavior. Ellis and Walsh observe: "Social learning theory is im-pressive in terms of the number of treatment programs it has helped to inspire. The most unique feature of [these] programs . . . is a heavy emphasis on rewarding pro-social ("good") behavior rather than trying to punish antisocial behavior" (2000, 346). As a result, in the Skinnerian behavioral approaches, the role of discipline in home and school is important, particularly focusing on the practices of parents and teachers. Thus, the social learning version of the theory involves varieties of resocial-ization, individual and family counseling, development of new behavioral options, and the provision of new "proper" role models (Patterson 1997).

In summary, the policy of many of these learning approaches argues for strength-ening the family to encourage children to make noncrime choices, teaching appro-priate parental socialization of children into responsible moral behavior, and teaching children right from wrong, which are all part of positive reinforcement. For its part in policy, social learning and behavioral modeling theory also implies a heavy monitoring of media, and developing societal mechanisms to control and filter the kind of television children watch, and for restricting the kind of video games that they are allowed to play. The cognitive learning perspective, which we turn to next, is less mechanistic than simple learning theory and goes beyond the modeling patterns of social learning theory to consider how social learning is a creative activity.

Cognitive Theories

Founded on the ideas of Wilhelm Wundt (1832–1920), William James (1842–1910), and Swiss child psychologist Jean Piaget (1896–1980), cognitive psychology captures the idea that human reasoning processes and meaning construction about the world shape the way humans act and orient them to behavior meaningful to their lives. There are several strands of cognitive theory relevant to criminology, notably those by Lawrence Kohlberg, Aaron Beck, Todd Feinberg, and Albert Bandura.

Piaget's ideas are seen in the notion of progressive moral development outlined by Lawrence Kohlberg (1969). Here cognitive theory has as its major theme how mental thought processes are used to solve problems—to interpret, evaluate, and decide on the best actions. These thought processes occur through mental pictures and conversations with ourselves. The assumption is that individuals' future orientation to action and to their environment will be affected by the knowledge they acquire and process. For Piaget ([1923] 1969, [1932] 1965, [1937] 1954), children develop the ability to use logic, to construct mental maps, and eventually to reflect on their own thought processes. He argued that this cognitive development occurs in stages, with each new stage of intellectual development emerging as a resolution to the contradictions between different and competing views of the same events.

Kohlberg (1969) applied Piaget's ideas to moral development, finding that children develop through six stages. They progress from a premoral stage, in which morality is heavily influenced by outside authority, through levels of convention in which decisions about right and wrong are based on what significant others expect, to full social awareness, combining a sense of personal ethics and human rights. Most people never make it to the last stage.

Cognitive theory emerged in criminology through several strands, notably the work of Samuel Yochelson and Stanton Samenow (1976, 1977; Samenow 1984, 2006), whose explanation of the criminal personality integrated free will, rational choice, and thinking patterns. These clinical psychologists, who had to abandon all their clinical training (Freudian and behaviorist), argued that faulty learning produces defective thinking, which results in criminal behavior choices. Yochelson and Samenow developed a theory rejecting the idea of determinism, arguing, "The essence of this approach is that criminals choose to commit crimes. Crime resides within the person and is 'caused' by the way he thinks, not by his environment. Criminals think differently from responsible people" (Samenow 1984, xiv). Criminal thinking is different from a very early age. In general, criminals think concretely rather than abstractly; are impulsive, irresponsible, and self-centered; and are motivated by anger or fear. These characteristics describe a person with a "criminal personality" who is difficult to change or rehabilitate. These underlying psychological emotions lead the criminal to view him- or herself as being worthless and to feel that others may come to see him or her the same way and that the condition is permanent. Criminals thus commit crimes to avoid reaching this state and to avoid having their worthlessness exposed. The fear that it might be exposed produces intense anger and hatred toward certain groups, who may be violently attacked for not recognizing the individual's inflated sense of superiority or for injuring his or her sense of pride.

A second line of cognitive theory applied to the criminology of violence is by Aaron Beck, who is seen as the father of modern cognitive therapy. In his book *Prisoners of Hate*, Beck links human thinking processes with emotional and behavioral expressions. Put simply, the way we think shapes our feelings and our actions. Beck argues that extreme forms of violence—from verbal abuse, domestic violence, rape, and hate crime to terrorist bombing and genocide—are exaggerations of patterns of everyday thought. These dysfunctional patterns of thinking Beck calls "hostile framing." They are the fundamental ways in which humans both see themselves as morally right and classify others with whom they are frustrated and in conflict, as "less than us," as "dangerous, malicious and evil" (1999, 8). Once negatively framed, the other's past and present words and actions are seen as challenging, hurtful, and demeaning and produce anger and hostility as we perceive ourselves the victim of the other's attack. We deal with these problems by further dehumanizing the other into an exaggerated caricature of his or her negative aspects, which leads to an endless cycle of disrespect, resulting in a desire for preemptive elimination of the other. Beck, like the other cognitive theorists, sees patterns of thinking developing over time and says that those of us who employ "hostile framing" are at an earlier stage of thinking that he calls "primal thinking," but that once locked into these patterns, they become a prison of reaction to the image we have constructed of the other rather than to the person: "They mistake the image for the person. . . . Their minds are encased in 'the prison of hate'" (ibid.).

A related approach that relies on cognitive analysis is found in the work of S. Giora Shoham (1979) and Jack Katz (1988). These authors are concerned with understanding how individuals strive to make a meaningful world when confronted with strong feelings of fear, anxiety, and alienation. Unlike Beck, who sees primal thinking as one stage in a sequence, Shoham sees it as emanating from a specific event: birth, which is seen as a cosmic disaster leading to ego formation and ego identity. Deviance is an attempt to deal with the trauma of birth separation through the negation of ego identity. Katz, in particular, was concerned with identifying how offenders make their world meaningful in ways that provide the moral and sensational attractions leading to crime. But both authors recognized that these approaches lack empirical verification and point only to vague policy objectives such as participatory democracy (Shoham and Seis 1993; Faust 1995, 56).

In yet another interesting and fruitful endeavor, De Coster and Heimer (2001) have integrated symbolic interactionism (discussed later) and psychology. They show that depression and law violation are not only related but also the interactive product of social-structural-psychological mechanisms (e.g., stressful events, family relationships, reflected appraisals). At this point, it is questionable whether these various cognitive "psychologies" are not just as arguably social constructionist sociologies.

In the previous chapter we showed that most serious biosocial theorists consider biological organisms to be in an interactive relationship with their environment. In this chapter we have increasingly seen how psychologists have moved from a trait-based to a learning, and ultimately a cognitive-environmental, view of the mind. A recent development in psychology that could have important implications for the psychological study of crime attempts to explain the interrelationship of brain-mind-environment. In his book *Altered Egos: How the Brain Creates the Self*, neurologist and psychiatrist Todd Feinberg shows that the physical workings of the brain's various and separate biological functions can produce a synthesis or unified self that produces meaning, purpose, and a sense of being from the world around it. He argues that the self and mind emerge from the many parts of the material (physical) brain. He says that the "self can be understood as a nested hierarchy of meaning and purpose," where the levels of self, and the many parts of the brain that contribute to the self, "are nested within all the other levels of the hierarchy" (2001, 138, 149). The implications of this approach are to recognize the irreducibility of mind to biology or to see the functions of the brain as disconnected from the mind.

We mentioned earlier Albert Bandura's contribution to social learning theory, but he has also developed a social cognitive theory and applied it to understand the processes involved in controlling antisocial, or "transgressive," behavior. Bandura criticizes those approaches that present a passive model of humans as products of their environments or as inheriting certain traits. In contrast, he presents an "agentic" view in which people play an active role in producing their environments and shaping their life course. He says, "The capacity to exercise some measure of control over one's thought processes, motivation, affect, and action operates through mechanisms of personal agency" (Bandura et al. 2001, 125). A core concept in Bandura's theory is "self-efficacy," also called "personal efficacy" (1999, 2001). Self-efficacy is the belief in one's ability to achieve goals that one has set for oneself: "The core belief that one has the power to influence one's own functioning and life circumstances." He argues, "A strong sense of efficacy oriented toward positive self-development can affect transgressive behavior. It does so, in large part, by promoting prosocialness, curtailing the propensity to disengage moral self-sanctions from socially alienating and harmful conduct, and countering ruminative and vengeful affectivity" (Bandura et al. 2001, 125). (We will have more to say about Bandura's ideas concerning the propensity to disengage moral self-sanctions, a process that has parallels with neutralizing moral norms, in a later chapter.) A good illustration of Bandura's social cognitive theory is his application of it to explain substance abuse. He argues that recovery from addictions is a process through which people increasingly act in ways that build their self-efficacy, and those with the greatest self-efficacy are those most likely to succeed in recovery.

Limitations and Policy
Implications of Cognitive Theory

Cognitive theory in criminology has received some empirical support, but also has some inherent weaknesses. Some psychologists have developed instruments to measure the different "thinking styles" thought to be associated with serious criminal activity (e.g., Psychological Inventory of Criminal Thinking Styles; see Walters 1995). Others, such as Catherine Blatier (2000), have examined the locus of control, stability, self-esteem, and controllability in a study of convicted offenders. Blatier found support for cognitive theory. Not surprisingly, the longer one is incarcerated, the lower one's self-esteem and the more powerless one feels. This has policy implications, since a higher self-esteem is related to a lower rate of recidivism. Similarly, a study by Henning and Frueh (1996) found that treatment intervention involving a "cognitive self-change program" designed to correct "criminogenic thinking errors" among incarcerated offenders supported the value of such therapeutic intervention.

However, as with several of the psychological theories we have examined so far, cognitive theorists, such as Yochelson and Samenow, do not explain why some offenders think criminally and others do not. They also used no control groups in their evaluation and provided little evidence of systematically gathered data. Perhaps most important, they overgeneralized from a highly selected group of problem-suffering clients or hospitalized hard-core adult criminals and serious juvenile offenders to the general population of offenders (Vold [1958] 1979, 155).

At a broader level, cognitive theory has been criticized for ignoring psychobiological explanations, disregarding the effects of emotions, and the same circular reasoning that was seen as a defect in trait-based theory: "It seems that behaviors are taken to indicate cognitive processes, and that in turn, the cognitive processes are given as explanations for the behaviors" (Faust 1995, 54).

Consistent with their assumptions about "stinking thinking" leading to crime, cognitive-oriented theorists' policies for crime control involve the identification and elimination of dysfunctional thought processes or reasoning ability. For example, Yochelson and Samenow's interventions (1977) were designed to identify and destroy current destructive criminal patterns of decision making by confronting offenders directly and by creating new thought processes. Yochelson and Samenow believed that criminals can be confronted with their behavior as victimizers of society in an attempt to increase feelings of guilt and self-disgust that eventually deter their criminal thinking. But these theorists also claimed to teach the suppression of criminal thoughts and substitution of noncriminal ones. Thus, Samenow argued, "We are as we think. It is impossible to help a person give up crime and live responsibly without helping him to change what is most basic—his thinking" (1984, 257). For these theorists, "The criminal must learn to identify and then abandon thinking patterns that have guided his behavior for years. He must be taught new thinking patterns that are self-evident and automatic for responsible people but are totally foreign to him" (ibid., 6–7). To do this, Yochelson and Samenow got criminals to write down their day-to-day thinking and report it to a group. Then the therapists would point out the errors in this thinking and suggest how to correct it. They claimed that eventually those treated developed new patterns of thought and behavior and discovered the rewards of behaving responsibly, without deception or intimidation. Cognitive behavioral therapy has become widely used in correctional institutions.

Similarly, Beck's cognitive therapy concentrates on correcting biased thinking patterns in order to "reframe their negative images" (1999, 8). Unfortunately, Beck also celebrates the work of those, such as Dodge (1993), who screen kindergarten children in high-poverty areas for aggressive behavior and subject them to social and cognitive skill training from first through tenth grade. Clearly, there are serious moral questions about preventative intervention, some of which we looked at in the last chapter.

In the next section we look at how far psychologists have come to embrace a broader social perspective, by considering those who focus on the environment as a significant factor in shaping the mind.

Ecological Psychology

Ecological psychology is the study of how environmental factors, such as unemployment and social settings, prevail on a person's mind to affect behavior. Ecological psychology developed as a reaction against the narrow clinical approach to treatment and disenchantment with psychotherapy, and it is considerably more eclectic in its assumptions. Ecological psychologists argue that psychotherapy has not demonstrated its effectiveness. Traditional psychology is accused of using a medical model with "a passive help giver who waits for the client to define his or her own need and then to request help" (Levine and Perkins 1987, 36).

The focus of community psychology is not to find out what is wrong with the individual. Rather, the emphasis is on looking at what is right with the person and his or her fit with the culture and environment (Rappaport 1977). Thus, this approach is much more encompassing than traditional psychological clinical approaches. Several factors that reflect the changing social context led to the development and growth of the perspective.

The social context of the mid-1960s was one of turbulence and change. First, the Kennedy-Johnson War on Poverty stimulated attention to many related social problems, such as crime, unemployment, poor education, mental retardation, and welfare inequities. Community psychology was one way of welding these problems into one cohesive mass. Second, with the large deinstitutionalization of mental health patients in the 1960s, it was recognized that new service-delivery models were needed. This recognition was spurred on in part by the efforts of then-president Kennedy (who had a mentally challenged sister). Furthermore, the recognition of the inability of the mental health community to keep pace with the demands society places on it called for a greater emphasis on prevention. Finally, empirical research documented that emotional problems are much more severe in areas (communities) of social disorganization (Levine and Perkins 1987). As a result, in 1961 President John F. Kennedy's Joint Commission on Mental Health suggested the following:

(1) There should be a broader definition of who could deliver mental health services, (2) early intervention was critical, and (3) intervention should occur in the community. Ecological psychology is called community psychology because it actively seeks out those who require help in their own environment or community.

According to Levine and Perkins, the people and settings within a community are interdependent (ibid., 95). First, change occurs in a whole social system, not just in an individual, and thus a variety of different problem definitions and solutions are possible in any situation. Second, community systems involve resource exchanges among persons and settings involving commodities such as time, money, and political power. Third, the behavior that we observe in a particular individual always reflects a continuous process of adaptation between that individual and his or her level of competence and the environment, with the nature and range of competence it supports. Adaptation can thus proceed by changing the environment as well as the person. Finally, change occurs naturally in a community, as well as by intentional design, and change represents an opportunity to redefine and reallocate resources in ways that facilitate adaptation by all populations in the community.

In a recent contribution to criminology that integrates learning theory and community and environmental psychology, Julie Horney criticizes criminology for not recognizing the diversity of psychological perspectives. She focuses on learning theory and states that psychological perspectives are often reduced to trait theory, with some people seen as possessing "a set of global traits that predispose behavior" (2006, 4–5). Instead, her approach "emphasizes the situational specificity of behavior"— that is, situations such as the separate spheres of work, home, school, bar, and the street (ibid., 2)—that provides a way of analyzing the disposition to offend that is manifest when opportunities arise. Thus, crime is understood through "particular patterns of behavior-situation contingencies" (ibid., 4–5). She argues that although behavioral learning is a valuable component of understanding crime, the context of "learning" is also important. Horney argues that organisms must be understood not just as learning new behaviors but also as maintaining certain behaviors over the long term. Horney's work challenges simplistic understandings of the "criminal mind" (ibid., 6), focusing instead on the specificity of and the environmental consistencies evident in individual lives. Consistent with the community and environmental view, Horney's approach "leads psychological criminology to a greater appreciation of longitudinal and life-course understandings of criminal behavior that interweave with social and environmental contexts" (Henry and Lukas 2009).

Evolutionary Psychology

A growing area of psychological inquiry involves evolutionary psychology (EP) (Thornhill and Palmer 2000; Barkow, Cosmides, and Tooby 1992). This version of psychology stresses that behavior is either directly or indirectly related to inherited mechanisms that increase survival odds while dealing with natural selection. As we saw in the previous chapter, the first to apply this idea to criminology via what they describe as r/K selection theory were the evolutionary biosocial criminologists Lee Ellis (1987; Ellis and Walsh 2000) and William Rushton (1990, 1995). Others have since applied the concept to violence and have emphasized the interactive aspects of development over the long term of human evolution (Bloom and Dess 2003). Evolutionary psychologists strongly dispute the idea that the mind is a general learning and problem-solving apparatus. Instead, the mind or brain is the result of millions of years of evolutionary processes meeting environmental challenges, which led to "specific cognitive functions to meet those challenges through the process of natural selection and sexual selection" (Ellis and Walsh 2000, 147). Our brain is composed of specific "modules" or areas that are geared to solving different adaptive problems. The "Genetic Evolutionary Psychology Perspective" proposes four ways or routes whereby behavior is maintained or changes over time: (1) biology, meaning that "one's genetic makeup, as expressed through various physical structures, systems, and processes, has an impact that varies depending on the behavior and the other three routes"; (2) psychology, "the ever-changing conscious, preconscious, unconscious and nonconscious mental activity of thought, emotion, and motivation"; (3) culture, which "denotes the sum total of ways of living developed by people through time and the social transmission of these ways within and across generations"; and (4) environment, which can limit or facilitate the other three as well as be affected by them (Bloom 2003, 10–11). What it does not propose is that social behavior is genetically determined, that behavior is resistant to change, that all behavior is the best possible for human functioning at any point in time, that "people are motivated to spread their genes far and wide." These myths have contributed to misunderstanding the value of the theory for public policy, particularly that dealing with violence (ibid., 12).

Some of the problems that evolutionary psychology has faced can be illustrated by looking at Thornhill and Palmer's argument (2000, also argued by Ellis, in his book *Theories of Rape* [1989]) that rape is best understood in the context of mate selection and adaptive processes:

> Males and females faced quite different sexual-selection problems in the Pleistocene period. More specifically, for females selecting a mate was a major decision as they typically invested long periods of time in the upbringing of their young. Therefore, selecting a male who was likely to invest his resources in her children was critical to ensuring their survival. Women evolved to choose their mates extremely carefully and placed a premium on traits such as reliability, kindness, and high status (i.e., access to more resources). Because males were typically more eager to have sex than females, it was possible to choose from a range of possible mates. However for males, sex was a low-investment activity; all they had to contribute was a small deposit of sperm and a few minutes of their time. In addition, finding a mate was an intensely competitive process with high quality males likely to dominate the sexual arena and secure exclusive sexual access to females. Therefore, males with the highest status and most resources were more likely to obtain sexual access to females, thereby increasing the

chances that their genes would be passed on and their offspring survive. (Ward and Siegert 2002, 151)

Other males were left to forcibly take their mates in order to pass on their genes. Having sex with as many women as possible further increased the male's chances of reproductive success (see also Ellis's "cheater theory" of crime in the previous chapter). The acquisition of multiple partners for males was also due to the fact that women conceive internally and males could never be certain of their paternity. Under the EP paradigm, people are just another form of animal. This perspective has understandably been criticized (Ward and Siegert 2002) and is especially challenging to the feminist perspective (discussed later).

Limitations and Policy Implications of Ecological and Evolutionary Psychology

Ecological psychology has been faulted for "lack of a well-articulated, widely shared conceptual model or set of theoretical principles" (Levine and Perkins 1987, 63). It has also been criticized for being more sociological than psychological. But as with the other theories we have examined, this has not stopped the formulation of policy.

Ecological psychology advocates a policy of manipulating environmental factors, specifically by making resources available. According to Levine and Perkins, "In the ecological perspective, human behavior is viewed in terms of the person's adaptation to resources and circumstances. From this perspective, one may correct unsuccessful adaptations by altering the availability of resources. Thus new services may be created, or existing strengths in social networks may be discovered and conditions created to enhance the use of such resources" (ibid., 5). Community psychology also recognizes that "before any individual appears his society has had a specific social life organized and systematized, and the existence of this life will exercise a tyrannical compulsion on him" (Saranson 1981, 832). Although the individual may need specialized attention, the preventive objective is to reduce the incidence of individuals requiring such attention. Ecological psychologists are thus concerned with neighborhood-level preventive interventions. Providing material, educational, and psychological resources to help people fit in diverse or different societies is the objective.

One strategy is community policing. Using an approach based on ecological psychology, the basic components of any theory must be identified, operationalized, and tested using psychometric procedures. For example, among the stated objectives of community policing are to reduce fear of crime and increase community cohesion, in part through decreasing physical and social disorder. Thus, scales, or instruments, were developed to measure cohesion, disorder, and fear of crime (Lanier and Davidson 1995). The next step would be to implement community policing and evaluate the impact using psychometric measures. The lack of resources is a major problem with this approach, however. It is difficult to make resources available to those in need when the political climate does not support such efforts.

Evolutionary psychology has been criticized on a number of grounds (Ward and Siegert 2002). First, it does not consider other competing theories. The thesis of how the brain is organized has also not been proven or is incomplete (Gilbert 1998). Further research on rapists shows that they view women differently than nonrapists—a learned behavior (Ward, Keenan, and Hudson 2000). Ward and Siegert (2002) also question whether the rapist during the Pleistocene era would have been harmed or killed by the females' relatives. Empirical research shows that many rapists have difficulty with erections and fail to ejaculate—further damaging the EP argument. Finally, humans can modify their behavior and learn from their mistakes. It is unclear what policies would fit with EP. The obvious one suggests that if men were castrated, the crime rate would be cut by 90 percent! Presumably, equal access and opportunities would, over millions of years of evolutionary process, lead to the diminishing need for rapists to rape.

Summary and Conclusion

The psychological perspective has added a rich and important dimension to criminological theory. In spite of mixed empirical support, it has raised serious questions with both the mechanical determinism of biological theories and the open vistas of individual freedom claimed in classical models. It has sensitized criminology to the importance of individual development, unconscious processes, and the consolidation of behavioral characteristics during childhood development. Most important, it has explored the way the human mind engages its environment toward self-preservation or destruction. Differences between the various psychological approaches have also enriched our understanding of how the environment may be translated into both constructive and destructive behavior. Ultimately, psychological criminology has provided a window to our mind and an opening to individualized treatment. Its attention to therapy has fostered understanding of the nature of our actions and the consequences of past relationships on future behavior, and how we may intervene at the individual level to make a difference to our relational world.

As the world has changed, one may ask, "How has psychology impacted the world? In this new era, do people learn in the same ways or interact in the same manner? How has globalization impacted the field? Has psychology itself evolved to meet the changing world?" Clearly, the answer is that things have changed and continue to change, both in the discipline of psychology and in the broader world. Look around you in class—how many laptops do you see? How many professors rely on PowerPoint or distance learning? When was the last time you took pen and paper and wrote a letter? When was the last time you sent a text message? Do your grandparents know what "IM" is? Do your parents? As technology has evolved, our means of learning have also changed. When you conduct a literature review for a class project, do you still go to the library or do you rely only on Google? Psychology provides insight into how these changes, and many others, impact us and affect how we learn, interact, and ultimately make sense of our environment and the changing world we live in.

Summary Chart:
Psychological Theories of Crime

Basic Idea: People have personalities formed through parental socialization. Some are inadequately socialized or are traumatized during development and form crime-prone personalities or behavioral tendencies or criminal-thinking patterns.

Human Nature: Humans are seen as biological entities but with personalities that are shaped by childhood developmental experiences in the family. Humans therefore are malleable. Their behavior reflects a combination of biological attributes and early socialization experiences that are mediated through cognitive processes of the "mind." Psychoanalytical theory believes the key to the mind is its unconscious process. Behaviorists believe human minds are a blank slate. Trait-based approaches fall somewhere between the two, seeing adult personality formation emerging from socialization with distinct traits. Social learning and cognitive theories assume perception, self-identity, and rational decision making. Existential and phenomenological approaches assume the importance of socially constructed meanings, emotions, and feelings absent in the behavioral learning models. Finally, ecological psychology is concerned with identifying the fit between individuals and their environment, seeing how the latter can shape an individual's mind. This has parallels to evolutionary psychology where adaptations occur with changing social mores and practices, but evolutionary psychology sees humans as more genetically determined.

Society and the Social Order: Generally seen as a consensus, with the exception of social learning theory, which sees conflicting social norms. Law is seen as the rules designed to protect the ongoing development of society. Crime is one form of abnormal behavior manifested by those with personality problems or defective personalities. Psychologists prefer the nonlegal definition of crime as aggressive or antisocial behavior, reflecting norm violation rather than law violation. Criminals, especially in trait theory, differ from noncriminals. Criminals in cognitive theory are those who have learned incorrect ways to think or behave in society.

Causal Logic: Most attribute cause to defective socialization by primary groups, principally the family, although some recognize modeling on significant others or even images of significant groups or role models. Specific causes vary depending on the variety of psychological theory: (1) Psychoanalytic theory argues that offensive behavior or antisocial behavior is the outcome of early childhood frustrations. Primitive drives of the id combine with weak ego and superego development because of (a) failed parental socialization, (b) unconscious guilt, (c) oedipal conflict, and (d) aggression. The result is frustration, and an unconscious search for compensatory gratifications leads to aggression and delinquency. Weak superego and riotous id cause breach of social controls; overdeveloped superego or damaged ego can also cause crime. (2) Trait-based personality theory believes the development of a criminal or psychotic personality is sometimes a result of extroversion or low IQ, affecting ability to learn rules, perceive punishment, or experience pain, as in biological theory. (3) Behavioral learning theory sees crime as the outcome of learning that under certain circumstances will be rewarded. A key concept is operant conditioning, whereby behavior is controlled through manipulation of the consequences of previous behavior. A central idea is reinforcement, which can be positive, in cases where past crimes are rewarded for their commission, or negative, where punishment or other consequences are avoided by committing the offense. (4) Social learning theory says observation and experience of poor role models produce self-reinforcement of observed deviant behavior, leading to imitation and instigation of the same. Violent behaviors are seen as acceptable behavioral options, and the imitation of others' criminal behavior is experienced as rewarding. (5) Cognitive interpretive processes explain why criminals and noncriminals behave differently, even when they have similar backgrounds. Applied to crime, the theory argues that faulty learning produces defective thinking, which produces criminal behavior. Existential and phenomenological variants of the theory focus on individual construction of meaning that triggers criminal activity. (6) Ecological or community-based psychology looks at the fit between individuals and the environment and attempts to manipulate the environment to prevent offending. (7) Evolutionary psychology argues that people evolve, just like other animals, based on the changing environment.

Criminal Justice Policy: Depends on version, but most involve some prediction and prevention and some kind of therapeutic intervention, assisted by drugs to correct and control traits.

Criminal Justice Practice: Psychoanalytic theory involves evaluation and treatment to help offenders uncover the childhood root causes, bring these to consciousness, and train to effectively control or correct problems of parental or "maternal" deprivation. Behavioral models require rewarding conventional behavior and not rewarding deviant behavior; the role of discipline in the home and school is important. Social learning theory involves varieties of resocialization, individual and family counseling, development of new behavioral options, and provision of new "proper" models. Cognitive theory involves learning new ways to think and replacing destructive thought processes with constructive ones. The environmental approach involves manipulation of community resources to prevent problems from arising at the outset. The various intervention techniques are largely focused at the individual level of treatment and include psychoanalysis, group therapy, counseling, family therapy, drug treatment, and environmental manipulation.

Evaluation: Psychoanalytical theory is criticized for being male oriented and seeing females as inherently abnormal. The theory is difficult to test, and ideas about "basic instincts" and "unconscious forces" cannot be verified or falsified. Trait theory provides an alternative to Freud and behaviorism; it promotes empirical research to find personality traits but ignores situational structuring of traits and so is too narrow.

Both theories have problems of circular reasoning. Behavioral approaches oversimplify the learning process by excluding cognitive processes such as interpretation, memory, and perception. Behaviorism based on stimulus-response is too mechanical. Cognitive theory also suffers from circular reasoning: Behavior is taken to indicate cognitive processes, and the processes are taken as explanations for the behavior. Phenomenological approaches lack scientific verification and policy implications. Environmental psychology does not deal with the wider political structures that shape the environment. Overall, psychological perspectives tend to do better at explaining sexual and violent crimes. But the approach has important implications for the way we discipline children and the public consumption of media messages, as in sex and violence on TV. This approach fails to explain individual differences in response to learning and provides only weak causal connections between factors.

Notes

1. There are four legal bases for the insanity defense. The M'Naghten Rule (established in 1843) requires that it be proved that the accused either did not know the illegal act was wrong or did not know its nature because of defective reasoning resulting from disease of the mind. The Durham Rule (established in 1871) is broader in that it allows an accused to escape criminal responsibility if the illegal act was the product of mental disease or defect, a definition that permits greater input by psychiatric expert witnesses. The Irresistible Impulse Test requires evidence to prove that the defendant could not control his or her behavior because of mental illness. Finally, the Substantial Incapacity Test says a person is not criminally responsible if at the time of the illegal act a mental disease or defect resulted in a lack of substantial capacity to appreciate the wrongfulness of the conduct or to conform to the law. Several states have established a compromise guilty but insane plea in which the person is first sent to a secure hospital or psychiatric center for treatment and when cured completes the remainder of the sentence in prison.

6

Learning Criminal Behavior
Social Process Theories

What we call human nature in actuality is human habit.
—Jewel [Kilcher], *Pieces of You* (1994)

Military and vampire cultures appear to be at opposite ends of the moral and behavioral spectrum. The military represents discipline, uniformity, respect for authority, high ethical standards, hierarchical status, and the promotion and protection of American values. Goth and vampire (or "vampyre") cults represent anarchy, individualism, disregard for authority, and little in the way of ethics; they challenge the most deeply held religious and social values. They both, however, share some similarities that can socialize their members into ways of thinking that can result in crime. Consider first the case of William Calley, then the case of Charity Keesee, and finally the case of Bernard Madoff.

On March 16, 1968, in Vietnam, as many as five hundred men, women, and children were killed by U.S. Army platoons in what was to become known as the My Lai massacre. A squad sergeant from one of the platoons testified, "We complied with the orders, sir" (Calley 1974, 342). Lt. William Calley, who gave the order for his squad to "get rid of 'em," reasoned: "Well everything is to be killed. . . . I figured 'They're already wounded, I might as well go and kill them. This is our mission'" (ibid., 347, 342). Dead Vietnamese were part of a GI's "body count." As Calley explained, these people were not seen as human beings: "We weren't in My Lai to kill human beings really. We were there to kill ideology that is carried by—I don't know. Pawns. Blobs. Pieces of flesh, and I wasn't in My Lai to destroy intelligent men. I was there to destroy an intangible idea. To destroy communism" (ibid., 343). Calley did not learn this on the street in a criminal gang but in U.S. schools, brought up as a "run of the mill average guy." As he explained:

I went to school in the 1950s remember, and it was drilled into us from grammar school on, "Ain't is bad, aren't is good, communism's bad, democracy's good. One and one's two," etcetera: until we were at Edison High, we just didn't think about it. The people in Washington are smarter than me. If intelligent people told me, "Communism's bad. It's going to engulf us. To take us in," I believed them. I had to. Personally, I didn't kill any Vietnamese that day: I mean personally. I represented the United States of America. My country. (ibid., 342–344)

Prior to her incarceration, Charity Lynn Keesee, at fifteen years of age, gained notoriety by belonging to a vampire cult that resulted in the notorious "Vampire Clan Killings," which have been the topic of several books, movies, and television documentaries. Although not typically resulting in violence and death, more than 4,000 are estimated to practice this black art. Unlike most, Charity's cult committed one of the most publicized crimes of the twentieth century. The leader of her cult, her boyfriend, Roderick (Rod) Ferrell, sixteen, and Scott Anderson, seventeen, broke into the home of cult member Heather Wendorf, fifteen, and beat her parents to death using a crowbar. Cigarette burns in the shape of a "V" were found on the victims. Charity, Heather, and Dana Cooper, nineteen, were across town visiting with friends during the attack. After the brutal satanic murder Ferrell and Anderson stole the family SUV and picked up the girls. After successfully eluding the police for days, Charity phoned her mother from a hotel in Louisiana. According to Charity, she had her mother notify the authorities as to their whereabouts (personal correspondence, November 2002). Others dispute this claim, stating that she was simply tying to get money. In either case, this phone call resulted in the arrest of the group in Baton Rouge. On June 15, 1996, Charity Lynn Keesee was convicted of being an accessory to first-degree murder and sentenced to fifteen years in Florida correctional institutions. After meeting with her numerous times my (Lanier's) impression was that she was still in many ways a lost sixteen-year-old. She was shy, sweet, and very open about her life and activities. She was very willing to please, anxious to improve her life, and looking forward to an education. There was also an undercurrent of strength, anger, and defiance. Though not criminal, Charity seeks refuge through self-mutilation. Her recollections of her problems go back to 1995 as the culmination of a traumatic upbringing.

In May 1995 Charity Keesee was fifteen years old and a runaway from rural Kentucky. She weighed ninety-five pounds and was pregnant. She was a lonely, shy girl, intelligent but rebellious. She was also a member of a group of kids who belonged to a vampire cult. Charity, in her own words, describes her entry into and life in the world of "darkness and evil":

I don't know exactly where to start in where I went wrong. I used to blame it on my parents, but now realize I can't do that. I was my own person. I was a bad girl.

My rebellionsness [*sic*] started out with my stepfather and mother. My stepfather, Harold, started sexually abusing me when I was seven years old. My mother worked the night shift at a communications company, which left me home alone with Harold from the time I got out of school until about one in the morning. The sexual abuse went on for a few months short of five years.

When I was twelve I finally told my grandparents what he was doing to me, despite Harold's threats if I ever told anyone. My mother told me I was lying, but later after Harold admitted to her what he had been doing she said I asked for it. Later that year a judge gave my mother a choice: have her child in the house with her, or have Harold. She chose Harold.

I was sent to Kentucky to live with my father. I wanted to stay with my dad because I know I'd be spoiled, but I still resented my mother because I felt like she abandoned me.

When I got to Kentucky my mind was a swirl of confusion. I trusted no one. Not even my father. All men were a threat to me. I would shrink away if my father got too close or if he even tried to hug me.

Daddy was gone a lot in those days, which left me home alone in our country house fifteen miles out of town. I didn't have many friends—by my own choice—and the ones I did have were all a few years older.

I met Rod that year. At the time he was a kindred spirit, a victim of sexual abuse himself, as well as someone with as many resentments as I had. Maybe more.

Rod wasn't always around. He would disappear sometimes for a week at a time. I was very lost and alone when he wasn't there. I was hurting inside and could find no way to stop it. Then I found a way. I would find razor blades in my dad's auto shop out back and slice my skin for hours. The physical pain and sight of blood made me forget that I was hurting inside. Dad was rarely home, so he'd never notice.

When I was thirteen Rod brought some acid, weed, and other drugs to my house. I was hooked. I discovered with acid I didn't have to think. Didn't have to feel. I was numb. Nothing mattered.

When I was fifteen, I started spending most of my time at Rod's apartment. Of course my father didn't know that, but what could he have done even if he found out? Nothing. I was out of control.

Rod and I started using heroin that year. It made him very violent. I would sit quietly, but inside the burning flames of rage were overtaking me. I was tired of life. I was tired of hurting. I found out I was pregnant in June. I told Rod, and he only said he was going to literally kill me. He didn't want a child. We had a fight and I left. I didn't see him for two weeks after that. Later that month Rod came out to my house. He was crying, saying he decided he wanted the baby, and ordered me to stop my current drug spree. He didn't stop, though.

In September, a week after my birthday, I came back to the apartment later than Rod thought I should, and wearing clothes he said were too tight—too revealing. He met me at the door at the top of the stairs and beat me, then proceeded to knock me down two flights of stairs. I lost the baby.

After that I really didn't care anymore. Life didn't mean anything. My drug habit worsened. I skipped school, and when I did go I was high. I couldn't get away from Rod either, despite that I hated him more than I'd ever hated anyone.

Right before my sixteenth birthday, Rod started talking about how he wanted us to come to Florida. We were going to pick up his friend Zoey (Heather), and the three of us would run away to New Orleans. I don't know how he intended us to survive there— all of us were under eighteen, from another state, knew no one there, and I was pregnant. Again.

I'm not going to go into the details about what happened once we got to Florida. All I will say is there was two murders, a burglary, and a week's worth of running from the cops. We did make it to New Orleans; however, we didn't stay.

That was seven years ago. I can't say I've changed completely. I still can't stand to be alone in a room with any man. Even my father. I still tend to try to cover up my inner pain with physical. However, I have figured out that if I've made it this far, there isn't anything that's going to tear me down now. (Interviewed by Mark Lanier, January 27, 2003)

Now consider the corporate "Ponzi scheme" perpetrated by Bernie L. Madoff illustrated in the box.

BOX 6.1 Global Capitalism, Corporate Culture, and Affinity Fraud
An Unequal-Opportunity Ponzi Scheme
STUART HENRY

"A Wall Street powerbroker for nearly 50 years who commanded billions of dollars in investments and built an influential firm has confessed to a fraud of historic proportions, admitting he squandered more than $50 billion and was likely doomed to prison, federal authorities say" (Associated Press 2008b).

Bernard L. Madoff, born in 1938, admitted to his employees, including his two sons, that his operations were "all just one big lie" and, "basically, a giant Ponzi scheme." On December 10, 2008, U.S. federal agents from the Securities and Exchange Commission arrested Bernie Madoff, a former chairman of the NASDAQ Stock Exchange, a member of the Yeshiva University's Board of Trustees, and founder of Bernard L. Madoff Investment Securities based in New York, for securities fraud. He was released on $10 million bail, subject to house arrest because of insufficient support for his bail. Prosecutors alleged that the seventy-year-old Madoff ran a Ponzi (or pyramid) scheme in which he hid losses on his investments and paid off some (particularly influential and early investors) from the principal that he received from newer investors. As soon as the harsh economic climate and the global economic crisis of 2008 struck, new investors dried up, and the scheme collapsed. The collapse and revelations were "triggered after investors whose fingers had been burnt by the financial crisis asked Madoff for their money back—they wanted $7 billion, but there was only $300 million in the bank. The system of sucking in new money to pay existing investors, which federal investigators allege had gone on since at least 2005, could not continue" (Quinn 2008). Initial losses to investors were estimated, by Madoff himself, at $50 billion—making it the largest individual fraud in global history.

Madoff, a father of three who immigrated to the United States from South Africa more than three decades ago for a better life, has been described as a "market maker." He created an exclusive investor group that attracted members of elite country clubs and other high-flying investors into his "invitation-only" marketing scheme. He promised (and to create trust delivered to some investors) consistently high-yield

CONTINUES

BOX 6.1 (CONTINUED)

interest earnings of 8–12 percent, regardless of the state of the economy. Madoff was able to do this because American capitalism is, or at least was, a "high-trust" investment culture. Madoff built trust among his big-name corporate clients, including Frank Lautenberg, New York Mets owner Fred Wilpon's charity (the Judy and Fred Wilpon Family Foundation), Hollywood producer Steven Spielberg, Elie Wiesel, Mort Zuckerman, and major global investors, including several European banks such as Britain's HSBC with $1 billion invested and a French bank whose funds manager, René-Thierry Magon de La Villehuchet, committed suicide shortly after it was revealed that his $1.4 billion investment with Madoff had been lost: "He locked the door of his Madison Avenue office and apparently swallowed sleeping pills and slashed his wrists with a box cutter, police said. A security guard found his body Tuesday morning, next to a garbage can placed to catch the blood" (Associated Press 2008a). As one commentator lamented, "It's ironic that a man who campaigned for greater transparency within NASDAQ should end up being charged with fraud and losing billions for innocent investors. What could possibly have driven him to risk his family's name in a world (Wall Street) that depends on the sanctity of the promise, 'My word is my bond'?" (Gagnier 2008).

The Picower Foundation, which was a charity that supported medical research and education, was one of several forced to close because of the loss of $1 billion in assets managed by Madoff. Barbara Picower, its president, said, "This act of fraud has had a devastating impact on tens of thousands of lives as well as numerous philanthropic foundations and nonprofit organizations" (Reuters 2008, A6). As others have commented, Madoff "has gutted an entire generation of Jewish philanthropic wealth, destroyed trust within the Jewish philanthropic world but, far more important, impoverished widows, orphans, and the elderly and, in so doing, endangered and shamed the Jewish people at a time when we have many real, not merely neurotically imagined enemies" (Chesler 2008).

This might seem to be a simple case of fraud, but think about the ordinary people caught in its flow:

> Sure, you could argue these investors should have known better than to believe in an investment strategy that seemed too good to be true, or that they should have seen the signs of wrongdoing. But most people—I'd venture to say at least 90% of us—don't have time to manage our money or to keep tabs on the "professionals" we hire to do just that. We know little about options trading, a cornerstone of Madoff's supposed strategy. We are too busy doing our jobs, now maybe even looking for work. Our energy is spent keeping our families fed and clothed. We are homework cops. We are caregivers tending to children who can't sleep . . . as well as loved ones who are sick. For Working Parents, we are chauffeurs, personal chefs, investment bankers, police, and personal assistants all wrapped up in one. If we are very lucky, we find a little time to take care of ourselves, too. (Young 2008)

CONTINUES

BOX 6.1 (CONTINUED)

Particularly vulnerable to Madoff's schemes were members of cultural communities: "Armenian-Americans, Baptist Church members, Jehovah's Witnesses, African-American church groups, Korean-Americans. In each case, the perpetrator relied on the fact that being from the same community provided a reason to trust the sales pitch, to believe it was plausible that someone from the same background would give you a deal, that if offered by someone without such ties would sound too good to be true" (Cass 2008). In Madoff's case, he targeted his own Jewish community: "Yeshiva University, one of the nation's foremost Jewish institutions of higher education, lost $110 million; Hadassah, the Women's Zionist Organization of America, lost $90 million; director Steven Spielberg's Wunderkinder Foundation acknowledged unspecified losses; and a $15 million foundation established by Holocaust survivor and writer Elie Wiesel was wiped out. Jewish federations and hospitals have lost millions and some foundations have had to close" (Peltz 2008).

References

Associated Press. 2008a. "N.Y. Investor Kills Himself After Losing over $1 Billion in Alleged Madoff Scam." http://www.haaretz.com/hasen/spages/1049644.html (accessed December 26, 2008).

———. 2008b. "SEC: Wall Street Kingpin with LI Ties Admits $50B Fraud." December 12. http://www.newsday.com/business/ny-bzfraud1213,0,3666375.story (accessed December 25, 2008).

Cass, Ronald A. 2008. "Bernard Madoff and Affinity Fraud." http://www.speroforum .com/a/17332/Bernard-Madoff-and-affinity-fraud (accessed December 22, 2008).

Chesler, Phyllis. 2008. "Madoff the Jew: The Media's Hypocritical Obsession with the Fraudster's Faith." *Jewcy News,* December 23. http://www.jewcy.com/tags/jewish _philanthropies (accessed December 26, 2008).

Gagnier, Monica. 2008. "The Rise and Fall of Bernard L. Madoff." *BusinessWeek,* December 12. http://www.businessweek.com/blogs/recession_in_america/archives/2008/12/ the_rise_and_fa.html (accessed December 19, 2008).

Peltz, Jennifer. 2008. "Some Jews Fear Madoff Case Stokes Anti-Semitism." Associated Press. http://www.google.com/hostednews/ap/article/ALeqM5jSLnvHBSvCHcE20bpw 41yDZqrthAD959SJ081 (accessed December 25, 2008).

Quinn, James. 2008. "Bernard Madoff 'Fraud': Betrayed by Their Best Friend; Bernard Madoff Wooed the Jet Set, but Few Knew How Much Was at Stake." *Daily Telegraph,* December 20. http://www.telegraph.co.uk/finance/financetopics/bernard-madoff/ 3853113/Bernard-Madoff-fraud-Betrayed-by-their-best-friend.html (accessed 26 December 2008).

Reuters. 2008. "Foundation to Close, Says Fund Manager Madoff to Blame." *San Diego Union-Tribune,* December 21, A6.

Young, Lauren. 2008. "Why I Hate Bernie Madoff." *BusinessWeek,* December 12. http:// www.businessweek.com/careers/workingparents/blog/archives/2008/12/its_2_am _and_i.html (accessed December 25, 2008).

Let's consider these three cases in more detail. Calley grew up in the 1950s as a privileged white male in a segregated patriarchal society. Calley represented America, discipline, success, and honor. Charity Keesee belonged to "Gen X" and was an abused, powerless, rural girl—individualistic, outside the mainstream, and a rebel. Madoff was brought up in a working-class ethnic Jewish family whose capitalist values were driven predominantly by profit making based on building trusted relationships. Yet all three participated in some of the most publicized crimes of our times. Is there a common set of characteristics that could explain these very different types of crimes and types of people? What do Lt. William Calley, Charity Keesee, and Bernie Madoff have in common?

Each case represents a segment of a learning matrix. The individual has either a "normal" or a "traumatic" upbringing and/or is subject to a "normal" or systemically problematic organizational learning environment. In the first case, Calley had a normal family socialization and a normal, if highly disciplined, organizational socialization. He learned through these processes that following orders for an ideal was the right thing to do, regardless of whether the outcome was harmful to others; Calley learned to follow orders, and not to question authority, and, therefore, did not see his slaughter of these Vietnamese citizens—old men, women, and children—as his responsibility.

Charity Keesee was subject to the opposite childhood extreme. Having been brought up in an abusive family, Charity first found relief through self-mutilation. She became an active participant in role-playing games such as Dungeons and Dragons and Masquerade. Over time, she increasingly sought refuge with what she calls "kindred spirits"—similarly abused youth who were into the Goth scene; her particular band, however, went further than most. Like William Calley, Charity Keesee belonged to an organized, hierarchically structured group. Cults and clans, though less formal than the military, still follow specific rituals, demand allegiance, and promote "values." Like William Calley, Charity complied with whatever her "commander" demanded. Goths and vampire cults, like the military, also dress in a uniform of sorts. Despite their professed desire to be unique, they all wear black, have pale skin, and follow Victorian clothing styles (one of Lanier's former students makes and sells fake teeth for vampires in Orlando and Virginia Beach and has a thriving business). Goths look alike. The fantasy role-playing games and obedience to authority practiced by many self-proclaimed vampires is not so different from small children who play soldier and carry toy guns (like Calley did as a child). Also like the military, Goths are law-abiding citizens the vast majority of the time. They work, eat, and pay bills like everyone else. Occasionally, they "drift" into crime. They also learn justifications for their deviant behavior. Charity, then, was subject to the cultural norms of a deviant organization (the cult); the result was harm without conscience to others.

Finally, Bernie Madoff, a "self-made man," experienced a normal childhood socialization and was also socialized into the norms of capitalist greed; the result was that he harmed massive numbers of others through a classic Ponzi scheme. Madoff, like Calley, came from a stable family, was not abused, but nonetheless was accused of the world's most costly fraud. At age twenty-two, in 1950, he invested $5,000 that he'd earned from his summer job as a Long Island lifeguard and from installing refrigeration systems to start his own investment firm. Madoff attended, but did not graduate from, Hofstra Law School. His brother was a part of his investment company, but it was his sons, who were partners in his firm, who turned him in.

These three different examples illustrate the central theme of this chapter: Ordinary human beings can become criminal offenders as a result of social processes through which they learn harmful behaviors and attitudes and rationalizations that excuse or justify harm to others. Whether they are conforming to the military objectives of the government, the code and conventions of a vampire cult, or the rules and practices of capitalist culture, what they learn can result in criminal harm. In this chapter, we examine several perspectives on social learning, called social process theories, that explain how this comes about: "Social process theories hold that criminality is a function of individual socialization. These theories draw attention to the interactions people have with the various organizations, institutions and processes of society" (Siegel 2004, 214).

This chapter and the next mark a transition from the individually oriented rational choice, biological, and psychological principles outlined in the previous chapters toward theories that explain criminal behavior based on social and group interactive factors. We thus move our understanding of crime and criminality toward the cultural, sociological, and structural principles that follow in the rest of the book. The two social process theories considered in this chapter, differential association and neutralization and drift, each in different ways addresses the important contribution of social interaction in the process of becoming criminal. But they each also make different assumptions about humans and the role of socialization in learning. As we shall see, "differential association theory" views crime and delinquency as the outcome of normal learning processes whereby youth learn the "wrong" behavior. "Neutralization and drift theory" views delinquency and crime as a result of juveniles learning to excuse, justify, or otherwise rationalize potential deviant and even criminal behavior (which allows them to be released from the constraints of convention and drift into delinquency). Let us look at these social process theories in more detail.

Common Themes and Different Assumptions

In the previous chapter, we discussed some psychological explanations about how human minds learn to think criminally and to develop "criminal" personalities. We also saw that other psychological theories explained how criminal thinking and criminal behavior could be learned. Similarly, several sociological theorists, notably Edwin Sutherland and his colleague Donald Cressey (1966), in their theory of differential association, rejected the psychological criminal personality analysis that criminals were different; instead, they argued that delinquents or criminals are no different from noncriminals. Criminals do not have different personalities and do not think or learn differently from noncriminals. Criminals learn to commit crimes just as they learn any other behavior and just as anyone else learns any type of behavior. Learning comprises "habits and knowledge that develop as a result of the experiences of the individual in entering and adjusting to the environment" (Vold and Bernard 1986, 205). Psychological learning theories provided a basis for social learning theory: "There are two basic modes of learning. People learn by experiencing the effects of their actions and through the power of social modeling" (Bandura 2001b, 170). As we saw in the previous chapter, behavioral psychologists have largely focused on the positive and negative response consequences of their behavior, but as Bandura showed us, people also learn vicariously through observation of others' behavior and consequences. Indeed, "much human learning either occurs designedly or unintentionally from the models in one's immediate environment" (ibid.).

The primary learning mechanism occurs in association with others. Most responsible for learning are those we are in close association with, usually through informal small groups, such as parents, family, friends, and peers. We learn through our interactions with these significant others and adapt to their social conventions. In addition, "a vast amount of knowledge about people, places, and styles of thinking and behaving is gained from the extensive modeling in the symbolic environment of the electronic mass media [where] a single model can transmit new ways of thinking and behaving simultaneously to many people in vastly dispersed locales. Video and computer delivery systems feeding off telecommunication satellites are now rapidly diffusing new ideas, values and styles of conduct worldwide" (ibid., 170–171).

What is crucially different between lawbreakers and law abiders then is not the learning process but the content of what is learned, as the examples provided by Bernie Madoff, Charity Keesee, and William Calley illustrate. Both law abiders and lawbreakers are socialized to conform to social norms. The norms that law abiders learn are those of conventional mainstream society, whereas the norms learned by delinquents and criminals are those of a delinquent subculture with values opposed to the larger society.

Early on, some sociologists, such as David Matza (1964) and Gresham Sykes (Sykes and Matza 1957; Matza and Sykes 1961), in their theory of neutralization and drift, argued that early social learning theory in criminology presented a too simplistic picture, one that was also overly deterministic. First, the theory assumed that humans are passive social actors, or blank slates, to be filled in with good or bad knowledge about how to behave. Second, it drew too stark a contrast between conventional mainstream values and delinquent subcultural values. Instead of being separate, these values are interrelated; delinquency forms a subterranean part of mainstream culture. Instead of being immersed in and committed either to convention or to delinquency, individuals are socialized to behave conventionally but can occasionally be released from the moral bind of law to drift between these extremes. Charity, for example, comes across as sweet, conforming, and innocent—most of the time. However, she belonged to one of the most ostracized of all social groups, the satanic cult. William Calley followed the rules he learned in school and in military training, yet he killed innocent civilians. Bernie Madoff followed the rules of capitalist investment banking, particularly options trading, yet suckered people into a Ponzi scheme that cost them $50 billion. Part of the contribution of social learning theory in criminology is to consider how these processes of learning occur and how their conflicting and often contradictory content is cognitively negotiated by humans to allow them to believe that what they are doing is, at least at the time of the acts, justifiable under the circumstances.

We begin our analysis of these two social process perspectives by considering the work of Edwin Sutherland, who has been described as "the leading criminologist of his generation" and "the most prominent of American criminologists" (Martin, Mutchnick, and Austin 1990, 139).

Sutherland's Differential Association Theory

Edwin Hardin Sutherland (1883–1950) was the son of a Baptist college president. He earned a doctorate from the University of Chicago, with a double major in sociology and political economy, and eventually went on to chair the Sociology Department at Indiana University. He first presented his theory of differential association in the third edition of his textbook *Principles of Criminology* (1939). He subsequently revised and developed the theory and presented the final version in the next edition, published in 1947.

Sutherland discounted the moral, physiological, and psychological "inferiority" of offenders (Jacoby 1994, 78) and rejected "internal" psychological theories (Martin, Mutchnick, and Austin 1990). His perspective explained crime by learning in a social context through interaction and communication (influenced by the symbolic interactionist tradition discussed later). Differential association is an abbreviation for "differential association with criminal and anti-criminal behavior patterns" (ibid., 155; see also Cressey 1962). Its central concept parallels Gabriel Tarde's ideas ([1890] 1903) that behavior is imitated in proportion and intensity to the social closeness between people.

According to Vold, Bernard, and Snipes ([1998] 2001), there are two basic elements to understanding Sutherland's social learning theory. First, the content of what is learned is important. This includes the specific techniques for committing the crime, motives, rationalizations, attitudes, and, especially, evaluations by others of the meaningful significance of each of these elements. Second, the process by which learning takes place is important, including the intimate informal groups and the collective and situational context where learning occurs. Reflecting aspects of culture conflict theory (discussed in Chapter 8), Sutherland also saw crime as politically defined. In other words, people who are in positions of power have the ability to determine which behaviors are considered criminal. Thus, Sutherland said we have "the differential implementation of the laws" (1949b, 513). More important for our present purposes, he argued that criminal behavior itself is learned through assigning meaning to behavior, experiences, and events during interaction with others.

The systematic elegance of Sutherland's theory is seen in its nine clearly stated, testable propositions:

1. Criminal behavior is learned.
2. Criminal behavior is learned in interaction with other persons in a process of communication.
3. The principal part of the learning of criminal behavior occurs within intimate personal groups.
4. When criminal behavior is learned, the learning includes (a) techniques of committing the crime . . . [and] (b) the specific direction of motives, drives, rationalizations, and attitudes.
5. The specific direction of motives and drives is learned from definitions of legal codes as favorable and unfavorable.
6. A person becomes delinquent because of an excess of definitions favorable to violation of law over definitions unfavorable to violation of law.
7. Differential associations may vary in frequency, duration, priority, and intensity.
8. The process of learning criminal behavior by association with criminal and anti-criminal patterns involves all of the mechanisms that are involved in any other learning.
9. Though criminal behavior is an expression of general needs and values, it is not explained by those general needs and values since non-criminal behavior is an expression of the same needs and values. (Sutherland [1939] 1947, 6–8)

The core of differential association is found in proposition 6. According to this proposition, learning an excess of definitions favorable to committing crime over those that are unfavorable results in people choosing the criminal option. As Martin, Mutchnick, and Austin have noted, "The situation most conducive to the development of criminality is that in which there is association with criminal behavior patterns and an absence of association with anti-criminal patterns" (1990, 157–158).

Both criminal and anticriminal associations can be affected by: (1) priority of learning: how early this is learned in life; (2) frequency: how often one interacts with groups encouraging the behavior in question; (3) duration: the length of exposure to particular behavioral patterns; and (4) intensity: the prestige or status of those manifesting the observed behavior. If each of these four aspects is favorable toward law violation, then there is a high probability of the person choosing criminal behavior. Associating with groups that value law violation can lead to learning criminal behavior.

A final aspect of Sutherland's theory is the shift from the concept of social disorganization to differential social organization. Social disorganization theory (discussed more fully in Chapter 8) says that those who become criminals are isolated from the mainstream culture and are immersed in their own impoverished and dilapidated neighborhoods, which have different norms and values. Differential social organization suggests that a complex society comprises numerous conflicting groups, each with its own different norms and values; associations with some of these can result in learning to favor law violation over law-abiding behavior. A good illustration of this is Sutherland's explanation of crimes by businesspersons, those he termed *white-collar criminals*:

> Respectable business men who violate the law are seldom in poverty and seldom manifest social and personal pathologies. The General Motors Corporation does not violate the law because of an Oedipus complex, the General Electric Company because it is emotionally unstable, the Anaconda Copper Company because of bad housing conditions, Armour and Company because of a broken home, the Standard Oil Company because of a lack of recreational facilities or any of them because of poverty. . . . We should attempt to explain white collar crimes and any other crimes in terms of processes that are common to both of them. These common factors are to be found in the "laws of learning" and in the modern social organization, with its specificity of cultural relations. (1949b, 514)

Sutherland argued that illegal practices that increase profits are diffused within business groups that are in conflict with others in society. This conflict is particularly strong in relation to specific practices, described as "just doing business." These practices within business groups are accompanied by definitions favorable to the violation of certain laws: those laws that are restrictive of business. At the same time, businesses are "isolated from and protected against definitions which are unfavorable to such crime" (ibid., 247). For example, being raised in a home where honesty is a virtue does not carry over to the specific cultures of corporations.

Empirical Support and Limitations of Differential Association Theory

The biggest problem with the original version of differential association theory is that some of its central concepts were not clearly defined and depended on a simple, passive definition of social learning. We saw in Chapter 5 that cognitive psychologists showed that learning is a creative and active process. Indeed, by focusing on learning in small groups, Sutherland ignored what social learning theorist Albert Bandura (1977, 1986, 2001b) later found to be significant modeling of images glorified in the media. As Bandura acknowledged, this is not surprising because most of these theories were crafted "long before the advent of revolutionary advances in the technology of communications" (2001b, 171).

Furthermore, Laub (2006) found that Sutherland failed to consider vital features of crime that opposed his theory. Early on, Sheldon Glueck (1956) raised another concern, asking if all criminal behavior is learned from others or if some people invent their own criminal behavior. If not, then, how does criminal behavior begin?

Differential association may explain why some people in high-crime areas commit crime. Indeed, several research studies have illustrated this. But it does not explain how criminal behaviors originate or who starts them. Nor does it explain how some individual crimes are committed without associates. It does not explain what counts as an excess of definitions. Nor does it explain irrational acts of violence or destruction. It does show how patterns of criminal behavior can persist over time, however, and how social and organizational groups of both the powerful and the powerless can sustain these.

Methodologically, research on differential association has been criticized on several counts. Glueck (1956) questioned the ability to test differential association, although others argued that it is testable (DeFleur and Quinney 1966), and considerable empirical research on the theory would seem to support this belief.

A further criticism is that most studies rely on asking subjects about their relationships with significant others. This method does not determine causality, and thus researchers are unsure if differential associations cause deviant behavior or result from deviant behavior. In addition, most of the studies rely on cross-sectional rather than longitudinal samples, which makes it impossible to know whether learning came before, after, or during criminal behavior.

Research on differential association has generally not been able to empirically validate the claims made, although it has received some support. Short (1960) was able to identify a connection between membership in a delinquent group and criminal acts. Higgins, Tewksbury, and Mustaine (2007) found evidence of a link between peer association and binge drinking among sports fans. Likewise, Monroe's research (2004) supports the relationship between differential association with smokers and adolescent smoking. Orcutt (1987) linked marijuana use to peer influence, but Johnson, Marcos, and Bahr (1987) found little support for differential association, in that adolescent drug use is influenced by drug use rather than attitudes and definitions of close peers, and hardly at all by parents. Indeed, the general conclusion of this research is that peer influence increases with age during adolescence and especially in relation to drug use and delinquent behavior (Gorman and White 1995). Wright and Cullen (2004) found that employment with prosocial coworkers may reduce rates of criminal behavior and drug use among young adults. Baier and Wright (2001) conducted a meta-analysis that examined the effects of religion on criminal behavior. Based on concepts from differential association, religion should provide an excess of definitions unfavorable to crime through "social selection and socialization" (Burkett and Ward 1993; Wright et al. 1999). Their reanalysis of sixty prior studies found that religious practices and belief do show a significant, moderate inhibiting effect on crime commission. However, Sellers, Cochran, and Branch (2005) found only modest support for differential association in their study of partner violence. In another study Costello and Vowell stated that "a major reconceptualization of differential association theory would be necessary" for doubts to be removed about its efficacy (1999, 829). In summary, the empirical research provides mixed support for differential association.

Modifying Differential Association: Differential Reinforcement Theory and Differential Identification Theory

In an attempt to overcome some of the early limitations of Sutherland's original theory, C. Ray Jeffery (1965) and Robert Burgess and Ronald Akers (1966; Akers [1977] 1985, 1998; Akers and Sellers 2008) developed versions of a differential reinforcement theory of crime based on a combination of Skinner's ideas of operant conditioning and Sutherland's ideas of differential association. Jeffery's version of differential reinforcement argues that individuals have differences in their reinforcement history with respect to being rewarded and punished: For some, being rewarded for minor rule breaking can lead to more serious law violation; for others, being punished may be interpreted as "attention receiving," and rather than reducing the tendency toward crime, punishment can actually increase it. Moreover, Jeffery claims that once a criminal behavior is learned, it can become self-reinforcing.

Rather than seeing a simple mechanical relationship between stimulus and response, Burgess and Akers (1966; Akers [1977] 1985, 2008), like Bandura, see a more complex relationship that depends on the feedback a person receives from the environment. Akers explains how people learn criminal behavior through operant conditioning and argues that people evaluate their own behavior through interaction with significant other people and groups. Burgess and Akers (1966) present a revised version of the propositional statement of Sutherland:

1. Criminal behavior is learned according to the principles of operant conditioning.
2. Criminal behavior is learned both in nonsocial situations that are reinforcing or discriminative and through that social interaction in which the behavior of other persons is reinforcing or discriminative for criminal behavior.
3. The principal part of the learning of criminal behavior occurs in those groups that make up the individual's major source of reinforcement.
4. The learning of criminal behavior (including specific techniques, attitudes, and avoidance procedures) is a function of the effective and available reinforcers and the existing reinforcement contingencies.
5. The specific class of behaviors that are learned and their frequency of occurrence are a function of the reinforcers that are effective and available and the rules or norms by which these reinforcers are applied.
6. Criminal behavior is a function of norms that are discriminative for criminal behavior, the learning of which takes place when such behavior is more highly reinforced than noncriminal behavior.
7. The strength of criminal behavior is a direct function of the amount, frequency, and probability of its reinforcement. These interactions rely on norms, attitudes, and orientations.

Tim Akers most recently linked this to the developing study of epidemiological criminology (Akers and Lanier 2009). Burgess and R. Akers are particularly interested in the role of punishment and who provides it. They see punishment as "positive" when it follows a behavior and causes it to decrease and as "negative" when it takes the form of a reduction or loss of reward or privilege. Burgess and Akers argue that differential reinforcement occurs when the rewards are given to two behaviors but one is more highly rewarded than the other.

Moreover, this differential rewarding is particularly influential when it comes from others who are significantly identified with, such as parents, teachers, peers, and so on. Furthermore, in his version of social learning theory, Akers, like Bandura, acknowledges that modeling can arise based on the rewards one sees others getting. Daniel Glaser (1956) called this identification with others, particularly the generalized characteristics of favored social groups or reference groups, differential identification theory.

Policy Implications of Differential Association and Social Learning Theory

The policy implications associated with differential association theory are relatively straightforward. If socialization in small groups provides an excess of definitions favorable to law violation, the implication for prevention is to keep young and suggestible people away from such groups and educate and train them to resist the messages of such groups. For those already influenced, "treatment" intervention involving resocialization is consistent with the theory's general principles. Specific prevention programs that follow from this theory include peer-led interventions, resistance-skills training, and personal and social skills training. In a review of research on such programs, however, Gorman and White noted that these "were shown to be of minimal effectiveness and conceptually limited in that they fail to address the complexity of the relationship between group associations and delinquency" (1995, 149). Gorman and White argued that because the relationship is reciprocal, it is insufficient to intervene at the adolescent peer-group level since doing so ignores the parent-child interaction in earlier years that led to involvement with antisocial peers in the first place. They suggested that family-based and community programs seem to be more conceptually consistent with differential association theory than the school-based skills programs, but the effectiveness of such programs has not yet been adequately demonstrated.

Also overlooked in the policy arena is the role of the law and public policy in influencing definitions favorable or unfavorable to law violation. For example, clearer and simplified laws provided by the dominant mainstream culture are indicated. A related policy would be to publicly proclaim the law and reasons for following it; the media may provide an effective format for delivering this message.

Limitations of Differential Reinforcement Theory

Empirical research has extensively tested differential reinforcement theory. Several large-scale studies (Akers et al. 1979; Krohn et al. 1985) have found it to be supported. Sellers et al., however, criticize narrative studies, stating that "the theory appears to have attracted a great deal of consensus on its predictive accuracy. This conclusion, however, has been based primarily on narrative reviews of numerous, widely disparate empirical tests of the theory," which can be compromised by subjective factors (2000, 1). Nevertheless, their own meta-analysis summarizing 140 other studies confirmed this support.

In spite of this empirical efficacy, this theory does not explain how people rewarded for conventional behavior (e.g., economically affluent youths) still commit crimes. Also, like Sutherland, Akers does not explain where the values transmitted through differential reinforcement come from in the first place, although he does point out that the social environment one is exposed to contains different content, some more conducive to illegal behavior than others. Indeed, in more recent work he has developed the macrolevel social structural side of this argument, proposing that environments impact individuals through learning (1998, 302).

Social learning theory's greatest merit is that not only does it draw together the psychological process components examined in the previous chapter of learning by role modeling and reinforcement of that learning, but "most significant, Akers contended that definitions and imitation are most instrumental in determining initial forays into crime" and that "continued involvement in crime, therefore, depends on exposure to social reinforcements that reward this activity. The stronger and more persistent the reinforcements . . . the greater the likelihood that the criminal behavior will persist" (Lilly, Cullen, and Ball 2002, 46), and the more conducive the social environment to providing this reinforcement, the more likely are such structures to contribute to such criminogenesis (Akers 1998). Indeed, as Sampson states in an evaluation of Aker's latest magnum opus, "Heir apparent to Sutherland's differential association theory, Ron Akers long ago made his mark in criminology. . . . There is also little doubt that social learning theory is one of the titans battling it out for supremacy in the etiology of delinquency wars" (1999, 438).

Going beyond Sutherland, Cressey, and Akers, we need to take into account Albert Bandura's significant contribution to social learning theory in its application to explain crime and deviance (1986, 1997, 2001a).

Cognitive Social Learning Theory

In the previous chapter we introduced the significant contribution to cognitive social learning made by Albert Bandura through his research on observational learning. Bandura's cognitive social learning theory was part of cognitive psychology that has revolutionized the field of psychology (Bruner 1987, 1990) and that includes Festinger's concept of cognitive dissonance (1957) and the treatment approach designed to correct errors in thinking known as cognitive therapy. Indeed, commenting on the application of cognitive theory in correctional settings, Maruna and Copes say, "The premise behind much cognitive programming owes a considerable debt to the neutralization idea: offending is partially facilitated by a cognitive mind-set that justifies and rationalizes criminal behavior" (2004, 21).

To recap, Bandura argues that people learn from others not just directly by being punished or rewarded but also through observation of others' behavior and through mass-mediated images of others' behavior. He says, "Virtually all behavioral, cognitive, and affective learning from direct experience can be achieved vicariously by observing people's actions and the consequences for them" (2001b, 170). In watching others they both imitate but also innovate behaviors that they see others do. He says there are four elements in observational learning that comprise a series of subprocesses: (1) attention to the behavior in question that involves perception, arousal, and awareness—"Attentional processes determine what people observe in the profusion of modeling influences and what information they extract from what they notice"; (2) retention of the behavior that involves classification, memory, and interpretation—"Retention involves an active process of transforming and restructuring the information conveyed by modeled events into rules and conceptions for memory representation"; (3) behavior reproduction (motor responses) that involves physical capability and skills—"Symbolic conceptions are translated into appropriate courses of action"; and (4) motivation, including stimuli from self and others, as well as from vicarious sources (ibid., 171).

From Bandura's "agentic" perspective, people act reflectively, purposefully, and in a self-regulating way, based partly on experience but also on the context or situation, such that "human action, being socially situated, is the product of a dynamic interplay of personal and situational influences." Humans integrate, but they also act on the world they experience rather than just reacting to it: "In social cognitive theory, people are agentic operators in their life course not just onlooking hosts of internal mechanisms orchestrated by environmental events. They are sentient agents of experiences rather than simply undergoers of experiences." Indeed, Bandura says, in contrast to biological or determinist accounts: "By regulating their own motivation and the activities they pursue, people produce the experiences that form the neurobiological substrate of symbolic, social, psychomotor and other skills" (ibid., 155).

Consistent with the interactive-reciprocal view of causation (Einstadter and Henry 1998, 2006), Bandura uses the term *emergent interactive agency* in which "persons are neither autonomous agents nor simply mechanical conveyers of animating environmental influences" (2001b, 156). By this he means that people are more than their constituent parts in that they develop in an ongoing way as a result of the variety of interactions that they have with their experiences and observations. This occurs not through linear causation but through "triadic reciprocal causation," such that there is "reciprocal causality" between (1) "internal personal factors in the form of cognitive, affective and biological events"; (2) "behavioral patterns"; and (3) "environmental events," all of which interact to influence each other, such that changes in one result in changes in the other (ibid., 156–157).

He says that the "environment" comprises an "imposed environment" about which little control can be exercised but can be interpreted, as well as a "selected environment" and a "constructed environment," through which we can filter the effects of the imposed environment to moderate and even change the reality of what is experienced compared with what might potentially be experienced: "People construct social environments and institutional systems through their generative efforts. The construal, selection and construction of environments affect the nature of the reciprocal interplay among personal, behavioral and environmental factors" (ibid., 157).

Unlike more limited views of causality, Bandura's reciprocal-interactive model recognizes not only that persons and situations affect each other but also that the behavior they produce can also affect feedback and interact with the persons and situations. Thus, people's "behavior plays a dominant role in how they influence situations which, in turn, affect their thoughts, emotional reactions and behavior. In short, behavior is an interacting determinant rather than a detached by-product of a behaviorless person-situation interchange" (ibid.). People "function as contributors to their own motivation, behavior, and development within a network of reciprocally interacting influences" (ibid., 169).

Bandura argues that through their symbolic representation of the world they are able to think about likely courses of action and select or discard them in their mind before actually enacting them. This can result in expanded possibilities or limited and distressful projected outcomes resulting from self-doubt and "self-defeating ideation." In their behavioral choices people not only are guided by expectations but also have the capacity for self-direction and, importantly, for self-regulation. "Once the capability for self-direction is developed, self-demands and self-sanctions serve as major guides, motivators, and deterrents" (ibid., 175). Self-regulation "operates through . . . self-monitoring, judgmental, and self-reactive subfunctions" (1999b, 213).

People are selectively attentive in monitoring aspects of their own behavior, and whether they perform an action will depend on how they judge it against personal guidelines and standards, in reference to the behavior of others, and in relation to values and a sense of personal adequacy: "People pursue courses of action that give them self-satisfaction and a sense of self-worth, but they refrain from behaving in ways that result in self-censure" (ibid., 176). Moreover, they seek to reduce the disparity between their perceived performance and the desired standard partly by taking corrective action but also by producing new discrepancies or new challenges to be achieved. We will return to the implications of these ideas after looking at the process of neutralization.

Neutralization Theory: Learning Rationalizations as Motives

One very important element of the behavior learned in intimate social groups and considered by Sutherland was the rationalizations that accompany behavior. These rationalizations are related to Sutherland's idea ([1939] 1947) about how law violations can be defined as favorable or unfavorable, and they were especially important to Donald Cressey. Cressey (1953, 1970), in a study of the "respectable" crime of embezzlement, found that three key elements were necessary for a violation of financial trust to occur: (1) a nonsharable financial problem (meaning a problem the offender feels embarrassed to tell others about, such as gambling debts); (2) the perception of their legitimate occupation as a solution to the problem, typically through using funds to which they have access; and (3) verbalizations, or words and phrases that make the behavior acceptable (such as "borrowing" the money and "intending" to pay it back). It is this third element and the possibility that such words and phrases may be found in the common culture that make the crime possible. As Cressey said: "I am convinced that the words and phrases that the potential embezzler uses in conversations with himself are actually the most important elements in the process that gets him into trouble" (1970, 111).

For Cressey, verbalizations were not simply rationalizations occurring after the fact of crime to relieve an offender of culpability. Instead, they were words and phrases that could, as C. Wright Mills (1940) had earlier argued, be "vocabularies of motive." They could inhibit someone from engaging in a criminal act by showing the potential offender that using such excuses or justifications after a criminal act might not be honored as acceptable. Alternatively, the excuses and justifications could be honored by future questioners, allowing the potential offender a sense of "freedom" that it might be acceptable to violate the law under the particular situation or circumstances described. The most sophisticated development of these ideas came from David Matza (1964) and Gresham Sykes (Sykes and Matza 1957; Matza and Sykes 1961) in their studies of juvenile delinquency. Indeed, they stated that techniques of neutralization "make up a crucial component of Sutherland's 'definitions favorable to violation of law.' . . . It is by learning these techniques that the juvenile becomes delinquent" (Sykes and Matza 1957, 667).

Drifting In and Out of Delinquency: Matza and Sykes's Neutralization Theory

The central idea behind neutralization theory is that "the excuses and justifications that deviants use to rationalize their behaviors might themselves be implicated in the etiology of deviant behavior" (Maruna and Copes 2004, 2). In Matza and Sykes's terms, neutralizations "precede deviant behavior and make deviant behavior possible" (1957, 666), though not inevitable, as Matza was later at pains to point out through his concept of "drift," discussed below.

In 1957, while at Princeton University, Gresham Sykes teamed up with his former student David Matza to develop a new theory of crime that extended Sutherland's learning theory (Sykes and Matza 1957). The analysis originated in Sykes's studies of prison inmates and guards learning to rationalize rule breaking (Martin, Mutchnick, and Austin 1990). Matza argued that existing theories, whether biological, psychological, or sociological, were too deterministic. These theories presented the adolescent as either committed to conventional behavior or committed to delinquency. Matza believed that not only was this an overstatement, but it also left out the classicist element of the choice to commit crime. He argued that existing theories predict too much crime. Most juvenile delinquents do not continue their criminal behavior into adulthood; in other words, most desist from crime. If a biological or psychological factor "caused" crime, why would its influence diminish after adolescence? If delinquent subcultures were so compelling at socializing youths to define crime as acceptable, then what accounts for their maturational reform—the tendency for juvenile delinquents to relinquish their delinquency as they age into their twenties and thirties? Matza sought to combine these observations to explain most delinquency (which he called mundane delinquency), arguing, "The image of the delinquent I wish to convey is one of drift; an actor neither compelled nor committed to deeds nor freely choosing them; neither different in any simple or fundamental sense from the law abiding, nor the same; conforming to certain traditions in American life while partially unreceptive to other more conventional traditions; and finally, an actor whose motivational system may be explored along lines explicitly commended by classical criminology—his peculiar relation to legal institutions" (1964, 28).

How Matza sought to combine these many orientations was, in part, by making a case for soft determinism. According to Matza, positivistic criminology (the scientific study of crime that had prevailed since the late nineteenth century, as discussed in Chapter 4) "fashioned an image of man to suit a study of criminal behavior based on scientific determinism. It rejected the view that man exercised freedom, was possessed of reason, and was thus capable of choice" (ibid., 5). Conversely, soft determinism argues that "human actions are not deprived of freedom because they are causally determined" (ibid., 9). The amount of freedom each person has varies. Some are more free than others and have a greater range of choices available. Moreover, this freedom varies according to circumstances, situations, and context.

Most important to understanding Matza and Sykes's argument is the concept of the "subculture of delinquency," which they prefer to the idea of a "delinquent subculture." As traditionally conceived, delinquent subcultures are considered separate and oppositional; their norms and values are different from those in the mainstream culture. The gang is the best example. For Matza and Sykes (1961), however, this was a false distinction. Most delinquents, they argued, are not full-fledged gang members but "mundane delinquents" who express remorse over their actions. Many admire law-abiding citizens. Furthermore, most differentiate between whom they will victimize and whom they will not. Finally, delinquents are not exclusively criminal; they also engage in many noncriminal acts. These factors suggest that delinquents are aware of the difference between right and wrong and are subject to the influence of both conventional and delinquent values.

Rather than delinquency and mainstream culture being separate, argue Matza and Sykes, mainstream culture has an underbelly of "subterranean values." These exist side by side with conventional values. Consider the example of sensation seeking: "Kicks, big time spending and rep have immediate counterparts in the value system of the law abiding" (ibid., 717). A good illustration of subterranean values can be found in the school setting.

When a teacher presents the class material on social studies, she or he teaches the knowledge content of the subject; when the teacher deals with students with favoritism, using gender or racial bias, or emphasizes grades as more important than understanding, she or he simultaneously sends a different message. Students learn how society works. They learn that there are public statements and private practices; they learn that beneath the rhetoric, what matters is getting ahead by whatever means, including cheating if necessary. This is useful knowledge, albeit informal knowledge. When these students get to the workplace, they will encounter formal rules and informal rules, such as the company policy on health, safety, and hygiene, as well as the preferred unspoken practice, which may be to cut corners and suspend rules in order to make a profit, regardless of who gets hurt. This kind of knowledge does not require the exclusivity of a gang of delinquents; it is there beneath the surface of every formal institution, policy, and practice. It is part of the subterranean subculture of delinquency.

This subterranean subculture of delinquency makes it unnecessary for adolescent youths to join gangs or other subcultural groups to learn delinquent values. Instead, simply by learning and being socialized into conventional values and norms, adolescents are simultaneously socialized into the negation of those values. Nowhere is this more evident than in legal codes.

Legal codes are inconsistent and thus vulnerable. As Matza wrote, "The law contains the seeds of its own neutralization. Criminal law is especially susceptible [to] neutralization because the conditions of applicability, and thus inapplicability, are explicitly stated" (1964, 60). This means people can claim various kinds of exemptions in the belief that they are, under certain mitigating circumstances, not bound by the law. The classic example is "self-defense." Another example is the idea that criminal intent (mens rea) must be present for an act to be criminal; Lorena Bobbitt, among others, used this rule to her advantage, as we illustrated in Chapter 5. Not only is this ambiguity present in the law, but in U.S. society it is reflected in contradictions resulting from trying to balance freedom of the individual and the collective interests of society. Take the example of speeding laws. It seems that only in the United States would the law ban speeding while allowing the sale of radar detectors—and these detectors are even sold by police at auctions of unclaimed recovered stolen property! Consider the laws in many states prohibiting gambling—yet Native Americans can run casinos and the states can run lotteries. Little wonder, then, that the ordinary Joe asks, "Why shouldn't I be able to use my local bookie to place bets? Why is that any different from the state-run lottery? I can afford it and do so to relax."

Such legal contradictions, and the implicit claims for exemption that follow from them, allow the possibility for choice and freedom because they render juveniles and others intermittently free to choose to commit delinquent acts. Whether youths break the law depends not so much on their being in a delinquent subculture but, first, on whether they are freed into a state of drift and released from the larger culture's moral bind, and, second, on whether they then exercise free choice: "Drift stands midway between freedom and control. Its basis is an area in the social structure in which control has been loosened. The delinquent transiently exists in a limbo between convention and crime, responding in turn to the demands of each, flirting now with one, now with the other, but postponing commitment, evading decision. Thus he [or she] drifts between criminal and conventional action" (ibid., 28).

This "loosening" of control, or release from moral convention into a state of drift, may initially be accidental, and it occurs through neutralization. For Matza, neutralization comprises words and phrases that excuse or justify lawbreaking behavior, such as claiming an action was "self-defense." Unlike rationalizations, which come after an act to avoid culpability and consequences, and verbalizations that come after contemplating an act to allow oneself to commit it, neutralizations come before an act is even contemplated. Thus, for Matza, they are "unwitting," something that occurs to an actor that results from the unintended duplication, distortion, and extension of customary beliefs relating to when and under what circumstances exceptions are allowed: "Neutralization of legal precepts depends partly on equivocation—the unwitting use of concepts in markedly different ways" (ibid., 74; see also L. Taylor 1972). Neutralization frees the delinquent from the moral bind of law so that he or she may now choose to commit the crime. Crucially, whether or not a crime occurs no longer requires some special motivation.

Sykes and Matza (1957) classified excuses and justifications that provide a moral release into five types, which they called "techniques of neutralization":

1. *Denial of responsibility* (e.g., "It's not my fault—I was drunk at the time"): In this technique offenders claim their questioned behavior was not in their control, or that it was accidental. Offenders may list reasons such as alcohol, peer pressure, bad neighborhood, and so on that caused them to commit the act. In a study of offenders with mental health problems, Green, South, and Smith (2006) found that denial of responsibility was a common factor among subjects.
2. *Denial of injury* (e.g., "No one got hurt"): Here the extent of harm caused is minimized or negated. Offenders may deny that anyone or anything was harmed by their action. For example, shoplifters might claim that stores have so much money and insurance that "they can afford it," or employee thieves may claim their company wastes so much that "it'll never miss it." Embezzlers are simply "borrowing the money," and joyriders are "borrowing" the car.
3. *Denial of victim* (e.g., "They had it coming to them"): Some offenders may claim that although someone got hurt, he or she deserved it. For example, corporations may treat their employees badly, paying them too little or instituting a stringent dress code. Employees may pilfer goods out of resentment "to get back at the company," saying they are the real victims of the corporation's abuse. Women who harm physically or psychologically abusive

spouses may claim that the "victim" was actually an offender who had therefore forfeited his rights to victimhood and was finally getting what he deserved. Absent or abstract victims are also easy to deny victim status, which is another reason it is morally less challenging to steal from large diffuse organizations than the clearly identifiable "mom and pop" store owner.

4. *Condemnation of the condemners* (e.g., "Law enforcement is corrupt"): This technique involves negating the right of others to pass judgment. Offenders may reject the people who have authority over them, such as judges, parents, and police officers, who are viewed as being just as corrupt and thus not worthy of respect: "Even ministers steal from the collection box." For example, the 2001 revelations of sexual abuse of children by Catholic priests and the cover-up by the Catholic Church provided considerable fuel for the denial of their moral authority to judge others.

5. *Appeal to higher loyalties* (e.g., "I didn't do it for myself"): Many offenders argue that their loyalties lie with their peers (homeboys, fellow gang members, fellow employees, fellow police officers, and others), and that the group has needs that take precedence over societal moral demands. Female embezzlers claim to have stolen for their families, and mothers have committed arson to provide work for their unemployed firefighter sons. Indeed, included are "corporate offenders who argue that their actions were conducted for 'higher' goals including profit for their stockholders and financial stability for their families" (Maruna and Copes 2004, 13). As price-fixing executives have said, "Customers are your enemies; corporations are your friends."

Since Matza and Sykes's original studies on delinquency, researchers have applied neutralization theory to a variety of other crimes, including adult crime, especially to offenders who maintain a dual lifestyle and are both part of the mainstream yet also engage in crime, as in employee theft (Ditton 1977; Hollinger and Clark 1983; Hollinger 1991) and buying and selling stolen goods (Klockars 1974; Henry [1978] 1988). In a study of corporate crime, Nicole Leeper Piquero, S. G. Tibbetts, and M. B. Blankenship (2005) found that respondents used neutralizations in making decisions for a drug company about producing a drug that was harmful to consumers. As a consequence of this extended research, at least five additional types of neutralization have been identified (Henry 1990; Pfuhl and Henry 1993; Maruna and Copes 2004, 14):

1. *Metaphor of the ledger* (e.g., "I've done more good than bad in my life"): This was used by Klockars (1974) to show how the professional fence believed himself to be, on the balance of his life, more moral than immoral ("Look at all the money I've given to charity and how I've helped children. If you add it all up, I've got to come out on the good side").

2. *Claim of normality* (e.g., "Everyone is doing it"): This suggests that the law is not reflecting the popular will, and since everyone engages in, say, tax evasion, pilfering from the office, extramarital sex, and so on, then such acts are not really deviant and therefore are not wrong.

3. *Denial of negative intent* (e.g., "It was just a joke"): Henry (1990; Henry and Eaton 1999) found this was used by college students to justify their use of explosives on campus, among other things ("We were only having some fun"). The neutralization is partial denial, accepting responsibility for the act but denying that the negative consequences were intended.

4. *Claim of relative acceptability* (e.g., "There are others worse than me"), also called justification by comparison (Cromwell and Thurman 2003): Unlike condemning the condemners, this appeals to the audience to compare the offender's crime to more serious ones and can go so far as claiming to be moral. For example, Los Angeles police officers claimed that the beating of African American Rodney King, after being stopped for a traffic violation, helped prevent him from being killed by nervous fellow officers (Pfuhl and Henry 1993, 70).

5. *Claim of entitlement* (e.g., "For the sacrifices that I've made I deserve some special reward"): This was used by deployed naval officers to justify cheating on their wives back home (Shea 2007). Neutralization has also been used by veterinarians who, in certain circumstances, question whether rules in the dominant normative system governing their professional ethics apply to their day-to-day roles as practicing veterinarians (Gauthier 2001).

The important point about these techniques of neutralization is their timing in the cognitive process. All could be used as techniques or devices (1) *after* an illegal act to seek to reduce blame or culpability or (2) *before* committing the act while contemplating it in order to seek self-conscious approval that it is acceptable to go ahead. But for Matza and others (Taylor 1972; Henry 1976), the critical point is that they can also occur (3) *before contemplating the act*, releasing the actor to be morally free to choose the act. In the latter case, the context, situation, and circumstances provide a neutralizing discourse that removes the moral inhibition, releasing a person to commit criminal acts, as they would any other act.

Maruna and Copes argue that not only are the original five techniques of neutralization not necessarily the most important techniques, and are anyway somewhat overlapping (e.g., denial of injury and denial of victim), but also "researchers have identified dozens (even hundreds, depending how finely one cuts them) of techniques that seem to serve the same function as neutralization techniques. What is interesting about neutralization theory is this function (what the neutralizations do), not the flavors it comes in." Indeed, they maintain that "the individual use of specific neutralizations should be understood within the wider context of sense making that is the self narrative process" (2004, 64). It is toward understanding this process that we now turn.

Bandura's Moral Disengagement Theory

In the context of his discussion of self-regulation Bandura comes close to Matza's concept of neutralization of morality. He describes the process of moral disengagement as one that uses psychological maneuvers or mechanisms for disengaging moral control, and he identifies two types. The first type is justificatory: "Investing harmful conduct with high moral purpose not only eliminates self-censure, but it engages self-approval in the service of destructive exploits as well. What was once morally condemnable, becomes a source of self-pride" (2001b, 178). Within the first type, three justificatory moral disengagement mechanisms are identified:

1. *Moral justification*, whereby harmful, inhumane, or otherwise detrimental conduct is made "personally and socially acceptable by portraying it as serving socially worthy or moral purposes" (ibid., 177).
2. *Sanitizing euphemistic language* is used to make harmful conduct personally respectable and more acceptable.
3. *Exonerating comparison* compares the questioned behavior to more harmful behavior such that "the more flagrant the inhumanities against which one's destructive conduct is contrasted, the more likely it will lose its repugnancy or even appear benevolent" (ibid., 178).

The second type of moral disengagement mechanism is that which diminishes a person's active human agency both to himself and others. This is a form of excuse, which Bandura calls "*displacement and diffusion of responsibility.*" Here someone or something is held responsible for the harm committed or when an individual sees him or herself as a fragment of a much larger framework. He says that in this form of moral disengagement, "personal agency is obscured by diffusing responsibility for detrimental behavior by group decision making, subdividing injurious activities into seemingly harmless parts, and exploiting the anonymity of collective action" (ibid., 178), a form prevalent among corporate and government offenders.

Weakened moral control also comes about by:

1. *Disregarding or distorting harm*, which has similarities to Matza's denial of injury by ignoring, minimizing, distorting, or disbelieving in the harm caused.
2. *Blaming others* for harm "becomes a justifiable defensive reaction to perceived provocations," which is similar to Matza's denial of the victim (Bandura 2001b, 179).

Bandura also argues, "Self-censure for cruel conduct can be disengaged by dehumanization that strips people of human qualities. Once dehumanized, they are no longer viewed as persons with feelings, hopes and concerns but as subhuman objects. If dispossessing one's foes of humanness does not weaken self-censure, it can be eliminated by attributing demonic or bestial qualities to them. It is easier to brutalize people when they are viewed as low animal forms" (ibid.). As others have noted, there are clearly close parallels between the major tenets of neutralization theory and Bandura's moral disengagement theory, even though Bandura does not acknowledge Matza's work in his own development of these ideas.

Policy Implications of Neutralization and Moral Disengagement Theory

Although neutralization theory explains certain kinds of criminal behavior, it also presents difficult policy questions. It suggests that contradictions in the dominant culture, injustice, and double standards need to be eliminated to lessen the possibility of people being able to neutralize. Cressey ([1965] 1987) was one of the few writers to specify the policy implications of this theory, at least at the level of institutional control. He suggested that to reduce the probability of verbalizations allowing embezzlement, employers should adopt educational programs that allow employees to discuss emerging financial problems from losses and that phrases used to excuse and justify such behavior should be repeatedly corrected to reveal their harm and crime. Some retail stores implement this suggestion through weekly meetings with sales staff, pointing out to them the precise losses from internal theft and how the company suffers. The aim is to undermine any neutralizing use of "denial of injury" by employees tempted to steal from the store.

Others have shown that it is not just the words and phrases that need constant monitoring and replacing but the conditions that give rise to them. Take, for example, the finding that employee resentment is highly correlated with employee theft and that high levels of job satisfaction are inversely correlated with employee theft (Hollinger and Clark 1983). Research by Jerald Greenberg (1990) has shown that although rates of employee theft typically rise if wages are cut, this can be avoided if employers use words and phrases to explain why the cuts are necessary and if they involve and inform the employees about what is happening. This way, the neutralizing effect of "denial of victim" is preempted and the justification for employee theft is undermined. Of course, whether such a policy would be effective depends on whether the theory is correct. Some have recommended incorporating techniques to combat neutralization and their associated belief systems into their crime prevention programs to "stimulate feelings of conscience at the point of contemplating the commission of a specific kind of offense" (Clarke 1997, 24).

Similarly, neutralization theory has led to "campaigns designed to make tax cheaters feel guilty about their behaviors," which can "reduce the prevalence of tax fraud" (Maruna and Copes 2004, 21; see also Thurman, St. John, and Riggs 1984) and to prevent rape "by exposing cultural stereotypes that rapists use as neutralizations and by replacing these myths with interpretations of reality that are not as conducive to crime" (Maruna and Copes 2004, 21). More broadly, in a study of risk neutralization and lay epidemiology by injecting drug users, P. G. Miller (2005) recommended that in order to craft more effective strategies to treat drug users, practitioners need to focus on cultural contexts rather than individual factors.

Maruna states, "Nowhere is the influence of this theory more apparent than in correctional practice, where the notion that habitual excuse-making promotes criminal behavior is largely taken for granted. Interventions as diverse as cognitive-behavioural therapy and restorative justice conferencing are all premised explicitly on overcoming rationalisations and encouraging offenders to take responsibility for their behaviour. Yet, does the research on neutralization theory over the last 50 years justify the faith in this theory?" (2003). However, one of Maruna and Copes's central arguments is that, particularly in the corrections and rehabilitation fields, the application of neutralization theory has been narrowly interpreted to define neutralization techniques as "bad" and as "criminal thinking errors," which need to be exposed through varieties of confessionals, or processes designed to accept responsibility. They point out that this "universal condemnation" contradicts the findings of some neutralization research that demonstrates that neutralization serves to protect a person's ego, and that for some offenders, recovery or desistance from crime requires an intact ego and a strong sense of self-efficacy: "Pathologizing excuse making and trying to prohibit the use of neutralizations in correctional programming, then, seems an iatrogenic strategy for the creation of widespread personality 'sickness.' If the only criterion for the diagnosis is an external locus of control in regard to wrongdoing, then all of us suffer from 'criminal thinking' and 'criminal personalities'" (2004, 67). At the same time, other research shows that neutralization can contribute to persistence in crime. As such, then, neutralization may have a complex relationship with crime, enabling it originally but subsequently facilitating the change toward desistance that might otherwise not occur. This again suggests that neutralization is a more reciprocal and interactive cognitive process between self-identity and the social construction of meaning or sense making, over time, which we look at in more detail in the next chapter.

Limitations and Evaluation of Neutralization Explanations

Maruna and Copes (ibid., 3–4) survey five decades of neutralization theory, in which the scope and application of the theory is demonstrated to include a wide variety of deviant and criminal behavior, from delinquency to homicide, sex offenders to corporate offenders, domestic violence survivors to Holocaust survivors, and, as we have seen, policy and practice, such as in cognitive therapy, reintegrative shaming, and restorative justice. Indeed, they describe it as "one of the earliest, fully articulated sociocognitive or narrative accounts of deviant behavior. . . . As such, neutralization theory might be considered one of the most creative and visionary (if flawed) theoretical developments in twentieth-century criminology" (ibid., 5).

How much it is flawed depends on how it is represented and evaluated. The critical issue when evaluating neutralization theory is whether offenders are committed to conventional values and norms in the first place. If they are not committed, neutralization is unnecessary, a point made by control theory, which we discuss in the next chapter. Topalli (2006) found that neutralization was effective only in predicting the behavior of socially attached individuals. Even Matza accepted that not all delinquents were committed to conventional values, since a minority were compulsive in their behavior, committed to unconventional values, and differed from the majority of mundane "drifters" (I. Taylor, Walton, and Young 1973, 180–181).

Early empirical research found little support for the idea that delinquents share mainstream values (Ball and Lilly 1971). Indeed, Michael Hindelang (1970, 1974) found that delinquents are committed to different values from those held by non-delinquents. Moreover, in an overview of the studies, Agnew (1994) found that most research shows that delinquents are more likely to accept techniques of neutralization than are nondelinquents. Copes (2003) researched auto thieves who were on community supervision and found that the socially attached subjects had a higher rate of neutralization than those subjects who were socially less attached. A self-report study by Landsheer, Hart, and Kox (1994) found that some delinquents viewed their acts as unacceptable yet committed them anyway, which tends to support neutralization theory, since this scenario requires some means for the delinquents to deal with their own moral objections. Moreover, in a study of street-offender decision making, Topalli (2005) found that offenders endeavored to maintain an image consistent with "a code of the streets" mentality. In other words, street offenders are committed to delinquent values and actually neutralize "good" rather than delinquent behavior.

Research on neutralizations also faces a causality problem, particularly in establishing when the neutralizations occur—before or after the criminal act. As Maruna and Copes summarize it: "There is little empirical evidence that individuals ascribe to neutralizations in advance of behaving criminally, and it is difficult to imagine how evidence of this could be reliably collected . . . [but] neutralization techniques may play an important role in maintaining persistence in crime" (2004, 7). For Hamlin (1988), neutralizations are produced after the act as motives attributed to behavior in response to questions about why it happened. However, in a study of shoplifters, Cromwell and Thurman (2003) found delinquent behavior occurring before neutralization a more plausible theory. Similarly, Agnew's analysis of the National Youth Survey's longitudinal data suggests that neutralization precedes violent acts, "may be used as both after-the-fact excuses and before-the-fact justifications," and "has a moderately large absolute effect on subsequent violence" (1994, 572).

Ultimately, like Sutherland's theory of differential association, neutralization theory does not explain how neutralization originates or who invents the extensions of the words and phrases that are learned.

Many of the studies that find relationships between neutralizations and delinquency suffer from methodological problems, such as using cross-sectional rather than longitudinal data, which does not allow the researcher to know whether neutralization preceded or followed the act. Maruna and Copes "question the reliability of interview methods for testing neutralization theory." They also question whether neutralizations stemming from interviews conducted after the fact in various different settings are not simply an artifact of the interview, since people vary their presentational selves and projected identities through narrative accounts depending on the audience and situation. They conclude that qualitative studies on neutralization "cannot be considered a test of the central neutralization premise because they almost never include a comparison group" (2004, 41).

Other "supporting" research has sampling problems. For example, Minor (1981), whose research provided limited support, relied on college criminal justice students for his sample. In an earlier study using a better sample, he could not support neutralization theory, concluding that in many cases, "Neutralizations and rationalizations are simply unnecessary" (1980, 115). Other studies have failed to distinguish neutralization from unconventional beliefs. However, Maruna and Copes also point out that the sample is typically unrepresentative, often being a "convenience sample," and that artificial and abstract measures of neutralization, typical of survey-based questionnaires, are not going to obtain insight into or evidence of the cognitive process in effect at the time of the crime (2004, 48). They summarize the findings of the empirical testing of neutralization theory as follows: "Research directed at measuring the effect of neutralizations on deviance has typically used one of two research strategies, both of which tend to find weak but positive relationships between acceptance of neutralizations and participation in delinquency" (ibid., 44).

Matza's ideas about "drift" have also come under attack. One commentator stated, "As with techniques of neutralization, drift theory does not have a solid foundation in empirical research, and this is a serious drawback" (Moyer 2001, 148). Part of the problem with Matza's drift theory, says Moyer, is that it has not been possible to develop a good operational definition, which has inhibited research.

Maruna and Copes identify what is "the thorniest methodological problem to date: how to measure the acceptance of neutralization techniques prospectively rather than simply in retrospect" (2004, 7). Again, it is clear that longitudinal research is the only answer in order to see whether, over time, words and phrases are learned and created in certain contexts and subcultures prior to engaging in deviant and criminal acts, and in ways that are documented as part of the discourse among predeviant or predelinquent members. They say, "Without longitudinal designs, there is no way to determine whether neutralizations precede criminal behavior or are merely after-the-fact rationalizations" (ibid., 45). Indeed, in one of the few well-designed longitudinal studies of neutralization, Agnew found that, at least in relation to violent acts, the majority of respondents disapproved of violence and "accept one or more neutralizations for violence" (1994, 573). He concluded, "Taken as a whole, the longitudinal data suggest that neutralization may be a relatively important cause of subsequent violence" (ibid., 572).

Finally, Maruna and Copes criticize criminologists who have used neutralization theory as a toolbox of individual discrete techniques that can be applied to a variety of behaviors, without seeking to explore the cognitive mechanisms whereby they are generated and the personal self-identity system or narrative identity within which they fit. Thus, they argue for the interrelationship between accounts that serve as neutralizations, the construction of personal identity, and future action:

> The narrative identity can be understood as an active information processing structure, a cognitive schema, or a construct system that is both shaped by and later mediates social interaction. People construct stories to account for what they do and why

they do it. These narratives impose order on our actions and explain our behavior with a sequence of events that connect up to explanatory goals, motivations, and feelings. These self-narratives act to shape and guide future behavior, as people act in ways that agree with the stories or myths they have created about themselves. (2004, 33)

This takes us into interactionist and social constructionist theory, which we consider in detail in the next chapter.

Summary and Conclusion

In this chapter, we have focused on theories that examine the interactive social processes involved in learning and becoming criminal. We move from theories offering a passive model of human nature to ones in which people actively learn criminal behavior from others. We explored the various elements in the learning process and, in particular, looked at the importance of learning words and phrases that form excuses and justifications that can serve to neutralize the moral inhibition to crime, releasing people into a state of drift wherein crime becomes simply a behavior to choose, like any other. We've looked at cognitive social learning and at moral disengagement theory. Each of these theories, in spite of its relatively different empirical validity, offers some insight and implication for how we might better parent children and how we may minimize the impact of negative social practices on their development. We have also looked at ways that organizations can better communicate with their members to render neutralization less likely, while recognizing that as an ego defense, neutralization may offer the best escape from a life of crime.

Summary Chart: Social Process Theories

1. Differential Association and Social Learning Theory

Basic Idea: People learn to commit crime as a result of exposure to others' criminal behaviors, ideas, and rationalizations that are favorable to violating the law.
Human Nature: Humans are social blanks until socialized into healthy social roles by families, education, and society. No difference between offenders and nonoffenders. All seen as rule following; which rules they follow depends on which groups socialize them.
Society and the Social Order: Society seen as a conflict of values. Law consists of behavioral prohibitions. Criminals are those who learn that under certain circumstances law violation is acceptable.
Causality: Sutherland's version: Individuals participate in both conventional and criminal groups and use the same process to learn behavior in both. In these groups or learning situations, they learn patterns of conventional and criminal behavior and the rationalizations that accompany them as well as the skills to carry them out. Learning an excess of definitions favorable to committing crime over those unfavorable

results in people being free to choose crime. Akers's version of social learning considers the importance of psychological learning by modeling and operant conditioning in a facilitative social environment.

Criminal Justice Policy: Keep children away from bad influences. Publicly and frequently proclaim the law and reasons for following it. Challenge all excuses and justifications. Rehabilitate through reeducation and resocialization of offenders. Segregate offenders.

Criminal Justice Practice: Preference for restitution and reparation and social rehabilitation. Group therapy and counseling for children of immigrants to provide them with coping skills needed to survive the clash of cultures. Clearer and simplified laws provided by the dominant culture. Greater flexibility of law when dealing with other or lower-class cultural contexts. Parental skills training. Decreased policing of streets. A tariff system that can be negotiated down in exchange for guilty pleas.

Evaluation: Explains why some people in high-crime areas refrain from crime but does not explain how behaviors originate or who starts them; does not explain individual crimes committed without associates in group; does not explain what counts as an excess of definitions; does not explain irrational acts of violence or destruction; does not explain why those rewarded for conventional behavior, such as middle-class youths, commit crimes; does not explain why some delinquent youths do not become adult criminals, despite being rewarded for crime. Assumes a passive and unintentional actor who lacks individuality or differential receptivity to criminal learning patterns.

2. Drift and Neutralization Theory

Basic Idea: Crime can become a behavioral option for people when their commitment to conventional values and norms is neutralized by excuses and justifications that render them morally free.

Human Nature: Humans are rational actors who choose behavior out of free will in a context of more or less commitment to convention and are capable of much moral ambiguity. Rules and acceptable behavior are open to interpretation.

Law: Contains both the imperatives for action and the principal exceptions—"seeds of its own neutralization"; law is thus ambiguous.

Criminals: No different from noncriminals; all are subject to neutralization by context and circumstance, and on those occasions all excuse or justify lawbreaking. Criminals may have highly developed abilities for neutralizing or may have learned words and phrases by which they can convince themselves that whatever they want to do is justified.

Causal Logic: Youths (and others) learn ways to neutralize moral constraints in the company of others, but these are not phrases absent from the wider society or words unique to delinquent subcultures; rather, they form a subculture of delinquency throughout the whole society. Invocation of words and phrases can occur in many circumstances. Timing is critical. Simply excusing or justifying after the act is not neutralization but merely rationalization; doing so before the act is committed (as in Cressey's verbalization) is motivating through removal of inhibition (even if by design). Crucial for Matza is the unwitting extension and distortion of excuses and justifications before contemplation of the act, such that it simply appears morally justified (e.g., working for an unfair boss builds up the neutralization of denial of victim). Neutralization releases the individual to a "moral holiday," free to choose or drift into delinquency. Neutralization occurs through use of several techniques: (1) denial of responsibility, (2) denial of injury, (3) denial of victim, (4) condemnation of condemners, (5) appeal to higher loyalties, (6) metaphor of the ledger, (7) claim of normality, (8) denial of negative intent, (9) claim of relative acceptability, and (10) claim of entitlement.

Criminal Justice Policy: Prevention to clarify property ownership and identify how people are harmed so that offender or potential offender accepts responsibility for his or her actions.

Criminal Justice Practice: Public exposure and declaration of excuses and justifications. Education in ethics and how we deceive ourselves into honest dishonesty, cognitive behavioral therapy, and restorative justice.

Evaluation: Explains why delinquents undergo maturational reform, why people can participate simultaneously in both conventional and unconventional behavior, and how people can maintain illegal, self-destructive behavior. Difficult to test since it cannot easily be established whether neutralization occurs before or after law violation. Does not explain why some people drift and others do not.

7

Failed Socialization
Control Theory, Social Bonds, and Labeling

An abandoned child manifests evil instincts in his early childhood.
—Jean-Paul Sartre, *Saint Genet: Actor and Martyr*

Robbie Hawkins's early years were filled with the trauma of witnessing physical violence between his parents, as well as being molested as a child. By the age of four he was manifesting repeated physical violence against other children at school and attacked the teachers when they disciplined him. Psychiatrists said that the four-year-old's violent behavior reflected his erratic family life, and they impressed on his parents the importance of a stable, nurturing family environment. Instead, Robbie got to witness a bitter divorce and custody battle that culminated in the arrest of his mother, Molly, for threatening behavior toward father Robert's new wife, Candice, who accused Molly of child endangerment. After this and after remarrying herself, Molly gave up visitation rights to Robbie. Now it was his stepmother, Candice, who was subjected to Robbie's anger and violence. To try to control it, Robbie's father and stepmother used various forms of restrain and violence:

> Rob's father preferred to handle his outbursts by pinning him on the floor, sometimes for longer than an hour, until he would calm down. But when it was her turn to control him, Candice, an Air Force vet, used the back of her hand. Growing up on a steady diet of psychiatric medicine and corporal punishment, Rob became more violent and withdrawn. When he was 13, his ongoing battle with Candice went nuclear. She searched his backpack for cigarettes, and Rob flipped out on her. In response she slapped him across the face so hard that her ring cut his forehead. He balled up his fist and said "I'm going to kill you." (Boal 2008, 75)

After psychiatric hospitalization for his further violence, his father gave Robbie up to juvenile court. The Nebraska "State Department of Health and Human Services became Rob's legal guardian. . . . At 16 Rob was now a veteran of institutions, having spent the last 24 months in group homes because he resisted the reconciliation with Candice that would have allowed him to rejoin the family" (ibid., 75). Robbie had now been further sexually molested and suffered suicidal ideation: "Over the years he kept trying to buck the rules and talk to his biological mother, with whom he held out hopes of a reunion, but he was never allowed to call her. By now his psychological profile included the darker, more exotic ailment that would lie behind his future crimes: anti-social personality disorder, a condition that makes it difficult, if not impossible to feel empathy for strangers. It is the underlying pathology of most serial killers" (ibid., 75–76).

After two years of therapy, when Robbie was finally persuaded to apologize to Candice, she refused to accept his apology, saying that she'd never feel safe in the house and threatened to divorce Robert if he allowed his son to return home: "My stepmother is evil—she has no heart, Rob told his roommate" at the highly disciplined group home for boys where he now lived, and to whom he admitted that he missed his biological mother deeply (ibid., 76). After a period in a foster home, where he was also engaged in a variety of relatively minor crimes, including selling marijuana and gas station stickups, Robbie successfully contacted his mother: "Molly threw herself into his life as if the separation and abandonment had just been a big misunderstanding." He later had an intense relationship with a girlfriend, Kaci, who reported that he'd describe his childhood as "shitty" and his mother as "fickle." Kaci said, "He cried all the time. It was really sad because he had, like, no family. He was the saddest about his mother" (ibid., 77).

Robbie once again called his mother, Molly, and this time was allowed to visit and spent Thanksgiving 2007 with her. He was photographed smoking pot, which he shared with her, and apparently enjoying the festivities, in spite of a pending court hearing on a drunk-driving charge and the fear that Molly would take his Jeep away from him as a punishment.

One week later, on December 5, 2007, after having dinner the previous night at his mother's house, Robbie Hawkins, now an eighteen-year-old, entered the Von Maur department store in the Westroads Shopping Mall in Omaha, Nebraska, and rode the elevator to the third level, where he randomly shot eleven people, killing eight, with an AK-47 assault rifle taken from his stepfather's closet the previous night, before killing himself.

In this chapter we explore the problems of failed socialization dramatically illustrated in the case of Robbie Hawkins. First we look at the effects of inadequate parental socialization by focusing on social control theory; later we examine the negative effects of labeling by social control agents and agencies of criminal justice.

In his theory of bonding and social control and in his later theory of self-control, Travis Hirschi (1969; Gottfredson and Hirschi 1990) rejected the ideas discussed in the previous chapter: either that some people learn criminal behavior or that everyone is socialized into conformity from which some are occasionally released from the moral bind of law, to offend. Indeed, Hirschi and Gottfredson have said, "We reject the idea that 'criminal activity' requires learning in any meaningful sense of the term. . . . nor do the 'learning processes' described by Sutherland and Akers account for 'conformity' as we define it." In contrast, Hirschi argued that some people are not socialized adequately in the first place. Socialized, in control theory, is not about learning behavior, but about knowing and caring about the consequences of behavior. Indeed, "A central element of our self-control theory (and of all control theories) is the assumption that behavior is governed by its consequences" (Hirschi and Gottfredson 2006, 115). Hirschi maintained that law abiders and lawbreakers are the same in that they are all *potential* offenders. What distinguishes us is how effectively we are socialized not to break the law, that is, how far control is instilled in us as children.

Hirschi (1969) claimed that inadequate socialization processes in children and youth allow, or even foster, the formation of unconventional attitudes that can result in crime and delinquency. When socialization works adequately, a tie or bond is created with conventional society that prevents law violation by insulating people from temptation. Learning self-control is a crucial element in the process of resisting the impulse to law violation. What significantly affects socialization are the social bonds of attachment, commitment, involvement, and belief formed between children and conventional others, such as teachers and parents. If these bonds are weak, or do not form, children will lack self-control and will be free to violate the law. Bonding, social control, and self-control theories, then, examine the connections and controls that link people to conventional society and lead them to care about the consequences of what they do.

Control Theory: Learning Not to Commit Crime

Whereas Sutherland ([1939] 1947) and Akers (1998) focused on learning kinds of behavior, and sought to explain how some people are introduced to and adopt lawbreaking behavior, control theory (like classical theory) assumes a universal motivation to crime and deviance and instead asks why most people conform (Hirschi 1969). Control theorists' answer is that attachment and commitment to conforming people, institutions, and values produce a loyalty that protects against the temptation to deviate.

> What distinguishes social control theory as a distinct framework is (a) its focus on restraints rather than the conventional criminological focus on motivations as the key to explaining crime, and (b) its assumption that the motives or impulses for most criminal acts are relatively normal and universal (rather than aberrant or pathological). Thus, social control theory reverses the usual explanation of crime by viewing criminal behavior as less explainable in the presence of something (deviant motivations) than in the absence of something (effective restraints). (Rankin and Wells 2006, 119)

Considering the issue of the presence or absence of restraint, it is possible to distinguish between two types of control theory, one where restraints are present but either break down or are eroded and the other where they are absent. We call the first type *broken-bond theory* and the second type *failure-to-bond theory.*

Kinds of Social Control Theory: Broken Bonds or Failure to Bond?

Most social control theories assume that socialization into convention occurs from an early age but something breaks or weakens the bonds to convention, freeing a person to deviate. This type of control theory can be called broken-bond theory. For example, the neutralization of the moral bind of law discussed in the last chapter has been considered by some criminologists to be a version of this type of control theory (Akers 1994, 114). Another example of broken-bond theory is social disorganization or social ecology theory (discussed in the next chapter), which argues that the isolation and breakdown of communities can undermine a person's commitment to conform to the dominant or mainstream culture (Kornhauser 1984). Of course, when children are raised in a disorganized and fragmented community, separated from mainstream culture and values, they may not form bonds to convention in the first place, which leads us to the second type of control theory.

The second kind of control theory, which is the one considered in this chapter, assumes that the creation of a commitment to convention is problematic. It is very difficult to persuade humans to conform to socially approved norms and values, and it requires much investment of time and energy and considerable maintenance (Box [1971] 1981). Inducing conforming social behavior requires certain kinds of socialization and can easily go wrong: "Differences in nurturing account for variations in attachment to others and commitment to an ordered way of living" (Nettler 1984, 290). Without this attachment and commitment forming in the first place, humans are more likely to deviate and to break the law. We call this type of control theory failure-to-bond theory.

One of the earliest versions of failure-to-bond theory is John Bowlby's "attachment theory" (see Chapter 5). Bowlby (1951) conducted research on forty-four juvenile delinquents who were referred to his child guidance clinic (which he compared to forty-four controls). He found that children who have frequent breaks in relations with their mother in the early years of development up to the age of eight, or who have factors that mitigate against secure maternal bonding, such as child abandonment, foster care, or child abuse, develop anxiety and have difficulty forming relationships with others. The result is "affectionless characters" who lack the ability to empathize with others and do not see or feel the pain that harm may cause others. The desirable state, according to Bowlby's revised theory of attachment, is "secure attachment," which requires a responsible, lovingly responsive, and sensitive mother figure who is empathetic and able to satisfy childhood needs for emotional and physical security. In contrast, people like Robbie Hawkins represent the failure of the attachment process: "Attachment theory predicts that the most problematic individuals will be those who were abandoned at an early age, who experienced multiple placements (in foster homes and so on), who had to deal with the early absence of one or both parents, and who faced traumatic conditions in early childhood (physical, sexual or other abuse)" (Schmalleger [1999] 2002, 186).

Several other early versions of failure-to-bond theory also laid a foundation for this perspective. Drawing on Albert Reiss's ideas (1951) about offenders' failure to internalize personal self-control and the absence of direct external social controls such as law and informal social control, F. Ivan Nye (1958) distinguished between three kinds of controls: (1) direct control from the threat of punishment; (2) indirect control, which protects youths from delinquency through their wish to avoid hurting intimates, such as parents; and (3) internal control, which relies on an internalized sense of guilt.

Another early version of failure-to-bond theory was Walter Reckless's containment theory ([1950] 1973, 1961). He argued that adolescent youths are motivated toward delinquency by "pushes" from the pressures and strains of the environment and "pulls" provided by peers. Juveniles will violate the law unless protected by both internal and external controls, which he called inner and outer containments. Outer containment comes from parents and school discipline, whereas inner containment comes from a strongly developed sense of guilt and a positive self-concept. The interplay of these forces could produce more or less delinquency. In particular, a positive self-concept can be enhanced by external social approval, and this, in turn, binds the youths to the community and to conventional behavior. Conversely (and anticipating labeling theory, discussed in the next section), negative reaction from society would result in a negative self-concept through which a reciprocity of disrespect leads to a failure to adopt conventional behavior.

Ruth Kornhauser summarized how both internal and external controls and rewards influence acts of conformity: "Social controls are actual or potential rewards and punishments that accrue from conformity to or deviation from norms. Controls may be internal, invoked by self, or external, enforced by others" (1984, 24). Kornhauser added, "Social bonds vary in depth, scope, multiplicity, and degree of articulation with each other" (ibid., 25). Travis Hirschi has been celebrated for his development of an elaborated version of the failure-to-bond version of control theory. Hirschi drew on several dimensions of these earlier theories to develop his social control theory.

Hirschi's Social Control Theory

Hirschi's book *Causes of Delinquency* (1969) is most often associated with recent social control theory, and his version of failure-to-bond theory has stimulated the most research. Like the early control theorists, Hirschi drew on an idea developed by Jackson Toby (1957), who argued that the key to forming commitment was developing an investment in convention, which he called a "stake in conformity." Once invested, the cost of losing this stake serves as a barrier to law violation. The underlying assumption in Hirschi's argument is that all people would break the law if they did not fear the damage and consequences of getting caught. Ties or bonds to conventional parents, school, friends, employers, and so on make crime too much of a risk for most people.

For Hirschi, the "social bond" consists of several components: attachment, commitment, involvement, and belief, each of which has a very precise meaning, different from its conventional or even psychological understanding. *Attachment* is defined as caring about others, including respecting their opinions and expectations, and is based on mutual trust and respect that develop from ongoing interactions and intimate relations with conventional adults. *Commitment* refers to the individual's investment in conventional behavior, including a willingness to do what is promised and respecting the expectations others have that it will be done. Commitment implies that "the interests of most persons would be endangered if they were to engage in criminal acts" (1969, 21). In other words, commitment involves a cost-benefit analysis of what degree of previous investment or "stake in conformity" would be lost if one were to participate in the act. *Involvement* is the time and energy spent on participation in conventional activities. This can be interpreted as a simple ratio. Since time and energy are limited, the more time spent doing conventional activities, the less time is available for deviant acts. Finally, the bond is solidified by *belief* in the moral validity of conventional norms and on the child's respect for the authority of those limiting their behavior. This is a fundamental and explicit assumption of control theory, which "assumes the existence of a common value system within the society or group whose norms are being violated" (ibid., 23). More broadly, belief refers to an ongoing conviction that conventional behavior and respect for its underlying principles, norms, and values are important and necessary. Finally, the elements of bonding in Hirschi's theory are interrelated, such that "the chain of causation is thus from attachment to parents, through concern for persons in positions of authority, to the belief that the rules of society are binding on one's conduct" (ibid., 200).

By way of illustrating Hirschi's theory, let us consider the example of two college seniors, Trevor and Shantell, who have fallen in love, feel like soul mates, spend a lot of time together, respect each other, and plan to get married upon graduation. In a new criminology class, Trevor meets an attractive sophomore, Donna, who "just wants to have fun." The opportunity arises for a date during which Trevor would be tempted to cheat on his longtime girlfriend, Shantell. How do Hirschi's key concepts explain what might unfold? Strong attachment means that Trevor would not go on the date, because he knows it would be disrespectful toward Shantell, who would feel upset and betrayed. Strong commitment means that Trevor has led Shantell to trust him. Such a date, especially given whom it would be with, would be cheating on his relationship. This would undermine the trust between Trevor and Shantell and risk the breakup of their relationship and cancellation of their planned marriage. Strong involvement in the relationship with Shantell would mean that Trevor was so busy doing activities with her that there literally would not be time for anyone else. Finally, strong belief in their relationship would include reference to certain values such as honesty, safety, monogamy, stability, security, and maybe even the belief that taking risks is unwise. In short, Hirschi's bonded conventional student, Trevor, would probably reject the date, recognizing that it threatened his valued relationship with Shantell. Of course, if he justified the act to himself with the arguments that the date with Donna would be a onetime kind of thing, that his steady would not know about it, and that she would be working anyway, he would be not a Hirschi-bonded student but a Matza-neutralizing drifter off on a moral holiday, free to date Donna, at least on this occasion!

Hirschi's bonding theory, which still stands alone as a viable explanation for crime, raises the question of whether the reason some people fail to form connections with conventional others has to do with their capacity for self-control, itself affected by parental socialization practices. These questions led Hirschi and his colleague Michael Gottfredson to a further refinement of control theory, to *self-control theory*, which we consider next.

Hirschi and Gottfredson's Self-Control Theory

In 1990, Travis Hirschi and Michael Gottfredson published *A General Theory of Crime*. This book has enjoyed wide circulation. Cohn and Farrington (1999) found that the book had the second-highest number of citations of all criminology books published in the 1990s. In this text, Gottfredson and Hirschi moved away from the four-component version of social bonding theory to focus on self-control, or the lack of it, that results in impulsive behavior. Impulsive behavior is a tendency in all humans; all are motivated to break rules and make a rational choice decision of whether or not to do so. Indeed, Hirschi and Gottfredson say, "All of us, it appears, are born with the ability to use force and fraud in pursuit of our private goals." Moreover, "everyone is capable of criminal or deviant acts. . . . However . . . some are more likely than others to actually commit them" (2001, 88). "The quality that prevents crime among some people more than it does among others . . . we call 'self-control,'" which is "the tendency to consider the broader or longer term-consequences of one's acts" (2006, 114) and "the tendency to avoid acts whose long-term costs exceed their immediate or short-term benefits" (2001, 82). They identify juvenile delinquency as just one of a wide range of crimes, including embezzlement and fraud, that can be explained not so much by the absence of bonds as by a lack of self-control on the part of the offender, especially in circumstances of increased opportunity and heightened situational temptation. "Those who have a high degree of self-control avoid acts potentially damaging to their future prospects, whatever current benefits these acts seem to promise. Those with a low degree of self-control are easily swayed by current benefits and tend to forget future costs. Most people are between these extremes, sometimes doing things they know they should not do, other times being careful not to take the unnecessary risks for short-term advantage" (ibid., 82).

> The difference between offenders and non-offenders is in their awareness of and concern for the long-term costs of crime—such things as arrest, prison, disgrace, disease, and even eternal damnation. . . . What distinguishes offenders from others is not the strength of their appetites but their freedom to enjoy the quick and easy and ordinary

pleasures of crime without undue concern for the pains that may follow them. . . . We thus infer the nature of criminality. People who engage in crime are people who neglect long-term consequences. They are, or tend to be, children of the moment. They have what we call low self-control. (ibid., 90)

However, they say that "something built into people is responsible for their continued involvement or lack of involvement in such acts" (2006, 113). Criminals, according to Gottfredson and Hirschi, lack self-control because they have been poorly trained as children, as a result of low parental investment in child rearing and poor monitoring and disciplining practices. This explains "the differential tendency of people to avoid criminal acts whatever the circumstances" (1990, 87). Matt DeLisi succinctly outlined Gottfredson and Hirschi's view of the outcome of such failed socialization:

Abject parenting nullifies successful childhood socialization. The outcome, in persons exposed to such an environment, is low self-control. Persons with low self-control (a) prefer immediate gratification of desires, (b) pursue simple tasks rather than activities that require tenacity, (c) value physical rather than verbal or cognitive experiences, (d) enjoy quick returns instead of long-term commitments such as marriage or occupational and educational careers, (e) are employed in low-skilled versus academic endeavors, and (f) are self-centered and generally insensitive to the feelings of others. (2001, 1)

Indeed, Grasmick has developed a profile of the characteristics of poor self-control (see table 7.1). The difference is in people's ability to suppress or restrain such urges and drives and in their needs for excitement, risk taking, and immediate gratification. Most people do not engage in criminal acts because they have been effectively socialized by parents to exercise self-control over their behavior. Those who fail to be properly socialized have a lack of control that can also be related to "low self-esteem." Pratt and Cullen add that this "increases the likelihood that individuals will be unable to resist the easy, immediate gratification that crime and analogous behaviors seductively, and almost ubiquitously, present in everyday life" (2000, 932). Hirschi and Gottfredson describe how people develop self-control over offensive behavior: "By the age of 8 or 10, most of us learn to control such tendencies to the degree necessary to get along at home and at school. . . . Low self-control is natural and . . . self-control is acquired in the early years of life. Children presumably learn from many sources to consider the long-range consequences of their acts" (2001, 90).

Developing self-control over one's behavior comes mainly from parenting practices:

But the major sources of self-control, in our view, are the actions of parents or other responsible adults. Parents who care for their children, watch them as best they can. When they see their children doing something they should not do, they correct, admonish, or punish them. The logical structure of successful socialization thus has four necessary conditions: care, monitor, recognize (deviant behavior) and correct. When all of these conditions are present, the child presumably learns to avoid acts with long-term negative consequences, whatever their legal or moral status. When any one of them is missing, continued low self-control may be the result. (ibid.)

TABLE 7.1 Grasmick's Characteristics of Low Self-Control

Impulsive
Seeks Instant Gratification
Low Levels of Diligence, Tenacity, and Persistence
Seeks Sensation and Excitement
Prefers Simple Physical Tasks over Complex Intellectual Tasks
Self-Centered
Insensitive to Others' Needs
Low Tolerance to Frustration
Addresses Conflict Through Confrontation

SOURCE: Grasmick 1994.

For some people, then, the socialization process is defective, providing little protection against committing crime. Their socialization is defective not because of something biological or psychological within the individual, not because of patterns of behavior that have been copied from others, but because the parents have failed to use adequate child-rearing practices and as a result have failed to instill self-control. Thus, early childhood is where this lack of self-control is manifested as "conduct problems" (Pratt and Cullen 2000).

Let's look in more detail at the failings of parenting that produce such lack of self-control characteristics. As we've indicated, for Hirschi and Gottfredson, parenting involves, among other things, the control of deviant behavior or normative regulation that "requires that someone (1) monitor behavior, (2) recognize deviant behavior when it occurs, and (3) correct or punish it" (2006, 115). Rankin and Wells add, "Normative regulation is the process of 'laying down the law' and making clear what children can and cannot do. . . . Monitoring children's behaviors for compliance or noncompliance entails supervision and surveillance. . . . Discipline and punishment of noncompliance comprise the application of unpleasant outcomes to sanction children's misbehaviors negatively" (2006, 122–123).

"Monitoring" refers to parents or guardians watching children's behavior. Monitoring can be ineffective because of lack of care, lack of time, or the periodic physical absence of the child from its parents, due, for example, to hospitalization of the child or parental work commitments. Recognizing refers to the parents' or guardians' conception of the norms, rules, and laws of society and their readiness to identify behavior as consistent with or deviant from them. Parents may not recognize deviant behavior for several reasons, including the popular child-rearing philosophy that this practice is harmful for healthy child development (we discuss labeling theory in more depth in the second half of this chapter). They may also not recognize it because they are themselves unaware or do not believe that such behavior is deviant.

Finally, even if they watch and recognize, parents may not provide effective punishments for deviant behavior or adequate rewards for conforming behavior. Together, inadequate monitoring, inappropriate recognition, and ineffective punishment result in dysfunctional child rearing. This will have a serious impact on children through their formative years (ages six to eight) and reduce the effectiveness of other socialization through formal schooling or informal peer groups.

Policy Implications of Control Theory

Control theory implies policy interventions based on preventive socialization designed to protect and insulate individuals from the pushes and pulls toward crime. Part of this protection comes from supervision, surveillance, and control. But rather than control being provided by the formal criminal justice system—which should remain as the punitive last resort—the major focus on preventive policy, according to control theory, should be through the informal control of children by their parents. This implies strengthening bonds to convention through developing more effective child-rearing practices and adequate childhood socialization. Early on in his comments about policy Hirschi argued that allowing adolescents to be employed undermines the family's ability to control its youth:

> How, if at all, does the employment of the youth affect the family's ability to punish his deviant behavior? The power of the family in this situation will depend on the resources available to it relative to the resources available to the child. . . .
>
> If the child does not want to go to college, his family does not own a car, and the money he earns provides him a level of living equal or superior to that of his family, he is by definition no longer dependent on them. His parents no longer have the material means to punish him, and the entire system of family control is vulnerable to collapse. Henceforth, the adolescent is free to come and go as he pleases. . . . The "child rearing" days are over. It is time to hope for the best. (1983, 6)

Although family size and single working parents may seem to present challenges to effective parental supervision, Gottfredson and Hirschi say that "responsible adults committed to the training and welfare of the child" can carry out the child rearing, and it may be accomplished in properly run day-care facilities where children are under supervision (1990, 273). Indeed, they argue that schools can be more effective than parents or families in providing the kind of supervision and control necessary to those not properly socialized by the family: "First it can more effectively monitor behavior than the family, with one teacher overseeing many children at a time. Second, as compared to most parents, teachers generally have no difficulty recognizing deviant or disruptive behavior. Third, as compared to the family, the school has such a clear interest in maintaining order and discipline that it can be expected to do what it can to control disruptive behavior. Finally, like the family, the school in theory has the authority and means to punish lapses in self-control" (ibid., 105).

   In addition, early intervention programs include parent training and functional-family therapy that seek to reduce family conflict through dispute settlement and negotiation, reduce abuse and neglect, promote positive parent-child interaction, and teach moderate discipline (Morton and Ewald 1987). When family problems are irresolvable, it has even been suggested that youths be placed in surrogate families and group homes with trained "teaching parents" (Braukmann and Wolf 1987; Agnew 1995b).

BOX 7.1 The Potential for Delinquency Among Victims of Human Trafficking
      MARK LANIER

One of the most heinous underreported crimes in a global context is that of human trafficking. After drug dealing, human trafficking is tied with the illegal arms industry as the second-largest criminal industry in the world today, and it is the fastest growing (Wilson and Dalton 2007). The U.S. Department of State defines human trafficking as modern-day slavery, involving victims who are forced, defrauded, or coerced into labor or sexual exploitation. This modern-day form of slavery is being reported with increasing frequency throughout the world. According to the 2008 *Trafficking in Persons Report*, approximately 800,000 people are trafficked across national borders annually, with an estimated 14,500 to 17,500 victims being trafficked into the United States each year. In a special presentation at the University of Central Florida on January 12, 2009, Allen Beck, senior statistician at the Bureau of Justice Statistics, reported only 61 convictions and 140 suspects for a twenty-one-month period ending September 2008 in the United States. Why such a large disparity between arrests and the reported number of victims?

   The police are the government agency most likely to first contact victims. Unfortunately, this initial contact is often the result of a criminal offense—committed by the victim. For example, many young women are forced into prostitution; others may be forced to sell or transport drugs. When the police respond to a criminal act, they are obligated by legislative mandate to arrest the prostitute or drug runner or user. As first responders, law enforcement agencies play a key role in identifying and rescuing victims of human trafficking, but in most cases, they do not have the proper training to be able to differentiate many of these victims from criminals. This inability to identify many individuals as victims fuels a vicious cycle that allows this modern-day slavery to remain an underground phenomenon. The cycle begins with traffickers' psychological bondage of victims—constantly threatening victims that if they try to reach out to authorities, they will be arrested and deported back to their home country. At the same time, any bond the victim had to their prior life is destroyed. With every "faulty" arrest law enforcement makes, the traffickers' hold on their victims grows exponentially, leaving victims isolated, too afraid to come forward, and further alienated from conventional society.

CONTINUES

BOX 7.1 (CONTINUED)

Two compounding and interactive factors help perpetuate the problem and crime. One tragic consequence is that the victims, especially those taken at an early age, have inadequate positive socialization and an overabundance of improper socialization. Bonds to conventional society, if ever formed initially, become ruptured due to the victimization. Second, victims may actually view conventional society, especially the government, as the enemy since they are repeatedly told by captors that the government will simply arrest or deport them. Sadly, too often this has been the case. The bonds that Hirschi and many others have found to reduce delinquency are thus impossible to form in victims. This vicious cycle suggests that the *victims* will actually be more likely to become delinquent—even if taken from their captors. Many have become drug addicted, many have engaged in dysfunctional sex acts, and most suffer from self-esteem issues. Finally, a life of crime may be all that they have ever bonded to!

Human trafficking is a unique problem because it transcends borders and police jurisdictions. A broad international solution is thus required. The solution must also be grounded in sound theoretical principles. If, as many empirical studies have shown, Hirschi is correct, a bond must be either established or reestablished. The first step is to make the government, especially the police, a friend and ally to the victims. The Florida Department of Law Enforcement (FDLE) and other international and national law enforcement agencies have recognized the problem and begun training officers to render aid rather than arrest "victims." In the United States, in October 2000, the Trafficking Victims Protection Act (TVPA) was enacted; before this, there was no federal law that existed to protect victims or to prosecute their traffickers. The three main goals (or the three p's) of the TVPA are to prevent human trafficking overseas, protect victims, and prosecute the traffickers. Another significant change that resulted from this law was the establishment of the "T-visa," which allows victims of human trafficking to become temporary residents of the United States. After three years of having a T-visa, victims are then allowed to receive permanent residence status. Previous law would result in the deportation of many human trafficking victims, but with the TVPA and the T-visa in place, we can now even offer victims eligibility for the witness protection program. This small first step should help the victim form positive ties (bonds) to society. In addition, the William Wilberforce Trafficking Victims Protection Reauthorization Act of 2007 makes a number of additions to the TVPA, including the allowance of prosecution for sex trafficking without proof of force or coercion (Spadanuta 2008). In 2006, the governor of Florida signed statute 787.06, which made it mandatory for law enforcement officers and prosecutors to go through basic training in human trafficking crimes (Florida Department of Law Enforcement 2006). This statute also added racketeering to the list of offenses, which makes human trafficking a first-degree felony with a maximum prison sentence of thirty years. It is hoped these efforts and assisting victims with bonding to conventional society will show positive results.

CONTINUES

BOX 7.1 (CONTINUED)

References

Florida Department of Law Enforcement. 2006. *Violent Crime and Drug Control Council.* Tallahassee: Florida Department of Law Enforcement.

Spadanuta, Laura. 2008. "Cracking Down on Sex Trafficking." *Security Management* 52, no. 8: 24.

Trafficking in Persons Report. 2008. U.S. Department of State. http://www.state.gov/g/tip/rls/tiprpt.

Wilson, Jeremy, and Erin Dalton. 2006. "Human Trafficking in the Heartland: Variation in Law Enforcement Awareness and Response." *Journal of Contemporary Criminal Justice* 24, no. 3: 296–313.

A second level of intervention for some control theorists is directed toward those "at risk" of engaging in antisocial activities. Policy here can focus on providing counseling and problem-solving and social-skills training (Goldstein, Krasner, and Garfield 1989; Hollin 1990), especially in the school context. Gottfredson and Hirschi (1990) argue that unless this kind of intervention occurs early in the child's development, it is already too late to make much difference.

A RAND study shows that both parent-based and school-based programs are more cost-effective in prevention than merely relying on incarceration. The study compared crime prevention programs that (1) sent child care professionals into homes of children from just prior to their birth up to the age of two to monitor their behavior and provided four subsequent years of day care, (2) provided parent training and therapy to families of children between ages seven and eleven who showed signs of aggressive behavior, (3) provided disadvantaged high school children aged fourteen to eighteen with cash incentives to graduate, and (4) provided twelve and thirteen year olds special counseling and supervision programs. The study found that high school graduation incentives were the most cost-effective, followed by parent-training programs, with delinquency supervision programs and prison being less cost-effective (Greenwood 1996).

These kinds of preventative interventions also have serious moral implications that go beyond the issue of economics to raise questions about the relationship between the state and the family that would need to be resolved before any such programs could be implemented on a wide scale. Admittedly, in spite of earlier statements that might appear to contradict this, Hirschi and Gottfredson have recently said, "We no longer accept the idea of obvious and necessary links to social policies. . . . Most contemporary theories, including control theory, are efforts to understand the origins of delinquency. They are not rooted in concerns about how to fix the problem or reduce its impact. . . . As a result they should not be judged by their alleged policy implications" (2006, 117).

Evaluation of Social Control and Self-Control Theory

Overall, social control theory has been one of the most tested of all theories. Moreover, as Rankin and Kern have noted, "Among the various social control perspectives, Hirschi's (1969) version is probably most responsible for developments in family and delinquency research. It is relatively explicit, well developed, and amenable to empirical tests" (1994, 495). The bonds to convention outlined by Hirschi have been extensively studied. In one study examining the social bonds Hirschi described, Costello and Vowell found the bonds to have "important direct effects" (1999, 815). Moreover, a study by Mack, Leiber, and Featherstone (2007) found that maternal attachment was the primary factor in determining levels of delinquency. One commonly identified element of the bond is religion. One of the more robust means of assessing theory quantitatively is through the use of meta-analysis. Baier and Wright conducted a meta-analysis (a summary and comparison of all the previous studies) of sixty studies examining religion and delinquency and concluded that "religious behavior and beliefs exert a significant, moderate effect on individuals' criminal behavior" (2001, 12). LaGrange and White (1985) pointed out that the strength of the bond to convention varies based on a number of factors, particularly age.

Similarly, studies of low self-control have produced considerable support for self-control theory. Nofziger (2008) found that the level of self-control of the mother will affect her choices of punishments as well as her degree of surveillance, thus impacting the self-control of her child. When Pratt and Cullen (2000) conducted a meta-analysis of twenty-one research studies on low self-control they found that self-control, or lack thereof, is a strong predictor of crime. Likewise, DeLisi (2001), Vazsonyi et al. (2001), and Hay (2001) found self-control to be inversely related to criminal offending. Further, those who exhibited low self-control were, indeed, found to be impulsive and risk takers, and were more serious criminals (DeLisi 2001). One study found that low self-control was related to negative interactions among offenders and criminal justice personnel, which "potentially affects discretionary outcomes" (DeLisi and Berg 2006). Overall, the research on self-control theory is fairly conclusive. In another summary of existing studies, Hay found that, "with few exceptions, these studies indicate that low self-control, whether measured attitudinally or behaviorally, positively affects deviant and criminal behavior" (2001, 707).

Although research has revealed much support for the various versions of this theory, it has also exhibited some flaws. Krohn (1991) has pointed out that Hirschi's original bonding theory fails to adequately distinguish between different elements of the bond and is unclear about the causal direction of bonding. Thus, although a lack of parental attachment can affect delinquency, delinquency can also affect parental attachment (Liska and Reed 1985). In other words, social control theory doesn't explain whether the reason that some parents fail to bond with their children is because the children themselves are the problem: "No recognition is given to evidence that children come into the world with different personalities and temperaments, and in so doing affect the behavior of parents from a very early age" (Ellis and Walsh 2000, 326). A study by Wong (2005) found that the type of conventional activity one is involved in affects the level of delinquency. More broadly, research conducted by Latimore, Tittle, and Grasmick (2006) found evidence that family socialization alone was inadequate to explain levels of delinquency and that other factors needed to be considered.

Others have criticized social control theory for failing to explain gender differences in delinquency—in other words, for failing to explain "why parents, schools, and churches throughout the world would socialize children in ways that make males form weaker bonds and have less self-control than females" (Ellis and Walsh 2000, 326). Nor does the theory gain as much support for explaining serious adult crime. Indeed, control theory ignores the insight of Matza and Sykes concerning the subterranean values of conventional society. As a result, the theory ignores the finding that effective bonding to convention and self-control do not protect against some serious deviance. In particular, where those who have leading roles in conventional society, including parents, also indulge in unconventional behavior, from drug taking to corporate fraud, then being bonded to "convention" can also mean being bonded to crime. Those who engage in pleasing the conventional employer, from President Richard Nixon to corporate presidents (such as Pharmor's Micky Monus or Enron's Kenneth Lay), may come to realize that their commitment to convention necessarily involves a commitment to crime and deviance. Indeed, recognizing the value of their "stake in conformity" as an instrument of compliance was no better expressed than by Richard Nixon's comment about loyalty that allowed moral and criminal laws to be broken: "Catch them by the balls [high salaries, high mortgages, investment in kids' college education], and their hearts and minds will follow" (meaning they'll do any risky, or immoral, behavior that you ask of them).

The more recently developed self-control theory has also been subject to similar critical assessments, not least for ignoring micro- and macrocontexts that affect self-control. For example, a study by Wright and Beaver (2005) concluded that genetic factors need to be considered in the explanation of those with low self-control. Indeed, one study of the relationship between testosterone levels and risk taking among stock market traders found that traders with higher levels of testosterone take more risks and are more profitable, and that the self-control comes from higher levels of the hormone cortisol, the imbalance between the two leading one commentator to explain the financial frauds of Bernie Madoff, something that clearly he was unable to control (Parikh 2008; Palmer 2008). At a more macro level Pratt, Turner, and Piquero (2004) found that the "structural characteristics of communities" were essential to the development of self-control. Furthermore, the parental controls that feature so prominently in Gottfredson and Hirschi's self-control theory (1990) can counteract the effects of bonding and work in different and complex ways (Wells and Rankin 1988; Rankin and Wells 1990). According to Rankin and Wells, "Many forms of social control operate in a curvilinear fashion such that the greatest reduction in delinquent behavior is produced by a moderate amount of control; thus the researchers demonstrated that more control is not necessarily better. Indeed, increasing direct control beyond a medium amount can yield negative behavioral outcomes. Excessive control may generate more delinquency rather than more obedience because it can prompt anger, rebellion, and the acting out of behaviors" (2006, 123).

Moreover, Akers (1994, 123) has argued that self-control theory is untestable because it is tautological: "Propensity toward crime and low self-control appear to be one and the same thing." However, Pratt and Cullen disagree arguing that "the charge of tautology does not apply to studies that measure self-control with attitudinal scales that were developed to assess self-control independently of criminal behavior" (2000, 945).

As with social control theory, it is not surprising that Curran and Renzetti (1994) observe in self-control theory that the narrow range of white-collar crimes Gottfredson and Hirschi examined for their general theory of crime relying on low self-control explanations omits the majority of crimes committed in corporate entities and government structures by executives and managers who are loyal to conventional values. Like Lieutenant Calley's role in the My Lai massacre and Bernie Madoff's financial fraud described at the beginning of the previous chapter, these persons believe they are supporting conventional values as they commit their crimes. In Madoff's case he was a trusted member of his local community and a pillar of the global financial community. To be fair, Hirschi and Gottfredson argue that their self-control theory deals with whole categories of people "rather than particular acts by named individuals" and that they are drawn more to abstract, simplified constructions and logical systems of explanation than to taking into account "the TV criminal of the day, however much he or she may offend our moral and political sensibilities" (2006, 116). That said, the question remains how the theory explains a whole category of white-collar offenders, particularly financial investors, socialized effectively by parents into valuing community, convention, and capitalism and acting in the long term with full awareness of the consequences of their actions. As Rabbi David Wolpe commented after the Madoff case was revealed, "Jews have these familial ties. . . . It's not solely a shared belief; it's a sense of close communal bonds. . . . I'd like to believe someone raised in our community, imbued with Jewish values, would be better than this" (Pogrebin 2008).

Labeling Theory:
A Special Case of Failed Socialization?

This second half of this chapter deals with the effect that society's agents of social control, such as police, schoolteachers, social workers, and probation officers, have on creating crime and criminals. Consider a second example. Author Mark Lanier first met Nick during his sophomore year at the University of Central Florida. He stood out in a class of more than one hundred due to his happy, friendly disposition. He came from a prominent, well-educated family in south Florida. Though bright, studying was not Nick's forte. This nineteen-year-old was on the five-year plan toward his criminal justice major and a career in law enforcement and never skipped class. The previous year, Nick became involved in a minor barroom altercation, which he did not start, with another drinking patron. Unfortunately for Nick, the other person was an off-duty police officer. Nick was arrested for "assaulting a police officer," underage drinking, and a few other minor charges. The officer walked away laughing with his friends. Nick accepted a plea bargain and pleaded guilty to one charge—unfortunately for Nick, the assault charge. He pleaded guilty rather than notify his parents and accepted the small fine and probation. The unanticipated long-term effects have been serious, however. Nick was arrested three more times before graduating from college. Most recently, Nick was at a rugby team "keg" party where underage females were present. Either a neighbor called the police, or, during a routine drive-by, the police decided to drop in on the party. The police proceeded to check everyone's identification. Of the forty-plus people present, Nick was the sole arrestee, despite the fact that he was compliant; it was not his house, keg, or female friends. He is convinced that when his arrest record was pulled by the officers on the scene and "assaulting a police officer" appeared, he was singled out for "special treatment." Needless to say, Nick's dreams of working in law enforcement have ended. He now has a very successful landscaping business. However, his family still wonders (until reading this, that is!) what happened. Nick represents a case of how the control of minor rule-breaking behavior can produce a stigma that amplifies the original deviance to have life-changing effects; in extreme cases, these effects can be full-blown criminal careers.

Like control theorists, labeling theorists are concerned with the failure of socialization. However, instead of focusing on bonds, they examine the social reaction component of interaction with society's control agents. For labeling theorists, adequate socialization occurs when youthful indiscretions and minor rule violations are tolerated rather than labeled deviant. Labeling theorists argue that society—specifically through persons in powerful positions—creates deviance by overreacting to minor rule breaking. This results in negative socialization that, over time, can undermine a person's sense of self-worth and foster a commitment to deviance. Labeling theorists, such as Edwin Lemert (1951, 1967) and Howard Becker ([1963] 1973), have argued that social interaction with others is important in shaping whether people eventually become offenders. Humans are not passive but are actively engaged with others in the construction of their own social identities and in creating the meaning of their world. Not all others are equally significant in this interactive process, however. Those more significant are members of powerful groups and significant individuals who seek to ban certain behavior by passing laws that are enforced via social control agents. So powerful is the impact of social control agents that otherwise minor rule breaking is magnified through criminal justice processes to have a significant impact on some perpetrators. The impact of these meaningful encounters can transform fragile social identities into criminal careers. Although Nick has not become a serious criminal, his life has been dramatically altered by this exact process. Others have become the deviant actor that their label projected; whether this would have occurred without the labeling is the central question that labeling theorists address. Let us examine the interactionist labeling theory of failed socialization in more detail.

Like the control theorists we have just examined, labeling theorists believe that social interaction with others is important in shaping whether people become offenders. But whereas social control and bonding theory see clear recognition of deviant behavior as an important component in the process of preventing future deviance, labeling theory views this as an important component in creating future problems. For these theorists, the issue is not so much what this teaches us about the consequences of our behavior or how we bond to others but how our sense of self-identity is built on the views that others have of us and how this identity can be negatively impacted through other people's reactions to our behavior. Again, Nick's drama mimics what has happened to countless students who were on their way to conventionally defined success as college graduates until agents of social control intervened, particularly with alcohol or drug violations. One further quick example will suffice. A Michigan student, a senior with a 4.0 grade point average, was enjoying his final spring break. He was sharing a room with five or six of his fraternity brothers in Daytona Beach, Florida. A few had small quantities of marijuana. Someone smelled the burning cannabis and notified the police. Hours later, when the student returned from the beach alone, he entered the room and the police closely followed. They searched the room, put all the small bags of pot into one big pile, thereby greatly increasing the weight, and charged the student with a felony due to the (now) large quantity. Had a drug-detecting test been administered, the student would have been found drug free. Unfortunately, like Nick, he did not notify his parents and handled it himself, greatly hurting his case. His friends all left, and he remained in jail for several days. His lifelong dream of working in federal law enforcement abruptly ended that spring break.

According to interactionist theory that underlies labeling theory, we discover self-identity through symbolic communication in interaction and role-play with others in social contexts. For adolescent youths, what their peers think of them and what image they project to others are of utmost importance, resulting in a concentration on style, body image, and so on. Many people define themselves, and are defined by others, according to how they appear. Look around you in class, and you can readily identify the "Greeks" who always wear their "letters" on clothing, purses, and cars and wear T-shirts signifying significant parties and socials. Observe too the "Goths" with their pale skin and dark hair, the "surfers" with their golden hair, board shorts, flip-flops, and deep tans. You may even have some "bikers" with their tattoos, Harley shirts, chains, and boots. Can you identify the "ROTC" students in your class? The "athletes"? Do the students who dress differently from one another make eye contact, sit by, and speak to each other? Who did you sit by on the first day of class? Many of us love the academic environment because of this broad diversity of experiences; students, unfortunately, often take this for granted as part of the social landscape, without recognizing the serious consequences of the social labels they live by. Yet the impact of these labels can be destructive and deadly. The spate of school violence and homicides of 1994–1999 were fueled, if not directly caused, by the negative stereotypes applied to vulnerable children who were seen as "geeks" or "nerds" before their frustration from bullying exploded into violence, as occurred at Thurston High in Springfield, Oregon, and Columbine High in Littleton, Colorado (Newman et al. 2004; Larkin 2007). Following this spate of school homicides, social control agents created a moral panic to seek out these nonconforming "odd ball killers, labeled by 'jocks' as 'The Trench Coat Mafia'" in what John Katz described as nothing short of "Geek Profiling." He relates how these marginalized "teenagers traded countless stories of being harassed, beaten, ostracized and ridiculed by teachers, students and administrators for dressing and thinking differently from the mainstream. Many said they had some understanding of why the killers in Littleton went over the edge" (1999). Consider the following account of "Jay" from Katz's Web site Voices from Hellmouth:

> I stood up in a social studies class . . . and said I could never kill anyone or condone anyone who did kill anyone, but that I could, on some level, understand these kids in Colorado, the killers. Because, day after day, slight after slight, exclusion after exclusion, you can learn how to hate, and that hatred grows and takes you over sometimes, especially when you come to see that you're smart and different, or sometimes even because you are online a lot, which is still so uncool to many kids! After class I was called to the principal's office and told that I had to undergo five sessions of counseling or be expelled from the school as I had expressed "sympathy" with the killers in Colorado, and the school had to be able to explain itself if I "acted out." (ibid.)

The social interaction of observing differences in others, negatively stereotyping them, and then excluding, taunting, bullying, and teasing those who display these attributes, such as clothes, what they say, or how they speak, is the subject of labeling theory. This theory of how social selves, self-esteem, and social identity are formed itself is based on symbolic interactionist theory rooted in social psychology.

Symbolic Interactionist Roots of Labeling Theory

According to symbolic interactionists, we see ourselves through the mirror of others, as they react to what they see in us. Charles Horton Cooley (1864–1929) called this the "looking glass self" ([1902] 1964). Symbolic interactionism can be broken down into several easily understood propositions. The most important of these are as follows: First, we form our definition of self, or "self-identity," based on how others react to, or treat, us. Second, what people say and do are the result of how they interpret their social world. Third, humans communicate through the use of symbols—the most common symbol being language or speech. Fourth, the better a researcher can assume the role of another (the research subject) or have empathy, the better theory can be developed. To the symbolic interactionist ideas of George Herbert Mead (1863–1931), who devised the notion of the social self, or generalized other (1934), Mead's student Herbert Blumer (1969) added that humans are actively engaged with others in the construction of their own social identities. Once formed, these identities are not fixed but continually reformed and reinterpreted as actors interact with others. Not all others are equally significant in this interactive process, however.

The most significant "others" are those in powerful groups who ban certain behavior through passing laws and those social control agents, such as police, courts, social workers, psychiatrists, school administrators, teachers, counselors, and so on, who enforce these laws. So powerful is the impact on identity by agents of social control, according to labeling theorists, that otherwise minor rule breaking or difference is magnified through criminal justice processes to have a significant effect. The impact of these officially sanctioned meaningful encounters can transform fragile social identities into criminal careers through a process Frank Tannenbaum originally referred to as "the dramatization of evil." Either punishment or reform, argued Tannenbaum, can lead to the very "bad behavior it would suppress," such that "the person becomes the thing he is described as being" (1938, 19–20). The key to this process, according to Tannenbaum, is the "tag," or label, attached to the rule breaker.

During the 1950s, the early ideas of labeling theorists lay dormant because of the dominance of social and structural explanations (Shoemaker 1996, 191). By the 1960s, the social and political climate became very open to the view that humans are malleable. Consistent with the general criticism of tradition and established institutions of control, labeling theorists found a resonance in the idea that excessive control inhibited the potentially free human spirit that strove to be different. Along with other protest movements for women and civil rights, labeling theory, or, as some called it, the "New Deviancy Theory" (I. Taylor, Walton, and Young 1973), seemed, at times, to romanticize if not celebrate the lawbreaker.

Founding figures in this "radical" movement were Edwin Lemert (1951, 1967), Howard Becker ([1963] 1973), and Erving Goffman (1961); major contributions also came from Lofland (1969), Schur (1965), Mankoff (1971), and J. Young (1971). Space precludes an extensive coverage, but a good understanding of the central ideas of the perspective can be gained by examining the ideas of the early theorists.

Lemert's Primary and Secondary Deviance

Edwin M. Lemert (1951, 1967) argued that crime begins not with the activities of the rule breaker but with the social audience that passes laws banning certain behavior as immoral or criminal. Indeed, he maintained that rather than deviance leading to social control, "social control leads to deviance" (1967, v). For example, skateboarders have been singled out by the government as being an undesirable element. Many youth have bumper stickers stating that "skateboarding is not a crime."

Clearly, in the view of the participants a nonharmful recreational activity should not be criminalized.

Orlando, Florida, "the city beautiful," is a tourist mecca. Recently, the city government has become concerned with the image that its many homeless persons present. The homeless do not fit the Disney image. Consequently, many new ordinances have been passed aimed at correcting this "problem." No longer can one lie on a park bench or splash water on their face from a fountain. You cannot even stand still in certain places. Lemert called spontaneous and sporadic minor rule violations primary deviance. Primary deviance may stem from many different sources. In 2008 a student visiting the independently run Aztec Shops on San Diego State University's campus purchased a bagel but left the store without paying for the cream cheese. She was immediately detained by store detectives, placed in handcuffs, and led away by police. Starbucks, also on campus, does not charge extra for cream cheese but includes it with its bagel. San Diego also recently passed ordinances banning alcohol consumption on its beaches. Clearly, minor rule-breaking behavior is easy for anyone to do, and many of us do it, from speeding to drinking and driving to smoking in public places, which in several states, such as Illinois, is now also illegal and punishable by fines. Everyone engages in forms of primary deviance, and alone it has little consequence for a person's social identity, provided that the person has a strong self-image. For example, employees who steal office equipment, use the telephone for personal calls, or overclaim expenses rarely think of themselves as "employee thieves," or embezzlers. Importantly, primary deviance "has only minor consequences for a person's status, social relationships, or subsequent behavior. Primary deviance tends to be situational, transient and idiosyncratic" (Matsueda 2001, 225).

Secondary deviance, in contrast, refers to behavior that results after a person's primary deviance is reacted to by authorities, particularly social control agents of the criminal justice system. Secondary deviance is rule-breaking behavior that emerges from a person's social identity. This occurs partly as a result of having to deal with others' labeling and partly because of who the person has become as a result of the social reaction to the primary deviance. This reaction produces stigmatization. "Secondary deviance . . . is explicitly a response to societal reactions to deviance and has major consequences for a person's status, relationships and future behavior. Secondary deviance occurs when society's response to initial deviance (e.g. stigmatization, punishment, segregation) causes fundamental changes in the person's social roles, self-identity, and personality, resulting in additional deviant acts" (ibid.).

Those who are uncertain of their identity as a result of a weak self-image are vulnerable to what others think of them. Many of the homeless described above would fit into this category, as do the high school "geeks" so heavily criticized by those around them for being different. Repeated forceful negative definition of these people's identity can raise serious questions for them about who they are and can eventually result in "identity transformation" through self-labeling. They come to see themselves as a deviant type and engage in subsequent deviance *because* of the stigmatized deviants they have become. They sometimes join groups of similarly labeled deviants (e.g., the "Trenchcoat Mafia"), forming a deviant or criminal subculture in which the members provide support for each other. Some gay and lesbian groups, some juvenile gangs, groups of drug abusers, and prostitute collectives may be formed through such a process. In such subcultures, members normalize each other's behavior through role adjustments (Becker [1963] 1973; Sagarin 1969). In some cases, through a process of delabeling and relabeling, group associations may result in the abandonment of the original deviant behavior—although not the problem created by the stigma, as in the case of alcoholics and narcotics users, or the obese (Trice and Roman 1970; D. Robinson and Henry 1977; Pfuhl and Henry 1993).

Becker's Interactionist Theory: Social Reaction and Master Status

Howard S. Becker was a student of the interactionist Herbert Blumer and of Ernest Burgess and Everett Hughes at the University of Chicago. Becker began participant observation studies (living in the daily lives of the group being studied) in graduate school by keeping a diary on barroom musicians at the Chicago tavern where he played jazz piano (Martin, Mutchnick, and Austin 1990, 350; Debro 1970, 159). His major book on deviance, *Outsiders* ([1963] 1973), was begun in 1954, just after Lemert's early works were written, but without knowledge of them (Debro 1970, 165). Becker combined a theoretical analysis with the early case studies of musicians and marijuana users. He found that the effects of an activity were a consequence of how a person interprets his or her experience. Although this work has become a classic in the field (*Outsiders* is the top-selling book on crime and delinquency by a sociologist, selling more than 100,000 copies; see Gans 1997), Becker himself admits to being only marginally involved in the study of deviance and then just as a diversion from his studies of occupations, education, and, more recently, the social organization of art (Debro 1970, 167).

Becker, like Lemert, shifted the causality of rule breaking from the actor to the audience, arguing that "deviance is not a quality of the act a person commits but rather a consequence of the application by others of rules and sanctions to an 'offender.'" He suggested that rule breaking is the outcome of a three-stage process: Social groups create deviance by (1) "making the rules whose infraction constitutes deviance," (2) "applying those rules to particular people," and (3) "labeling them outsiders." The deviant actor is the product of this process, "one to whom that label has been successfully applied; deviant behavior is behavior that people so label" ([1963] 1973, 9).

The first stage of Becker's labeling process may involve actors engaging in behavior that an audience finds offensive, such as drug use, but it need not. Some people, such as minority youths, for example, may be arrested on suspicion by police for minor rule-breaking behaviors such as "loitering" or DWB (Driving While Black). What is crucial is that the audience selects a behavior that it defines as offensive. As we saw in Chapter 2 on defining crime, this can be a very arbitrary decision and shows considerable variation culturally and historically. Importantly, Becker recognized that what becomes defined as deviant behavior and what may be criminalized depend on who has the power and whose interests they represent.

Becker coined the term *moral entrepreneur* to refer to those with more power to shape the law with their own ideas of what is offensive. This is one reason the offenses of adolescents become labeled delinquency, whereas the offenses of corporations and governments more often remain violations of administrative regulations.

The second stage in the deviance process—in which control agents select people whose behavior is offensive and label their behavior—also depends on power. The process involves identifying some people's behavior as different, negatively evaluating it as offensive, finding the appropriate offense category, and supplying an interpretation of why the person's behavior is an example of that category. As Becker said in an early interview, "The whole point of the interactionist approach to deviance is to make it clear that somebody had to do the labeling. It didn't just happen. . . . The court labeled him or his parents labeled him or the people in the community" (Debro 1970, 177).

In the third stage, the contested definition over the meaning of the signified behavior depends on who has the greater power to influence the labeling process and whether an accused has the power to resist the application of a deviance label. Young, lower-class, urban minority offenders typically do not have the resources for resistance. In contrast, middle- and upper-class offenders are typically able to redefine their activities as acceptable. Chambliss (1973), for example, found that although middle-class adolescents engage in similar delinquent activities as their lower-class counterparts, they are able to do so in greater secrecy and even when caught are protected because of their demeanor and family or community connections.

Once successfully labeled, a person is subject to the negative effects of the label itself, which provides what Becker called a "master" status. Being caught and publicly labeled as an offender "has important consequences for one's further social participation and self-image" (Becker [1963] 1973, 31). The status of "deviant" highlights certain characteristics of the person as central to his or her identity while diminishing others. This interaction with others, wrote Becker, produces a "self-fulfilling prophecy" that "sets in motion several mechanisms which conspire to shape the person in the image people have of him [or her]" (ibid., 34). Part of this process involves closing off legitimate forms of activity, which restricts the opportunities for the labeled offender to behave differently. The label also leads others to engage in retrospective interpretation.

Retrospective interpretation occurs when a review of a person's past activity highlights previous instances that can be reinterpreted as consistent with the new deviant master status. Such actions further lead to a new narrow focus by the audience, now with heightened sensitivity toward the labeled individual. This, in turn, results in more deviance being discovered. Wilkins (1965) and J. Young (1971) described this as "deviancy amplification," since it leads to even more secrecy and interaction with similarly defined others. Deviancy amplification may eventually result in an individual accepting the label, adopting a deviant or criminal career, and joining an organized deviant group (Becker [1963] 1973, 37).

For Becker, then, the central issue was not the normal rule breaking that everyone sometimes engages in as part of human freedom and curiosity. Rather, it was others' transforming that activity into a negative, restricted force that results in new and additional offenses. In clarifying his account, Becker ([1963] 1973) argued that the secret deviant, who on the surface seems to contradict his idea that deviance does not exist until it is labeled (J. Gibbs 1966), actually refers to evolving definitions of behavior. Becker noted that at one point in time the powerful do not provide the procedures for determining a behavior's standing, yet at a subsequent time they do.

If Lemert's and Becker's work sensitized us to the power of the definition process, Erving Goffman led us to the force of stigma and spoiled identities that can result from institutionalization.

Goffman's Stigma and Total Institutions

Erving Goffman (1922–1983) was a sociologist in the interactionist tradition of George Herbert Mead. He used his fieldwork on a Scottish island community to write his doctorate at the University of Chicago, where he was a fellow student of Howard Becker (Martin, Mutchnick, and Austin 1990). Although most of his work described and analyzed everyday, face-to-face interaction in a variety of noncriminological settings, his work on stigma and on mental hospital institutionalization has direct relevance to criminological discussions of labeling theory. Goffman used the metaphor of drama: The world is a stage, and we are all players bringing off performances and demonstrating our strategic gamesmanship to the audience. His book *Stigma* (1963) distinguishes between the physical, moral, and racial forms of stigma, each of which is based on identified differences that others negatively evaluate and construct into "spoiled identities." The person with disabilities or suffering schizophrenia would be an example of a spoiled identity. Through interactive situations, individuals classify others into categories, some of which may be stigmatized ones. Once people are classified, we treat them as a spoiled or "virtual" identity rather than as who they actually are. For example, those with physical or mental disabilities are seen as blemished and treated as though they have numerous other deficits—and as less than human. Similarly, those racially or ethnically different from a dominant group are typically treated as deficient and inferior. Consider our discussion in Chapter 3 of immigrants to the United States from Europe around 1900 and how they were seen as paupers and degenerates. Finally, those whose behavior may indicate a character flaw, such as criminal offenders, are treated as morally bankrupt, dishonest, evil, and so forth. As a consequence of this process, the stigmatized are uncomfortable with their classifiers, who they feel have unjustly exercised social and political power to deny them their full humanity.

Applied to inmates of mental hospitals or correctional settings, it is clear that the stigma process reduces the ability of those stereotyped as "spoiled" to return to a mainstream or noncriminal life (Goffman 1961). Research conducted by Bernburg, Krohn, and Rivera (2006) found that stigma increased the probability of subjects' socializing with delinquent social groups. Furthermore, a study by Funk (2004) found that stigmatization increases recidivism. The result may be an effort by the stigmatized to conceal their physical and socially constructed defects by constructing a "front" in order to pass as "normal," that is, as persons appearing to have no defects. For example, consider men who abuse their wives in the privacy of their home who in public appear to others as perfectly charming.

Goffman's notion of "total institutions," which was formulated in his study of a mental hospital, *Asylums* (1961), has had considerable impact on labeling theory generally and especially on understanding the way prisons dehumanize the inmate. A total institution is a place where similarly classified people are forced to live, work, and play together around activities consistent with the goals of the institution. This takes place under formal supervisory control governed by strict rules and procedures and within a restricted environment. The inmates in total institutions are separated formally and socially from the staff and have no input into decision making about their activities or outcomes. According to Goffman, this process is designed to force inmates to fit the institutional routine. When continued over time, the process results in inmates' dehumanization and humiliation. As a result of the adaptive behaviors inmates have to adopt in order to cope, the inmates' behavioral patterns become solidified. This changes their moral career and renders them unfit for a return to life outside the institution (ibid., 13). Goffman argued this results in a "mortification" of the self. How permanent such identity change is has been subject to controversy, but there is no question that Goffman's work added considerably to our understanding of the impact of social and institutional effects on the labeling process.

Particularly important, in light of the theories discussed in this and the previous chapter, is that labeling demonstrates the dangers inherent in attempts to intervene to change people. This is most pronounced when punitive interventions are falsely presented as reform programs that suggest a "spoiled identity."

Braithwaite's Reintegrative Shaming

John Braithwaite is an Australian criminologist whose earlier studies were on white-collar crime in the pharmaceutical industry. He is one of the most recent contributors to the labeling perspective, agreeing that the kind of stigmatization Goffman described is certainly destructive. In his book *Crime, Shame, and Reintegration* (1989), Braithwaite defined this negative stigmatization as disintegrative shaming and argued that it is destructive of social identities because it morally condemns people and reduces their liberty yet makes no attempt to resolve the problem by reconnecting the accused or convicted with the community. Braithwaite described a second, positive, kind of stigmatization, which he called reintegrative shaming. This is actually constructive and can serve to reduce and prevent crime. Reintegrative shaming, while expressing social disapproval, also provides the social process mechanisms to bring those censured back into the community, reaffirming that they are morally good—only a part of their total behavior is unacceptable. Braithwaite believed this explains why numerous different communitarian societies that use a positive reintegrative form of shaming, such as Japan, have low crime rates, whereas those that use disintegrative shaming have high crime rates. In the latter cases, offenders are cut off from the mainstream society and are free from informal controls to recidivate. A number of studies have found some support for Braithwaite's theory and the detrimental effects of stigmatization (Losoncz and Tyson 2007; Murphy and Harris 2007).

Although labeling processes are a major component of Braithwaite's analysis, several commentators (Akers 1994; Gibbons 1994; Einstadter and Henry 2006) see his ideas as an integrated theory linking several of the social process theories we have discussed in this and the previous chapters (learning, control, differential association, and labeling) with those we shall discuss in the next two (cultural, subcultural, and strain). We shall briefly return to these again in Chapter 11.

Matsueda's Informal Negative Labeling and Differential Social Control

Ross Matsueda (1992, 2001) and colleague Karen Heimer (Heimer and Matsueda 1994) have recently developed labeling theory to explain not only secondary deviance but also primary deviance, which for a long time was argued to be one of the weaknesses of labeling theory. This is based on their interactionist view of the social self: "The self arises through role-taking, the process of taking the role of the other, viewing one's self from the perspective of the other, and controlling one's behavior accordingly. . . . Moreover, because role-taking involves considering lines of action from the standpoint of reference groups, it follows that behavior is controlled by social groups. Self-control is actually social control" (Matsueda 2001, 224).

Matsueda (1992) argued that important parts of the labeling process occur through unofficial control agents such as parents, peers, and teachers. Matsueda's contribution suggests that the informal labeling process starts much earlier than the formal, and may continue in tandem with it. He asserted that because "the self is a reflection of appraisals made by significant others," such informal negative labeling "would influence future delinquency through the role-taking process." Heimer and Matsueda "expanded the role-taking process to include learned definitions of delinquency, anticipated reactions to delinquency, and delinquent peers" (1994, 366–368). They called this process "differential social control," arguing that it can result in a "conventional direction (e.g. when taking the role of conventional groups) or a criminal direction (e.g. when taking the role of criminal groups)" (Matsueda 2001, 235).

Policy Implications of Labeling Theory

Labeling theory has had a considerable impact on criminal justice policy, especially with regard to juveniles. It has even impacted popular culture through the use of person-preserving politically correct terms such as a *person with disabilities* as opposed to a *disabled person* and *visually challenged* rather than *blind* and *metabolically challenged* rather than *fat*.

With regard to criminal behavior, since the central tenet of labeling theory is that social reaction to minor rule breaking creates extra deviance and crime, the policy is clear. If repeated negative definition by official social control agencies transforms ambivalent social identities into criminal ones, the policy must involve reducing social reaction. This will minimize the production of secondary (or extra) rule breaking and, in particular, prevent minor rule breakers from entering criminal careers. Edwin Schur (1973) defined this overall approach as "radical nonintervention." Einstadter and Henry summarized four policy components of this perspective identified in the literature: (1) decriminalization, (2) diversion, (3) decarceration, and (4) restitution or reparation (2006, 229–232).

Decriminalization is the legalization of crimes involving consent, which, as we saw in Chapter 2, are also called victimless crimes (Schur 1965) and include activities such as drug use, homosexuality, gambling, and prostitution. Not only is banning these activities morally questionable (Duster 1970), but their illegality in the face of a wide public demand for them provides a basis for organized crime, gang activity, police corruption, and bribery, together with the accompanying violence necessary for "market" protection (Schur and Bedau 1974; Curran and Renzetti 1994).

Diversion is a policy that redirects those engaged in minor law violations, especially status offenses such as truancy, runaways, and curfew violation, away from the courts through informal processes leading to noncorrectional settings. The approach is credited with being responsible for the existence of the parallel system of juvenile justice, separate from and less formal than the criminal justice system for adult offenders. Juvenile justice is designed to be less stigmatizing. It involves settlement-directed talking, such as conflict resolution, mediation, and problem solving, rather than punishment.

Decarceration attempts to deal with the stigma effects of total institutions by minimizing their use and letting numerous people, such as those convicted of substance abuse offenses, out on alternatives such as probation or electronic tethers. Instead of calling for more prisons, this strategy involves stopping prison building and stopping the sentencing of offenders to prison terms for nonviolent offenses. In particular, juveniles in institutions such as reform schools and training schools were deinstitutionalized into community-based programs (Akers 1994, 131–132).

Restitution and reparation are designed to make the offender responsible for the crime by repaying or compensating either the victim (restitution) or the community or society (reparation) for the harm done. This can involve working to pay back the offender or forms of community service.

Finally, the policy implications of Braithwaite's analysis of reintegrative shaming (1989) involve providing both public exposure of harmful behavior and informal rehabilitation programs designed to bring the accused back as acceptable members of society. Like programs for the recovering alcoholic, these programs can be used as an example of how problems can be worked through. Braithwaite (1995) described this as a move toward new forms of "communitarianism" that is both a social movement and family focused. Finally, his ideas are consistent with the notion of "restorative justice," which involves bringing together offenders and victims in mediation programs designed to reintegrate both back into the community and allow both a participative role in determining the appropriate level of restitution or reparation. Restorative justice will be discussed further in the policy section of the next chapter since it is an emerging policy for how communities are coping with juvenile crime.

In many ways, the policy implications of labeling theory are very radical and are not acceptable to most Americans, who have been fed a media diet of punishment and the quick fix ("Three strikes and you're out") from politicians. As a result, the practice of such measures as stopping prison building is confronted with the reality of massive prison-building programs. Mandatory prison sentences for first-time drug dealers, however, such as college students occasionally selling cocaine to friends and then getting eight years in prison, with all that involves for their potential identity, suggest that labeling theorists may have a point, especially in the case of some kinds of offenders.

Evaluation of Labeling Theory

Labeling theory, with its commonsense truth of a "self-fulfilling prophecy," has been subject to much controversy, not least from its seemingly outrageous basic suggestion that attempts to control crime can actually make it worse. The first major criticism was that the theory does not explain why people engage in primary deviance and why some people engage in more of it than others (Gibbs 1966). Second, if deviance is only a product of public labeling, why do some, such as white-collar offenders, employee thieves, embezzlers, and so on, and some violent offenders, such as abusive husbands, engage in careers of crime without ever having been publicly labeled (Mankoff 1971)? One study found that the label applied by parents was strongly related to conceptions of delinquency, a factor that may explain more than the "official" labels that are applied. A study conducted by Johnson, Simons, and Conger (2004) found that although labeling may be one determining factor in deviance, the type of social reaction involved was also critical. Moreover, if the effects of labeling are so strong on vulnerable identities that such persons become locked into criminal careers, how do some reform? The question ultimately raised is, How resilient is the label, and is it only a coping strategy for the institutionalized?

Some critics even contest that control agents are arbitrary in their selection of offenders (Akers 1968; Wellford 1975). One researcher (Jensen 1972a, 1972b, 1980) found that the label applied differentially affects youths based on race or ethnicity.

Whites accept the labeling consequences of official sanctions more than African Americans. Moreover, in a study of probationers in Texas, Schneider and McKim (2003) found that although probationers were stigmatized by others, this did not lead to self-stigmatization.

Finally, why does labeling theory tend to focus largely on the agencies of social control and on certain labeled groups—"the nuts, sluts and perverts" (Liazos 1972)—but ignore the wider structure of society and the power of the state and corporate interests in shaping the public policy of the agencies that enforce the labeling (I. Taylor, Walton, and Young 1973; J. Young 1981)? All these questions and more are not helped by the empirical evidence largely failing to offer support for the theory, although some question the validity of these studies (Plummer 1979; Paternoster and Iovanni 1989).

A major feature of this research is the relative lack of support for the notion that being labeled produces a negative self-image among those labeled (Shoemaker 1996). As a result, as one of its founding critics observes, it became far less dominant in the 1970s, has little to distinguish it, has lost its influence, and "no longer generates the interest, enthusiasm, research and acceptance it once did as a dominant paradigm two or three decades ago" (Akers 1994, 137). However, in the past ten years the work of Ross Matsueda has created renewed interest in the theory.

Summary and Conclusion

In this chapter, we have looked at two social process theories that present a mirror image of the two we examined in the previous chapter. Social control theory rejects the neutralization idea that interactive communications may release us from the moral bind of law and instead suggests that more important is the fact that bonds form in the first place. Failure to bond to convention and ineffective socialization practices produce low self-control and allow deviance to go unchecked. For control theorists, particularly self-control theorists, if children are not socialized into thinking about the long-term consequences of their behavior, they will not develop self-control and will exhibit impulsive behavior. The key for self-control theorists is for parents to identify and call attention to the unacceptability of deviant conduct by punishing the consequences of that behavior as soon as it appears. But for labeling theorists, the very fear of the diversity of human behavior may lead to social processes of control that limit the assumed creativity of human lives, bringing about and sustaining careers focused on the very acts the controllers wish to prevent. Thus, for labeling, learning the wrong values is not the issue, nor is bonding to convention or being released from it. For labeling theorists, the issue is how difference is reacted to; how deviants are rejected and labeled is most devastating to their future sense of self, leading them to acquire deviant identities.

Although all these social process theories sensitize us to the importance of adequate socialization and symbolic interaction, they disagree about what is helpful and what is not. Moreover, they do not offer an understanding of the wider cultural and structural forces that shape the contexts in which these social relations take place. It is toward these theories that we turn in the next chapter.

Summary Chart: Control Theory and Labeling Theory

1. Control Theory

Basic Idea: Explains why we do not all commit crime; claims we do if the controls never form or are worn away.

Human Nature: Humans are seen as rationally calculating, self-interested, and selfish actors (as in classical theory) whose behavior is limited by connections and bonds to others who are significant reference groups for them. People learn the consequences of their behavior and develop greater or less self-control

Society and the Social Order: Consensus. Law is an expression of the rules of the conventional society. Criminals are those for whom bonds of caring for others never formed or are removed. We are all potential criminals.

Causal Logic: Crime is the result of a failure of people to be socialized into a bond with society and develop a stake in conformity. Social bonding consists of four elements: (1) attachment to teachers, parents, friends, and others and the desire not to lose them or hurt them; (2) commitment to conventional behavior, with a willingness to do what one has expressed in trust; (3) involvement in conventional activities, especially school related; and (4) belief in the need to obey conventional rules and in the institutions of society. Children who do not develop an awareness and concern about the consequences of their actions lack self-control and will act impulsively.

Criminal Justice Policy: Ensure an adequate level of bonding between youths and conventional society through intensive socialization in traditional and conventional values. Ensure adequate parental socialization of children through (1) monitoring their behavior, (2) recognizing deviance, and (3) ensuring there are consequences when the behavior departs from norms.

Criminal Justice Practice: Prevention and rehabilitation through increased bonding. Strengthened families and increased commitment to conventional occupations by work-training schemes. Reinforced participation in conventional activities at school, and through more effective parenting to instill self-control. Schools can also assist in this process, but generally if the lack of self-control persists, the criminal justice system is too late to make changes.

Evaluation: Explains crime by all social classes. Has been empirically tested and has highest level of support of all theories of crime causation, but fails to explain differences in crime rates or whether a weakened bond can be strengthened. Does not distinguish relative importance of different elements of the bond; does not explain how those highly bonded to convention commit crime or how bonding can actually be used as leverage to coerce offenders who are committed to the high rewards of other jobs and will do anything to keep them; and does not explain ethnic and class influences on beliefs or school performance. Does not consider role of delinquent peers and subcultures in breaking bond; does not consider biological and psychological differences in generating impulsive behavior.

2. Labeling Theory

Basic Idea: As a result of negative labeling and stereotyping (especially by society's control agents), people can become criminal; crime, then, is a self-fulfilling prophecy rooted in the fear that people might be criminal.

Human Nature: Humans are malleable, pliable, plastic, and susceptible to identity transformations as a result of interactions with others and based on how others see them. Human behavior is not fixed in its meaning but open to interpretation and renegotiation. Humans have a social status and are inextricably social beings who are creative and free to interact with others but when they do so become subject to their controls.

Society and the Social Order: A plurality of groups dominated by the most powerful who use their power to stigmatize others less powerful. Law is the expression of the power of moral entrepreneurs and control agents to determine which behaviors are criminalized and which are not. Rules are made that impute ancillary qualities to the deviator. Conflict over legal and public definitions of crime and deviance. Crime is a status. "Criminal" is a socially constructed public stereotype or "master status" for those whom control agents identify as breaking the rules of those in power. We can all become criminals if we have the misfortune of becoming subject to processing by the criminal justice system.

Causal Logic: Social control agents cause crime by their dramatizing of it and by their excessive reaction to people's expression of individuality. Powerful groups ban behavior and then selectively enforce the ban through control agents, such as the police, psychiatrists, social workers, and so on. Some people's banned behavior is seen as significant, reacted to, and made subject to official agency processing. Lemert distinguished between primary and secondary rule breaking, or deviance. Primary deviance is the incidental and occasional rule breaking that we all do; selective application of rules to some offenders produces stigma, which Goffman described as a spoiled identity and a master status; this results in a deviant and negative self-image. Others engage in "retrospective interpretation," perceiving the actor as having always been deviant and reinterpreting past behavior for "signs" and "cues" of current status. Attempts at stereotypical designation may initially be negotiated or bargained over, as in psychiatric assessments or police discretion, but if the designation is pursued to formal processing, the result is individual role engulfment in a deviant career. Secondary deviance is the repeated rule breaking that comes from our believing that we are now the people that we have been labeled. "Deviancy amplification" comes from the expansion of deviant behavior as we now engage in other deviance in order to conceal our deviant identity and commit acts because we are not that person governed by this master status and committed to a criminal career. Parents and others exercise informal labeling that begins before formal labeling, which can have similar effects in the generation of secondary deviance.

Criminal Justice Policy: Social function of existing system is seen as moral degradation of offender's status; the alternative is to prevent the condemnation and degradation of the defendant by limiting social reaction through radical nonintervention. The perspective is critical of this process, of the shaming and social degrading of defendants as morally inferior, and of agents' control over the process. Preferred alternatives are (1) participant control over the process, (2) victim-offender interaction, (3) mediation and conciliation, and (4) action taken against defendants being influenced by their past relationships with others.

Criminal Justice Practice: Radical nonintervention, tolerance to replace moral indignation, and restitution, reparation, and rehabilitation. Minimalist approach: (1) decriminalize victimless crime; (2) diversion programs to avoid stigmatizing adolescents; (3) stop building prisons; (4) decarcerate prison population, especially nondangerous offenders; (5) develop alternative programs that allow offenders to be rehabilitated from the label; and (6) imprison only the most serious offenders.

Evaluation: Does not explain primary deviance, unless peer group and deviant group social control are incorporated; does not explain how in spite of labeling attempts, some never perceive self as stigmatized; does not explain perpetuity of the label (how long does it last?); does not spend enough time on the reasons for banning behavior in first place. Some policy implications are impractical. Overemphasizes relativity of rules and laws. Does not explain common-law crimes or differences between groups or individuals in the same stigmatized category.

8

Crimes of Place

Social Ecology and
Cultural Theories of Crime

Edward James Olmos's movies *The Family: Mi Familia* and *American Me* provide stirring documentaries of Hispanic gang life in California. In East Los Angeles, there have been Latino "gangs" for more than fifty years. These gangs are often generational in nature; current members typically have relatives who were members of the same gang in years past. The gangs have a strong affiliation with certain neighborhoods, staking out turf lines that coincide with neighborhood boundaries. To their members, the gangs serve several functions in the "hood." "The gang has practical and symbolic meaning for its members, fulfilling functions of protection, solidarity and, for some, becoming an alternative family" (Hagedorn 2004, 330). They preserve the ethnic quality and provide "rites of passage" for young males entering adulthood. In addition, they provide an alternative means of earning income in high-unemployment areas, a means to gain social respect, and, at least for older members, a feeling of being "protected and loved" (Knox, Harris et al. 1997).

Data gathered by the annual U.S. National Youth Gang Survey for 2006 reveal that nationwide there are an estimated 26,500 gangs containing 785,000 members; law enforcement agencies report gang problems are more prevalent in large cities (86 percent) compared with suburban communities (51 percent), smaller cities (33 percent), and rural counties (15 percent) (Egley and O'Donnell 2008). Studies of gangs in Los Angeles, New York, Washington, D.C., St. Louis, and Milwaukee show that gang members are variably involved in irregular employment in the drug economies of the area. Although drug sales are the most frequently reported informal economic activity of gangs (Huff 1998), "other research reveals mixed findings with regard to the role of the gang in drug sales. Research . . . suggests that the recreational use and sale of drugs may be part of gang-life, but that gang-related drug sales are not highly organized or entrepreneurial" (Henry and Nurge 2007, 90). Although they are the exception and perhaps growing, more organized and profitable gang-based drug structures can provide a significant source of income (Jankowski 1991; Decker and

Van Winkle 1996; Venkatesh 2000). These structures produce an income ranging from $300 to $3,700 per month in areas of cities that have little formal employment (Fagan 1991; MacCoun and Router 1992; Hagedorn 1998; Decker and Van Winkle 1996). The amount earned depends on the organizational sophistication of the gang and a member's rank in the gang hierarchy: "Higher level gangs which are more organizationally sophisticated . . . have formalized rules, often their own argot or gang language, and exist in different areas. These gangs have members who are youths and adults, but the top leaders are for the most part adults with long tenure in the gang" (Knox, Tromanhauser, et al. 1995).

But many male gang members desire to "mature out" into conventional U.S. lifestyles: They want to settle down in a conventional job, live with a wife and kids, and, most of all, leave the street life (Hagedorn 1994, 211). This is particularly the case for Latino gangs of the East Los Angeles barrios who value work, church, and family (J. Moore 1991). Indeed, Knox, Harris et al. (1997) report that 44.8 percent of gang members they interviewed have tried to quit gang life, and 79.6 percent would quit the gang if given a "second chance in life." For many of these members, gang identity is only one of multiple roles: "One can be a gang member, a father, a student, a breadwinner, American, Mexican and Catholic, all at once" (Hagedorn 2007b, 299).

In this chapter we seek to explain what it is that makes some geographical areas more prone to certain kinds of crime than other areas—why are certain cities, and certain areas of those cities, more prone to gang activity than other areas? Paul Bellair summarized this phenomenon, stating, "The concentration of crime within a small number of urban communities is an unfortunate, yet enduring, social fact" (2000, 137). A major explanation for this "social fact" is social ecology theory.

Social ecology theory seeks to explain why such patterns of criminal activity occur in specific geographical areas such as cities, and why they persist over time, even when the original members move out, mature into legitimate work, are incarcerated, or die. Criminologists, like Bellair, who examine the connection between crime and geographical space are known as social or human ecologists (from *oikos*, the Greek word for "household" or "living space"). Their criminology is based on the idea that the way plant and animal species colonize their environments can be applied to the way humans colonize geographical space. As a criminological theory, social ecology involves the study of "criminal" places. Certain neighborhoods, homes, and places remain crime problem areas for years, regardless of the particular people who live there. These places gain bad reputations, such as "Sin City," and are known as areas with high levels of street crime, such as robbery, drug dealing, and prostitution. People know better than to walk there alone at night, to park their car there, or to look lost or confused when passing through. Omitted from the commonsense and media accounts, however, are explanations of the economic and political forces that work to create and maintain these criminal areas.

In this chapter, we look at the main themes of social ecology as well as related cultural and subcultural theory, each of which contributes to our understanding of how crime becomes spatially concentrated. We also examine recent theoretical developments that take a more critical analysis of ecological driving forces. Importantly, we note that what began as a spatially specific societal phenomenon has now taken on a global dimension, as the structural forces of globalization—cultural forces conveyed through mass communication and national government policies, such as the U.S. government policy of deporting immigrants convicted of crimes, particularly gang crimes—have resulted in the export of the U.S. gang problem to cities in other nations (Vittori 2007; Hagedorn 2005, 2007a, 2007b, 2008; Flynn and Brotherton 2008). Finally, we note that through developments in the technology of mapping, particularly Geographical Information Systems (GIS), crime mapping and its analysis have made major advances in our understanding of the environmental context of crime (Paulsen and Robinson 2008).

The Historical Roots of Social Ecology Theory

Social ecology theory examines the movement of people and their concentration in specific locations. In Western nations, the most significant transformation of populations occurred when agricultural workers moved into the cities during eighteenth- and nineteenth-century industrialization (see Chapter 3 for further discussion on population migrations). This flow of people to the city and its tendency to be associated with areas of criminal activity were first described by nineteenth-century social reformers such as Henry Mayhew and Charles Booth, who provided rich descriptions of the criminal areas of London known as "rookeries" (Mayhew [1861] 1981). Belgian mathematician-astronomer Adolphe Quételet and French lawyer-statistician André Michel Guerry of the "cartographic school" were the first to gather quantitative data on the residential addresses of delinquents and show how they were associated with locality.

During the late nineteenth and early twentieth centuries, the U.S. economy, like that of Europe, was shifting from agriculture to industry, and consequently cities like Chicago were growing at a rapid and unprecedented rate. In the fifty-seven-year period from 1833 to 1890, Chicago grew from 4,100 residents to 1 million and just twenty years later had reached 2 million, largely fueled by waves of immigration from Europe, from the South, and from farmlands (Lilly, Cullen, and Ball 2002, 32, citing Palen 1981). Chicago faced exaggerated growth, social opportunities, and prosperity, but also mushrooming poverty and social problems. These changes, coupled with the presence of the first U.S. sociology department (established in 1892 at the University of Chicago), led to Chicago becoming a natural laboratory for sociological research in what became known as the "Chicago School." (James Short [2002], a sociologist from the University of Chicago, has described the department and many of its members, themes, and contributions.) Chicago sociologists gathered both statistical and qualitative data that seemed to demonstrate that crime was a "social product" of urbanism. This shifted the theoretical focus from an emphasis on individual pathology (biological and psychological differences) as the cause of crime, which had been dominant in the late eighteenth and early nineteenth centuries, to social pathology: the social, cultural, and structural forces accompanying the massive social changes taking place. We discuss the Chicago School's contribution in more detail later, but before doing so it will be helpful to examine the core themes and assumptions that characterize the overall position of social ecology in explaining "crimes of place."

Common Themes and Assumptions

Social ecologists see humans as social beings, shaped by their interdependence on each other, their dependence on the resources of their environment, and the functions that they perform for the system within their localized communities. Indeed, the central hypothesis of social ecologists is that human organization "arises from the interaction of the population and the environment" (Hawley 1968, 330). Within these constraints, humans make rational choices, but their choices are "environmentally structured" (Einstadter and Henry 2006, 131).

Social ecology holds both a conflict and a consensus view of the social order. Individuals make up community and neighborhood units competing with each other for scarce resources. This results in conflict. Yet these different units also exist in a symbiotic balance with each other and with the society as a whole. Nowhere is this more evident than in the notion of a dominant or "mainstream" culture, implying a consensual U.S. culture containing a diversity of ethnic subcultures. Humans conform to their own groups and subcultures as these form in certain areas, yet they also conform to the U.S. cultural identity in terms of ideology and law.

Early social ecologists believed that the driving forces of social change that brought together different groups in the cities would subside and that the dominant or mainstream culture would absorb the diversity of differences. The failure of this to happen and the permanence, rather than transience, of criminal areas led to later revisions in the theory to account for this tendency.

Sociologist Rodney Stark has provided a helpful summary of the main themes of social ecology in answer to his fundamental question: "How is it that neighborhoods can remain the site of high crime and deviance rates despite a complete turnover of their populations?" He believed that "there must be something about *places* as such that sustain crime" (1987, 893; emphasis in the original). Concentrations of population, argued Stark, result in increased population density, which brings together people from different backgrounds. This coming together increases the level of moral cynicism in a community, as what previously were private conflicts become public knowledge and poor role models become highly visible. Dense neighborhoods have crowded homes, resulting in a greater tendency for people to congregate in the street and in other public places, which raises the opportunities for crime. Crowding also lowers the level of child supervision, which in turn produces poor school achievement and a reduced commitment to school and increases the tendency for conflict within the family, which further weakens children's commitment to conformity. High-density neighborhoods also tend to mix commercial and residential properties, with the former threatening to take over the latter.

Sampson and Wilson (1993; W. Wilson 1996) showed that changes in economic patterns produce inequality and an "underclass" of the poor. The more successful move out to the suburbs, leaving the least able concentrated and isolated in the inner city, where they increasingly fail to achieve common values (what Kornhauser [1978] referred to as "attenuated culture") and may develop values oppositional to those of mainstream culture (E. Anderson 1999).

Mixed-use neighborhoods that evolve, unlike those planned for gentrification, increase the opportunities for those congregating on the street to commit crime. Such neighborhoods, partly because of the commercial property ownership and partly because of the creation by residential property owners of cheap, run-down, dilapidated rental property, have high transient populations, which in turn further weakens family attachments in the community, undermines informal and formal controls, and reduces levels of surveillance. This produces neighborhoods that people want to leave—neighborhoods further stigmatized by visibly high rates of crime and deviance. Further reductions in residents' commitment to their neighborhood come when the most successful flee and conventional and successful role models fail to replace them. As Bursik and Grasmick have argued, not only are there isolation and a lack of integration and organization, but crime becomes "an alternative means of gaining economic and social sustenance from the environment" (1993b, 266), an observation first made by human ecologist Amos Hawley (1950). This results in a concentration of those who have failed to leave becoming demoralized and more vulnerable as victims. As formal policing gives up on the defeated neighborhood, moral cynicism further increases, together with crime and deviance, which draws in more people who are looking to participate in crime. The outcome is even more crime, with consequences including higher levels of fear, criminal victimization, and involvement of family members with the criminal justice system. All of these developments normalize crime as part of everyday life, as a visible and "normal" way of succeeding in the inner city (Stark 1987; R. Taylor 2001).

For Wesley Skogan (1986), a similar pattern can begin from a series of fear-driven events that cause people to withdraw from community life, in turn weakening informal social controls. Fear also produces a reduction in organizational life and business activity.

Three major dimensions left undeveloped in early social ecology theory but taken up in recent theorizing are as follows: (1) the political economic forces that cause populations to concentrate in the first place, (2) the dynamics of these forces within a neighborhood, and (3) how these forces impact the systemic relationships among neighborhood networks, extracommunity networks, and social control. We discuss these issues later in this chapter. First, we review the contribution of the Chicago School researchers who developed what has been described as "one of the most ambitious data collection projects ever attempted in the United States," and whose "key innovative aspect . . . was the interpretation of the spatial patterns within the context of human ecology and social disorganization theoretical frameworks" (Bursik and Grasmick 1995, 108).

The Chicago School

Robert Park, a newspaper reporter who became a sociologist and chair of the University of Chicago's Department of Sociology, made some important initial observations. First, he deduced that like any ecological system, a city does not develop randomly. Park (Park and Burgess 1920; Park 1926; Park, Burgess, and McKenzie 1925) believed that the distribution of plant and animal life in nature could provide important insights for understanding the organization of human societies. Just like plant and animal colonies, a city grows according to basic social processes such as invasion, dominance, and accommodation. These produce a "biotic order" within which exist competing "moral orders." Park and his colleagues' second major contribution was the argument that social processes could best be understood through careful, scientific study of city life. Park's students and contemporaries built on these two themes and developed the very influential Chicago School.

Among Park's most important followers were Clifford R. Shaw and Henry D. McKay, two researchers employed by a child guidance clinic in Chicago. Shaw and McKay ([1942] 1969) used an analytical framework developed by Ernest Burgess (a colleague of Park's) to research the social causes of crime. This framework is known as "Concentric Zone Theory." Burgess (1925) used five concentric zones, each two miles wide (see figure 8.1), to describe the patterns of social development in Chicago. He argued that city growth was generated by the pressure from the city center to expand outward. Expansion threatened to encroach on the surrounding areas and did so in concentric waves, or circles, with the center being the most intense, having the highest density and highest occupancy. These concentrations become progressively less intense and of lower density with greater distance from the center.

At the heart of a city was Zone One, composed of the central business district (in Chicago this was known as the "Loop" because it was where the commuter trains turned around). This was a commercial area that had valuable transportation resources (water and railways). Zone Two was a transitional zone, because it was an area of previously desirable residences threatened by invasion from the central business district and industrial growth. The residences, which were already deteriorating, were allowed to further erode by slum landlords who were waiting to profit from increased land values. They did not want to invest money in repairing their properties, however, and so were able to attract only low-income renters, those least able to afford a place to live. These were typically newly arrived immigrants and African Americans from the rural South, who found it convenient to live close to factories in the hope of obtaining work. This zone was an area of highly transient people, and those who were able to move up and out to more desirable homes did so. Zone Three was made up of workers' homes. Most of these people had "escaped" from Zone Two and were second- and third-generation immigrants. Zone Four was a

FIGURE 8.1   Concentric Zone Theory

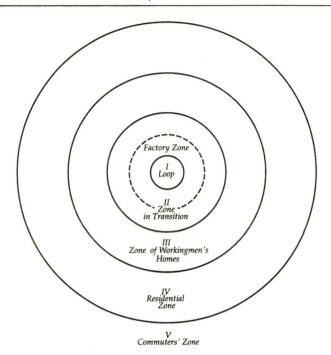

SOURCE: Burgess 1925, p. 51.

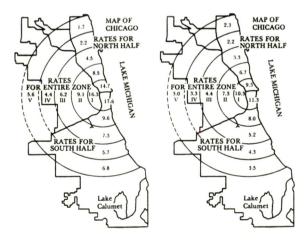

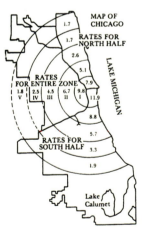

| Zone rates of male juvenile delinquents, 1900–1906 series | Zone rates of male juvenile delinquents, 1917–1923 series | Zone rates of male juvenile delinquents, 1927–1933 series |

SOURCE: Shaw and McKay [1942] 1969, p. 69.

residential suburban area of more expensive homes, condominiums, and apartments. Zone Five contained the highest-priced residences and was called the commuter zone. This zone contained single-family dwellings and was most desirable because of its distance from the hustle of downtown, pollution from factories, and the poor. The most influential white middle- and upper-income residents lived here and were imbued with the dominant mainstream culture and values.

According to social ecology theory, these concentric zones were based on patterns of invasion and dominance common in plant life. Within each zone or circle were specific defined areas, or natural neighborhoods, each with its own social and ethnic identity: African American, German, Irish, Italian, Polish, Chinese, and so on. How could this ecological analogy explain crime?

In nature, order is found to be stable in settled zones and unstable in transitional areas where rapid changes to the ecostructure take place. Applying this observation to the social ecology of the city, Shaw and McKay's primary hypothesis ([1942] 1969) was that Zone Two, the transitional zone, would contain higher levels of crime and other social problems such as drug abuse and alcoholism, suicide, tuberculosis, infant mortality, and mental illness. This would be the case regardless of which racial or ethnic group occupied the area, independent of its economic impoverishment, and primarily because of its level of "social disorganization."

Social Disorganization

Social disorganization was a concept first developed by W. I. Thomas and Florian Znaniecki to explain the breakdown of community among second-generation Polish immigrants to Chicago. They defined it as the "decrease of the influence of existing social rules of behavior on individual members of the group" (1920, 1128). More generally, social disorganization refers to a situation in which there is little or no community feeling, relationships are transitory, levels of community surveillance are low, institutions of informal control are weak, and social organizations are ineffective. Unlike an organized community, where social solidarity, neighborhood cooperation, and harmonious action work to solve common problems, socially disorganized neighborhoods have several competing and conflicting moral values. Immigrant children in these areas can become increasingly alienated from their parents' ethnic culture as they adapt more rapidly to aspects of the dominant culture, which in turn weakens parental control over the children. A further problem associated with social disorganization is the conflict in these impoverished areas between various ethnic groups over scarce resources. Finally, delinquency patterns themselves become a competing lifestyle as a means of surviving and as a way of obtaining income, intimacy, and honor. This makes it an area ripe for the formation of gangs.

Frederic M. Thrasher (1927), another Chicago School sociologist, demonstrated in his classic study *The Gang* that gang membership provides a substitute for the disorganized and fragmented community, one that develops its own values and traditions of loyalty and support for fellow gang members. Once formed, these gangs are self-sustaining as a source of "conduct, speech, gestures, and attitudes." It is from existing gang members that a child "learns the techniques of stealing, becomes involved in binding relationships with his companions in delinquency, and acquires the attitudes appropriate to his position as a member of such groups" (Shaw and McKay [1942] 1969, 436).

Given Edwin Sutherland's presence at the University of Chicago during this period, it is not surprising that there are parallels between this gang research, pointing to the "cultural transmission" of criminal behavior patterns, and Sutherland's differential association theory ([1939] 1947, discussed in Chapter 6). In short, the argument is that the environment provides the context not only for the cultural transmission of criminal behavior patterns but also for the failure to transmit the necessary socialization that results in conventional behavioral patterns (the central point of control theory, discussed in Chapter 7). Social disorganization within certain areas of a city creates the conditions for crime to flourish, independent of the individuals who live there or their ethnic characteristics. The lack of community integration and social control together with the presence of contradictory standards and values allow residents the freedom to choose crime (Walker 1994). We will return to the ways this impacts the creation and maintenance of gangs later in the chapter.

Shaw and McKay's Landmark Research

To test their hypotheses, Shaw and McKay (1931, [1942] 1969) examined 56,000 official court records from 1900 to 1933 and created "spot maps" based on 140 square-mile areas (see figure 8.1). On these maps, they located the residences of juveniles (aged ten to sixteen) who were involved in various stages of criminal justice adjudication. They then created other maps, or overlays, that showed community factors such as demolished buildings and the incidence of tuberculosis and vagrancy. Rate maps were then constructed indicating the rate of male delinquency for each zone. The final step was to create zone maps. These confirmed that community problems were concentrated in the zone of transition, that is, Zone Two.

The results of Shaw and McKay's research showed that official crime rates were greatest in Zone Two (in the 1927–1933 series ranging from 7.9 to 11.9 percent), declining with distance outward from the city (being as low as 1.7 to 1.9 percent in Zone Five), and that the pattern persisted over forty years, no matter which ethnic group or nationality moved into the area during each new wave of immigration. Shaw and McKay also found that official delinquency rates varied within a zone. For example, Zone Three (working-class homes) varied between 2.6 percent on the North Lakeshore side of Chicago, but was nearly double at 5.7 percent on the South Side of the city. Indeed, subsequent research confirmed the same patterns in eighteen other cities (Shaw and McKay [1942] 1969) and over a period of sixty years has demonstrated that "official rates of delinquency decline with movement away from the inner city" (Shoemaker 1996, 80). Other evidence has also supported the Shaw and McKay analysis. For example, in a study of low-income youth, Fauth, Leventhal, and Brooks-Gunn (2005) found that overall, youth who relocated to middle-class neighborhoods experienced less crime and victimization. Moreover, Mustaine, Tewksbury, and Stengel (2006) concluded that registered sex offenders were often consigned to living in areas with higher levels of social disorganization. The results of a number of studies have also been consistent with social disorganization theory (Appiahene-Gyamfi 2007; Zhang, Messner, and Liu 2007).

As some commentators have observed, the fact that delinquency areas persisted after the immigration waves of the 1930s subsided eventually caused Shaw and McKay to change their explanation of delinquency. They subsequently emphasized the importance of economic pressure and the response to "strains experienced by economically deprived people in a society that encouraged all citizens to aspire to [monetary] success goals" (Gibbons 1994, 30; see also Finestone 1976). This anticipated Merton's strain theory, which we discuss in the next chapter. Nevertheless, the Chicago School's contribution was to move criminology away from individual pathology and personality traits and toward social pathology and the view that "crime and deviance were simply the normal responses of normal people to abnormal social conditions" (Akers 1994, 142).

Policy Implications of the Chicago School's Social Ecology

The policy implications associated with the Chicago School's social ecology theory are massive in nature and would require dramatic changes in economic structuring to be fully implemented. To their credit, members of the Chicago School, especially Clifford Shaw, applied their theories to reducing delinquency by attempting to strengthen the sense of community and increasing the levels of social organization in disorganized neighborhoods (Kobrin 1959).

In 1932, Shaw developed the Chicago Area Project (CAP) to assist with developing social organizations through involving neighborhood residents in setting up local groups and clubs for youths. Adults in the affected communities ran these groups (to prevent imposing a dominant alien middle-class culture), and through them the programs attempted to combat neighborhood disorganization in several ways. First, they organized recreational activities such as athletic and youth leagues and summer camps. Then they sought to reduce physical deterioration in the neighborhoods. CAP staff members also tried to help juveniles who came into conflict with the criminal justice system. Finally, they provided curbside counseling to troubled residents. The objective was to allow local residents to organize activities that would reduce crime at the local level.

The Chicago Area Project met with mixed success. The project was not subject to controlled empirical evaluation. Thus, scientific verification was impossible. Schlossman and his colleagues (1984) provided a comprehensive evaluation, however, which concluded that the project had been successful in reducing reported delinquency, although other evaluations of similar projects have found little success (W. Miller 1962).

Overall, a major limitation of Shaw and McKay's research was their unwillingness or inability to act on the economic and political realities of inner cities. Indeed, the very business owners who drove the engine of environmental deterioration themselves sat on the Chicago Area Project and contributed financially to it (Curran and Renzetti 1994, 141; Snodgrass 1976). Similarly, the "natural" areas of the city were actually planned for and governed by statutes and ordinances (Suttles 1972). This suggests that any ecological criminology has to account for the role of economic and political power in order to explain how the environment causes crime. What is needed—and to some extent has been provided by recent contributions to social ecology theory—is a political economy of urban ecology. As Shoemaker has observed, "The theory of social disorganization, as principally developed by Shaw and McKay, has merit in that it has pointed to social causes of delinquency that seem to be located in specific geographical areas. . . . The theory would appear to be generally accurate, but incomplete" (1996, 89). As we will see shortly, more recent developments in social ecology theory have come some way toward addressing this deficit.

Evaluation of the Chicago School's Social Ecology Theory

Despite the considerable impact that the Chicago School has had on criminology and on U.S. social policies (discussed later), there are several notable criticisms. For example, Alihan (1938) argued that the use of plant ecology was based on a series of false analogies that resulted in the fallacious error of using aggregate-level data to explain individual actions. This criticism questions the entire theoretical basis of the ecological theory of the Chicago School. Known as the ecological fallacy, this major defect involves making assumptions about individuals based on group characteristics. The Chicago School primarily relied on aggregate, group-level data to explain deviance.

Another major criticism is the Chicago School's failure to show that residents living in low-crime, desirable areas were more organized than their counterparts in high-crime areas (Kobrin 1971). However, subsequent research has offered support in this regard. Sampson and Groves (1989) in a study of 10,000 respondents to the British Crime Survey found that structural factors—such as low socioeconomic status, low levels of heterogeneity, high residential mobility, family disruption, and increased social disorganization—produced weakened friendship networks, low participation in community organizations, and unsupervised teens, and that crime rates were higher in such areas than in organized areas. The results of a number of other studies have also been consistent with social disorganization theory (Appiahene-Gyamfi 2007; Zhang, Messner, and Liu 2007).

The Chicago School's analysis has also been criticized on logical and methodological grounds. Kobrin (1971) pointed to the weakness of some of the data concerning the claims that a delinquent cultural tradition resulted from conflicting moralities. A related criticism is the tautological (circular) nature of Shaw and McKay's logic in which neighborhoods with a high rate of delinquency are the result of the existence of a tradition of delinquency (Bursik 1988).

A further methodological criticism leveled at Shaw and McKay is their reliance on official police and court records to document delinquency rates (Robison 1936). No account is taken of self-report data or victimization data. When these are included, the results can be different. For example, a self-report study by Johnstone (1978) revealed that most delinquency was found in Chicago among lower-class adolescents living in better-class neighborhoods rather than in the transitional areas. Furthermore, white-collar and corporate crimes conducted in corporate offices in the inner city or the residences of the outer zones were not included, begging the question of what kind of crime counts as real crime (Henry and Lanier 2001).

Shaw and McKay also argued that different racial and ethnic groups would experience similar rates of delinquency if subjected to the same physical environment. Yet contemporaneous research found that "Oriental" residents had lower rates of delinquency (Hayner 1933; Jonassen 1949). Conversely, and perhaps most important in terms of crime and its control, the model was unable "to account for the existence of highly stable, well-organized neighborhoods that appear to have fairly uniform and consistent cultural systems yet have traditionally high rates of delinquency nonetheless" (Bursik and Grasmick 1995, 111; see also Schwartz 1987). Indeed, this problem has also been raised by research on cities outside the United States (DeFleur 1967; Ebbe 1989), which suggests that, at best, Shaw and McKay's research may apply only to the structure of U.S. cities. Others, such as Valier (2003), taking a broader perspective, have claimed that changes in society, including globalization, question the Chicago School's theory for its myopic ethnocentric perspective.

However, in spite of these criticisms, the Chicago School's social ecology, especially its cultural and social disorganizational components, has continued to have a major presence in criminology. It is to its developing new directions that we now turn.

The New Social Ecology Theories

Since the 1960s, social ecology theory has gone in three distinct, although related, new directions. The first, which we call *urban design and environmental criminology*, relates to the issue of space, land use, and physical design and how these impact crime. The second new direction, which we call *critical ecology*, tries to take into account the political and economic forces in creating and shaping the space that is used to facilitate crime. The third new direction we call *integrated and systemic ecology* because it suggests a systemic approach to explain crime that focuses on the interrelationship among social ecological, biological, social learning, routine activities, rational choice, and cultural theories and on the regulatory capacities of relational networks in neighborhoods and between them. Let us look briefly at each of these new directions in social ecological theory.

Social Ecology, Urban Design, and Environmental Criminology

In the 1960s while working for the Chicago Housing Authority, Elizabeth Wood thought that it was important for residential security to design housing to include natural surveillability. She may have been influenced by the thinking of Jane Jacobs, the editor of *Architectural Forum*, whose classic book, *The Death and Life of Great American Cities*, published in 1961, laid the foundation for crime prevention through urban and environmental design movements of the 1970s. Jacobs criticized urban planners and their urban-renewal programs for destroying community integration, and in the process undermining its informal networks of social control. She pointed out that "crime flourished when people did not know and meaningfully interact with their neighbors, for they would thus be less likely to notice an outsider who may be a criminal surveying the environment for potential targets or victims. . . . High levels of natural surveillance created a safe environment. . . . Residential streets which promote multiple land uses promote natural and informal surveillance by pedestrians, and therefore, potentially increase residents' safety." Jacobs said that three primary qualities were needed in order to make them safer: "a clear demarcation between public and private space; diversity of street use; and fairly constant sidewalk use, which translated into 'eyes on the street'" (M. Robinson 1996).

Acknowledging their debt to Jacobs, during the early 1970s, several urban planners and some criminologists claimed that the physical design characteristics of urban neighborhoods could be manipulated in such a way that street crime would be reduced (Jeffery 1971). While C. Ray Jeffery concentrated on general environmental design characteristics and their interaction with the biosocial individual, it was Oscar Newman (1972, 1973), an architect and city planner from New York, who argued that crime prevention should be part of the architect's responsibility through urban design and the built environment. He believed that crime prevention should create areas of "defensible space." Reflecting Jacobs, Newman argued that to prevent crime it is necessary to enhance feelings of territoriality among neighborhood residents, which in turn leads to residents' own desire to protect their neighborhoods through self-policing. His planning and design strategies are aimed at reassigning "ownership" of residential space to reduce the amount of common multiple-user open space because residents cannot assert responsibility for these areas, leaving them open to crime and vandalism (Newman 1996). Newman claims to demonstrate that the physical environment can be used to define zones of influence, clearly separate public from private zones, and provide facilities within zones to meet occupants' needs. Re-creating a sense of ownership by dividing areas, and assigning them to individuals and small groups to use and control, isolates criminals because their turf is removed (ibid.). To achieve this aim, city architects and planners should include a significant component of physical security elements, such as restricted pedestrian traffic flow, single rather than multiple entrances, regulated entry, and clear boundary markers. Newman maintains that physical design can also be used to improve surveillance through better windows and lighting and altered traffic flow. Planning safe residential zones next to other safe facilities adds to the overall effect of crime reduction. Finally, according to Newman (1973), distinctiveness of design, such as height, size, material, and finish, can reduce the stigma of a neighborhood.

The impact of the defensible space theory has been enormous, and it has recently been merged with rational choice and routine activities theories (Gardiner 1978; Clarke and Mayhew 1980), which we discussed in Chapter 3, to become a major movement: Crime Prevention Through Environmental Design (CPTED). This term, coined by Jeffery, took urban design beyond the built environment, although not as far as Jeffery desired. Indeed, Robinson has argued that it was Newman's rather than Jeffery's restricted concept that prevailed (M. Robinson 1996).

Research in the area of environmental design suggests that crime and its fear can be reduced by paying attention to four key sets of physical features: (1) housing design or block layout, (2) land-use and circulation patterns, (3) resident-generated territorial features, and (4) physical deterioration (R. Taylor 1988; R. Taylor and Harrell 1996; Weisel and Harrell 1996). Each can "influence reactions to potential offenders by altering the chances of detecting them and by shaping the public vs. private nature of the space in question" (R. Taylor and Harrell 1996, 3). But the evidence to date leaves researchers unable to distinguish whether crime reductions result from physical changes or from the social and organizational changes that accompany the effort at redesign. Moreover, design ecology and environmental design take no account of the political and economic forces that create and sustain existing environmental contexts.

Critical Ecology

A second new direction taken in the social ecology literature, which we call critical ecology, tries to take into account the political and economic forces that create and shape the space that is used to facilitate crime. Research has revealed that there are three kinds of political decisions that affect the formation of criminal areas: local government planning decisions, local institutions, and public policing decisions. Local government can exacerbate social disorganization by concentrating problem residents in older, less desirable housing, which results in delinquent areas (T. Morris 1957; Gill 1977). Mustaine, Tewksbury, and Stengel (2006), for example, found that registered sex offenders were often consigned to living in areas with higher levels of social disorganization. Other studies, however, show that the concentration of problem families, even in new and well-maintained privately owned but subsidized "Section 8" housing, can also result in criminal areas. Such low-income housing becomes a refuge for drug trading, associated criminal activity, high levels of domestic violence, and child neglect. But this concentration is not simply a natural development, for "without the forces of political economy and state, those affected most by economic transformations would remain relatively dispersed" (Weinstein et al. 1991, 54).

Local institutions can also impact the extent of collective efficacy, social capital, and, thereby, social control. Communities that do not take the political initiative to develop coordinated action between their businesses, schools, and voluntary organizations to implement alternative programs for youth run the risk of allowing gangs to flourish, which creates further fear that undermines collective efficacy (Markowitz et al. 2001). In these disorganized neighborhoods research has also shown that the presence of features such as a concentration of alcohol outlets, which reflects business power, correlates with increases in violent crime (Costanza, Bankston, and Shihadeh 1999; Peterson, Krivo, and Harris 2000). This supports the assertion proposed by Concentric Zone Theory that the farther one moves from the city core, the weaker the relationship between alcohol availability and violent crime (Costanza, Bankston, and Shihadeh 1999). It also supports the critical ecology argument that business decisions that are not regulated by community planners can result in increased crime problems.

Finally, as well as informal social control, communities need the resources of public formal control, which means an effective police presence. Collier (2006) found that many political decisions made for economic reasons have adverse effects on the quality of policing. Research has shown that without adequate levels of formal policing, criminal gangs and drug operations can readily locate in a neighborhood (Klinger 1997). As Siegel points out:

> The police presence is typically greatest when community organizations and local leaders have sufficient political clout to get funding for additional law enforcement personnel. . . . In more disorganized areas, the absence of political power brokers limits access to external funding and protection. Without money from outside, the neighborhood lacks the ability to "get back on its feet." In these areas there are fewer police and those that do patrol the area are less motivated and their resources are stretched more tightly. These communities cannot mount an effective social control effort. (2004, 189)

Clearly, the critical ecological perspective suggests that a combined effort by local political leaders is necessary to make a difference in effective social control. However, for some, such as Hagedorn (2007a, 2007b, 2008), the political analysis of social ecology theory is limited. We'll have more to say about this when we look at the explanation of gangs in the last section of this chapter. Before doing so, let's consider some attempts at an integrated approach to social ecology.

Integrated and Systemic Ecology

A third development of social ecology theory attempts to bring together various aspects of previous developments. One version, integrated ecology, is an attempt to integrate ecological, biological, social learning, routine activities, rational choice, and cultural theories. This began with Lawrence Cohen and Richard Machalek's evolutionary ecological theory (1988) and was extended by Bryan Vila (1994). Like early social ecology, it looks at human adaptation to the environment but pays particular attention to cultural traits based on socially learned information and behavior, the evolution of which can be "guided." This approach enables criminologists to "integrate ecological factors that determine what opportunities for crime exist, micro-level factors that influence an individual's propensity to commit a criminal act at a particular point of time, and macro-level factors that influence the development of individuals in society over time" (ibid., 312). We consider this version of ecology theory in Chapter 12 when we examine integrated theory.

Systemic ecology moves away from the idea that social disorganization demands a policy response of social organization and instead suggests that what is required is a "systemic model that focuses on the regulatory capacities of relational networks that exist within and between neighborhoods" (Bursik and Grasmick 1995, 107–108; see also 1993a, 1993b). We call this systemic ecology, and it draws heavily on the idea of "social capital." Systemic theory focuses on ecological dimensions of social order (Capowich 2003). Under this theory, the composition of a neighborhood can help or hinder the development of "social networks" (Bellair 2000). Systemic social disorganization impacts control at the neighborhood level "through its effects on the private (primary relationships among family), parochial (informal networks of friends and acquaintances), and public (neighborhood links with public agencies) dimensions of social order" (Capowich 2003, 41). The systemic crime model is shown in figure 8.2.

Drawing their theoretical framework from Walter Buckley's systems theory (1967), Robert Bursik and Harold Grasmick (1995) note four components of their expanded social ecology of neighborhood-based networks and crime. First, they argue that it is necessary to take into account the totality of complex interrelations among individuals, groups, and associations that make up a community. We must consider (1) how these networks and ties serve to integrate residents into intimate, informal, primary neighborhood groups that operate to privately control behavior (Bursik and Grasmick 1993b) and (2) how a parochial level of control operates to signpost external threats and supervise neighborhood children in a general way and through community organizations.

Second, Bursik and Grasmick argue that the degree of systemness will vary across social structures in a community depending on factors such as size and density of the networks, with many-member small-location networks tending to have lower crime rates; scope (closure) of crosscutting ties, with increased ties across different cultural, ethnic, and racial groups helping to reduce the crime level; reachability, or the real ability of network members to meet; the content, or nature, of the network ties; durability, or the length the network has existed; intensity of the obligation of network

FIGURE 8.2 Bellair's Systemic Crime Model

Social Networks ---------+---------Informal Control--------- - ---------Street Crime members; and frequency with which members use the network (1995, 115–116). The hypothesis here is that neighborhoods with large dense networks, minimal barriers between groups, and members who meet regularly and have intense mutual obligations will have the highest level of crime control and the lowest rates of crime. In other words, areas with high social capital will be areas of low crime rates.

Third, the system components of a community can change without destroying the network of relations, for they exist in a larger system of relationships that "bind them into the broader ecological structure of the city" (ibid., 117). This component of the theory allows, in contrast to Shaw and McKay's earlier work ([1942] 1969), consideration of the wider transformation of cities through the "urban dynamics" of postindustrial societies, including the effects of economic polarization.

Fourth, like critical ecology, systemic ecology does not ignore the forces that create these "unfortunate" movements of industry and the resultant concentrations of poverty and power. It takes an open systems approach, allowing for external factors, including the political, social, and economic contexts in which the communities are embedded (Bursik and Grasmick 1995, 118; Bursik 1989). Drawing on Hunter (1985), Bursik and Grasmick refer to the effect of such forces on the "public level of control . . . the ability to secure public and private goods and services that are allocated by groups and agencies located outside the neighborhood" and the effects this ability has on a community's regulatory capacity (1995, 118).

Sampson, Raudenbush, and Earls (1997) further developed the idea of the failure of a community to enact informal social control building on their notion of "collective efficacy." This is a measure of social cohesion among residents and their willingness to act to control unacceptable behavior. The degree to which neighborhood residents intervene in response to unacceptable behavior by others in their community, whether by personally stepping in or calling authorities for assistance, varies. Sampson, Raudenbush, and Earls say that it depends on the extent to which neighbors trust one another. A variety of structural and cultural factors (such as population stability or instability and economic advantage or disadvantage) affects whether there is a high degree of trust that leads to a high level of social capital (networks of connected neighbors), which in turn results in a high degree of collective efficacy and thereby informal social control. As Lilly, Cullen, and Ball state, collective efficacy is distinctive because of its "focus not merely on the degree of neighborhood disorganization but also the willingness of neighbors to activate social control. . . . 'Efficacy' implies not merely a state of being socially organized but rather a state of being ready for *social action*" (2002, 43). Indeed, Bursik has gone on to define social organization as "the regulatory capacity of a neighborhood that is imbedded in the structure of that community's affiliational, interactional and communication ties among the residents" (1999, 86).

The problem with the existing systems model is that it is predominantly designed around structural organizational factors. Barbara Warner (2003) argues that we need to consider *both* structural and cultural weaknesses that work together to reduce informal social control, freeing residents to engage in varieties of law-violating behavior. She states that cultural weaknesses (attenuated culture) affect social control because residents do not perceive their neighbors as holding conventional values, do not see themselves as similar, and therefore do not see their neighbors intervening to control crime.

Systemic Ecology Policy

Bursik and Grasmick's, Sampson, Raudenbush, and Earls's, and Warner's systemic ecology draws on considerable existing research, but many of its new ideas remain to be tested. In one recent analysis, Capowich (2003) examined eight Chicago neighborhoods and found empirical support for the theory. However, systemic ecology has significant policy implications that go beyond early social ecology theory, particularly at the level of public control. Especially important is how the development of crime-preventive networks is related to the perceived effectiveness of crime control and the relations between local community representatives and law enforcement agencies. Bursik and Grasmick argued, "The development of extracommunity networks for the purposes of crime control presupposes at least a minimal set of private, parochial, and public control structures that can familiarize local residents with the operations of public and private agencies and can represent the community to these constituencies so that the relationship can be developed" (1995, 120–121). Where these do not exist because of past police action or lack of trust between police and neighborhood residents (typically found in economically deprived, low-class minority neighborhoods), higher rates of crime can be expected. Law enforcement agencies have recognized this and have also embraced the idea that social and physical disorder can result in crime. Wilson and Kelling (1982) first presented this "broken windows" thesis in 1982. As visible disorder increases, so do fear and isolation (Kelling and Coles 1996). Eventually, more serious forms of crime will increase in these areas (Skogan 1990; Cordner 1981, 1998).

Also crucial to the development of crime-preventive networks is the solicitation of other resources, such as those for public works, those providing financial and mortgage activity conducive to residential improvement and mobility, and those affecting daily services such as garbage collection, sewer repair, environmental protection, and so on, all of which improve the physical ambiance of neighborhoods (e.g., see D. Kennedy 1996; and Weisel and Harrell 1996). In short, it may well be that organized neighborhoods that fail to integrate into the wider political, social, and economic systems are vulnerable to high crime and delinquency, and that this can be counteracted only through fostering intracommunity linkages and networks among constituencies of heterogeneous neighborhoods and paying attention to how resources can be channeled to them. Finally, Warner argues that "building stronger communities will require, not only strengthening the structural arrangements therein, but also strengthening the culture . . . creating opportunities for residents of all neighborhoods to live out conventional values such that those values are visible and alive within the community" (2003, 94).

Under the Clinton presidency the U.S. government supported several programs that meet the criminal justice policy implications of the new social ecology theory for a more coordinated community-based approach to crime prevention (Conly and McGillis 1996). Through the Office of Justice Programs, funding was provided to communities to bring together government officials, service providers, businesspeople, and residents to identify crime-related problems and mobilize a broad spectrum of community resources. For example, Project PACT (Pulling America's Communities Together) was established in four states. Its goal was to "empower local communities to address youth violence by developing broad-based, coordinated anti-violence strategies" (L. Robinson 1996, 5). Another community-based program, SafeFutures, operated in six sites and included components such as after-school mentoring, family strengthening programs, mental health services, and gang prevention intervention and suppression for schools (ibid.; Conly and McGillis 1996). Project Safe Childhood, established in 2006, under the Bush presidency, brings together federal, state, and local authorities with community leaders and nonprofit organizations in order to combat sexual crimes against children (U.S. Department of Justice 2008).

Let us now turn to cultural theory, which in many ways came out of the early social ecology and, as we have seen from the previous discussion, intersects and interrelates with later versions, particularly through the integrated systemic ecological theory.

Cultural Theories of Crime and Deviance

Ecological theorists argue that environmental conditions in certain places create or encourage crime. Cultural theorists (not to be confused with cultural criminology, which we consider in a later chapter) observe that people from different origins and ethnic groups have distinct cultural heritages. One group may numerically or economically dominate, and their culture is then considered "normal" or mainstream. Members of a "minority" culture may have values and cultural norms that are in conflict with the dominant culture. Sometimes, these behaviors are criminalized by the dominant culture, creating criminals of people who are doing what they would normally do: conforming. For example, some southwestern Native Americans have traditionally used peyote, a cactus containing a hallucinogen, in their religious rites. The State of California legislated against "peyotism," arguing that "it seemed to threaten the Indians' relationship to larger society" and "to be a reversion to uncivilized practices, wholly out of place in modern times" (H. Morgan 1981, 162).

The norms and behavior patterns of each culture are taught by a process of socialization and social learning in the manner we described in Chapter 6. Thus, people are seen as being born equal and are thought to acquire behavioral patterns through learning from others in their culture. Regardless of whether a culture is dominant or subordinate, the means of learning behavior are the same. We consider culture conflict theory below, before exploring how cultural theory, and social ecology more generally, has been applied to explain gang activity.

Sellin's Culture Conflict Theory

The first substantial culture conflict theory was presented by the Swedish-born criminologist Thorsten Sellin in 1938. As we have already seen, in this period the United States was being urbanized and saw an influx of many immigrants from southern and eastern Europe. These new arrivals had very different cultures from previous immigrants to the United States. In *Culture Conflict and Crime* (1938), Sellin argued that legal definitions are relative, changing over time as a result of changes in conduct norms. Conduct norms are associated with a culture and define some behavior as acceptable and other behavior as unacceptable. These norms regulate an individual's daily life and behavior. However, different cultural groups have different ideas about what behaviors are appropriate or inappropriate, what is acceptable or unacceptable, and what should be considered criminal. In other words, conduct norms are different for different cultures. For example, Herzog and Rattner (2003) found that culture conflict caused differences in the public perception of crime between native-born and immigrant ethnic groups. In U.S. society, behavior defined as criminal by those sharing conduct norms of the majority culture is legislated against by its members who dominate the legislature and the institutions of government. The differences in cultural norms between the dominant and subordinate cultures create conflict. Conflict occurs when following the norms of one's own culture causes a person to break the legislated conduct norms of the dominant culture. In this theory, then, crime is a result not of deviant individuals but of conforming individuals who happen to belong to cultures with norms that conflict with the dominant ones. Religious cults, such as David Koresh's cult in Waco, Texas, which in 1993 ended with the death of eighty-two Davidians, including adults and children, after a three-month standoff with ATF officers (four of whom also died in the initial conflict), provide excellent illustrations of culture conflict theory.

Sellin distinguished between two types of culture conflict: primary and secondary. Primary culture conflict refers to those cases where the norms of the subordinate culture are considered criminal in the new (dominant) culture. Secondary culture conflict refers to instances where segments within the same culture differ as to the acceptability of conduct norms. In other words, one social group defines something as deviant or criminal, yet others in the same culture consider this behavior normal and noncriminal. Sellin argued, "The more complex a culture becomes, the more likely it is that the number of normative groups which affect a person will be large, and the greater is the chance that the norms of these groups will fail to agree, no matter how much they may overlap as a result of a common acceptance of certain norms" (1938, 29). In a study of Maori and crime in New Zealand, Bull (2004) found that drastic increases in Maori crime were partially due to secondary culture conflicts with regard to alcohol consumption.

We consider secondary culture conflicts and subcultures as causes of crime in the following chapter. Next we look at the ways that the social ecology of the Chicago School and the political economy of cities have merged with aspects of cultural theory to produce a new approach to understanding crime in spaces and places.

Beyond Social Ecology:
The Politics of the City, Gangs, and Crime

> Gangs, in the most straightforward sense, mint power for the otherwise powerless
> from their control of small urban spaces: street corners, slums, playgrounds, parks,
> schools, prison dormitories, even garbage dumps. For poor youth lacking other re-
> sources, these informal spatial monopolies, if successfully defended and consolidated,
> provide some measure of entrepreneurial opportunity as well as local prestige and war-
> rior glamour.
>
>   —Mike Davis, "Reading John Hagedorn"

We started this chapter talking about gang crime in inner cities. Several of the social ecology, social disorganization, and cultural theories of crime discussed above
have been drawn on to explain the phenomenon of gangs in the United States and,
more recently, globally. In this section we conclude the chapter by examining how
"critical gang studies" go beyond the early theories to explain gangs and "ganging."

We saw earlier that Chicago School sociologist Frederic Thrasher had argued that
gangs are likely to form in natural spatial areas surrounding industrial employment
where there is an absence of integrating values, and where there is separation, marginalization, and isolation of a community and ethnic groups from mainstream organizational life. Thrasher saw gangs as a problem of industrialization, immigration,
and adaptation rather than one of race and marginalization. In 1927 he defined the
"immigrant colony" as an "isolated social world" and said that those who move in it
know little of the world outside. Thrasher saw the youth gang as a boyish peer group
"formed spontaneously" in the marginal areas of the city, the in-between urban
spaces, whose members become "integrated through conflict." He said the gang was
characterized by meetings, group movement through space, conflict, and planning:
"The result of this collective behavior is the development of tradition, unreflective
internal structure, esprit de corps, solidarity, morale, group awareness, and attachment to a local territory" (1927, 46). He found that gang membership provided a
substitute for the disorganized and fragmented community, one that develops its
own values and traditions of loyalty and support for fellow gang members. Once
formed, these gangs are self-sustaining as a source of "conduct, speech, gestures, and
attitudes." Gangs, for Thrasher, were partly a generational cultural adjustment, "a
way to work out the masculine anxieties of immigrant boys, yearning to be free of
the traditional bonds of their old world parents" (Hagedorn 2004, 329), and partly a
temporary response to the social disorganization of the changing industrial landscape of the city and its separating residential districts. This view, consistent with the
Chicago School's social ecology, saw gangs as "fundamentally interstitial, adolescent
groupings in the process of going out of existence, residues of the irrationalities of
modernism" (Hagedorn 2008, 301).

Consistent with the social ecology perspective, Elijah Anderson (1990, 1999) has
examined the key features of "street culture" and found that some youth whose fam-

ilies are cut off from conventional culture, suffering from a range of economic and social problems and inconsistently monitored and disciplined, become alienated from the mainstream society that they have little hope of joining. A central theme of these youth is to establish respect from others through a "street reputation" for toughness, and mediated by a code that demands a violent response to any challenge to their reputations and any act of disrespect, however slight. This code prevails in the urban environment and applies to all who live there, even those who are not alienated and from morally decent backgrounds. If they do not follow the code, they become victims.

Others, such as Jeff Ferrell and Clinton Sanders (1994), describe a similar set of conditions that lead to a cultural abandonment of the mainstream in favor of cultural values of erotic excitement and cheap fun that can lead to destructive behaviors, such as graffiti signing, that annoy the guardians of the mainstream. This in turn can also indicate and celebrate activities such as the presence of ethnic gangs. Ferrell's work is part of critical criminology's new school of "cultural criminology" that we consider in the last chapter.

John Hagedorn (1994, 2007a, 2008) was one of the first to challenge the social ecological Chicago School view of gangs. He first argued that gangs are not simply youthful organizations but angry, alienated political reactions to a loss of identity and community, reflecting both the economics and the politics of deindustrialization (1994). Later, he tied this to the ways societies exclude and marginalize segments of their populations as a result of making political and economic decisions based on race and ethnicity (2007c). Most recently, he has argued that gangs are the result of the combined effects of globalization, the declining power of the state, political policies that reinforce marginalization, and mass communication and exploitation of the hip-hop gangsta-rap culture that feed the formation of resistance identities (2008). He argues that the more organized gangs are engaged in informal economic activity, largely around a drug economy, that is enforced through violence to settle disputes of honor. Hagedorn says that powerful interests, rather than natural organic development, built cities, brokered real estate deals, and built railroads and highways that "had particularly devastating consequences on African Americas and implications for the nature of gangs," and he sees these "institutional gangs" as structurally related to politics and race (2007a, 14–16). "To say that a gang has institutionalized is to say that it persists despite changes in leadership (e.g., killed, incarcerated or 'matured out'), has organization complex enough to sustain multiple roles of its members (including roles for women and children), can adapt to changing environments without dissolving (e.g., as a result of police repression), fulfills some needs of its members (economic, security, services), and organizes a distinct outlook of its members (rituals, symbols and rules)" (2005, 162).

Hagedorn acknowledges the Chicago School's legacy for combating the inherent racism of the early twentieth century through dispelling stereotypes of immigrants but criticizes its social ecology for ignoring the significance of race in land use, residence, and housing. He points out that in Chicago, land values have skyrocketed because of advancing gentrification of slum areas, forcing black and Latino residents into the southern and western suburbs: "Massive spatial upheavals have also accompanied the tearing down of housing projects . . . creating social disruptions that have powerfully influenced the nature and behavior of gangs" (2007, 19). Instead of integrating ethnic and racial groups, these changes have brought increasingly segregated gentrified communities that use a variety of measures such as public surveillance, gated communities, zero tolerance, and community policing to protect from and reduce the fear of crime, "policies that are more often exclusive rather than inclusive processes" (ibid., 20). Based on his overall analysis, Hagedorn (2006, 2007c) sees gangs as "social actors" in the globalized city: "Gangs are organizations of the socially excluded. While gangs begin as unsupervised peer groups and most remain so, some institutionalize in barrios, fevelas, ghettos and prisons. Often these institutionalized gangs become business enterprises within the informal economy and a few are linked to international criminal cartels. Most gangs share a racialized or ethnic identity and a media-diffused oppositional culture. Gangs have variable ties to conventional institutions and, in given conditions, assume social, economic, political, cultural, religious or military roles" (2007b, 309).

Some insight into gangs as social actors is their informal economic activities, revealed in the analysis of the financial operations of one gang in one area of a midwestern city, over a four-year period during the late 1980s (Levitt and Venkatesh 2000). This was a "corporatized" African American gang involved in drug dealing as a source of revenue generation operating in a 99 percent African American community of the city. Income from drug distribution varied depending on a variety of factors, in particular the degree of organizational sophistication of the gang and the gang member's position in the gang hierarchy. Levitt and Venkatesh found that the average wage in the gang was a little above the legitimate market alternative; street-level sellers earned the equivalent of minimum wage, with "high-level gang members earning far more than their legitimate market alternative." This fact provided the primary economic motivation for low-level gang members, who believed in the possibility of "rising up through the hierarchy" (ibid., 756–757). Gang wars over honor and economic turf were found to be costly, not only in deaths but in the loss of customers in an area, dropping the price of drugs some 20–30 percent. There was also evidence that frequent gang wars were "the result of . . . the desire of low-level gang members to build a reputation for toughness" (ibid., 758).

Hagedorn argues that the shift to institutionalization and economic corporatization of gangs in the informal economy, particularly in Chicago, came about partly because of the abandonment by the middle class of the 1960s revolutionary politics that had made attempts to incorporate black gangs into the political and economic structure but was seen as threatening by city and federal authorities. As a result of orchestrated aggressive police tactics against gangs, the liberal organizations that sought to empower them collapsed: "Disillusionment with the broken promises of civil rights leaders led to a strengthening of a radicalized gang identity that was related more to 'hustling' than to politics" (Hagedorn 2007a, 22–23). This led gangs to restructure and reorganize to form new centrally run economic enterprises that produced vast sums of money, and only an occasional charity for the community in which they operated.

The mass incarceration of gang leaders in the 1990s also fueled this reorganization. Many gangs are run by incarcerated gang leaders from their prison cells, and some were formed in prison and exported to the city streets: "Gangs today might best be defined as organizations of the socially excluded simultaneously occupying the spaces of both prison and ghetto." As a result of these changes, "Many of today's gangs are an institutional bricolage of illicit enterprise, social athletic club, patron to the poor, employment agency for youth, substitute family, and nationalist, community, or militant organization" (ibid., 25).

Global Policy Implications of Critical Gang Studies

In reviewing Chicago School social ecology theory we saw that in the long term, consistent with their social disorganization perspective, gangs would supposedly disappear with the assimilation of immigrants into the wider society. In the short term they could be controlled and assimilation facilitated by social programs and by organizing and empowering communities to become urban villages. However, recent work, particularly that of Robert Sampson (Sampson 2006) and Paul Bellair (1997, 2000), rejects the old idea that strong and dense social ties are the solution to problems of crime and gangs because (as Hagedorn argues) they exclude. Sampson argues that the close-knit dense networks, idealized in the urban village model of neighborhoods as independent islands in a city, "bear little resemblance to those of contemporary cities, where weak ties prevail over strong ties and social interaction among residents is characterized more often by instrumentality than by altruism or affection," and where social networks "frequently criss-cross traditional ecological boundaries, many of which are permeable and vaguely defined" (2006, 132). In this view, communities with weak ties (rather than no ties) reflect more frequent interaction among neighbors because they "integrate the community by way of bringing together otherwise disconnected groups . . . [and] are predictive of lower crime rates" (ibid., 134; Bellair 1997, 2000). Sampson maintains that "collective efficacy" involving a combination of loose social cohesion of the collective and shared expectations of control within the collective can effectively maintain public order and reduce crime (2006, 135). He believes that we can no longer consider policies to deal with crime and gangs that "focus solely on the internal characteristics of neighborhoods. . . . Neighborhoods themselves are part of a spatial network encompassing the entire city—not only are individuals embedded but so are neighborhoods" (ibid., 138–139). He continues: "The characteristics of surrounding neighborhoods are crucial to understanding violence in any given neighborhood. . . . In short, crime is affected by the characteristics of spatially proximate neighborhoods, which in turn are affected by adjoining neighborhoods in a spatially linked process that ultimately characterizes the entire metropolitan system" (ibid., 138).

Importantly, and perhaps not surprisingly, both Sampson and Hagedorn see the future direction of understanding the policy necessary for dealing with crime in cities as crucially tied to a wider global analysis. Sampson states, "The future of neighborhood research will probably be increasingly cross-national and comparative. Efforts are now underway seeking to examine the general role of spatial inequality and neighborhood efficacy in cities around the world." He argues that we need a general approach to policy that "emphasizes ameliorating neighborhood inequality in social resources, including metropolitan spatial inequality, and enhancing social conditions that foster the collective efficacy of residents and organizations" (ibid., 139). However, Hagedorn goes further, saying that we cannot limit our analysis to local conditions but must look at crime and gangs in a global context, as part of a global phenomenon in which global economics has led to the redivision of city spaces across the globe, and urbanization in nations worldwide has provided the prime conditions for the growth of gangs (2005, 154). Indeed, he says that gangs and other organizations of the socially excluded need to be considered in the context of the globalized city: "Gangs cannot be understood outside their global context, not reduced to epiphenomena of globalization or cogs in an international terrorist conspiracy. . . . Gangs are being reproduced throughout this largely urban world by a combination of economic and political marginalization and cultural resistance. We ignore organizations of the socially excluded at great risk. . . . How we deal with the reality of gangs and others among the socially excluded is one of those markers that will shape the future of civilization" (ibid., 163–164).

What began as a study of neighborhood crime and gangs in the developing mod-ernist city has ended with the study of worldwide gangs in the globalized city. Its policy implications are much larger than can be dealt with by local neighborhood program initiatives alone (see box 8.1).

BOX 8.1 City Gangs and Public Policy
DANA NURGE

Policy measures in relation to gangs are often the result of knee-jerk reactions to dra-matic personal tragedies. Rather than relating policy to research findings and analysis, activist "moral entrepreneurs" often seek to pass laws that seem to offer simple technopanaceas in the mistaken belief that these will solve the problem. In response to the deaths of two teens due to gang violence in San Diego on Friday, December 12, 2008, a member of the community wrote to the San Diego Gang Commission at-tempting to rally the city and community to support legislation to have GPS tracking for all documented gang members. The proposed legislation would be called "Monique's Law," in honor of the seventeen-year-old girl, Monique Palmer, who was killed in the incident. Here is the response of Dr. Dana Nurge, an adviser to the San Diego Gang Commission, based on a memo she sent to the Gang Commission:

The deaths this weekend (and again last night) were tragic and warrant the City's and Commission's attention, but I absolutely do not think that GPS moni-

CONTINUES

BOX 8.1 (CONTINUED)

toring of all documented gang members would be an appropriate, rational or effective response.

Incidents like this one can help bring us together (through our grief and despair) to create effective solutions or they can ignite "moral panics," which lead to (more) Draconian responses, driven by fear, exclusivity and/or vindictiveness, rather than practical policy sense. Such responses distract us from the real issues. The hopelessness—which breeds recklessness and lack of respect for life—among some of our community's young adults (and is exemplified through gang violence) has its roots in myriad social issues including, but not limited to: poverty; unemployment and underemployment; discrimination, marginalization, and social exclusion (all of which have contributed to the breakdown of the family); inadequate educational opportunities; lack of legitimate opportunities for youth to build self-esteem and establish an identity; a lack of positive adult role models; and a broader culture that promotes hyper-consumerism, individualism, violence, and excessive self-gratification.

Responding to the symptoms of these problems, such as gang-related violence, is extremely costly, largely ineffective, and diverts attention and resources away from the root causes. There is no doubt that the fear in these communities is real and that kids are navigating dangerous streets and schools (and sometimes homes) on a daily basis, but tracking (alleged) gang members will not quell those fears or alter those realities. Pure, deterrence-based gang policies, such as this one, haven't worked (gangs continue to exist and proliferate) and there is no empirical evidence to suggest they will.

I'm hopeful that the sadness, frustration and outrage that this tragedy has sparked in our community can be channeled and directed towards addressing the root causes of the problems, rather than attempting to manage the symptoms. Let's ask ourselves why this happened? Some have questioned whether laws and law enforcement can and should do more to monitor and control gang members. But let's go deeper than that and question how/why gangs remain a problem: why are some of our young people joining gangs, arming themselves, and engaging in acts of violence against their peers and community? How/why does a child transform into an adolescent or adult who's willing to kill in the name of their gang or "hood" or reputation? What can we do to detract our youth from gangs and violence and keep them safe, healthy and future-oriented? In short, how can we provide more opportunities for our youth to succeed?

Our responses to those questions would direct our attention away from further attempts to control gang members in our community, and towards the issues that contribute to youths' desire to join gangs. Research on gangs consistently reveals that kids join gangs in hopes of gaining: (1) protection/safety, (2) family/belonging/love, and (3) status/identity. Our efforts to address gang violence have to begin with an understanding of why/how youth are attracted to them and what purpose they serve in their lives. The desire for protection/safety, love, and self-identity and meaning are universal and well-established (e.g., Maslow's Hierarchy of

CONTINUES

BOX 8.1 (CONTINUED)

Needs). Let's look at how our community falls short in providing opportunities for all youth to attain those needs through legal, healthy, pro-social means. Instead of creating increasingly harsh laws that are constitutionally questionable, impossible to enforce, cost prohibitive, and ultimately ineffective, let's look to address the root causes of gang involvement and find ways to address our youths' desire/need to seek fulfillment/meaning through a gang. Let's direct our community's grief, despair and need to "do something" in response to these tragedies towards the roots: building healthier communities and fostering community involvement in youths' lives, making safer and more effective school environments, generating and promoting opportunities for youth to be involved in pro-social, identity-enhancing activities (sports, jobs, arts, etc.), strengthening families, expanding job opportunities (that pay a living wage).

While it is clearly understandable why community activists want action now in order to prevent death and destruction in which kids are living imperiled lives, it is unlikely that these actions will have their intended effects. Programs developed by reformers that take time to implement and have mixed results seem like a distant prospect to those directly affected. Yes, something must be done now, but something must also be done for the future. The "now" part must include a cease-fire, probably supported by a show of respect, threat of oppressive control, promise of collaboration, and future opportunity. But this approach will not address the root causes. To do this it is necessary to build a coalition, to prevent wrong-headed ideas from gaining traction, and to start down a fruitful path that addresses the long-term issues. Coalition-forming means listening to all concerns, compromising, and doing some things individual interests don't want to do. In the end, such a coalition must reach beyond the local community to deal with the structural causes of the inequalities, exclusions and marginalization that create the fertile conditions for gangs to take root. In order to deal with these realities it is necessary that coalition partners include the very organizations and corporations that create these conditions, on both a local, national and global level.

Dana Nurge is Associate Professor of Criminal Justice at San Diego State University and technical adviser to the San Diego Gang Commission.

Summary and Conclusion

In this chapter, we have moved from the notion in the previous chapters that crime is a product of individual choices, causes, or processes to the idea that places, networks, and cultural adaptations create criminal opportunities. We have seen how economic and political forces can produce massive social changes and population movements, which can result in highly volatile concentrations of people that accentuate their problems. We have seen, too, that once formed, these patterns are self-sustaining and reinforcing. We have also seen that the conditions that create these forces are much larger than the city and are part of a globalized urbanization process.

The global, political, and economic forces that serve to shape specific areas and the social exclusions that they generate can also provide the context for the learning of behavior (as we discussed in connection with differential association theory) and the formation or lack of attachments (discussed previously under bonding theory). Regardless of the "causality" (perhaps learning or bonding) of individual effects, the downward spiral of certain places can carry with it those who are unable to escape, who may violate laws simply by conforming to their culture or subculture or in order to survive the hardships of their neighborhood. Once the process begins, fear and limited resources undermine a community's ability to control its own members, which results in further crime and more fear. This leads to the departure of those best able to escape, leaving behind those least able to cope in conventional ways. Angry with their situation but politically rudderless, some form gangs that compete with each other for their own survival and create an identity of resistance at the only level they can control.

Although preventive efforts and ideas have become increasingly sophisticated, one of the major omissions from social ecology and cultural theories of crime is what drives the movements that make places criminal. In the next chapter, we look at one of the ways sociologists have tried to fill this gap by examining structural forces at a societal and ultimately at a global level and how these forces shape spatial, cultural, and subcultural responses.

Summary Chart:
Social Ecology Theory and Culture Conflict Theory

1. Social Ecology Theory

Basic Idea: Rooted in geography and notions of space, population movement, and density and how these are shaped by the physical environment. Crime is a product of the geopolitical environment found in certain areas of a city.

Human Nature: Human actions are determined by major social trends that affect the physical and social environment. The choices and moral sense they have emerge in environmentally structured contexts. People are seen as conformist and act in accordance with values and norms of the groups with which they self-identify.

Society and the Social Order: Early theories emphasized consensus yet implied group conflict and the plurality of values and norms that are found more explicitly in later theories. Law is taken for granted but reflects the norms, values, and interests of the dominant culture. Criminals are those who are in a state of transition through fragmented social organization; criminality is not a permanent state. In later versions of these theories, criminality, in the form of organizations of the excluded, is seen as a permanent, institutionalized, and globalized phenomenon.

Causal Logic: Social change, such as immigration, rural-urban migration, high social mobility, and growth of cities, undermines traditional coping behaviors and especially traditional control institutions: family networks destroyed, extended family fragmented, ethnic culture lacking authority. This produces social disorganization in which people compete rather than cooperate as a community. At the same time, these neighborhoods are insulated from values of the dominant culture. Parents lose the respect of their children, who are in conflict with them over mixed values systems, and this results in a loss of parental control over children. Social disorganization leads to personal disorganization. This leads to crime, delinquency, and mental illness, especially suicide. Insulated from the dominant culture and alienated from parents, some immigrant youths form their own new primary subcultures, or gangs. Gangs develop their own delinquent traditions, which are passed on to new members. The areas where this disorganization is most intensely felt are inner-city zones of transition where property values are low but rising and slumlords neglect properties while waiting for the rise in value. These low-income housing areas have the highest numbers of immigrants. Some immigrant subcultural groups, such as the Chinese, are able to resist the wider disorganization of neighborhood by maintaining their original strong culture and traditions. Some argue that disorganized areas are not all the same but may have as many as three or more subareas of disorganization. More recent theory sees these processes set in motion and sustained by interested political and economic decisions.

Criminal Justice Policy: Some in the 1930s felt areas would eventually improve as immigration stopped and the city stabilized, so little needed to be done. Others argued that it was necessary to move those most affected by disorganization to new geographical areas. Yet others argued for strengthening community organization. More recent theorists believe in a systemic or integrated approach to strengthen both internal informal networks and their connection with wider political, social, and economic networks and resources. Rather than develop close community ties, loose community networks are seen as the more realistic ways that neighborhoods demonstrate a "collective efficacy" and build social capital to resist crime. The importance of the globalized city as a focus of social change is seen as vital.

Criminal Justice Practice: Structural and institutional changes. Community mobilization (e.g., the Chicago Area Project). Facilitation of the process of assimilating both immigrants and the disorganized into mainstream society. More recently, facilitate collaborative partnerships to maximize collective efficacy and more equitable distribution of resources. Involve corporate social actors with community and gang actors to work toward removing structural causes.

Evaluation: Explains some inner-city street crime and why crime rates are highest in cities and slums. Undermines argument of biological and psychological theories, since they would predict more random occurrence of crime geographically. Criticized for accepting official crime statistics as valid, ignoring white-collar crime in suburbs and excessive policing of inner cities. Fails to explain corporate crime, fails to explain insulation of some youths in the inner city from delinquency, and fails to account for how people in disorganized areas disengage from crime as adults.

2. Culture Conflict Theory

Basic Idea: Some people have cultural heritages that differ from those of the dominant culture, and they are often in conflict with it; they become criminal simply by following their own cultural norms.

Human Nature: Humans are seen as equal, sociocultural blanks who are socialized into norm- and rule-following actors.

Society and the Social Order: Divided by culture into dominant and a diversity of subordinate or ethnic minority cultures, which are in conflict. Law is the rules of the dominant groups of a particular society. Criminals are those caught breaking another culture's laws; no different from noncriminals, in that both are rule following, except that they follow different rules.

Causal Logic: Socialization into the norms of another culture through the family produces three ways that lawbreaking may occur: (1) In Sellin's version, the other culture is the native country of the immigrant, and when its norms are followed and they clash with the norms of the dominant culture, this "normal" behavior is defined as criminal, and punishment may result. (2) When immigrant parents enforce standards of behavior of their native country on their children, who react because of their indoctrination in the adoptive country, the resulting strife and alienation may cause delinquency. (3) Because complex societies have multiple social groups and a pluralism of subcultures, including corporate culture, norm and law violation can result when the behavior of one group or subculture conflicts with that of the dominant culture.

Criminal Justice Policy: Some argue that crime will melt away when the United States becomes "one culture" after assimilation of immigrants into the mainstream, so we need to do very little. Others believe we need acculturation programs and policies.

Criminal Justice Practice: Education and cultural socialization in schools and community. Increased opportunities for assimilation and changing values of diverse ethnic groups. Counseling for children of immigrants to provide them with coping skills needed to survive the clash of cultures. Clearer and simplified laws provided by the dominant culture. Greater flexibility of law when dealing with other or lower-class cultural contexts. Decreased policing of streets.

Evaluation: Useful to explain some aspects of racial and ethnic crime and Chinese, Cuban, Haitian, Vietnamese, and Latino gangs. Explains resistance identity and cultural exploitation by corporate interests that take gang phenomena into the globalized world. Does not explain adult crime in lower-class neighborhoods or middle- and upper-class crime.

The Sick Society

Anomie, Strain,
and Subcultural Theory

In the previous chapter we saw how gang crime can form in areas of a city that are the product of political and economic marginalization and exclusion. But what about a whole society that produces excluded and marginalized categories of people? Can groups form in the society at large and then move to other areas of the society, perhaps inner city, perhaps outer suburbs, where there are better opportunities, for both legitimate and underground economic activity? The 1991 movie *New Jack City*, starring Ice-T, Mario Van Peebles, Judd Nelson, Chris Rock, and Wesley Snipes playing the "Cash Money Brothers," was based on the activities of the Chambers brothers gang that operated in the mid- to late 1980s in Detroit and was recently documented in the BET American Gangster series *The Chambers Brothers* (2007). What started as a legitimate liquor and party store, selling homegrown marijuana on the side, escalated to selling crack cocaine across the street and eventually from entire apartment blocks. At the peak of their empire, the Chambers brothers controlled half of Detroit's crack trade, ran two hundred crack houses, and supplied five hundred others, allegedly earning between $1 and $3 million a week ("I'm Going to Detroit" 1988), although others have said the extent of their operation was greatly exaggerated in the charges in their indictment (W. Adler 1995). It was described as a franchise operation, "the McDonald's of crack cocaine operations in Detroit" (BET 2007). But the four Chambers brothers (from a family of fourteen) did not come from the rapidly declining city of Detroit, with its boarded-up storefronts and failing auto industry, a city that at the time was losing 250,000 jobs and 20 percent of its population. They came from the economically depressed rural delta town of Marianna, Arkansas, with a population of 6,200, located in Lee County, the nation's sixth poorest county, where unemployment for young black males was 50 percent and the per capita income was $6,387 ($10,013 in 2007 adjusted for inflation). Earlier in the century African Americans from the rural South went north to work in the Detroit auto plants for Henry Ford, General Motors, and Chrysler. In the mid-1980s these same young black males escaped the poverty of southern unemployment or backbreaking work in the cotton fields for something better: to work in the "land of opportunity," the slums of Detroit, for the Chambers brothers' drug "franchise" operation, which recruited around 150 seventeen- to twenty-one-year-olds to work as runners, couriers, foot soldiers, and dealers at $2,000 a month. What led the Chambers brothers and those who followed them to make this journey, to make a "rational career choice" (W. Adler 1995), and to eventually take up illegitimate rather than legitimate work is instructive and gets at the heart of strain theory.

In 1979 B. J. Chambers left Marianna to continue his high school education; he stayed with another Arkansas family in Detroit and first learned the marijuana business while there. His brother Willie Chambers had also moved to Detroit, where he worked as a mail carrier. Consistent with the American Dream, Willie saved his post office wages and by 1982 was able to buy a house on the Lower East Side and a small party store selling liquor, beer, wine, chips, and so on. B. J. went to work for Willie, selling marijuana on the side until a police raid resulted in his moving across the street to a house purchased cheaply in the Detroit economic downturn. He added cocaine to the product range, and by 1984 business was booming (W. Adler 1995, 80–83).

As criminologist Carl Taylor says, "These guys had a great work ethic. They were hungry. . . . They handled their business like a distributorship. It's like Pizza Pizza, except it was Dope Dope" (cited in BET 2007). A former DEA agent said, "They were resourceful, opportunistic. . . . If these guys had taken the skills that they had, put that into a legitimate business environment," they would have been successful. "They recognized a market. They advantaged the market, and they outcompeted everybody" (ibid.). Indeed, William Adler points out in *Land of Opportunity: One Family's Quest for the American Dream in the Age of Crack* (1995) that with no more than a high school education, the Chambers brothers "identified a market niche, mastered wholesale buying, mass production and risk analysis, monitored cash flows, devised employee benefit plans, performance bonuses and customer incentive plans" (cited in Will 2001, 131).

What led the Chambers brothers to turn their work ethic in pursuit of the American Dream into these increasingly illegitimate means to achieve it? The Chambers brothers illustrate the main themes of the sociological ideas of strain theory: They accepted U.S. society's cultural goals and objectives for success (high monetary rewards, material wealth, owning a home or a business). They even exhibited its strong work ethic as a means to achieve these goals. They did not, however, use the other legitimate normatively accepted means (student loans, delayed gratification, legal methods) to achieve those goals, but instead innovated with illegitimate means.

But strain theory is not restricted to explaining conventional street crime, nor is it confined to the lower reaches of the social structure. It has also been applied to corporate and organizational crime, as the following analysis illustrates:

> Corporations, like all organizations, are primarily oriented towards the achievement of a particular goal—profit—at least in the long run. This defining characteristic

makes a corporation inherently criminogenic, for it necessarily operates in an uncertain and unpredictable environment such that its purely legitimate opportunities for goal achievement are sometimes limited and constrained. The contradictions between corporate goal-achieving behaviour and environmental uncertainties create a strong strain towards innovative behaviour. Examples [include]: espionage, arson, patent copying; bribery and corruption to influence those in new and expanding markets, such as government officials in developing economies[;] refusal to make work conditions safe or properly inspected/maintained[;] fraudulent advertizing, misleading sales behavior; false labelling of products; manufacture and distribution of dangerous products. (Box 1983, 35–37)

Nor is this connection between the entrepreneurial character of the street offender and the corporate offender surprising to leading anomie and strain theorists. Consider the late 1980s convicted insider trader Michael Miliken who developed junk bonds and created cheap credit working for Wall Street investment bank Drexel, Burnham, Lambert. The Michael Miliken story illustrates the paradoxes inherent in the sources of and responses to crime in the United States:

The very qualities in which Miliken took pride and for which he was praised—his daring, energy, intelligence, and, most important, his ability to create and willingness to use innovative solutions for conventional problems—also led to his crimes and punishment. These qualities are not merely the personal traits of a particular criminal. . . . They are the elements of social character rooted in broad value orientations within American culture that help shape both the archetypal American hero and the archetypal American villain. To understand fully the nature and level of crime in a society, therefore, it is essential to consider the distinguishing features of that society, particularly its distinctive cultural imagination. (Messner and Rosenfeld 2006, 2)

In this chapter, then, we begin to consider the ideas of theorists who argue that the structure of society, that is, how society is organized, can affect the way people behave. In particular, we examine the idea that "some social structures exert a definite pressure on certain persons in the society to engage in nonconforming conduct rather than conformist conduct" (Merton 1938, 672). We examine the theories of the sociological functionalists, principally Émile Durkheim and Robert Merton, who argued that the organization of industrialized societies produces divisions between people and between groups based on social position in a hierarchy and occupational role within the system (known as the division of labor). Functionalist sociologists believe that social roles become specialized and work interdependently to serve the system as a whole.

Social institutions are complexes of particular elements of culture and social structure that perform these basic functions of adaptation, goal attainment, integration, and pattern maintenance. . . . Adaptation to the environment to meet the physical and material needs of a population is the chief function of the economy. Political institutions, or the "polity," enable a population to attain collective goals. Responsibility for social integration and the maintenance of cultural patterns falls to religion, education, and the family system. The interrelations among these institutions constitute a society as an ongoing concern and distinguish it from other societies. (Rosenfeld and Messner 2006, 165)

French sociologist Émile Durkheim first presented the basic components of this functionalist analysis of crime in 1893 when he was trying to explain how society could change from the stability of its preindustrial order to the potential chaos that the capitalist industrial system could produce. He argued that in times of rapid change, the moral regulation of behavior is undermined by structural divisions and by a cult of the individual, which promotes unlimited aspirations, some of which involve criminal behavior.

In the twentieth century, these ideas were applied to the United States by Robert Merton (1938, [1957] 1968), who examined society after the Great Depression and found that its culturally defined goals, such as "the American Dream," could be met by illegal means by those denied access to approved means. These approved means would include legitimate opportunities such as formal education and economic resources. Development and extension of these ideas included the seminal work of Albert Cohen (1955) and Richard Cloward and Lloyd Ohlin (1960) on collective rather than individual adaptations by working-class populations to societal strain; Robert Agnew (1992, 1995a, 2006) on strategies of avoiding the frustration and anger produced by strain, based on a variety of social-psychological variables; Steven Messner and Richard Rosenfeld's ideas (1994, 2006) about the role of U.S. economic institutions in dominating other social values and undermining strong social controls; and, most recently, Nikos Passas's theory of global anomie (2000, 2006) in which unlimited global economic trade creates vast disparities of wealth and removes safety nets, magnifying relative deprivation and promoting deviant responses. Before we explore the different forms that anomie, or strain theory, has taken and its criminal justice policy implications, let us look at its core underlying common themes and assumptions.

Common Themes and Assumptions

Anomie theory, more recently called strain theory, has gone through several transitions in its hundred-year development and has proven remarkably resilient in explaining crime in changing societies. During this process, many of its underlying assumptions have remained constant, although others have changed and become subject to disagreement. All versions of strain theory agree that deviant behavior is a normal response to abnormal conditions. Furthermore, humans are socialized to behave in certain, often predictable, ways. Strain theorists may disagree over what the specific goals are, but they agree that seeking to achieve goals is a normal human trait. Finally, strain theorists agree that society's structure and culture cause strain by their form of organization, by the kinds of goals they prescribe, and by their alloca-tion of resources; more recent theorists disagree about the extent that individual be-havioral characteristics can mitigate these forces. Let us consider these assumptions in greater detail, first looking at their similarities and complementary aspects and then looking at how they diverge.

In addition to strain theorists assuming that crime is a normal reaction to abnor-mal social conditions, strain theory also emphasizes "the problem-solving functions" served by nonconforming, antisocial, delinquent, and criminal behavior (Brezina 1996, 39). Strain theories link macrolevel variables, such as the organization of soci-eties (especially capitalism), to the microlevel behavior of individuals. In other words, strain theory "links the macro-structural organization of society to the micro-social choices of its individual members" (Holman and Quinn 1992, 217). Thus, it is often termed a mesolevel explanatory framework (or what Merton [(1957) 1968] called a theory of the "middle range").

Taken as a whole, strain theory describes the interplay among social structures, cultural context, and individual action. Different strain theorists disagree over some fundamental dimensions of their theory, however, and therefore emphasize different aspects of its components. For example, Durkheim's original theory of anomie as-sumes a view of humans born with insatiable appetites to be "heightened or dimin-ished by the social structure." In contrast, versions of strain theory in the Merton mold assume individual appetites are "culturally rather than structurally induced," but societal strain comes from differential opportunities in the social structure that have not met the culturally raised appetites (Einstadter and Henry 2006, 155).

Individual appetites also include an instrumental component (Orru 1990). This means that crime is seen as an instrumental act of goal seeking. Whether committed by individuals or corporate entities, crime serves a purpose. Mertonian theory as-sumes that humans act rationally and have self-serving motivations for their behav-ior, but this is "not in the utilitarian sense of having 'free will,' but as actors whose behavioral choice is influenced by societal structures, cultural definitions, and inter-active processes" (ibid., 154). Mertonian conceptions of a structured human choice also reflect the results of socialization in families, schools, and particularly through the media. These are the ways that cultural values are communicated. Strain theorists also assume that "under normal conditions people are naturally inclined to abide by social norms and rules" (Paternoster and Bachman 2001, 141).

Combining the ideas of Merton and Durkheim in a formulation known as tradi-tional strain theory reveals a shared concept of humans as engaged in goal-oriented, achievement-directed behavior shaped by social structure and culture. For Mertoni-ans, the culture, most vividly expressed through the mass media, encourages people to achieve the goals of monetary success—that is, "Go for it!" and express "No fear!" and "Have it all!" At the same time, the culture fails to place limits on acceptable means of achievement, and the structure does not provide equal opportunities for all to achieve these societal goals. Such a society is described as suffering strain because of (1) a dysfunctional mismatch between the goals or aspirations it sets for its mem-bers and the structure of opportunities it provides for them to achieve these goals

(Merton 1938), (2) an unleashing of individual aspirations without a corresponding provision of normative or moral guidelines to moderate the level of raised aspirations (Durkheim [1897] 1951), and (3) the failure to match people's skills and abilities to the available positions in the society (known as a "forced" division of labor) (Durkheim [1893] 1984). A society experiencing such structural strain is unable to retain a meaningful sense of moral authority with regard to normative controls on behavior and is referred to as being in a state of anomie, or normlessness (Durkheim [1897] 1951). In a word, the society is "sick."

Societal strain can affect people, groups, and organizations in different ways as they seek to adapt to solve the problems that strain creates. One of these adaptations is crime, whereby people attempt to achieve societal goals of money, material success, and social status (a house, expensive cars, jewelry, and electronic equipment) regardless of the means used (as in the example of dealing drugs presented at the start of this chapter) to achieve them. In short, they cheat. Crime, then, is one way of both responding to the structural strain and realizing common goals espoused by the larger dominant culture.

The Durkheim-Merton tradition of strain theory seems to be useful for explaining property crimes among the economically disadvantaged, who may experience greater personal stress as a result of structural strain, as Merton pointed out, and the disadvantaged are not equally impacted. Indeed, "crime is unevenly distributed across individuals within certain collective groups, therefore, because some persons experience more strain than others" (Paternoster and Bachman 2001, 142). But Merton ([1957] 1968) recognized that the theory also explains how the economically powerful commit economic crimes using illegal or unethical innovations, illustrated by the analysis of corporate crime at the start of the chapter. Indeed, "If 'success' is far more heavily emphasized in the higher strata of society, and if its measurement is virtually open-ended in these strata, then Merton's theory of anomie is even more applicable to white-collar and corporate crime than it is to conventional crime" (Friedrichs 1996, 232; see also D. Cohen 1995; Waring, Weisburd, and Chayet 1995; and Schoepfer and Piquero 2006). This too is what led Durkheim ([1897] 1951) "to focus on the top social stratum as the primary location of anomie, for it was power not poverty that facilitated too easily the personal achievement of socially inculcated cultural ambitions" (Box 1983, 40). Nowhere is this better illustrated than in the 1980s insider-trading crimes linked to the "unbridled pursuit of pecuniary rewards" (Lilly, Cullen, and Ball [1989] 1995, 67) and the men at Enron Corporation, whose corporate and individual greed from 1995 to 2001 became emblematic of an era (McLean and Elkind 2003). As one commentator of the movie *Enron: The Smartest Guys in the Room* observed: "Former executives are candid, and company audiotapes and videotapes illustrate the ethically challenged corporate culture of the Houston-based concern. . . . It was as though everyone wanted to believe in the power of people to outsmart the system—the American dream of overnight success" (Puig 2005).

Also shown in the earlier corporate illustration are the numerous illegal strategies corporations use to achieve goals of financial profit that they are unable to achieve legitimately (Vaughan 1983; Passas 1990). Moreover, as Passas (1990) argues, the commission of crimes by the more wealthy sections of society, combined with their immunity from prosecution, produces a cynicism among the population. Such cynicism feeds the general state of anomie, as those in less privileged positions become confused about what moral rules really apply (Friedrichs 1996, 232).

Newer versions of strain theory, such as Agnew's revised strain theory (1985, 2006), may be less compatible, since Merton's notion of goal-seeking actors is partially replaced by a view of humans invested in behavior designed to follow a particular rule of justice. For example, adolescents may be more concerned with the fairness of a process of job hiring than whether they get the job. Moreover, this response can be modified by individuals' different cognitive and behavioral attributes. Those who have doubts about their identities and capabilities may be more satisfied with less than those without such doubts, who may become more frustrated with injustices and choose crime to escape their frustrations. As we will see later, differences in the assumptions made about humans are some of the main features that distinguish the different versions of strain theory.

Another assumption over which strain and revised strain theorists disagree is the extent to which a consensus exists on societal goals, their nature, and diversity. Since Durkheim's original anomie theory, the types of goals have increased, so that in the most recent theoretical revisions the goals held by people are very different, depending on their social influences, peer groups, gender, race, and age. Let us examine in more detail the ideas of the specific versions of strain theory that have emerged over the past hundred years.

Founders of Anomie and Strain Theory

In this section, we consider the ideas of the founding theorists in the strain theory tradition. We begin with Durkheim's anomie theory and then look at Merton's adaptation of these ideas to the twentieth-century United States before discussing how their approaches were supplemented by the research of Merton's students Albert Cohen and Richard Cloward.

Durkheim's Original Concept of Anomie

French sociologist Émile Durkheim (1858–1917) was one of the three founders of sociology who at the turn of the nineteenth century sought to explain the transformation that was taking place as societies changed after the Industrial Revolution (Max Weber and Karl Marx, whose ideas we discuss in the next chapter, were the other two founders). Durkheim's view of humans was not unlike that of the classical philosopher Hobbes and later control theorists (discussed in Chapter 7). He believed people were born with potentially insatiable appetites, which can be heightened or diminished by social structure and its cultural values. In a well-ordered society, a cohesive set of values and norms regulates the levels of aspiration and expectation. As a result, levels of crime are relatively low.

For Durkheim ([1895] 1950), crime was any action that offends the collective feelings of the members of society—that shocks their common conscience. He believed that some level of crime is normal and necessary for several reasons. First, even in a well-ordered society (even a society of saints), crime is necessary (functional) to remind the community of its values and standards. Second, crime serves to create a sense of solidarity among law-abiding citizens; the criminal or crime presents an occasion to bring people together to celebrate their values by denigrating those they oppose. Third, society can make moral messages about which rules are most important by adjusting the severity of punishment. Fourth, the punishments given to criminals help to force compliance with the law; fear of shame, humiliation, and lack of liberty motivates people to obey the laws. Finally, and important for Durkheim, there was the idea that crime functioned to warn a society that something may be wrong with the overall way it operates—that is, with its social structure. Crime is the pain of a sick society. It serves as a stimulus for innovation and social change.

For Durkheim, then, some level of crime was inevitable, if only because of those he saw as born biological and psychological misfits (I. Taylor, Walton, and Young 1973, 84). Crime is inevitable because of "the incorrigible wickedness of men" ([1895] 1982, 98). But Durkheim also saw excessive levels of crime as a result of change from the small-scale face-to-face society with a low division of labor and everyone doing similar tasks and sharing common (religious and traditional) values to a large-scale industrial society with a high division of labor and diverse beliefs. In modern industrial society, people become highly specialized in their tasks. Moreover, they are encouraged to act as competitive individuals rather than as members of a common group in pursuing their different occupational roles and to aspire to individual rather than social desires (which he called egoism). Under these circumstances, the moral authority of the collective conscience loses much of its force, and people aspire to positions and levels for which they are ill-suited and that do not satisfy them. Their "greed is aroused" and opens up an insatiable "thirst for novelties, unfamiliar pleasures and nameless sensations, all of which lose their savor once known" (Durkheim [1897] 1951, 256). Such a society is in a state of anomie: a "breakdown in the ability of society to regulate the natural appetites of individuals" (Vold and Bernard 1986, 185), "a situation in which the unrestricted appetites of individual conscience are no longer held in check" (I. Taylor, Walton, and Young 1973, 87). In a condition of anomie, rates of all kinds of nonconformity increase, including crime and suicide, as "individuals strive to achieve their egoistic desires in a way that is incompatible with social order and incommensurate with their biologically given abilities" (ibid., 85). Durkheim's analysis implies that a society explicitly committed to competitive individualism should, therefore, expect a high level of crime; indeed, for such a society, high levels of crime are normal:

> There is nothing necessarily "sick," pathological, dysfunctional, or disorganized about a society organized to produce high rates of crime. . . . A particular level and type of crime are a normal outcome of a specified set of cultural and social arrangements. . . . A low level of predatory crime would be a sign of "something wrong" with a society

that places a premium on the individual competitive pursuit of financial gain, encourages people to create ever more efficient means of besting others, and offers comparatively little protection or comfort to the unsuccessful. We would be on the lookout for something out of the ordinary, something abnormal, about unusually low or falling crime rates in a society organized for crime. (Rosenfeld and Messner 2006, 168)

For Durkheim, this was a societal problem that could be avoided by new forms of moral regulation; its analytical value was that it drew attention to the important role in crime played by changing social structures (e.g., feudalism to capitalism) that generated the social pressure that Merton was later to call strain. The impending eruption of crime and suicide from this misalignment could be avoided, not to go back to a face-to-face society but to advocate new secular values that would acknowledge the rise in individualism but provide appropriate constraints on aspirations. He saw this secular morality as being built around occupations (perhaps professional ethics) but dealt little with how conflicts between these moralities would be resolved.

BOX 9.1 Global Anomie: Hidden Consequences of Globalization
NIKOS PASSAS

Globalism and neoliberalism seem to be indistinguishable empirically or even conceptually (Cox 1993; Stewart and Berry 1999). Nevertheless, I think it is useful to try to separate them analytically. Globalism refers to the degree of interconnectedness and the increase or decrease of linkages. By contrast, neoliberalism refers to an economic and political school of thought on the relations between the state, on the one hand, and citizens and the world of trade and commerce, on the other. Because it espouses minimal or no state interference in the market and promotes the lifting of barriers to trade and business transactions across regional and national borders, it certainly becomes a motor of globalization.

Globalization in the past two decades shows clear signs of deeper and thicker interconnections that affect many more people than ever before. The effects are now much faster, as shown by the financial crisis in Thailand in 1997 and the global fiscal crisis of 2008–2009. The world has shrunk and become "one place," with global communications and media, transnational corporations, supranational institutions, and integrated markets and financial systems that trade around the clock (McGrew 1992; Sklair 1995). The cultural landscape has changed under the influence of mass media. Through their ads, TV programs, movies, and music, they contribute to cultural globalism, target young children, and foster consumerism (e.g., "Image Is Everything," "Just Do It," or "Coke Is It"). Information technology is making for "distant encounters and instant connections" (Yergin and Stanislaw 1998). Fresh normative and comparative ideals are thus promoted, legitimated, and presented as attainable.

The ideological underpinning of globalization, thus, has been the primacy of economic growth, which is thought to be benefiting the whole planet. Consistent with

CONTINUES

BOX 9.1 (CONTINUED)

that prime directive, country after country have been persuaded (or forced) to pro-mote "free trade" and consumerism, to reduce government regulation of business, and to adopt the same economic model, regardless of local specificities and differences be-tween industrialized and developing countries (Bello 1999; Mander 1996).

The Consequences of Global Neoliberalism

Throughout the world, the expectations raised by neoliberal theorists have not mate-rialized, despite the extensive application of their policy recommendations. Instead, most economies "fell into a hole" of low investment, decreased social spending and consumption, low output, decline, and stagnation. Both the World Bank and the In-ternational Monetary Fund retreated from structural adjustment programs and ac-knowledged their failure (Bello 1999; Katona 1999; Watkins 1997).

Criminogenic Effects: Systemic Strains and Global Anomie

What makes the ideology of the American Dream unique is a focus on money and material goods, a strong emphasis on "winning" (often, by all means), and success for everyone in a society where many opportunities for material advancement are available and plenty of "rags to riches" stories lend legitimacy and credibility to the egalitarian discourse. Legal opportunities, however, for achieving the lofty goals are inaccessible to most Americans. In such a consumption-driven culture, which highly values com-petition and individualism, the means-ends disjunction has entailed a significant crim-inogenic risk, much greater than in the rest of the world. Crime has been the flip side of economic growth, innovation, and better living standards for certain segments of the population. What sheltered other countries from this negative potential were things absent or minimized in the United States, such as rigid social stratification, low rates of social mobility, less materialism and time spent before TV boxes, safety nets for the underprivileged, more emphasis on other priorities (e.g., solidarity), and more. The "American Dream" through globalization has fared even worse elsewhere in coun-tries such as China, India, Argentina, Russia, and others (see Passas 2006, where the global anomie framework is applied to Iraq and central Asian republics).

The Consequence: Means-Ends Discrepancies

The worldwide consequences of neoliberal policies were replicated in Russia. How-ever, the effects have been far more disastrous than elsewhere: lower productivity, high unemployment, much steeper inequalities, increased levels of absolute poverty, disap-pearance of familiar safety nets, and administrations paralyzed by ineptness and cor-ruption. The ensuing means-ends discrepancies are far more than a theoretical construct. They are painfully experienced by large numbers of people who realize that they simply cannot attain their goals. Within one year, inflation wiped out most

CONTINUES

BOX **9.1** (CONTINUED)

people's life savings, while the buying power of most wages dropped to the level of the 1950s. In the winter of 1993, funds were often insufficient to heat residential buildings (Burbach, Nunez, and Kagarlitsky 1997; Handelman 1993).

Repressed nationalism, globalism, and bad times have jointly contributed to several armed conflicts and rebellions in the former USSR (the Caucasus, Moldova, Crimea, Tajikistan, and Chechnya). Rebellion and illegal markets become interconnected, as armed conflicts necessitate training, weapons, intelligence, and financing. The cases of Chechnya, Tajikistan, Afghanistan, and Colombia show how political revolts are associated with corruption; money laundering; the traffic in arms, drugs, and even nuclear material; and other crimes that go unpunished (Kuznetsova 1994, 445; Lee 1999; Naylor 1999; OGD 1996). Chechnya, which survives thanks to donations from criminal organizations based in other parts of Russia, has become such a paradise for these activities that some depict the war there as "a crusade against a 'mafia republic,'" while others think of it as "a conflict between opposing criminal elites for the control of oil and the financial resources held by the government in Grozny" (Politi 1998, 44).

"Retreatism" is often the only option left to those lacking access to illegal opportunities or who are unwilling to assume the associated risks of violence and arrest. Hence, expressive crimes could be expected. More important, the rates of alcohol and drug abuse (further facilitated by the decriminalization of drug use in Russia in 1991) increased geometrically, especially in the cities, and fueled the demand for things provided in illegal markets (Lee 1994; OGD 1996).

Conclusion

Tremendous structural strains have overwhelmed even the usually patient Russians. The economic situation deteriorated further, hopes were dashed, opportunities for criminal gain and for looting the former USSR's assets multiplied, and the anomic societal context offered no assistance to anyone seeking to restore some law and order. In Russia and around the world, the neoliberal operation was successful, but the patients are being systematically frustrated, are starving, and are subject to exploitation by corporations, criminal enterprises, and corrupt politicians. In short, globalization and neoliberalism spread analytically similar criminogenic processes that were once unique to the U.S. culture of the American Dream in a context of structural inequalities. Just as the world supposedly became freer, wealthier, more democratic, more enjoyable, and more equal, people find themselves poorer, more exploited, and facing increased hardships. Just as the need for strong normative guidance grows, norms break down or lose their legitimacy. Just as effective controls become necessary to slow down or stop the vicious cycle leading to higher rates of crime, a dysnomic regulatory patchwork remains in place largely because of nationalist insistence on sovereignty and states' unwillingness to allow the introduction of common principles and law enforcement mechanisms.

Nikos Passas is Professor at Northeastern University, College of Criminal Justice, in Boston, Massachusetts.

CONTINUES

BOX 9.1 (CONTINUED)
This insert was reproduced from an article: "Global Anomie, Dysnomie, and Economic Crime: Hidden Consequences of Neoliberalism and Globalization in Russia and Around the World," *Social Justice* 27, no. 2 (Summer 2000): 16–45.

References

Bello, W. 1999. "Is the 'Structural Adjustment' Approach Really and Truly Dead?" *Business-World,* Internet edition, November 8. http://www.bworld.com.ph/current/today.html.

Burbach, R., O. Nunez, and B. Kagarlitsky. 1997. *Globalization and Its Discontents.* London: Pluto Press.

Cox, R. W. 1993. "Structural Issues of Global Governance: Implications for Europe." In *Gramsci, Historical Materialism, and International Relations,* edited by S. Gill. Cambridge: Cambridge University Press.

Handelman, S. 1993. "Why Capitalism and the Mafia May Mean Business." *New York Times,* January 24.

Katona, D. 1999. "Challenging the Global Structure Through Self-Determination: An African Perspective." *American University International Law Review* 14: 1439–1472.

Kuznetsova, R. W. L. F. 1994. "Crime in Russia: Causes and Prevention." *Demokratizatsiya* 2, no. 3: 442–452.

Lee, R. W. 1994. "The Organized Crime Morass in the Former Soviet Union." *Demokratizatsiya* 2, no. 3: 392–411.

———. 1999. "Transnational Organized Crime: An Overview." In *Transnational Crime in the Americas,* edited by T. Farer, 1–38. London: Routledge.

Mander, J. 1996. "Facing the Rising Tide." In *The Case Against the Global Economy,* edited by J. Mander and E. Goldsmith, 3–19. San Francisco: Sierra Club Books.

McGrew, T. 1992. "A Global Society?" In *Modernity and Its Futures,* edited by S. Hall, D. Held, and T. McGrew, 62–102. Cambridge: Open University Press.

Naylor, R. T. 1999. *Patriots and Profiteers: On Economic Warfare, Embargo Busting, and State-Sponsored Crime.* Toronto: McClelland and Stewart.

OGD [Observatoire Geopolitique des Drogues]. 1996. *The Geopolitics of Drugs.* Boston: Northeastern University Press.

Passas, Nikos. 2000. "Global Anomie, Dysnomie, and Economic Crime: Hidden Consequences of Neoliberalism and Globalization in Russia and Around the World." *Social Justice* 27, no. 2 (Summer): 16–45.

Politi, A. 1998. "Russian Organised Crime and European Security." In *Illicit Trade and Organised Crime: New Threats to Economic Security?* edited by EU Directorate-General for External Relations, 31–57. Luxembourg: European Communities.

Sklair, L. 1995. *Sociology of the Global System.* 2d ed. New York and London: Prentice-Hall and Harvester Wheatsheaf.

Stewart, F., and A. Berry. 1999. "Globalization, Liberalization, and Inequality: Expectations and Experience." In *Inequality, Globalization, and World Politics,* edited by Ngaire Woods and A. Hurrell, 150–186. Oxford: Oxford University Press.

Watkins, K. 1997. *Globalisation and Liberalisation: Implications for Poverty, Distribution, and Inequality.* Occasional Paper 32. New York: UN Development Program.

Yergin, D., and J. Stanislaw. 1998. *The Commanding Heights: The Battle Between Government and the Marketplace That Is Remaking the Modern World.* New York: Simon and Schuster.

Merton's Instrumental Anomie and Differential Opportunity Structures

Robert K. Merton, the sometimes-delinquent son of eastern European Jewish immigrants, whose father was a carpenter and truck driver in South Philadelphia, rose from part-time magician to become a leading contemporary sociologist at both Harvard and Columbia universities (Martin, Mutchnick, and Austin 1990). He presented the first contemporary anomie theory in 1938, having witnessed the Great Depression. Although relying heavily on Durkheim and his concept of anomie, Merton made different assumptions about humans and society. In contrast to the class-stratified structure of Durkheim's nineteenth-century France, twentieth-century U.S. society was founded on a supposed equality among people, an ethic whereby hard work and innovation were rewarded, and an overall utilitarian ideology. In Durkheim's France, it was normal for people to be told, "You must go no further"; in Merton's United States, the cultural motto was "Never stop trying to go further" (Passas 1995, 94–95), and an ideology that "promotes insatiability (unlimited aspirations, 'the sky's the limit') through a cultural emphasis on a universal ability to succeed" (Einstadter and Henry 2006, 153). Merton appropriately shifted the emphasis of anomie from a breakdown of, or a failure to develop, adequate moral or normative regulation to "differential access to opportunity structures" that, combined with the egalitarian ideology, produced relative deprivation (Box [1971] 1981, 97–99; Merton [1957] 1968; Passas 1995).

Relative deprivation is the condition in which people in one group compare themselves to others (their reference group) who are better off, and as a result they feel relatively deprived, whereas before the comparison no such feeling existed. Merton ([1957] 1968) used reference group theory and differential experience of the effects of structural strain to explain why some people in anomic situations do not resort to deviance, whereas others do (Shoemaker 1996, 96).

Unlike Durkheim, Merton argued that human "appetites," or desires, are not natural. Rather, they are created by cultural influences (Passas 1995). For example, in the United States heavy emphasis is placed on monetary and material success, such as owning one's own home and car(s). Societal institutions, such as parents, families, schools, government, and the media, impose this pressure. This is known as the "American Dream." In the United States, people with money are generally held in high esteem. In other cultures, different characteristics are valued, such as old age or religious piety. As a Japanese commentator on the American Dream observed, it can look to others like selfishness: "The American Dream is about keeping the rest of the world at bay. Achievements are measured not so much by wealth itself, but by one's ability to hold on to that wealth. . . . 'Moving up' is the American way. . . . Because it can all change tomorrow and not everyone can achieve the dream (though everyone is supposedly free to pursue it), protecting that dream is very important. . . . 'Extreme materialism' . . . is worth fighting for" (Brasor 2003).

Merton pointed out that he was using monetary success only as an illustration, and in his later arguments he asserted that "cultural success goal" could be substituted for money with the same results ([1957] 1968; 1995, 30). It is "only when a system of cultural values extols, virtually above all else, certain common symbols of success for the population at large while its social structure rigorously restricts or completely eliminates access to approved modes of acquiring these symbols for a considerable part of the same population, that anti-social behavior ensues on a considerable scale" (1938, 680).

In the United States, as in other capitalist societies, the approved modes of acquiring success symbols are the institutionalized means used for achieving society's goals. These means are emphasized in the "middle-class values" of saving, education, honesty, hard work, delayed gratification, and so on, but the means are not evenly distributed. This is because the society is divided into a class hierarchy in which access to the approved means is restricted for most of the population; it is "differentially distributed among those variously located in the social structure" (ibid., 679). In a well-integrated society there are adequate means available for all who desire to successfully pursue the culturally prescribed goals: "A well regulated, or stable, society has a balanced equilibrium between means and goals. In a stable society, both means and goals are accepted by everyone and are available to all. Social integration occurs effectively when individuals are socialized into accepting that they will be rewarded for the occasional sacrifice of conforming to the institutionalized means and when they actually compete for rewards through legitimate means. Malintegrated, or unstable, societies stress the goals without stressing the means, or vice versa" (Beirne and Messerschmidt 2000, 129). It is this mismatch between "certain conventional values of the culture" and "the class structure involving differential access to the approved opportunities for legitimate, prestige bearing pursuit of the cultural goals" that "calls forth" antisocial behavior (Merton 1938, 679). This condition, or disjunction, creates the strain that produces anomie. The resolution of this strain can include deviance and crime.

Thus, in contrast to Durkheim's original conception, Merton's anomie "is used to clarify the contradictory consequences of an overwhelming emphasis on the monetary success-goal coupled with the inadequacy of the existing opportunity structure" (Orru 1987, 124). Nor are these contradictions restricted merely to class divisions, since, as Merton argues, the structural sources of differential access to opportunity "among varied social groups (not, be it noted, only social classes)" are "in ironic conflict with the universal cultural mandate to strive for success" in a "heavily success-oriented culture" (1995, 11).

When individuals are socialized to accept the goals of material wealth and upward social mobility but due to their disadvantaged economic position are unable to obtain the resources (means) to achieve these goals, they may cope in several ways, some of which involve crime. It should be noted that Merton emphasized that the differential opportunity structure (not merely confined to economic opportunities) is the cause of strain rather than the cultural goals (ibid., 27–28).

Merton identified five ways in which individuals respond or adapt to "selective blockage of access to opportunities among those variously located in the class, ethnic, racial, and gender sectors of the social structure" (ibid., 12). These five adaptations are all based on an individual's attitudes toward means and goals. These five adaptations are conformity, innovation, ritualism, retreatism, and rebellion (see table 9.1).

Conformity. The conformist accepts the goals of society and the legitimate means of acquiring them. The means include delayed gratification, hard work, and education: "'The American Dream' may be functional for the substantial numbers of those with the social, economic, and personal resources needed to help convert that Dream into a personal reality" (ibid., 16). Illustrative of this adaptation are people from lower-economic-class families and those against whom considerable institutional discrimination exists who succeed due to extra effort or education. Actual success is not necessary, so long as the conformist continues to make the effort and plays by the rules: "Access need not mean accession" (ibid., 8).

But, continues Merton, the dream "may be dysfunctional for substantial numbers of those with severely limited structural access to opportunity and under such conditions it invites comparatively high rates of the various kinds of deviant behavior—socially proscribed innovation, ritualism, and retreatism" (ibid., 16).

Innovation. Innovators accept the goals but significantly reject or alter the means of acquiring the goals; put simply, they cheat. They innovate and seek alternative means to success—often illegitimate. This mode of adaptation accounts for the majority of the crime explained by strain theory. Persons who want goals, say, wealth and status, but who lack legitimate means of acquiring them may find new methods through which wealth can be acquired. Crime is one option. Some common examples of this mode of adaptive behavior would be theft, drug dealing, white-collar crime, and organized crime. A good illustration of white-collar innovation is the case of the prospective graduate students who in 1996 paid $6,000 to be part of a scam to take the Graduate Record Examination, better known as the GRE. The test was taken on

TABLE 9.1   Merton's Individual Modes of Adaptation

	Cultural Goals	*Institutionalized Means*
I. Conformity	+	+
II. Innovation	+	−
III. Ritualism	−	+
IV. Retreatism	−	−
V. Rebellion	±	±

SOURCE: Merton 1938, p. 676.
NOTE: (+) signifies acceptance, (−) signifies elimination or rejection, and (±) signifies rejection and substitution of new goals and standards. Replacement represents a transitional response that seeks to institutionalize new procedures oriented toward revamped cultural goals shared by the members of society. It thus involves efforts to change the existing structure.

the West Coast after expert test takers had taken the same test three hours earlier on the East Coast and phoned the correct answers to the West Coast, where they were inscribed on pencils given to the cheating students.

Ritualism. The third type of adaptation to structural strain is ritualism. Ritualists reject the societal goals but accept the means. These people recognize that they will never achieve the goals due to personal inability or other factors. The bureaucrat who becomes obsessed with the rules but loses sight of the objectives of the organization is one example of a ritualist. Another is the "terminal student" who has no expectation of ever finishing college but continues to take courses. Merton argues that this action is deviant because the culture demands striving to get ahead, not accepting failure or doing only enough to get by.

Retreatism. This is an adaptation whereby the individual rejects both the goals of society and the legitimate means to attain them. This mode of adaptation is most likely to be chosen when the socially approved means are perceived as being unlikely to result in success and the conventional goals are seen as unattainable. Retreatism becomes an escape device for such people. Examples of retreatist behavior would include chronic alcoholism, drug abuse, and vagrancy, behavior that reflects giving up the struggle. The retreatist is "in society but not of it" and may even go on to commit suicide (1964, 219).

Rebellion. The final mode of adaptation is rebellion. Rebels not only reject the goals and means but replace them with new ones. Members of street gangs and motorcycle gangs may fit into this category, as do right-wing militia groups. Another form of rebellion can be seen among members of religious orders who seek certain states of consciousness and reject material gain and members of religious cults such as Heaven's Gate, whose core members committed mass suicide in 1997.

Critique. There have been some notable criticisms of Merton's version of strain theory: that it falsely assumes a universal commitment to materialistic goals; that it ignores violent, passionate, or spontaneous crime; that it cannot explain middle-class, corporate, or white-collar crime; that it relies on official crime statistics; and that it fails to differentiate between aspirations (desired goals) and expectations (probable accomplishments) (F. Adler and Laufer 1995). These have been addressed by recent developments and extensions, as we show next.

Cohen: Status Frustration and Delinquent Subcultures

Albert Cohen, a student of Merton's and Sutherland's, went on to integrate the Chicago School's ideas on culture, differential association, and crime with Merton's anomie theory. He used Merton's theory to answer the criticism that differential association fails to explain how patterns of delinquent behavior originate (discussed in

Chapter 7). But he criticized Merton for overemphasizing the individual dimension of adaptation to strain. Albert Cohen (1955), looking exclusively at delinquent boys, observed that most delinquent behavior not only occurs in interactive group or gang settings rather than alone but also originates there. Each member stimulates the others into behavior they would not commit individually: "Deviant as well as nondeviant behavior is typically not contrived within the solitary individual psyche, but is a part of collaborative social activity, in which the things that other people say and do give meaning, value and effect to one's own behavior" (1955, 8). He also observed that most of this collective action among juvenile delinquent boys was "nonutilitarian, malicious, and negativistic" in nature (ibid., 25). He also criticized Merton's individualistic version of anomie theory for failing to explain the nonutilitarian nature of delinquency. He argued that lower-class male delinquent behavior was the result of a collective adaptation or adjustment to the strain caused by the disjunction between culturally induced goals and differential opportunity structure.

Cohen claimed that for juvenile boys, the central value was achievement or success that brought social status. The socially approved context for this was the school, which provides status based on the middle-class values of accomplishment, display of drive and ambition, individual responsibility and leadership, academic achievement, deferred gratification, rationality, courtesy, self-control over violence and aggression, constructive use of leisure time, and respect for property (J. Hagan 1994; Shoemaker 1996). But many lower-class youths, prior to entering school, have low ascribed status (which is conferred by virtue of one's family position). Nor do they have the socially relevant means and background skills to legitimately achieve status by accomplishing the goals that would bring success in the school setting. Such youths are judged by middle-class standards and typically cannot measure up to their middle-class counterparts. This places lower-class youths under severe strain, from which they experience "status frustration." This is a psychological state involving self-hatred, guilt, self-recrimination, loss of self-esteem, and anxiety. To resolve their status frustration, lower-class youths seek achieved (aspired) status, but since they are unable to achieve this by legitimate means, they collectively rebel (as in Merton's fifth mode of adaptation to strain) through a process that Cohen calls "reaction formation."

Reaction formation involves "(1) redefining the values among similarly situated peers; (2) dismissing, disregarding, and discrediting 'school knowledge'; and (3) ridiculing those who possess such knowledge" (Einstadter and Henry 2006, 168). These youths rebel against the middle-class values by inverting them and thereby creating their own peer-defined success goals, which form the basis of the delinquent subculture. Thus, argues Cohen, these oppositional values are often negative and destructive, involving behavior such as fighting, vandalism, and any acts that provide instant gratification. For Cohen's delinquent boys, "Middle-class standards are not only to be rejected, they are to be flouted. Thus, 'good' children are to be terrorized, playgrounds and gyms are to be taken over for aimless use, golf courses are to be torn up, library books are to be stolen and destroyed and so on" (Shoemaker 1996, 106). Status for conducting such activities is achieved among like-minded peers, ultimately in gang membership. In the gang context, others who hold the same negative values respect the deviant lawbreaker. Cohen argues that "the delinquent's conduct is right by the standards of his subculture precisely because it is wrong by the norms of the larger culture" (1955, 28).

Cohen recognized that his theory was not all-inclusive and did not explain all juvenile crime, particularly crimes by females. He also argued that, as well as the delinquent subculture, there were two other collective responses, the nondeviant "college boy" subculture, whose members struggle against all odds to achieve conventional success, and the dropout "corner boy" subculture. The corner boy parallels Merton's individual retreatist in that he is unable to succeed and believes he is destined to fail at school. But instead of suffering his fate alone, he joins collectively with others for emotional support and engages in marginally deviant activities, which are driven by fatalistic motives rather than the rational goal-directed ones of the delinquent subculture. Subsequent theorists used this analysis as a transitional point and examined these groups.

Cloward and Ohlin: Differential Opportunity Structures and Alienated Youths

Like Cohen, Richard A. Cloward and Lloyd Ohlin saw collective rather than individual action as a key feature of delinquent behavior. In contrast to Cohen, however, their major insight was the notion that rather than rejecting middle-class values, working-class male youths are rational, goal seeking, and oriented toward these values, particularly economic success. They also added an important new dimension, which involved differential access to success goals by illegitimate means. This implied the parallel existence of an illegitimate opportunity structure (Cloward 1959); this idea first appeared in Cloward's doctoral dissertation on military prison completed under Merton and Ohlin at Columbia University. In 1960, Cloward and Ohlin presented their classification scheme to explain the formation of three types of delinquent gangs, showing how these varied depending on the illegal opportunity structures.

The basis of gang formation was rooted in the alienation of some adolescent youths from conventional society as a result of what they perceived as being unjustly denied access to the legitimate means to succeed. Gangs formed as a result of interaction with other similarly affected youths. The way they formed depended on the neighborhood characteristics. Reflecting Chicago School ideas (discussed in Chapter 8), opportunity was also ecological in nature. Different neighborhoods had different resources and opportunity structures available—both legitimate and illegitimate. Concepts central to differential association were vital because youths identify with neighborhood role models and pattern their behaviors after these significant others. (Consider the Chambers brothers example.)[1] Cloward and Ohlin's explanation successfully integrated the ecology theories of the Chicago School, Sutherland's differential association ([1939] 1947), and Merton's anomie.

Like Merton, Cloward and Ohlin agreed that strain and anomie exist because of a "discrepancy" between aspirations and opportunities. Their view, more consistent with Merton's than Cohen's, was that crime may be the result of "differential opportunity structures." Cloward and Ohlin argue that lower-class youths are "led to want" "conventional goals" but find they are unavailable. Because of the "democratic ideology espousing equality of opportunity and universally high aspirations for success," and "faced with limitations on legitimate avenues of access to these goals, and unable to revise their aspirations downward, they experience intense frustrations; the exploration of nonconformist alternatives may result" (1960, 108, 86). Moreover, these frustrations are likely to be more intensely felt among those in social positions where the discrepancy causing the frustration is most acute (ibid., 108).

What further distinguishes Cloward and Ohlin from Cohen is that the frustration produced by the differential opportunity systems is not interpreted by adolescent youths as their own fault or failing. Rather, they perceive their failure as the fault of the system: "It is our view that the most significant step in the withdrawal of sentiments supporting the legitimacy of conventional norms is the attribution of the cause of failure to the social order rather than to oneself." Thus, youths view their failure not as "a reflection of personal inadequacy" but as a result of "unjust or arbitrary institutional arrangements" (ibid., 111). Although such youths do internalize conventional goals, they do not internalize the failure to accomplish these goals as the result of their own inadequacy but as a result of an unjust cultural and social system.

For Cloward and Ohlin, the strain producing frustration does not lead automatically to collective delinquent solutions but depends first on alienation. Whether this alienation from the conventional system converts into subcultural delinquency depends on the outcome of a complex interactive and dynamic evolutionary process among peers. Indeed, those who aspire to economic success are more likely to take part in serious criminal conduct than those who aspire to a middle-class lifestyle (Hoffmann and Ireland 1995, 248–249). Anticipating subsequent renditions of control and neutralization theory (discussed in Chapters 6 and 7), Cloward and Ohlin argued that before delinquent subcultures can form, four conditions must be met: "First, [youths] must be freed from commitment to and belief in the legitimacy of certain aspects of the existing organization of means. Secondly, they must join with others in seeking a solution to their adjustment problems rather than attempt to solve them alone. Thirdly, they must be provided with appropriate means for handling the problems of guilt and fear. Finally, they must face no obstacles to the possibility of joint problem-solving" (1960, 110).

Cloward and Ohlin identified three primary types of deviant subcultures that form in response to the shared perception of injustice. They argued that subcultures develop in relation to the legitimate and illegitimate neighborhood opportunities in which youths grow up. Members of the criminal subculture are primarily interested in crimes that bring material gain: theft, drug dealing, numbers rackets, and so on. These groups are likely to form in neighborhoods where there exists a connection between both conventional activity and theft and various moneymaking rackets. This mutual interdependence provides a relatively stable illegal opportunity structure.

Here, adult criminal role models exemplify an alternative career path and appropriate criminal skills for the juveniles who, like Merton's innovators, are goal-directed instrumentalists rather than impulsive, irrational actors (Shoemaker 1996, 113). The members of these gangs avoid irrational crimes involving violence because such acts would threaten their criminal careers (again consider the Chambers brothers as an example of Cloward and Ohlin's criminal subculture).

In contrast, conflict subcultures form where stable organized criminal activity fails to develop. This is because of a variety of ecological factors, including a transient population, few adult role models, and isolation from conventional opportunity structures. Conflict subcultures have parallels with Merton's rebellion and Cohen's delinquent subcultures. Members of conflict subcultures are involved in violent or "expressive" crimes essentially motivated by an angry war against society for the injustice and humiliation it has bestowed on them. These subcultures may be gangs who fight to preserve territorial boundaries and honor. Here, self-worth, or "rep," is developed through establishing oneself as a risk taker, a hard-ass, being cool, and having a violent macho image. Being "quoted," or beaten by gang members as an initiation rite, illustrates this value. Part of the reason for this alternative status or honor hierarchy is the absence of stable illegitimate opportunity structures.

Finally, retreatist subcultures, which have parallels to Merton's retreatist mode of adaptation and Cohen's "corner-boy subculture," are composed of dropouts involved with excessive alcohol and drug use, sexually promiscuous behavior, and survival activities such as pimping. Members of these subcultures are deemed "double failures" because they have also failed in other types of gangs (criminal and conflict) as well as in conventional society. The retreatist reflects the important point of blockage by both the legitimate and the illegitimate opportunity structures.

Policy Implications of Traditional Strain Theory

There are two broad policy approaches addressing the structural-cultural causes of strain. First, the raised cultural aspirations emphasizing monetary acquisition produced by a society can be tempered, reduced, or otherwise lowered. Second, the unequal opportunity structure can be addressed by making it more equitable. By far the majority of policy suggestions and implementations from traditional strain theories have attempted to increase access to legitimate opportunities. We will see later that one version of the new strain theory attempts to deal with the cultural question.

At the macro policy level of dealing with problems of differential opportunity structure, it is clear that if juveniles lack the means to achieve "middle-class" success, then the means should be provided to them. Educational programs such as Head Start help disadvantaged children from an early age to succeed in the school setting. Providing resources and mobilizing disorganized communities are also suggested by strain theorists. Unlike many criminological theories, these policies have been implemented—although not completely and not with much success, with the exception of Head Start, which was implemented in 1965 and by 2003 had enrolled 20 million children.

In the early 1960s, Robert Kennedy was appointed attorney general of the United States by his brother and then-president John F. Kennedy. Robert Kennedy had read Cloward and Ohlin's book and as a result asked Ohlin to help devise a new federal policy for dealing with juvenile delinquency. The Juvenile Delinquency Prevention and Control Act of 1961 was designed to provide employment and work training for disadvantaged youths. The act also directed resources to social services and community organizations. Despite good intentions, the act is generally considered to have failed, in part, according to some, because it did not go far enough. For example, Ohlin advocated strikes against schools and lawsuits against landlords as a means of promoting change. The act was much less ambitious, incorporating only piecemeal solutions. But it was the forerunner of Lyndon Johnson's War on Poverty, announced in 1964, including the Office of Economic Opportunity (Gilsinan 1990; Sundquist 1969). From that office emerged numerous social engineering programs, such as Mobilization for Youth, Head Start, Job Corps, Vista, Neighborhood Legal Services, and the Community Action Program. Again, some have argued that the $6 billion spent on these programs between 1965 and 1968 was a gross underfunding given the magnitude of the problems and claim that up to $40 billion would have been more appropriate (Curran and Renzetti 1994, 170; Empey and Stafford 1991). Others maintained that the programs underestimated the extent of political resistance reflected in the fact that those who challenged the political and economic structure of their communities saw their funds withdrawn (Empey and Stafford 1991). The outcome was more certain: "Contrary to expectations, the crime rate, rather than decreasing appeared to increase. Moreover, as legitimate opportunities seemed to expand, the demand for even greater opportunity increased and urban riots became a commonplace spectacle on the nightly news" (Gilsinan 1990, 146). By the 1980s, most of Johnson's War on Poverty programs had been dismantled (Curran and Renzetti 1994, 172), with the exception of Head Start, which was still receiving funding in 2008.

In summary, traditional versions of strain theory have drawn attention to the interplay between structural and cultural forces and individual and collective adaptations to their misalignment and the deviant and criminal outcomes that result. Policy suggestions have been implemented with some success, if limited resources. What has been omitted from the theory and the policy are an analysis of increasingly diverse social values, variation among individuals' perceptions, and the contribution from institutions to these developments. The various revisions to strain theory attempt to fill these gaps and begin to make policy recommendations but as yet have received only limited empirical evaluation.

Evaluation of Traditional Strain Theory

Most criticisms of Merton's original strain theory have been addressed by subsequent theorists such as Cohen and Cloward and Ohlin, but several have proved resilient. These include (1) the omission of major segments of the population whose social characteristics lead them to not share in dominant cultural goals of economic success, notably women (Leonard 1982) and minorities (LaFree, Drass, and O'Day 1992); (2) confusion over the definition of goals and means (Sanders 1983); (3) oversimplification of the process of gang formation, gang types (Spergel 1964; Campbell 1984), and what motivates gang members (Jack Katz 1988; Hagedorn [1988] 1994/1998); and (4) failure to allow for humans' being creative and interpretive enough to overcome the social structure and transform it (Suchar 1978). Although some have acknowledged that Merton's theory has been "reborn" as "a viable and promising theory of delinquency and crime," primarily because of recent attempts to develop and extend it (discussed later), even these new ideas are subject to challenge (Farnworth and Leiber 1989, 273).

The empirical evidence for strain theory demonstrates conditional support, although support is growing for the various revised versions of the theory. However, the theory has fared less well in its hypothesis that crime is related to pursuing a goal of material success, and is less supported in its prediction that Americans attach greater importance than other cultures to financial success and the willingness to ignore rules to pursue goals (Jensen 2002; Cao 2004). In contrast, Baron (2006), while finding mixed support for strain theory, did conclude that the cultural stress on economic success was related to crime. Baumer and Gustafson (2007) found partial support for anomie theory, but concluded that additional research and refinement were necessary. The incorporation of the dimensions of other theories improves the likelihood of empirical support. For example, Featherstone (2003) found that although strain theory was a possible explanation for deviant behavior, it was not the only possible explanation. The ecological ideas of Cloward and Ohlin about neighborhood organization and gang formation are better supported. But the balance of evidence suggests that both Cohen's and Cloward and Ohlin's theories are not generally supported by the empirical data, especially Cohen's idea of youths' joining with others to commit offenses in opposition to middle-class values as a result of school failure. However, Sharp, Aldridge, and Medina (2006) found that membership in a delinquent youth group was associated with delinquent behavior. Nor has Cloward and Ohlin's notion that lower-class youths blame the system for their failures or their typology of gangs received much empirical support (Shoemaker 1996, 111, 114–115, 120). However, evaluation of policy applications of the theory has shown some positive results. For example, the Head Start program over its history has demonstrated positive results, both for educational achievement, employment prospects, and participation in crime. A seventeen-year follow-up controlled group study of 622 young adults aged twenty-two in Colorado and Florida found that those who participated in Head Start achieved greater school success than those who did not. Importantly, however, female but not male participants in Head Start did much better educationally, with 95 percent graduating or obtaining a general equivalency diploma compared to 81 percent of nonparticipants. For Head Start programs using the High Scope program (based on the principle that active learners learn best from activities that they plan and carry out themselves and then reflect upon), there were only half as many convictions as nonconvictions among all participants compared to nonparticipants (Oden, Schweinhart, and Weikart 2000). Indeed, an evaluation of the High Scope/Perry School Project determined that 7 percent of adults who had participated in the program had been arrested five or more times, compared with 35 percent of those who had not, and that participants were four times more likely (29 percent) to earn $2,000 or more per month than were nonparticipants (7 percent) by the time each reached adulthood (Schweinhart 2003). Another study that randomly assigned 123 African Americans living in poverty to either the program or no program and evaluated the crime-prevention effects of this program through age forty found that "the program group significantly surpassed the no-program group in tested ability and performance throughout childhood; higher adult earnings and rates of employment and home ownership; half as many lifetime arrests, including fewer lifetime arrests for violent, property, and drug crimes; and fewer convictions and months sentenced" (Schweinhart 2007, 141). The study showed that among the program group, compared with the nonprogram group, 14 percent compared with 34 percent were arrested for drug offenses, 33 percent compared with 48 percent were arrested for violent offenses, and 36 percent compared with 58 percent were arrested for property offenses. Moreover, 45 percent of program males had five or more arrests by age forty compared with 63 percent of no-program males. Finally, whereas only 10 percent of High Scope participants had been arrested for a felony, 39 percent of those who received conventional instructional methods had been arrested for a felony (Schweinhart 2007).

Overall assessment of the policy implications of traditional anomie and strain theory varies depending on which version is followed. Since all relate the source of crime to the strain produced by structural (means) and cultural (goals) contradictions, crime-control policy must attend to removing or reducing these strains or improving the legitimate ways that those affected cope.

Recent Revisions to Anomie and Strain Theory

Several contemporary criminologists have presented revised versions of traditional strain theory. For example, while retaining the core elements of strain theory, Elliott and his colleagues (Elliott, Ageton, and Canter 1979; Elliott, Huizinga, and Ageton 1985) asserted that juveniles have varied goals that differ among individuals and groups. Moreover, juveniles may hold multiple goals that they consider important. These may include having an active social life, being a good athlete, getting good grades, and having a good physical appearance and an attractive personality (Agnew 1984; 1995a, 114–115). However, like the original versions of strain theory, this version has a very limited scope, since it examines the behavior of delinquent boys only in urban environments (Broidy 2001).

Passas (1995, 101) extended the original formulation by arguing that anomic trends apply "at all levels of the social structure" and showed especially how they apply to corporate deviance (1990, 1993). He pointed out that in "achievement-oriented societies" where people are encouraged to compete, "they do not compete for the same things." Thus, we do not necessarily need comparisons between different classes; comparisons can occur with more successful peers, which may be upsetting and "generate frustrations and bring about a breakdown of normative standards" (ibid., 101–102).

Perhaps the most visible contributor to the revised strain theory is Robert Agnew (1985, 1992, 1995a, 1995b, 2006), who also argued for a general strain theory able to explain crime and middle-class delinquency, and has sought to identify the conditions that cause strain (2001) and the interrelation between personality traits or "negative emotionality" and strain (Agnew et al. 2002).

Agnew's General (or Revised) Strain Theory

Whereas Merton sought to explain how macrolevel influences produce strain that bears on individual choices, Robert S. Agnew's "general strain theory" (1992) argued that there are also microlevel stresses emanating from negative interpersonal, peer group, or familial relationships that produce strain and that these may be more important. Not only that, but the two kinds of strain, structural and psychological strain, are interrelated. Thus, strain first "can refer to characteristics of a society: a situation in which the social structure fails to provide legitimate means to achieve what the culture values. Second, it can refer to feelings and emotions that an individual experiences; feelings of stress or frustration or anxiety or depression or anger. The line of argument connecting these two meanings is that people in situations of 'social structural strain' . . . may feel 'strained' . . . and feelings then are the actual cause of higher crime rates associated with these people" (Vold, Bernard, and Snipes 2001, 147).

For example, Agnew argued that juveniles not only seek societally valued goals but experience stress and exercise pain-avoidance behavior as a goal. For Agnew, strain triggers negative emotions and anger that necessitate coping strategies. But legitimate avenues of avoidance may be blocked: "Adolescents who are abused by parents, for example, may be unable to legally escape from home. Or adolescents who are harassed by teachers may be unable to legally escape from school. This inability to escape from painful situations, or this blockage of pain-avoidance behavior, [is] another major type of strain" (1995a, 115–116; 1985; 1989). In other words, Agnew focuses on social psychological variables instead of social structural variables that were considered by earlier versions of strain theory (Broidy 2001).

Agnew presents four sources of strain: (1) "strain as the actual or anticipated failure to achieve positively valued goals" (e.g., failure to get into college); (2) "strain as the actual or anticipated removal of positively valued stimuli" (e.g., being kicked off the high school basketball team or thrown out of a budding local hip-hop group); (3) "strain as the actual or anticipated presentation of negatively valued stimuli" (e.g., experiencing domestic violence, or being subjected to school bullying); and (4) strain produced by the failure of achievements to meet expectations (e.g., failing to meet a desirable boyfriend or girlfriend and always ending up with the loser, or getting into an average college but not the top college that friends have achieved) (1992, 47). Strain resulting from each of these sources manifests in negative emotions such as anger and frustration, which "creates pressure for corrective action, with delinquency being one possible response" (1995a, 116; see also Brezina 1996). Agnew talks of an "aversive situation" for adolescents, which may include the following indicators of "environmental adversity": (1) the extent to which parents scream, slap, threaten, nag, ignore, and withdraw love privileges; (2) the extent to which teachers lose their tempers, make negative comments, and talk down to students; and (3) the extent to which students find school boring and a "waste of time" (1991b, 282). Thus, Agnew's theory here implies an unequal distribution of power within the social structure that is based on gender or age. Indeed, it is a distinguishing feature of adolescents that they lack power and are often compelled to remain in situations that they find aversive. They are compelled to live with their family in a certain neighborhood, to go to a certain school, and, within limits, to interact with the same group of peers and neighbors (1985, 156). Adolescents, then, are considered more constrained by institutional structures than, say, adults (although adults receive different kinds of constraints) and, as a result, have goals that are directed to the avoidance of pain rather than achieving pleasure. For Agnew, delinquency operates as one way of coping with these power imbalances, experienced as "negative social relations" and as uncomfortable psychological states (e.g., anger and frustration) (1995a, 113).

Agnew has subsequently refined this position, arguing that vicarious and anticipated strain in addition to directly experienced strain are also important (2002). Vicarious strain "refers to the real-life strain experienced by others around the individual. . . . The individual may directly witness the strain experienced by these others (e.g., such as an assault), may hear these others' experience of strain (e.g., gun shots, screams) or may hear about the strain of these others (e.g., from victims of in the media)" (2001, 604). Anticipated strain is the person's expectation that the current strain will continue into the future. Agnew also posits that some types of strain will not be related to crime (2001).

What Agnew contributed to traditional strain theory, then, is an analysis of the psychological processes that convert structurally induced frustrations and negative emotions (especially anger) into delinquent action, focusing on cognitive, behavioral, and emotional coping strategies (1995b, 63). Put simply, he argued that the unique contribution of strain theory is its essential insight that "if you treat people badly, they might get mad and engage in delinquency" (1995a, 132; 1995b, 43) and that "the ultimate source of crime is negative treatment by others" (2001, 171). Moreover, he asserted that people, particularly adolescents, are more likely to get mad if they have personality traits that include ineffective problem-solving skills, emotional sensitivity, low tolerance to adversity, and poor self-control (Agnew et al. 2002). Agnew (2001) identified the range of potential strains most likely to be responsible for crime and delinquency: (1) strain perceived as being unjust (e.g., being "picked on" for punishment by a teacher for behavior that others get away with); (2) strain of high magnitude (e.g., consistently experiencing abuse at home or continually witnessing parents' fighting); (3) strain accompanied by low social control (e.g., family abandoned by a loved father and having to accept a hated stepfather); and (4) strain creating pressure to engage in criminal coping (e.g., viciously fighting back against a bully, or against those who allow bullying to continue such as teachers and other students). However, Agnew is fully aware that not all strains or "stressors" lead to crime but recognizes the "centrality of anger" that follows strain. Anger short-circuits the ability to reason with others, reduces the awareness of the consequences of committing crime, and allows the person to feel that the crime is justified under the circumstances, thereby increasing the probability of crime. He states that "people are more likely to engage in criminal coping when they lack the ability to cope in a legal or constructive manner, when they perceive the costs of crime are low, and when they are disposed to criminal behavior patterns" (2006, 158). In short, from Agnew's perspective, crime is a coping mechanism: "Crime may be a means to reduce strains or escape from them (steal the money one desires, run away from abusive parents); seek revenge against the source of the strain or related targets; or make oneself feel better (through illicit drug use)" (ibid., 155).

Policy Implications of General Strain Theory

General strain theory sees the problem of crime in sociopsychological terms and, therefore, prefers microlevel individual policy solutions. Since Agnew simplifies the problem of strain as "treating people badly," whereupon they "get mad" and commit crimes, he not surprisingly sees policy suggestions as relatively straightforward. At this level general strain theory has two core policy recommendations. First, "reduce the likelihood that people will treat one another badly" by introducing family, school, and peer group programs that teach people "prosocial skills so that they will be less likely to provoke negative reaction from others." Second, "reduce the likelihood that people will respond to negative treatment with delinquency" by providing them with social support and teaching them better coping skills (1995b, 43). In particular, Agnew provides four concrete policy proposals for juveniles: (1) Reduce the adversity in youths' social environment by providing them with more participation in the decisions that affect their lives. This will increase their sense of "distributive justice." Provide academic and social monitoring and support and rewards for pro-social behavior while helping them overcome adverse environments, whether this involves changing schools or families. (2) Provide social skill–training programs to reduce youths' likelihood of provoking negative social reactions in others. (3) Provide social support such as advocates or counselors and mediation programs to increase youths' ability to solve problems legitimately, particularly in stressful times of transition. (4) Increase social skill–training, problem-solving, and anger-control programs to increase the ability of youths to cope with adversity without resorting to delinquency (ibid., 64). It is important to point out, as Agnew did, that none of these coping strategies remove the forces causing strain in the larger environment and influencing the success or failure of particular programs. As he acknowledged, "It is difficult for parent training programs to be successful, for example, when parents face multiple stressors such as the lack of good jobs, poor housing, and neighborhoods plagued by a host of social problems" (ibid., 61). Agnew left this level of policy intervention to others, however.

Evaluation of General Strain Theory

As a result of its focus in psychological, behavioral, and cognitive processes, Agnew's general strain theory is seen by some as reductionist, undermining the major structural tenets of the original theory (Farnworth and Leiber 1989, 272; Shoemaker 1996, 96). But Agnew (1995b) himself argues that his revision is intended not to displace the structural dimension but to complement it (indeed, there could be no better complement to it than the work of Messner and Rosenfeld, discussed below, who combined broad social-structural processes and, in particular, examined the shift toward an extreme emphasis on material goals and the impact this has on institutions of social control).

The basic tenets of general strain theory are supported by recent empirical research (Arter 2008; Bao, Haas, and Pi 2007; Brezina, Piquero, and Mazerolle 2001; N. Piquero and Sealock 2000). It is also quite robust and allows extension and modification. Extensions have included Arter (2008), who successfully applied strain theory to explain police behavior, while Ellwanger (2007) has used strain theory to explain traffic delinquency. Walsh (2000) incorporated strain theory in an integrative behavioral genetics and biology to explain individual criminal behavior. Johnson and Kercher (2007) found that ADHD could decrease individuals' ability to cope with psychological strain, making them more prone to criminal behavior. Hinduja (2007) applied Agnew's strain theory to explain harassment in the workplace. Froggio and Agnew (2007) examined the relationship between subjective versus objective strain and criminal behavior. Aspects of Agnew's general strain theory concerning the negative effects of multiple sources of strain on social bonds and increased delinquent peer associations have also received some empirical support. Overall, "there is consistent empirical evidence that exposure to strain increases the likelihood of criminal offending" but "less support for the idea that adaptations to strain are conditioned by a range of other factors," yet "some evidence indicates that the combination of strain and anger increases the risk of criminal conduct" (Lilly, Cullen, and Ball 2002, 61).

Messner and Rosenfeld's Institutional Anomie Theory

Unlike Agnew's microtheoretical interpretation of strain theory, Messner and Rosenfeld's book *Crime and the American Dream* (1994) presents the macrotheoretical idea of institutional anomie to explain the uniquely U.S. obsession with crime. This revised interpretation of Merton's strain theory includes elements of control theory not dissimilar to Durkheim's original argument. It focuses, however, on what the authors claim is the unique character of U.S. culture, embodied in the "American Dream" and its relationships with U.S. economic institutions. Messner and Rosenfeld argued that all societies have their own internal institutional balance of power, with some institutions more dominant than others. The particular balance in American society is dominated by the "free market economy" that favors economic institutions over the rest:

> Non-economic institutions "bend" to the economy as plants to sunlight; their rewards and routines conform to economic requirements, and the very language used to describe them has economic overtones. Think of the accommodations families make to economic requirements, how work hours determine household meal and vacation schedules, how an employer's permission is needed to tend to a sick child, how having a family above all requires having a job. Think of how the economy dominates American political life, how much attention during elections is devoted to the candidates' "tax and spend" policies, how much more efficient government would be, we are told, if it were run like a business. (Rosenfeld and Messner 2006, 165–166)

This predominantly individualized competitive free-market ideology colors the American Dream. Rosenfeld and Messner defined the American Dream as "a commitment to the goal of material success, to be pursued by everyone in society, under conditions of open, individual competition" (1995b, 164). The American Dream promotes never-ending individual achievement as a measure of social worth. It emphasizes winning over the way we play the game, as in 1960s Green Bay Packers football coach Vince Lombardi's famous quote, "Winning isn't everything; it's the only thing." In their view, Americans are motivated to succeed or "win" by a competitive desire to meet their material and other needs via the system of economic inequality that distinguishes winners from losers: without this, "it is difficult to see how people could be motivated to participate with any enthusiasm in the sometimes harsh and unforgiving competitive race to success. The promise of 'making it' keeps the players in the game, and is it possible to 'make it,' to compete successfully, unless at least some other players are unsuccessful?" (Rosenfeld and Messner 2006, 168). Their view of American society implies that institutions shape people's actions and that the particular market-driven configuration of American society "reinforces 'anomic' cultural tendencies that elevate the goal of material success above others and de-emphasizes the importance of using the legitimate means for attaining success" (ibid., 165).

Messner and Rosenfeld maintained that social institutions, such as schools and the family, serve to perpetuate the economic status quo of competitive material success by failing to stimulate alternative means of self-worth and, as a result, are unable to tame economic imperatives: "In short the institutional balance of power is tilted toward the economy" (Rosenfeld and Messner 1995b, 170). They stated that this economic dominance over social organizations is manifest in three different ways: "(1) in the devaluation of non-economic institutional functions and roles; (2) in the accommodation to economic requirements by other institutions; (3) in the penetration of economic norms into other institutional domains" (ibid., 171). For example, in U.S. culture, education becomes a means to jobs rather than an end in itself; educational curricula reflect the accommodations to economic needs, and educational practice is penetrated by economic norms reflected in grading schemes, individual learning, and program assessment. Similarly, occupational roles are seen merely instrumentally as a means to economic rewards. Even the political institutions are reduced from their role of setting collective goals to facilitating ways to obtain material possessions. This is well captured in the Clinton-era political campaign slogan on what was the priority issue: "It's the economy, stupid!" Institutional anomie theory "holds that culturally produced pressures to secure monetary rewards, coupled with weak controls from non-economic social institutions, promote high rates of instrumental criminal activity" (Chamlin and Cochran 1995, 413). This is because under the particular insatiable demands of the American Dream, no amount of money obtained from legal sources is ever enough: "Illegal means will always offer further advantages in pursuit of the ultimate goal. There is a perpetual attractiveness associated with illegal activity that is an inevitable corollary of the goal of monetary success" (Rosenfeld and Messner 1995b, 175). Moreover, the authors believed that not only is the effect of anomie ameliorated by the strength of noneconomic social institutions, but without them crime knows no bounds (Messner and Rosenfeld 1994).

Rosenfeld and Messner's institutional anomie theory has particular relevance for explaining crime in a late-modern or postmodern society where there is a celebration of the "culture of consumption." As they say, the American Dream is fulfilled through consumption, and consumption is often not possible without crime: "The consumer role is the principal structural locus of anomic cultural pressures in modern market societies" (1995a, 2). Whether the anomic tendencies of the consumer role lead to crime depends on the embeddedness of consumption. In community-based societies such as Japan, the anomic pressures are subdued in market relations with strong noneconomic content and control. Market relations "are embedded in non-economic institutional domains" that foster trust and networks of interpersonal relations (ibid., 6). In late-modern or postmodern societies such as the United States, where the economic "bottom line" pervades all institutional arenas and social standing and personal worth are defined primarily in terms of individual material acquisition, anomic pressures to engage in crime are stimulated. This point is nicely illustrated by Siegel, who in discussing institutional anomie theory stated, "Economic language, standards, and norms penetrate into noneconomic realms. Economic terms become part of the vernacular. People want to get to the 'bottom line'; spouses view themselves as 'partners' who 'manage the household; we 'outsource' home repairs instead of doing them ourselves. Corporate leaders run for public office promising to 'run the country like a business'" (2004, 195).

Messner and Rosenfeld (1994, 2001, 2006), therefore, saw the cause of crime in the structural, cultural, and institutional conditions of society. They argued that for each configuration of society's balance of institutions, there is a corresponding rate of crime or deviance. Their argument is that American capitalist society, dominated by a market-driven economy, which permeates all social institutions, allows an unfettered pursuit of needs and desires that pays little attention to the legitimacy of the methods used to achieve them:

> We maintain that the dominance of the free-market economy in the institutional structure reinforces "anomic" cultural tendencies that elevate the goal of material success above others and de-emphasize the importance of using the legitimate means for attaining success. Under such cultural conditions, people tend to cut corners, and they may disobey the law when it impedes the pursuit of economic gain. At the same time, the social control exerted by the polity, family, education, and religion is diminished when the institutional balance of power favors the economy. The social support institutions provide also weakens. . . . Diminished social control frees people from normative restraints; weakened social support pushes people to meet their material and other needs however they can. Both lead to high rates of criminality. (2006, 166)

They said their own research (Messner and Rosenfeld 1997) indicated that societies with stronger welfare safety nets, designed to protect their members from the harshness of unemployment and mitigate the effects of inequality, have lower crime rates than those with weaker social support systems.

Policy Implications of Institutional Anomie

With regard to policy questions in relation to strain theories, theorists have rarely suggested addressing the cultural problem of raised aspirations. Rosenfeld and Messner, however, did just that. As they observed, "Americans live in a society that enshrines the unfettered pursuit of material success above all other values. Reducing these crimes will require fundamental social transformations that few Americans desire and rethinking a dream that is the envy of the world" (1995a, 176–177). Indeed, they said, "Permanent reductions in criminality, as opposed to the stabilization of high crime rates, will require a tempering of the extreme materialism and competitive individualism of the American Dream. Those cultural changes, in turn, must be accompanied by a corresponding shift in the institutional balance of power that strengthens the social control and social support functions of noneconomic institutions" (2006, 171).

As part of their policy for ameliorating the extreme effects of capitalist inequalities, Messner and Rosenfeld (2001, 2006) suggested initiatives designed to protect and insulate youth from delinquency by providing socialization for the young in the responsibilities and obligations of adulthood, paid family leave for parents, and even universal national service. For those already in trouble with the law, they suggested reductions in sentence length and increased support for prisoner reentry programs designed to integrate offenders into their communities. But with regard to delivering more fundamental social change, they believed it is necessary to go beyond policy makers to social movements: "organized groups of citizens dedicated to transforming conventional outlooks and institutional practices" (Rosenfeld and Messner 2006, 171).

Thus, although antithetical to U.S. cultural values of individualism and material gain, stressing the values of cooperative activity, social rather than instrumental relations, sharing rather than consuming, and humility and satisfaction with the inner self as opposed to monetary success, physical beauty, and material trappings would reduce or eliminate the insatiable desire to pursue instrumental goals. Indeed, some have suggested shifting the culture toward increased social support at the very time when it appears to be moving away from this value (E. Currie 1985; Cullen 1994). However, rather than simply providing welfare, addressing the pervasiveness of market principles would require a massive restructuring of capitalist society. For example, Einstadter and Henry pointed to one aspect of what such a policy might entail: "Limiting the extent to which we create a demand for unnecessary consumption through advertising in the mass media. Controls might include laws minimizing advertising to informational claims, reducing the length of advertisements to one or two line announcements as currently occurs on Public Broadcasting Service sponsorship, and vigorously controlling any 'hyping' of product that is not substantially supported by independent consumer research" (2006, 177).

Ultimately, of course, this kind of approach begins to challenge the very foundation of American capitalist society, and as we shall see in the next chapter, that is precisely what some feel it should do. Indeed, critical theorists, beginning with Marxists, argue that the ultimate failure of the strain approach is that it is reformist; the system is rigged, and no amount of adjustment is going to remove the strain that stems from its basic inequalities.

Evaluation of Institutional Strain Theory

Messner and Rosenfeld's contribution could be said to have shifted our attention back from the psychological interpretation of Agnew to the economic structuralist argument focusing on the centrality of the materialist American Dream. Merton (1995), however, rejected an exclusive focus on structure as too limited. Indeed, focusing on the formal economic institutions of society as the dominant shaping forces of U.S. culture and formal social institutions as ameliorators ignores the force of the often very differently focused informal institutions and informal and hidden economies of social support and mutual aid (Robinson and Henry 1977; Henry [1978] 1988, 1981; Ferman, Henry, and Hoyman 1987) that we saw in the previous chapter were so significant in marginalized communities. That these informal institutions focus on social support and reciprocity as central organizing themes of their members and exist as part of the subculture of U.S. society has only recently been addressed by strain theorists (Cullen 1994; Colvin, Cullen, and Vander Ven 2002).

However, institutionalized strain theory has received some empirical support. Trahan, Marquart, and Mullings (2005) found that the acceptance of capitalistic values was an important factor in criminal behavior, particularly fraud. Jukka Savolainen used data from the World Health Organization to show that economic inequality is related to homicide in nations with weak collective institutions of social protection.

Specifically, "the positive effect of economic inequality on the level of lethal violence is strongest in nations where the economy dominates the institutional balance of power" (2000, 1026). As we argue in the next chapters, this may also support conflict and radical theory, but Savolainen prefers an explanation based on institutional anomie and strain. Similarly, Cernkovich, Giordano, and Rudolph (2000) found that white Americans in particular who believed in the American Dream but failed to achieve economic success were more crime-prone than either whites who have achieved success, whites who didn't believe strongly in the American Dream, and African Americans who had lower expectations because of their unique history. Bernburg (2002) and Deflem (1999) added excellent commentary on this. In spite of the support, Chamlin and Cochran (2007) in contrast stated that not only does Messner and Rosenfeld's theory not lend itself easily to falsification, but it may also apply only to developed Western societies. However, as we will see, Nikos Passas has shown that it does apply globally.

Global Anomie Theory and Crime

In his analysis of anomie theory, Nikos Passas (2000, 2006) went beyond American society to locate anomie in the wider structural context of a global economic system that he saw as the cause of the inequalities that cause crime. He argued that neoliberal economics promotes relatively unlimited free trade, and as a result is a polarizing force dividing the rich from the poor based on the unequal distribution of income and wealth. At the same time, the free-market economy destroys social safety nets because any nation investing in them is unable to compete in the world economy with those who have no such social supports. In order to compete in the global marketplace, corporations have to reduce costs, which means cutting health insurance, pension benefits, welfare benefits, as well as wages. In this neoconservative liberal global order, nation-states are necessarily forced to shrink their "government" in the interests of cutting taxes on the global competitive producers, which results in a lack of services at the very time that those worst affected need them most. The result is extreme relative deprivation, and in order to survive without state support, the disadvantaged have to seek deviant solutions. The same drive for global competitiveness pressures national governments to cut their regulation of corporations, with the result that increases in corporate and white-collar crime also occur. Passas argued that the vast deregulation fueled by neoliberalism's desire to encourage free trade has failed to limit the effects of global corporate greed:

> Neo-liberal policies have been applied to both rich and poor countries with the promise of economic growth, prosperity, freedom, democracy, self-sufficiency and consumerism, even though the short-term could be characterized by painful austerity measures. In this process, safety nets and welfare state arrangements were reduced or abolished through waves of privatization and deregulation. Global anomie theory argued that economic misconduct and vulnerabilities to both exploitation and victimization are expected outcomes of the systematic frustration of raised expectations and

widening inequalities (economic, political, technological, power asymmetries). Some state protections were cut and others were allowed to wither at the very time they were needed most. Simultaneously, international rules were undermined precisely when normative firmness and legitimacy became critical. (2006, 175–176)

The effects of the "competitive consumerism" of the global market economy withdraws public support from and undermines informal networks that otherwise cushion the deprivation and disadvantages of those who struggle to make it. Indeed, as we've seen in the previous section, evidence suggests that in capitalist nations where a safety net of welfare, pensions, and health care is provided, extreme economic deprivation is avoided and crime rates are lower (Savolainen 2000). Others have indicated that social support is generally preventive of crime, whereas coercion is criminogenic (Colvin, Cullen, and Vander Ven 2002). Insofar as the reduction of state support is experienced as coercive, evidence suggests that the shift to global anomie will also be criminogenic (Colvin 2000). Indeed, Konty argued that a society that promotes self-interest in the anomic sense of celebrating competitive individualism becomes criminogenic only in the absence of social interest that prevents the pursuit of self-interested goals: "Anomie at the individual level can this be understood as the presence of strong self-interest in the absence of social interest," a condition of imbalance called "microanomie" (2005, 111). Clearly, a global anomie can foster a societal anomie that creates the conditions for microanomie.

Passas (2000, 2006), therefore, located the cause of crime not only at the societal level in the shrinking or retracting state but also, importantly, at the global macrolevel of economics. He related societal-level conditions to global conditions, claiming that the free-market economy has permeated societies around the world, which in turn has raised people's expectations for improved lifestyles and conditions, while simultaneously undermining the ability of most of the world's citizens to share in the increased wealth brought about by globalization. This has created a global as well as a societal strain. The only realistic policy to reverse this global anomic economic trend is to move toward recognizing the value of global collective social interests.

Summary and Conclusion

In this chapter, we have examined the ideas that a society's culture, combined with its social organizational structure, sets the conditions for human behavior. Under certain circumstances, these structural forces present some sections of the population with problems to which they have to adapt. The problems, experienced as anger and frustration, are dealt with either individually or collectively. We have examined the several individual and collective ways—often criminal—that people, particularly youths, react to these forces and the different patterns of behavior that emerge. We went on to examine recent revisions to these ideas that expand their breadth and provide a more detailed analysis of their social-psychological components. We also presented extensions of strain theory to corporate and white-collar crime. We also explored how the U.S. capitalist system represents an extreme version of institutional anomie that might account for its having the highest violent crime rate among industrialized nations. We explored the policy implications of these theories and evaluated their theoretical and empirical adequacy, concluding that the more recent revisions tend to be more supported than the original statements. Perhaps the most significant concluding observation is that the contribution of anomie and strain theorists to our understanding of social and structural forces in shaping the context for individual actions has been considerable. They have, however, been less helpful in explaining why societies put up with the maladaption, malintegration, strain, and stresses of social structure and have been more inclined to accept the conditions as inevitable. In the next chapter, we examine theories observing the same trends by advocates who believe that the solution is to eliminate the inequitable social conditions that create crime.

Summary Chart:
Anomie and Strain Theory

Basic Idea: The kind of organization a society adopts, particularly the nature and distribution of occupational roles, opportunities, and the means to obtain them, can contradict its cultural goals. The resulting strain created by differential opportunity structures creates problems, frustration, and anger for people whose adaptive solutions may include illegitimate behavior. Subcultural versions argue that strain is adapted to collectively rather than individually by the formation of groups that may have different values from the wider society from which the individual defects; through "peer pressure" new members learn behavioral patterns, skills, and rationales or justifications for committing crime.

Human Nature: Humans are born as rational beings with the ability to learn and be socialized into goals and values and have the capacity to learn the necessary norms and skills to achieve those values; they have a tendency toward conformity. Subcultural version emphasizes youthful susceptibility to "peer pressure" and "pressure of the group" in the socialization process.

Society and the Social Order: A moral consensus on class hierarchy and on goals and values, although later versions recognize the diversity of goals. Law for Durkheim is an expression of a society's collective conscience; for Merton, it serves the function of integrating the members of the society and maintaining order necessary for the smooth functioning of occupational mobility. Criminals for Durkheim appear as four types: (1) biological, (2) egoistic (those subject to unbridled emphasis on satisfying selfish ends or goals), (3) anomic (those without moral guidance who are "rudderless"), and (4) rebellious (those who show structure is in need of change). For Merton, most criminals are no different from us all. They have followed society's success goals but have been frustrated in their attempt and so have adapted. Subcultural versions see some criminals learning different oppositional values and norms that replace those of dominant culture; they are various kinds of defectors rather than defectives.

Causal Logic: For Durkheim, the cause of crime is a combination of (1) the breakdown of traditional moral regulatory structures of the family, kinship networks, the community, and traditional values coexisting with (2) a "forced" division of labor (rather than "spontaneous"); (3) celebration of the individual, or the "cult of individualism" raising aspirations to insatiable levels; and (4) the failure to adapt the social structure fast enough to accommodate rapid social change. For Merton, there are four modes of deviant adaptation to the fundamental cause, which he sees as structural strain and the maladaption of cultural goals and values in society to the means available to achieve them. A society shares and promotes common values and goals; in the case of the United States this is captured in the notion of the American Dream, meaning acquisition of wealth and display of material (monetary) success. Unequal access to the legitimate means to achieve these goals, expressed by the unequal access to education or other credentials and the unequal availability of good jobs, places strain on conformity to the legitimate goals-means package. Individuals adapt to this strain in different ways. Merton identifies four nonconforming modes of adaptation: (1) innovation—rejecting the legitimate means but maintaining the same societal goals, which explains lower-class property, white-collar, and even corporate pecuniary crime; (2) ritualism—rejecting the goals by giving up the attempt to achieve more than one has but conforming to the legitimate means, which explains some petty bureaucratic deviance; (3) retreatism—rejecting both goals and means, which explains some dropout forms of deviance, such as tramps, vagrancy, and drug and alcohol abusers; and (4) rebellion—rejecting prevailing values and the legitimate means and substituting new goals and using new means, which explains terrorism and revolutionary and even political crimes. In subcultural versions, the American Dream is combined with inadequacies of lower-class socialization and preparation for claimed educational meritocracy, which leaves lower-class youths with impaired ability to compete with middle-class counterparts and decreased achievement against middle-class educational standards. For Cohen, this leads to loss of self-esteem and "status frustration" as the failure within the dominant middle-class system is reacted to, rejected, or replaced by a negative subculture. Identification with those in the same situation results in the formation of a "delinquent subculture" with inverted values of dominant classes: versatile, malicious and negativistic, nonutilitarian behavior and the desire for immediate rather than deferred gratification. Two other responses are those of the "corner boy," who makes the best of the existing situation, and the "college boy," who strives to achieve middle-class standards despite adverse conditions. In the case of Cloward and Ohlin, the situation of the American Dream and blocked opportunities produces alienation that is perceived as injustice. If adolescent blames self, then solitary solutions and dropping out result; if system is blamed, support for it is withdrawn, and it is replaced by one of three subcultures, depending on neighborhood conditions: (1) a criminal rationalistic subculture that emphasizes illegitimate means to achieve societal goals, such as drugs, trading, numbers running, and burglary; (2) a conflict subculture emphasizing violence and protest; or (3) a retreatist subculture escaping into drug use. Agnew's revised version of strain introduces strategies for avoiding the pain of strain, based on a variety of social-psychological variables. Messner and Rosenfeld centralize Merton's concept of the American Dream, showing the importance of the dominant role of U.S. economic institutions in undermining strong social institutions and their moral controls. Passas takes this to the global level, seeing the free market creating extreme divisions between rich and poor, retracting back the protective state, and weakening regulation of corporate greed.

Criminal Justice Policy: Change the social organization of society to better integrate members to socioeconomic roles available. Do not overpromote goals or raise people's aspirations beyond their capabilities. Reduce the sources of strain. Balance the overemphasis on market principles at the expense of other values. Change the global free-market system toward one that reflects principles of social interest.

Criminal Justice Practice: Provide economic opportunities for lower classes. Create jobs, education, welfare and child care programs, and War on Poverty and Head Start programs. Organize local communities to have an investment in conventional society. Community and youth-participation programs. Include programs to accept more wide-ranging skills and knowledge in the educational system. Draw school-teachers from a broader social base. Teach legitimate social and coping skills but also provide legitimate opportunities at school and workplace. Group discussion on change and growth for youths.

Evaluation: Points out how the organization of society can affect individual behavior; supported by studies of better-integrated societies with high family values having low crime rates, such as Japan and Switzerland. Shows how strain can create criminal solutions in anyone. Explains both lower-class crime resulting from strain and middle- and upper-class crime. Fails to explain why people choose particular crime patterns and fails to explain violence and senseless acts. Subcultural version shows how conditions of inequality of opportunity can produce frustration and crime. Explains violent behavior and destructive acts. Indicates how people become involved in different types of crimes. Cohen's version has received inconclusive empirical support; ignores rational profitable delinquency and does not explain middle-class crime. Cloward and Ohlin's version also fails to account for middle-class crime (unless middle classes see themselves as relatively deprived), and subcultural specialization argument is contradicted by evidence. Later versions apply to corporate and white-collar crime. Agnew's revised general strain theory has empirical support. Messner and Rosenfeld's institutional anomie theory is gaining growing support.

Notes

1. Consider how Billy Joe (B. J.) in the Chambers brothers example learned the marijuana trade from his Detroit host family. Also consider the Chambers brothers' Detroit reputation as described by their fellow students: "I graduated with Otis in the Lee Senior High School class

of 1986 so I lived this story firsthand. There is no exaggeration that he received a standing ovation during the graduation ceremonies. He was considered a hero among many of my classmates" (el-detroit 2003). "I lived through this period ([during my] late teens) in Detroit and can attest to the influence of the Detroit Drug organizations. . . . Billy Joe, White Boy Rick, Larry, and some of the others were definitely celebrities. As a high school student, we knew who they all were" (14-karat 2005).

10

Capitalism as a Criminogenic Society
Conflict and Radical Theories of Crime

Strongly identified with violent criminality by skin color alone, the anonymous young black male in public is often viewed first and foremost with fear and suspicion, his counterclaims to propriety, decency, and law-abidingness notwithstanding. Others typically don't want to know him, and in public seek distance from him and those who resemble him.

Shawn's experience is instructive. A law student in Washington, D.C., Shawn grew up in Philadelphia. He comes from the inner city but was able to attend private schools, where he did very well, and went on to college and a prestigious law school. He and the handful of other black law students were the only nonwhite residents of the affluent neighborhood near the law school. One evening after classes, Shawn was waiting for a bus to go home. His apartment was only a ten-minute walk, but he had just stopped by the local grocery store, so he had groceries and books to carry, and he decided to take the bus that stopped just across the street from the law school. Shawn was talking to his girlfriend on the phone as he waited for the bus when he noticed a police car drive slowly by. Then it drove by again, and circled for a third time. On the fourth pass, the officer pulled up behind him and sat for approximately three minutes, with the car floodlight shining on the bus stall in which Shawn sat. Then Shawn was startled to hear a blow-horn order for him to put his hands out where they could be seen and to turn slowly toward the light. Shawn did so with his phone still in his hand. As he turned toward the officer, who had stepped out of his cruiser, he saw that the officer was reaching for his holster and drawing his gun. Another law student, a white female whom Shawn did not know but who had also been waiting for the bus, yelled out to the officer that what he had in his hand was only a cell phone. The officer yelled for Shawn to drop it, which he did. The officer then told Shawn to place his hands against the wall and not to move. The officer immediately handcuffed and frisked him.

Shawn asked what was happening and explained that he was a student at the law school just across the street and was waiting for the bus to go home. The officer ignored his explanation and continued frisking him. By this point, approximately seven other police cars had arrived and had blocked off the street to traffic. At the same time, students and professors from Shawn's law school began to form a crowd across the street, but no one made a move to assist him. He was humiliated. The police cursed at him and yelled at him to cooperate. He did so, confused by what was going on. They repeatedly kicked his legs and ankles, forcing his legs farther and farther apart until he was spread-eagled. They kept pushing his face against the wall or down toward his chest, telling him to keep his head down and stop resisting. He was frisked two more times and his wallet taken. His schoolbooks and laptop were dumped on the sidewalk; his grocery bags were emptied as well. He was restrained by three officers who held his handcuffed hands together with the slack from the back of his shirt and pants to prevent him from running away. They questioned him roughly, showing no respect for him as a law-abiding citizen.

When Shawn again asked what was going on, he was told he fitted the description of someone involved in a shooting a few blocks away. Just then, one of the officers' radios crackled, "Black male, five-foot-eight, blue button-down shirt, khaki-tan dress pants, brown dress shoes." The description fitted Shawn exactly. Having heard himself being described over the radio, he was convinced he was going to jail. After ten minutes of being forced to stand straddled, physically restrained, and handcuffed in front of his peers and professors, another radio announcement let the officers know that the suspect had been arrested. Shawn was uncuffed and told to have a seat. The officers who were standing around returned to their vehicles and drove off. The officer who made the initial stop took down Shawn's information for the police report. As the officer filled out the form, he attempted to make small talk with Shawn, who felt humiliated and still afraid, but mostly angry at the lack of respect he had received and the clear racial profiling that had just taken place.

Shawn realized it was the neighbors who had called the cops and provided the description. They had heard that there was a shooting in the neighborhood and when they saw Shawn, who had been living in the neighborhood for three years, standing on the corner at night, they called the police, having concluded that this black male must be the suspect. These were the neighbors who had stared at him every day and avoided eye contact as he walked by them on the sidewalk on his way to and from law school.

Because the young black male is essentially disenfranchised and considered a troublemaker or at best a person of no account, his is a provisional status. Every black male is eligible for skeptical scrutiny, which renders him vulnerable to harassment for any infraction, real or imagined. His credibility is always shaky. The constant confusion between the street-oriented and the law-abiding black male means that all are subject to suspicion in white eyes, and such public reception then encourages many blacks not to trust whites. Thus, both blacks and whites assign provisional status to the other, deepening the racial divide (E. Anderson 2008, 3, 19–21).

Racial profiling is at the forefront of serious examination of police practices (Barkley 2006). *Police Quarterly* (2002) devoted an entire issue to the topic. Traditionally, profiling has been a frowned-upon, ignored, denied, and vilified practice. This is particularly true of the racial profiling of African Americans while driving: "Blacks and white liberals have been decrying the situation for several years. Many conservatives, on the other hand, dismiss such complaints as the exaggerations of hypersensitive minorities. Or they say that if traffic cops do in fact pull over and search the vehicles of African Americans disproportionately, then such 'racial profiling' is an unfortunate but necessary component of modern crime fighting" (W. Anderson and Callahan 2001). However, since the World Trade Center terrorist attacks of September 11, 2001, profiling has enjoyed increased support. Much like the Japanese Americans who were detained during World War II due solely to their racial profile, the new "ethnic" threats to America, those who came here from the Arab world and who are Muslim, are now being targeted.

Clearly, racial profiling is nothing new in America. It began to receive attention following the Civil War when African Americans were the target of increased police attention. This is not just a perception: Recent research shows that while African Americans and Hispanics are stopped about the same amount as others, African American and Hispanic drivers are more than twice as likely to be searched and are issued more tickets than whites (E. Robinson 2007). The practice that flourished with the profiles of drug couriers in the 1980s and 1990s has now shifted toward those suspected of terrorist threats (John Jay College of Criminal Justice 2001).

Many people of color still feel victimized by this practice and have coined the term DWB: "Driving While Black" (Meehan and Ponder 2002, 400; W. Anderson and Callahan 2001). As Michael Smith and Matthew Petrocelli noted, "Historically, minorities, particularly African Americans, have had physical force used against them or have been arrested or stopped by police at rates exceeding their percentage in the population" (2001, 5). Although African Americans make up less that 13 percent of the total U.S. population, they are arrested for nearly a third of all crimes. Hispanics are stopped by police even more often than African Americans (M. Smith and Petrocelli 2001). For example, the Arizona Department of Public Safety's own data from 2006 and 2007 "showed that Hispanic drivers were much more likely to be ticketed and less likely to receive warnings for infractions. Native Americans and black drivers also were 'significantly more likely' to be arrested and searched" ("Our Opinion" 2009). Law enforcement officials often counter, "Well, they commit more crime!" In fact, "many law enforcement officers view racial profiling as an appropriate form of law enforcement" (Barlow and Barlow 2002, 337). The issue is not so clear-cut, however. Social standing may also play a role. Meehan and Ponder noted that "disparate treatment by the police may not be the product of race alone—the racial and class composition of a neighborhood influences police behavior" (2002, 400).

Thus, the issue has become contested terrain as each group and its advocates try to get the upper hand in the conflict. Again, Arizona is illustrative. The Arizona Chapter of the Civil Liberties Union released a report in 2008 confirming that Latinos and African Americans are stopped more and receive the largest number of fines for traffic violations, and filed a class action suit on their behalf. This report came five years after a 2003 federal court ruling ordered the Arizona Department of Public Safety to stop its racial profiling practices. Following the 2003 lawsuit, then-governor Janet Napolitano, subsequently nominated as President-elect Barack Obama's secretary of U.S. homeland security, appointed a committee to review and recommend new police procedures for traffic stops. They teamed up with the University of Cincinnati Policing Institute and implemented changes: "Officers now must get a driver's consent before searching a vehicle—by signature, an audiotape or on video. The officer must complete a form enumerating what factors raised suspicion about the vehicle. If a driver won't consent to a search, the officer can try to get a warrant" ("Our Opinion" 2009). Although this seems to settle the issue, the more realistic view is that this is just the latest move in the struggle between conflicting groups that will likely be played out in an ongoing way in the future, just as it has in the past.

The crimes and laws resulting from the conflict between different racial and ethnic groups in a society, and the political and legal struggle surrounding how this is played out, are not easily explained by the theories that we have examined so far (with the exception of social constructionist and labeling theories). Radical and conflict theorists, however, provide a theoretical explanation for this and other similar collective struggles, as we illustrate in this chapter and as Engel, Calnon, and Bernard (2002) noted. Radical and conflict theorists are centrally concerned with social inequity, with class differences, and with the power used by the ruling class to define what counts as crime and what does not (Schwendinger and Schwendinger 2001).

Conflict and radical theorists consider how social structure and the agencies of government, referred to as "the state," impact human behavior. As the profiling example illustrates, certain disempowered groups or immigrant groups are targeted, begin to feel resentment, and eventually solidify in a social or political movement that leads to either progress or crime. Martin Luther King Jr. harnessed such resentment and effectively channeled it into social change (Barkley 2006). Fidel Castro utilized peasant resentment to overthrow the former Cuban government. However, as the discussion above makes clear, the point about struggle is that it rarely ends with one party in victory; rather, each advance by one party is then countered by a move from the other party so that what we see are battle victories and setbacks but rarely an outright victory, even when the matter seems settled by the courts; no better illustration of this is the 1973 Supreme Court "victory" in *Roe v. Wade* on the legalization of abortion, which seemed like a definitive victory for the prochoice coalition over the right-to-life coalition. Subsequent legal challenges and changes have shown that even such a political victory is not necessarily permanent.

As well as conflict over race, ethnicity, and gender issues, conflict and radical theorists are also very interested in issues involving economic power and so are interested in corporate and government crimes because they bring out features of the structural causes that are not immediately apparent when criminologists look at conventional street crime. Conflict and radical theorists suggest that crime is not simply an individual but also a societal phenomenon. They argue that law, crime, and law enforcement are often political acts rooted in the conflict between groups or classes in society and see the source of crime in the conflict that stems from the inequalities produced by capitalist society (Schwendinger and Schwendinger 2001; Turk 2006).

Although some theorists use the terms *conflict* and *radical* interchangeably, others (ourselves included) make a clear distinction. There is no one "radical" or "conflict" view of crime, and "no firm consensus or precise definition of radical criminology, either with respect to its key concepts or its primary theoretical emphasis" (Lynch and Groves 1986, 4) exists. But it is useful to differentiate between conflict and radical theories based on their different conceptions of inequality (Vold, Bernard, and Snipes [1998] 2001; Einstadter and Henry 2006). In general, conflict criminologists draw their analysis from the ideas of the nineteenth-century German sociologists Max Weber and Georg Simmel: "Conflict theorists emphasize that the needs and interests of different people and different groups are often incompatible and contradictory, especially with regard to the distribution of scarce material or financial resources" (D. Johnson 2008, 367). Conflict theorists see inequality based on differences in wealth, status, ideas, religious beliefs, and so forth. These differences result in the formation of interest groups that struggle with each other for power. Radical criminologists, who instead draw on the ideas of the German social theorist Karl Marx, believe that the fundamental conflict is economic. This conflict is between capitalists, or propertied classes (the bourgeois), who own the "means of production" (i.e., wealth and the capital used to make it), and wage earners, or nonpropertied classes, who own only their labor, which they sell to make a living. The result is a class-divided society, with those in the lower classes being exploited by those in the upper classes. Radical theorists argue that the conflict over economic inequality is at the root of all of the conflicts that the conflict theorists identify. As we enter the worst economic crisis America and the world have experienced since the Great Depression in the 1930s, pay particular attention to what Marx predicted about capitalist societies as you read this chapter.

Not only does capitalist society generate vast inequalities of wealth, but those who own the wealth, who head large corporations and financial and commercial institutions, influence the decisions of those who hold political power. As we saw in Chapter 2, both conflict and radical theorists reject the restricted legal definitions of crime because they take power for granted. Indeed, "the role of power in the definition of crime is the central focus of conflict criminology" (Vold and Bernard 1986, 267).

In the first half of this chapter, we look briefly at the roots of conflict theory in the sociology of Max Weber and Georg Simmel and the resulting "conservative" view of conflict theory found in Ralf Dahrendorf (1959). Then we discuss its criminological application through the ideas of George Vold ([1958] 1979), who explored group conflict; Austin Turk (1964, 1966, 1969), who questioned authority and subject roles and their relationship to legal norms; and the early ideas of Richard Quinney (1970), who analyzed societal constructions of crime by powerful segments of society.

In the second half of the chapter we explore the ideas of radical theorists, beginning with Marx and Engels, and the first application of radical theory to crime by Dutch criminologist Willem Bonger. Among contemporary radical theorists, we look at the ideas of William Chambliss (1975, 1988), the later works of Richard Quinney (1974, 1977), and the radical criminology of Ian Taylor, Paul Walton, and Jock Young (1973, 1975). Before we focus on these particular theorists, however, let us see what ideas conflict and radical theorists contribute to our understanding of crime.

Common Themes and Assumptions and Some Key Differences

Conflict and radical theorists share a view that humans are active, creative agents who invest their energy to build the social structure. Conflict theorists see individuals cooperating with like-minded others to form groups, which then compete in the struggle over resources, ideas, ideologies, and beliefs. There are also similarities between conflict and radical theories over the cause of crime. Each views crime as being the result of the way society is organized. Furthermore, both conflict and radical views share a macrolevel perspective. Thus, each looks to structural causes of crime in the conflict within society; most crime is seen as the result of large forces (e.g., economic, form of government, and so forth) and not individual pathologies.

Conflict and radical perspectives also share a concern with the possession of power and closely examine "law creation, interpretation and enforcement" (Holman and Quinn 1992, 289; see also Chambliss 1989). Consistent with their ideas about society, however, conflict theorists see law as a social control mechanism, a resource and weapon in the struggle for power intended to help those who capture it to maintain or increase that power (Turk 1969). Conflict theorists recognize that law has a symbolic role, publicly representing the social standing of the ideas of those in power (Gusfield 1963). They argue that groups who have power over others (whether it is economic, social, ideological, moral, or religious) typically define which behaviors are criminal and which are not. Thus, laws reflect the values and interest of the dominant group(s). As a result, laws mainly criminalize crimes of the powerless, leaving harms caused by the powerful (such as corporations and government) as lesser administrative or regulative offenses. Similarly, the powerful organize the system of criminal justice to benefit those with money (Barkley 2006). What sanctions are given to powerful offenders are usually civil or restitutive in nature. Thus, although severe prison sentences are given on rare occasions to the powerful who commit exceptional crimes and corporations are sometimes given large fines, the majority of such offenders receive relatively little punishment. For example, the average corporate fine is the equivalent of $8 for a person earning $35,000 per year (Ermann and

Lundman [1992] 2001, 46). Economic differences are only one point of concern. Radical and conflict theorists also agree that there are other types of limited resources, both material and social.

Despite these important similarities, there are some important differences. Conflict theorists view human nature as amoral rather than good or bad. Radicals view human nature in a more positive light: People are born with a "perfectible" nature, but forces serve to shape them in imperfect, deviant, and criminal ways. If humans behave badly, therefore, it is not their doing alone but how their nature is shaped by the social structure. Humankind is assumed to be basically good, and the structure of society is what creates or causes evil people. Marx thus believed human nature is "perfectible," but perfection requires a society that celebrates social and communal connections over individuality.

Radical theorists also see humans as social beings who use their energies to transform the world. They are thus purposeful. In the course of transforming the world, they are themselves shaped and formed. As Marx insightfully observed, "Humans are both the producers and products of history" (J. Young 1981, 295; Marx [1859] 1975). Marx also believed people are shaped more by their society's economic organization than by their own individuality.

Although both versions see the idea of consensus as a myth, their ideas about the nature of conflict differ. Conflict theorists recognize that society is composed of many different groups that have differing, and often competing, interests, values, and norms. They acknowledge a plethora of interest groups (women versus men, ethnic group versus ethnic group, rich versus poor, liberal versus conservative, Greek students versus non-Greek, and so on) and issues (more government versus less government, antiabortion versus choice, proenvironment versus proconsumption, and others). Since there are limited resources (both material and social) available in any given society, competition between these different groups for resources inevitably results in conflict—don't you compete with the other students for used textbooks until those are gone and then those who lose have to buy their books new at full price? In California students have to compete with each other to get into classes; those who don't succeed have then to compete with other students to get an override, known as "crashing," and once the room is at capacity, those who don't get in have to wait until another semester to take the class. This sets up a conflict between students with "priority registration" and those who register late. As a result, some students will resort to a variety of competitive resource manipulations, such as registering for more classes than they are actually going to take (hoarding) or kissing up to an instructor to outcompete their fellow students.

Although more conservative conflict theorists (Simmel [1908] 1955; Coser 1956; Dahrendorf 1959) believe the competition among interest groups produces a balance and compromise that can actually prove functional to society, others believe that some groups emerge as dominant and that such domination can be destructive (Vold [1958] 1979). In particular, those who control the resources and those who have authority positions also have power in society (Turk 1966, 1969). This is because over time humans in subordinate positions learn to follow those who dominate them.

Based on Marx's analysis, radical theorists offer a more dichotomous view of the source of conflict and see this rooted in economic inequalities: Those who own and control the "means of production" (capitalists) are in conflict with and control the lives of those who do not—the labor providers (workers). The radical analysis, therefore, is primarily focused on economic structure and class stratification (I. Taylor, Walton, and Young 1973; Quinney 1974), with all other conflicts being an outcome of the basic economic struggle between the capitalist and working classes. Radical theorists believe either that the law represents the machinery of capitalist repression, directly controlling those who challenge the economically powerful (instrumentalists) (Quinney 1975b, 1977), or that the law is an ideological device that mystifies, or renders opaque, the power of the dominant classes by pretending to be neutral in its protection of individuals, regardless of their power (structuralists) (J. Young 1981). Radical criminologists define crime much more broadly than do legal definitions to include all acts that create harm, including those that violate human rights. Consequently, crimes of domination such as "imperialism, racism, capitalism, sexism and other systems of exploitation" are defined as criminal by those sharing a radical perspective (Platt 1974, 6; Schwendinger and Schwendinger 1970, 2001; Quinney and Wildeman 1991).

There are also other differences. Methodologically, "radical criminologists are more specific than conflict theorists in their identification of the explanatory variables that presumably account for crime" (Bohm 1982, 566). Radicals look to the political and economic structure of society, whereas conflict theorists consider stratification as the culprit. Radicals see the capitalist structure as forcing humans into competitive hostility with one another rather than helping people to be cooperative partners. Crime is the outcome of this competition and an expression of the anguish that exploitation imposes on the powerless (Engels [1845] 1958; Bonger [1905] 1916). As a result, some crime is also an expression of political protest at the capitalist system (I. Taylor, Walton, and Young 1973).

The Roots of Conflict Criminology

Social conflict is present in all societies and occurs at all levels, from individuals to groups. It has been defined as "a struggle over values or claims to status, power, and scarce resources, in which the aims of the conflicting parties are not only to gain the desired values but also to neutralize, injure, or eliminate their rivals" (Coser 1968, 232). In Chapters 2 and 8, we discussed Sellin's ideas of culture conflict (1938) and will not reiterate these again, except to say that culture conflict is an integral part of conflict theory's intellectual roots. Here, we are concerned with the ideas of those who look at crime as resulting from structural rather than cultural differences, although the two are clearly interrelated, as we have just seen. Early ideas about broad notions of structural conflict can be found in the work of Max Weber.

Weber's Class, Status, and Party

Max Weber (1864–1920), a German lawyer and sociologist, is considered one of the three founders of sociology and a major contributor to the understanding of the sources of conflict. At age thirty-four, he suffered acute depression and did not recover to resume his academic writing until he was thirty-nine, when he made major contributions. Weber did not present a theory of crime causation, but he did lay the basis for others to do so by explicating sources of conflict.

Weber's discussion of conflict emerges in his analysis of the role played by charismatic leaders in the transition from traditional society to modern capitalist society ([1922] 1966). Weber identified three important dimensions of inequality: (1) power, represented by party; (2) wealth, which relates to economic position, represented by class; and (3) prestige, which is attached to those in high-status groups. Conflict, according to Weber, is most likely to occur when these three major kinds of stratification coincide—when those who have wealth also have status and power. Conflict is also likely when only a few are allowed access to the privileged positions or when social mobility to these positions is highly restricted. Such a merger produces tensions and resentment among those without power, prestige, and wealth who engage in conflict with the privileged group. Those excluded also become receptive to charismatic leaders who organize conflict groups to challenge traditional authority (Turner 1986, 146–149). Whether this new challenge simply restores another form of traditional authority, itself eventually producing a new privileged group, depends on whether a rational-legal bureaucratic system is instituted.

A rational system establishes authority based on formal rules applied equally to all without taking into account privilege and allows social mobility based on performance and ability. According to Weber, the increasing rationalization of society prevents conflict by freeing the individual to pursue personal goals, but this comes at a price: "Rationalization of life brings individuals a new freedom from domination by religious dogmatism, community, class, and other traditional forces; but in their place it creates a new kind of domination by impersonal economic forces, such as markets and corporate bureaucracies, and by the vast administrative apparatus of the ever-expanding state" (ibid., 149).

Simmel's Functions of Group Conflict

Like his friend Max Weber, Georg Simmel (1858–1918) was a German sociologist, but he was far more optimistic about the nature of modern society and the role of conflict. For most of his life, he taught at the University of Berlin, becoming a professor only four years before his death. Simmel was one of the first sociologists to explain conflict as a common and stable form of interaction. Conflict to Simmel was one of several patterns of reciprocal relations, along with competition and coopera- tion, that underpin complex social behavior. Indeed, for him "conflict and competi- tion are often interwoven in subtle and complex ways with processes of cooperation and social integration" (D. Johnson 2008, 367). Unlike Weber, Simmel looked at the interrelationships between individual meanings attributed to social action and the transpersonal meanings that people construct. His major contribution to conflict theory was a short but influential essay in which he argued that conflict is both in- evitable and functional in its ability to resolve contradictions and leads to a unity of the systemic whole ([1908] 1955). Simmel believed that biological differences are natural, and he believed they are exacerbated by differences of interest but could also be placated by harmonious relations. Simmel believed that conflict is a variable phe- nomenon and that some levels of less violent conflict serve a functional "tension- reducing" process that "promoted the solidarity, integration and orderly change of systems" (Turner 1986, 140). Simmel saw violent conflict occurring where different groups have a high degree of harmony, emotional involvement, and solidarity among their members and where the nature of conflict is beyond the members' individual interests. The violent actions of some right-to-life groups who define abortion as murder provide a clear contemporary crime illustration. For example, in June 2003 Eric Rudolph was caught and convicted for bombing an abortion clinic in Birming- ham, Alabama. But this example in the abortion conflict also seems to undermine another of Simmel's arguments: As specific goals of interest groups become clarified, violence is replaced by other means to achieve the same ends.

Dahrendorf's Dialectical Conflict Perspective

Ralf Dahrendorf, a sociologist who taught at the University of Hamburg and Stan- ford University and later became director of the London School of Economics, went into politics when he was appointed as a life-peer in the British House of Lords. In a critique of functionalism, which he saw as utopian and unrealistic, Dahrendorf (1959) presented a "pluralistic" version of conflict in which he showed two faces of society, both consensus and conflict, existing in a dialectical relationship. This was based on Hegel's notion that a society produces contradictions (seen here as conflicts between opposing forces) whose resolution results in a new organization different from its original (seen here as consensus) (Balkan, Berger, and Schmidt 1980, 336).

By examining conflict between economic interest groups and a variety of groups that compete for authority, Dahrendorf incorporated Weberian ideas, although some say as a result he ultimately reproduced a conservative-consensus perspective (I. Tay- lor, Walton, and Young 1973, 238; Turner 1986). Dahrendorf described groups as having an organization of social roles whereby some people exercise power over oth- ers whom they can coerce to conform. Thus, people exist in relations of domination and subordination. But these relations of domination and subjugation need not mean people are totally dominated, because they may hold different positions in different groups or organizations: "Since domination in industry does not necessarily involve domination in the State or a church, or other associations, total societies can present a picture of a plurality of dominant (and conversely, subjected) aggregates" (1959, 171). Dahrendorf argued that such power relationships become accepted by members as legitimate authority (1958, 1959). Simultaneously, power and authority are seen as resources to be won and over which subgroups within the organization fight. Those who acquire power coerce groups without power to conform. This creates two basic types of social groups, each contesting authority: the rulers and the ruled, the former trying to preserve their power, the latter trying to redistribute it. Should those who are dominated take control, the whole cycle repeats, resulting in further polarization around new interests, followed by further conflict and resolution (Dahrendorf's dialectical process of social change). Thus, conflict is continually coming and going as conflicting groups first win control and then stabilize before again reverting into conflictual relations.

For Dahrendorf, conflict is not a matter of a particular underlying inequality of economic interests but can be based on any kind of difference. For him, the existence of inequality is inevitable because humans evaluate each other as different rather than equal. Therefore, some will always be dominant over others in terms of a rank-ordered social status. Inequality, then, is a function of organizational processes that produce legitimate authority roles of domination and subordination. Like some other founding conflict theorists, Dahrendorf did not specifically address crime, but his ideas greatly influenced later conflict criminologists, particularly Austin Turk, as we shall see later.

Vold's Group Conflict Theory

George Vold (1895–1967) was one of the first criminologists to systematically apply the conflict ideas presented by Weber, Simmel, and Dahrendorf to the study of crime. Vold, who taught at the University of Minnesota and was a contemporary of Dahrendorf, published his highly respected *Theoretical Criminology* in 1958. Later editions of this book are still much in use today, and the work has become a standard text on criminological theory, currently in its sixth edition ([1958] 1979; Vold and Bernard 1986; Vold, Bernard, and Snipes 2001, 2009). Vold was especially influenced by the work of Simmel. He presented a view of certain crimes being caused by conflict and argued that it was absurd to explain these acts using individual-level theories. He pointed out that humans are group-involved beings and that society is a continuity of group interaction "of moves and countermoves, of checks and cross-checks" ([1958] 1979, 283). Society exists in a state of equilibrium and relative stability, not because of consensus among all its members but because of "the adjustment, one to another of the many groups of varying strengths and of different interests" (ibid., 284). However, Vold argued that groups come into conflict because of overlapping interests and encroachments over territory that lead to competition. Group members must protect against the danger of being taken over or replaced.

Members of groups are invested in defensive activity, which they express through acts of identification, loyalty, and self-sacrifice, each intensified by conflict. In the conflict between groups, the weak are generally overwhelmed and absorbed, whereas the strong may either increase their power, be vanquished, or meet with compromise.

Applying these ideas to crime, Vold argued that in the conflict between groups, each seeks the support of the state to defend its rights and protect its interests, with the result that "the whole political process of law making, law breaking, and law enforcement directly reflects deep-seated and fundamental conflicts between interest groups and their more general struggles for the control of the police power of the state" (ibid., 288). Those who win dominate the policies that define crime. With regard to crime, Vold noted a prevalence of group involvement, from organized crime to delinquent gangs, each fighting for turf, markets, and social honor in ways that are in conflict with those of organized society. In a study of deviant driving behavior in South Africa, Khoza and Potgieter (2005) used Vold's theory to explain how the conflict of group interests is reflected in criminal traffic law.

The group also provides definitions of its members' behavior as acceptable, even honorable. Vold described how much criminal activity is a product of the clash of interests between groups and their members' attempts to defend against challenges to their control. Obvious examples are violence as a result of disrespect or turf infringements by members of different gangs, violence between rival organized drug-distribution networks, and violence protesting dominant systems of justice, as in the Los Angeles race riots following the police beating of African American Rodney King. This latter protest represents a more general case of crime as a political expression against the dominant groups in society. Vold concluded, "There are many situations in which criminality is the normal, natural response of normal, natural human beings struggling in understandably normal situations for the maintenance of the way of life to which they stand committed" ([1958] 1979, 296).

Contemporary Conflict Criminology

Since Dahrendorf and Vold, others have sought to develop and extend the ideas of these founding conflict theorists to crime and the law (Box [1971] 1981; Hills 1971; Chambliss and Seidman [1971] 1982; Krisberg 1975; Pepinsky 1976; Reiman [1979] 1995; Schwendinger and Schwendinger 2001). Here, we focus on two illustrative contributors: Austin Turk (1969), whose ideas closely follow those of Dahrendorf, and Richard Quinney (1970), whose theory was more derived from Vold's approach.   •

Turk and the Criminalization of Resisting Subordinates

Austin Turk's major contribution to conflict criminology, *Criminality and the Legal Order* (1969), was deeply indebted to Dahrendorf's dialectical conflict theory of society. Turk (1966, 1969) attempted to show how people in subordinate positions of authority are subject to the values, standards, and laws of those in authority positions. Unless the subordinates learn to be deferential to authority, their behaviors will be defined as criminal and they will be given the status of criminals. Turk argued that people continually learn to interact with each other as holders of superior or inferior social status. The learning is never complete or stabilized but is in constant adjustment and conflict because of individual differences. Turk defined the norms learned in this process as "norms of domination" and "norms of deference." People who learn norms of domination believe they are superior to others and destined to command them. In Turk's view, the extent to which a person relates to norms of domination is related to sociocultural factors such as age, race, and gender. Most people, however, learn norms of deference, meaning that they see themselves as inferior, destined to obey others, and subject to their authority: "Criminality is a label imposed on subjects who resist the claims and impositions of authorities" (2006, 186). "Norm resisters" are found to be those relatively unsophisticated in the "knowledge of patterns in the behavior of others which is used in attempts to manipulate them" (1966, 348). In short, for Turk, crimes are the acts of those who have not been "conditioned to accept as a fact of life that authorities must be reckoned with," and it is such conditioning that underlies social order in all societies (1969, 44).

Turk went on to identify the conditions that make conflict between authorities and subjects over different norms and values more likely: (1) when cultural values and social actions of authorities are in close agreement and a similar congruence exists in the case of subjects, (2) when authorities and subjects are organized, and (3) when authorities or subjects are less sophisticated. He then described the conditions under which conflict will lead to subjects' being criminalized. Again three major factors are involved: (1) when law enforcers (police) and the courts (prosecutors and judges) agree on the serious nature of the offenses and are committed to enforcing the law, (2) when there is a large power differential between enforcers and resisters, and (3) the realism or lack of realism of each party's actions in relation to their chances of success, which for resisters is avoiding criminalization and for enforcers is imposing norms and stopping resistance (2006, 186). He suggested that over time the authority-subject relationship becomes less coercive and more automatic, as new generations of people are born into the existing set of laws, rules, and definitions of reality, which they are less likely to contest. Schwendinger and Schwendinger's (2001) analysis of student protest and the government's response is an excellent illustration of Turk's conflict-type analysis.

In his later work, Turk (1976, 1982) examined how legal orders generate or aggravate or alternatively resolve conflicts. Here he defines law as a form of power that is mobilized in five ways and combinations to shape legal institutions and processes, often fostering rather than preventing conflicts: "(1) violence, i.e., police or military power; (2) production, allocation, and use of material resources, i.e., economic power; (3) decision-making processes, i.e., political power; (4) definitions of and access to knowledge, beliefs, and values, i.e., ideological power; and (5) human attention and living time, i.e. diversionary power." He continued: "Gaining law power becomes itself a goal of conflict insofar as the law facilitates defending or advancing the interests or values of some parties against those of others. . . . Law may preclude or hinder the informal resolution of disputes by explicitly pitting contending parties against one another, legitimating inequalities, and producing symbolic rather than acceptable decisions on issues in dispute. In sum, law is, at best, a mixed blessing in its impact on the formation and sustenance of social order" (2006, 187). Unlike many conflict and radical criminologists who want revolutionary change to solve these problems, as we show in the policy section below, Turk believed that "conflict criminology's postulates imply the radical transformation of our current system through specific policy initiatives" (ibid., 188).

Importantly, in his most recent work Turk (2003, 2004) develops his analysis in relation to global political issues, not least to global political conflict and terrorism. He uses a model to explain the escalation and de-escalation of political violence that has a remarkable application to conflicts in the Middle East, Northern Ireland, and elsewhere. He sees these political conflicts escalating and de-escalating through three stages: (1) *coercive violence*, using coercion to try to send a persuasive message to those they oppose—where authorities through law enforcers suspend civil liberties, while norm resisters vandalize symbols of authority through riots and property destruction; (2) *injurious violence*, designed to punish the failure to learn from the messages and comply with the coercive violence—which can involve extreme torture and other physical brutality; and (3) *destructive violence*, intended to exterminate opponents—which for authorities is military search-and-destroy operations and for norm resisters involves terrorist attacks. As he says, "In the final analysis, my position is that criminology necessarily becomes embedded in political sociology as we deal with the increasingly murky distinctions between legal and illegal, crime and not-crime, authority and power" (2006, 189).

Quinney's Social Reality of Crime

As a contemporary of Austin Turk's in the University of Wisconsin's Sociology Department, Richard Quinney has become one of the most prolific critical theorists in criminology. Although beginning as a functionalist in the anomie and strain mold, Quinney was to metamorphose through interactionism, social constructionism, conflict theory, and instrumental and structural Marxism and eventually reach a spiritualist-informed peacemaking approach (discussed in the next chapter). During each phase, he wrote one or more passionately committed books on the perspective (Martin, Mutchnick, and Austin 1990). His contribution to conflict sociology came with his 1970 book, *The Social Reality of Crime*. Drawing on several of the conflict traditions discussed previously, particularly Simmel's and Vold's work, Quinney saw humans as rational, purposeful actors subject to an unequal distribution of power that produces inevitable conflict. This conflict is between competing groups or "segments" of society, whose members' actions are designed to maintain or advance their position (1970, 8–14).

Segments of society share norms, values, and ideology, but unlike Vold's interest groups, they need not be organized (Vold [1958] 1979, 302). Those who have the power to shape public policy act through authorized agents in society (such as legislators and judges) to formulate definitions of crime that contain, or control, the behaviors of members of those segments with whom they are in conflict. Recall the discussion of racial profiling. The conflict need not be organized political struggle but can consist of individual acts of resistance by members of powerless segments. Criminalization is done with a view to maintain the current balance of power or increase a segment's position of control.

BOX 10.1 Private Security Contracting and Its Contradictions on the New Frontiers of Capitalist Expansion

ROBERT P. WEISS

The latest edition of *Essential Criminology* begins with a discussion of globalization and its impact on crime and justice issues. In a special double issue of *Social Justice* (34, nos. 3–4 [2007–2008]), I began an examination of the expansion and globalization of private security. The enterprise serves capitalist interests and provides a disturbing illustration of the type of globalization that Lanier and Henry describe. The following is taken from the introduction to this special issue.

The security-industrial complex emerging today involves many different services for an unprecedented variety of clients, including NGOs, corporations, governments, and even local citizen groups (Kempa et al. 2000; Avant 2006). What they have in common is state failure. In contrast to nineteenth- and twentieth-century imperialism, which denied sovereignty to its colonies and protectorates, neoliberal globalization, or the "new imperialism" (Harvey 2003), utilizes weak or failed client states that are exploited through dispossession and the tyranny of the market. Primitive accumulation under neoliberalism is a violent affair, igniting political resistance as well as intensifying organized crime and a wide array of labor discipline problems (Cha 2004; Bacon 2005). Hence, neoliberalism reprises the process of policing social junk and social dynamite (Spitzer 1975).

The U.S. occupation of Iraq, for instance, has attracted more than 126,000 private security operatives, contracted to help reestablish police, prison, and even judicial functions through companies such as DynCorp. Along with Blackwater and Global Risk Strategy, DynCorp also has a major security presence in Afghanistan. The private prison and detention industry is also making significant inroads internationally. After a business slump around 2000, the prison business has rebounded in the United States and is being reinvigorated and transformed internationally. Homeland security and immigration control are the fastest-growing markets for detention services in the United States (Crary 2005; Kolodner 2006), and the private prison industry has

CONTINUES

BOX 10.1 (CONTINUED)

revived under neoliberal penality (Weiss 2001). Individual states are turning to private companies to help run a vast array of public-sector services, including management of correctional, detention, and mental health and residential treatment facilities in the United States, Australia, South Africa, the United Kingdom, and Canada. The entire private security sector has grown more than 20 percent in the United States alone over the past decade, and now comprises more than 13,000 companies employing more than 1.5 million workers (Bureau of Labor Statistics 2006).

On the surface, commercial security would appear to be the perfect neoliberal institution because private force thrives in an environment of heightened insecurity, currently aggravated by a U.S. neoconservative foreign policy favoring intransigence over diplomacy (Meyer 2007), and within weak and failed states that are unable or unwilling to provide governmental security (Goldsmith 2003; Liu 2005a, 2005b). On closer examination, however, commercial security harbors several contradictions. Neoliberal "shock therapy" increases violence and the threat of terrorism by destroying public welfare provisions that foster true social security. And in advanced capitalist nations, fear can be stoked. The desire for security will always exceed the available supply when politicians engage in the "discourse of fear" (Altheide 2006, 78–85) concerning crime, disorder, and terrorism. Following neoclassical economics, which favors exchange over production, the value of a good is determined by its subjective scarcity of supply rather than by costs of production. Increasing fear leads to increasing security demand and rising prices without inflation.

Robert P. Weiss is Professor of Sociology and Criminal Justice at the State University of New York at Plattsburgh.

References

Altheide, David L. 2006. *Terrorism and the Politics of Fear*. Lanham, MD: AltaMira Press.

Avant, Deborah. 2006. *The Market for Force: The Consequences of Privatizing Security*. Cambridge: Cambridge University Press.

Bacon, David. 2005. "CAFTA's Vision for the Future: Privatization at Gunpoint." Truthout/Perspective, May 7. http://www.americas.org/item_19488.

Bureau of Labor Statistics. 2006. "Security Guards and Gaming." In *Occupational Outlook Handbook, 2006–07 Edition*. http://www.bls.gov/oco/ocos159.htm.

Cha, Ariana Eunjung. 2004. "Underclass of Workers Created in Iraq." *Washington Post*, July 1, A1.

Crary, David. 2005. "Private Prisons Experience Business Surge." *Washington Post*, July 31.

Goldsmith, Andrew. 2003. "Policing Weak States: Citizen Safety and State Responsibility." *Policing and Society* 13, no. 1: 3–21.

Harvey, David. 2003. *The New Imperialism*. Oxford: Oxford University Press.

Kempa, M., R. Carrier, J. Wood, and C. Stenning. 2000. "The Evolving Concept of 'Private Policing.'" *European Journal of Criminal Policy and Research* 7, no. 1: 197–223.

CONTINUES

BOX 10.1 (CONTINUED)

Kolodner, Meredith. 2006. "Private Prisons Expect a Boom: Immigration Enforcement to Benefit Detention Companies." *New York Times*, July 19, C1.

Liu, Henry C. K. 2005a. "The Business of Private Security." Pt. 3 of World Order, Failed States, and Terrorism. *Asia Times*, March 3. http://www.atimes.com.

———. 2005b. "The Failed-State Cancer." World Order, Failed States, and Terrorism. *Asia Times*. http://www.atimes.com.

Meyer, Josh. 2007. "In Terrorism Fight, Diplomacy Gets Shortchanged." *Los Angeles Times*, March 18, A1.

Spitzer, Steven. 1975. "Toward a Marxian Theory of Deviance." *Social Problems* 22: 638–651.

Weiss, Robert P. 2001. "'Repatriating' Low-Wage Work: The Political Economy of Prison Labor Reprivatization in the Postindustrial United States." *Criminology* 39, no. 2 (May): 253–292.

———. 2007. "From Cowboy Detectives to Soldiers of Fortune: Private Contracting and Its Contradictions on the New Frontiers of Capitalist Expansion." *Social Justice* 34, nos. 3–4 (2007–2008): 1–19.

Definitions of crime are not merely legislated but become part of the public psyche and popular culture as a result of their dissemination through the mass media. In other words, some rather than other meanings of a crime have "social reality" because they are defined, illustrated, elaborated, and sensationalized in the media. For example, bank robbers are demonized as violent criminals, whereas savings and loan swindlers or fraudulent investors are presented as engaging in "financial irregularities."

Quinney further argued that criminal definitions are then applied by the authorized agents (police, judges) of those segments of society having power. This is done in relation to the degree of threat that the powerful perceive from the powerless and in proportion to the degree of visibility of their crime(s). Thus, crimes most visible and most threatening to the powerful are those most subject to criminal processing. In response, those who are relatively powerless develop patterns of behavior in relation to the definitions imposed on them (Quinney 1970, 15–23). For example, African Americans may avoid taking shortcuts through affluent white neighborhoods because of a fear of being stopped, searched, and ticketed. From this, Quinney concluded that the social reality of crime in a politically organized society is a political act designed to protect and perpetuate a particular set of interests over others. In support of Quinney's theory, Olaussen (2004) stated that crime is the result of societal agreements on moral behavior that are institutionalized and thus empower certain people. Furthermore, in a study of emerging criminal justice policies, Bernard, Calnon, and Engel (2005) found that although new policies reduce overt differential processing of offenders, they increase veiled differential processing by focusing criminal justice resources on high-crime groups.

Policy Implications of Conflict Theory

The policies advocated by conflict theorists range from reform to transformation rather than revolution. Conflict theorists do not necessarily see revolution as helpful or even likely to happen in the short term and believe that something needs to be done to reduce the harm of crime in the meantime. (We look at one group of these radical reformists, known as "left realists"—founded by one of the original radicals, Jock Young—in the next chapter.) Of all the conflict theorists, Austin Turk has perhaps gone furthest to detail the changes to criminal justice consistent with the essence of conflict theory. With regard to policy, Turk is to be commended for at least specifying the concrete measures about which most conflict and radical theorists are silent. In a 1995 article, "Transformation Versus Revolutionism and Reformism: Policy Implications of Conflict Theory," Turk identified five general principles on which he based his program for structural transformation: (1) Policy making is a political process aimed at minimizing human casualties, not merely the application of technical fixes; (2) reducing crime and criminalization requires changing structural relationships, not merely persons; (3) policies must fit within a broad strategy of change rather than being piecemeal programs and reforms; (4) policy should recognize "field controls," emphasizing environmental changes rather than "command" proclamations and moral invectives and threatening punishment; and (5) policy should aim for a more viable rather than a more docile society (18–21). Based on these five principles, Turk identified eleven concrete measures to reduce crime:

1. Establish a public information resource center on crime and justice to organize research favoring structural transformation.
2. Establish gun control nationwide.
3. Abolish capital punishment.
4. Indefinitely incarcerate heinous violent offenders.
5. Stop building prisons.
6. Create paid part-time community service jobs for all young people.
7. Decriminalize drug possession and use, returning control to medical authorities.
8. Decriminalize all consensual sexual activities.
9. Decriminalize all forms of recreational gambling.
10. Declare a moratorium on all mandatory sentencing.
11. Establish community policing and community development. (ibid., 21–24)

In addition, Turk proposed the establishment of national commissions to oversee every level of government, to meet the health and economic needs of families, to promote educational excellence, to develop communities, to promote progressive and eliminate regressive taxation, and to encourage socially conscious economic and technological development. These policy proposals and practices are designed to eliminate the structural barriers that "pit classes and groups against one another" and to minimize "the conflicts among them" (ibid., 26).

Most of these policies have not been enacted in the United States, and many doubt that they ever will be, although it will be interesting to see if they gain a new lease on life during President Obama's term of office. Part of the reason for this lies in conflicting value systems. Libertarians, for example, feel strongly that we need *fewer* government agencies and "national commissions," as Turk advocates. They make a series of forceful arguments on both philosophical, legal, and economic grounds (http://www.lp.org). To provide another area of conflict, Americans and citizens elsewhere (South Africa, for example) are deeply divided on issues related to gun control. Many feel that guns are a "natural and constitutional right" and are the primary means of personal protection from criminals as well as from the government itself (http://www.GunFacts.info). For example, had one professor been armed at Virginia Tech when, in April 2007, an armed student attacked students and faculty, killing thirty-two and wounding many others, it could have saved lives or had the long-term effect that perpetrators of subsequent planned rampage shootings come more armed and better protected.

Evaluation of Conflict Theory

Conflict theory has been criticized on a number of grounds. Some of this criticism has come from radical criminologists. For example, Quinney's theory has been criticized both by others (I. Taylor, Walton, and Young 1973) and by himself (1974). One primary criticism is that the theory is overly pluralistic and fails to acknowledge that powerful segments are actually economically powerful classes. I. Taylor, Walton, and Young criticized Turk for accepting "the retrenchment of existing orders of domination and repression" and for being a manual for oppressors aiming to maintain inegalitarian social orders (1973, 266). They also criticized conflict theory generally for being limited to exposing ruling-class interests in the criminal justice system while ignoring how law and the crimes of the poor and rich are connected to the structure of capitalism. As Lynch and Groves pointed out, in contrast to the pluralistic ideas of conflict theorists, radicals "emphasize structured inequalities as they relate to the distribution of wealth and power in capitalist society, and hence define power in terms of class affiliation, rather than diffuse interest groups or segments" (1986, 40). Overall, conflict theory does an effective job of identifying sources of conflict and discrimination and for this has received empirical support. For example, E. B. Sharp (2006) found support for the theory when applied to race and police strength. A. Brown (2007) concluded that defendants were disadvantaged by their criminal status throughout the criminal justice process. Esqueda, Espinoza, and Culhane (2008) found the same results, specifically for Mexican Americans. As we saw at the outset, racial profiling has been substantially demonstrated in research and reports, even by those in positions of power and authority. However, with the exception of Turk's analysis of crime as resistance and oppression, conflict theory does not really explain crime. In contrast, radical criminology locates the cause of crime in the structure, inequality, and class struggle of capitalist society.

The Roots of Radical Theory: Marx's Analysis of Capitalist Society

German Jewish philosopher, sociologist, and historian Karl Marx (1818–1883) is one of the most influential social thinkers of all times. Entire governments and social systems have been developed from his ideas (China, Vietnam, North Korea, Cuba, and Venezuela remain communist governments). Marxist theory has also been one of the major frameworks of study in all the social sciences. It is therefore surprising for students to learn that Marx wrote very little about crime! What Marx and his colleague cotton mill owner Friedrich Engels (1820–1895) did write about was the economic class conflict that exists in capitalist societies that they believed would ultimately result in those societies' downfall. Their analysis was based on the concept of *historical materialism*, which is a method of study and explanation for understanding how past empirical events shape future social systems. Unlike the German philosophical idealist Georg Hegel (1770–1831) (who believed humans created the world from their own thoughts and ideas), Marx and Engels adopted the opposite, materialist view that human consciousness was created by the concrete conditions of productive work (labor). But Marx's notion of materialism was not the traditional one that saw humans laboring as isolated individuals but a new "historical" materialism that recognized the social relations of productive activity in different historical eras (Carver 1987, 105). Thus, in one of Marx's most frequently quoted passages, he argued:

> In the social production of their existence, [humans] inevitably enter into definite relations, which are independent of their will, namely relations of production appropriate to a given stage of development of their material forces of production. The totality of these relations of production constitutes the economic structure of society, the real foundation, on which arises a legal and political superstructure and to which correspond definite forms of social consciousness. The mode of production of material life conditions the general character of the social, political, and intellectual life. It is not the consciousness of [humans] that determines their existence, but their social existence that determines their consciousness. At a certain stage of development, the material productive forces of society come into conflict with the existing relations of production. Then begins an era of social revolution. ([1859] 1975, 425–426)

Marx believed that different historical periods typically have a dominant or characteristic mode of production (e.g., slavery, feudalism, capitalism, socialism). This is a particular combination of the forces or means of production (e.g., technology, resources, tools, energy, knowledge, and skills) and the relations of production that compose "the network of social roles encompassing the use and ownership of productive forces and of the products that emerge" (e.g., employer, worker, investor, dependent) (Carver 1987, 109). Curran and Renzetti helpfully translate this nineteenth-century terminology: People "make a living" through a productive process that we call the economy. Economies can be of different types in different periods of history depending on the resources, technology, and environment in which they operate and the relationships they enter into in order to do productive work. We are now shifting from a service-based economy to an information-based economy, just as we went from an agricultural to an industrial or manufacturing one, and this latest shift has been termed by some as the "postmodern era," which we look at in more detail in a later chapter. The important point Marx makes is that "people do not make their living in isolation, but rather in association with other people. The production process is not just physical or material, it is also social" (Curran and Renzetti 1994, 25).

According to Marx, throughout history the relations of production have been class relations, and the history of existing society is a history of class conflict. In capitalist society, these social relations exist between owners of the means of production and those who own only their labor. Conflict is rooted in the contradictions of the capitalist system, which at its heart is a system of economic exploitation. One simplistic, yet insightful, summary of this conflict is that it is "inherent in the nature of social arrangements under capitalism, for it was capitalism that generated the vast differences in interests and capitalism that gave the few at the top so much power over the many at the bottom" (Lilly, Cullen, and Ball [1989] 1995, 134). Class conflict is based on the inequality in the ownership of wealth whereby those capitalists who own the means of production (capital, plants, equipment, machinery) exploit workers who merely own their labor, which they must sell to capitalists for a wage in order to make a living. The providers of labor, whom Marx called the proletariat, sell their labor to the capitalists, who prosper through paying the laborers less than the value of their work and keep the difference as profit ("surplus value"; see Lynch 1988).

To enable profit to be made, it is necessary to keep wage levels low. This is achieved by retaining a "surplus population" of unemployed to be drawn on whenever the competition between employers increases the cost they have to pay for workers. This *lumpen proletariat*, as Marx put it, occupies the lowest strata of society: underemployed or unemployed persons who do not contribute to society in any meaningful way other than as a reserve source of labor, should capitalist business require it (Lynch and Groves 1986, 10). Capitalism's need for keeping a reserve labor force that will gladly work for low, rather than no, wages also produces the contradiction of poverty, disease, and social problems as these people struggle to survive on very little (Lanier 2009). To live, some of the lumpen proletariat devise nefarious and tenuous means, including begging, prostitution, gambling, and theft. They thus form "criminal classes" that are seen as a danger and a threat to the capitalist system. From this point of view, crime is an inevitable product of the inherent contradictions of capitalism.

It may be asked, Why do the masses of underemployed remain complacent? Why don't they riot against the capitalist system? For that matter, why don't exploited workers strike or revolt if they are so exploited? To Marx, one answer was ideology, which among other meanings "is a process whereby beliefs, deriving from real social relationships, hide or mask the precise nature of such relationships, masking from exploited classes the nature of their oppression and its precise source" (Beirne and Messerschmidt [1991] 1995, 342). Marx described this as "false consciousness" and said it results in part from capitalist society's superstructure. One's awareness or consciousness is shaped in a way that is consistent with one's class position. Institutions of society's superstructure (i.e., the political institutions, the legal institutions, the church, the educational system) instill into people certain values and ideas. For example, most religions teach that it is good to be humble and accept your position in life since you will be rewarded in the afterlife. For this reason Marx called religion the "opiate of the masses." The actual quote is more expressive: "Religion is the sigh of the oppressed creature, the heart of a heartless world, and the soul of soulless conditions. It is the opium of the people" ([1844] 1975, 175). Education in capitalist societies stresses delayed gratification and hard work as the means to monetary and emotional reward. One of the most important ideological components of the superstructure is provided by law.

Marx's Paradox of Law and Capitalism as Crime Producing

The capitalist system of law, bourgeois legality, as a part of the superstructure, reflects the particular mode of production of capitalist society. Bourgeois law serves the capitalist power holders, or *bourgeoisie*, who use it and other means to retain or increase their power and control. This is done not simply as a coercive instrument of power but as ideological domination in which workers are both controlled and defined by law. People are simultaneously "protected" by law from the dangerous classes and from extreme excesses of exploitation created by the capitalist system. Law, therefore, controls by the assent of the majority. As Jock Young pointed out, state law under capitalism exists in a dual relation: It limits excessive exploitation but allows the system of exploitation to remain, it controls all of the population but exercises greater control over some classes than others, and it provides the freedom for the worker to sell his or her labor while preventing the worker from owning the means of production (1981, 299).

In addition to the crimes committed by the lowest strata, Marx and Engels also recognized that the capitalist system of production was "criminogenic" (crime-prone) overall because of the way it impoverished all those within it. One way it does this is through alienation. According to Marx ([1844] 1975), alienation refers to the way the capitalist system of production separates and isolates humans from their work, from its products, from themselves, and from each other. It estranges (separates) them from (1) the products of their labor since they contribute to only a part of the production process, the outcome or products over which they have no ownership or control (the Harley-Davidson company recognized the problems with this, and now has a group of three workers completely build each of its Sportster-model motorcycles); (2) their own work process, which loses all personal ownership and intrinsic worth as it is sold to owners and carried out under their control; (3) their own unique creativity and intellectual possibilities, which are lost to the instrumental purpose of work; and (4) other workers and capitalists, with whom they are set in conflict and competition. Thus, workers in a capitalist society—"in their alienation from the product of their labor, from their capacity to freely direct their own activities, from their own interests and talents, from others and from human solidarity—are alienated from their deepest human needs, that is, their needs for self-determination and self-realization" (Bender 1986, 3). This impoverishment by capitalism renders humans "worthless." Through the alienated work process they learn to view one another as isolated individuals and potential enemies rather than social beings with mutual interests (Jaggar 1983, 58). This leads to a lack of human caring and concern for others. Alienation therefore makes the harm of crime more tolerable to the society and to those who may offend.

Engels ([1845] 1958) argued that crime also emerged as a reflection of the inherent strains and pressures that capitalism creates. One way the conditions of crime are created by the capitalist system is through its use of technology. As technology is improved and production is made more efficient, there is less need for workers and they are replaced by machines, a process that intensifies their feelings of worthlessness.

Another way criminogenic conditions are generated is from capitalist competition, which serves to further disempower members of the working class since they must "not only compete with the capitalist over working conditions, but are forced to compete with each other for a limited number of jobs and a limited livelihood. Consequently, Engels viewed crime as the result of competition over scarce resources" (Lynch and Groves 1986, 52). Engels viewed crime as a result of the brutalization, impoverishment, and dehumanization of workers by the capitalist system. They turn to crime because capitalism undermines their morality to resist temptation; crime is an expression of their contempt for the system that impoverishes them and an exercise in retaliatory justice. As Engels pointed out, when everyone looks to his or her own interests and fights only for him- or herself, whether "he [or she] injures declared enemies is simply a matter of selfish calculation as to whether such action would be to his [or her] advantage or not. In short, everyone sees in [his or her] neighbor a rival to be elbowed aside, or at best a victim to be exploited for [his or her] own ends" ([1845] 1958, 145–146).

Finally, Marx and Engels also saw crime, like any other activity, as sustained and exploited by the capitalist system while at the same time being a productive aspect of it. Marx pointed out that in addition to the ideological function, crime actually served those who live parasitically off the crime industry: "The criminal produces not only crime but also the criminal law the professor who delivers lectures on this criminal law, and even the inevitable text-book in which the professor presents his lectures. The criminal produces the whole apparatus of the police and criminal justice, detectives, judges, executioners, juries, etc." ([1862] 1964, 158–160). The rapid increase of students majoring in criminal justice programs illustrates this, as do the huge numbers of people employed by the criminal justice apparatus, especially in the United States. Consider this recruitment ad from just one agency: "The California Department of Corrections and Rehabilitation (CDCR) is the world's largest correctional employer. The CDCR team is comprised of more than 60,000 dedicated employees, working in over 40 locations throughout California" (CDCR 2009).

Marx and Engels's criminological contribution was, as we have noted, tangential to their analysis of the capitalist system. The first systematic Marxist consideration of crime was attempted by Dutch criminologist Willem Bonger.

Bonger's Criminality and Economic Conditions

Willem Bonger (1876–1940) built on Marx's and particularly Engels's concern about the impoverishment that capitalism brings on society. This impoverishment sets the economic and social conditions for crime. But whereas Marx and Engels focused on the conditions conducive to working-class crime, Bonger extended the analysis to include crime at all levels of society. This included crime among the capitalist classes and a wide range of other crimes, including sex offenses, crimes of vengeance, and political crimes. Bonger saw crimes as the acting out of a "criminal thought." People are more likely to have criminal thoughts when a society promotes egoism rather than altruism. In a notion somewhat reminiscent of Durkheim's anomie theory, Bonger suggested that altruism was a predominant theme in traditional precapitalist societies where the simple productive process for consumption rather than exchange and shared conditions and problems of living promoted a sense of community among the people, "a uniformity of interest" that "obliged them to aid one another in the difficult and uninterrupted struggle for existence" ([1905] 1916, 35). The result of altruism was to suppress the criminal thought.

The change in the mode of production to capitalism brought with it the misery of impoverishment, a condition that was demoralizing and dehumanizing, but it also promoted egoism, which for Bonger meant individual greed, selfishness, and fervent excitement. The climate of egoism favors the criminal thought. The fragmentation of community brought by the capitalist system has a diminished capacity to curtail this destructive thought. The capitalist celebration of egoism is not reflected in official crime rates, argued Bonger, because the upper economic classes determine the shape of the criminal law to legalize the crimes of the rich and criminalize those of the poor, with the result reflected in the title of one radical's book, *The Rich Get Richer and the Poor Get Prison* (Reiman [1979] 1995).

In spite of Bonger's attempt to bring Marx's work alive in criminology, his ideas and those of Marxism generally did little to stimulate criminologists until the advent of radical criminology some sixty-five years later.

Contemporary Radical Criminology

In returning to Marxist criminology in the 1970s, radical criminologists such as Richard Quinney, William Chambliss, Steven Spitzer, Raymond Michalowski, Ian Taylor, Paul Walton, and Jock Young developed a composite critique of the criminogenic nature of capitalist society that has continuities with earlier conflict and Marxist theories. The reason for the reappearance of radical criminology cannot be divorced from the historical period of growing social conflict and unrest.

The 1960s were a turbulent era in the United States. Radicals prospered in the climate of revolution and change. There were many legitimate social grievances, such as the Vietnam War, the sexual revolution, drug legalization efforts, and so on. University faculty members and students at Berkeley, California, were at the forefront of the protest movement. The most notable Marxist movement in criminology occurred at the University of California at Berkeley, where the first Department of Criminology had been established in 1950. Many leading U.S. Marxists and radicals were taught there or served as faculty members. Since radicals advocate social change and action (praxis) rather than just passive empirical observation and measurement (like most positivist criminologists), they actively and aggressively spearheaded a social movement. It is not insignificant, then, that funding for the School of Criminology was eliminated by then-governor Ronald Reagan as a consequence of their ideas, which were seen as too radically left. The demise of the school for political reasons is a fascinating story and illustrates several principles (or lack thereof), such as academic freedom (see Geis 1995; Morn 1995; and Schwendinger, Schwendinger, and Lynch 2002). The abolition of this academic program by the State of California was interpreted by some as confirmation of these critical arguments. By way of a summary, let us look at the basic ideas of these contemporary radical theorists.

Central Themes and Assumptions

Radical criminologists reject individual-level theories of crime that place humans apart from their society and thereby fail to take into account the structural context of human action. They also reject reformist structural-functionalist theories that inadequately account for capitalism's criminogenic nature. The primary impetus here came in the book *The New Criminology* by British criminologists Ian Taylor, Paul Walton, and Jock Young, which was eventually translated into twenty languages. This devastating criticism of all previous "positivist" criminology and even the early "interpretive" and conflict criminology marked a resurgence of radical Marxist criminology. The authors called for a "new" criminology adequate for grasping the connection between the capitalist "society as a totality," its system of inequality, the class conflict within it, the crime resulting from this conflict, and the social reaction to crime from its structures of power expressed in law (1973, 278).

They argued that, caught in a "dialectic of control and resistance to control," humans are simultaneously "creatures and the creators of a constraining structure of power, authority and interest" within which they weave a diverse range of responses, consciously making choices "freely chosen albeit within a range of limited alternatives" (ibid., 248). A new criminology must account for this duality of freedom and constraint, not by separating humans from the political economy that forms the social structure but by bringing the parts together that form the dynamic social whole. As these authors acknowledged, "This 'new criminology' will in fact be an old criminology, in that it will face the same problems that were faced by the classical theorists" (ibid., 278). Indeed, for this reason, "It is perhaps more accurate to refer to the emergence of radical criminology as a renaissance rather than a 'New Criminology'" (Bohm 1982, 569). Together, these authors did not develop the radical theory beyond their critique, although separately they have done so with others (I. Taylor et al. 1975; I. Taylor 1981; J. Young 1981), whose central ideas we summarize now.

1. *Capitalism shapes social institutions, social identities, and social action.* The mode of production comprising the means of production and the relations of production, facilitated by the ideology promulgated through social institutions, shapes the character of the institutions through which it operates; it encourages divisions of class, race, and gender and shapes identities and the activities of the individuals subject to it (Michalowski 1985).

2. *Capitalism creates class conflict and contradictions.* Capitalist society forces humans into class conflict based on the inequalities of ownership and control of the means of production (Spitzer 1975; Quinney 1977). These classes are divided because the capitalist owners and employers want to maintain the existing power relations or improve them in their favor by increasing profits, whereas workers want to change the system and increase their share of the fruits of production by increasing wages. These desires produce two fundamental contradictions. The wages, profits, and consumption contradiction requires workers to have sufficient income to make consumption purchases and thereby increase economic growth. Too much growth, however, is undesirable, as profits and investment possibilities are undermined. The wages–labor supply contradiction requires that a surplus population of unemployed workers be maintained to keep labor costs down, but these people are not so impoverished that they create problems and costs for capitalism (Chambliss 1988).

3. *Crime is a response to capitalism and its contradictions.* Crime is a rational response to the objective conditions of one's social class (Chambliss 1975, 1988). Capitalism creates crime directly through generating and maintaining a surplus labor force of the unemployed and underemployed, or "underclass" (resulting from technological replacement), who are necessary for keeping wages low, but who also may commit crimes to survive (Spitzer 1975; Chambliss 1988). Capitalism creates problems indirectly through education, necessary for managing increased technology and for learning how

to labor, but with the unintended consequence of raising consciousness (Spitzer 1975). Predatory crimes of theft, robbery, and burglary and personal crimes such as murder, assault, and rape are the result of the oppressive conditions of capitalism to which those exploited have to accommodate. Crimes such as sabotage and political violence are the result of resistance to and even rebellion against capitalist domination. Crimes of both accommodation and resistance may be more or less politically conscious acts (Quinney 1977; Michalowski 1985; I. Taylor, Walton, and Young 1973). Crimes among the dominant economic classes also result from capitalists' attempting to resolve the contradiction of wages, profits, and consumption by cheating to get illegally what they cannot get legally in ways that harm other capitalists (Chambliss 1988).

4. *Capitalist law facilitates and conceals crimes of domination and repression.* Capitalist law as part of its methods of domination inflicts harms on those subject to control, including violence and violations of human rights. As well as such "crimes of control," capitalism facilitates "crimes of government," including corruption and graft; "crimes of economic domination" such as corporate fraud, price-fixing, dangerous production methods and products, and toxic pollution, which are undertaken in response to its basic contradictions; and social harm or injury to human rights resulting from institutionalized racism and sexism, which are reflective of the hierarchy of domination in the capitalist system as a whole (Quinney 1977).

5. *Crime is functional to capitalism.* Crime provides work for the surplus population and for others in the crime-control industry, mystifies the capitalist exploitation of workers (Chambliss 1975), and justifies the need for the very law that maintains that system of exploitation (J. Young 1981).

6. *Capitalism shapes society's response to crime by shaping law.* The ruling economic class defines the content of criminal law in order to control the subordinated classes, which threaten or create problems for capitalism's accumulation of wealth and its system of domination (Chambliss 1975; Spitzer 1975; Quinney 1977). These problems include threats to the capitalist system of ownership of the products of work (e.g., theft), threats to the production process (e.g., unemployment, vagrancy, drug use, mental illness), threats to the system of distribution and consumption (e.g., substance abuse, theft), threats to the system of reproduction of workers (e.g., truancy, homosexuality), and threats to the institutions promoting the dominant ideology (e.g., alternative schools, cooperatives). For the purpose of management, these threats fall into one of two problem populations: the relatively harmless "social junk," which has to be carried by the system, and the relatively dangerous "social dynamite," which must be controlled and undermined. (Spitzer 1975)

Many of these concepts have been addressed by contemporary researchers together with those assessing conflict theory. The role of the state or government in relation to the management of crime resulting from the contradictions of capitalism has led to two divergent radical positions, which we now explore.

The Capitalist State and Crime Control: Instrumental Versus Structural Marxism

Radical theorists have taken two directions, identified as instrumental and structural Marxism, the difference between them having to do with the role of the state in relation to capitalism (Beirne 1979). Instrumental Marxists see a direct and crude relationship between the ruling economic classes and the government (Chambliss 1975; Quinney 1974; Krisberg 1975); the political administration is dominated by, and serves the will of, the economically powerful. Instrumental Marxists argue that the law and criminal justice system are coercive instruments used to control the lower classes. This control serves to maintain the existing social, political, and economic system. Members of the dominant capitalist ruling class make laws and devise a criminal justice system that promotes their own economic interest. Instrumental Marxists see two major classes: a capitalist elite and the mass of the proletariat. For example, in his study of crime in South Africa, Breetzke (2008) discusses the relationship between government policy and economic and racial inequality and its positive relationship with crime. Furthermore, he shows how policies and public officials in South Africa discriminate against refugees who must "face abuse, xenophobia, intolerance and conflict with local citizens, as well as human rights violations, and social and economic insecurity" (Pretorius 2004, 141).

In contrast, structural Marxists see a much more autonomous role for government, which acts on behalf of the long-term interests of capitalism rather than in the short-term interests of powerful corporations (Kinsey 1979; J. Young 1981; Greenberg [1981] 1993; Chambliss and Seidman [1971] 1982; Chambliss 1988). They view the instrumental perspective as being too simplistic. For example, "If law and justice were purely instruments of the capitalist class, why would laws controlling corporate crimes, such as price fixing, false advertising, and illegal restraint of trade, have been created and enforced?" (Siegel 1995, 248). Furthermore, instrumentalists suggest a single "homogenous capitalist ruling class" when it is clear, even in Marx's original analysis, that capitalists compete with each other and undermine each other (Chambliss and Seidman [1971] 1982).

Structural Marxists argue, "The functions of the state are presumed to be determined by the structures of society rather than by the particular people who occupy positions of state power or by individual capitalists" (Bohm 1982, 576; Michalowski 1985). The contradictions of capitalist society create a force of disturbance that needs to be contained. In light of these contradictions, criminal law cannot exclusively represent the interests of a ruling elite to repress the lower classes. If it did so, it would risk revolt and would need to divert wasteful energy into social control. Thus, in order to retain ideological dominance rather than use coercive dominance, it must enact and enforce laws that also benefit the less powerful. Furthermore, "Legislation is designed to prevent any single capitalist from dominating the system. One person cannot get too powerful at the expense of the economic system" (Siegel 1995, 248).

Recent Developments: Toward a Global Radical Criminology

Since the late 1980s, in response to a bias in mainstream criminology that emphasizes crime among the lower classes and underemphasizes crimes of the powerful, and in response to charges that radical criminology lacked empirical support, several radical criminologists "became more empirically oriented" and have shifted their focus from local to more global concerns (Lynch and Stretesky 2006, 193, 200). These empirical studies from the radical perspective have produced, for example: (1) tests of social structures of accumulation that predict trends in incarceration and crime rates and show how structures of accumulation affect the impact of unemployment on crime and imprisonment (Michalowski and Carlson 1999); (2) studies that demonstrate how economic cycles affect criminal justice cycles (Box and Hale 1986; Barlow, Barlow, and Chiricos 1993; Lynch, Hogan, and Stretesky 1999); (3) studies of crime in the media (Barlow, Barlow, and Chiricos 1995; Altheide and Michalowski 1999); and (4) empirical studies of corporate and white-collar crime "focusing on four areas: environmental justice hypotheses, the enforcement of corporate crime regulations, environmental contaminants that influence criminal behavior, and media reporting of corporate crime" (Lynch and Stretesky 2006, 195; Lynch, Stretesky, and Hammond 2000). As Lynch and Stretesky say, "The empirical studies generated by radical criminologists use a variety of advanced empirical applications and complicated methodologies," including time-series and GIS data analyses (2006, 195–196). Moreover, they point out that the radical criminology, in addressing issues like environmental pollution, addresses issues that affect global rather than simply local concerns:

> Environmental issues are, in short, a major concern for the citizens of the world. Within the U.S., for example, 100 million people are exposed to dangerous levels of smog every day. Meeting the challenge of devising and instituting policies, laws and enforcement practices (as well as non-legal responses) to address these issues will require the reorganization of society, and the reorganization of the focus of academic research. Scientific evidence on a number of environmental issues suggests an ever increasing threat to the world presented by environmental pollution and the impending oil crisis. In contrast, in two thousand years, crime has not undermined society. The near future will tell whether orthodox criminology is up to the challenge of reorienting its approach away from its focus on ordinary crimes to produce research more responsive to the major harms that victimize the public. (ibid., 200)

Indeed, some radical/critical criminologists have begun to systematically explore the global dimensions of crime (R. Weiss 2000; Barak 2000). Barak argues, "Critical criminologists are trying to understand the comparative effects that the development, globalization, and increasing inequalities are having" on crime and crime control (2001, 58). He relates crime, crime control, and justice to modernization, opportunity, and world system theory and says that "the roots of both crime and crime control may be found in the interplay between the local, national and global forces" (ibid., 70). For example, world system theory (I. Wallerstein 1974) "contends that the dependence of developing nations on developed nations is fundamental to the trends in crime and crime control" (Barak 2001, 61). He points out that world system theory takes a broad view of crime that sees it grounded in relations of production and power as well as social injuries and harms, including global corporate crime, human rights violations, and acts against global treaties and universal covenants. He argues that the combined effects of globalization in reducing the planet to a global village "create excess opportunities for capital(ist) and criminal(ist) expansion, or for the exchange of both licit and illicit goods and services" (ibid., 66). At the same time, there has been both deregulation of control of the commanding heights of the economy as well as a privatization of crime and punishment such that "as part of the process of globalization, both the legitimate and illegitimate fields of criminal enterprise have been freed up for the exploitation of all humankind" (ibid., 70).

Crimes embodied in globalization include "fraudulent and unfair trade practices . . . laundering of unauthorized drug and arms trade profits, the smuggling of illegal immigrants . . . the dumping of toxic wastes and other forms of ecological destruction . . . the acts of terrorism . . . and the behavior of multi-nationals to move capital and technology to exploit cheap labor . . . and illicit commodities of international productivity and service delivery" that involve "organized networks functioning in local, regional, national, and international markets" (ibid., 66). In short, "world system theory analyzes the state, law, and crime in terms of both political and class struggle, and in terms of the developing modes of capitalist production. . . . Crime and crime control are viewed are viewed as products of inequality, poverty, and political oppression that accompany development based on exploitation and dependency" (ibid., 61). Clearly, this global analysis adds a new dimension to the policy implications of conflict and radical theory, to which we now turn.

Policy Implications of Radical Theory

The policy implications of radical theory are clear. If social structure is the cause of class conflict resulting in exploitation and crime, the only solution is to change the social structure. Criminal justice cannot be the focus, because this "does little to alter the fundamental economic inequalities which structure social relationships" (Lynch and Groves 1986, 108). Instead, it is necessary to change the system of capitalist production to another that does not reproduce the conditions that generate crime. This involves revolution. Marx and Engels thought that the masses would eventually recognize their plight as an oppressed class and revolt. As Marx and Engels wrote in *The German Ideology* ([1845] 1964), revolution is necessary because "the ruling class cannot be overthrown in any other way, but also because the class overthrowing it can only in a revolution succeed in ridding itself of all the muck of ages and become fitted to found society anew" (Tucker 1978, 193). For Marx and Engels, this revolution would be followed by a period of state-run socialism before arriving at a final stage of communism. In this final stage, the private ownership of property would be abolished, and humanity would be emancipated from exploitation. As Engels put it, where all people have their basic material and spiritual needs satisfied, where hierarchy ceases to exist, "we eliminate the contradiction between individual man and all others, we counterpose social peace to social war, we put the axe to the root of crime" ([1845] 1958, 248–249).

Many contemporary radical theorists are also convinced that socialist revolution is the only solution to the crime problem. Illustrative is Quinney's statement: "Only with the collapse of capitalist society and the creation of a new society, based on socialist principles, will there be a solution to the crime problem" (1975a, 199). In his most recent writings, however, Quinney has abandoned this call for revolutionary socialism in favor of a spiritual inner-peace revolution, which we discuss in a later chapter under peacemaking criminology. The policy solutions advocated by radicals have also been criticized as being utopian and unrealistic. These criticisms have led to the development of various revisions by leading radicals and other critical criminologists that we consider in the next two chapters.

Evaluation of Radical Theory

Earlier, we saw that conflict theorists have been criticized for having a limited view of the structural causes of conflict and for failing to show the precise links between crime, conflict, and capitalism. We also saw that instrumental Marxists were criticized for their crude, overly deterministic conception of class structure. Indeed, much of the criticism of radical theory is really a criticism of instrumental Marxism, not structural Marxism. Thus, when radical Marxists are criticized for lacking realism, for being imprecise, for misrepresenting reality, for making untestable claims, and for being insufficiently supported by empirical evidence (Klockars 1980; Mankoff 1978; Turk 1980), what we see is further criticism of instrumental rather than structural Marxism. When Klockars argued that the state does empower oppressed people and provides them with genuine rights they otherwise would not have, this too is part of the structural Marxist critique (not that Klockars was a structural Marxist, but they also make this argument against instrumental Marxism). Similarly, radicals are criticized for demanding controls on crimes of repression and domination, since that would serve only to increase the state's power and control, not lead to a "withering away of the State" (Lynch and Groves 1986, 30). But this was a call from conflict theorists rather than Marxists who, as we have seen, want to change the social structure, not criminalize more behavior.

Criticisms by Klockars and others that the class divisions of capitalist society, rather than being harmful, can actually be helpful and that interest groups allow valuable connections across class boundaries apply to structural Marxism and conflict theory, however. A further criticism offered by Klockars to both versions of Marxist criminology is that radicals romanticize the freedom from crime under socialism while ignoring the relative freedom from crime enjoyed in capitalist countries like Switzerland and Japan. If capitalism is criminogenic, he asks, why are these capitalist societies relatively crime free? More recent criticisms have included the charge that because national socialism has failed, particularly with the fall of the Soviet Union in 1989, the theory must also have failed. However, developments such as the dramatic increase in organized crime in Russia since the introduction of free-market capitalism and the revelations of massive corporate and government corruption in Japan tend to weaken these criticisms. So too does the observation that both Japan and Switzerland are very strong collective societies.

Radical criminology has also been criticized because it is too abstract and cannot be empirically tested, and, therefore, it lacks empirical support. However, as we saw above in the section on recent developments, the past thirty years have produced considerable empirical research supporting some of the perspective's core arguments, and as a result "some orthodox criminologists have begun to appreciate and recognize the contribution that radical criminology can make to the study of crime and justice" (Lynch and Stretesky 2006, 193–194).

As we have already seen, it is not the orthodox critique of Marxism so much as the structural Marxist critique of crude instrumental Marxism that is perhaps the most devastating, and it has been supplemented by the arguments of left realists. We discuss their theoretical position in later chapters but point out here that left realism is rooted in former radical criminologist Ian Taylor's "practical socialism" (1981) and Jock Young's (1981) critique of the "left idealist" versions of radical theory (1981). Robert Weiss (1983) pointed out that structuralism itself has problems and tends toward a "super determinism" that denies and confines the contribution of human ability to social action and the structures that emerge from it. However, in spite of the various criticisms, most of which were launched more than thirty years ago, radical criminology, at least in its expanded "critical criminological" form, which we will discuss in a later chapter, has not only remained but expanded in interesting new directions. Indeed, it not only has divisions within the two major professional associations for criminological studies (the American Society of Criminology and the Academy of Criminal Justice Sciences) but also has its own journal, *Critical Criminology*, and is highly influential in the ethos of other journals such as *Crime, Law, and Social Change* and *Social Justice* (Lynch and Stretesky 2006). If anything, conflict and radical criminology is stronger now than it has ever been, even if its dispersal into these fragmented forms does not please all of its advocates. Indeed, Stuart Russell has called for critical criminologists "to redirect their attention back to Marxist theory by developing and extending its tools of critical theoretical analysis" (2002, 113), and others have launched blistering attacks on some of the critical criminological dissenters within the Marxist orthodoxy (Cowling 2006).

Summary and Conclusion

The summary chart below provides the key elements in the assumptions and arguments of conflict and radical theories. Their major contribution is to force criminologists to look beyond simple individual behaviors to the deeper causes of crime contained in the social structure of society—particularly capitalist society. Although we have presented here three somewhat different approaches (conflict and instrumental and structural Marxist), the disagreements between them may be less problematic for critical theory than they at first seem. A resolution may be found in the recognition that each theoretical model, including the functionalist anomie and strain theory model examined in the previous chapter, may actually represent a snapshot of a different stage in the dialectical historical development process of capitalism. Roberto Unger (1976; Collins 1987) has suggested a cyclical development process in which conflict and "legitimacy crisis" are recurrent stages between various more stable states. Thus, we begin with the elite-domination model (described by instrumental Marxists) relying on coercive domination that was characteristic of early capitalism, followed by a legitimacy crisis and a breakdown into conflicting interest groups. This is succeeded by the dual-power model (described by structural Marxists) in modern capitalism as the state becomes more autonomous. As we shall see, the implications of this kind of historical analysis are that the crisis of legitimacy for modern capitalism and the relative increase in societal conflict it has seen herald a move from modern capitalist society to advanced capitalist, late modernist, and even postmodernist society that requires further revisions to the critical framework.

Summary Chart: Conflict Theory and Radical Theory

Basic Idea: The structure of capitalism involving the private ownership of property and vast differences in inequality creates conflict and contradictions that provide the conditions for crime. Conflict theorists see the source of conflict in different group interests; radicals (Marxists) see the source of conflict in the class structure of capitalism's exploitative system of economic production.

Human Nature: Humans are basically a social species, connected to others and shaped by their social structural contexts as well as their own human agency. They can join with others depending on their interests (conflict theory) or their objective class position (radical theory).

Society and the Social Order: Conflict theory sees divisions and competition based on a variety of different interests (class, status, power, gender, race, and so on). Radical theorists see a major conflict in capitalist society based on class interests between owners of wealth and owners of labor. Instrumental version sees the state as a tool of the ruling economic class. Structuralist version sees the state as semiautonomous, protecting the long-term interests of society against threats from particular interests, whether powerful or powerless. Conflict between the two major classes (owners and workers) is repressed by either coercive (instrumental Marxist) or ideological (structural Marxists) means of domination.

Law: Conflict theorists see the law as rules enforced by the powerful to maintain their economic, political, and social positions. Content of law and what counts as crime are set by the powerful. Instrumental Marxists see law as a coercive instrument of repression used by the dominant classes. Structuralists see the law as both a protector of the capitalist system and an ideological vehicle mystifying class exploitation and building consensus for capitalism by providing genuine rights and protections.

Criminals: Those who challenge the powerful (conflict theory) and threaten the capitalist mode of production, especially the surplus labor population or underclass (radical theory). There is no difference between criminals and noncriminals except that the latter are better able to get around the criminal justice system and can steal through quasi-legal means. Criminals are rationally responding to their objective situation of exploitation and see crime as a solution.

Causal Logic: Conflict theory argues that capitalism is criminogenic because it intensifies differences in positions of domination and subordination and produces the conditions for humans to commit crime: the demoralization of the human cooperative spirit and the celebration of egoistic tendencies over those of altruism, which free the criminal thought. Radical theory sees capitalism as criminogenic because it produces fundamental contradictions, the resolution of which includes crime. Capitalism causes inequality, division of labor, specialization, and the alienation of humans from themselves, the products of their labor, the labor process, and their own species. Demoralization, brutalization, and dehumanization result in crime as an unconscious expression of anger and revolt against those who dominate politically and economically. Law and the criminal justice apparatus add to frustration through their use to repress legitimate expressions of injustice. They facilitate crimes by the powerful in the course of repressive control as both capitalists and workers attempt to overcome capitalism's inherent contradictions.

Criminal Justice Policy: Conflict theorists want to reduce the causes of conflict and restructure the society to be less conflicting and more cooperative. Radicals want to reduce conflict born of inequalities of wealth by removing or considerably reducing economic inequality in society.

Criminal Justice Practice: Restructure the distribution of wealth and ownership, move ownership to the employees, create a world in which people are concerned with each other's welfare, create and enforce laws equally against wealthy and poor, and decriminalize consensual crimes, minor property theft, and drug offenses. Structural change needed to prevent crime in future involves revolution and move to socialist or communist society.

Evaluation: Analysis of law and injustice related to social structure helpful but criticized for being unrealistic and idealistic and assuming crime does not occur in socialist countries. Some capitalist countries have very low crime rates, and this is not explained. Criticized for a lack of practical concern for current crime victims.

11

Patriarchy, Gender, and Crime
Feminist Criminological Theory

Isis Sapp-Grant, twenty-nine, a girl gang member from New York, told the following story to Sue Russell:

> I was fourteen when I first saw the power of violence. . . . There was violence everywhere when I was in high school. Your survival depended on letting people know that you wasn't gonna be punked. There were lots of cliques and posses. My group mostly came from single-parent backgrounds, were dirt poor, felt powerless and as if nobody was really listening to their struggles. We got together to watch each other's backs because a group of bad-ass girls was bullying everybody. Within a few months we went from just trying to protect ourselves to looking for trouble. . . . A few of us girls were riding the trains with a group of guys that robbed people. The group just got bigger until there were 35 or 40 kids running through the subways. Whoever was in the way got run down or beat up or robbed. It was totally out of control. . . . I was a piece of this big mob. People looked petrified but they understood to mind their own business and hope that it wasn't them we were coming after. . . . My heart was racing, it was a full adrenaline rush. It was almost like being on a real emotional high where you could just do whatever you wanted and it didn't matter. A total wilding experience . . . For once, I felt really powerful and invincible. It was a really good feeling. I also saw I had the potential to be the best at robbing and beating people up. . . . To sharpen our fighting skills, we made up this game, "one punch knockout." We would randomly pick someone as they left the train station . . . and just try to knock them out. You never knew if they'd pull a gun on you or fight back. I hit men and women, it didn't really matter. . . . I was known for being able to knock people out on the first punch, and that made me happy. I wanted to be the best girl fighter. . . . If you really don't care about yourself, you don't care about anyone else. People become objects. I felt nothing for them. I could watch somebody cry or bleed and it wouldn't touch me.

We liked to dress nice and we prided ourselves on the fact that you'd never know we were gang members. . . . [We] were known for carrying baseball bats and hammers. We put them up our sleeves or down our trousers when we were getting ready to fight another group. You'd go meet them and battle. . . . We didn't plan on living past eighteen, we expected to go out like soldiers, eventually. Partly it was being willing to die for the cause; also, so many of our peers were dying. . . . I didn't know how a bullet would feel but I kind of welcomed the feeling. That's the sick, suicidal kind of thoughts that a lot of us had, though we never thought of it as suicide. (2000)

Women have traditionally been portrayed as more empathic and caring than men. The types of crimes they typically commit, such as shoplifting, prostitution, and embezzlement, reflect being less violent; when they are violent, it is often a response to repeated abuse by men. However, examples of violent and callous crimes by girls and women are a reality, as illustrated in the example above. Consider another example. While driving home, Chante Mallard, a twenty-seven-year-old nurse's aide, hit thirty-seven-year-old Gregory Biggs, who was walking along a freeway in Texas. Rather than stopping to render aid, she drove home with him lodged in her windshield. Once home, she closed her garage door and left him in the windshield, where he bled to death over the next few hours. The next day she had two male friends dump his body in a park. They then burned the passenger seat of her car to conceal the crime. When one of the two men told his girlfriend of a "caper they had gotten away with," the girlfriend called the police. On June 26, 2003, a Texas jury found Mallard guilty. She received a fifty-year sentence for murder and ten years for tampering with evidence. Under Texas state law she will be eligible for parole in 2028. She accepted responsibility for her actions but blamed drugs and alcohol for her poor judgment. She had been drinking and smoking pot and had one ecstasy pill prior to driving home that fateful day.

How do criminologists explain crime committed by women? How do they explain women's relatively low rates of arrest and conviction compared to men? How do they explain the maleness of most crime? For years, they were not able to because all theories of crime were theories of male crime rather than female crime due "to the repeated omission and misrepresentation of women in criminology theory and research" (Chesney-Lind 2006, 7).

In this chapter, we consider the contribution of feminist theory to the explanation of crime. Feminist theorists seek to explain why women like Isis Sapp-Grant and Chante Mallard engage in serious crime, and why women form gangs. Importantly, they seek to explain some interesting recurring patterns of crime. They try to explain why most violent crime is committed by men, and why women are far less likely to be involved in criminal activity, a phenomenon known as the "gender-ratio problem." Why is it that when some men decide to commit suicide, they kill their wife or girlfriend first, but when women decide to commit suicide, they almost never kill their husband or boyfriend, although they may kill their children (Polk 2003)? Why are many women "linked to serial killers as victims but rarely as perpetrators"

(Skrapec 2003, 235; Kelleher and Kelleher 1998)? Although the exception, those who do kill, such as Eileen Wuornos, the Florida prostitute-turned–serial killer who killed seven men in Florida between 1989 and 1990, later claiming they raped or attempted to rape her, constitute only 10–15 percent of all serial murderers. Yet women terrorists have existed throughout the world. Why are all cases of rampage shootings in schools committed by boys, not girls? Why do some men kill their female partners out of jealousy, yet women almost never do? Why do some men feel compelled to use lethal force to defend their honor or resolve disputes, whereas "women almost never feel that they must use exceptional violence to defend their sense of honor. And . . . they rarely employ lethal violence as way of resolving . . . personal conflicts" (Polk 2003, 136)? As we shall see, feminist scholars believe that traditional mainstream criminology is unable to explain these patterns of behavior because it ignores the structuring of society by gender that results in patriarchy and its theories are almost exclusively designed and applicable to explain male crime, which is known as the "generalizability problem." In contrast, as Jody Miller has argued, "Feminist criminology . . . situates the study of crime and criminal justice within a complex understanding that the social world is systematically shaped by relations of sex and gender" (2003, 15). Indeed, feminist criminologists take gender as the central concept in explanations of social relationships, processes, and institutions that produce law, power, crime, and victimization.

Common Themes and Assumptions

According to Kathleen Daly and Meda Chesney-Lind's seminal article on feminist criminology, there are five key aspects that distinguish it from mainstream criminology, and these relate to the nature of gender: (1) Gender is a social, historical, and cultural construct built on biological sex differences and reproductive capacities; (2) gender and gender relations are fundamental organizers of social institutions and social life; (3) gender relations and the social constructs of masculinity and femininity are based on assumptions that men are superior to women, and this is reflected in male dominance in social, economic, and political institutions; (4) what is taken for granted as knowledge of the natural and social world is men's knowledge, the production of which is gendered; and (5) women should be at the center of intellectual inquiry, not peripheral, invisible appendages to men (1988, 504). Failure to acknowledge the politics of gender has resulted in a myopic view of crime and criminal justice that also fails to address some of its most distinctive features. Indeed, Chesney-Lind (2006) described the unique political climate in which feminist criminology emerged and continues to struggle, which includes political backlash, right-wing agendas, moral agendas, and public and governmental policies that are hostile to women's rights, all of which has resulted in an attempt to minimize feminist criminology and its efforts at challenging patriarchy.

One of the major criminological findings that has remained consistently unexplained by mainstream criminologists is that although women do occasionally commit serious, and especially violent, crimes, they generally commit far fewer of them than men and are rarely arrested or convicted for their crimes (Cain 1989). Indeed, "gender—specifically being male—is one of the strongest correlates of criminal offending. This is especially the case, the more serious and more violent the crime in question" (Jody Miller 2003, 17). Some simple statistics demonstrate the point. In the United States, according to the Uniform Crime Reports data, annually around 80 percent of all persons arrested are men, and men make up 95 percent of inmates in state and federal correctional facilities. Similarly, victimization data reveal that the offender was male in 85 percent of single-offender victimizations. As Polk says, "Across many different countries and in many research studies, official crime, especially violent crime, involves mostly male offenders. In the case of homicide for example, typically males make up between 85 and 95 per cent of known offenders" (2003, 133). Even in the case of crimes typically associated with women, such as sexual offending, women are less frequently convicted. For example, in Canada there were 4,545 inmates convicted of sexual offenses in the early 1990s, only 19 of whom were female (Syed 1996).

What does the gender-ratio problem, this preponderance of male offenders over female offenders, say about the causes of crime? Is crime caused by something to do with being a man, such as differently wired brains, differences between male and female hormones, or the socially constructed identity of masculinity? Is this identity rooted in the customary and legal historical content of Western societies or in biological, cultural, or structural forces? Or is crime created by those who make the laws, which feminists argue have been enacted by men for men, in order to perpetuate their privilege? Research suggests that gender differences for certain types of crime (e.g., drug offenses and some violent crimes) do not vary significantly between men and women (Alarid, Burton, and Cullen 2000). Further, the small group of offenders who commit the most crimes do not vary significantly by gender (A. Piquero 2000). Some self-report data also suggest less distinct levels of offending (Campbell, Muncer, and Bibel 1998; Chesney-Lind 1997). However, serious violent crime is consistently a male activity.

Responses to observations about gender differences in both levels of crime and arrest rates by feminist criminologists began with critical works by Dorie Klein ([1973] 1980), Rita Simon (1975), Freda Adler (1975), and Carol Smart (1976). But the feminist perspective in criminology did not become firmly established until the 1980s, and serious consideration of feminist criminological theory did not even begin to appear in textbooks on theory until the 1990s (e.g., Einstadter and Henry 1995). Part of the explanation for this omission and delay was that mainstream criminology was really "malestream" (i.e., dominated by men). These theorists were very slow to respond to feminist theory and tended to marginalize feminist contributions and exclude them (Menzies and Chunn 1991; Messerschmidt 1986). Also, as Simpson (1989) pointed out, some of the early accounts by women were less involved with developing their own theoretical position than with criticizing the lack of attention by male criminologists to women and gender issues (e.g., Leonard

1982). Flavin postulates that "many criminologists' dismissal of feminism stems as much from ignorance and misinformation as deliberate, ideological resistance" (2001, 271).

BOX 11.1 Feminist Criminology in a Global Context

NICOLE HAHN RAFTER AND FRANCES HEIDENSOHN

The meaning of "feminist" is changing. What began as an egalitarian "women's liberation" movement expanded to include the recognition of gender as a basic element in social structures throughout the world. The goal of feminism broadened to embrace an understanding of how gender shapes verbal interactions, education, identities, organizations and other aspects of culture, such as crime rates, definitions of crime and social control traditions. What began with concern about "sexism" grew to include the social construction of femininity and enlarged again to include masculinity. . . . Feminists now investigate how multiple dimensions of power—age, geographical location, race, sexuality, social class and so on—combine with gender to affect human lives. These investigations have fractured the notion of gender, turning it into one of multiple "femininities" and "masculinities.". . . Feminism has rendered problematic concepts whose meanings not long ago seemed self-evident: gangs, Mafia, rape, victims, violence (even "feminism" itself). It has also challenged the epistemological status of theories of crime. . . .

Throughout the world . . . feminists have challenged others' pronouncements about the nature and causes of crime. They have questioned some basic concepts of the discipline and revitalized others. . . . Domestic violence, sexual abuse, rape—these issues cut across national boundaries. Sharing fears of male violence, women around the globe are already bound by strong ties. But recent years have witnessed an internationalization of women's concerns about crime and justice. More than a recognition and acknowledgement of mutual interests, this phenomenon is self-consciously feminist. And it aims explicitly at creating transnational and transcultural alliances that will respect diversity.

One factor encouraging globalization is the collapse of old political orders in Eastern Europe . . . the Balkans and South Africa. . . . In country after country, patriarchal regimes that silenced dissent have been overthrown. Out of the rubble are emerging a host of new minorities—ethnic, feminist, nationalist—contending for participation in the new regimes. Internationalization has also been fostered by the trend toward postmodernism—the fragmentation of old explanatory structures and acceptance of multiple perspectives. Interest in discourses, identities, representations; these facets of postmodernist thought have all contributed to a renewed interest in the origins and effects of cultural difference. Globalization has been further promoted by the simple fact that, throughout the world, feminists and their allies have entered work in criminology and criminal justice, creating a critical mass capable of giving

CONTINUES

BOX 11.1 (CONTINUED)

voice to women's concerns. Throughout the world we now find crusades against domestic violence and other forms of victimization of women. Participants in these
movements now constitute an international audience for information on gender,
crime and social control.

Nicole Hahn Rafter is Professor and Senior Research Fellow at the College of Criminal
Justice at Northeastern University and an affiliated faculty member in the Law, Policy, and
Society program in Boston, Massachusetts. Frances Heidensohn is a visiting Professor at
the Mannheim Centre for Criminology, Department of Sociology, at the London School
of Economics and Political Science.

Extract from Nicole Hahn Rafter and Frances Heidensohn, eds., *International Feminist Perspectives in Criminology: Engendering a Discipline* (Philadelphia: Open University Press,
1995), 3–4, 8–9.

Early on, feminist criminologists argued that the history of criminological theory
is a history of the study of men behaving badly: Criminology has been "gender
blind." Omitted has been significant research or discussion on women as victims or
offenders (A. Morris 1987; Gelsthorpe and Morris 1988). Criminological research,
for the most part, has been about males, and criminology has been shaped by a male
view of the world (Leonard 1982; Heidensohn 1985). Traditional criminological
theories also neglect "gender-related factors such as patriarchal power relations"
(Alarid, Burton, and Cullen 2000, 172). Criminological theory "has either ignored
women—focusing exclusively or implicitly on explaining male participation in
crime and defining females as unimportant or peripheral—or has ignored gender"
(Miller 2003, 16). Further, as Gaarder and Belknap note, "Traditional theories of
crime causation, which tend to be based on male models of crime and behavior, cannot adequately explain the experiences of delinquent girls" (2002, 482) or, for that
matter, those of criminal women. Moreover, applying theories of male crime to
women but not theories of women's crime to male offending makes "women a sub-
category of men" (Miller 2003, 16). Rather than assertively committing crime,
mainstream constructions of "the female offender" embody the traditional stereotype that "women's greater emotionality, passivity and weakness . . . account for both
their involvement (or lack thereof) in crime and the nature of their criminal activities" (ibid., 17).

Recent research on female murderers challenges this view and suggests that biased
portrayals in the media, in the law, and even in feminist discourse that present
women murderers as victims deny their agency and freedom to be human (Morrisey
2003). Indeed, as Carol Smart (1976) observed thirty years ago, as a result of gender-
biased criminology, women are denied not only their individuality through subordination but also their criminality and their victimization. Through rape, prostitution,
and domestic battering, women are seen to "deserve" or "ask for" their problems. In-

deed, victimization studies reveal that some of the previously most hidden victims of men's harm are women. Studies show that violence toward women and rape have been, until relatively recently, grossly underreported (Brownmiller 1975). Self-report studies have also shown that women are not merely passive accomplices of men but actively engage in independent criminal acts alone and with others.

The crimes of women are not restricted to status offenses, sex offenses, shoplifting, and poisonings, as in the typical media stereotype. They include robbery, violence, child abuse, drug abuse, drug dealing, and gang activity as well as certain kinds of white-collar crime, as the Martha Stewart case illustrates (Campbell 1984, 1993). But the data on such crimes have largely been gathered from studies of men, which means any differences of gender are disregarded, and generalizations are less about crime and more significantly about masculinity (Daly and Chesney-Lind 1988; Leonard 1982; Messerschmidt 1993).

In seeking alternative explanations, some feminist writers have suggested that there are different "pathways to crime" for women. Certain events or life experiences increase one's risk of offending (Heimer and De Coster 1999). Pathways, or life-course, research suggests that child neglect and physical and sexual abuse of young girls is often related to their incidence of "doing" crime (Gaarder and Belknap 2002), and this is consistent with the reciprocal interactive theory of violence (Barak 2003, 2006). Also, developmental pathways may significantly affect the ways girls and boys respond to situational triggers. Heimer and De Coster (1999) note that direct family controls, such as supervision and coercive discipline, are gender structured such that young girls are more likely to be subject to indirect controls, such as emotional bonding, whereas boys are subject to direct controls, such as physical discipline. Similarly, they argue that boys are more likely to associate with peers who are risk takers and who have a favorable view of violence than are girls. Clearly, the "pathways" approach also explains that the crimes of men and women have a foundation in different childhood developmental processes.

In the years following the initial critiques, feminist criminology moved into several different theoretical strands and is currently moving toward a reintegration of its diverse positions. What are the areas of crime and justice that feminist scholars have focused on, and what are the different ways their scholarship theorizes the causes of crime by both men and women? Flavin describes three directions that most scholarship and practice involving women have taken. First, feminist criminology criticizes the criminological mainstream's omission of women: "Most . . . scholarship focuses on men or extends theorizing based on men's experiences to women without offering any reconceptualization" (2001, 273). This is simply adding women to the mix and "stirring." Jody Miller (2003) calls this the "generalizability approach," which she says cannot explain men's disproportionate involvement in crime (the gender ratio of offending), and also ignores the confluence and amplification effects of class, race, and gender.

A second movement of feminist scholarship has been to focus on crimes that adversely affect women more so than men. Domestic violence is given as a prime example, though sexual violence is also commonly studied in this manner. This type of research is still guilty of treating men as the norm and women as anomalies, according to Flavin. In addition, such an approach has been criticized by other feminists for assuming the concept of a "universal woman," and thereby not accounting for the different experiences of women, such as those affected by race and class, that lead to different outcomes of offending and victimization (ibid., 22–23).

Finally, feminist scholars are beginning to study women "on their own terms" and to recognize a "multiplicity of factors and offer a richer contextual analysis" (Flavin 2001, 273). As part of this trend, feminist scholarship has also moved toward a more general analysis of gender and difference that is more inclusive of other differences, experiences, and inequalities (Smart 1990; Caulfield and Wonders 1994; Schwartz and Milovanovic 1996; Daly and Maher 1998).

BOX 11.2 The Changing Status and Role of Women
Katy Hancock

The twenty-first century has seen changes and advances for women around the world. The new century has seen several American states, including Massachusetts, Vermont, and Virginia, elect their first female sheriffs. Harvard University named its first female president in 2007. An investment company in Saudi Arabia, recognizing the opportunity presented by female investors, has now appointed its first female chief financial officer. For the first time, females are piloting for airlines in South Korea. The entertainment industry has seen a broader and more positive representation of women as law enforcement professionals in such television shows as *CSI*, *Law and Order*, and *The Closer*. In addition, 2008 was a landmark year for women. The U.S. Army promoted its first female four-star general. Indy driver Danica Patrick became the first woman to win a race in a top-level racing series. The United States reached a milestone for women with the 2008 presidential election, not only with Hillary Clinton's presidential campaign but also with the second female vice-presidential candidate, Sarah Palin.

At the same time, on the other side of the spectrum, the world has seen women more and more as the perpetrators of crime. In one of the most publicized cases of white-collar crime since the Enron scandal, Martha Stewart was convicted of insider trading in 2003. Moreover, 2008 saw media coverage of Orlando, Florida, resident Casey Anthony being first arrested for check forgery and then for murdering her child.

Over the past decade, the media has increasingly been covering cases involving women as perpetrators of murder and child abuse. For example, in 2008, Samantha Rothwell was convicted of second-degree murder for stabbing a friend at a birthday party over an argument about God. Other examples are those of Andrea Yates, who murdered her children, and Lisa Nowak, the NASA astronaut accused of attempted

CONTINUES

BOX 11.2 (CONTINUED)

kidnapping. As terrorism has become a more prominent issue since September 11, 2001, we have also heard more about female terrorists and suicide bombers, not only in the United States but also in strife-ridden areas, such as Iraq, Palestine, and North Korea. In addition, we now see many advocacy groups, including victim services on college campuses, working to raise awareness for men as victims of abuse from their wives or girlfriends. While the prison inmate population is still largely male, the percentage of incarcerated women is growing.

At a time when women are accomplishing greater things and have more options than ever before, why do we also see an increase in female crime? One argument is that, although globalization has created many opportunities for careers, education, diversification, and worldwide networking, it has also created pressures and obligations for women, who feel they must compete in a global workplace and still have time for family. An emphasis on global issues such as world hunger, political unrest, the environment, and violence against women and children has also created more pressure on individuals to fulfill obligations to an overwhelming number of social issues. Furthermore, the increasing impersonality of society has led to many people, including women, feeling isolated and angry. The question still remains how to reduce or even eliminate the negative effects of globalization while still reaping its many benefits.

Katy Hancock is a Research Graduate Assistant in the Department of Criminal Justice and Legal Studies at the University of Central Florida in Orlando.

An important contribution made by feminist theory is the concept of "blurred boundaries" (Daly 1992; Daly and Maher 1998). This points to an overlap between women as victims and women as offenders (for example, abused women who kill their partners, described by Raeder 2006), or women who escape violent homes only to pursue street-survival strategies, including drug use and prostitution). The notion of blurred boundaries suggests that patterns of past victimization can result in future violent offending. The emphasis on gendered victimization as a cause of future offending is a special case of the pathways approach discussed earlier. For example, in a study of women inmates in Texas, Pollock, Mullings, and Crouch (2006) concluded that violent women were more likely to come from a background of childhood abuse. However, simply citing past abuse and economic stresses may not fully capture the etiology of female offending since it again presents a passive view of women and ignores their intentionality and resistance (Gaarder and Belknap 2002; Maher 1997; Miller 2003). Although Simmons, Lehmann, and Craun (2008) found that the majority of women arrested for intimate-partner violence came from abusive backgrounds, past abuse was not adequate to explain female offending.

Before examining recent theoretical developments such as the integration of a variety of feminist ideas in gendered theory, we briefly survey the differences between the four main feminist positions that developed in the 1980s and 1990s: liberal feminism, radical feminism, Marxist feminism, and socialist feminism (Jaggar 1983; Daly and Chesney-Lind 1988; Simpson 1989; Alleman 1993; Tong 1998). As we explore each of these varieties of feminist theory, it is important to consider how gender relations shape crime and criminal justice and how patriarchy (a society whose organization is dominated by men and masculine ideas and values) is as powerful a force as class and race. It also important to bear in mind that whereas some feminist criminologists want to abandon the classification of feminism into liberal, radical, Marxist, and socialist perspectives, others continue to use it (e.g., Chesney-Lind and Faith 2001).

Liberal Feminism

In response to the core question, "What causes crime?" liberal feminists answer, "Gender socialization and sexual discrimination." They argue that the subordinated position of women and the criminal tendencies of men result from the way boys and girls are socialized into different masculine and feminine identities and from male discrimination against feminine identities. Men are socialized to be risk-taking, self-interested individuals and to use coercive power to win; women are socially controlled. Lo and Zhong (2006) concluded that women are more susceptible than men to relational factors that control deviant behavior. Furthermore, many young males are encouraged to engage in physically demanding sports such as hockey, football, and wrestling. Young girls more often play soccer or softball. Newer forms of recreation such as wakeboarding and surfing are much less gender specific, and many young women excel at these sports. Even traditional male activities like motorcycling are showing large increases in the number of women who participate. For example, at "Bike Week" in Daytona Beach, Florida, and at the annual Sturgis, South Dakota, rally, women once were relegated to riding on the back, but now many own and ride their own Harley-Davidsons. Will this mean that women will engage in the newer forms of crime (e.g., computer crimes and credit card fraud) at rates equal to males? Will women also begin to engage in more violent forms of crime as equality is realized?

The official arrest data on crime and gender show that, like male crime, women's crime is also the result of social and cultural factors. Liberal feminists reject the traditional claims of Lombroso and Ferrero (1900) that women are biologically averse to crime and that their criminality is the product of being a flawed person (Klein [1973] 1980). Nor is women's participation in certain kinds of crimes, typically petty property offenses, shoplifting, check fraud, welfare fraud, and embezzlement, a result of their "deceptive" and manipulative sexuality, as Pollak (1950) claimed, or of their pathological sickness or hormonal imbalances. Rather, liberal feminists believe that the difference between men's and women's crime rates is a result of differences in

(1) sex-role expectations, (2) socialization, (3) criminal opportunities, (4) recruitment to delinquent subcultures based on sex role, (5) the way crimes are defined, and (6) the way males and females are socially controlled (Hoffman-Bustamente 1973). These findings not only apply to the United States but also have global applicability. For example, according to laws in South Africa, "It is only women who can be charged with crimes related to prostitution and it is only men who can be labeled as serial killers" (Beukman 2000, 52). Furthermore, the nature of laws in South Africa (Kent 2007) limits their ability to serve women. If the liberal arguments hold true, then social changes that reduce these distinctions and remove discrimination also mean that women's crime rates will inevitably increase. Let us look at this superficially appealing argument.

Masculinization and the Emancipation Thesis

The argument that women's crime rates reflect their changing social position began with two books: Freda Adler's *Sisters in Crime: The Rise of the New Female Criminal* (1975) and Rita Simon's *Women and Crime* (1975). When these books were written, the media had picked up the "alarming" statistic that women's official rate of crime was increasing from 10 percent of all crime to 15–20 percent. Adler (1975) explained this by the liberation thesis, which is based on women's social masculinization. This thesis proposed that as a result of the 1960s women's movement, women were adopting male roles, becoming socially and culturally more like men, becoming more competitive with men, working more, encountering more economic opportunities, and fighting as aggressively as men to establish themselves. Moreover, as a result of similar strains to those experienced by men, this would produce similar patterns of crime and higher female crime rates—which would eventually reach the levels of men's crime rates (ibid.; Figueira-McDonough 1980). For example, a study of female serial killers reveals that "the modus operandi of these women is evolving to incorporate more overt, traditionally 'male' forms of violence" (Skrapec 2003, 235; 1999; 2001). In short, an increase in women's criminality was seen as a consequence of social masculinization and a cost of liberation. Simon (1975) pointed out that increased involvement in the workforce meant that women would not only get more opportunities for employment but also have more opportunities for crime. This was known as the emancipation thesis, although both masculinization and emancipation are interrelated in this liberal explanation of the perceived expansion of women's crime.

A subcultural and social learning version of this liberation thesis argument explains the gender-ratio problem of different gender involvement in crime in relation to differential exposure to delinquent peers, with females having less exposure and therefore less opportunity to have criminal role models or learn delinquent skills than males. The argument also sees males as more influenced by peers than females, not least because females are more institutionally and morally controlled, and are therefore less suggestible.

With regard to the implications for criminal justice policy, liberal feminists are less concerned with rising rates of women's crime than with working within the mainstream arguing for equal rights for women. They believe discrimination and oppression can be reduced by social and legal reforms to the existing system designed to increase opportunities for women in education, employment, and politics and reduce gender-role socialization. In other words, liberal feminism wants society to deal with the problems of discrimination based on sex or gender "through education, integration and litigation" (Chesney-Lind and Faith 2001, 291, citing Lorber 1998, 19). Specifically, they would like to see action "correcting the differentially severe treatment that women receive for minor deviances . . . providing equal protection against violence and coercion (e.g. rape, harassment, assault), having equal access to legal representation and due process, and receiving equal correctional treatment in comparably equipped facilities" (Einstadter and Henry 2006, 277–278). They see this occurring through government action: "The liberal feminist program calls for state reform to bring about those changes necessary to promote women's rapid integration into the backbone of society" (Beirne and Messerschmidt [1991] 1995, 516).

Evaluation of Liberal Feminism

Liberal feminists have come under attack for such liberation-causes-crime arguments, both from mainstream theorists and from other feminists. In an analysis of official crime rates of property offenses between 1965 and 1977, Steffensmeier (1978, 1980) found that increases in female crime occurred prior to the women's movement of the late 1960s. He also found that the subsequent increase was a result of increases in traditional women's crimes of shoplifting and check and welfare fraud and not in new crimes of opportunity, as suggested by the emancipation version of liberal feminist theory. Nor are women's rates catching up with those of men (Messerschmidt 1986).

Carol Smart (1979) rejected both the liberal-feminist argument and Steffensmeier's interpretation. She argued that the biggest increase in crime is not in property crime but in violent crime, which is not a traditional area, and that any comparative increase is misleading because of the small absolute figures. For example, a 500 percent increase in murder can occur when the figures go from one to five, but that need not be as significant as an increase in absolute figures from 1,500 to 2,000, which is 500 more murders but only a 25 percent increase in the murder rate (a point also made by Steffensmeier). Smart pointed out that analyzing data from earlier decades, such as 1935–1946 and 1955–1965, shows a more rapid increase in women's crime than when the women's movement supposedly occurred. Finally, she argued that official crime arrest statistics are biased, overrepresent the working class and minorities, and are affected by changes in police and prosecution policy, including the attitudes of police officers.

According to what is known as the *chivalry hypothesis*, in the past women have been less likely to be featured in the official crime statistics not because they are less criminal but because of "knightly virtue" and kindly treatment of women by police, district attorneys, and judges, most of whom have typically been male. In recent years, this has changed because of greater numbers of women entering criminal justice professions who are less likely to treat women offenders lightly. Also, attitudes toward women as active agents are changing. As Smart (1976) argued, the increase in women's crime rates is only a product of women's liberation insofar as liberation makes enforcers such as police, social workers, and judges believe in liberated women and more prepared to arrest them, charge them, and sentence them. This is particularly true for women's violent offenses (Box 1983). For instance, Carrington (2006) attributes the rise in female juvenile delinquency since 1960 partially to changes in legislation and juvenile justice policy that label more girls as delinquent.

In short, the pattern of female criminality is an artifact of the selectivity shown by the police and courts and other agencies toward women, which is based on sexist assumptions and perceptions (Campbell 1981; Box and Hale 1983; A. Morris 1987). In many types of crimes, sentencing results in women getting tougher sentences (Chesney-Lind 1986; Chesney-Lind and Sheldon 1992). This is particularly true for single women, who compete with men for jobs, challenging the male-dominated (patriarchal) society's gender norms. Not least of these norms is patriarchy's need to control young single women. This can result in young women whose status offenses include running away from home to avoid being doubly victimized, first by their male caretaker abusers and second by the criminal justice system, which may unwittingly return these daughters to abusive parents, compounding their harm.

Similarly, the more recent power-control thesis, which implies that a mother's liberation explains increases in her daughter's crime, has been criticized for falsely "assuming that working in an authority position in the labor market translates into power and authority in the home" (Beirne and Messerschmidt [1991] 1995, 549). Power-control versions of liberal feminism have also been criticized on the basis that they are not supported by the evidence, because although women's participation in work has increased, all measures of female delinquency show stability (Chesney-Lind 1989, 20).

Radical feminists such as MacKinnon (1987, 1989) are critical of liberal feminists' attempts to change the law to bring about equality and for buying into male culture. They argue that liberal feminists' attempts at legal reform miss the central problem of patriarchy. Worse, it leaves it intact under the veil of formal equality.

Finally, socialist feminists have argued that rather than liberation leading to increases in crime among women, any real increase in property crime is due to women's economic marginalization in a patriarchal society. This means more women are either unemployed or employed in insecure, part-time, unskilled, low-paid jobs, at a time when welfare has been increasingly cut back, "so they are less able and willing to resist the temptations to engage in property offenses as a way of helping solve their financial difficulties" (Box 1983, 198–199; Box and Hale 1983).

Because of the limitations of the liberal feminist analysis, several other feminist criminologists have argued that it is not enough to pursue equality for women through reform—what is needed is a change in the whole system away from patriarchy. Most vigorous in this criticism are the radical feminists, whose position we examine next.

Radical Feminism

According to radical feminists, the explanation for the gender ratio in crime is self-evident. Crime is men's behavior, not women's behavior. It is in men's biological nature to be aggressive and dominate. Crime is simply an expression of men's need to control and to dominate others. This occurs in numerous forms, including imperialism, racism, and class society, but most of all men seek to dominate women, forcing them into motherhood and sexual slavery (Barry 1979). Men are born to be sexually dominant, and it is this biological difference that directly causes their criminality (Brownmiller 1975) and also explains why the gender crime ratio is universal across time, space, and cultures. Thus, rape is the ultimate expression of women's subordination, because it is "an act of aggression in which the victim is denied her self-determination" (Griffin 1979, 21) and through which all men keep all women in a state of fear (Brownmiller 1975, 5). Similarly, "the serial killing of women, like rape, is essentially a crime of domination and power; serial killers resemble perpetrators of domestic homicides who kill the intimate female partners they have typically dominated, controlled and battered, often for long periods of time" (Websdale 2003, 236).

As a result of prioritizing patriarchy, radical feminists see their role as "thinking about the way in which the sex/gender system affects and shapes crime, victimization and criminal justice . . . to systematically think about the links between the observed patterns of women's victimization, women's offending and women's experience with the criminal justice system within the context of patriarchy" (Chesney-Lind and Faith 2001, 290). Chesney-Lind, for example, has argued that the victimization of girls and their response to harm are shaped by their subordination in a male-dominated family context that defines and accepts dominant definitions of their daughters as sexual property. Girls who commit status crimes such as running away and getting involved in drugs and prostitution are criminalized rather than protected for their attempts to survive their hostile and abusive family environments. Chesney-Lind (1989) sees these delinquent acts as "survival strategies" necessary in a patriarchal system that oppresses females and stretches from the home to the legal and judicial system.

A distinguishing feature of radical feminism is its focus on patriarchy and human reproduction and how this is used as a basis to force women into subordination (Jaggar 1983). Women are subordinated to men through a sexual division of labor in which women are assigned all the work necessary to rear children, and the "sexual division of labor established originally in procreation is extended into every area of life" (ibid., 249). The sexual division of labor is reinforced by male aggression, which is used to define and control the culture and institutions of society, including (1) the state and its institutions of government; (2) employment (where men's ideas dominate industry and commerce), and especially work relationships; and (3) social institutions, especially the family, which provides the root of this "law of the father." In each of these arenas, men control women through psychological, economic, sexual, and physical abuse and manipulation, often linked to controls over their sexuality and reproduction through the family structure and the law. Indeed, Lauritsen and Schaum (2004) found that family structure is a critical factor in understanding the domestic abuse of women. In addition, the male-constructed law has limited consideration of the ways women's bodies and activities are controlled through the law and the state, both of which are male dominated, in ways far more repressive than the laws affecting men. Not surprisingly, because of the male domination of family and law, women's culture reflects their servile status and fosters an attitude of self-sacrifice. Even in areas of society where women have increasingly been employed to do equivalent work to men, the way they perform those tasks reflects this repressive control. For example, in a study of New York police officers, Eterno (2006) found that even though both male and female officers showed the same levels of aggression in weapons-search situations, female officers were more likely than men to follow legal restrictions with regard to such situations.

There is an interesting parallel between the radical feminist analysis and the biological and evolutionary psychology perspective we discussed in Chapter 4, which argues that male violence contributes to successful human evolution by ensuring the most able and successful males reproduce with the best-suited females. Indeed, Campbell's "staying alive" thesis argues that evolutionary logic requires passing on to future generations the genetic structure that has proved to be effective in both survival and reproduction. As a result, females avoid risky behavior that threatens their survival, which affects the kind of crime females select and why they avoid those involving physical harm: "The evolved mechanism by which the costs of aggression (and other forms of risk taking) are weighted more heavily for females may be a lower threshold for fear in situations which pose a direct threat of bodily injury. . . . Hence among females, disputes do not carry implications for status with them as they do among males, but are chiefly connected with the acquisition and defence of scarce resources" (1999, 203).

Policy Implications of Radical Feminist Theory

Radical feminists believe that they can be free from male domination only by liberating themselves from male definitions of reality and of women's roles and place in society, particularly in the family. Since male domination shapes the state and its laws, if they hope to advance their cause women must take power from men in these institutions (MacKinnon 1989). This means replacing men in powerful positions, in particular in the law and the courts and other institutions of criminal justice.

Furthermore, women should become sexually autonomous in reproduction and involve themselves in women-centered and women-only organizations, developing their own values and culture rooted in women's traditional hidden culture. It is because radical feminists want to exclude men from social life that they are also referred to as separatist feminists (T. Young 1995, 287).

Radical feminists believe that once women have obtained power, the objective is to abolish gender, hierarchy, and the distinction between the public and private spheres of society (Jaggar 1983, 254–255). Ultimately, argue radical feminists, patriarchy must be replaced by *matriarchy* (rule of mothers), "a society in which production serves the interests of reproduction; that is, the production of goods is regulated to support the nurturance of life" (Love and Shanklin 1978, 186). Only then will crime, that is, men harming others, diminish. Among modern-day matriarchal societies, such as the Minangkabau people of West Sumatra, Indonesia, studied by Peggy Reeves Sanday (2002), it is not so much that the women rule, even though their power extends into economic and political realms of the society and women control land inheritance. Rather, men and women are seen as complementary, with emphasis in the society placed on nurturing growth, and on the maternal in daily life. "While we in the West glorify male dominance and competition, matriarchy in this society is about making the maternal the center, origin, and foundation, not just of life but of the social order as well" (Sanday 2003). Most important, Sanday describes a peaceable, almost violence-free Minangkabau society among the population of 4 million.

On a more pragmatic level than a revolution toward matriarchy, radical feminists have "lobbied for shelters and more effective legislation, and actively confronted cultural norms that accepted man's right to discipline, control, and punish his family anyway he chose" (Chesney-Lind and Faith 2001, 293; Faith and Currie 1993). One of the problems faced by radical theorists, and for that matter other feminist theorists, in relation to policy is their expressed desire for increased criminalization of sexual assault and domestic violence. These were initially thought of as a positive for women, but this development placed many feminists and victim advocates into unholy alliance with police and prosecutors; it also meant men learned how to use the new system to further intimidate and harass their victims (Chesney-Lind 2006).

Evaluation of Radical Feminist Criminology

Criticism of the radical-feminist agenda has come from numerous sources, including other feminists (Danner 1991; Messerschmidt 1993; Munro 2003). One of the primary objections is that it assumes a biological determinism in which men are destined to be harmful, aggressive, and controlling. Catharine MacKinnon, a leading radical feminist, has been particularly criticized on deterministic as well as essentialist issues (Munro 2003). Research suggests that women's abuse by men is not always for control.

Second, radical feminism ignores differences among men and among women, perceiving gender as a "sex-caste." This "assumes a universality and commonality of women's subordination that does not exist. Important power differentials among women are ignored" (Danner 1991, 52). For example, in a study of prostitution, Weitzer (2005) found that radical feminism was too one-dimensional to explain gender inequality in the sex trade.

Third, the argument about men controlling women through physical force and violence in the best interests of societal evolution fails to explain how the criteria of being successful have changed, such that those who are most successful "in the competition for resources in fact are the least likely to employ serious forms of violence as a tactic in their interpersonal negotiations, including dealing with competitors either for economic resources or in terms of the reproductive capacities of women" (Polk 2003, 138).

Fourth, in its instrumental conception of the state as a means to power, radical feminism assumes that men are the sole problem rather than power itself being problematic. In attempting to use the state to protect women against male violence, radical feminists risk increasing the power of the male state against women (Pitch 1985; D. Currie 1989; Smart 1989). Furthermore, by ignoring the construction of differences among people, radical feminism presents a naive view that women in institutions would be able to create a nurturing society devoid of power relations. For many, particularly Marxist and socialist feminists, the radical position is inadequate without a more profound analysis of social structure and the state.

With regard to positive contributions, radical feminism demonstrates the various ways that women are victimized through physical, sexual, and emotional violence (Chesney-Lind and Faith 2001, 293).

Marxist Feminism

The Marxist-feminist perspective emerged in the late 1960s as an attempt to explain women's oppression using Marxist analysis (Messerschmidt 1993). Marxist feminism, like radical feminism, sees society structured as a patriarchy but argues that this patriarchy is rooted in the kind of economy a society has, in particular in its class relations of production. Historically, capitalist societies based on private ownership of the means of production and male inheritance have created class-divided societies in which men dominate. Gender differences are used as a means to subordinate and exploit women as a "reserve army of labor" used as free domestic labor to keep capitalist wage costs down. As Engels (1884) argued, women's place in the family is based on the master-slave relationship, which exploits women through their subordinate and dependent relationship to men. Their role, and the role of the family, is to reproduce and socialize compliant workers who will sell their labor to capitalists. Thus, although capitalist class society oppresses the majority, "women are doubly oppressed through their tie to a domestic sphere that is inconsequential in terms of its power and influence. The essence of the Marxist-feminist position, therefore, is that women, like men, are oppressed economically but, unlike men, women are once again enslaved by their domesticity" (Alleman 1993, 27) and have been marginalized by being kept ignorant of financial and business matters.

Thus, it is the double oppression of women, argue Marxist feminists, that leads both to their victimization and to their criminality. In contrast to radical feminists, Marxist feminists see male crime against women not as the result of inherent qualities of male nature but as a product of men's molding to exploitative relations by a capitalist system. Men see others as competitive threats that need to be controlled in order to retain their own position of relative power and to keep women economically dependent. It is for this reason that men rape women, a phenomenon not typically found in noncapitalist societies, and women feel guilt, blaming themselves for being raped (Schwendinger and Schwendinger 1983; Sanday 1981).

The class-patriarchy analysis also explains spousal battering, which victimizes women at three times the rate of male victimization (Bureau of Justice Statistics 1993, 25). This is explained as men's attempt to control women who are trying to liberate themselves from economically dependent domesticity (Saunders 1988). Finally, the increasing international problems related to human trafficking show women to be, by far, the primary victims and include sexual abuse, slavery, and subordination to men as primary components (Virtual Center for Epidemiological Criminology 2009).

The relative lack of women's criminality and the nature of women's crimes are also explained from the Marxist-feminist perspective. Their control of economic exploitation explains why women, like slaves, commit very few crimes. Moreover, the crimes women do commit are reflections of their class-defined dependency or attempts to break from it. For example, unlike men, when women commit embezzlement, it is typically to help solve economic problems confronted by their families for which they alone feel responsible since virtually anything justifies maintaining the welfare of their husbands, children, or parents (Zietz 1981). Similarly, unlike men who kill women intimates, "women who kill their partners typically do so only after years of enduring various forms of physical, sexual, and psychological abuse. Typically, these women have used up all available forms of social support, perceive that they cannot leave their abusive relationships, and fear for their lives" (DeKeseredy and Schwartz 1996, 291; DeKeseredy 1993; Dobash et al. 1992). Other petty property crimes are also the result of women's oppressed position in a capitalist economic system that attaches them to the subordination of family servitude (Balkan, Berger, and Schmidt 1980).

As with most Marxist analysis, since these problems are rooted in the capitalist system of production, the policy implication is that capitalism must be replaced by socialism, which does not exploit its workers or allow the economic exploitation of women by men.

Evaluation of Marxist Feminism

The major criticism of Marxist feminists comes from socialist feminists who disagree with the priority given to class over patriarchy. In particular, Marxist feminism has been criticized for explaining women's domestic labor in relation to capital but not in relationship to men (Messerschmidt 1993, 52). Instead, socialist feminists address the class-patriarchy relationship, as we show in the next section.

Given the priority of class over patriarchy in Marxist feminists' analysis, it is not surprising that their solution involves changing the capitalist class structure to involve women as full and equal, independent, productive members of society. This means eliminating male-dominated inheritance of property, paying women for housework, and providing house care and child care services. The only way all this is possible is to replace the capitalist system with a democratic socialist one (Daly and Chesney-Lind 1988).

Radical feminists also criticize Marxist feminists for buying into male culture. They argue that prioritizing the economic sphere (as in Marxist feminism) is accepting male standards of what is important while doing nothing about patriarchy.

Socialist Feminism

Socialist feminism is an attempt to merge Marxist feminism and radical feminism (Jaggar 1983; Danner 1991; Einstadter and Henry 2006; DeKeseredy and Schwartz 1996). It examines the interrelated and interdependent forces of capitalism and patriarchy that lead to men's crime and women's oppression, subordination, and dependency. It does this without prioritizing one over the other (Eisenstein 1979; Hartmann 1981).

A major statement from a socialist feminist on the cause of crime came from James Messerschmidt, a criminologist at the University of Southern Maine. In his book *Capitalism, Patriarchy, and Crime* (1986), Messerschmidt argued that relationships between owners of capital and workers result in the workers' exploitation by the owners (based on class inequality). Intertwined with class oppression is a system of "relations of reproduction." Through these relations, men exploit women's labor power and control their sexuality in order to reproduce the existing social order (including its sex-role divisions and hierarchy of power relations). The relatively powerful position of men results in their having greater opportunities for crime and a greater ability to create harm, as, for example, human trafficking shows (Virtual Center for Epidemiological Criminology 2009). In contrast, women's relatively subordinate position affords them less opportunity to offend, just as it affords them less opportunity to benefit from legitimate opportunities. In short, class patriarchy not only creates crime but subordinates women.

Whereas the other versions of feminism see women's subordination resulting from one or another determining force (evolutionary, liberal-socialization, radical-biology, Marxist-capitalist class relations), socialist feminism sees humans as shaped and transformed by cooperative productive activity "in which human beings continuously re-create their physiological and psychological constitution" (Jaggar 1983, 303). As Jaggar noted, "socialist feminism's distinctive contribution is its recognition that the differences between men and women are not pre-social givens, but rather are socially constructed and therefore alterable" (ibid., 304).

John Hagan and colleagues (1989, 1990; Hagan, Simpson, and Gillis 1987) illustrate a version of socialist feminism in their power-control theory in which they combine patriarchy and class in relation to gender-role socialization. They suggest that class relations in the workplace and gender relations in society come together in the domestic context of the family, producing two basic types of families with different consequences for female crime. Where the husband/father works in a powerful authority position and the wife/mother stays at home, this "patriarchal family" reproduces a sexual division of labor in their children, with daughters becoming homemakers and sons being active in the labor force. This is because in such families girls are subject to "instrumental" control and supervision in the belief that they need greater protection from their vulnerability to crime victimization. Mothers also exert more relational control over their daughters, using the constraints of emotional attachment (Hagan 1990). Thus, "parents socialize girls into domestic roles, in order to limit their risk-taking, to restrict their sexual activity, and to reduce any inclination to look for deviant role exits from their family structures. Girls, therefore, are controlled relationally, by both male domination and by female role modeling and supervision and, therefore, are less likely to engage in crime than boys" (Einstadter and Henry 2006, 322). Hagan (1990) argues, like Chesney-Lind, that girls in patriarchal families are forced to either endure or escape their domestic oppression and will look for deviant-role exits such as suicide or running away, resulting in their designation as deviant or delinquent. However, boys in patriarchal families are given greater freedom to take risks and are socialized to control others and as a result are relatively free to deviate. In contrast, where both parents work and share domestic chores, this "egalitarian family" produces daughters and sons equally prepared to work. These daughters of egalitarian families, unlike those in patriarchal families, are socialized to be greater risk takers and are just as likely to be involved in crime as are the sons.

When gender and class-power dimensions are combined, four types of families result, each with different probabilities that their children will be involved in crime. Higher class-power egalitarian families, such as dual-career professional families, are likely to show the least difference between delinquency among their sons and daughters: "Daughters become more like sons in their involvement in such forms of risk taking as delinquency" (Hagan 1989, 158). Dual-career working-class egalitarian families show a higher difference, but lower than the difference in delinquency between sons and daughters of higher-class patriarchal families, since patriarchy is more differentiating than class power. Each of these families can be expected to show a lower difference than traditional working-class patriarchal families since they experience the combined negative effects of both class and gender. Importantly, Hagan (1989) argues that "the greater access to power and resources renders those in the highest economic positions the most liberated to commit (white collar and corporate) crime using either the corporation or their occupational resources, and they are the most able to afford the means to separate and protect themselves from prosecution" (Einstadter and Henry 2006, 322–323).

As a result of the critical evaluations that Hagan's power-control theory has received over the past twenty years (see below), there have been some significant developments and modifications. One of the most interesting is John Hagan and his colleagues' analysis of the influence of mothers on their sons (McCarthy, Hagan, and Woodward 1999). Interestingly, their study confirmed that in patriarchal families, males supported gendered activity concerning appropriate and inappropriate behaviors, which includes their "freedom" to offend, but they also found that mothers in less patriarchal families have affected their sons' patriarchal views, suggesting that sons in these families are less likely to offend. Also, by looking at informal controls Sims-Blackwell (2000) found that males in less patriarchal families felt more shame than females because in such families the fathers engage in child care duties and through these were able to have a greater influence on their sons.

Policy of Socialist Feminism

The policies advocated by socialist feminists are based on the idea that if productive activity creates differences, then "the power of sharing" (Winfree and Abadinsky 2003, 273) can also be used to reduce the differences between men and women. Thus, socialist feminists see the solution to women's subordination as replacing capitalism with a collective political and legal order based on equality between class and gender. They want to expose and eliminate male-dominated power hierarchies and the wage-based capitalist system and foster male attitudes and behaviors. In short, they want to abolish both class and gender. Socialist feminists believe that of central importance in any new order is reproductive freedom (i.e., women's control over whether, and under what circumstances, they bear and rear children) and sexual freedom. They also believe that there should be an end to compulsory motherhood. They believe in the availability of paid maternity leave and of publicly funded, community-controlled child care. These policies are designed to liberate women from alienated motherhood and allow them the freedom to be economically independent of men. But the socialist-feminist collective order requires more than an absence of hierarchy. As Einstadter and Henry (2006) argue, it requires equality based on the recognition of differences of experience while at the same time not discriminating on the basis of these differences.

Evaluation of Socialist Feminism

Socialist-feminist analyses have been subject to criticism, again largely from other feminists. Some claim the theory is still essentially Marxist and deterministic in that the double vision for patriarchy and capitalism leaves no room for the meaningful construction of human action (Smart 1987). Radical feminists criticize both Marxist and socialist feminism for failing to explain why capitalism requires women to be subordinate. Furthermore, they argue that there is no guarantee that a socialist revolution would liberate women (Hartmann 1981).

Hagan's power-control theory, which is perhaps one of the most theoretically elegant attempts to combine class and patriarchy, has received some qualified empirical support. For example, one study found that "boys are more likely to be both victims and offenders, girls are more likely to engage in role exit behaviour, and victimization significantly increases role exit behaviour in more patriarchal families" but that the effects on victimization and delinquency are different and that although delinquency effects are supported, patriarchy and class power have no effect on victimization or on the search for exits, with boys and girls being affected in the same way (Sims-Blackwell, Sellers, and Schlaupitz 2002). However, Hagan's theory has also been subject to the most criticism, not least by other feminist theorists. The theory has been compared with the emancipation-causes-crime arguments that blame the working absence from the home as responsible for females' increased delinquency and therefore that increased participation by women would result in increased crime rates for young girls. They asked instead why sons wouldn't become more like daughters and commit less crime (Naffine 1987; Chesney-Lind 1989; Chesney-Lind and Sheldon 1992). Also, why should those in authority positions at work be in authority positions at home, and why are class and gender power intertwined (Messerschmidt 1993)? In contrast to Hagan's predictions, Singer and Levine (1988) found greater differences in parental controls, risk taking, and delinquency among boys and girls in egalitarian than in patriarchal households and found that mothers in egalitarian households exerted more control than those in patriarchal households. Some, including Hagan, now recognize that gender power and patriarchy might have separate and more important impacts than class power. Indeed, Messerschmidt asserted that by concentrating on gender differences in crime, "power control theory . . . ignore[s] gender similarities in crime between men and women and disregard[s] the differences among men and boys as well as among women and girls. . . . Consequently, power control . . . miss[es] what must be acknowledged: Women and girls also construct masculine practices that are related to crime" (2006, 217).

Hagan's power-control theory has also been criticized for ignoring racial, ethnic, and cultural differences. For example, Curran and Renzetti argued that the theory ignores differences of race and ethnicity and the quality of the child-parent relationship in different families (1994, 274). Messerschmidt stated that by constructing an "essentialist criminology" that collapses gender into sex roles, Hagan's power-control theory ignores cross-cultural differences and also ignores differences in masculine and feminine practices by men and women, within any particular society, "constructed according to class, race, age, sexuality and particular social situation" (2006, 117).

The failure of socialist feminism in general to acknowledge the race and ethnicity dimension has resulted in the accusation that it is exclusionary. For example, Beverly Brown (1988) contended that the concept of patriarchy fails to recognize the historical variation within women and within men. Others also found the concepts of patriarchy and gender to be racist and ethnocentric since they are based on the experiences of white women and exclude women of color (Ahluwalia 1991; Barrett and McIntosh 1985; Mama 1989; Rice 1990).

In response to some of these charges, feminist theory, during the 1990s, shifted toward dissolving the previous categories and analyzing the following: (1) the ways gender was represented, (2) the gendered production of feminist knowledge, and (3) the interconnections among all dimensions of hierarchy. Theorists also acknowledged the concept of difference: "The crux of the socialist-feminist concern with the intersection of gender, class, and race is the recognition of difference. . . . Patriarchy cannot be separated from capitalism, neither can racism, imperialism or any other oppression based on 'otherness'" (Danner 1991, 53). This shift to "difference" rather than particular structural forms occurred in multiple new epistemological directions, including standpoint, poststructural, postcolonial, postmodern, and critical race theories, "each of which drew attention to the discursive power of criminological and legal texts in representing sex/gender and women" (Daly 2006, 206) and led to a cluster of feminist criminologies (Daly 2001).

Gendered Theory

Although there are different approaches to feminist analysis discussed above (Caulfield and Wonders 1994), they are increasingly united around the need to "develop a gendered theory of crime, that is a theory that explicitly takes into account the effects of gender and more significantly, gender stratification, on women's lives and development [and] the recognition that people's perceptions, opportunities and experiences are shaped not only by the mode of production under which they live, but also by the form of gender relations dominant in their society" (Curran and Renzetti 1994, 272). Indeed, Daly has summarized three core areas of concern for feminist theorists concerned with crime and justice: "(1) the intersections of class, race, and gender; (2) sex/gender as an accomplishment or a production—referred to as 'doing gender'; and (3) sexual difference and the relation it has both to gender and the institutionalization of cultural and structural categories—referred to as 'sexed bodies'" (Daly 2006, 206; see also 1997). She argued that there is now less interest by feminist scholars in developing general theories of crime and more interest in building theories "about women's lawbreaking and victimization, the gendered qualities of crime and victimization, and the discursive power of dominant discourses (criminological and legal)" (2006, 206).

One of the implications of gendered theory is that we consider how both women's femininity and men's masculinity are formed by their experiences. In this context, Messerschmidt has revised his earlier socialist-feminist position toward one of structured action theory: "Crime by men is a form of social practice invoked as a resource, when other sources are unavailable, for accomplishing masculinity" (1993, 85). This is almost like saying that crime is the result of blocked opportunities to be a man. Messerschmidt argued that the concept of patriarchy obscures real variations in the construction of masculinity. He noted that there are differing masculinities, just as there are different femininities. Committing crimes depends on class, age, and situation but is also an example of "doing gender" (the social construction of gender), or building masculinity or femininity. In other words, doing crime is part of manliness (Polk 2003). Indeed, Messerschmidt asserted:

> Gender is a situated social and interactional accomplishment that grows out of social practices in specific settings and serves to inform such practices in reciprocal relation—we coordinate our activities to "do" gender in situational ways. . . . Because individuals realize that their behavior may be held accountable to others they configure their actions in relation to how these might be interpreted by others in the particular context in which they occur. . . . We facilitate the ongoing task of accountability by demonstrating that we are male or female through concocted behaviors that may be interpreted accordingly. Consequently, we do gender (and thereby crime) differently, depending upon the social situation and social circumstances that we encounter. (2006, 217–218)

Messerschmidt pointed out that "doing gender" does not occur in a vacuum but is shaped by social structural constraints. Principal among those structures that constrain and enable action are race and class, which interrelate with gender and play out in space and time. The dynamics of gendered theory are well illustrated in the work of Jody Miller on girls in gangs and on their everyday suppression by men. In her first work, *One of the Guys* (2000), Jody Miller discussed the gender-structured way girls enter and take part in gangs that makes them subject to victimization as part of their participation. Certain girls identify with boys in their gangs and see each gang as a male operation. Indeed, Isis Sapp-Grant's gang, whose example opened this chapter, was called "the Deceptinettes" after the boy gang that they ran with, called "the Decepticons."

> My group officially became a gang, the Deceptinettes, after we joined up with these guys, the Decepticons. They got the name from the bad guys in *The Transformers*, a cartoon about robots that could transform their appearances. . . . The Deceptinettes grew from about ten girls to forty or fifty. There were a few hundred Decepticons, mostly male. . . . I never slept around but some girls had such low self-esteem they slept with guys for the protection. If you were "sexed in" to our gang, you never got respect. No one was raped but to get in, you did have to prove that you knew how to fight. There were blacks and hispanics and a couple of white guys in the Decepticons. . . . I was going out with the leader of Decept and I thought I was going to marry him and have the Decepticon children and we was just gonna have a Decept world. We were going to be like the mafia. (S. Russell 2000)

Miller, in *One of the Guys*, said that mixed-gender gangs have unequal gender relations and that some girls stand out from other girls by embracing a "masculine identity." Similarly, Messerschmidt, commenting on his gender and adolescent work (2004), stated that "some of these girls 'do' masculinity by, in part, displaying themselves in a masculine way, by engaging in what they and others in their milieu consider to be authentically masculine behavior, and by outright rejection of most aspects of femininity" (2006, 219).

In her most recent work, *Getting Played*, Miller looks at these combined effects of class, race, gender, place, and experience in the ecological context of disadvantaged areas of a city. Focusing on the much understudied African American girls' lives in a poor neighborhood of St. Louis, Miller revealed how they are daily vulnerable to violent abuse and victimization. Victimization ranges from harassment to gang rape, running "trains," and "gang banging," and the perpetrators of this oppression are male family members, friends, and relatives who themselves often also have a history of abuse. These men "play" the girls and young women for prestige, "macho rep," and social status among their male peers, and do so in public contexts that themselves are gender structured to rationalize and justify male oppression of women. Grounded in gender-based stereotypes, these African American girls are seen as responsible for their own victimization, and neither bystanders nor authorities assist in preventing their violent and sexual oppression because of this racial and cultural acceptance. The outcome of this failure of support is isolation, despair, and anger. This results in the girls' withdrawing their support for social institutions and turning to self-help survival that often reinforces their own oppression; these girls find themselves alone and powerless to change the situations that cause them such pain and become increasingly self-deprecating. In her analysis Jody Miller investigates "how the structural inequalities that create extreme—and racialized—urban poverty facilitate both cultural adaptations and social contexts that both heighten and shape the tremendous gender-based violence faced by African American girls" (2008, 3).

Epistemological Issues and Postmodern Feminism

Epistemology is "theories of what knowledge is, what makes it possible, and how to get it" (Harding 1991, 308; see also Flavin 2001). Epistemology is how we create knowledge. As such it involves the methods we employ. Part of the difficulty confronted by gendered theory is that the available social science methodology is based on male culture's definitions and ways of obtaining knowledge and truth through positivism; in other words, our commonsense knowledge and "ways of knowing" are gendered (Hatty 2000). Such approaches are arguably incapable of appreciating the diversity of gender constructions. In contrast, some feminist theorists have developed an alternative research method called "standpoint epistemology," which claims, "The construction of knowledge requires many voices; especially those that have been marginalized by racism, sexism or class privilege. No one standpoint is given greater honor over others; together they give a rough understanding of the many ways to grasp the incredible complexity and ever-changing patterns of social life. Standpoint epistemology reveals a neglected or forgotten point of view, it empowers those excluded" (T. Young 1995, 730). Flavin adds that "standpoint feminists try to construct knowledge from the perspectives of the persons being studied on the grounds that the perspective of the oppressed or marginalized tends to be less distorted" (2001, 274). This attention to a diversity of experiences, multiple knowledges, and the social construction of difference has led some to the view that a new nonexclusionary paradigm is necessary. One such approach is postmodernism (which we discuss in more detail in the next chapter).

Briefly, postmodernism "emphasizes the importance of alternative discourses and accounts and frequently takes the form of examining the effects of language and symbolic representations" (ibid., 274). Postmodern feminists who write about crime, law, and social control, such as Carol Smart (1989), Alison Young (1990, 1996), and Adrian Howe (1994), go further than the standpoint feminists, although their positions may at first seem similar. Both celebrate the legitimacy of discounted knowledges. Standpoint feminism wants to replace male truths with truths based on the diversity of women's experiences. Postmodern feminists prefer multiple knowledges rather than new truths, because these tell different stories. This continuing diversity offers resistance to any domination, particularly from identities formed in hierarchical contexts that tend to produce further domination (Smart 1990; Grant 1993). Postmodern feminists reject notions of class, race, and gender and note that the early white Western feminist notions of the universal subordination of women neglected differences among women, particularly women of color, third world women, lesbian women, and others. The notions of "woman" and "women" themselves have been questioned as inadequate by feminist postmodernism (Howe 1994, 167; Smart 1992; Bordo 1990). The assumption that each person has one fixed sex, one sexuality, and one gender is replaced by crosscutting sex, sexuality, and gender constructs that capture the complexity of gendered experience (Lorber 1996). Postmodernism criticizes early feminist criminology for taking for granted assumed gender distinctions between men and women, masculine and feminine, without questioning them (B. Brown 1990). Consideration of alternative discourses is thus critical.

A third way of creating knowledge is through traditional social science methods: positivism. Although most feminists have rejected this methodology, some have embraced it. For example, Campbell, Muncer, and Bibel conducted a sophisticated statistical analysis on the female evolutionary perspective (1998). These types of researchers and theorists are called feminist empiricists, and their position is considered "the most conservative" feminist approach (Flavin 2001).

Summary and Conclusion

In this chapter we reviewed the contribution of dominant feminist theories and theorists. We conclude by noting that the primary feminist contribution has been to show that "gender inequalities exist in society and that these inequalities should be addressed" (ibid., 272). We have shown how feminist scholarship has focused on core issues that highlight the importance of the difference between men's and women's patterns of crime and victimization. We showed how feminist theory moved from a liberal critique of differences and a call for equality through radical, Marxist, and socialist forms before reintegrating around a set of issues having to do with the gendering of crime and justice, and of crime as the practice of "doing gender." Several social policies have been examined in this vein, each offering a way in which gender, together with race and class, needs to be incorporated into justice in order to correct the deficits of a male-dominated theoretical tradition. Indeed, feminist criminology "has provided major insights about the process of offending and victimization and it has presented major challenges to established criminological assumptions and analysis" (Einstadter and Henry 2006, 278). Moreover, "feminist criminologists have reminded criminology that men also have a gender, and that thinking about gender and male criminality could offer new insights" (Chesney-Lind and Faith 2001, 298).

In the next chapter we extend this "critical" discussion and focus on left realism, postmodernism, anarchism, and peacemaking theories. As you read the next chapter you will note that it is really an extension of the basic critical assumptions that began this chapter on feminism.

Summary Chart: Feminist Theory

Human Nature: Humans are (1) in liberal feminism, social blanks socialized into gender roles through family, media, education, and work; (2) in radical feminism, biologically determined—men are aggressive and competitive, and women are cooperative and nurturing; (3) in Marxist feminism, creatively different but oppressed and exploited for class interests, which creates artificial divisions and accentuates competitive male characteristics; (4) in socialist feminism, "gendered identities"—gender, like race and ethnicity, comprises socially constructed categories imposed on biology that create women as secondary, marginal beings, a view reinforced by socialization.

Society and the Social Order: Represents male interests in its structure, organization, institutions, and operation and excludes women's interests: (1) in liberal feminism, hierarchy with unequal opportunity for women; (2) in radical feminism, patriarchy with male gender dominating all institutions of power, including state; (3) in Marxist feminism, class hierarchy based on inequalities of wealth in which women are dependent and reproductive of male labor; (4) in socialist feminism, class-based patriarchy with coalescing inequalities of class, gender, and race, with state seen as relatively autonomous. Crime is men's domination and control over women, who are devalued; in socialist feminism, doing crime is doing masculinity. Law reflects male definitions: (1) In liberal feminism, law upholds inequalities; (2) in radical feminism, law is an extension of male power; (3) in Marxist feminism, law reflects capitalist interests and works to maintain dominant class interests, which are male; (4) in socialist feminism, law bolsters male supremacy and reinforces appearance of women's inferiority as natural but also affords women some protection. Criminals manifest the gendered identity of masculinity.

Causal Logic: (1) In liberal feminism, women's liberation as women becomes more androgynous; (2) in radical feminism, male aggression, dominance, and control contribute to women's subjugation; (3) in Marxist feminism, class exploitation and subordination of women leave them dependent, weak, and vulnerable; (4) in socialist feminism, the interaction of forces of class and gender subordinates women, creating them as a category of "otherness" that is part of a general social construction of difference; masculinity is used by some to dominate others through patriarchy. Feminist empiricism accepts traditional models of causality.

Criminal Justice Policy: (1) In liberal feminism, it seeks to end gender discrimination through changes to law, increasing women's opportunities and fights for equal treatment in law; (2) in radical feminism, it seeks to replace patriarchy with matriarchy in which production serves reproduction and nurturance and sees the state as major resource to be captured; (3) in Marxist feminism, it seeks to replace capitalist class hierarchy with a socialist society; (4) in socialist feminism, it seeks to replace class-patriarchy with decentralized socialism, providing equal control over decision making to the disempowered (women, minorities, and others), to eliminate power based on difference and allow women to define themselves, and to demystify gender constructions of masculinity and femininity to show diversity within.

Criminal Justice Practice: Encourage increased reporting of violence against women at home and at work. Pass new laws banning sexual harassment, stalking, date rape, pornography, and so forth. (1) In liberal feminism, acquire more control over men's power through stronger police force, stricter laws, and regulating men's violence; (2) in radical feminism, replace men in institutions of power with women; (3) in Marxist and socialist feminism, decentralize democratic institutions of justice and replace rational male principles with women's principles of caring, connection, and community.

Evaluation: Radical feminism criticized for assuming biological determinism and sex castes composed of dominant men and subordinated women; liberal and radical feminism accused of strengthening power of the male state and denying entry points for women to make change. Radical-feminist view of men as criminal and women as victim ignores women as offender, reinforcing view of women as passive and men as active. All criticized for being blind to race and ethnicity and for ignoring unique worldviews of persons of color.

12

New Directions in Criminological Theory

In this concluding chapter we consider several new criminologies that attempt to address crime from a wider, more holistic, and globally aware perspective. The theories discussed in this chapter in several cases build on or incorporate insights and ideas from throughout the text, but they do so in a way that produces exciting new insights on crime and criminal justice. Most have emerged during the closing quarter of the twentieth century, though a few can trace their roots further. All are considered to be on the cutting edge of criminology in the twenty-first century. We consider three clusters of new theories. The first cluster, "Critical Criminologies," builds on the critical perspectives that we examined in the previous two chapters. Included here are left realism, postmodernism, constitutive theory, edgework, anarchism, abolitionism, peacemaking, restorative justice, and cultural criminology, to which we have added critical race theory. The second cluster, known more generally as "Integrative Criminologies," brings together mainstream and critical theories in various combinations in an attempt to provide greater explanatory power than any single theoretical approach. The third group, "Reciprocal-Interactive Integrative Criminology," is a subset of integrative theory but also goes beyond to produce new theoretical directions and takes a developmental approach that looks at crime as the ongoing outcome of a time-structured interactive process. This cluster includes life-course theory, developmental or pathways theory, and reciprocal interactive theory. Let's begin with those theories that are an extension of the ideas presented in the last chapter.

Critical Criminologies

Like interactionism, labeling theory, and social constructionism, which we considered in Chapter 7, and radical, Marxist, and feminist theories, considered in Chapters 10 and 11, the theories considered here are "critical" for at least four reasons.

First, they do not accept state definitions of crime at face value or for that matter as a fact of social reality. Instead, they define crime as social harm and/or as violations of human rights. Second, critical criminologies do not necessarily assume that the cause of crime is to be found within the individuals who commit crime, but rather look for it in the system and social structure of society. Elliot Currie, for example, says the research evidence shows that violence in America comes "from certain fundamental fault lines in our society—especially the effects of economic and racial inequality and, in particular, the absence of hope and opportunity in the inner cities" such that the "high level of violent crime is a *cost* of certain kinds of social arrangements. . . . It is part of the price we pay for maintaining societies that are wracked by a constellation of larger social ills—including extremes of inequality, economic deprivation and insecurity, and a pervasive culture of predatory competition" (2006, 299). So any analysis of crime causation needs also to "consider how offenders have themselves been 'victimized,' first by society, and subsequently by the criminal justice system through its selective processing of the powerless" (Einstadter and Henry 2006, 235). Critical criminologies not only challenge definitions of crime and standard theories of crime causation, but, third, they also oppose power hierarchies based on inequality, regardless of whether it is based on class power, political power, social power, or cultural power. Therefore, fourth, they see the criminal justice system as ineffective as a means to correct injustice and, rather than being an instrument for reform or change, as a semiautonomous partner of the capitalist system of production, with the overall objective of maintaining that system's dominant power structure. Instead of tinkering with criminal justice policy and practices, which often feeds the monster of domination and disciplinary control, critical criminologies demand a radical transformation of the total social and political organization of society: "While critical criminology emphasizes the crucial importance of social structure, it also considers human agency to be significant, and sees society as a distinctly human product that can be changed through human actions, albeit ones shaped by structural and cultural forces. Thus social structure only has the appearance of a fully external force; critical criminology's role is to demystify that appearance to facilitate human agents to make social change" (Henry 2006, 347). Believing that reforms are of limited value and can even be counterproductive to getting real change accomplished, critical criminologists' policies advocate broad societal-level changes.

However, critical criminology does not speak with one voice, a point that has been subject to angry contention, particularly by some radical Marxist criminologists (see especially S. Russell 2002; and Cowling 2006). Just as feminist criminological thought on crime and justice initially fragmented into a variety of different feminist theories and then came together around core issues of class, race, and gender, so too is there a proliferation of critical criminologies that have gone beyond the original conflict, radical, and feminist theorizing. As Henry and Lukas (2009) have said, these include: (1) "left realist" challenges to a romantic vision of the criminal as protorevolutionary, which sees a reversion to a strain-type relative-deprivation analysis of marginalized populations and police oppression; (2) postmodernist-inspired "constitutive criminology" that shares an anarchist anathema with power, seeing the expression of power as the root of harm production, whether it is by the state, corporations, or individuals, and cultural criminology's concern for a holistic intervention focused on changing the cultural discourse; (3) "cultural criminology" that "emphasizes the essential role of meaning, image, and representation in shaping the reality of crime and the range of collective responses to it" (Ferrell 2006, 247); (4) anarchist "peacemaking criminology" and "restorative justice" criminology that challenge the power of government with the implication that people can solve their own problems and that the state only accentuates power differentials and exacerbates conflict, which merges into Scandinavian abolitionist roots to develop a variety of restorative justice mechanisms that replace the use of power to solve crime and conflict; and (5) "critical race theory" that focuses on the overrepresentation of marginalized groups in the criminal justice system and racism in its institutions. Not surprisingly, these multiple voices of critical criminology, though agreeing that change to society and its system of justice is necessary, have different views on the extent and ways in which change should occur. Having said that, we start with a review of left realism, which actually challenges extreme radical criminology for not making enough concrete change in the short term, on the way to the long-term change that it advocates.

Left Realism

Left realism took form in the 1980s when Jock Young, one of the coauthors of the radical criminological milestone *The New Criminology* (I. Taylor, Walton, and Young 1973), and his colleagues began to analyze the results of a local-area victimization study (see, especially, Jones, MacLean, and Young 1986; Matthews and Young 1986, 1992; Young and Matthews 1992; and MacLean 1991). To their amazement, working-class Londoners were not so bothered about crimes of the powerful; they cared more about the crimes occurring in their own neighborhoods, committed by their own "working-class villains," and they wanted something done about them.

Young had earlier criticized criminology "of the left" for being too idealistic and termed it "left idealism" (J. Young 1979; Lea and Young 1984). It was idealistic because it started from abstract concepts rather than concrete realities (MacLean 1991, 11). Lea and Young (1984) argued that left idealism's exclusive focus on corporate and white-collar crime, its romantic celebrations of street criminals as working-class revolutionaries, and its assertions about the need for broad revolutionary policies ignored the feelings of most working-class crime victims—who most feared crimes by members of their own class.

In contrast, left realism takes crime victims seriously, arguing that crime destroys the quality of urban community life (Matthews 1987). But left realists, as critical criminologists, are also acutely aware of the harm caused to victims suffering from crimes of inequality. Advocates believe that the polarizing effects of capitalism divide societies into the "haves" and "have nots" while simultaneously promoting competitive individualism and greed. This "exclusive society" (J. Young 1999) marginalizes and abandons its poor, who suffer relative deprivation, frustration, and anger, which they express through disrespect and violence toward each other.

To complete the picture of crime, left realism argues that it is essential to include both victims and offenders in their relationships to each other, to the state's criminal justice agencies, and to the general public. Left realists call this set of relationships the "square of crime" (J. Young and Matthews 1992). More like strain theorists (discussed in Chapter 9) than Marxists, they argue that the capitalist system promotes competitive individualism and feeds off patriarchy and racism, creating inequalities between people that lead to relative deprivation (J. Young 1999). This suggests that income, standard of living, or quality of life "experienced as being unfairly low compared to that of the rest of society creates a feeling of economic disenfranchisement" (DeKeseredy and Schwartz 2006, 308–309). Those at the bottom of the heap, in *relative* poverty to their peers, experience relative deprivation because they cannot afford the pleasures of life enjoyed by others: "These are people who watch the same TV ads as everyone else and who are hustling to obtain products and status symbols such as color TVs, fancy cars, and expensive gold jewelry—desires created almost solely by capitalism" (DeKeseredy and Schwartz 1996, 250). Capitalism is the source of discontent and a perceived sense of injustice. Jock Young (1999) contends that many Americans and Europeans now live in "exclusive societies" "where an alarming number of people are excluded from the formal labor market, where thousands of people have to live on the street or in dilapidated public housing estates, and where inner-city violence is endemic" (DeKeseredy 2003, 39). These ghettos and ghost towns were produced by capital concentrations but were abandoned as capitalism "winged its way elsewhere" to new global locations "where labor was cheaper and expectations lower" (J. Young 1999, 20). Since those isolated at the bottom of the hierarchical heap are politically powerless to change their situation, they become angry and violent and beat up on each other, producing violent crime incidents. Some of their numbers also turn to stealing the very symbols (TVs and so forth) they cannot afford to buy. In this context, crime is an unjust individualistic solution to the experience of injustice among people who lack the legitimate means of solving the problem of relative depravation (J. Young 1999; DeKeseredy 2003). Moreover, it is also a collective solution because "people who lack legitimate means of solving the problem of relative deprivation may come into contact with other frustrated disenfranchised people and form subcultures, which, in turn, encourage and legitimate criminal behaviors" (DeKeseredy and Schwartz 2006, 309).

Rather than protect them from crime, police agencies tend to reinforce the inequalities, and the class-biased criminal justice system produces its own casualties within already impoverished neighborhoods where it targets primarily lower-class and minority males, the most vulnerable of the excluded, who are then punished. Thus, the "excluded" become victimized from all directions, from their oppression in the society, from the crimes of their fellow oppressed, from the crimes of corporations, and from the injustice and punitive actions of the criminal justice system.

Left realism, as its name suggests, is, therefore, critical of capitalism for creating and sustaining the inequalities and divisions that turn people against each other, favoring instead some form of socialist society (hence the term *left*). However, rather than waiting for the revolution, left realists propose to do something immediate, practical, and concrete to alleviate the suffering (this accounts for *realism*). Unlike the "left idealists" (whom we considered under radical criminology in Chapter 10) who romanticize the crimes of the poor, or "progressive minimalists" who are seen as downplaying the problems of the poor (D. Currie 1992), left realists do not believe in waiting for a socialist revolution before implementing policies that reduce the suffering from crime caused by the capitalist system and its agencies of social control. They argue that to do so is irresponsible because it allows the sole voice in the policy debate to be the right realist "law and order" lobby (Matthews 1987). (In contrast to left realists, right realists tend to view crime as the result of individual choice and include many of the ideas and policy recommendations we discussed in Chapter 3.)

Instead of tougher sentences and more prisons, left realists prefer alternative practical policy interventions that deal with both the immediacy of the crime problem and people's fear of it (Lea and Young 1984). These include preventive policies that (1) introduce problem solvers into working-class neighborhoods to defuse problems and to address residents' concerns through local crime surveys, (2) use alternative sanctions such as restitution and community service to "demarginalize" offenders and reintegrate them back into the community, and (3) encourage community involvement and democratically accountable control of the police by community citizens.

In general, left realists "seek short-term gains while remaining committed to long-term change. That is why they propose practical initiatives that can be implemented immediately and that 'chip away' at patriarchal capitalism" (DeKeseredy 2003, 36). These include efforts aimed at "reducing poverty and unemployment, curbing violence against women, and building strong communities" (ibid., 37). In this regard, left realists are increasingly acknowledging the value of "collective efficacy" or "social capital" in which strong community networks of social support and informal social control play a significant role, though not without meaningful employment and effective social programs (ibid., 39; see the ecology perspective in Chapter 8).

A good illustration of left realism can be found in the work of Elliot Currie, whose early work *Confronting Crime: An American Challenge* (1985) drew on international and comparative data to demonstrate that "serious violent crime was not simply a function of individual proclivity or, as some writers argued, of the universal effects of prosperity and democracy: it varied according to what kind of society you lived in. And that by looking at why we in the United States suffered this affliction more than nearly every other country in the world, we could understand something not only about how to deal more effectively with our own problem but about how to understand the roots of violence generally" (2006, 301). He argued that violent crime is still with us because we spend money on futile punishment programs but have not, as a society, fully committed to removing the extremes of inequality, particularly poverty. In his 1993 work *Reckoning: Drugs, the Cities, and the American Future*,

Currie argued that neither punishment nor treatment alone, without dealing with the underlying causes, is going to win a war on drugs: "The American drug problem was not, as some suggested, solely a creation of the drug war itself: it was also a cost, once again, of the enduring structures of inequality and deprivation that distinguished the U.S. from many other advanced societies" (2006, 302). In further development of these ideas, Currie (1997, 1998) took a holistic, multilevel analytical approach to explore the causes of crime and punishment in America, which he found in the core variables of market society, driven by the pursuit of profit for private gain, an economy that has been called "turbocharged capitalism." In contrast to other capitalist market economies, according to Currie, the United States, with its extremes of inequality and lack of social support, is becoming a global model with serious implication for crime worldwide (see box 12.1).

BOX 12.1 The Global Market Context of U.S. Crime and Punishment
ELLIOTT CURRIE

The United States was distinctive among the advanced nations in the extent to which its social life was shaped by the imperatives of private gain—my definition of "market society"—and it was not accidental that it was also the nation with by far the worst levels of serious violent crime, for market society created a "toxic brew" of overlapping social effects. It simultaneously created deep poverty and widened inequality, destroyed livelihoods, stressed families and fragmented communities. It chipped away at public and private sources of social support, while promoting a corrosive ethos of predatory individualism that pitted people against each other in a scramble for personal gain. . . . The empirical research of the past seven years . . . confirms the importance of inequality and insecurity as potent breeding grounds for violent crime; so does the evidence of experience, as the spread of these problems under the impact of "globalization" has brought increased social disintegration and violence across the world in its wake. . . . Violence has been reduced in many other advanced capitalist societies, without resorting to correspondingly high levels of incarceration, to levels that seem stunningly low by U.S. standards. The variation among those societies in street violence remains extraordinary, and I'd argue that it is largely due to the systematic differences in social policy that can coexist within the generic frame of modern capitalism. It is true that some of these differences in levels of crime (and in the response to crime) are narrowing, especially to the degree that other countries have adopted parts of the U.S. social model. But it also remains true that the United States isn't Sweden, or even France or Germany, when it comes to violent crime, or rates of imprisonment. And this difference isn't merely academic: it translates into tangible differences in the risks of victimization and the overall quality of life. . . . Social policy in the United States, and in many other countries as well, has, if anything, gone backwards on many of the issues raised by this line of thinking about crime. We continue

CONTINUES

BOX 12.1 (CONTINUED)

to chip way at our already minimal system of social supports for the vulnerable, while pressing forward with economic policies that, by keeping wages low and intensifying job insecurity, foster ever-widening inequality and deepen the stresses on families and communities that many of us have singled out as being crucial sources of violence. We continue to rely on mass incarceration as our primary bulwark against crime, despite an abundance of evidence that doing so is not only ineffective but also self-defeating. . . .

These tendencies are especially troubling because they are increasingly taking place on a worldwide scale. What we somewhat misleadingly call "globalization"—really the spread of "market" principles to virtually every corner of the world—threatens to increase inequality, instability, and violence wherever it touches, while simultaneously diminishing the political capacity for meaningful social change. Formerly stable and prosperous countries in the developed world are busily dismantling the social protections that traditionally helped to keep their rates of violent crime low: parts of the developing world that were once relatively tranquil are becoming breeding grounds for gang violence, official repression, and a growing illicit traffic in drugs and people. The world will not be able to build enough prisons to contain this volatility. The future under this model of social and economic development does not look pretty. Fortunately, it is not the only future we can envision.

Elliott Currie is a Professor of Criminology, Law, and Society in the School of Social Ecology at the University of California–Irvine.

Extracted from Elliott Currie, "Inequality Community and Crime," in *The Essential Criminology Reader,* edited by Stuart Henry and Mark M. Lanier (Boulder, CO: Westview Press, 2006), 299–306.

It is perhaps ironic, then, that the School of Criminology that founded left realism at Middlesex University in England has since dispersed and many of its advocates have now gone into a series of different critical theories. Jock Young, who founded the perspective with Roger Matthews at Middlesex, has turned his attention to developing a new critical perspective called cultural criminology, which we discuss next, and has abandoned further left realist writing. In the United States the perspective still has some committed supporters, particularly Elliott Currie, Nikos Passas, and Marty Schwartz, but even here left realist concerns are integrated with other theoretical positions, such as anomie theory and feminist theory. However, in Canada, the perspective has taken root not only at Simon Frazer University with the work of John Lowman, but most recently at the new Center for Criminological Studies at the University of Ottawa Institute of Technology, which has gathered together key Canadian and international criminologists who have become leaders in developing left-realist research. We now turn to a critical criminological perspective that is almost the polar opposite of left realism in that it is abstract, holistic, and somewhat idealistic; it even challenges the existence of truth and reality, which it sees as socially constructed.

Postmodernism

Postmodernism is more a movement than a theory. It is also much larger than crime, criminal justice, and criminology (Kraidy 2002). Among other things, it encompasses art, architecture, literature, and social movements as well as the study of crime and crime control. The concept of postmodernism is inherently abstract, broad, and multifaceted. Postmodern ideas mark a major break from those we have so far examined. As one commentator noted, "Postmodernism and poststructuralism are difficult to both define and comprehend" (Bohm 1997a, 134). Thus, it is important to consider their contribution to our understanding of crime at the outset.

What unites advocates to the "postmodernism turn" (Best and Kellner 1997) is the "idea of making space for different ways of knowing and being" (Longstreet 2003, 11). Put simply, postmodernist theory alerts us to the socially constructed (and thus somewhat arbitrary) nature of society's rules, norms, and values, and, further, "postmodernism rejects the possibility of an agreed upon version of objective reality . . . and it postulates instead that all accounts of reality are in fact interpretive" (Mason 1995).

Within criminology, a postmodernist view of crime not only includes challenges to legal definitions but also sees the total society, particularly its discourse, as a source of crime. As we saw in Chapter 2, a postmodernist definition of crime involves a much wider range of harms than a legal or even a sociological definition, in that it includes harms created by the routine practices of our society's institutions, such as work, bureaucracy, government, law, and family (as will be further elaborated below). Furthermore, unlike previous theories, which identify a causal force, whether this be at the level of individual, family, institutions, community, culture, or social structure, postmodernism sees the "cause" of crime in the interplay of all of these elements as expressed through the prevailing ways of describing our world, called discourses. Finally, postmodernism agrees with Greek philosopher Heraclitus, who observed that you can't step in the same river twice. Things are in a state of flux and change, as we will learn later when we discuss chaos theory. Postmodernism also is consistent with Heisenberg's uncertainty principle, that reality is affected by the observer, even in subatomic particles, such that what is real and true is less certain, less decidable.

The policy implications of postmodernist theory (unlike for previous theories) do not involve changing individuals, institutions, or central features of society such as structural features. Rather, "policy," which is not a word postmodernists use, involves changing our whole set of societal practices and our current mode of discourse and replacing them with other less harmful discourses. In short, it "is not this or that" that is wrong with modern industrial society but the way we conceive of and approach everything we do. We can make a difference to what is currently problematic only by changing it all, together. Let us look at this theory in more detail, remembering our caution about complexity.

Postmodernism refers to a school of thought that has emerged out of a period of intense skepticism with science. Scientific method and rational thought were, as will be recalled from Chapters 3 and 4, an outcome of the eighteenth-century Enlightenment and prevail to this day. Science assumes that rational and objective methods can be used to discover knowledge and truth, which can then be applied to solve society's problems and to control nature. The concept of such scientific "progress" has characterized the "modern era." Disenchantment with modernism, linked to the suffering that its hierarchies, divisions, and exclusions have brought to many (through imperialism, sexism, racism, and class oppression), together with its increasing inability to solve society's problems (e.g., pollution and poverty), has led to a questioning of its values, particularly the value of scientific analysis and rational thought (Hunt 1991; Best and Kellner 1991, 1997; Borgmann 1992) as well as the source of that knowledge. Many modern problems have been exacerbated by science and technology; for example, consider the threat of nuclear devastation, germ warfare, pollution, ozone depletion, the Holocaust, and so on. The creators of this technology have also been subject to critical examination:

> Communities that were custodians of that knowledge were called into question as well. A shift away from the dominance of scientific knowledge, largely controlled by military, industrial, and governmental communities, occurred in favor of a plurality of different communities. Many of these communities were avowedly unscientific and subjective. Indeed, they frequently interpreted the claims to objectivity and the universality of science as a subterfuge giving power to a military, industrial, and institutional complex that was anything but objective. (Longstreet 2003)

Postmodernists see rational thought as a form of elite power through which those who claim to have special knowledge earn the right to decide the fate of those who do not share this knowledge. Indeed, postmodernists fundamentally disagree that there is such a thing as objective truth. Instead, all knowledge is subjective, shaped by personal, cultural, and political views. Whereas feminism's standpoint epistemology maintains that many oppressed versions of truth are valid, postmodernists argue instead that all knowledge is made up simply of "claims to truth" (Foucault 1977, 1980). They believe that knowledge and truth are "socially constructed." This means that they have no independent reality outside the minds and practices of those who create them and re-create them. Knowledge is artificial, an outcome of humans making distinctions and judging one part of any distinction as superior to another, one set of ideas as superior to another, and so on. These distinctions are conceptual and are made through communication, particularly but not exclusively written or spoken language, referred to by postmodernists as discourse or "texts" (Manning 1988; Arrigo 2003).

One of the major causes of conflict and harm in societies, according to postmodernists, results from people investing energy in these "discursive distinctions," believing in their reality and defending them and imposing them on others. Distinctions made in discourse, such as middle class and working class, citizen and offender, white and black, teacher and student, convict and ex-convict, good guys and bad guys, and so forth, result in categories that exclude and marginalize. For example, the gender distinctions "men" and "women" exclude the differences within these categories and preclude connections between them; so too with "black," "brown," and "white," distinctions based on race that exclude others. As a result, postmodernists point to the centrality of language use (i.e., discourse) in shaping social reality (Arrigo 2003).

Postmodernists reject the self-evident reality of distinctions. They reject the idea that distinctions should be made between different kinds of knowledge, especially between "scientific knowledge" (book smarts) and "commonsense knowledge" (street smarts). One of their principal tools of analysis is to expose the soft, socially constructed "belly" of privileged knowledge through what they call "critique." This is different from criticism, which involves arguments against a particular position and policy suggestions to arrive at a solution. Critique is a continuous process of challenge to those who claim to know or hold the truth; it uses "deconstruction" (Derrida 1970, 1981) to expose the socially constructed, rather than real, nature of truth claims. Deconstruction is a form of analysis that exposes unquestioned assumptions and internal contradictions in language and arguments. Postmodernists adhere to an "aura of unmaking the old—decentering, deconstructing, demystifying" (Longstreet 2003). Put simply, deconstruction is the reverse of construction, where that is taken to be the often accepted process of creating social reality by making assumptions and distinctions and imposing them on the world. For example, if we distinguish between offenders and nonoffenders, we can then distinguish between places for offenders and nonoffenders, and if we have the power to create them, we can construct those places first through policies and on paper, then through plans and designs, and then through institutions that provide money and resources and staff, and finally through physical or built environments. We can then put those people whom we conceptually defined as different from us into the physical places that we constructed to house them. Those places can be given a name: prison. Deconstruction would be to expose the process of prison as an autonomous reality independent of us and show how it is tied to all those conceptual and linguistic distinctions.

Deconstruction then is a method of analysis that seeks to "undo" constructions, to demolish them, but to do so in a way that exposes how they are built and why they appear to be real (Rosenau 1992; S. Cohen 1990). As T. R. Young explained, "Whereas modern science privileges objectivity, rationality, power, control, inequality and hierarchy, postmodernists deconstruct each theory and each social practice by locating it in its larger socio-historical context in order to reveal the human hand and the group interests which shape the course of self-understanding" (1995, 578–579). Arrigo said that the deconstruction or "trashing" of a text, or a discourse, whether it is written or spoken, involves a careful, critical reading designed "to unveil the implicit assumptions and hidden values . . . embedded within a particular narrative":

> Deconstruction shows us how certain truth claims are privileged within a given story while certain others are disguised or dismissed altogether. Because deconstruction focusses on the actual words people use to convey their thoughts, it attempts to uncover the unconscious intent behind the grammar people employ when writing or speaking. Thus language or entire systems of communication are put under the microscope for closer inspection. In a sense, then, trashing a text entails reading between the lines to ascertain the meanings (ideology) given preferred status in a particular language system. (2003, 48)

Indeed, part of the postmodern critique involves the "resurrection of subjugated knowledges," the excluded, neglected, and marginal knowledges discounted by dominant social constructions. It involves including others' voices: "The postmodern challenge invites us to embrace articulated differences, making them part of the social fabric of ongoing civic interaction . . . of evolving possibilities" (ibid., 49).

Commentators have argued that there are numerous versions of postmodernism (M. Schwartz and Friedrichs 1994). For example, Peter McLaren (1994) offered "resistance postmodernism," where difference is the "recognition that knowledges are forged in histories that are riven with differentially constituted relations of power" (cited in Kraidy 2002, 15). However, for the sake of brevity, it is helpful here to distinguish two broad types: skeptical and affirmative (Rosenau 1992; Einstadter and Henry 1995). Skeptical postmodernism refers to the work of those who believe there is no basis for objectivity and no way truth either exists or can be discovered. They use deconstruction simply to undermine all claims to truth, revealing its underlying assumptions and disrupting its acceptance as fact. In some cases, they imply an extreme relativism that has no standards and accepts anything as valid. They do not believe in suggesting alternatives because they would themselves then be making truth claims and be subject to their own criticism (hence, skeptics are also called nihilists; nihilism is the rejection of any view or idea or position that requires faith because doing so means it has no verifiable objective substance, which includes anything from theology to science).

Affirmative postmodernism, in contrast, refers to those who believe deconstruction also implies reconstruction, or rebuilding: "Exposing how an edifice is built, and how it stands, in spite of opposition, also implies how it can be rebuilt or built differently" (Einstadter and Henry 2006, 288). In deconstruction, affirmative postmodernists show how humans actively build their social world rather than being passive subjects of external forces. They also show how people could invest their energies to build new social worlds, albeit ones that are ever changing and always in the process of being built. To understand the relevance of postmodernism to criminology, we shall briefly illustrate how postmodernism has been applied by Henry and Milovanovic's constitutive criminology.

Constitutive Criminology

According to its founders, "Constitutive Criminology is a broad sweeping, wide-ranging holistic perspective on crime, criminals and criminal justice . . . whose objective is to help build a less harmful society" (Henry and Milovanovic 2003, 57). The core of the constitutive argument is that crime and its control cannot be separated from the totality of the structural and cultural contexts in which it is produced (Henry and Milovanovic 1994, 1996, 1999, 2003). It rejects the argument of traditional criminology that crime can be separated from that process and analyzed and corrected apart from it. Crime is an integral part of the total production of society, and insofar as societies are interconnected through globalization processes, crime is a global production. It is a coproduced outcome of humans and the social and organizational structures that people develop and endlessly (re)build. Therefore, criminological analysis of crime must relate crime to the total social and, ultimately, global picture rather than to any single part of it. This is not an easy task.

To accomplish their project, constitutive theorists start out by redefining crime, victims, and criminals (Milovanovic and Henry 2001). They argue that unequal power relations, built on the constructions of difference, provide the conditions that define crime as harm. Thus, constitutive criminology redefines crime as the harm resulting from humans' investing energy in harm-producing relations of power. Humans suffering such "crimes" are in relations of inequality. Crimes are people being disrespected. People are disrespected in several ways, but all have to do with denying or preventing them from becoming fully social beings (and in this, the theory is similar to Marx's assumptions about human nature). What is human is to make a difference to the world, to act on it, to interact with others, and, together, to transform the environment and themselves. If this process is prevented, we become less than human; we are harmed. Thus, Henry and Milovanovic define crime as "the power to deny others their ability to make a difference" (1996, 116).

Constitutive criminologists see crime in relation to power differentials and to hierarchical relations. They distinguish between two kinds of crime: "crimes of reduction" and "crimes of repression." Harms of reduction occur when offended parties experience a loss of some quality relative to their present standing. They could have property stolen from them, but they could also have dignity stripped from them, as in hate crimes. Harms of repression occur when people experience a limit, or restriction, preventing them from achieving a desired position or standing. They could be prevented from achieving a career goal because of sexism or racism or meet a promotional "glass ceiling." Considered along a continuum of deprivation, harms of reduction or repression may be based on any number of constructed differences. At present, in Western industrial societies harms cluster around the following constructed differences: economic (class, property), gender (sexism), race and ethnicity (racism, hate), political (power, corruption), morality, ethics ("avowal of desire"), human rights, social position (status and prestige, inequality), psychological state (security, well-being), self-realization and actualization, biological integrity, and others (Milovanovic and Henry 2001).

Whatever the construction, actions are harms either because they reduce the offended from a position or state they currently occupy or because they prevent them from occupying a position or state that they desire, whose achievement does not deny or deprive another. (Clearly, one problem facing this theory is the current unequal distribution of power in most societies, which would imply that progressive taxation that redistributes wealth from the rich to the poor is a crime against the rich since they are being reduced from a position they currently have to a lesser one; however, the long constitutive view would argue that to accumulate their wealth, the rich committed harms of reduction and oppression to others, so their redistribution of wealth was returning them closer to where they were before their own exploitative actions.)

Constitutive criminology also has a different definition of criminals and victims. The offender is viewed as an "excessive investor" in the power to dominate others. Such "investors" put energy into creating and magnifying differences between themselves and others, in order to gain some advantage over others (again, the dimensions of what qualities are differentiated are wide ranging, from physical appearance, race, and ethnicity to ability, wealth, beauty, intelligence, morality, and so on). This investment of energy disadvantages, disables, and destroys others' human potentialities.

The victim is viewed as a "recovering subject," still with untapped human potential but with a damaged faith in humanity. Victims are more entrenched and more disabled and suffer loss. Victims "suffer the pain of being denied their own humanity, the power to make a difference. The victim of crime is thus rendered a non-person, a non-human, or less complete being" (Henry and Milovanovic 1996, 116). This reconception of crime, offender, and victim locates criminality not in the person or in the structure or culture but in the ongoing creation of social identities through discourse and discursive distinctions that are reinforced by social actions and institutions.

Not surprisingly, the constitutive analysis leads to a different notion of crime causation. To the constitutive theorist, crime is not so much caused as discursively constructed through human processes, of which it is one. Put simply, crime is the coproduced outcome not only of individuals and their environment but of human agents and the wider society, increasingly a global society, through its excessive investment, to the point of obsession, in crime, through crime shows, crime dramas, crime documentaries, crime news, crime books, crime films, crime precautions, criminal justice agencies, criminal lawyers, and, yes, even criminologists. All, as Marx noted, are parasitic on the crime problem, but as constitutive criminology suggests, they also contribute to its ongoing social and cultural production. They are the sustenance on which individual offenders feed and thrive.

If conventionally understood causality is rejected, what takes its place to explain how crime happens? Constitutive theorists, due to their observations about the indeterminate nature of causal relations, look to chaos theory to help reveal alternative ways of knowing. Chaos theory, also known as "nonlinear dynamics," argues that "orderly disorder governs the behavior of all natural systems," such that while exhibiting patterned regularity, they are simultaneously random and unpredictable (Arrigo 2003, 50; Henry and Milovanovic 1996; Milovanovic 1997; Williams and Arrigo 2001). Constitutive theorists argue that the complexity of social relations needs an explanation framed in terms of dialectical causality, such as interrelationships or coproduction rather than "the linear and deterministic concept of single or multiple causality" (Henry and Milovanovic 2003, 65). Indeed, "these processes comprise relationships that are not deterministic but dialectical, a dialectic that assumes nonlinear development and a movement, through human agency, toward instability of social forms. . . . Whether a particular situation or interrelationship will result in criminality cannot be determined with any precision since the dynamics of human relations are indeterminate, can be altered by seemingly small events, and are part of a historically situated, ongoing process that is also indeterminate" (Colvin 1997, 1449).

Given this interrelated yet indeterminate nature of social structures and humans, the question remains as to how these affirmative postmodernists recommend reducing harms that are crime. Constitutive criminology calls for a justice policy of replacement discourse "directed toward the dual process of deconstructing prevailing structures of meaning and displacing them with new conceptions, distinctions, words and phrases, which convey alternative meanings. . . . Replacement discourse, then, is not simply critical and oppositional, but provides both a critique and an alternative vision" (Henry and Milovanovic 1996, 204–205). In terms of diminishing the harm experienced from all types of crime (street, corporate, state, hate, and others), constitutive criminology talks of "liberating" discourses that seek transformation of both the prevailing political economies and the associated practices of crime and social control. Replacement discourse can be implemented through attempts by constitutive criminologists to reconstruct popular images of crime in the mass media and through engaging in news-making criminology (Barak 1988, 1994). It can also be induced through narrative therapy (Parry and Doan 1994). Narrative therapy developed as part of family therapy as ways to enable offenders (excessive investors in power) to construct more liberating life narratives, and through these reconstitute themselves. As we shall see later, yet another form of replacement discourse comes in the form of peacemaking approaches to conflict. Although this and abolitionism developed independently from postmodernism, they are resonant with it. Before discussing these developments, we first consider the application of constitutive theory to penology and then a related development known as "edgework" studies by one of the cofounders of constitutive theory, Dragan Milovanovic.

In their latest work *Revolution in Penology*, constitutive criminologists Bruce Arrigo and Dragan Milovanovic (2009) return to the original constitutive statements (Henry and Milovanovic 1991; Milovanovic and Henry 1991) to develop ideas about constitutive penology. Their book "intends to be a flash of light, a poetic spark, a fleeting epiphany, a coupling moment. It intends to communicate that subjectivity can be recovered for anyone or group in which dispossession or alienation prevails. It intends to communicate that becoming other can be resuscitated for any one or group in which oppression and disenfranchisement triumphs" (Arrigo and Milovanovic 2009, xix).

Arrigo and Milovanovic set out to deconstruct penological thinking and challenge society to reconstruct the world in nonpunitive, less harmful ways. At its core, their vision is premised on the constitutive holistic conception of humans-in-the-world rather than seeing them as separate individuals. They argue that prison and penology are internal human social and symbolic processes that have real external harmful consequences both for prison populations and for nonprison populations. They share Loc Wacquant's view of penality as the ensemble of categories, discourses, practices, and institutions concerned with enforcement of the sociocultural order that has become a major engine of urban and social change in the twenty-first century. Arrigo and Milovanovic (2009) suggest replacing penology's existing view of crime control with one that reconnects the components, parts, and segments to the whole in dynamic configurations.

After outlining their core assumptions, the authors explore how expressions of power "emerge from within historically mediated socio-cultural conditions," which give rise to penal forms that sustain the social structures that produce them in a dynamic relationship of mutual coproduction. They show how the discourse of penology, penal policy, and penal practice has a pivotal role in this regenerative process and through them how all in society are victimized, as they are limited from what they might otherwise have become.

To avoid falling into the same trap as those they criticize, Arrigo and Milovanovic adopt the strategies of the "criminology of the shadow" and the "criminology of the stranger." The criminology of the shadow unveils the structural harms embodied in penal institutions. The authors "demonstrate how the recursive activities of existing correctional abstractions, categories, and practices work to co-produce and reify the prison form, its constitutive parts, and the whole of society that legitimizes and essentializes the discourse of penology" (ibid., 71). Applying their analysis to desistance theory, whereby over time many offenders mature out of crime, Arrigo and Milovanovic go beyond the view that prison disrupts the process of going straight to show that such analysis is merely reconstitutive of the existing institutional forms. In contrast, the criminology of the stranger offers a "trans-desistance" approach that "examines how the activities of the recovering subject (being) and the transformative subject (becoming) recast the character of human agency as constituents of a replacement discourse and logic" (ibid., 70). Here the authors are able to untangle the difficult problem of acknowledging the harm of the offense without bringing harm to the offender. They argue that human subjects "should be seen as a multiplicity of lives, and one that cannot be confined to the narrow framework prescribed by the release plan. . . . What needs to be recognized is the multiple forms of expression of the human subject" (ibid., xii). In other words, radical trans-desistance theory seeks to open up the multiplicity of avenues for those reentering society to reconnect with it.

Arrigo and Milovanovic also examine the self-fueling system of incarceration-release-reincarceration, known as the "pains of imprisonment" thesis. In a critical assessment of modernist penology's account of the punitive violence of prison, they show how the roles of prison actors (prisoners, correctional officers, public officials, and the general public) take center stage in the production of their violent conditions of confinement. Current approaches offer an inadequate account of the penological problem. In contrast, Arrigo and Milovanovic (2009) apply a probing constitutive critique to the images and the various messages these hyperrealistic images convey. They argue that such representations do not allow us to distinguish between authentic reality and representational illusion. The authors demonstrate the key role that existing institutional processes play in normalizing violence and limiting the process of human transformation, thereby amplifying the criminological shadow. This curtailing of possibilities affects not only prisoners but all those involved in prison work, and ultimately the whole society for failing to realize its own transcendent potential.

Overall, Arrigo and Milovanovic challenge penology to stand outside itself and, in doing so, herald the possibility of the postpenological society, one that calls for us to "accept the potentials that inhere within each of us" and to resist the tendency to "limit these becomings." Arrigo and Milovanovic envision not only a revolution in penology but also a release of possibility toward the liberation of humanity.

Edgework Studies

Edgework is the term coined by Steven Lyng (1990, 2005) to describe and explain the high-risk "adrenaline-rush" behavior of those who engage in a variety of deviant activities such as skydiving, BASE jumping, hang gliding, surfing, downhill skiing, and other extreme sports. He and his colleagues are particularly interested in how and why these edgeworkers invoke a high degree of control and skill to avoid the extreme dangers, possibly death, in order to reap the "pleasures of sensation and emotion" of the body (Milovanovic 2006). We saw in Chapter 4 that biological and psychological explanations for such behaviors describe them as "sensation seeking." The central issue is what motivates people to pursue dangerous and risky behaviors. Edgework theorists reject biopsychological arguments and rational choice explanations. Instead, they invoke a nonmaterial explanation for deviant motivation as an end in itself, as a place of freedom from constructed limits and borders, in which humans experience their own humanity, enjoyed as one approaches "the invitational edge" that most control systems prevent humans from approaching (Matza 1969).

Jack Katz (1988) explored the phenomenology of subjective experience and emotions in his book *Seductions of Crime*. He focused on the idea that a significant dimension of the human subject's experience is emotional excitement, adrenaline rushes, the sensual, the visceral experienced through the body. Katz explained the attraction to crime, from "sneaky thrills" to murder, as a person's attempt to overcome what is perceived as an intolerable moral challenge or dilemma, typically a humiliation, in order to a reestablish his or her own humanism and self-respect. Thus, paradoxically, murder is seen as "righteous slaughter" as a subject attempts to reassert control over his or her own moral dilemma through a "moral transcendence." They regain their own humanity through the sense of righteousness provided by rage that justifies their act, only to lose control to the consequences of the act as they cross the edge. Yet it is approaching the edge that attracts. The edge is the borderline, or order and disorder, "some boundary between ordered and chaotic social reality, consciousness and unconsciousness, sanity and insanity and the line between life and death. . . . Go over the edge and you die or suffer serious injury. . . . The high is overcoming this extreme challenge" (Milovanovic 2006, 237). Here the body experiences the "rush"—the sensation of intense bodily pleasures: "It is the play of being in and out of control at the edge that provides the moments for the expression of bodily desires" (Milovanovic 2003, 8). The edge may be a moment in time, an event, but it is experienced as more real than everyday reality.

Lyng (1990) suggested that the structural context for such a search for meaning is the meaninglessness of the mundane, routine, alienated life of capitalism, although this was not consistent with the research (Ferrell, Milovanovic, and Lyng 2001). O'Malley and Mugford related these ideas to the structural context of late capitalist society, seeing a "phenomenology of pleasure" rooted in the nineteenth-century romantic period in history (eventually replaced by the material rationality of capitalism). A second force was the civilizing process that laid down moral boundaries for appropriate action, order, and rational behavior that create barriers to spontaneous emotional expression. They argued that "within modern cultures there is a steady and increasing pressure toward emotionally exciting activities, including leisure activities, as a source of transcendence and authenticity with which to offset the suffocation of an over controlled, alienated existence within the mundane reality of modern life" (1994, 206). They saw Lyng's work as describing situations approaching but not crossing the limit, whereas Katz's study described situations of going beyond the limit.

Drawing on previous postmodernist, particularly Lacanian and constitutive theory, Milovanovic, together with Lyng and Jeff Ferrell (Ferrell, Milovanovic, and Lyng 2001; Milovanovic 2003), developed these ideas into a postmodernist-informed study of desire that situated sensation seeking in the context of meaning construction, framed by wider cultural production, information technology, and mass media.

The attempt by some postmodernist and constitutive theorists to locate the motivation for crime and deviance between the human desire for pleasure framed in a historical and cultural period illustrates again how this perspective seeks to show the connectedness of people to each other that transcends the simple reductionist accounts of earlier theories. Postmodernism and edgework laid the foundation for the more recent developments in cultural criminology.

Cultural Criminology

Cultural criminology "places criminality and its control in the context of culture; that is, it views crime and the agencies and institutions of crime control as cultural products—as creative constructs" (Hayward 2007). Cultural criminology as a field of study emerged in the mid-1990s (Ferrell and Saunders 1995), although its ideas had been percolating in criminological thought longer than that.[1] In addition to its connection with edgework and Katz's studies of the shared thrill, pleasure, excitement, and sensuality that are the emotion and seduction of crime, cultural criminology has its roots in several theoretical perspectives, including symbolic interaction and sociological phenomenology, with their emphasis on the social construction of situated meaning in everyday existence; Birmingham cultural studies, which had shown the importance of the politics of resistance through youth subcultures and the cultural significance of public mass-mediated displays of the contested politics of crime control through state policing; and the anarchist antipower and control theme found in Pepinsky and Ferrell's politics of the disenfranchised youth and their creative and destructive displays of resistance through style. "In other words, cultural criminology seeks to fuse a 'phenomenology of transgression' with a sociological analysis of late modern culture" (Hayward 2007). Using ethnography, its advocates study "the situated meaning and subtle symbolism constructed within criminal subcultures and events" (Ferrell 2007). What cultural criminology captures through its qualitative engagement is the richness of the experience of crime and its control as a contested arena of symbolic representation: "Cultural criminology explores the many ways in which cultural dynamics intertwine with the practices of crime and crime control in contemporary society; put differently, cultural criminology emphasizes the centrality of meaning and representation in the construction of crime as momentary event, subcultural endeavor, and social issue. . . . They . . . explore the looping circulation of images, the representational hall of mirrors, that increasingly define the reality of crime and justice" (ibid.).

Cultural criminology sees a blurring of the boundaries between image and reality in a variety of representational arenas, not least in popular culture, advertising, news, and films. As Ferrell said, the appropriate subject matter must include "not simply 'crime' but the many images of crime and criminality that are produced and circulated by the mass media, and, likewise the recurring campaigns of symbolic threat and moral panic that political and legal authorities orchestrate" (2006, 247). Indeed, it is the stratified strain between these arenas of mediated display that captures the nexus between the cultural production and the spontaneity of human creativity:

> It is this very tension that accounts for various contemporary confluences of crime and culture: the aggressive policing of alternative subcultures and their styles; the mediated consumption of crime as commodified titillation and entertainment; and the shifting and always contested boundaries between art and pornography, music and political provocation, entertainment and aggression, crime and resistance. In all of these cases, cultural criminologists attempt to account for the political economy of crime by locating it inside the dynamics of the everyday, amidst the ambiguities of day-to-day transgression and control. (Ferrell 2007)

Mike Presdee's analysis *Cultural Criminology and the Carnival of Crime* (2000) demonstrates crime's formation as a cultural spectacle. Drawing on Mikhail Bakhtin's analysis of the carnival as licensed misrule (1984), in which dominant authority is defied, Presdee sees transgression and crime experienced as pleasure and risky performance breaking out beyond containment in legitimate festivals "but as an enjoyable part of popular everyday life and as a site of resistance to rationality . . . as a playful resistance to authority where those normally excluded from the discourse of power celebrate their anger at their exclusion" (2006, 32–33). Although we now expect the fragments of carnival dispersed into the fabric of society as transgression and crime, Bakhtin's return to order and integration is less a reality than it is itself a performance. Thus, cultural criminology highlights the numerous ways that social control attempts to limit and channel these raw carnivalesque experiences and expressions of freedom through mass-mediated imagery: "Cultural criminology emphasizes the permeability of images as they flow between the mass media, criminal subcultures, and crime control agencies, and likewise the essential role of image and ideology in constructing crime control policies and practices. Following this line of analysis, cultural criminology suggests that everyday criminal justice has now become in many ways a matter of orchestrated public display, and an ongoing policing of public perceptions regarding issues of crime and threat" (Ferrell 2007).

In a broader sense, mass-mediated cultural productions and consumption of crime talk have become global phenomena, as they are communicated transnationally and play a part in the constitution of the urban and the global city: "The political demonstration 'the Carnival against Capitalism' that erupted at the . . . 1999 meeting of the World Trade Organization in Seattle . . . evidenced the global carnival of crime and pleasure, partly organized through the Internet, that showed that practical politics . . . can cause widespread disruption; can be criminal yet immensely pleasurable to the participants" (Presdee 2006, 33). Here we see the emergence of a globalized economy that includes and excludes through its polarizing effects on rich and poor, questioning identities and unraveling social embeddedness, as demonstrated in Jock Young's departure from left realism, signposted in *The Exclusive Society* (1999) and more fully developed in *Cultural Criminology: An Invitation* (Ferrell, Hayward, and Young 2009). This identifies a

> globalized economy of image and consumption, the tension between late modern patterns of social inclusion and exclusion, and the uncertain dynamics of personal and cultural identity within these arrangements. . . . In this context cultural criminologists highlight especially the importance of the global city to the understanding of crime and crime control. With its contested cultural spaces of consumption and display, its amalgam of illicit subcultural dynamics, and its spatial and symbolic practices of everyday policing, the city seems an essential embodiment of contemporary social and cultural trends. (Ferrell 2007)

And it is the global city that is the nexus of the contests taking place, the city as the area for late modernity's spectacle of crime, as articulated by Keith Hayward's *City Limits: Crime, Consumer Culture, and the Urban Experience* in which he explored "the 'crime-city nexus,' with the specific aim of identifying the myriad forms of relationships that exist between the contemporary 'urban experience,' certain forms of criminal behaviour seen as expressive criminality, and the particular social forces and cultural dynamics that one associates with late modern consumer culture" (2004, 1). He stated that in its concreteness and representation of the distinct and interrelated spheres of urban existence, late-modern consumer culture is bringing change that contributes to the contemporary urban crime problem. Indeed, in this context crime has new meaning "as a technique for resolving certain psychic and emotional conflicts that are in turn viewed as being indelibly linked to various features of contemporary life" (2007).

For these reasons, cultural criminology challenges the "slippery politics" or representational codes that together with their meaningless, abstract, "voodoo" quantitative methodology pass for the science of mainstream criminology in its conspiratorial dance with the power of state control and its administration of justice, and seeks to enrich its arid prose with the humanism of its subjects' daily existence while keeping criminologists honest in their subject matter (J. Young 2004; Ferrell, Hayward, and Young 2009).

With regard to direct policy implications, clearly in the long term the structural inequalities of exclusion and the consumerist global culture need to be addressed. However, in general the perspective does not advocate a policy position. Part of the reason is because it sees the social construction of "crime fighting" as part of "crime talk" that invests energy into the spectacle of crime as a media production, a war movie played out on our streets, rather than a genuine attempt to reduce harm production. In other words, instead of defusing the thrill of crime, crime-fighting discourse adds to crime's continued production. What cultural criminology does is provide a framework for making changes in society that reduce the desire for thrills from crime by replacing the meaninglessness of consumerist interaction and commodified relationships with meaningful and substantial alternatives. In Durkheim's terms, it reverses the extremes of anomie by providing a meaningfully and morally grounded set of social relations; in Baudrillard's terms, it reduces the hyperreality of late modernity.

In pragmatic terms it is difficult to see what concrete measures can be adopted as policy, since without fundamental changes in society's orientation toward increasingly sensationalized consumption, any piecemeal practices will more likely add to the accentuation of the existing carnival of crime than make a difference to it. Having said this, it is clear that social policies that provide a general reduction of fear and risk, such as health care provision, social support, and mutual aid, allow people to build socially meaningful relationships and social capital that can insulate us from competitive individualism and displays of identity competition. So cultural criminologists might defuel the investment in policies such as those of rational choice and situational crime-control theorists that increase target hardening through adding surveillance, fences, and sensors, which only raise the sophistication of the crime game for its players, and invest in programs that celebrate people's common identity and unique inherent value.

Anarchism, Abolitionism, Peacemaking, and Restorative Justice

The theories considered here, like those of postmodernism and constitutive theory, take a holistic approach to the problems of crime, connecting crime, offenders, victims, the community, and the wider structural issues of societies in their global contexts. They include *abolitionism*, which believes in removing punishment from criminal justice, *peacemaking*, which advocates nonviolent approaches to resolving the conflict of crime, and *restorative justice,* which calls for adopting practices that integrate offenders with victims and their community. The origin of this evolving perspective lies in anarchistic thinking applied to criminology and criminal justice, which led to the abolitionist movement.

Anarchy means a society without rulers. But it is not a society without order, although that is often assumed in the pejorative use of the term. Anarchism refers to those who oppose organizational and institutional authority. It has its intellectual roots in the nineteenth-century writings of Pierre-Joseph Proudhon (1809–1865), Mikhail Bakunin (1814–1876), and Pyotr Kropotkin (1842–1921) (Woodcock 1963, 1977). Proudhon believed that authority and power in any form are oppressive and that they are rooted in the private ownership of property, which he saw as theft. Bakunin, like Proudhon, vehemently opposed Karl Marx's communism, believing that his ideas for a dictatorship of the proletariat would simply result in another form of domination and re-create the state in a new form. He argued that privilege makes humanity depraved and can be removed only by destroying all forms of hierarchy. Kropotkin demonstrated, in contrast to Darwin, that successful societies are founded on cooperation and mutual aid rather than competition and that the government is unnecessary and destructive. These anarchists took the view that cooperative interactive relations are a natural human form that will emerge, provided people are allowed to engage in free and open interaction. Structures of power, whatever their form, are based on inequality and hierarchy, which create conflict and destroy the freedom necessary for constructive cooperation. More recently, these ideas have been applied to criminology through the works of Larry Tifft, Dennis Sullivan, Hal Pepinsky, and Jeff Ferrell. The anarchist theory of crime causation is that crime is caused by structures of power and domination. Thus, the anarchist criminologist spends more time trying to replace structures of power than developing analyses of how these actually cause crime.

Anarchist criminologists (Pepinsky 1978; Tifft and Sullivan 1980, 2006; Ferrell 1994; Ferrell and Websdale 1999) believe that hierarchical systems of authority and domination should be opposed. As Ferrell argued, nothing is more formidable than the unchallenged supremacy of centralized authority structures that feed off divisions of class, gender, and race. Recent anarchist criminology relates crime as a meaningful activity of resistance to both its construction in social interaction and "its larger construction through processes of political and economic authority."

Anything that fragments the state from its seamless hierarchies of authority and power is desirable. Thus, anarchists believe existing structures of domination should be replaced by a "fragmented and decentered pluralism" that "celebrates multiple interpretations and styles" (Ferrell 1994, 163). Like postmodernists, anarchists believe that knowledge and information are structures of domination to be discredited and replaced by embracing "particularity and disorder." Advocates are interested in "fostering social arrangements that alleviate pain and suffering by providing for everyone's needs" (Tifft and Sullivan 2006, 259).

State justice should be replaced by a decentralized system of negotiated, face-to-face justice in which all members of society participate and share their decisions (Wieck 1978; Tifft 1979, 397), a system of "collective negotiation as a means of problem solving" (Ferrell 1994, 162). This is designed to bring the individual to accept responsibility for his or her behavior by reminding offenders of their connectedness to other members of the society. The aim is to restore the wholeness of social existence to the collective after it has been breached by a person's failure to accept responsibility and connectedness. In the anarchist view, crime and deviance may be no more than indicators of difference. Such a view demands an "anti-authoritarian justice" that "would entail respect for alternative interpretations of reality" but would oppose "any attempt to destroy, suppress, or impose particular realities" (Ryan and Ferrell 1986, 193) and would encourage "unresolved ambiguities of meaning" (Ferrell 1994, 163). Clearly, the logic of the anarchist criminologists' position is that if power is the source of domination and thereby the source of crime, it is power and structures of power that should be removed. This is precisely where abolitionists argue that punishment, as an instrument of the state, should be removed.

Abolitionism has its origins in Norwegian criminology, particularly that of Thomas Mathiesen (1974, 1986) and Nils Christie (1977, 1981), and, more recently, in the work of Dutch criminologists Herman Bianchi and Rene Van Swaaningen (1986) and Willem de Haan (1990). Abolitionism is rooted in the notion that punishment is never justified. It is a movement not merely to reform prisons but to get rid of them entirely and replace them with community controls and community treatment that attempt to deal with crime as an outcome of relationship issues. Not only are prisons seen to fail to control crime and fail to prevent recidivism, but they are also viewed as an inhumane mechanism used mainly for controlling the least-productive members of the labor force. Abolitionists point out that the "cultural values embedded in the conception of prisons reflect a social ethos of violence and degradation. When prisons are expanded, so too are negative cultural values symbolizing acceptable strategies for resolving interpersonal conflict" (Thomas and Boehlefeld 1991, 242). For abolitionists, like constitutive theorists, social control should be about not inflicting more pain but reducing pain. To achieve this, it should be decentralized and broken up into democratic community control, and new concepts such as "redress" should be adopted (de Haan 1990). These concepts are based on redefining crimes as undesirable events, as problems to be solved. For example, Knopp pointed to the complete failure of the current system of punishment and argued for a system of "restorative justice" founded "on social and economic justice and on concern and respect for all its victims and victimizers, a new system based on remedies and restoration rather than on prison, punishment and victim neglect, a system rooted in the concept of a caring community" (1991, 183). Although rooted in a similar humanistic concern, peacemaking criminology goes beyond the limits of abolitionism.

The actions of Jesus Christ, Mahatma Gandhi, Martin Luther King Jr., and Nelson Mandela exemplify the fact that peacemaking is nothing new and not exclusive to criminology. Peacemaking as articulated in the teachings of Buddhism, Christianity, Judaism, Islam, Taoism, and Native American religions is thousands of years old. Yet there are interesting parallels with the ideas of postmodernism. Science and the Age of Enlightenment generally relegated religion to a secondary status, as a means of creating knowledge. Empiricism became the new God, with objectivity, determinism, and causality the new mantras. Postmodernism questioned this and opened the door for a reconsideration, if not reconceptualization, of ancient means of dispute resolution. According to Mason (1995), postmodernism is helpful for expanding our understanding of peace studies, to adjust planning and expectations to different societal conditions, and to be conscious of Western ethnocentric assumptions. Mason (1995) considered the conflict-resolution measures used by several cultural groups to provide some insight. By contrasting the United States with Japan, for example, one sees that Americans value individuality over age and even status. Americans are highly verbal, precise, and litigious, whereas the Japanese focus on expression and body language. The Hawaiian model of peacemaking focuses on a religious context, conciliation, and achieving harmony; in rural China the village as a whole resolves conflict (ibid.). Native Americans rely on restorative justice grounded in cultural beliefs (Winfree 2002). Each method is culturally specific, yet if adaptation is possible and if the human state is malleable, then each offers lessons for peacemaking. A caution is that if we are serious about respecting diversity, we may have to tolerate that which may offend our cultural or religious sensitivities. If peace could be obtained, this would be a small price to pay—much cheaper than the wars we wage. Can peacemaking replace the war on crime?

Based on a spiritual humanistic critique of Western civilizations, peacemaking criminologists Hal Pepinsky and Richard Quinney want to replace making war on crime with the idea of making peace on crime (1991; Pepinsky 2006). Like crimes, penal sanctions are intended harms, and, as Harris noted, we "need to reject the idea that those who cause injury or harm to others should suffer severance of the common bonds of respect and concern that bind members of a community. We should relinquish the notion that it is acceptable to try to 'get rid of' another person, whether through execution, banishment, or caging away people about whom we do not care" (Pepinsky and Quinney 1991, 93). Peacemaking criminologists argue that instead of escalating the violence in our already violent society by responding to violence and conflict with state violence and conflict in the form of penal sanctions such as death and prison, we need to de-escalate violence by responding to it through forms of conciliation, mediation, and dispute settlement: "The only path to peace is peace itself. Punishment merely adds heat. . . . Relief from violence requires people to indulge in democracy, in making music together" (Pepinsky 1991b, 109–110). By democracy, Pepinsky means a genuine participation by all in decisions about our lives that is achievable only in a decentralized, nonhierarchical social structure.

Bracewell (1990) articulated the central themes of peacemaking as follows: (1) connectedness to each other and to our environment and the need for reconciliation, (2) caring for each other in a nurturing way as a primary objective in corrections, and (3) mindfulness, meaning the cultivation of inner peace. To promote such a vision of justice, according to Quinney (1991), it is necessary to recognize connectedness, or "oneness," with other beings in the world, the inseparable connection between our personal suffering and the suffering in the world. To change the world, we must first change ourselves. This means not retaliating against others when they hurt us and not classifying others in ways that deny them freedom.

Inspired by the work of Pepinsky and Quinney, John Fuller (1998, 2003) contrasted the peacemaking perspective with the war-on-crime perspective. He showed how "peacemaking criminology is part of a larger intellectual enterprise that spanned the range from interpersonal issues to global concerns, thus demonstrating the interconnectedness of criminal justice to larger areas of social justice" (2003, 86). In his book *Criminal Justice: A Peacemaking Perspective* (1998), Fuller outlined six components: (1) advocating nonviolence in criminal justice responses, particularly opposing the premeditated violence of the death penalty; (2) social justice issues such as sexism, racism, and inequality need to be incorporated and corrected in criminal justice responses; (3) inclusion means that every stakeholder affected by and connected with a crime, such as the victim, families of the victim and offender, neighbors, and so on, needs to be involved in its solution rather than restricting criminal justice to the offender and the state; (4) correction entails involving the offenders in the settlement of their cases, rather than having them imposed, and removing mechanisms of enforcement, such as racial profiling, that contribute to further crimes rather than those that reduce tensions; (5) "ascertainable criteria" refers to the need for victims, offenders, and community members to fully understand the criminal justice process that they participate in, which means the use of nonlegalese and technical jargon; and (6) categorical imperative, which means throughout the criminal justice system all participants should be treated with respect and dignity. Fuller argued:

> As opposed to the war on crime perspective, the peacemaking perspective has the potential to provide lasting solutions to the problems that lead individuals to commit violations of law. The war on crime perspective, with its emphasis on punishment and retribution, ensures that offenders will strive only to commit their crimes in a more efficient manner so as not to get caught. The peacemaking perspective, on the other hand, seeks to address the conditions of society that foster crime and to address the problems of the individual offender. Additionally the peacemaking perspective seeks to understand and respond to the concerns of the victims. (2003, 88)

Restorative justice has its roots in several different cultural approaches throughout the world, including the restitution practices of the first-century Anglo-Saxons, Native

American and Aboriginal peoples', justice, Mennonite activism, victim movements, abolitionist and peacemaking criminology, and Braithwaite's ideas about reintegrative shaming (Sarre 2003; Menkel-Meadow 2007). The term *restorative justice* was first coined by psychologist Albert Eglash when he was writing about reparation (1977, 95; Sarre 2003, 100–101). Restorative justice emerged as a response to an "overly harsh criminal justice system that neither effectively deterred crime nor successfully rehabilitated offenders," and it includes the four *r*'s of repair, restore, reconcile, and reintegrate (Menkel-Meadow 2007, 10.3). Like peacemaking, restorative justice is concerned with rebuilding relationships after an offense rather than driving a wedge between offenders and their communities, which is the hallmark of modern criminal justice systems (Sarre 2003). Restorative justice "is a victim-centered response to crime that allows the victim, the offender, their families, and representatives of the community to address the harm caused by the crime" (Umbreit 2001). It focuses on "repairing the harm caused by the crime" (Daly 1997) and, like restitution, "seeks to restore losses suffered by crime victims and facilitate peace" (Coward-Yaskiw 2002). Rather than impose decisions about winners and losers through an adversarial system, "restorative justice seeks to a facilitate dialog between all agents affected by the crime . . . including the victim, offender, their supporters, and the community at large" (Brennan 2003, 6). It involves "a process whereby all parties with a stake in a particular offence come together to resolve collectively how to deal with the aftermath of the offence and its implications for the future" (Marshall 2002, 11). In the process of coming together,

> victims speak of how the crime affected them; offenders may be able to explain why they committed the offense, and community members can offer narratives on how the community may have been changed because of the crime. Supporters of both the victim and offender may offer their stories as well. By giving a voice to all parties involved it may help the victim understand why the offense was committed (perhaps the offender had a substance abuse problem and needed money for drugs) and find the compassion to forgive and find treatment. (Brennan 2003, 7)

According to one of the founders of this approach, "Restorative justice is about healing rather than hurting, moral learning, community participation and community caring, respectful dialogue, forgiveness, responsibility, apology, and making amends" (Braithwaite 2002, 11). Moreover, it "mostly works well in granting justice, closure, restoration of dignity, transcendence of shame, and healing for the victim" (ibid., 69). The approach is well summarized by Sarre: "A restorative system of criminal justice endeavors to listen to, and appease, aggrieved parties to conflict and to restore, as far as possible, right relationships between antagonists. In restorative models crime is defined as a violation of one person by another, the focus is on problem solving, dialogue and restitution (where possible), mutuality, the repair of social injury and the possibilities of repentance and forgiveness" (2003, 98).

In practice, restorative justice includes a whole host of forums, including family conferencing for juveniles (Braithwaite and Mugford 1994; Strang 2000), family violence court, victim-offender mediation conferences and programs, family group counseling, sentencing circles, healing circles, and "other practices such as 'reparation boards' in Vermont, services to crime victims, meetings between imprisoned offenders and victims (or their family members)" (Daly 2000, 170).

Unlike conventional criminal justice that focuses on the offense to the state by individuals but does nothing to deal with the consequences of the harm to the victims and the community, restorative justice builds community trust and adds to a community's "social capital," thereby providing protection against future crimes (Coleman 1988). "Restorative justice builds on social capital because it decentralizes the offense from merely the act of an offender breaking the law, to a breach in a community's trust in its members. This in turns allows the community along with the offender and victim to *collectively* look for a resolution" (Brennan 2003, 8).

Critical Race Theory

Although the ideas of critical race theory have been around since the 1960s, it is only since 1989 that the theory has been more formally constituted and not until 1998 that it has been seriously applied to criminology and criminal justice (see especially K. Russell 1998; K. Russell and Milovanovic 2001; Mann and Zatz 1998; and Mann, Zatz, and Rodriguez 2006), though it was first applied to law and was seen as part of critical legal studies. Indeed, in that context, like radical theory, it questioned law and the courts, whose judicial conclusions were seen as the outcome of dominant power structures. There are similarities to anarchist theory in that critical race theory in law also criticizes all forms of domination and subordination. One of its more controversial statements translated into practice is its advocacy that black juries acquit black defendants not seen as a danger to the community on the grounds that their time would be more usefully spent with their families in their communities.

The first critical race theory workshop was held at a convent outside Madison, Wisconsin, in the summer of 1989. As Richard Delgado and Jean Stefancic have pointed out, critical race theory was founded by lawyers who had realized that civil rights gains were not being realized and in some cases were being rolled back. It was designed "to deal with the new types of colorblind, subtle, or institutional racism that were developing" (2005). Like feminists, whose theories we examined earlier, critical race theorists point out that not only is academic scholarship (and that would include academic criminology) dominated by white academics doing "imperial scholarship," but "they took little or no notice of the work of the emerging minority scholars" (ibid.). It is ironic then that the beginnings of critical race theory emerged in 1982 from the politics of university struggles going on at two stellar academic institutions, Berkeley and Harvard. Each was subject to protests by "students of color" at the lack of representation by "professors of color" on their faculties, and they fought to establish diversity. At Harvard the students ran their own alternative Saturday class, with guest lectures from minority faculty from around the country presenting papers. Some of their papers ended up becoming leading statements of critical race theory (Crenshaw et al. 1995), and several book-length treatments now exist (Delgado 1995; Delgado and Stefancic 1998, 2001).

In their presentation to the John Jay College of Criminal Justice in 2005, Delgado and Stefancic said that critical race theory "provides a new and different lens and way of systematizing the search for knowledge. It helps avoid the search for easy answers, focuses attention on social construction and mind-set, asks us to attend to the material factors underlying race and racism, and to go beyond the ordinariness of racist action and treatment." They identified several of its core beliefs both in their presentation and in their 1993 article. These include:

1. Racism is ordinary, not exceptional, meaning that it is the usual way that society does business and thus represents the common, everyday experience of most people of color.

2. Because racism can advance the interests of both white elites as well as white working-class people, large segments of society have little incentive to eradicate it (interest convergence).

3. The social construction of race, and the related idea of differential racialization, holds that race and races are products of social thought, categories that dominant society invents as it racializes different minority groups for particular purposes. Recent commentary has also explored the social construction of "whiteness."

4. Intersectionality and antiessentialism mean that no person has a single, easily stated, unitary identity. Everyone has potentially conflicting, overlapping identities, loyalties, and allegiances. Race is not a simple essence, which you either have or don't have.

5. Discontentment with incremental color-blind liberalism as a cure for the nation's racial ills because it has served only to sidestep the major issues. Racism is not an accident or matter of ignorance that will go away with education or better enforcement.

6. The need to develop a story, storytelling, and a "voice of color" and the virtues of "naming one's own reality."

7. Support for cultural nationalism: black separatism, black nationalism, and black power.

8. The importance of multiple cumulative disadvantages necessitating the study of the intersections of race, gender, and class.

When applied to criminal justice, critical race theorists raise a series of questions related to these issues, such as what is crime and how it should be redefined to take into account race (K. Russell 1998, 2001) and why our country tolerates "a criminal justice system that results in a prison population that is seventy percent black and brown" (Delgado and Stefancic 2005). They point out, like critical criminologists generally, that this is because the fear of black street crime is distorted and exaggerated, and the reality of harm from white-run corporate and white-collar crime, for example, is grossly understated. They oppose punitive drug policy exemplified in the war on drugs and instead advocate "complete legalization of at least some of the

milder drugs." With regard to the issue of interest convergence, a social constructionist approach is taken:

> Differential racialization theory could look at how society has constructed and stereo-
> typed the typical black offender, the typical Latino offender, the typical Asian of-
> fender, and the typical Indian offender, and assigned each group a different role in the
> national imagination, one the mugger, another the sneak, another the drunk and so
> on. It could look as well at how police officers engage in different forms of profiling
> for members of the different groups. If, in the past, we racialized groups differently
> based, essentially, on what we wanted from each—from the Indians, land; from the
> blacks, labor; from the Asians, railroad building and mining technology; and so on, it
> stands to reason that we might be racializing them differently now in terms of what
> we do not want to see from them in the way of crime. We might be treating them dif-
> ferently in the way defense attorneys interact with—or "construct" them as clients—
> in whether we accept plea bargains from them, and what kind of bargains; and how
> we supervise them when they are on probation or parole. (ibid.)

Evaluation of Critical Criminology

Each of the critical criminological positions considered here has been subject to critical evaluation, and we give a summary overview of some of the main criticisms below.

Left realism has been subject to several criticisms, not least of which is the charge
that it lacks originality, taking us little further than previous theory with regard to
causation. Moreover, as both Gibbons (1994, 170) and Shoemaker (1996, 219)
pointed out, left realist policy proposals are similar to those that emerged from social
ecology theory (discussed in Chapter 8), strain theory (discussed in Chapter 9), and
mainstream sociological criminology in general. Michalowski (1991) also cautioned
that left realists use a loose concept of community that could result in right-wing
populist and racist control of the police. He warned of the contradictions in pursuing criminal justice reform without accompanying structural changes from the capitalist system to a socialist form.

Another major criticism of left realism is that it excludes feminist concerns, remaining "gender blind" and "gender biased." It makes no attempt to explain women's
experiences of crime, victimization, or justice (Carlen 1992). Some argue that its
policies calling for a strengthening of the power of the oppressive state work to
strengthen patriarchy and to defeat women's interests (M. Schwartz and DeKeseredy
1991; DeKeseredy and Schwartz 1991).

Finally, left realists have been criticized for ignoring crimes of the powerful such as
corporate or white-collar crime (Henry 1999) and for advocating so-called progressive policies that include reinforcing the very structures of capitalist oppression that
they are critiquing, such as "job creation programs," "entrepreneurial skills training
in schools and linking schools and private businesses" (DeKeseredy 2003, 37).

Postmodernism has been sharply criticized by mainstream criminologists and even
critical criminologists (M. Schwartz and Friedrichs 1994). It is criticized for being

(1) difficult to understand, not least because of its complex language (M. Schwartz 1991); (2) nihilistic and relativistic, having no standards to judge anything as good or bad, thus fostering an "ideology of despair" (Melichar 1988, 366; see also Hunt 1990; S. Cohen 1990, 1993; and Handler 1992); and (3) impractical and even dangerous to disempowered groups (D. Currie 1992; S. Jackson 1992). In one specific example of how the disempowered may need more than a change in the discourse to protect their interests, Lisa Miller found that more than fifty local organizations in Seattle opposed the federally funded operation "Weed and Seed" because it had the potential to further empower police to target and harass minorities while also deflecting "attention from underlying economic issues" (2001, 177). At the same time, Weed and Seed illustrates the way official agencies can replace the discourse of, say, "rehabilitation" with the more punitive concept of "Weed and Seed" (see Kappeler and Kraska 1999 on how this was also done with the concept of "community policing").

The criticism that disempowered groups are targeted has been made particularly of postmodernist feminism by socialist feminists and radical feminists. Stevi Jackson (1992) and Lovibond (1989) argued that deconstructing gender categories may result in women being denied a position from which to speak, allowing men to continue to dominate through their control. Yet postmodernist feminists "insist that the challenge women confront is to construct a contingent method of communicating feminine ways of knowing freed from the trappings of masculine logic, sensibility and discourse" (Arrigo 2003, 52). Constitutive criminology offers a solution to these problems, but it is too soon to know whether its ideas will stand the test of critical assessment and practical application.

Finally, postmodernism has not been well understood and thus received by practitioners working in criminal justice. It has most often been applied to correctional issues, where it refers to the discursive transformation of the penal process away from rehabilitation and toward a "new penology," designed to control "the risk society" through the use of actuarial techniques to target offenders as social types who represent different amounts of risk (J. Simon 1993; Feeley and Simon 1998; D. Garland 1996; Lucken 1998).

Yet even in the corrections arena, "postmodern penal trends remain subordinate to modern penal trends that are still in place" (Hallsworth 2002, 145). It is less often mentioned with regard to law enforcement (but see Kappeler and Kraska 1999). Lisa Miller (2001) did, however, provide an excellent, simplistic, example of the critical power of postmodernist criminology in her analysis of the Seattle Weed and Seed program that does deal with crime, politics, law enforcement, and neighbors. Perhaps the greatest affinity of postmodern and constitutive theory is with the theorists who have developed an approach that not only recognizes the general interconnection of people but also seeks to redesign the criminal justice system to address this. This field comprises three related humanitarian ideas: abolitionism, peacemaking, and restorative justice. In each case the idea is to develop a response to crime that brings offenders and victims together in a peaceful, community-oriented context to resolve the conflict and mitigate the harm caused by their crimes.

Both anarchism and abolitionism have been criticized, even by sympathizers, for their romantic idealism, lack of conceptual clarity, failure to develop a well-grounded theoretical analysis of their opposition to punishment, and the absence of concrete practical strategies for dealing with dangerous offenders (Thomas and Boehlefeld 1991).

Not surprisingly, the ideas of peacemaking criminologists have also met with considerable criticism from commentators who point out that "being nice" is not enough to stop others from committing harm, that peacemaking is unrealistic, and that it can extend the power of the state, resulting in widening the net of social control (S. Cohen 1985). Others have suggested that its value lies in sensitizing us to alternatives to accepting violence (DeKeseredy and Schwartz 1996). One of the most extensive criticisms of peacemaking was offered by Akers (2000), who claimed that the perspective is not open to empirical scrutiny, is contradictory to Marxist and feminist ideas that claim to inform it, offers nothing new that has not been offered by traditional mainstream criminology, and does not offer a solution to address wider structural causes of violence. Advocates such as Fuller accept that the theory needs to be developed to be testable and agree that although peacemaking policies "such as non-punitive treatment of offenders, mediation, restitution, offender reintegration, rehabilitation, and so on have been advocated by traditional criminology, unfortunately, with the war on crime mentality that dominates the criminal justice system today, these policies have fallen into disuse. . . . The peacemaking perspective provides a coherent web to weave together all of these progressive policies" (2003, 94).

One way of conceiving of peacemaking that avoids some of the more obvious pitfalls, developed by constitutive criminologists, has been called social judo: "Judo means 'gentle way' and is based on the seeming paradox that the best defense is non-fighting and that one gains victory over an opponent by yielding—gentle turns away the sturdy opponent. . . . It is a method whereby the energy of the violent is redirected against the opponent to diffuse the violence" (Einstadter and Henry 1995, 315; see also Henry and Milovanovic 1996). As Bohm pointed out, "The judo metaphor is apt here because, on the one hand . . . using power to reduce the power of others only replaces one excessive investor with another. On the other hand, when using judo as a means of self-defense, the power of the aggressor is turned back against the aggressor" (1997b, 16). Although this model might release us from the punitive trap, as yet it remains underdeveloped, particularly as to how in practice energy invested by offenders can be turned back on them in peaceful ways. Gregg Barak has suggested explicit ways of achieving peace. In American society, for example, the media play a huge role in influencing perceptions. Unfortunately, rather than a positive force for peace, "organizationally and managerially, mass media overemphasizes interpersonal violence . . . while it ignores or downplays institutional and structural violence" (2003, 11). He continues to make a strong case for conflict resolution and peacemaking based on mutuality, human rights, and a "need-based justice."

Overall, peacemaking approaches have one common theme that is consistent with several other of the critical approaches that we have examined: connections and the social nature of humans and the world we construct. All would agree that the analytical approaches that separate individuals from their social context are deficient for leaving out much of what is important. As we have seen, the approach that has been most developed in this regard is that of restorative justice, though it too has received its share of critical evaluation.

Sarre identified several criticisms that have been leveled at restorative justice that explain a reluctance to adopt it more widely. These include the following views: (1) It is really rehabilitation in disguise; (2) it excuses violence, particularly against women and children; (3) it contradicts the principle of public open justice and legal protections by use of private forums and co-option techniques on participants; (4) it is soft on crime, ignoring the public's retributive attitudes; (5) its community justice and informal judgments undermine the standards of traditional legal reasoning; (6) it contradicts the legal notion of equal treatment of like cases and the certainty and consistency of outcomes (which under restorative justice are necessarily variable); and (7) restoration assumes that the status quo is the desired outcome rather than a transformative outcome that changes the situation of those offending and those harmed (2003, 101–102). In addition, it has been pointed out that restorative programs deal with less serious offenses. At the same time, there is an emerging set of principles that mitigate against some of the problems that have been identified. These include ensuring that all parties are present voluntarily, that victims are treated with sensitivity and that they have the control lost through the crime restored, that the offender be sufficiently coerced to not use the system for self-preservation but to help solve the problems created by their offense, that trained and unbiased facilitators be used, and that facilitators be flexible toward the solutions proposed by the participants (Umbreit 2001; Umbreit and Coates 1998; Umbreit et al. 2002).

There is also growing evidence that restorative justice approaches are being increasingly adopted even for violent offenders. Ironically, Texas, one of the most punitive states, developed a victim-offender protocol for violent offenses in 1993, and similar ones have since been adopted by twelve states (Umbreit et al. 2002). Umbreit and his colleagues suggested that "many of the principles of restorative justice can be applied in crimes of severe violence, including murder, with clear effectiveness in supporting both the process of victim healing and offender accountability" (ibid., 2). However, although evidence is building, at present "there is a lack of definition and a lack of data," and "we need to find out about the performance of each restorative model in order to determine whether it can 'support the hopes of its proponents . . . or succumb to the criticisms of its detractors'" (Strang 2000, 31; Sarre 2003, 107).

Carrie Menkel-Meadow reviewed the growth of restorative justice, discussed its variations and tensions, and assessed whether, as a practical alternative, this outcome of critical criminology actually works in dealing with issues of harm, peace, and justice. She said that restorative justice "has moved into larger national and international arenas of reintegration in political and ethnic conflicts" (2007, 10.1). Critiques of restorative justice have been numerous, ranging from empirical, philosophical and sociological, and legalistic to anthropological and political concerns.

Menkel-Meadow believed that it should be rigorously evaluated, including its effectiveness in reducing recidivism.

In the final section of this chapter we examine integrative criminology, an approach that, like peacemaking and restorative justice, seeks to work from the assumption that crime is interconnected with the wider society.

Integrative Criminologies

Since 1979, a trend in criminology has emerged that many find exciting and fitting with our changing global situation. Instead of developing new theories that compete to supersede all those previously existing, some theorists have engaged in attempts to combine what they see as the best elements of these diverse positions (R. Johnson 1979; Elliott, Huizinga, and Ageton 1985). Those engaging in integration have done so for a variety of reasons, not least because of a desire to arrive at central anchoring notions in theory, to provide coherence to a bewildering array of fragmented theories, to achieve comprehensiveness and completeness to advance scientific progress, and to synthesize causation and social control (Barak 1998, 2009). By way of conclusion, we want to briefly explore the integration of criminological theories, beginning with a simple definition, critically exploring some of the issues in integration and then illustrating integration. We provide two examples of different kinds of integration— modernist and "holistic"—and give examples of these as they appear in developmental and interactive-reciprocal theory.

Theoretical integration has been defined as "the combination of two or more pre-existing theories, selected on the basis of their perceived commonalities, into a single reformulated theoretical model with greater comprehensiveness and explanatory value than any one of its component theories" (Farnworth 1989, 95). So, for example, one component of integrated theory may focus on the learning process, another on the impact of social control, and a third on the effects on both of the broad class structure or social ecology in which these different processes are located. This sounds relatively straightforward, logical, and even, as students often tell us, plain common sense. But it is fraught with difficulty. Let us see why.

First is the issue of what precisely is integrated. Do we integrate theoretical concepts or propositions? Integrating concepts involves finding those that have similar meanings in different theories and merging them into a common language, as has been done in Akers's conceptual absorption approach ([1977] 1985, 1994; Akers and Sellers 2008). Akers merged concepts from social learning and social control theory (among others) so that, for example, "belief," which in control theory refers to moral convictions for or against delinquency, is equated to "definitions favorable or unfavorable to crime," taken from differential association theory, and so on. Since this can reduce or absorb one or another concept to the other (Thornberry 1989; Hirschi 1979), even Akers asked whether it is integration or simply a "hostile takeover" (1994, 186).

Moreover, comprehensive attempts at conceptual integration can distort, even transform, the original concepts, as in Pearson and Weiner's attempt to integrate every theory (1985). So, for example, "commitment," which in control theory refers to the potential loss that crime may produce to those with whom one is bonded, is combined with more simplistic classical and learning ideas of rewards and punishment to become the new concept of "utility demand and reception"! But if the integrated concepts are not reduced, then simply including all the major concepts would become impracticably cumbersome.

If we integrate not concepts but merely their propositions, the problems can be worse. Propositional integration refers to combining propositions from theories or placing them in some causal order or sequence. As Shoemaker observed in considering the integration of differential association and social control theories, "If one were to include all major components of these two theories in one comprehensive model, there would be at least 13 variables, and most likely more than double that amount. If other theoretical explanations were included, such as anomie, social disorganization, psychological and biological theories, the number of potential variables in the analysis would soon approach 50!" (1996, 254). Testing such an integrated theory would be impractical on account of the difficulty of the large sample size required—that is, if we rely on positivistic principles of testing.

Beyond what is integrated is the issue of how propositions are logically related. Propositions may be related (1) end to end, which implies a sequential causal order; (2) side by side, which implies overlapping influences; or (3) up and down, which suggests that the propositions from one can be derived from a more abstract form (Hirschi 1979; Bernard and Snipes 1996).

A third related issue is the nature of causality that is assumed within the formal structure of any integrated theory. Does the integrated theory use linear causality, which takes the form of a sequential chain of events? Does it employ multiple causality, in which a crime is the outcome of several different causes or a combination of them together? Might interactive or reciprocal causality, in which the effects of one event, in turn, influence its cause(s), which then influence the event, be most appropriate? Alternatively, should the integrative theory use dialectical or reciprocal causality, such that causes and events are not discrete entities but are overlapping and interrelated, being codetermining (Einstadter and Henry 2006; Henry and Milovanovic 1996; Barak 1998)? Clearly, the interactive and dialectical models of causality suggest a dynamic rather than static form of integration (Einstadter and Henry 2006). Should different causalities be integrated such that some are dynamic and some static?

A fourth issue is the level of concepts and theories that are integrated. Should these be of the same level or across levels? In other words, should only theories relating to the individual level be combined with others at the individual level (microlevel integration), as in Wilson and Herrnstein's combination of biological and rational choice (1985), or in Hagan, Simpson, and Gillis's (1987) power-control integration of structural-cultural level Marxism with structural-cultural feminism (macrolevel) integration? Should integrationists cross levels (macro-micro integration), as in Colvin and Pauly's attempt to combine Marxist, conflict, strain subculture, social learning, and social control theories (1983)? Integrational levels to be considered then include (1) kinds of people, their human agency, and their interactive social processes; (2) kinds of organization, their collective agency, and their organizational processes; and (3) kinds of culture, structure, and context (Akers 1994; Barak 1998).

The level of integration may depend on what is to be explained, or the scope of integration, which is a fifth consideration. Is the integration intended to explain crime in general or a specific type of crime? Is it intended to apply to the population in general or only certain sectors of it (e.g., young, old, men, women, African American, Hispanic, and so on)? Yet another type of integration looks at particular problem (e.g., human trafficking) and applies various theories to explain different aspects of the problem (see box 12.1).

Some have argued that by combining theories, we lose more than we gain—that "theory competition" and "competitive isolation" are preferable to "integration." They point out that criminology shows a "considerable indifference and healthy skepticism toward theoretical integration" (Akers 1994, 195; see also Gibbons 1994). Yet others see "knowledge integration" as valuable (Shoemaker 1996; Bernard and Snipes 1996; Barak 1998).

Clearly, these are complex issues to resolve. The result, as Einstadter and Henry (2006) argue, may be that the original goal of reducing competitive theories is replaced by competition between different types of integrative theory as integrationists argue for their particular model as the best combination.

Although table 12.1 is not exhaustive of the range of integrative theories and conflates similar ones while leaving out others that are no more than developments of earlier theories, it does indicate that the most frequently included theories in integrated paradigms are social learning and social control, followed by anomie and conflict, and then Marxist, ecology, psychology/personality, and rational choice. With social learning most frequently incorporated, there is some justification to Akers's claim (2000) that all criminal behavior is based on social learning because almost all theories draw on social learning as a component; equally, the relatively low number of inclusions of feminist theory does little to challenge feminist views that gender has been left out of criminological theorizing. Kraska (2006) has even proposed combining criminological theories with those of criminal justice. Regardless, the above analysis suggests that the array of integrated theories is now as vast as the array of original theories, as Einstadter and Henry (2006) had predicted, which leads to some considerable confusion.

Recently, some have begun to point to ways out of this theoretical quagmire. These involve, first, the suggestion that there are really two broad approaches to integration—modernist and postmodernist—and, second, the notion that it is possible to provide an integration of integrated theory. We might call this *hyperintegration*.

Barak's book *Integrating Criminologies*, which provides the most comprehensive review of integration to date, suggests that modernist integration is in all its different guises really "aimed at the questionable objective of delivering some kind of positivist prediction of 'what causes criminal behavior,'" whereas in postmodernist

TABLE 12.1—Integrative Theories

Theory (ordered by year idea first introduced)	Theorists	Core Idea	Classical/ Rational Choice	Biological	Psychological Personality	Learning	Control Social Bonding	Labeling/Social Constructionism	Ecology/ Cultural	Subcultural	Strain Anomie	Conflict	Marxist Radical	Feminist	Postmodernist	Peacemaking Restorative
Integrated social theory	Elliott, Huizinga, and Agerton, 1979, 1985	Strain in family, school, community weakens social bonds, increases bonds with delinquent peers				X	X				X					
Social developmental model/theory	Weis and Hawkins, 1981; Weis and Sederstrom, 1979	Socialization in poorly bonded families reduces resistance to delinquency via peer subculture				X	X			X	X					
Integrated structural Marxist theory/ differential coercion theory	Colvin and Pauly, 1983; Colvin, 2000	Capitalist exploitation produces coercive family environment, strains family, weakens bonds, aggravated by coercive school				X	X			X	X	X	X			

(continues)

TABLE 12.1—Integrative Theories (continued)

Theory	Theorist(s)	Description												
Left realist/exclusion theory	Mathews and Young, 1986; Young 1999	Capitalist market economy creates poor underclass, excluded from share of wealth, experience relative deprivation and subcultural conflict	X							X	X	X			
Conceptual integration theory	Pearson and Weiner, 1985	Primarily considers all the factors that can affect social learning and lead to crime	X				X	X	X	X	X	X			
Human nature	Wilson and Herrnstein, 1985	Humans make decisions shaped by biological, psychological, and environmental interactive factors	X		X	X									
Power control theory	Hagan, Simpson, and Gillis, 1987	Capitalism and patriarchy affect men and women in workplace, resulting in differential control over girls and boys at home with different delinquency outcomes	X				X						X	X	X

(continues)

Theory (ordered by year idea first introduced)	Theorists	Core Idea	Classical/ Rational Choice	Biological	Psychological Personality	Learning	Control Social Bonding	Labeling/Social Constructionism	Ecology/ Cultural	Subcultural	Strain Anomie	Conflict	Marxist Radical	Feminist	Postmodernist	Peacemaking Restorative
Network analysis theory	Krohn, 1986	Differential reinforcement of convention or deviant acts depending on extent and density of network contacts				X	X										
Interactional theory	Thornberry, 1987	Adolescence weakens conventional bonds, peers in disorganized communities become influential, but diminish with work and marriage			X	X	X		X								
Delinquency development/ age-graded/life course/ pathways	Farrington, 1988; Loeber and LeBlanc, 1990; Sampson and Laub, 1993	Poor parental interaction, poor role models shape criminal personality, reinforced by criminal career, or limited by social capital			X	X	X		X								

TABLE 12.1—Integrative Theories (continued)

Theory	Source	Concept																
Reintegrative shaming theory	Braithwaite, 1989	Strain affects bonding, which if weakened makes labeling a shaming and excluding process rather than reintegrating and normalizing			X	X	X		X	X			X			X
Edgework theory	Lyng, 1990; O'Malley and Mugford, 1994; Milovanovic, 2002	Historical and cultural limits on the expression of human desire lead to pursuit of emotional expression via approaching the edge					X							X			
Constitutive theory	Henry and Milovanovic, 1991, 1996	Power and inequality build socially constructed differences through which harm deprivations imposed on the subordinated					X				X	X	X	X	
General ecology theory	Vila, 1994	Desire for resources interacts with socio-cultural and ecological factors in a chaotic, nonlinear way	X	X	X				X							

	Control balance theory	Integrated systems theory	Total Number of inclusions by Integrated Theorists
Theorists	Tittle, 1995	Robinson, 2004	
Core Idea	Imbalance between amount of control exercised relative to amount subjected to leads to crime	Crime is the outcome of a combination of risk factors, from biological through organism, group, community, and societal	
Classical/Rational Choice	X	X	6
Biological		X	3
Psychological Personality	X	X	6
Learning	X	X	12
Control Social Bonding	X	X	11
Labeling/Social Constructionism		X	5
Ecology/Cultural	X	X	6
Subcultural		X	5
Strain Anomie		X	7
Conflict	X	X	7
Marxist Radical			6
Feminist			2
Postmodernist	X		4
Peacemaking Restorative			2

integration, "everything, at both the micro and macro levels, affects everything else, and where these effects are continuously changing over time" (1998, 188). In what is reminiscent of the old criminological division between functionalist and conflict theories, we are here confronted with a clash between modernist and postmodernist approaches (Henry and Milovanovic 1996; Milovanovic 1995).

This division is now applied to integration. Modernist integrative schemes, of the kind discussed so far, whatever form they take, are propositional and predictive, use linear or multiple causality, and are particularistic and static. Postmodernist integrative schemes, in contrast, are conceptual and interpretive, use interactive or reciprocal causality, and are holistic and dynamic. Barak argues that it is these holistic integrative models (e.g., "interactional," "ecological," "constitutive") of crime and crime control that hold out the most promise for developing criminology. But rather than stopping there, Barak's hyperintegration model attempts to integrate these integrations, arguing that bringing together both modernist and postmodernist sensibilities is necessary to capture the "whole picture" of the social reality of crime.

A direction in integrated theory was provided by Matthew Robinson. He attempted to integrate all the factors from human "cell to society" (clustered in twenty-two groups) in a developmental interactive sequence to show how antisocial behavior is more or less likely. He stated, "The integrated systems theory of antisocial behavior attempts to advance the state of theories . . . past its myopic state by illustrating how risk factors at different levels of analysis from different academic disciplines interact to increase the probability that a person will commit antisocial behavior" (2004, 271). Instead of discussing theories in historical sequence (he believed criminology is "stuck in the past") and instead of dividing them by disciplines (which he said reinforces "artificial boundaries in knowledge about crime" and "limits our understanding of it") and instead of discussing the merits of different theories (which he believed creates false divisions), he examined the meaningful (tested) contribution to our understanding of crime made by each discipline (ibid., x–xi). How far this theory stands up to empirical testing remains to be seen, but this is perhaps the most ambitious, comprehensive, interdisciplinary attempt so far made to move integration of criminological theory to new heights.

In one of the most recent developments within integrated theory, researchers have begun integrating academic fields that are already multidisciplinary. For example, Mark Lanier developed the Virtual Center for Epidemiological Criminology (VCEC) (see http://www.epidemiologicalcriminology.com) based on the work of Akers and Lanier (2009), Lanier (2009), and Lanier, Lucken, and Akers (2010). Epidemiological Criminology, or EpiCrim, seeks to link public health issues with criminal justice issues. At the same time, methodological and theoretical integration is achieved by linking epidemiology with criminology. The Web site states:

> There is an increasing overlap and blurring of distinctions between public health and criminal justice. Many other academic units such as sociology and social work share

these commonalities as well. While integration between all the social sciences is possible, probable and inevitable, for now we are focusing on criminal justice and public health. Each discipline works with marginalized populations; people at high risk to multiple dangers including drug use, health problems and incarceration. Numerous research reports and funding trends document this merging. However, explicit theoretical and methodological linkages between the two have been rare. Through the VCEC we are helping with the development of a new paradigm that links methods, and statistical models of public health, to that of their criminal justice counterpart. We further link epidemiological analogies, theories and models, to that of their criminological equivalent. (2008)

This enterprise has gained considerable support from students, researchers, and policy makers. Several research studies dealing with human trafficking and HIV/AIDS are already under way linking public health and criminal justice agencies and researchers.

Since its initial development, integrative theory has resulted in some major innovative theoretical approaches to the study of crime. In our closing section we explore some of the exemplars of this approach that we call reciprocal-integrative criminology. Within this overarching framework we review two specific theories, the first illustrating the modernist microlevel integrative analysis and the second illustrating a macrolevel integrative analysis.

Reciprocal-Interactive Integrative Criminology

During the past twenty years there has been increasing attention given to theories taking a developmental approach that look at crime as the ongoing outcome of a time-structured interactive process. These theories often draw on more than one discipline and more than one level of analysis to explain how life develops across the life course. This cluster of theories includes life-course theory, developmental or pathways theory, control-balance theory, differential coercion and social support theory, and reciprocal-interactive theory. What these theories have in common is that they document how people interact with others, social institutions, cultures, and structures over time and how, in the process, the way people act changes in ways that can be more or less criminal or more or less harm producing. These theories are called reciprocally interactive because people take on aspects of the social world around them and are changed by it. In the process, they interact with the social world and change it, in an ongoing process of mutual influence. In order to study crime over the life course it is necessary to conduct longitudinal research.

In the 1980s there was a debate over whether eventual offenders were more crime-prone than nonoffenders, as argued in the "criminal propensity thesis" (Gottfredson and Hirschi 1989) or whether offenders developed "criminal careers" as a result of a

series of events across their life courses (Blumstein et al. 1986). Some would continue from the onset of their first offense to become "life-course persistent offenders," while others may begin but then desist from crime, and these were called
"adolescent-limited offenders" (Moffitt 1993). The work of Albert Blumstein,
Jacqueline Cohen, David Farrington, and Terrie Moffitt came from the mainstream
of criminology and tended to be psychologically oriented. However, over the next
fifteen years it became increasingly recognized that a life-course or developmental
theory of crime could accommodate a wider range of variables and multiple levels of
analysis, beyond those at the individual psychological developmental level, to include organizational-, neighborhood-, community-, and societal-level influences,
and that these could build into pathways toward or away from crime. Although
there is an important literature on the psychological factors and childhood profile
characteristics that affect career or noncareer pathways to crime, and "keystone" behaviors or triggers, turning points, or catalysts, and although there are disagreements about how many pathways exist and at what ages or developmental stages
these become critical (Nagin and Land 1993; Loeber and Hay 1994; Loeber and
Stouthamer-Loeber 1996, 1998), here we illustrate the approach with a few milestone theories.

Developmental or Life-Course Criminology

The concept of developmental criminology first appeared in Loeber and LeBlanc's
analysis (1990) of individual careers as a means to understanding the pathways to
delinquency, although other criminologists, from Wolfgang, Figlio, and Sellin
(1972) through Farrington (1989), LeBlanc (LeBlanc and Fréchette 1989), and Rutter (Robbins and Rutter 1990), had been working on similar kinds of longitudinal
studies using related developmental concepts such as "delinquency development"
and "pathways" to conformity or deviance. In addition, Terence Thornberry (1987,
1997) had been developing an interactive theory of crime.

A major milestone in integrative developmental theory came with Robert Sampson and John Laub's seminal *Crime in the Making: Pathways and Turning Points
Through Life* (1993), which was based on a reanalysis of data from Sheldon Glueck
and Eleanor Glueck's classic longitudinal study (1950) of five hundred juvenile
delinquent boys matched with five hundred nondelinquent boys from childhood
through age thirty-two. Glueck and Glueck found that not only did stable family life
insulate against involvement in delinquency and crime, but the aging process, with
its life-course effects, also promoted desistance from crime (the "aging out" process),
although the earlier the onset of crime, the longer in the life course did it persist.

In their reanalysis, integrating social control and labeling theories, Sampson and
Laub (1993) found that social bonding operated over the life course and was part of
a long-term trajectory or a short-term transition or both. What developed and how a
person moved along these pathways and between statuses depended on the stage that
a person was in their development (or age-graded status). Although past involvement

in delinquency was found to predict future involvement, factors that brought change were important. Principal among these was "social capital" that strengthened the commitment to conformity, and resilience to crime becoming persistent, even for those adolescents involved in youthful and adult delinquency. Having the networks of social capital created opportunities to return to a stable life of noncrime. In contrast, being cut off from these pathways or transitory events that can serve as turning points to desistance, such as occurs when juveniles or adults are channeled into detention or prison, can promote crime persistence. As a result, life-course theory insists that crime-prevention programs involving parent training, job-skills training, and education- and community-based intervention are more effective policies than incarceration (Laub, Sampson, and Allen 2001).

Reciprocal-Interactive Theory

In his book *Violence and Nonviolence: Pathways to Understanding,* Barak (2003) recognized his debt to several developmental, life-course, or reciprocal theories in criminology that reflect examples of integrated theorizing, particularly Terence Thornberry's interactional theory of delinquency (1987), Terrie Moffitt's adolescent-limited and life-course-persistent explanation of antisocial behavior (2001), Robert Sampson and John Laub's social development theory of antisocial behavior (2001a, 2001b), and Mark Colvin's reciprocal differential coercion theory (2000). In his "reciprocal theory of violence and non-violence" Barak argued that pathways to violence (and nonviolence) that span "across the spheres of interpersonal, institutional and structural relations as well as across the domains of family, subculture and culture are cumulative, mutually reinforcing, and inversely related" (2003, 169). He pointed out that "most explanations of the etiology of violence and nonviolence . . . emphasize the interpersonal spheres to the virtual exclusion of the institutional and structural spheres" (ibid., 155). In contrast, he said we need to take into account the dynamic interrelations of these different levels in order to understand the pathways to violence: "The interpersonal, institutional and structural levels of society are, indeed, part and parcel of the same cultural relations" (ibid., 170). In an extension of this theory, Barak (2006) argued that we need to consider the full range of behavioral motivations and sociocultural constraints that intersect with the spheres of interpersonal, institutional, and structural communication. Indeed, he stated, we need also to recognize that those in schools are not immune to the processes of violence in the wider society that he referred to as "structural violence: postcolonial violence, corporate violence, underclass violence, terrorist violence and institutional-structural violence" (2003, 134). Although these wider manifestations of cultural and structural violence are rarely considered when examining specific forms of violence, he said that such acts of structural violence "are the products of a complex development of social and psychic forces that have allowed masses of people the ability to deny, with only minimal, if any feelings of shame and guilt, the humanity of whole groups of people, that their actions or inactions victimize. In sum, these states of cultural and institutional denial of victimization contribute to the socialized lack of empathy for, and dehumanization of, the Other, each a prerequisite for the social reproduction of structural violence" (ibid., 135).

The major contribution Barak made to the integrative literature was to advance our analysis of crime to include the macrocultural and structural factors and collective images and how these can impact the life course of offenders and nonoffenders and feed into the more microlevel analyses that we considered above. Barak's analysis has been applied by Henry (2009) to explain school violence in general and rampage school shootings in particular.

Conclusion

We began this book by reviewing how the world has undergone major changes, indeed, a great transformation during the past twenty years, which has involved a globalization of economics, health, politics, and social and cultural life. We showed how this change has impacted production, consumption and distribution, communications, technology, transportation, and privatization. We showed how the world's societies now face changing kinds of threats from disease, security, and terrorism that are changing our physical and emotional landscapes. Underlying these changes is an increased interdependence with others in societies across the world. We argued that traditional criminological approaches that fail to acknowledge this global interconnectedness and criminal justice approaches that adopt a war metaphor against crime are inadequate to address the emerging problems, harms, and crimes of the twenty-first century. Throughout the text we have shown how this global change impacts crime and our theorizing about crime. In this final section we reiterate that context shapes not only perception but also behavior. We anticipate even greater, and more rapid, changes in the future as globalization and technology spread and as the limits of the market economy are reached. Changing positions of world dominance (the European Commonwealth, China, India, Russia, and the United States, for example), trade and the economy, and global fiscal crises will inevitably affect all societies and all people. Anticipating this change is one challenge we leave you with.

In this final chapter, we explored new approaches that are sensitive to the global context in ways that earlier theories could not comprehend, including left realism, postmodernism and constitutive theory, peacemaking criminology, and restorative justice. These theories have in common the view that criminology needs to take a holistic, integrative approach that brings offenders, victims, and the community back together. Although these new approaches hold much promise for the future, others believe that in order to fully comprehend the complexity of the individual's relationship with global society, we need first to incorporate and integrate the divisions in criminological thinking. In view of this, we saw how several criminologists have begun to examine the reconnection of criminology to itself under the umbrella term *integrated theory*.

At the beginning of the twentieth century, criminology had but two very different paradigms to rub together, classical (free will) versus positivism (determinism). As the twentieth century progressed, the number and diversity of theories proliferated, and calls for integration abounded. In the twenty-first century, we are invited to reconstitute the criminological enterprise anew from the perspective of a postpostmodernist, hyperintegrative theory. How much this will take hold remains to be seen. As to what causes crime, we leave that for you to ponder, but each of the theories presented in this book makes a contribution, and we hope that now that you have read them you will have an enhanced understanding of the complexity of crime and criminality.

Likewise, we do not conclude this book with a solution to the crime problem. There is no single policy solution, and there are no easy answers. As should be apparent from reading the often contradictory theories presented here, there is no consensus on how to address crime. Even if a consensus did exist, it would be problematic, because without conflict and differences of opinion, evolutionary progress is not possible. This book is descriptive, not prescriptive. It is ultimately up to readers—the future criminological scholars and policy makers—to arrive at future crime solutions. Our goal has been to show what has transpired and where future directions in theory are leading us. Good luck!

Summary Chart

1. Left Realism

Human Nature: Humans are shaped by hierarchical power structures of class, race, and gender, which produce differentials in wealth and relative deprivation. Humans are repressed and co-opted for the benefit of dominant interests.

Society and the Social Order: Capitalist class hierarchy uses the state to resolve contradictions; gains legitimacy by co-opting the powerless. Crime is harm to others; it is divisive and undermines community, which helps maintain capitalist system. Law is a system of maintaining power that provides genuine protection against harm in order to gain legitimation for wider capitalist system. Law represents a history of victories over the powerful, curbing their crude, arbitrary, and coercive will. Criminals are structurally powerless, commit genuine harm, and create real fear through victimizing others, especially others who are powerless; criminals are also victims of capitalism's structural contradictions and of the state via the criminal justice system.

Causal Logic: Relative deprivation from conspiring forces of class inequality, racism, and patriarchy causes crime as people feel injustice and anger and take these feelings out on those closest to them. Other crime results from state inequities in justice and labeling of offenders.

Criminal Justice Policy: Ultimately should work toward democratic socialist society, but until then pragmatic approach to do something now to prevent suffering from crime rather than waiting for the revolution. Restructure rather than replace criminal justice. Strengthen and control the criminal justice system of capitalist society and correct bias that leaves structurally powerless more vulnerable to street crime. Belief that law can provide the structurally powerless with real gains, if not ideal victories. Protecting the structurally weak through improving social justice helps to re-create community necessary to replace the existing capitalist system with decentralized socialism.

Criminal Justice Practice: Protect rights of victims. Essential to provide equal justice to powerless through state protection, community policing, and neighborhood-watch groups. Democratize police and subject them to community controls. Defends treatment, rehabilitation, and welfare against attacks from the political Right.

Evaluation: Criticized by the radical Left for abandoning socialist cause, being reformist, and being co-opted by capitalist system, which its policies seek to strengthen, particularly its bureaucratic apparatuses. In supporting working-class victimology, distracts from crimes of powerful. Focus little different from mainstream criminology. Feminists argue it is gender blind, treating women as victims rather than active human agents.

2. Postmodern/Constitutive

Human Nature and Society: Interrelated and coproductive of each other. Humans are socially constructed "subjects" whose energy and active agency build the very social structures that limit and channel their actions and transform them and thereby change society in an ongoing dialectical fashion. Both are socially constructed, although treated as if real. Crime is harm produced through the exercise of power that denies others the ability to make a difference. Crimes of repression keep people from becoming what they might have been; crimes of reduction undermine what they already have become (e.g., by removing something from them, whether physically through violence, material assets through theft, or status, identity, belief, and so forth). Law is myth: an exaggeration of one narrowly defined kind of rule to the exclusion of others, such as informal norms, customs, and so on. Criminals are "excessive investors" in the use of power to dominate others; expropriate the ability to make a difference by denying others theirs. Victim is a "recovering subject" contingent on becoming fulfilled but never completing the process, damaged through having that progress interrupted.

Causal Logic: Crime is not so much caused as coproduced by the whole society through its investment in social construction of difference and expert knowledge and in building power based on this. Process of crime production is manifested through symbolic and harmful discourse that imbues social constructions with the appearance of objective realities and then treats them as such.

Criminal Justice Policy: Deconstruction of existing truth claims through exposing their arbitrary constitution. Reconstruction of less harmful discourses. Work toward decentralized superliberal democratic structure that accommodates a diversity of voices.

Criminal Justice Practice: Replacement discourse, through media. Nonviolent settlement-directed talking. Peacemaking alternatives such as mediation, restorative justice, and narrative therapy. Empowering ordinary people through accepting their voices.

Evaluation: Unclear and complex. Excludes others through use of highly abstract jargon. Nihilistic, lacking standards. Not open to conventional empirical testing. Romantic about possibility of transformation.

3. Abolitionist/Peacemaking/Restorative

Human Nature: Humans are products of power structures, repressed from being their true humanistic cooperative selves and encouraged by hierarchical divisions to be competitive individualists. Can restore their humanity by being reconnected with others.

Society and the Social Order: A hierarchical system of power and authority regardless of the basis. Socialist and even communist as bad as capitalist, as each is dominated by a powerful centralized, bureaucratic state. All hierarchical societies feed off and exploit divisions of class, race, and gender. Crime is a reflection and an expression of broken social relations and harms other individuals and communities. Law is the enforcement arm of state, itself a force of conflict that divides rather than unites communities. Criminals are the distorted product of power structures who can be reintegrated to the community, provided they are treated with respect and allowed to actively make amends for their harms.

Causal Logic: Concentration of power creates hierarchies that divide people and pit them against one another in an unnatural competitive struggle in which they lose respect and see each other as objects and obstacles in the way of personal, often material, goals. The hierarchical system of power and authority is the cause of the harm that is crime.

Criminal Justice Policy: Replace systems of hierarchical power. Abolish state coercion, especially prisons, and replace with fully participatory genuine democracy based on consensual decision making. Achieved through a spiritual awakening. Philosophy is to reintegrate offender, victim, and community, which provides an opportunity to correct problems in wider social relations. Encourage diversity and difference and leave ambiguities of meaning unresolved.

Criminal Justice Practice: Replace existing form of justice with a peacemaking, restorative, decentralized system of negotiated face-to-face informal justice in which all members participate and share their decisions as fully responsible members. Justice should be about peacemaking and healing wrongs through mediation and negotiation, with sanctions of collective persuasion and shaming. Responsibility for offense is shared with community.

Evaluation: Seen as untestable and with an air of conspiracy theory by mainstream critics; seen as supporting rather than challenging the status quo by radical critics, but as part of an overall solution by moderate supporters.

Notes

1. Since 2004 cultural criminology has expanded in England, specifically at the University of Kent, which has drawn together its leading theorists, Young, Presdee, Ferrell, Hayward, and Hale.

References

Abbott, Jack Henry. 1981. *In the Belly of the Beast*. London: Hutchinson.

Abrahamsen, David. 1944. *Crime and the Human Mind*. New York: Columbia University Press.

———. 1960. *The Psychology of Crime*. New York: Columbia University Press.

———. 1973. *The Murdering Mind*. New York: Harper and Row.

Acker, James R. 1991. "Social Science in Supreme Court Death Penalty Cases: Citation Practices and Their Implications." *Justice Quarterly* 8: 421–446.

Adams, A. Troy. 2000. "The Status of School Discipline and Violence." In "School Violence," edited by William Hinkle and Stuart Henry. Special issue, *Annals of the American Academy of Political and Social Science* 567.

Adler, Alfred. 1931. *What Life Should Mean to You*. London: Allen and Unwin.

Adler, Freda. 1975. *Sisters in Crime: The Rise of the New Female Criminal*. New York: McGraw-Hill.

Adler, Freda, and William S. Laufer, eds. 1995. *The Legacy of Anomie Theory: Advances in Criminological Theory*. Vol. 6. New Brunswick, NJ: Transaction Publishers.

Adler, Freda, Gerhard O. W. Mueller, and William S. Laufer. 1995. *Criminology*. 2d ed. New York: McGraw-Hill.

Adler, William F. 1995. *Land of Opportunity: One Family's Quest for the American Dream in the Age of Crack*. New York: Atlantic Monthly Press.

Ageton, Suzanne S., and Delbert S. Elliott. 1974. "The Effects of Legal Processing on Delinquent Orientations." *Social Problems* 22: 87–100.

Agnew, Robert S. 1984. "Goal Achievement and Delinquency." *Sociology and Social Research* 68: 435–451.

———. 1985. "A Revised Strain Theory of Delinquency." *Social Forces* 64: 151–167.

———. 1989. "A Longitudinal Test of Revised Strain Theory." *Journal of Quantitative Criminology* 5: 373–387.

———. 1991a. "The Interactive Effects of Peer Variables on Delinquency." *Criminology* 29: 47–72.

———. 1991b. "Strain and Subcultural Crime Theories." In *Criminology: A Contemporary Handbook*, edited by Joseph F. Sheley, 273–294. Belmont, CA: Wadsworth.

———. 1992. "Foundation for a General Strain Theory of Crime and Delinquency." *Criminology* 30: 47–87.

———. 1994. "The Techniques of Neutralization and Violence." *Criminology* 32: 555–580.

———. 1995a. "The Contribution of Social-Psychological Strain Theory to the Explanation of Crime and Delinquency." In *The Legacy of Anomie Theory: Advances in Criminological Theory*, edited by Freda Adler and William S. Laufer. Vol. 6. New Brunswick, NJ: Transaction Publishers.

———. 1995b. "Controlling Delinquency: Recommendations from General Strain Theory." In *Crime and Public Policy: Putting Theory to Work*, edited by Hugh D. Barlow. Boulder, CO: Westview Press.

———. 2001. "Building on Foundation of General Strain Theory: Specifying the Types of Strain Most Likely to Lead to Crime and Delinquency." *Journal of Research in Crime and Delinquency* 38: 319–361.

———. 2002. "Experienced, Vicarious, and Anticipated Strain: An Exploratory Study on Physical Victimization and Delinquency." *Justice Quarterly* 19: 603–629.

———. 2006. "General Strain Theory." In *The Essential Criminology Reader,* edited by Stuart Henry and Mark M. Lanier, 155–163. Boulder, CO: Westview Press.

Agnew, Robert, Timothy Brezina, John Paul Wright, and Frances Cullen. 2002. "Strain, Personality Traits, and Delinquency: Extending General Strain Theory." *Criminology* 40: 43–72.

Agnew, Robert, and Helen Raskin White. 1992. "An Empirical Test of General Strain Theory." *Criminology* 30: 475–499.

Ahluwalia, Seema. 1991. "Currents in British Feminist Thought: The Study of Male Violence." *Critical Criminologist* 3: 5–6, 12–14.

Aichhorn, August. 1935. *Wayward Youth.* New York: Viking.

Akers, Ronald L. 1968. "Problems in the Sociology of Deviance: Social Definitions and Behavior." *Social Forces* 46: 455–465.

———. [1977] 1985. *Deviant Behavior: A Social Learning Approach.* Belmont, CA: Wadsworth.

———. 1990. "Rational Choice, Deterrence, and Social Learning Theory: The Path Not Taken." *Journal of Criminal Law and Criminology* 81: 653–676.

———. 1994. *Criminological Theories: Introduction and Evaluation.* Los Angeles: Roxbury Press.

———. 1998. *Social Learning and Social Structure: A General Theory of Crime and Deviance.* Boston: Northeastern University Press.

———. 1999. "Social Learning and Social Structure: Reply to Sampson, Morash, and Krohn." *Theoretical Criminology* 3: 477–493.

———. 2000. *Criminological Theories: Introduction, Evaluation, and Application.* 3d ed. Los Angeles: Roxbury Press.

Akers, Ronald L., Marvin D. Krohn, Lonn Lanza-Kaduce, and Marcia Radosevich. 1979. "Social Learning and Deviant Behavior: A Specific Test of a General Theory." *American Sociological Review* 44: 635–655.

Akers, Ronald L., and Christine S. Sellers. 2008. *Criminological Theories: Introduction, Evaluation, and Application.* 5th ed. Oxford: Oxford University Press.

Akers, Timothy, and Mark Lanier. 2009. "'Epidemiological Criminology': Coming Full Circle." *American Journal of Public Health* 99, no. 3: 397–402.

Alarid, Leanne Fiftal, Velmer Burton, and Francis Cullen. 2000. "Gender and Crime Among Felony Offenders: Assessing the Generality of Social Control." *Journal of Research in Crime and Delinquency* 37: 171–199.

Albonetti, Celesta A., Robert M. Hauser, John Hagan, and Ilene H. Nagel. 1989. "Criminal Justice Decision Making as a Stratification Process: The Role of Race and Stratification Resources in Pretrial Release." *Journal of Quantitative Criminology* 5: 57–82.

Albrow, Martin. 1990. Introduction to *Globalization, Knowledge, and Society,* edited by M. Albrow and E. King, 3–13. London: Sage.

Alexander, Franz, and William Healy. 1935. *Roots of Crime.* New York: Alfred A. Knopf.

Alihan, M. A. 1938. *Social Ecology: A Critical Analysis.* New York: Columbia University Press.

Alleman, Ted. 1993. "Varieties of Feminist Thought and Their Application to Crime and Criminal Justice." In *It's a Crime: Women and Justice,* edited by Roslyn Muraskin and Ted Alleman. Englewood Cliffs, NJ: Prentice-Hall.

Allen, Craig M., and Henry L. Pothast. 1994. "Distinguishing Characteristics of Male and Female Child Sex Abusers." *Journal of Offender Rehabilitation* 21: 73–88.

Allport, Gordon, W. 1937. *Personality: A Psychological Explanation.* New York: Holt.
————. 1961. *The Person in Psychology.* Boston: Beacon.
Altheide, David L. 2006. *Terrorism and the Politics of Fear.* Lanham, MD: AltaMira Press.
Altheide, David L., and Raymond Michalowski. 1999. "Fear in the News: A Discourse of Control." *Sociological Quarterly* 40: 475–503.
American Friends Service Committee. 1971. *Struggle for Justice.* New York: Hill and Wang.
American Psychiatric Association. 1994. *Diagnostic and Statistical Manual of Mental Disorders.* Washington, DC: American Psychiatric Association.
Anderson, Elijah. 1990. *Streetwise: Race, Class, and Change in an Urban Community.* Chicago: University of Chicago Press.
————. 1999. *Code of Streets: Decency, Violence, and the Moral Life of the Inner City.* New York: W. W. Norton.
————. 2008. *Against the Wall: Poor, Young, Black, and Male.* Philadelphia: University of Pennsylvania Press.
Anderson, William, and Gene Callahan. 2001. "The Roots of Racial Profiling: Why Are Police Targeting Minorities for Traffic Stops?" *Reason Magazine* (August–September). http://www.reason.com/news/show/28138.html (accessed January 4, 2009).
Antonaccio, O., and C. R. Tittle. 2007. "A Cross-National Test of Bonger's Theory of Criminality and Economic Conditions." *Criminology* 45, no. 4: 925–958.
Appiahene-Gyamfi, J. 2007. "Interpersonal Violent Crime in Ghana: The Case of Assault in Accra." *Journal of Criminal Justice* 35, no. 4: 419–431.
Arrigo, Bruce, ed. 1997. *The Margins of Justice: The Maturation of Critical Theory in Law, Crime, and Deviance.* Belmont, CA: Wadsworth.
————. 2000. Introduction to *Forensic Psychology: Issues and Controversies in Crime and Justice.* New York: Academic Press.
————. 2003. "Postmodern Justice and Critical Criminology: Positional, Relational, and Provisional Science." In *Controversies in Critical Criminology,* edited by Martin D. Schwartz and Suzanne E. Hatty, 43–55. Cincinnati: Anderson.
Arrigo, Bruce, and Dragan Milovanovic. 2009. *Revolution in Penology: Rethinking the Society of Captives.* New York: Rowman and Littlefield.
Arrigo, Bruce A., and Stacey L. Shipley. 2004. Introduction to *Forensic Psychology: Issues and Controversies in Crime and Justice.* 2d ed. New York: Academic Press.
Arrigo, Bruce, and T. R. Young. 1996. *Postmodern Criminology: Theories of Crime and Crimes of Theorists.* Red Feather Institute Transforming Sociology. Weidman, MI: Red Feather Institute.
Arter, M. L. 2008. "Stress and Deviance in Policing." *Deviant Behavior* 29, no. 1: 43–69.
Associated Press. 2008a. "N.Y. Investor Kills Himself After Losing over $1 Billion in Alleged Madoff Scam." http://www.haaretz.com/hasen/spages/1049644.html (accessed December 26, 2008).
————. 2008b. "SEC: Wall Street Kingpin with LI Ties Admits $50B Fraud." December 12. http://www.newsday.com/business/ny-bzfraud1213,0,3666375.story (accessed December 25, 2008).
Aultman, Madeline G., and Charles F. Wellford. 1979. "Towards an Integrated Model of Delinquency Causation: An Empirical Analysis." *Sociology and Social Research* 63: 316–327.
Avant, Deborah. 2006. *The Market for Force: The Consequences of Privatising Security.* Cambridge: Cambridge University Press.

Bachman, Ronet, Raymond Paternoster, and Sally Ward. 1992. "The Rationality of Sexual Offending: Testing a Deterrence/Rational Choice Conception of Sexual Assault." *Law and Society Review* 26: 343–372.

Bacon, David. 2005. "CAFTA's Vision for the Future: Privatization at Gunpoint." *Truthout/ Perspective,* May 7. http://www.americas.org/item_19488.

"Bad Vibrations." 2002. *People Magazine,* September 2, 95–97.

Baier, Colin J., and Bradley R. E. Wright. 2001. "If You Love Me, Keep My Commandments: A Meta-analysis of the Effect of Religion on Crime." *Journal of Research in Crime and Delinquency* 38: 3–21.

Bailey, W. C., and R. D. Peterson. 1989. "Murder and Capital Punishment: A Monthly Time Series Analysis of Execution Publicity." *American Sociological Review* 54: 722–742.

Baker, Laura A., Wendy Mack, Terry E. Moffitt, and Sarnoff A. Mednick. 1989. "Sex Differences in Property Crime in a Danish Adoption Cohort." *Behavior Genetics* 19: 355–370.

Baker, Paul J., and Louis E. Anderson. 1987. *Social Problems: A Critical Thinking Approach.* Belmont, CA: Wadsworth.

Bakhtin, Mikhail. 1984. *Rebelais and His World.* Bloomington: Indiana University Press.

Balkan, Sheila, Ronald Berger, and Janet Schmidt. 1980. *Crime and Deviance in America: A Critical Approach.* Belmont, CA: Wadsworth.

Ball, Richard A. 1966. "An Empirical Exploration of Neutralization Theory." *Criminologica* 4: 22–32.

Ball, Richard A., and J. Robert Lilly. 1971. "Juvenile Delinquency in an Urban County." *Criminology* 9: 69–85.

Bandura, Albert. 1969. *Principles of Behavior Modification.* New York: Holt, Rinehart, and Winston.

———. 1973. *Aggression: A Social Learning Analysis.* Englewood Cliffs, NJ: Prentice-Hall.

———. 1977. *Social Learning Theory.* Englewood Cliffs, NJ: Prentice-Hall.

———. 1986. *Social Foundation of Thought and Acquisition: A Social Cognitive Theory.* Englewood Cliffs, NJ: Prentice-Hall.

———. 1997. *Self-Efficacy: The Exercise of Control.* New York: Freeman.

———. 1999a. "A Social Cognitive Analysis of Substance Abuse: An Agentic Perspective." *Psychological Science* 10: 214–217.

———. 1999b. "Social Cognitive Theory of Personality." In *The Coherence of Personality: Social-Cognitive Bases of Consistency, Variability, and Organization,* edited by Daniel Cervone and Yuichi Shoda, 185–225. New York: Guilford Press.

———. 2001a. "Social Cognitive Theory: An Agentic Perspective." *Annual Review of Psychology* 52: 1–26.

———. 2001b. "Social Cognitive Theory of Personality." In *Handbook of Personality: Theory and Research,* edited by Lawrence A. Pervin and Oliver P. John, 154–196. 2d ed. New York: Guilford Press.

Bandura, Albert, Gian Vittorio Caprara, Claudio Barbaranelli, Concetta Pastorelli, and Camillo Regalia. 2001. "Sociocognitive Self-Regulatory Mechanisms Governing Transgressive Behavior." *Journal of Personality and Social Psychology* 80, no. 1: 125–135.

Bandura, Albert, and R. Walters. 1963. *Social Learning and Personality Development.* New York: Holt, Rinehart, and Winston.

Bao, W., A. Haas, and Y. Pi. 2007. "Life Strain, Coping, and Delinquency in the People's Republic of China: An Empirical Test of General Strain Theory from a Matching Perspective in Social Support." *International Journal of Offender Therapy and Comparative Criminology* 51, no. 1: 9–24.

Barak, Gregg. 1988. "Newsmaking Criminology: Reflections on the Media, Intellectuals, and Crime." *Justice Quarterly* 5: 565–587.

———, ed. 1991. *Crimes by the Capitalist State: An Introduction to State Criminality.* Albany: State University of New York Press.

———, ed. 1994. *Media, Process, and the Social Construction of Crime: Studies in Newsmaking Criminology.* New York: Garland.

———, ed. 1996. *Representing O. J.: Murder, Criminal Justice, and Mass Culture.* Albany, NY: Harrow and Heston.

———. 1998. *Integrating Criminologies.* Boston: Allyn and Bacon.

———. 2000. *Crime and Crime Control: A Global View.* Westport, CT: Greenwood Press.

———. 2001. "Crime and Crime Control in an Age of Globalization: A Theoretical Dissection." *Critical Criminology* 10: 57–72.

———. 2003. *Violence and Nonviolence: Pathways to Understanding.* Thousand Oaks, CA: Sage.

———. 2006. "Applying Integrative Theory: A Reciprocal Theory of Violence and Nonviolence." In *The Essential Criminology Reader,* edited by Stuart Henry and Mark M. Lanier, 336–346. Boulder, CO: Westview Press.

———. 2009. *Criminology: An Integrated Approach.* 2d ed. New York: Rowman and Littlefield.

Barak, Gregg, Paul Leighton, and Jeanne Flavin. 2006. *Class, Race, Gender, and Crime: The Social Realities of Justice in America.* 2d ed. New York: Rowman and Littlefield.

Barkley, Charles. 2006. *Who's Afraid of a Large Black Man? Race, Power, Fame, Identity, and Why Everyone Should Read My Book.* New York: Riverhead Freestyle.

Barkow, J. H., L. Cosmides, and J. Tooby. 1992. *The Adapted Mind: Evolutionary Psychology and the Generation of Culture.* Oxford: Oxford University Press.

Barlow, David, and Melissa Hickman Barlow. 2002. "A Survey of African American Police Officers." *Police Quarterly* 5: 334–358.

Barlow, David, Melissa Hickman Barlow, and Ted Chiricos. 1993. "Long Economic Cycles and the Criminal-Justice System in the United States." *Crime, Law, and Social Change* 19: 143–169.

———. 1995. "Mobilizing Support for Social Control in a Declining Economy: Exploring Ideologies of Crime Within Crime News." *Crime and Delinquency* 41: 191–204.

Baron, S. W. 2006. "Street Youth, Strain Theory, and Crime." *Journal of Criminal Justice* 34, no. 2: 209–223.

Barrett, Michele, and Mary McIntosh. 1985. "Ethnocentrism and Socialist Feminism Theory." *Feminist Review* 20: 23–47.

Barry, Kathleen. 1979. *Female Sexual Slavery.* Englewood Cliffs, NJ: Prentice-Hall.

Bartlett, K. 1991. "Feminist Legal Methods." In *Feminist Legal Theory,* edited by K. Bartlett and R. Kennedy. Boulder, CO: Westview Press.

Bartol, Curt R. 1991. *Criminal Behavior: A Psychological Approach.* 3d ed. Englewood Cliffs, NJ: Prentice-Hall.

———. 1999. *Criminal Behavior: A Psychological Approach.* Upper Saddle River, NJ: Prentice-Hall.

Bartol, Curt R., and A. M. Bartol. 1994. *Psychology and Law: Research and Application.* Pacific Grove, CA: Brooks/Cole.

———. 2006. *Current Perspectives in Forensic Psychology and Criminal Justice.* Thousand Oaks, CA: Sage Publications.

Bartusch, Dawn Jeglum, and Ross L. Matsueda. 1996. "Gender, Reflected Appraisals, and Labeling: A Cross-Group Test of an Interactionist Theory of Delinquency." *Social Forces* 75: 145–176.

Baskin, Deborah, Ira Sommers, and Henry Steadman. 1991. "Assessing the Impact of Psychiatric Impairment on Prison Violence." *Journal of Criminal Justice* 19: 271–280.

Baumer, E. P., and R. Gustafson. 2007. "Social Organization and Instrumental Crime: Assessing the Empirical Validity of Classic and Contemporary Anomie Theories." *Criminology* 45, no. 3: 617–663.

Beccaria, Cesare. [1764] 1963. *On Crimes and Punishments.* Translated by Henry Paolucci. Indianapolis: Bobbs-Merrill.

Beck, Aaron T. 1999. *Prisoners of Hate: The Cognitive Basis of Anger, Hostility, and Violence.* New York: Perennial.

Beck, Ulrick. 1992. *Risk Society: Towards a New Modernity.* London: Sage.

Becker, Gary S. 1968. "Crime and Punishment: An Economic Approach." *Journal of Political Economy* 76: 169–217.

———. 2006. "On the Economics of Capital Punishment." *Economists' Voice* 3, no. 3. http://www.bepress.com/ev/vol3/iss3/art4.

Becker, Howard. [1963] 1973. *Outsiders: Studies in the Sociology of Deviance.* New York: Free Press.

Becker, Paul J., Arthur J. Jipson, and Alan S. Bruce. 2002. "*State of Indiana v. Ford Motor Company* Revisited." *American Journal of Criminal Justice* 26, no. 2: 181–202.

Beirne, Piers. 1979. "Empiricism and the Critique of Marxism on Law and Crime." *Social Problems* 26: 373–385.

———. 1991. "Inventing Criminology: The 'Science of Man' in Cesare Beccaria's *Dei Delitti e Delle Pene* (1764)." *Criminology* 29: 777–820.

———. 1993. *Inventing Criminology: Essays on the Rise of "Homo Criminalis."* Albany: State University of New York Press.

———. 1994. "The Law Is an Ass: Reading E. P. Evans' *The Medieval Prosecution and Capital Punishment of Animals.*" *Animals and Society* 2: 27–46.

Beirne, Piers, and Joan Hill. 1991. *Comparative Criminology: An Annotated Bibliography.* Research and Bibliographical Guides in Criminal Justice, no. 3. New York: Greenwood Press.

Beirne, Piers, and James Messerschmidt. [1991] 1995. *Criminology.* 2d ed. Fort Worth, TX: Harcourt Brace College Publishers.

———. 2000. *Criminology.* 3d ed. Boulder, CO: Westview Press.

Bellair, Paul E. 1997. "Social Interaction and Community Crime: Examining the Importance of Neighborhood Networks." *Criminology* 35: 677–703.

———. 2000. "Informal Surveillance and Street Crime: A Complex Relationship." *Criminology* 38: 137–169.

Bello, W. 1999. "Is the 'Structural Adjustment' Approach Really and Truly Dead?" *Business-World,* Internet Edition, November 8. http://www.bworld.com.ph/current/today.html.

Benda, Brent B., and Leanne Whiteside. 1995. "Testing an Integrated Model of Delinquency Using LISREL." *Journal of Social Service Research* 21: 1–32.

Bender, Frederic. 1986. *Karl Marx: The Essential Writings.* Boulder, CO: Westview Press.

Bennett, Richard R. 1991. "Routine Activities: A Cross-National Assessment of a Criminological Perspective." *Social Forces* 70: 147–163.

Bennett, Richard R., and Jeanne M. Flavin. 1994. "Determinants of Fear of Crime: The Effect of Cultural Setting." *Justice Quarterly* 11: 357–381.

Bennett, Trevor. 1986. "A Decision-Making Approach to Opioid Addiction." In *The Reasoning Criminal,* edited by Derek B. Cornish and Ronald V. Clarke. New York: Springer-Verlag.

Bennett, Trevor, and Richard Wright. 1984. *Burglars on Burglary.* Aldershot, UK: Gower.

Bentham, Jeremy. [1765] 1970. Introduction to *The Principles of Morals and Legislation,* edited by J. H. Burns and H. L. A. Hart. London: Athlone Press.

Berg, Bruce. [1989] 2000. *Qualitative Research Methods for the Social Sciences.* Boston: Allyn and Bacon.

Bernard, Thomas J., J. M. Calnon, and R. S. Engel. 2005. "Efficiency and the New Differential Processing." *Journal of Crime and Justice* 28, no. 1: 79–105.

Bernard, Thomas J., and Jeffrey B. Snipes. 1996. In *Crime and Justice: A Review of Research,* edited by Michael Tonry. Vol. 20. Chicago: University of Chicago Press.

Bernard, Thomas J., Jeffrey B. Snipes, and Alexander L. Gerould. 2009. *Vould's Theoretical Criminology.* 6th edition. New York: Oxford University Press.

Bernburg, Jon Gunnar. 2002. "Anomie, Social Change, and Crime: A Theoretical Examination of Institutional-Anomie Theory." *British Journal of Criminology* 42: 729–742.

Bernburg, Jon Gunnar, M. D. Krohn, and C. J. Rivera. 2006. "Official Labeling, Criminal Embeddedness, and Subsequent Delinquency: A Longitudinal Test of Labeling Theory." *Journal of Research in Crime and Delinquency* 43, no. 1: 67–88.

Best, Steven, and Douglas Kellner. 1991. *Postmodern Theory: Critical Interrogations.* Basingstoke, UK: Macmillan.

———. 1997. *The Postmodern Turn.* New York: Guilford Press.

BET. 2007. *American Gangster: The Chambers Brothers.* http://www.bet.com/onblast/?chan=3&id=582&itype=e (accessed December 31, 2008).

Beukman, Brenda. 2000. "Attitudes Toward Women and Crime." *Acta Criminologica* 13, no. 3: 131–140.

Bianchi, Herman, and Rene Van Swaaningen, eds. 1986. *Abolitionism: Toward a Nonrepressive Approach to Crime.* Amsterdam: Free University Press.

Biderman, Albert, and Albert J. Reiss Jr. 1980. *Data Sources on White-Collar Law-Breaking.* Washington, DC: U.S. Government Printing Office.

Billings, F. J., T. Taylor, and J. Burns. 2007. "Can Reinforcement Induce Children to Falsely Incriminate Themselves?" *Law and Human Behavior* 31, no. 2: 125–139.

Blackwater, USA. 2008. "2008 Training Course Catalog." http://www.blackwaterusa.com/images/pdf/Course%20cat.pdf (accessed March 17, 2009).

Blatier, Catherine. 2000. "Locus of Control, Causal Attributions, and Self-Esteem: A Comparison Between Prisoners." *International Journal of Offender Therapy and Comparative Criminology* 44: 97–110.

Blomberg, Thomas, and Stanley Cohen, eds. 1995. *Punishment and Social Control.* Hawthorne, NY: Aldine de Gruyter.

Bloom, Richard W. 2003. "The Evolution of Scientific Psychology and Public Policy: On Violence and Its Antidotes." In *Evolutionary Psychology and Violence: A Primer for Policymakers and Public Policy Advocates,* edited by Richard W. Bloom and Nancy Kimberly Dess, 1–22. Westport, CT: Praeger.

Bloom, Richard W., and Nancy Kimberly Dess, eds. 2003. *Evolutionary Psychology and Violence: A Primer for Policymakers and Public Policy Advocates.* Westport, CT: Praeger.

Blumer, Herbert. 1969. *Symbolic Interactionism: Perspective and Method.* Englewood Cliffs, NJ: Prentice-Hall.

Blumstein, Alfred, Jacqueline Cohen, Susan E. Martin, and Martin H. Tonry, eds. 1983. *Research on Sentencing: The Search for Reform.* Vol. 1. Washington, DC: National Academy Press.

Blumstein, Alfred, Jacqueline Cohen, and Richard Rosenfeld. 1991. "Trend and Deviation in Crime Rates: A Comparison of UCR and NCS Data for Burglary and Robbery." *Criminology* 29: 237–264.

———. 1992. "The UCR-NCS Relationship Revisited: A Reply to Menard." *Criminology* 30: 115–124.

Blumstein, Alfred, Jacqueline Cohen, Jeffery Roth, and Christy Visher, eds. 1986. *Criminal Careers and "Career Criminals."* 2 vols. Washington, DC: National Academy Press.

Boal, Mark. 2008. "Everyone Will Remember Me as Some Sort of Monster." *Rolling Stone,* August 21, 73–80.

Bogan, Kathleen M. 1990. "Constructing Felony Sentencing Guidelines in an Already Crowded State: Oregon Breaks New Ground." *Crime and Delinquency* 36: 467–487.

Bohm, Robert M. 1982. "Radical Criminology: An Explication." *Criminology* 19: 565–589.

———. 1989. "Humanism and the Death Penalty, with Special Emphasis on the Post-Furman Experience." *Justice Quarterly* 6: 173–195.

———. 1991. "American Death Penalty Opinion, 1936–1986: A Critical Examination of the Gallup Polls." In *The Death Penalty in America: Current Research,* edited by Robert Bohm. Cincinnati: Anderson.

———. 1993. "Social Relationships That Arguably Should Be Criminal Although They Are Not: On the Political Economy of Crime." In *Political Crime in Contemporary America: A Critical Approach,* edited by Kenneth Tunnell. New York: Garland.

———. 1997a. *A Primer on Crime and Delinquency.* Belmont, CA: Wadsworth.

———. 1997b. "Review of Stuart Henry and Dragan Milovanovic's Constitutive Criminology." *Criminologist* 22: 15–16.

Bohm, Robert M., and Keith N. Haley. 1999. *Introduction to Criminal Justice.* 2d ed. New York: Glencoe/McGraw-Hill.

Boies, Henry M. 1893. *Prisoners and Paupers.* New York: G. P. Putnam.

Boland, Barbara. 1996. "What Is Community Prosecution?" *National Institute of Justice Journal* 231 (August): 35–40.

Bonger, Willem. [1905] 1916. *Criminality and Economic Conditions.* Boston: Little, Brown.

Bonta, James, Moira Law, and Karl Hanson. 1998. "The Prediction of Criminal and Violent Recidivism Among Mentally Disordered Offenders: A Meta-analysis." *Psychological Bulletin* 123: 123–142.

Booth, Alan, and D. Wayne Osgood. 1993. "The Influence of Testosterone on Deviance in Adulthood: Assessing and Explaining the Relationship." *Criminology* 31: 93–117.

Bordo, Susan. 1990. "Feminism, Postmodernism, and Gender Scepticism." In *Feminism/Postmodernism,* edited by Linda J. Nicholson. New York: Routledge.

Borgmann, Albert. 1992. *Crossing the Postmodern Divide.* Chicago: University of Chicago Press.

Bottomley, A. Keith. 1979. *Criminology in Focus.* London: Martin Robertson.

Bourdieu, Pierre. 1977. *Outline of a Theory of Practice.* Cambridge: Cambridge University Press.

Bowers, William, and Glenn Pierce. 1975. "The Illusion of Deterrence in Issac Ehrlich's Research on Capital Punishment." *Yale Law Journal* 85: 187–208.

———. 1980. "Deterrence or Brutalization? What Is the Effect of Executions?" *Crime and Delinquency* 26: 453–484.

Bowlby, John. 1946. *Forty-four Juvenile Thieves: Their Characters and Home-Life.* London: Bailliere, Tindall, and Cox.

———. 1951. *Maternal Care and Mental Health.* Geneva: World Health Organization.

———. 1988. *A Secure Base: Clinical Applications of Attachment Theory.* London: Routledge.

Box, Steven. [1971] 1981. *Deviance, Reality, and Society.* New York: Holt, Rinehart, and Winston.

———. 1977. "Hyperactivity: The Scandalous Silence." *New Society* 42: 458–460.

———. 1983. *Power, Crime, and Mystification.* London: Tavistock.

Box, Steven, and Chris Hale. 1983. "Liberation and Female Delinquency in England and Wales." *British Journal of Criminology* 23: 35–49.

———. 1985. "Unemployment, Imprisonment, and Prison Overcrowding." *Contemporary Crises* 9: 209–228.

———. 1986. "Unemployment, Crime, and Imprisonment and the Enduring Problem of Prison Overcrowding." In *Confronting Crime,* edited by Roger Matthews and Jock Young. London: Sage.

Bracewell, Michael C. 1990. "Peacemaking: A Missing Link in Criminology." *Criminologist* 15: 3–5.

Braithwaite, John. 1989. *Crime, Shame, and Reintegration.* Cambridge: Cambridge University Press.

———. 1995. "Reintegrative Shaming, Republicanism, and Public Policy." In *Crime and Public Policy: Putting Theory to Work,* edited by Hugh D. Barlow. Boulder, CO: Westview Press.

———. 2002. *Restorative Justice and Responsive Regulation.* New York: Oxford University Press.

Braithwaite, John, and Steve Mugford. 1994. "Conditions of Successful Reintegration Ceremonies: Dealing with Young Offenders." *British Journal of Criminology* 342: 139–171.

Brantingham, Paul J., and Patricia L. Brantingham. 1991. *Environmental Criminology.* Prospect Heights, IL: Waveland Press.

Brasor, Philip. 2003. "Selfishness and Greed Motor the American Dream." *Japan Times,* April 6. http://search.japantimes.co.jp/cgi-bin/fd20030406pb.html (accessed January 1, 2009).

Brassett-Grundy, A., and N. R. Butler. 2004. "Prevalence and Adult Outcomes of Attention-Deficit/Hyperactivity Disorder: Evidence from a 30-Year Prospective." BG Occasional Paper, no. 2. London: Bedford Group for Lifecourse and Statistical Studies, Institute of Education.

Braukmann, Curtis J., and Montrose Wolf. 1987. "Behaviorally Based Group Homes for Juvenile Offenders." In *Behavioral Approaches to Crime and Delinquency: A Handbook of Applications Research and Concepts,* edited by Edward K. Morris and Curtis J. Braukmann. New York: Plenum.

Brayton, Steven. 2002. "Outsourcing War: Mercenaries and the Privatization of Peacekeeping." *Journal of International Affairs* 55: 303–330.

Breetzke, Gregory. 2008. "Exploratory Spatial Data Analysis (ESDA) of Violent, Economic, and Sexual Offenders in the City of Tshwane, South Africa." *Acta Criminologica: CRIMSA Conference* 1: 131–149.

Brennan, Luann. 2003. *Restoring the Justice in Criminal Justice.* Detroit: Wayne State University, Department of Interdisciplinary Studies.

Brezina, Timothy. 1996. "Adapting to Strain: An Examination of Delinquent Coping Responses." *Criminology* 34: 39–60.

Brezina, Timothy, Alex P. Piquero, and Paul Mazerolle. 2001. "Student Anger and Aggressive Behavior in School: An Initial Test of Agnew's Macro-Level Strain Theory." *Journal of Research in Crime and Delinquency* 38: 362–386.

Broidy, Lisa M. 2001. "A Test of General Strain Theory." *Criminology* 39: 9–35.

Bromberg, Walter. 1965. *Crime and the Mind: A Psychiatric Analysis of Crime and Punishment.* New York: Macmillan.

Brown, A. 2007. "The Amazing Mutiny at the Dartmoor Convict Prison." *British Journal of Criminology* 47, no. 2: 276–292.

Brown, Beverly. 1988. "Review of Capitalism, Patriarchy, and Crime." *International Journal of the Sociology of Law* 16: 408–412.

———. 1990. "Reassessing the Critique of Biologism." In *Feminist Perspectives in Criminology,* edited by Loraine Gelsthorpe and Allison Morris. Milton Keynes, UK: Open University Press.

Brownfield, David, and Ann Marie Sorenson. 1994. "Sibship Size and Sibling Delinquency." *Deviant Behavior* 15: 45–61.

Brownmiller, Susan. 1975. *Against Our Will: Men, Women, and Rape.* London: Secker and Warburg.

Brownridge, Douglas A. 2004. "Male Partner Violence Against Women in Stepfamilies: An Analysis of Risk and Explanations in the Canadian Milieu." *Violence and Victims* 19, no. 1: 17–36.

Bruinsma, Gerben J. N. 1992. "Differential Association Theory Reconsidered: An Extension and Its Empirical Test." *Journal of Quantitative Criminology* 8: 29–49.

Bruner, Jerome. 1987. "Life as Narrative." *Social Research* 54: 11–32.

———. 1990. *Acts of Meaning.* Cambridge, MA: Harvard University Press.

Buckley, Walter. 1967. *Sociology and Modern Systems Theory.* Englewood Cliffs, NJ: Prentice-Hall.

Bull, Simone. 2004. "'The Land of Murder, Cannibalism, and All Kinds of Atrocious Crimes?': Maori and Crime in New Zealand, 1853–1919." *British Journal of Criminology* 44, no. 4: 496–519.

Burbach, R., O. Nunez, and B. Kagarlitsky. 1997. *Globalization and Its Discontents.* London: Pluto Press.

Bureau of Justice Statistics. 1981. *Dictionary of Criminal Justice Data Terminology.* Washington, DC: U.S. Department of Justice.

———. 1983. "The Seriousness of Crime: Results of a National Survey." In *Report to the Nation on Crime and Justice.* Washington, DC: U.S. Department of Justice.

———. 1988. *Report to the Nation on Crime and Justice.* Washington, DC: U.S. Department of Justice.

———. 1993. *Highlights from 20 Years of Surveying Crime Victims: The National Crime Victimization Survey, 1973–92.* Washington, DC: U.S. Department of Justice.

———. 1994. *Sourcebook of Criminal Justice Statistics, 1993.* Washington, DC: U.S. Department of Justice.

———. 1995. *Sourcebook of Criminal Justice Statistics, 1994.* Washington, DC: U.S. Department of Justice.

———. 1996. *Sourcebook of Criminal Justice Statistics, 1995.* Washington, DC: U.S. Department of Justice.

———. 1998. *School Crime Supplement to the National Crime Victimization Survey, 1989 and 1995.* Washington, DC: U.S. Department of Justice, Office of Justice Programs.

———. 2006. *National Crime Victimization Study: Criminal Victimization, 2005.* NCJ 214644. Washington, DC: Department of Justice, Bureau of Justice Statistics.

Bureau of Labor Statistics. 2006. "Security Guards and Gambling." *Occupational Outlook Handbook, 2006–07 Edition.* http://www.bls.gov/oco/ocos159.htm.

Burgess, Ernest W. 1925. "The Growth of the City." In *The City,* edited by Robert E. Park, Ernest W. Burgess, and Roderick D. McKenzie. Chicago: University of Chicago Press.

———. 1950. "Comment to Hartung." *American Journal of Sociology* 56: 25–34.

Burgess, P. K. 1972. "Eysenck's Theory of Criminality: A New Approach." *British Journal of Criminology* 12: 74–82.

Burgess, Robert L., and Ronald L. Akers. 1966. "A Differential Association: Reinforcement Theory of Criminal Behavior." *Social Problems* 14: 128–147.

Burkett, Steven R., and David Ward. 1993. "A Note on Perceptual Deterrence, Religiously Based Condemnation, and Social Control." *Criminology* 31: 119–134.

Burkett, Steven R., and Mervin White. 1974. "Hellfire and Delinquency: Another Look." *Journal for the Scientific Study of Religion* 13: 455–462.

Bursik, Robert J., Jr. 1988. "Social Disorganization and Theories of Crime and Delinquency: Problems and Prospects." *Criminology* 26: 519–551.

———. 1989. "Political Decision-Making and Ecological Models of Delinquency: Conflict and Consensus." In *Theoretical Integration in the Study of Deviance and Crime,* edited by S. F. Messner, M. D. Krohn, and A. E. Liska. Albany: State University of New York Press.

———. 1999. "The Informal Control of Crime Through Neighborhood Networks." *Sociological Focus* 32: 85–97.

Bursik, Robert J., Jr., and Harold G. Grasmick. 1993a. "Economic Deprivation and Neighborhood Crime Rates, 1960–1980." *Law and Society Review* 27: 263–283.

———. 1993b. *Neighborhoods and Crime: The Dimensions of Effective Community Control.* New York: Lexington.

———. 1995. "Neighborhood-Based Networks and the Control of Crime and Delinquency." In *Crime and Public Policy: Putting Theory to Work,* edited by Hugh D. Barlow. Boulder, CO: Westview Press.

Bursik, Robert J., Jr., and Jim Webb. 1982. "Community Change and Patterns of Delinquency." *American Journal of Sociology* 88: 24–42.

Burton, Velmer S., Frances T. Cullen, David Evans, and R. Gregory Dunaway. 1994. "Reconsidering Strain Theory: Operationalization, Rival Theories, and Adult Criminality." *Journal of Quantitative Criminology* 10: 213–239.

Cadoret, R. J. 1978. "Psychopathology in Adopted-Away Offspring of Biologic Parents with Antisocial Behavior." *Archives of General Psychiatry* 35: 176–184.

Cadoret, R. J., W. R. Yates, E. Troughton, G. Woodworth, and M. Stewart. 1995. "Adoption Study Demonstrating Two Genetic Pathways to Drug Use." *Archives of General Psychiatry* 52: 42–52.

Cain, Maureen. 1989. *Growing Up Good: Policing the Behavior of Girls in Europe.* London: Sage.

Calavita, Kitty, and Henry Pontell. 1993. "Savings and Loan Fraud as Organized Crime: Toward a Conceptual Typology of Corporate Illegality." *Criminology* 31: 519–548.

Calhoun, Craig, and Henryk Hiller. 1986. "Coping with Insidious Injuries: The Case of Johns-Manville Corporation and Asbestos Exposure." *Social Problems* 35: 162–181.

Calley, William L. 1974. "So This Is What War Is." In *In Their Own Behalf: Voices from the Margin,* edited by Charles H. McCaghy, James K. Skipper Jr., and Mark Lefton. Englewood Cliffs, NJ: Prentice-Hall.

Campaign for Effective Crime Policy. 1998. *Three Strikes Five Years Later.* Washington, DC: Campaign for Effective Crime Policy.

Campbell, Anne. 1981. *Girl Delinquents.* Oxford: Basil Blackwell.

———. 1984. *The Girls in the Gang*. Cambridge: Basil Blackwell.

———. 1993. *Men, Women, and Aggression*. New York: Basic Books.

———. 1999. "Staying Alive: Evolution, Culture, and Women's Intrasexual Aggression." *Behavioral and Brain Sciences* 22: 203–214.

Campbell, Anne, Steven Muncer, and Daniel Bibel. 1998. "Female-Female Criminal Assault: An Evolutionary Perspective." *Journal of Research in Crime and Delinquency* 35: 413–428.

Canadian Law Commission. 2003. *What Is a Crime?* Ottawa: Canadian Law Commission.

Cao, Liqun. 2004. "Is American Society More Anomic? A Test of Merton's Theory with Cross-National Data." *International Journal of Comparative and Applied Criminal Justice* 28: 17–31.

Capowich, George E. 2003. "The Conditioning Effects of Neighborhood Ecology on Burglary Victimization." *Criminal Justice and Behavior* 30: 39–61.

Capowich, George E., Paul Mazerolle, and Alex Piquero. 2001. "General Strain Theory, Situational Anger, and Social Networks: An Assessment of Conditioning Influences." *Journal of Criminal Justice* 29: 445–461.

Caputo, Alicia A., Paul J. Frick, and Stanley L. Brodsky. 1999. "Family Violence and Juvenile Sex Offending." *Criminal Justice and Behavior* 26: 338–356.

Carey, Gregory. 1992. "Twin Imitation for Antisocial Behavior: Implications for Genetic and Family Research." *Journal of Abnormal Psychology* 101: 18–25.

Carlen, Pat. 1992. "Women, Crime, Feminism, and Realism." In *Realist Criminology: Crime Control and Policing in the 1990s*, edited by John Lowman and Brian D. MacLean, 203–220. Toronto: University of Toronto Press.

Carlisle, E. Moody, Thomas B. Marvell, and Robert J. Kaminski. 2002. *Unintended Consequences: Three-Strikes Laws and the Murders of Police Officers*. Washington, DC: National Institute of Justice.

Carmin, Cheryl, Fred Wallbrown, Raymond Ownby, and Robert Barnett. 1989. "A Factor Analysis of the MMPI in an Offender Population." *Criminal Justice and Behavior* 16: 486–494.

Carrabine, Eamonn. 2001. "Incapacitation." In *The Sage Dictionary of Criminology*, edited by E. McLaughlin and J. Muncie, 146–147. London: Sage.

Carrington, K. 2006. "Does Feminism Spoil Girls? Explanations for Official Rises in Female Delinquency." *Australian and New Zealand Journal of Criminology* 39, no. 1: 34–53.

Carver, Terrell. 1987. *A Marx Dictionary*. Cambridge: Polity.

Caspi, Avshalom, Terrie E. Moffitt, Phil A. Silva, Magda Stouthamer-Loeber, Robert F. Kruega, and Pamela S. Schmutte. 1994. "Are Some People Crime-Prone? Replications of the Personality Crime Relationship Across Countries, Genders, Races, and Methods." *Criminology* 32: 163–195.

Cass, Ronald A. 2008. "Bernard Madoff and Affinity Fraud." http://www.speroforum.com/a/17332/Bernard-Madoff-and-affinity-fraud (accessed December 22, 2008).

Caulfield, Susan L. 2000. "Creating Peaceable Schools." In "School Violence," edited by William Hinkle and Stuart Henry. Special issue, *Annals of the American Academy of Political and Social Science* 567.

Caulfield, Susan L., and Nancy Wonders. 1994. "Gender and Justice: Feminist Contributions to Criminology." In *Varieties of Criminology: Readings from a Dynamic Discipline*, edited by Gregg Barak. Westport, CT: Praeger.

CDCR [California Department of Corrections]. 2009. http://www.cdcr.ca.gov/ (accessed January 2, 2009).

Center for the Advancement of Human Rights. 2003. *Florida Responds to Human Trafficking.* Tallahassee: Florida State University.

Cernkovich, Steven A., and Peggy C. Giordano. 1987. "Family Relationships and Delinquency." *Criminology* 25: 295–319.

Cernkovich, Steven A., Peggy C. Giordano, and Jennifer Rudolph. 2000. "Race, Crime, and the American Dream." *Journal of Research in Crime and Delinquency* 37: 131–170.

Cernkovich, Steven A., N. Lanctot, and P. C. Giordano. 2008. "Predicting Adolescent and Adult Antisocial Behavior Among Adjudicated Delinquent Females." *Crime and Delinquency* 54, no. 1: 3–33.

Cha, Ariana Eunjung. 2004. "Underclass of Workers Created in Iraq." *Washington Post,* July 1, A1.

Chambliss, William J. 1973. "The Saints and the Roughnecks." *Society* 11: 24–31.

———. 1975. "Toward a Political Economy of Crime." *Theory and Society* 2: 149–170.

———. 1988. *Exploring Criminology.* New York: Macmillan.

———. 1989. "On Trashing Marxist Criminology." *Criminology* 27: 231–238.

Chambliss, William J., and Robert B. Seidman. [1971] 1982. *Law, Order, and Power.* 2d ed. Reading, MA: Addison-Wesley.

Chamlin, Mitchell B. 1989. "A Macro-Social Analysis of the Change in Robbery and Homicide Rates: Controlling for Static and Dynamic Effects." *Sociological Focus* 22: 275–286.

Chamlin, Mitchell B., and John Cochran. 1995. "Assessing Messner and Rosenfeld's Institutional Anomie Theory: A Partial Test." *Criminology* 33: 411–429.

———. 2007. "An Evaluation of the Assumptions That Underlie Institutional Anomie Theory." *Theoretical Criminology* 11, no. 1: 39–61.

Champion, Dean J. 1997. *The Roxbury Dictionary of Criminal Justice.* Los Angeles: Roxbury Press.

Chappell, Duncan, Gilbert Geis, Stephen Schafer, and Larry Siegel. 1971. "Forcible Rape: A Comparative Study of Offenses Known to the Police in Boston and Los Angeles." In *Studies in the Sociology of Sex,* edited by James Henslin. New York: Appleton Century Crofts.

Chermak, Steven. 1994. "Body Count News: How Crime Is Presented in the News Media." *Justice Quarterly* 11: 561–582.

Chesler, Phyllis. 2008. "Madoff the Jew: The Media's Hypocritical Obsession with the Fraudster's Faith." *Jewcy News,* December 23. http://www.jewcy.com/tags/jewish_philanthropies (accessed December 26, 2008).

Chesney-Lind, Meda. 1986. "Women and Crime: The Female Offender." *Signs* 12: 78–96.

———. 1989. "Girl's Crime and Woman's Place: Toward a Feminist Model of Female Delinquency." *Crime and Delinquency* 35: 5–29.

———. 1997. *The Female Offender: Girls, Women, and Crime.* Thousand Oaks, CA: Sage.

———. 2006. "Patriarchy, Crime, and Justice: Feminist Criminology in an Era of Backlash." *Feminist Criminology* 1, no. 1: 6–26.

Chesney-Lind, Meda, and Karlene Faith. 2001. "What About Feminism? Engendering Theory-Making in Criminology." In *Explaining Criminals and Crime,* edited by Raymond Paternoster and Ronet Bachman, 287–302. Los Angeles: Roxbury Press.

Chesney-Lind, Meda, and Randall G. Sheldon. 1992. *Girls, Delinquency, and Juvenile Justice.* Pacific Grove, CA: Brooks/Cole.

Chin, Ko-lin. 1990. *Chinese Subculture and Criminality: Non-traditional Crime Groups in America.* Westport, CT: Greenwood.

Chiricos, Theodore G., and Gordon P. Waldo. 1975. "Socioeconomic Status and Criminal Sentencing: An Empirical Assessment of a Conflict Proposition." *American Sociological Review* 40: 753–772.

Christiansen, Karl O. 1977. "A Preliminary Study of Criminality Among Twins." In *Biological Basis of Criminal Behavior,* edited by Sarnoff A. Mednick and Karl O. Christiansen. New York: Gardner.

Christie, Nils. 1977. "Conflicts as Property." *British Journal of Criminology* 17: 1–19.

Cilliers, Jakkie. 2003. "Peacekeeping, Africa, and the Emerging Global Security Architecture." *African Security Review* 12: 111–114.

Cintron, Ralph. 1981. *The Limits to Pain.* Oxford: Martin Robertson.

———. 2000. "Listening to What the Streets Say: Vengeance as Ideology?" In "School Violence," edited by William Hinkle and Stuart Henry. Special issue, *Annals of the American Academy of Political and Social Science* 567.

Clark, William L., and William L. Marshall. 1978. "Legal Definitions of Crime, Criminal, and Rape." In *Crime in Society,* edited by Leonard D. Savitz and Norman Johnston. New York: John Wiley.

Clarke, Ronald V., ed. 1997. *Situational Crime Prevention: Successful Case Studies.* Guilderland, NY: Harrow and Heston.

Clarke, Ronald V., and Derek B. Cornish, eds. 1983. *Crime Control in Britain: A Review of Policy and Research.* Albany: State University of New York Press.

———. 1985. "Modeling Offenders' Decisions: A Framework for Research and Policy." In *Crime and Justice and Annual Review of Research,* edited by Michael Tonry and Norval Morris. Vol. 6. Chicago: University of Chicago Press.

Clarke, Ronald V., and Patricia Mayhew. 1980. *Designing Out Crime.* London: Her Majesty's Printing Office.

Clear, Todd R. 1996. "Towards a Corrections of 'Place': The Challenge of 'Community' in Corrections." *National Institute of Justice Journal* 231 (August): 52–56.

Cleckly, Hervey. 1941. *The Mask of Insanity.* St. Louis: Mosby.

Clinard, Marshall B. 1983. *Corporate Ethics and Crime: The Role of Management.* Beverly Hills, CA: Sage.

Clinard, Marshall B., and Richard Quinney. 1973. *Criminal Behavior Systems.* New York: Holt, Rinehart, and Winston.

Clinard, Marshall B., and Peter C. Yeager. 1980. *Corporate Crime.* New York: Free Press.

Cloward, Richard A. 1959. "Illegitimate Means, Anomie, and Deviant Behavior." *American Sociological Review* 24: 164–176.

Cloward, Richard A., and Lloyd Ohlin. 1960. *Delinquency and Opportunity.* New York: Free Press.

CNN.com. 2007. "Wilson Released After Two Years Behind Bars for Teen Sex Conviction." http://www.cnn.com/2007/US/law/10/26/wilson.freed/index.html (accessed March 19, 2009).

Coccaro, E. F., and R. J. Kavoussi. 1996. "Neurotransmitter Correlates of Impulsive Aggression." In *Aggression and Violence: Genetic, Neurobiological, and Biosocial Perspectives,* edited by D. M. Stoff and R. B. Carns, 67–99. Mahwah, NJ: Lawrence Erlbaum Associates.

Cochran, John K., and Mitchell B. Chamlin. 2000. "Deterrence and Brutalization: The Dual Effects of Executions." *Justice Quarterly* 17, no. 4: 685–706.

Cochran, John K., Mitchell B. Chamlin, and Mark Seth. 1994. "Deterrence or Brutalization? An Impact Assessment of Oklahoma's Return to Capital Punishment." *Criminology* 32: 107–134.

Cochrane, Raymond. 1974. "Crime and Personality: Theory and Evidence." *Bulletin of the British Psychological Society* 27: 19–22.

Cohen, Albert K. 1955. *Delinquent Boys*. New York: Free Press.

———. 1965. "The Sociology of the Deviant Act: Anomie Theory and Beyond." *American Sociological Review* 30: 5–14.

———. 1966. *Deviance and Control*. Englewood Cliffs, NJ: Prentice-Hall.

Cohen, Albert K., Alfred Lindesmith, and Karl Schuessler, eds. 1956. *The Sutherland Papers*. Bloomington: Indiana University Press.

Cohen, Deborah Vidaver. 1995. "Ethics and Crime in Business Firms: Organizational Culture and the Impact of Anomie." In *The Legacy of Anomie Theory: Advances in Criminological Theory,* edited by Freda Adler and William S. Laufer. Vol. 6. New Brunswick, NJ: Transaction Publishers.

Cohen, Gary. 1998. "Bhopal and the New World Order." http://www.simplelife.com/FIND ORGANICCOTTON/31LINKSBHOPAL.html.

Cohen, Jacqueline, and Michael H. Tonry. 1983. "Sentencing Reform Impacts." In *Research on Sentencing: The Search for Reform,* edited by A. Blumstein, J. Cohen, S. E. Martin, and M. H. Tonry. Vol. 2. Washington, DC: National Academy Press.

Cohen, Lawrence E., and Marcus Felson. 1979. "Social Change and Crime Rate Trends: A Routine Activities Approach." *American Sociological Review* 44: 588–608.

Cohen, Lawrence E., and Richard Machalek. 1988. "A General Theory of Expropriative Crime: An Evolutionary Ecological Approach." *American Journal of Sociology* 94: 465–501.

Cohen, Stanley. 1985. *Visions of Social Control*. Cambridge: Polity.

———. 1988. *Against Criminology*. New Brunswick, NJ: Transaction Books.

———. 1990. "Intellectual Scepticism and Political Commitment: The Case of Radical Criminology." Bonger Memorial Lecture, University of Amsterdam, May 14.

———. 1993. "Human Rights and Crimes of the State: The Culture of Denial." *Australian and New Zealand Journal of Criminology* 26: 97–115.

Cohn, Ellen G., and David. P. Farrington. 1999. "Changes in the Most-Cited Scholars in Twenty Criminology and Criminal Justice Journals Between 1990 and 1995." *Journal of Criminal Justice* 27, no. 4: 345–359.

Coleman, J. W. 1987. "Toward an Integrated Theory of White-Collar Crime." *American Journal of Sociology* 93: 406–439.

———. 1988. "Social Capital in the Creation of Human Capital." *American Journal of Sociology* 94: 95–121.

Collier, P. M. 2006. "Costing Police Services: The Politicalization of Accounting." *Critical Perspectives on Accounting* 17, no. 1: 57–86.

Collins, Hugh. 1987. "Roberto Unger and the Critical Legal Studies Movement." *Journal of Law and Society* 14: 387–410.

Colvin, Mark. 1997. "Review of Stuart Henry and Dragan Milovanovic's *Constitutive Criminology.*" *American Journal of Sociology* 102: 1448–1450.

———. 2000. *Crime and Coercion: An Integrated Theory of Chronic Criminality*. New York: Palgrave Press.

Colvin, Mark, Francis T. Cullen, and Thomas Vander Ven. 2002. "Coercion, Social Support, and Crime: An Emerging Theoretical Consensus." *Criminology* 40: 19–42.

Colvin, Mark, and John Pauly. 1983. "A Critique of Criminology: Toward an Integrated Structural-Marxist Theory of Delinquency Production." *American Journal of Sociology* 89: 513–551.

Comby, Henry B., III. 1982. "Status Offender Treatment in the Juvenile Court: A Conflict Theory Approach." *Free Inquiry in Creative Sociology* 10: 105–107.

Conklin, John E. 1977. *Illegal but Not Criminal: Business Crime in America.* Englewood Cliffs, NJ: Prentice-Hall.

Conly, Catherine, and Daniel McGillis. 1996. "The Federal Role in Revitalizing Communities and Preventing and Controlling Crime and Violence." *National Institute of Justice Journal* 231 (August): 24–30.

Cooley, Charles Horton. [1902] 1964. *Social Organization: A Study of the Larger Mind.* New York: Shocken.

Copes, Heith. 2003. "Societal Attachments, Offending Frequency, and Techniques of Neutralization." *Deviant Behavior* 24, no. 2: 101–127.

Corbett, Claire, and Frances Simon. 1992. "Decisions to Break or Adhere to the Rules of the Road, Viewed from the Rational Choice Perspective." *British Journal of Criminology* 32: 537–549.

Cordella, Peter, and Larry Siegel, eds. 1996. *Readings in Contemporary Criminological Theory.* Boston: Northeastern University Press.

Cordner, Gary. 1981. "The Effects of Directed Patrol: A Natural Quasi-Experiment in Pontiac." In *Contemporary Issues in Law Enforcement,* edited by J. Fyfe, 37–58. Beverly Hills: Sage.

———. 1998. "Problem-Oriented Policing vs. Zero Tolerance." In *Problem-Oriented Policing,* edited by T. Shelly and A. Grant, 303–329. Washington, DC: Police Executive Research Forum.

Cornish, Derek B., and Ronald V. Clarke, eds. 1986. *The Reasoning Criminal.* New York: Springer-Verlag.

———. 1987. "Understanding Crime Displacement: An Application of Rational Choice Theory." *Criminology* 25: 933–947.

———. 2006. "The Rational Choice Perspective." In *The Essential Criminology Reader,* edited by Stuart Henry and Mark M. Lanier, 18–29. Boulder, CO: Westview Press.

Corrigan, Patrick W., Amy C. Watson, Gabriela Gracia, Natalie Slopen, Kenneth Rasinski, and Laura L. Hall. 2005. "Newspaper Stories as Measures of Structural Stigma." *Psychiatric Services* 56, no. 5 (May): 551–556.

Cortes, J. B., and F. M. Gatti. 1972. *Delinquency and Crime: A Biopsychosocial Approach.* New York: Seminar Press.

Corvo, K. 2006. "Violence, Separation, and Loss in the Families of Origin of Domestically Violent Men." *Journal of Family Violence* 21, no. 2: 117–125.

Coser, Lewis. 1956. *The Functions of Social Conflict.* New York: Macmillan.

———. 1968. "Conflict: Social Aspects." In *The International Encyclopedia of the Social Sciences,* edited by David L. Sills. Vol. 3. New York: Macmillan and the Free Press.

Costanza, S. E., William B. Bankston, and Edward Shihadeh. 1999. "Alcohol Availability and Violent Crime Rates: A Spatial Analysis." *Journal of Crime and Justice* 24: 71–83.

Costello, Barbara J., and Paul R. Vowell. 1999. "Testing Control Theory and Differential Association: A Reanalysis of the Richmond Youth Project Data." *Criminology* 37: 815–837.

Coward-Yaskiw, Stephanie. 2002. "Restorative Justice: What Is It? Can It Work? What Do Women Think?" *Herizons* 15 (Spring). http://web2.infotrac.galegroup.com.

Cowling, Mark. 2006. "Postmodern Policies? The Erratic Interventions of Constitutive Criminology." *Internet Journal of Criminology.* http://www.internetjournalofcriminology.com/Cowling%20-%20Postmodern%20Policies.pdf (accessed January 5, 2009).

Cox, R. W. 1993. "Structural Issues of Global Governance: Implications for Europe." In *Gramsci, Historical Materialism, and International Relations,* edited by S. Gill. Cambridge: Cambridge University Press.

Crary, David. 2005. "Private Prisons Experience Business Surge." *Washington Post,* July 31.

Crenshaw, Kimberle, Neil Gotanda, Gary Peller, and Kendall Thomas, eds. 1995. *Critical Race Theory: The Key Writings That Formed the Movement.* New York: New Press.

Cressey, Donald R. 1953. *Other People's Money.* Glencoe, IL: Free Press.

———. 1960. "Epidemiology and Individual Conduct: A Case from Criminology." *Pacific Sociological Review* 3: 47–58.

———. 1962. "The Development of a Theory: Differential Association." In *The Sociology of Crime and Delinquency,* edited by M. E. Wolfgang, L. Savitz, and N. Johnston. New York: John Wiley.

———. [1965] 1987. "The Respectable Criminal." In *Social Problems: A Critical Thinking Approach,* edited by Paul J. Baker and Louis E. Anderson. Belmont, CA: Wadsworth.

———. 1970. "The Respectable Criminal." In *Modern Criminals,* edited by James Short. New York: Transaction-Aldine.

Crews, Gordon A., and Jeffrey A. Tipton. 2002. "A Comparison of Public School and Prison Security Measures: Too Much of a Good Thing?" http://www.kci.org/publication/articles/school_security_measures.htm (accessed May 26, 2004). Available at http://www.ncjrs.gov/App/publications/Abstract.aspx?id=205572 (accessed March 20, 2009).

Cromwell, Paul, and Quint Thurman. 2003. "The Devil Made Me Do It: Use of Neutralizations by Shoplifters." *Deviant Behavior* 24: 535–550.

Croucher, Sheila L. 2004. *Globalization and Belonging: The Politics of Identity in a Changing World.* New York: Rowman and Littlefield.

Crowe, R. R. 1974. "An Adoption Study of Antisocial Personality." *Archives of General Psychiatry* 31: 785–791.

———. 1975. "An Adoptive Study of Psychopathy: Preliminary Results from Arrest Records and Psychiatric Hospital Records." In *Genetic Research in Psychiatry,* edited by R. R. Fieve, D. Rosenthal, and H. Brill. Baltimore: Johns Hopkins University Press.

CSP. 2009. *Center for Systemic Peace.* http://www.systemicpeace.org (accessed March 17, 2009).

Cullen, Francis T. 1994. "Social Support as an Organizing Concept for Criminology." *Justice Quarterly* 11: 527–559.

Cullen, Francis T., Bruce G. Link, Lawrence F. Travis III, and John F. Wozniak. 1985. "Consensus in Crime Seriousness: Empirical Reality or Methodological Artifact?" *Criminology* 23: 99–118.

Cullen, Francis T., William J. Maakestad, and Gray Cavender. 1987. *Corporate Crime Under Attack.* Cincinnati: Anderson.

Culley, M. R., M. Conkling, and J. Emshoff. 2006. "Environmental and Contextual Influence on School Violence and Its Prevention." *Journal of Primary Prevention* 27, no. 3: 217–227.

Curran, Daniel J., and Claire M. Renzetti. 1994. *Theories of Crime.* Boston: Allyn and Bacon.

Currie, Dawn H. 1989. "Women and the State: A Statement on Feminist Theory." *Critical Criminologist* 1: 4–5.

———. 1992. "Feminist Encounters with Postmodernism: Exploring the Impasse of the Debates on Patriarchy and Law." *Canadian Journal of Women and the Law* 5: 63–86.

Currie, Elliott. 1985. *Confronting Crime: An American Challenge.* New York: Pantheon.

———. 1993. *Reckoning: Drugs, the Cities, and the American Future.* New York: Hill and Wang.

———. 1997. "Market, Crime, and Community: Toward a Mid-range Theory of Post-industrial Violence." *Theoretical Criminology* 1: 147–172.

———. 1998. *Crime and Punishment in America.* New York: Metropolitan Books.

———. 2006. "Inequality, Community, and Crime." In *The Essential Criminology Reader,* edited by Stuart Henry and Mark M. Lanier, 299–306. Boulder, CO: Westview Press.

Dabbs, James M., and Robin Morris. 1990. "Testosterone and Antisocial Behavior in a Sample of 4,462 Men." *Psychological Science* 1: 209–211.

Dabbs, James M., Jasmin K. Riad, and Susan E. Chance. 2001. "Testosterone and Ruthless Homicide." *Personality and Individual Differences* 31: 599–603.

Dahrendorf, Ralf. 1958. "Out of Utopia: Toward a Reconstruction of Sociological Analysis." *American Journal of Sociology* 67: 115–127.

———. 1959. *Class and Class Conflict in an Industrial Society.* London: Routledge and Kegan Paul.

D'Alessio, Stewart J., and Lisa Stolzenberg. 1995. "The Impact of Sentencing Guidelines on Jail Incarceration in Minnesota." *Criminology* 33: 283–302.

Dalgard, Odd S., and Einar Kringlen. 1976. "A Norwegian Twin Study of Criminology." *British Journal of Criminology* 16: 213–232.

Dalton, Katharina. 1961. "Menstruation and Crime." *British Medical Journal* 3: 1752–1753.

———. 1971. *The Premenstrual Syndrome.* Springfield, IL: Charles C. Thomas.

Daly, Kathleen. 1992. "Women's Pathways to Felony Court: Feminist Theories of Lawbreaking and Problems of Representation." *Review of Law and Women's Studies* 2, no. 1: 1–42.

———. 1997. "Different Ways of Conceptualizing Sex/Gender in Feminist Theory and Their Implications for Criminology." *Theoretical Criminology* 1, no. 1: 25–51.

———. 2000. "Restorative Justice in Diverse and Unequal Societies." *Law in Context* 17, no. 1: 167–190.

———. 2001. "Feminist Criminologies." In *The Sage Dictionary of Criminology,* edited by Eugene McGlaughlin and John Muncie, 119–121. London: Sage.

———. 2006. "Feminist Thinking About Crime." In *Essential Criminology Reader,* edited by Stuart Henry and Mark M. Lanier, 205–213. Boulder, CO: Westview Press.

Daly, Kathleen, and Meda Chesney-Lind. 1988. "Feminism and Criminology." *Justice Quarterly* 5: 497–538.

Daly, Kathleen, and Lisa Maher. 1998. *Criminology at the Crossroads: Feminist Readings in Crime and Justice.* New York: Oxford University Press.

Dann, Robert. 1935. "The Deterrent Effect of Capital Punishment." *Friends Social Service Series* 29.

Danner, Mona J. E. 1991. "Socialist Feminism: A Brief Introduction." In *New Directions in Critical Criminology,* edited by Brian D. MacLean and Dragan Milovanovic. Vancouver, BC: Collective Press.

Danzig, Richard. 1973. "Toward the Creation of a Complementary Decentralized System of Criminal Justice." *Stanford Law Review* 26: 1–54.

Darwin, Charles R. [1859] 1968. *On the Origin of Species.* New York: Penguin.

———. 1871. *Descent of Man: Selection in Relation to Sex.* London: John Murray.

Davis, Mike. 2008. "Reading John Hagedorn." Foreword to *A World of Gangs: Armed Young Men and Gangsta Culture,* by John M. Hagedorn, xi–xvii. Minneapolis: University of Minnesota Press.

Debro, Julius. 1970. "Dialogue with Howard S. Becker." *Issues in Criminology* 5: 159–179.

Decker, Scott H., and Barrik Van Winkle. 1996. *Life in the Gang: Family, Friends, and Violence.* Cambridge: Cambridge University Press.

De Coster, Stacy, and Karen Heimer. 2001. "The Relationship Between Law Violation and Depression: An Interactionist Analysis." *Criminology* 39: 799–836.

Deffenbacher, J. L., T. L. Richards, and L. B. Filetti. 2005. "Angry Drivers: A Test of State-Trait Theory." *Violence and Victims* 20, no. 4: 455–469.

Deflem, Mathieu. 1999. Review of *The Future of Anomie Theory,* edited by Nikos Passas and Robert Agnew. *Social Forces* 78: 364–366.

DeFleur, Lois B. 1967. "Ecological Variables in the Cross-Cultural Study of Delinquency and Community." *Social Forces* 45: 556–570.

DeFleur, Melvin, and Richard Quinney. 1966. "A Reformulation of Sutherland's Differential Association Theory and a Strategy for Empirical Verification." *Journal of Research in Crime and Delinquency* 2: 1–22.

De Haan, Willem. 1990. *The Politics of Redress.* Boston: Unwin Hyman.

DeKeseredy, Walter S. 1993. *Four Variations of Family Violence: A Review of Sociological Research.* Ottawa: Health Canada.

———. 2003. "Left Realism and Inner City Violence." In *Controversies in Critical Criminology,* edited by Martin D. Schwartz and Suzanne E. Hatty, 29–41. Cincinnati: Anderson.

DeKeseredy, Walter S., and Martin D. Schwartz. 1991. "British and U.S. Left Realism: A Critical Comparison." *International Journal of Offender Therapy and Comparative Criminology* 35: 248–262.

———. 1996. *Contemporary Criminology.* Belmont, CA: Wadsworth.

———. 2006. "Left Realist Theory." In *The Essential Criminology Reader,* edited by Stuart Henry and Mark M. Lanier, 319–335. Boulder, CO: Westview Press.

Delgado, Richard. 1994. "Critical Race Theory." *Sage Race Relations Abstracts* 2: 3.

———, ed. 1995. *Critical Race Theory: The Cutting Edge.* Philadelphia: Temple University Press.

Delgado, Richard, and Jean Stefancic. 1993. "Critical Race Theory: An Annotated Bibliography." *Virginia Law Review* 79, no. 2: 461–516.

———. 1998. *The Latino/a Condition: A Critical Reader.* New York: New York University Press.

———. 2001. *Critical Race Theory: An Introduction.* New York: New York University Press.

———. 2005. "The Role of Critical Race Theory in Understanding Race, Crime, and Justice Issues." Address to John Jay College of Criminal Justice, CUNY, December 13. http:// www.jjay.cuny.edu/centersinstitutes/racecrimejustice/publishedpaper.pdf (accessed January 11, 2009).

DeLisi, Matt. 2001. "It's All in the Record: Assessing Self-Control Theory with an Offender Sample." *Criminal Justice Review* 26: 1–16.

DeLisi, Matt, and M. T. Berg. 2006. "Exploring Theoretical Linkages Between Self-Control Theory and Criminal Justice System Processing." *Journal of Criminal Justice* 34, no. 2: 153–163.

Dembo, Richard, Gary Grandon, Lawrence La Voie, James Schmeidler, and William Burgos. 1986. "Parents and Drugs Revisited: Some Further Evidence in Support of Social Learning Theory." *Criminology* 24: 85–104.

Denno, Deborah. 1985. "Sociological and Human Developmental Explanations of Crime: Conflict or Consensus." *Criminology* 23: 711–741.

———. 1989. *Biology, Crime, and Violence: New Evidence.* Cambridge: Cambridge University Press.

Derrida, Jacques. 1970. "Structure, Sign, and Play in the Discourse of Human Sciences." In *The Languages of Criticism and the Sciences of Man,* edited by Richard Macksey and Eugenio Donato. Baltimore: Johns Hopkins University Press.

———. 1981. *Positions.* Chicago: University of Chicago Press.

Dezhbakhsh, Hashem, Paul Rubin, and Joanna Shepherd. 2003. "Does Capital Punishment Have a Deterrent Effect? New Evidence from Postmoratorium Panel Data." *American Law and Economics Review* 5: 344–376.

Dickens, William T., and James R. Flynn. 2006. "Black Americans Reduce the Racial IQ Gap: Evidence from Standardization Samples." *Psychological Science* 17: 913–920.

Ditton, Jason. 1977. *Part-Time Crime: An Ethnography of Fiddling and Pilferage.* London: Macmillan.

———. 1998. "Public Support for Town Centre CCTV Schemes: Myth or Reality?" In *Surveillance, Closed Circuit Television, and Social Control,* edited by Clive Norris, Jade Morgan, and Gary Armstrong. Aldershot, UK: Ashgate.

Dobash, R., R. E. Dobash, M. Wilson, and M. Daly. 1992. "The Myth of Sexual Symmetry in Marital Violence." *Social Problems* 39: 71–91.

Dodge, K. A. 1993. "Social Cognitive Mechanism in the Development of Conduct Disorders and Depression." *Annual Review of Psychology* 44: 559–584.

Dollard, J., L. W. Doob, N. E. Miller, O. H. Mowrer, and R. R. Sears. 1939. *Frustration and Aggression.* New Haven, CT: Yale University Press.

Donohue, John J., and Justin Wolfers. 2006. "The Death Penalty: No Evidence for Deterrence." *American Law and Economics Review* 5: 344–376.

Douglas, Jack D., and Paul K. Rasmussen. 1977. *The Nude Beach.* Beverly Hills, CA: Sage.

Douglas, Mary. 1970. *Natural Symbols.* London: Crescent.

———. 1978. *Cultural Bias.* London: Royal Anthropological Institute.

Dowie, Mark. [1977] 1979. "Pinto Madness." *Mother Jones* 2 (September–October): 18–34. Reprinted in *Crisis in American Institutions,* edited by Jerome Skolnick and Elliot Currie. 4th ed. Boston: Little, Brown.

Drahms, August. [1900] 1971. *The Criminal: His Personnel and Environment—A Scientific Study.* Introduction by Cesare Lombroso. Montclair, NJ: Patterson Smith.

Dugdale, Richard Louis. [1877] 1895. *The Jukes: A Study in Crime, Pauperism, Disease, and Heredity.* 3d ed. New York: G. P. Putnam.

Durkheim, Émile. [1893] 1984. *The Division of Labor in Society.* New York: Free Press.

———. [1895] 1950. *The Rules of Sociological Method.* Edited by G. E. G. Catlin. Translated by S. A. Solovay and J. H. Mueller. Glencoe, IL: Free Press.

———. [1895] 1982. *The Rules of Sociological Method and Selected Texts on Sociology and Its Method.* Edited by Steven Lukes. Translated by W. D. Halls. London: Macmillan.

———. [1897] 1951. *Suicide: A Study in Sociology.* New York: Free Press.

Duster, Troy. 1970. *The Legislation of Morality.* New York: Free Press.

Ebbe, Obi N. I. 1989. "Crime and Delinquency in Metropolitan Lagos: A Study of 'Crime and Delinquency' Theory." *Social Forces* 67: 751–765.

Edelhertz, Herbert. 1970. *The Nature, Impact, and Prosecution of White-Collar Crime.* Washington, DC: U.S. Government Printing Office.

Edwards, Susan. 1990. "Violence Against Women: Feminism and the Law." In *Feminist Perspectives in Criminology,* edited by Loraine Gelsthorpe and Allison Morris, 144–159. Milton Keynes, UK: Open University Press.

Eglash, Albert. 1977. "Beyond Restitution: Creative Restitution." In *Restitution in Criminal Justice,* edited by J. Hudson and B. Galaway. Lexington, MA: Lexington Books.

Egley, Arlen, Jr., and Christina E. O'Donnell. 2008. *Highlights of the 2006 National Youth Gang Survey OJJDP Fact Sheet #05 (July).* Washington, DC: U.S. Department of Justice, Office of Juvenile Justice and Delinquency Prevention.

Ehrenkranz, Joel, Eugene Bliss, and Michael Sheard. 1974. "Plasma Testosterone: Correlation with Aggressive Behavior and Social Dominance in Man." *Psychosomatic Medicine* 35: 469–475.

Ehrenreich, Barbara, and Annette Fuentes. 1994. "Life on the Global Assembly Line." In *Crisis in American Institutions,* edited by Jerome H. Skolnick and Elliot Currie, 326–340. 9th ed. New York: Harper Collins.

Ehrlich, Isaac. 1973. "Participation in Illegitimate Activities: An Economic Analysis." *Journal of Political Economy* 81: 521–567.

———. 1975. "The Deterrent Effect of Capital Punishment: A Question of Life or Death." *American Economic Review* 65: 397–417.

———. 1982. "The Market for Offenses and the Public Enforcement of Laws: An Equilibrium Analysis." *British Journal of Social Psychology* 21: 107–120.

Einstadter, Werner, and Stuart Henry. 1995. *Criminological Theory: An Analysis of Its Underlying Assumptions.* Fort Worth, TX: Harcourt Brace College Publishers.

———. 2006. *Criminological Theory: An Analysis of Its Underlying Assumptions.* 2d ed. Boulder, CO: Rowman and Littlefield.

Eisenstein, Zillah. 1979. *Capitalist Patriarchy and the Case for Socialist Feminism.* New York: Monthly Review Press.

el-detroit. 2003. Customer review of *Land of Opportunity.* http://www.amazon.com/Land-Opportunity-Familys-Quest-American/dp/0871135930/ref=sr_1_1?ie=UTF8&s=books&qid=1230994841&sr=1-1 (accessed January 2, 2009).

Elias, Robert. 1986. *The Politics of Victimization: Victims, Victimology, and Human Rights.* New York: Oxford University Press.

Elliott, Delbert S., and Susan S. Ageton. 1980. "Reconciling Race and Class Differences in Self-Reported and Official Estimates of Delinquency." *American Sociological Review* 45: 95–110.

———. 1983. *National Youth Survey, 1976.* Ann Arbor: ICPSR.

Elliott, Delbert S., Susan S. Ageton, and R. Canter. 1979. "An Integrated Theoretical Perspective on Delinquent Behavior." *Journal of Research on Crime and Delinquency* 16: 3–27.

Elliott, Delbert S., Beatrice A. Hamburg, and K. R. Williams. 1998. *Violence in American Schools.* Cambridge: Cambridge University Press.

Elliott, Delbert S., and David Huizinga. 1983. "Social Class and Delinquent Behavior in a National Youth Panel, 1976–1980." *Criminology* 21: 149–177.

Elliott, Delbert S., David Huizinga, and Susan Ageton. 1985. *Explaining Delinquency and Drug Use.* Beverly Hills: Sage.

Elliott, Delbert S., and Harwin L. Voss. 1974. *Delinquency and Dropout.* Lexington, MA: Lexington.

Ellis, Lee. 1977. "The Decline and Fall of Sociology, 1975–2000." *American Sociologist* 12: 56–66.

———. 1987. "Criminal Behavior and r/K Selection: An Extension of Gene-Based Evolutionary Theory." *Deviant Behavior* 8: 149–176.

———. 1988. "Neurohormonal Bases of Varying Tendencies to Learn Delinquent and Criminal Behavior." In *Behavioral Approaches to Crime and Delinquency,* edited by E. K. Morris and C. J. Braukmann. New York: Plenum.

———. 1989. *Theories of Rape: Inquiries into the Causes of Sexual Aggression.* New York: Hemisphere.

———. 1990. "Introduction: The Nature of the Biosocial Perspective." In *Crime in Biological, Social, and Moral Contexts,* edited by L. Ellis and H. Hoffman. New York: Praeger.

———. 1995. "Arousal Theory and the Religiosity-Criminality Relationship." In *Contemporary Criminological Theory,* edited by Peter Cordella and Larry Siegel. Boston: Northeastern University Press.

———. 2005. "A Theory Explaining Biological Correlates of Criminality." *European Journal of Criminology* 2: 287–315.

Ellis, Lee, and H. Hoffman, eds. 1990. *Crime in Biological, Social, and Moral Contexts.* New York: Praeger.

Ellis, Lee, and Anthony Walsh. 1997. "Gene-Based Evolutionary Theories in Criminology." *Criminology* 35: 229–267.

———. 2000. *Criminology: A Global Perspective.* Boston: Allyn and Bacon.

Ellsworth, M. J. 1927. *The Bath School Disaster.* Bath, MI: Bath School Museum.

Ellwanger, S. J. 2007. "Strain, Attribution, and Traffic Delinquency Among Young Drivers: Measuring and Testing General Strain Theory in the Context of Driving." *Crime and Delinquency* 53, no. 4: 523–551.

Emory, L. E., C. M. Cole, and W. J. Meyer. 1992. "The Texas Experience with DepoProvera, 1980–1990." *Journal of Offender Rehabilitation* 18: 125–139.

Empey, Lamar T., and Steven G. Lubeck. 1971a. *Explaining Delinquency.* Lexington, MA: D. C. Heath.

———. 1971b. *The Silverlake Experiment.* Chicago: Aldine.

Empey, Lamar T., and Mark C. Stafford. 1991. *American Delinquency: Its Meaning and Construction.* 3d ed. Belmont, CA: Wadsworth.

Engel, Robin Shepard, Jennifer M. Calnon, and Thomas J. Bernard. 2002. "Theory and Racial Profiling: Shortcomings and Future Directions in Research." *Justice Quarterly* 19: 249–273.

Engels, Friedrich. [1845] 1958. *The Condition of the Working Class in England.* Oxford: Blackwell.

———. 1884. "The Origin of the Family, Private Property, and the State." In *Selected Works,* by Karl Marx and Friedrich Engels. Moscow: Progress Publishers.

Enzmann, Dirk, Werner Greve, and Daniela Hosser. 2001. "The Stabilization of Self-Esteem Among Incarcerated Adolescents: Accommodative and Immunizing Processes." *International Journal of Offender Therapy and Comparative Criminology* 45: 749–768.

"Epidemiological Criminology." 2008. http://www.epidemiologicalcriminology.com/index .htm (accessed on October 30, 2008).

Ericson, Richard, and Kevin Carriere. 1994. "The Fragmentation of Criminology." In *The Futures of Criminology,* edited by D. Nelken. London: Sage.

Ermann, M. David, and William H. Clements. 1984. "The Interfaith Center on Corporate Responsibility and Its Campaign Against Marketing Infant Formula in the Third World." *Social Problems* 32: 185–196.

Ermann, M. David, and Richard J. Lundman. [1992] 2001. *Corporate and Governmental Deviance.* 5th ed. New York: Oxford University Press.

Esqueda, C. W., R. K. Espinoza, and S. E. Culhane. 2008. "The Effects of Ethnicity, SES, and Crime Status on Juror Decision Making: A Cross-Cultural Examination of European American and Mexican American Mock Jurors." *Hispanic Journal of Behavioral Sciences* 30, no. 2: 181–199.

Estabrook, Arthur H. 1916. *The Jukes in 1915.* Washington, DC: Carnegie Institute.

Eterno, J. A. 2006. "Gender and Policing: Do Women Accept Legal Restrictions More Than Their Male Counterparts?" *Women and Criminal Justice* 18, nos. 1–2: 49–78.

Evans, T. Davis, Francis Cullen, Gregory Dunaway, and Velmer Burton. 1995. "Religion and Crime Reexamined: The Impact of Religion, Secular Controls, and Social Ecology on Adult Criminality." *Criminology* 33: 195–224.

Eysenck, Hans J. [1964] 1977. *Crime and Personality.* 2d ed. London: Routledge and Kegan Paul.

———. 1983. "Personality, Conditioning, and Anti-social Behavior." In *Personality Theory, Moral Development, and Criminal Behavior,* edited by S. Laufer and J. M. Day. Lexington, MA: Lexington.

Eysenck, Hans J., and G. H. Gudjonsson. 1989. *The Causes and Cures of Criminality.* New York: Plenum.

Fagan, Jeffrey. 1991. "Drug Selling and Licit Income in Distressed Neighborhoods: The Economic Lives of Street-Level Drug Users and Dealers." In *Drugs, Crime, and Social Isolation,* edited by Adele V. Harrell and George E. Peterson. Washington, DC: Urban Institute Press.

———. 2005. *Deterrence and the Death Penalty: A Critical Review of the Evidence.* Testimony to the New York State Assembly. http://www.deathpenaltyinfo.org/FaganTestimony .pdf (accessed March 20, 2009).

Faith, Karlene, and Dawn Currie. 1993. *Seeking Shelter: A State of Battered Women.* Vancouver, BC: Collective Press.

Farnworth, Margaret. 1989. "Theory Integration Versus Model Building." In *Theoretical Integration in the Study of Deviance and Crime,* edited by Stephen F. Messner, Marvin D. Krohn, and Allen Liska. Albany: State University of New York Press.

Farnworth, Margaret, and Michael J. Leiber. 1989. "Strain Theory Revisited: Educational Goals, Educational Means, and Delinquency." *American Sociological Review* 54: 263–274.

Farrell, Ronald A., and Victoria Lynn Swigert. 1988. *Social Deviance.* 3d ed. Belmont, CA: Wadsworth.

Farrington, David. 1989. "The Origins of Crime: The Cambridge Study of Delinquent Development." *Home Office Research and Planning Unity Research Bulletin* 27: 29–33.

———. 1998. "Psychological Factors in the Explanation and Reduction of Delinquency." *Today's Delinquent* 7: 44–46.

Farrington, David, and Brandon Welsh. 2002. "Improved Street Lighting and Crime Prevention." *Justice Quarterly* 19, no. 2: 313–342.

Farrington, David, and Donald J. West. 1993. "Criminal, Penal, and Life Histories of Chronic Offenders: Risk and Protective Factors and Early Identification." *Criminal Behavior and Mental Health* 3, no. 4: 492–523.

Fattah, Ezzat A. 1992. *Towards a Critical Victimology.* New York: St. Martin's.

Faust, Frederic L. 1995. Review of *A Primer in the Psychology of Crime,* by S. Giora Shoham and Mark C. Seis. *Social Pathology* 1: 48–61.

Fauth, R. C., T. Leventhal, and J. Brooks-Gunn. 2005. "Early Impacts of Moving from Poor to Middle-Class Neighborhoods on Low-Income Youth." *Journal of Applied Development Psychology* 26, no. 4: 415–439.

Fazel, Seena, and Grann Martin. 2006. "The Population Impact of Severe Mental Illness on Violent Crime." *American Journal of Psychiatry* 163, no. 8: 1397–1403.

Featherstone, Richard. 2003. "Anomie and Strain: Context and Consequences of Merton's Two Theories." *Sociological Inquiry* 73, no. 4: 471–489.

Feder, Lynette. 1995. "Psychiatric History, Due Procedural Safeguards, and the Use of Discretion in the Criminal Justice Process." *Justice Quarterly* 12: 279–305.

Federal Bureau of Investigation. 1992. *Uniform Crime Reporting Handbook: NIBRS Edition.* Washington, DC: U.S. Government Printing Office.

———. 1993. *Uniform Crime Reports.* Washington, DC: U.S. Government Printing Office.

Feeley, Malcom, and Jonathan Simon. 1992. "The New Penology: Notes on the Emerging Strategy of Corrections and Its Implications." *Criminology* 30: 449–470.

———. 1998. "The New Penology: Notes on the Emerging Strategy of Corrections and Its Implications." In *The Criminology Theory Reader,* edited by Stuart Henry and Werner Einstader. New York: New York University Press.

Feinberg, Todd. 2001. *Altered Egos: How the Brain Creates the Self.* Oxford: Oxford University Press.

Feldman, M. P. 1977. *Criminal Behavior: A Psychological Analysis.* London: John Wiley.

Felson, Marcus. 1986. "Routine Activities and Crime Prevention in the Developing Metropolis." In *The Reasoning Criminal,* edited by Derek B. Cornish and Ronald V. Clarke. New York: Springer-Verlag.

———. 1987. "Routine Activities, Social Controls, Rational Decisions, and Criminal Outcomes." *Criminology* 25: 911–931.

Felson, Marcus, and Lawrence E. Cohen. 1981. "Molding Crime Rate Trends: A Criminal Opportunity Perspective." *Journal of Research in Crime and Delinquency* 18: 138–164.

Felson, Richard B. 1992. "'Kick 'Em When They're Down': Explanations of the Relationship Between Stress and Interpersonal Aggression and Violence." *Sociological Quarterly* 33: 1–16.

Ferman, A. Louis, Stuart Henry, and Michele Hoyman, eds. 1987. "The Informal Economy." Special issue, *Annals of the American Academy of Political and Social Science* 493.

Ferrell, Jeff. 1994. "Confronting the Agenda of Authority: Critical Criminology, Anarchism." In *Varieties of Criminology: Readings from a Dynamic Discipline,* edited by Gregg Barak. Westport, CT: Praeger.

———. 1998. "Against the Law: Anarchist Criminology." *Social Anarchism,* no. 25: 5–15.

———. 2006. "Cultural Criminology." In *The Essential Criminology Reader,* edited by Stuart Henry and Mark M. Lanier, 247–256. Boulder, CO: Westview Press.

———. 2007. "Cultural Criminology." In *Blackwell Encyclopedia of Sociology.* Oxford: Basil Blackwell. http://www.culturalcriminology.org/papers/cult-crim-blackwell-ency-soc.pdf (accessed January 11, 2009).

Ferrell, Jeff, Keith J. Hayward, and Jock Young. 2009. *Cultural Criminology: An Invitation.* London: Sage.

Ferrell, Jeff, Dragan Milovanovic, and Steven Lyng. 2001. "Edgework, Media Practices, and the Elongation of Meaning." *Theoretical Criminology* 5, no. 2: 177–202.

Ferrell, Jeff, and Clinton Saunders, eds. 1995. *Cultural Criminology.* Boston: Northeastern University Press.

Ferrell, Jeff, and Neil Websdale. 1999. *Making Trouble: Cultural Constructions of Crime, Deviance, and Control.* Hawthorn, NY: Aldine de Gruyter.

Ferri, Enrico. 1901. *Criminal Sociology.* New York: D. Appleton.

Festinger, Leon. 1957. *A Theory of Cognitive Dissonance.* Stanford, CA: Stanford University Press.

Fiero, John W. 1996. *"Roe v. Wade."* In *Ready Reference: American Justice,* edited by Joseph M. Bessette. Englewood Cliffs, NJ: Salem Press.

Figueira-McDonough, Josephina. 1980. "A Reformulation of the Equal Opportunity Explanation of Female Delinquency." *Crime and Delinquency* 26: 333–343.

———. 1983. "On the Usefulness of Merton's Anomie Theory: Academic Failure and Deviance Among High School Students." *Youth and Society* 14: 259–279.

Finestone, Harold. 1976. *Victims of Change.* Westport, CT: Greenwood.

Fishbein, Diana H. 1990. "Biological Perspectives in Criminology." *Criminology* 28: 27–72.

———. 1998. "Biological Perspectives in Criminology." In *The Criminology Theory Reader,* edited by Stuart Henry and Werner Einstadter. New York: New York University Press.

Fishbein, Diana H., and Susan E. Pease. 1988. "The Effects of Diet on Behavior: The Implications for Criminology and Corrections." *Research in Corrections* 1: 1–44.

Fishbein, Diana H., and Melissa Reuland. 1994. "Psychological Correlates of Frequency and Type of Drug Use Among Jail Inmates." *Addictive Behaviors* 19: 583–598.

Fishbein, Diana H., and Robert W. Thatcher. 1986. "New Diagnostic Methods in Criminology: Assessing Organic Sources of Behavioral Disorders." *Journal of Research in Crime and Delinquency* 23: 240–267.

Fisher, Eric. 1975. "Community Courts: An Alternative to Criminal Adjudication." *American University Law Review* 24: 1253–1274.

Flavin, Jeanne. 2001. "Feminism for the Mainstream Criminologist: An Invitation." *Journal of Criminal Justice* 29: 271–285.

Florida Department of Law Enforcement. 2006. *Violent Crime and Drug Control Council.* Tallahassee: Florida Department of Law Enforcement.

Florida Freedom. 2008. "Empowerment for Victims of Modern Day Slavery." http://www.floridafreedom.org.

Flynn, Michael, and David C. Brotherton, eds. 2008. *Globalizing the Streets: Cross-Cultural Perspectives on Youth, Social Control, and Empowerment.* New York: Columbia University Press.

Fogel, David. 1975. *We Are the Living Proof: The Justice Model for Corrections.* Cincinnati: Anderson.

Forst, M. 1983. "Capital Punishment and Deterrence: Conflicting Evidence?" *Journal of Criminal Law and Criminology* 74: 927–942.

Foster, Jack D., Simon Dinitz, and Walter C. Reckless. 1972. "Perceptions of Stigma Following Public Intervention for Delinquent Behavior." *Social Problems* 20: 202–209.

Foster, Janet. 1990. *Villains: Crime and Community in the Inner City.* New York: Routledge.

Foucault, Michel. 1977. *Discipline and Punish.* Harmondsworth, UK: Allen Lane.

———. 1980. *Power/Knowledge: Selected Interviews and Other Writings, 1972–1977.* Edited by Colin Gordon. Brighton, UK: Harvester.

14-karat. 2005. Customer Review of *Land of Opportunity.* http://www.amazon.com/Land Opportunity-Familys-Quest-American/dp/0871135930/ref=sr_1_1?ie=UTF8&s =books&qid=1230994841&sr=1-1 (accessed January 2, 2009).

Fox, James Alan, and Jack Levin. 1994. "Firing Back: The Growing Threat of Workplace Homicide." *Annals of the American Academy of Political and Social Science* 563: 16–30.

Fox, Richard, G. 1971. "The XYY Offender: A Modern Myth." *Journal of Criminal Law, Criminology, and Police Science* 62: 59–73.

Frazier, Charles E., Donna M. Bishop, and John C. Henretta. 1992. "The Social Context of Race Differentials in Juvenile Justice Dispositions." *Sociological Quarterly* 33: 447–458.

Frazier, Charles E., and John K. Cochran. 1986. "Official Intervention, Diversion from the Juvenile Justice System, and Dynamics of Human Services Work: Effects of a Reform Goal Based on Labeling Theory." *Crime and Delinquency* 32: 157–176.

Free, Marvin D., Jr. 1994. "Religiosity, Religious Conservatism, Bonds to School, and Juvenile Delinquency Among Three Categories of Drug Users." *Deviant Behavior* 15: 151–170.

Freud, Sigmund. 1915. *Der Verbrecher aus Schuldbewusstsein. Gesammelte Schriften.* Vol. 10. Vienna: Internationaler Psychoanalytsischer Verlag.

———. 1950. "Criminals from a Sense of Guilt." In *Gesammelte Werke,* 14: 332–333. London: Imago.

Friedlander, Kate. 1947. *The Psychoanalytical Approach to Juvenile Delinquency.* London: International Universities Press.

Friedman, Jennifer, and Dennis P. Rosenbaum. 1988. "Social Control Theory: The Salience of Components by Age, Gender, and Type of Crime." *Journal of Quantitative Criminology* 4: 363–381.

Friedrichs, David O. 1991. "Peacemaking Criminology in a World Filled with Conflict." In *New Directions in Critical Criminology,* edited by Brian D. MacLean and Dragan Milovanovic. Vancouver, BC: Collective Press.

———. 1996. *Trusted Criminals: White-Collar Crime in Contemporary Society.* Belmont, CA: Wadsworth.

Froggio, G., and R. Agnew. 2007. "The Relationship Between Crime and 'Objective' Versus 'Subjective' Strains." *Journal of Criminal Justice* 35, no. 1: 81–88.

Fuller, John. 1998. *Criminal Justice: A Peacemaking Perspective.* Boston: Allyn and Bacon.

———. 2003. "Peacemaking Criminology." In *Controversies in Critical Criminology,* edited by Martin D. Schwartz and Suzanne E. Hatty, 88–95. Cincinnati: Anderson.

Funk, P. 2004. "On the Effective Use of Stigma as a Crime-Deterrent." *European Economic Review* 48, no. 4: 715–728.

Gaarder, Emily, and Joanne Belknap. 2002. "Tenuous Borders: Girls Transferred to Adult Court." *Criminology* 40: 481–517.

Gabor, Thomas. 1994. *Everybody Does It! Crimes by the Public.* Toronto: University of Toronto Press.

Gacono, Carl, and J. Reid Meloy. 1994. *The Rorschach Assessment of Aggressive and Psychopathic Personalities.* Hillsdale, NJ: Lawrence Erlbaum.

Gado, Mark. 2002. "Hell Comes to Bath: America's Worst School Violence Ever." http://www.crimelibrary.com/serial7/bath/.

Gagnier, Monica. 2008. "The Rise and Fall of Bernard L. Madoff." *BusinessWeek,* December 12. http://www.businessweek.com/blogs/recession_in_america/archives/2008/12/the_rise_and_fa.html (accessed December 19, 2008).

Gans, Herbert J. 1997. "Best-Sellers by Sociologists: An Exploratory Study." *Contemporary Sociology* 26: 131–135.

Gant, Andrew. 2008. "Brothers Wonder What Else Could Have Been Done to Save Mark Rohlman and the Deputy He Killed." *Northwest Florida Daily News,* July 23.

Garabino, James. 1999. *Lost Boys: Why Our Sons Turn Violent and How We Can Save Them.* New York: Free Press.

Gardiner, Richard A. 1978. *Design for Safe Neighborhoods: The Environmental Security Planning and Design Process.* Washington, DC: LEAA–U.S. Department of Justice.

Garland, Allen E. 2001. "The Biological Basis of Crime: An Historical and Methodological Study." *Historical Studies in the Physical and Biological Sciences* 31: 183–223.

Garland, David. 1985. *Punishment and Welfare: A History of Penal Strategies.* Brookfield, VT: Gower.

———. 1996. "The Limits of the Sovereign State: Strategies of Crime Control in Contemporary Society." *British Journal of Criminology* 36: 445–471.

———. 1997. "'Governmentality' and the Problem of Crime: Foucault, Criminology, Sociology." *Theoretical Criminology* 1, no. 2: 173–214.

————. 2001. *The Culture of Control: Crime and Social Order in Contemporary Society.* Oxford: Oxford University Press.

Garofalo, James, Leslie Siegel, and John Laub. 1987. "School-Related Victimizations Among Adolescents: An Analysis of National Crime Survey (NCS) Narratives." *Journal of Quantitative Criminology* 3: 321–338.

Garofalo, Raffaele. 1914. *Criminology.* Translated by Robert Wyness Millar. Boston: Little, Brown.

Gauthier, Deann K. 2001. "Professional Lapses: Occupational Deviance and Neutralization Techniques in Veterinary Medical Practice." *Deviant Behavior* 22, no. 6: 467–490.

Geerken, Michael, and Walter Gove. 1975. "Deterrence: Some Theoretical Considerations." *Law and Society Review* 9: 497–514.

Geis, Gilbert. 1995. "The Limits of Academic Tolerance: The Discontinuance of the School of Criminology at Berkeley." In *Punishment and Social Control: Essays in Honor of Sheldon L. Messinger,* edited by Thomas G. Blomberg and Stanley Cohen. Hawthorn, NY: Aldine de Gruyter.

Gelsthorpe, Loraine, and Allison Morris. 1988. "Feminism and Criminology in Britain." In *A History of British Criminology,* edited by Paul Rock. Oxford: Clarendon.

————, eds. 1990. *Feminist Perspectives in Criminology.* Philadelphia: Open University Press.

Gerlach, Neil. 2001. "From Disciplinary Gaze to Biological Gaze: Genetic Crime Thrillers and Biogovernance." *Canadian Review of American Studies* 31: 95–118.

Ghodsian-Carpey, Jilla, and L. A. Baker. 1987. "Genetic and Environmental Influences on Aggression in 4- to 7-Year-Old Twins." *Aggressive Behavior* 13: 173–186.

Gibbons, Don C. 1979. *The Criminological Enterprise: Theories and Perspectives.* Englewood Cliffs, NJ: Prentice-Hall.

————. 1994. *Talking About Crime and Criminals: Problems and Issues in Theory Development in Criminology.* Englewood Cliffs, NJ: Prentice-Hall.

Gibbs, Jack P. 1966. "Conceptions of Deviant Behavior: The Old and the New." *Pacific Sociological Review* 14: 20–37.

Gibbs, Leonard. 1974. "Effects of Juvenile Legal Procedures on Juvenile Offenders' Self-Attitudes." *Journal of Research in Crime and Delinquency* 11: 51–55.

Gibbs, W. Wayt. 1995. "Seeking the Criminal Element." *Scientific American* 272: 100–107.

Gibson, Mary. 2002. *Born to Crime: Cesare Lombroso and the Origins of Biological Criminology.* Westport, CT: Praeger.

Gibson, Mary, and Nicole Hahn Rafter. 2006. Introduction to *Criminal Man,* by Cesare Lombroso. Durham, NC: Duke University Press.

Giddens, Anthony. 1999. "Risk and Responsibility." *Modern Law Review* 62, no. 1: 1–10.

Gilbert P. 1998. "Evolutionary Psychopathology: Why Isn't the Mind Designed Better Than It Is?" *British Journal of Medical Psychology* 71: 353–373.

Gill, O. 1977. *Luke Street: Housing Policy, Conflict, and the Creation of the Delinquency Area.* London: Macmillan.

Gilsinan, James F. 1990. *Criminology and Public Policy.* Englewood Cliffs, NJ: Prentice-Hall.

Glaser, Brian A., Georgia B. Calhoun, and John V. Petrocelli. 2002. "Personality Characteristics of Male Juvenile Offenders by Adjudicated Offenses as Indicated by the MMPI-A." *Criminal Justice and Behavior* 29: 183–201.

Glaser, Daniel. 1956. "Criminality Theories and Behavioral Images." *American Journal of Sociology* 61: 433–444.

————. 1978. *Crime in Our Changing Society.* New York: Holt, Rinehart, and Winston.

Glueck, Sheldon. 1956. "Theory and Fact in Criminology: A Criticism of Differential Association." *British Journal of Delinquency* 7: 92–109.

Glueck, Sheldon, and Elinor Glueck. 1950. *Unraveling Juvenile Delinquency.* New York: Commonwealth Fund.

———. 1956. *Physique and Delinquency.* New York: Harper and Brothers.

———. 1968. *Delinquents and Nondelinquents in Perspective.* Cambridge, MA: Harvard University Press.

Goddard, Henry H. 1912. *The Kallikak Family: A Study in the Heredity of Feeblemindedness.* London: Macmillan.

Goffman, Erving. 1961. *Asylums.* New York: Doubleday Anchor.

———. 1963. *Stigma: Notes on the Management of Spoiled Identity.* Englewood Cliffs, NJ: Prentice-Hall.

Gold, Martin. 1970. *Delinquent Behavior in an American City.* Belmont, CA: Wadsworth.

Goldsmith, Andrew. 2003. "Policing Weak States: Citizen Safety and State Responsibility." *Policing and Society* 13, no. 1: 3–21.

Goldsmith, Douglas F., David Oppenheim, and Janine Wanlass. 2004. "Separation and Reunification: Using Attachment Theory and Research to Inform Decisions Affecting the Placements of Children in Foster Care." *Juvenile and Family Court Journal* 55, no. 2: 1–13.

Goldstein, Arnold P., Leonard Krasner, and Sol L. Garfield. 1989. *Reducing Delinquency: Intervention in the Community.* New York: Pergamon.

Goodstein, Lynne, and John R. Hepburn. 1986. "Determinate Sentencing in Illinois: An Assessment of Its Development and Implementation." *Criminal Justice Policy Review* 1: 305–328.

Goring, Charles. [1913] 1972. *The English Convict: A Statistical Study, 1913.* Montclair, NJ: Patterson Smith.

Gorman, D. M., and Helene Raskin White. 1995. "You Can Choose Your Friends, but Do They Choose Your Crime? Implications of Differential Association Theories for Crime Prevention Policy." In *Crime and Public Policy: Putting Theory to Work,* edited by Hugh D. Barlow. Boulder, CO: Westview Press.

Gottfredson, Michael R., and Travis Hirschi. 1989. "A Propensity-Event Theory of Crime." In *Advances in Criminological Theory,* edited by William S. Laufer and Fred Adler, 1: 57–67. New Brunswick, NJ: Transaction.

———. 1990. *A General Theory of Crime.* Stanford, CA: Stanford University Press.

Gould, Leroy, Gary Kleck, and Marc Gertz. 1992. "The Concept of 'Crime' in Criminological Theory and Practice." *Criminologist* 17: 1–6.

———. 2001. "Crime as Social Interaction." In *What Is Crime?* edited by Stuart Henry and Mark Lanier, 101–114. Boulder, CO: Rowman and Littlefield.

Gove, Walter, ed. 1975. *The Labeling of Deviance: Evaluating a Perspective.* New York: John Wiley.

Gove, Walter, and C. Wilmoth. 1990. "Risk, Crime, and Neurophysiological Highs: A Consideration of Brain Processes That May Reinforce Delinquent and Criminal Behavior." In *Crime in Biological, Social, and Moral Contexts,* edited by L. Ellis and H. Hoffman. New York: Praeger.

Grant, J. 1993. *Fundamental Feminism: Contesting the Core Concepts of Feminist Theory.* New York: Routledge.

Grasmick, Harold G., and Robert J. Bursik Jr. 1990. "Conscience, Significant Others, and Rational Choice: Extending the Deterrence Model." *Law and Society Review* 24: 837–861.

Grasmick, Harold G., Robert J. Bursik Jr., and John K. Cochran. 1991. "'Render unto Caesar What Is Caesar's': Religiosity and Taxpayers' Inclinations to Cheat." *Sociological Quarterly* 32: 251–266.

Green, Gary S. [1990] 1997. *Occupational Crime.* Chicago: Nelson-Hall.

Green, Gary S., N. South, and R. Smith. 2006. "'They Say You Are a Danger but You Are Not': Representations and Construction of the Moral Self in Narratives of 'Dangerous Individuals.'" *Deviant Behavior* 27, no. 3: 299–328.

Greenberg, David F., ed. [1981] 1993. *Crime and Capitalism: Readings in Marxist Criminology.* Palo Alto, CA: Mayfield.

Greenberg, Jerald. 1990. "Employee Theft as a Reaction to Underpayment Inequity: The Hidden Cost of Pay Cuts." *Journal of Applied Psychology* 75: 561–568.

Greenwood, Peter W. 1983. "Controlling the Crime Rate Through Imprisonment." In *Crime and Public Policy,* edited by James. Q. Wilson. San Francisco: Institute for Contemporary Studies.

———. 1996. *Diverting Children from a Life of Crime: What Are the Costs?* Santa Monica: RAND.

Griffin, Susan. 1979. *Rape: The Power of Consciousness.* San Francisco: Harper and Row.

Gross, Edward. 1978. "Organizational Sources of Crime: A Theoretical Perspective." In *Studies in Symbolic Interaction,* edited by Norman K. Denzin. Greenwich, CT: JAI.

Grossman, Dave. 1998. "Trained to Kill: Are We Teaching Our Children to Commit Murder?" *Christianity Today,* August 10.

Grossman, Dave, and G. DeGaetano. 1999. *Stop Teaching Our Kids to Kill: A Call to Action Against TV, Movie, and Video Game Violence.* New York: Crown Books.

Gusfield, Joseph R. 1963. *Symbolic Crusade.* Champaign: University of Illinois Press.

Haddock, Vicki. 2006. "Lies Wide Open: Researchers Say Technology Can Show When and How a Lie Is Created Inside the Brain." *San Francisco Chronicle,* August 6, E1.

Hagan, Frank E. 1986. *Introduction to Criminology.* Chicago: Nelson-Hall.

———. 1993. *Research Methods in Criminal Justice and Criminology.* New York: Macmillan.

Hagan, John. 1977. *The Disreputable Pleasures.* Toronto: McGraw-Hill Ryerson.

———. 1985. *Modern Criminology: Crime, Criminal Behavior, and Its Control.* New York: McGraw-Hill.

———. 1989. *Structural Criminology.* New Brunswick, NJ: Rutgers University Press.

———. 1990. "The Structuration of Gender and Deviance: A Power-Control Theory of Vulnerability to Crime and the Search for Deviant Role Exits." *Canadian Review of Sociology and Anthropology* 27, no. 2: 137–156.

———. 1993. "The Social Embeddedness of Crime and Unemployment." *Criminology* 31: 465–492.

———. 1994. *Crime and Disrepute.* Thousand Oaks, CA: Pine Forge Press.

Hagan, John, and Alberto Palloni. 1990. "The Social Reproduction of a Criminal Class in Working-Class London, Circa 1950–1980." *American Journal of Sociology* 96: 265–299.

Hagan, John, John Simpson, and A. R. Gillis. 1987. "Class in the Household: A Power-Control Theory of Gender and Delinquency." *American Journal of Sociology* 92: 788–816.

Hagedorn, John M. [1988] 1994/1998. *People and Folks: Gangs, Crime, and the Underclass in a Rustbelt City.* Chicago: Lake View Press.

———. 1994. "Homeboys, Dope Fiends, Legits, and New Jacks." *Criminology* 32: 197–220.

———. 2004. "Gang." In *Encyclopedia of Men and Masculinities,* edited by Michael S. Kimmel and Amy M. Aronson, 329–330. Santa Barbara, CA: ABC-CLIO.

————. 2005. "The Global Impact of Gangs." *Journal of Contemporary Criminal Justice* 21, no. 2: 153–169.

————. 2006. "Gangs as Social Actors." In *The Essential Criminology Reader,* edited by Stuart Henry and Mark M. Lanier, 141–151. Boulder, CO: Westview Press.

————. 2007a. "Gangs, Institutions, Race, and Space: The Chicago School Revisited." In *Gangs in the Global City: Alternatives to Traditional Criminology,* edited by John M. Hagedorn, 13–33. Champaign: University of Illinois Press.

————. 2007b. "Gangs in Late Modernity." In *Gangs in the Global City: Alternatives to Traditional Criminology,* edited by John M. Hagedorn, 295–317. Champaign: University of Illinois Press.

————, ed. 2007c. *Gangs in the Global City: Alternatives to Traditional Criminology.* Champaign: University of Illinois Press.

————. 2008. *A World of Gangs: Armed Young Men and Gangsta Culture.* Minneapolis: University of Minnesota Press.

Hale, Robert. 1992. "Arrest Rates and Community Characteristics: Social Ecology Theory Applied to a Southern City." *American Journal of Criminal Justice* 16: 17–32.

Hall, Jerome. 1952. *Theft, Law, and Society.* 2d ed. Indianapolis: Bobbs-Merrill.

Halleck, Seymour. 1971. *Psychiatry and the Dilemmas of Crime.* Berkeley and Los Angeles: University of California Press.

Hallsworth, Simon. 2002. "Case for a Postmodern Penality." *Theoretical Criminology* 6: 145–163.

Hamlin, John E. 1988. "The Misplaced Role of Rational Choice in Neutralization Theory." *Criminology* 26: 425–438.

Handelman, S. 1993. "Why Capitalism and the Mafia May Mean Business." *New York Times,* January 24.

Handler, Joel. 1992. "The Presidential Address, 1992—Law and Society: Postmodernism, Protest, and the New Social Movement." *Law and Society Review* 26: 697–731.

Harding, Sandra G. 1991. *Whose Science? Whose Knowledge? Thinking from Women's Lives.* Ithaca, NY: Cornell University Press.

Harris, Anthony R. 1976. "Race, Commitment to Deviance, and Spoiled Identity." *American Sociological Review* 41: 432–442.

Harris, Kay M. 1991. "Moving into the New Millennium: Toward a Feminist View of Justice." In *Criminology as Peacemaking,* edited by Harold E. Pepinsky and Richard Quinney. Bloomington: Indiana University Press.

Harris, Melissa, and Sandra Mathers. 2002. "Orlando Restricts Homeless." *Orlando Sentinel,* August 6.

Harris Poll. 2006. "Large Majorities of Public Support Surveillance of Suspected Terrorists." In *The Harris Poll,* no. 63. August 17. http://www.harrisinteractive.com/harris_poll/index.asp?PID=690 (accessed March 25, 2009).

Hartmann, Heidi. 1981. "The Unhappy Marriage of Marxism and Feminism: Towards a More Progressive Union." In *Women and Revolution,* edited by Lydia Sargent. Boston: South End Press.

Hartung, Frank. 1950. "White-Collar Offenses in the Wholesale Meat Industry in Detroit." *American Journal of Sociology* 56: 25–34.

Harvey, David. 2003. *The New Imperialism.* Oxford: Oxford University Press.

Hasking, P. A. 2007. "Reinforcement Sensitivity, Coping, and Delinquent Behavior in Adolescence." *Journal of Adolescence* 30, no. 5: 739–749.

Hathaway, Starke. 1939. "The Personality Inventory as an Aid in the Diagnosis of Psychopathic Inferiors." *Journal of Consulting Psychology* 3: 112–117.

Hatty, Suzanne E. 2000. *Masculinities, Violence, and Culture.* Thousand Oaks, CA: Sage.

Hawley, Amos H. 1950. *Human Ecology: A Theory of Community Structure.* New York: Ronald.

———. 1968. "Human Ecology." In *International Encyclopedia of the Social Sciences,* edited by David Sills, 4: 328–337. New York: Macmillan and Free Press.

Hay, Carter. 2001. "Parenting, Self-Control, and Delinquency: A Test of Self-Control Theory." *Criminology* 39: 707–735.

Hayner, Norman S. 1933. "Delinquency Areas in the Puget Sound Region." *American Journal of Sociology* 22: 314–328.

Haynes, Roger, Kevin Cole, and Jennifer Woll. 1994. *Federal Sentencing Guidebook.* New York: McGraw-Hill.

Hayward, Keith J. 2004. *City Limits: Crime, Consumer Culture, and the Urban Experience.* London: Glasshouse.

———. 2007. "Cultural Criminology." In *The Dictionary of Youth Justice,* edited by Barry Goldson. Cullompton, Devon, UK: Willan. http://www.culturalcriminology.org/papers/youth-justice-dictionary.pdf (accessed January 11, 2009).

Healy, William, and Augusta Bronner. 1926. *Delinquents and Criminals: Their Making and Unmaking.* New York: Macmillan.

———. 1936. *New Light on Delinquency and Its Treatment.* New Haven, CT: Yale University Press.

Heidensohn, Frances. 1985. *Women and Crime.* Basingstoke, UK: Macmillan.

Heimer, Karen, and Stacy De Coster. 1999. "The Gendering of Violent Delinquency." *Criminology* 37: 277–317.

Heimer, Karen, and Ross L. Matsueda. 1994. "Role-Taking, Role Commitment, and Delinquency: A Theory of Differential Social Control." *American Sociological Review* 59: 365–390.

Heineke, John M., ed. 1978. *Economic Models of Criminal Behavior.* New York: North-Holland.

———. 1988. "Crime, Deterrence, and Choice: Testing the Rational Behavior Hypothesis." *American Sociological Review* 53: 303–305.

Heinlein, Gary. 2002. "Michigan Eases Drug Sentences: Judges' Discretion Replaces Mandatory Terms for Offenders." *Detroit News and Free Press,* December 29, A1, A9.

Heitgerd, Janet L., and Robert J. Bursik Jr. 1987. "Extracommunity Dynamics and the Ecology of Delinquency." *American Journal of Sociology* 92: 775–787.

Henderson, Charles R. 1893. *An Introduction to the Study of the Dependent, Defective, and Delinquent Classes.* Boston: D. C. Heath.

Henning, K. R., and B. C. Frueh. 1996. "Cognitive-Behavioral Treatment of Incarcerated Offenders: An Evaluation of the Vermont Department of Corrections' Cognitive Self-Change Program." *Criminal Justice Behavior* 23, no. 4: 523–541.

Henry, Stuart. 1976. "Fencing with Accounts: The Language of Moral Bridging." *British Journal of Law and Society* 3: 91–100.

———. 1977. "On the Fence." *British Journal of Law and Society* 4: 124–133.

———. [1978] 1988. *The Hidden Economy: The Context and Control of Borderline Crime.* Oxford: Martin Robertson; Port Townsend, WA: Loompanics.

———, ed. 1981. *Informal Institutions.* New York: St. Martin's.

———. 1983. *Private Justice.* London: Routledge and Kegan Paul.

———. 1984. "Contradictions of Collective Justice: The Case of the Co-op Cops." *Howard Journal of Criminal Justice* 23: 158–169.

———. 1985. "Community Justice, Capitalist Society, and Human Agency: The Dialectics of Collective Law in the Co-operative." *Law and Society Review* 19: 303–327.

————, ed. 1990. *Degrees of Deviance: Student Accounts of Their Deviant Behavior.* Aldershot, UK: Avebury; Salem, WI: Sheffield.

————. 1991. "The Informal Economy: A Crime of Omission by the State." In *Crimes by the Capitalist State: An Introduction to State Criminality,* edited by Gregg Barak. Albany: State University of New York Press.

————, ed. 1994. "Employee Dismissal: Justice at Work." Special issue, *Annals of the American Academy of Political and Social Science* 536.

————. 1999. "Is Left Realism a Useful Theory for Addressing the Problems of Crime? No?" In *Controversial Issues in Criminology,* edited by John R. Fuller and Eric W. Hickey, 137–144. Boston: Allyn and Bacon.

————. 2000. "What Is School Violence? An Integrated Definition." In "School Violence," edited by William Hinkle and Stuart Henry, 16–29. Special issue, *Annals of the American Academy of Political and Social Science* 567.

————. 2009. "School Violence Beyond Columbine: A Complex Problem in Need of an Interdisciplinary Analysis." In "Columbine: Lessons Learned," edited by G. W. Muschert and J. W. Spencer. Special issue, *American Behavior Scientist* (April).

Henry, Stuart, and Roger Eaton, eds. 1999. *Degrees of Deviance: Student Accounts of Their Deviant Behavior.* 2d ed. Salem, WI: Sheffield.

Henry, Stuart, and Mark Lanier. 1998. "The Prism of Crime: Arguments for an Integrated Definition of Crime." *Justice Quarterly* 15: 609–627.

————, eds. 2001. *What Is Crime? Controversies over the Nature of Crime and What to Do About It.* Boulder, CO: Rowman and Littlefield.

Henry, Stuart, and Scott Lukas, eds. 2009. *Recent Developments in Criminological Theory: Toward Disciplinary Diversity and Theoretical Integration.* Farnham, UK: Ashgate.

Henry, Stuart, and Dragan Milovanovic. 1991. "Constitutive Criminology: The Maturation of Critical Theory." *Criminology* 29: 293–316.

————. 1994. "The Constitution of Constitutive Criminology: A Postmodern Approach to Criminological Theory." In *The Futures of Criminology,* edited by David Nelken. London: Sage.

————. 1996. *Constitutive Criminology: Beyond Postmodernism.* London: Sage.

————, eds. 1999. *Constitutive Criminology at Work: Applications to Crime and Justice.* Albany: State University of New York Press.

————. 2001. "Constitutive Definition of Crime: Power as Harm." In *What Is Crime?* edited by Stuart Henry and Mark Lanier, 101–114. Boulder, CO: Rowman and Littlefield.

————. 2003. "Constitutive Criminology." In *Controversies in Critical Criminology,* edited by Martin D. Schwartz and Suzanne E. Hatty, 57–70. Cincinnati: Anderson.

Henry, Stuart, and Dana Nurge. 2007. "Gangs and the Informal Economy." In *The Encyclopedia of Gangs,* edited by Louis Kontos and Dave Brotherton, 87–94. Westport, CT: Greenwoord Press.

Hepburn, John R. 1977. "The Impact of Police Intervention upon Juvenile Delinquents." *Criminology* 18: 121–129.

Hepburn, John R., and Lynne Goodstein. 1986. "Organizational Imperatives and Sentencing Reform Implementation: The Impact of Prison Practices and Priorities on the Attainment of the Objective of Determinate Sentencing." *Crime and Delinquency* 32: 329–365.

Herzog, S., and A. Rattner. 2003. "Public Perceptions of Crime Seriousness in Israel: Native-Born Versus New Immigrants." *International Journal of the Sociology of Law* 31, no. 4: 323–341.

Heumann, Milton, and Colin Loftin. 1979. "Mandatory Sentencing and the Abolition of Plea Bargaining: The Michigan Felony Firearm Statute." *Law and Society Review* 13: 393–430.

Hibbert, Christopher. [1963] 1966. *The Roots of Evil: A Social History of Crime and Punishment.* London: Weidenfeld and Nicolson.

Higgins, G. E., R. Tewksbury, and E. E. Mustaine. 2007. "Sports Fan Binge Drinking: An Examination Using Low Self-Control and Peer Association." *Sociological Spectrum* 27, no. 4: 389–404.

Hills, Stuart L. 1971. *Crime, Power, and Morality.* Scranton, PA: Chandler.

Hinckeldey, Christoph, ed. 1981. *Criminal Justice Through the Ages: From Divine Judgement to Modern German Legislation.* Translated by John Fosberry. Rothenburg, Germany: Medieval Crime Museum.

Hindelang, Michael J. 1970. "The Commitment of Delinquents to Their Misdeeds: Do Delinquents Drift?" *Social Problems* 17: 502–509.

———. 1973. "Causes of Delinquency: A Partial Replication and Extension." *Social Problems* 20: 471–487.

———. 1974. "Moral Evaluations of Illegal Behaviors." *Social Problems* 21: 370–385.

Hinduja, S. 2007. "Workplace Violence and Negative Affective Responses: A Test of Agnew's General Strain Theory." *Journal of Criminal Justice* 35, no. 6: 657–666.

Hinkle, William, and Stuart Henry, eds. 2000. "School Violence." Special issue, *Annals of the American Academy of Political and Social Science* 567.

Hirschi, Travis. 1969. *Causes of Delinquency.* Berkeley and Los Angeles: University of California Press.

———. 1979. "Separate and Equal Is Better." *Journal of Research in Crime and Delinquency* 16: 34–38.

———. 1983. "Crime and Family Policy." *Journal of Contemporary Studies* 4: 3–16.

Hirschi, Travis, and Michael R. Gottfredson. 2001. "Self-Control Theory." In *Explaining Criminals and Crime,* edited by Raymond Paternoster and Ronet Bachman, 81–96. Los Angeles: Roxbury Press.

———. 2006. "Social Control and Self-Control Theory." In *The Essential Criminology Reader,* edited by Stuart Henry and Mark M. Lanier, 111–118. Boulder, CO: Westview Press.

Hirschi, Travis, and Michael Hindelang. 1977. "Intelligence and Delinquency: A Revisionist Review." *American Sociological Review* 42: 471–586.

Hirschi, Travis, and Rodney Stark. 1969. "Hellfire and Delinquency." *Social Problems* 17: 202–213.

Hoffman-Bustamente, Dale. 1973. "The Nature of Female Criminality." *Issues in Criminology* 8: 117–136.

Hoffmann, John P., and Timothy Ireland. 1995. "Cloward and Ohlin's Strain Theory Reexamined: An Elaborated Theoretical Model." In *The Legacy of Anomie Theory: Advances in Criminological Theory,* edited by Freda Adler and William S. Laufer. Vol. 6. New Brunswick, NJ: Transaction Publishers.

Hoge, Robert D. 1999. "An Expanded Role for Psychological Assessments in Juvenile Justice Systems." *Criminal Justice and Behavior* 26: 251–266.

Hollin, Clive R. 1990. *Cognitive Behavioral Interventions with Young Offenders.* New York: Pergamon.

Hollinger, Richard C. 1991. "Neutralizing in the Workplace: An Empirical Analysis of Property Theft and Production Deviance." *Deviant Behavior* 12: 169–202.

Hollinger, Richard C., and John P. Clark. 1983. *Theft by Employees.* Lexington, MA: D. C. Heath.

Holman, John E., and James F. Quinn. 1992. *Criminology: Applying Theory.* St. Paul, MN: West.

Holmes, M. D., B. W. Smith, and A. B. Freng. 2008. "Minority Threat, Crime Control, and Police Resource Allocation in the Southwestern United States." *Crime and Delinquency* 54, no. 1: 128–152.

Holsinger, K., and A. M. Holsinger. 2005. "Differential Pathways to Violence and Self-Injurious Behavior: African American and White Girls in the Juvenile Justice System." *Journal of Research in Crime and Delinquency* 42, no. 2: 211–242.

Hood-Williams, John. 2001. "Gender, Masculinities, and Crime: From Structures to Psyches." *Theoretical Criminology* 5: 37–60.

Hooton, Ernest A. 1939. *The American Criminal: An Anthropological Study.* Cambridge, MA: Harvard University Press.

Horney, Julie. 1978. "Menstrual Cycles and Criminal Responsibility." *Law and Human Nature* 2: 25–36.

———. 2006. "An Alternative Psychology of Criminal Behavior." *Criminology* 44, no. 1: 1–16.

Horowitz, Donald. 1977. *Courts and Social Policy.* Washington, DC: Brookings Institution.

Horwitz, Allan, and Michael Wasserman. 1979. "The Effect of Social Control on Delinquent Behavior: A Longitudinal Test." *Sociological Focus* 12: 53–70.

Howe, Adrian. 1994. *Punish and Critique: Towards a Feminist Analysis of Penality.* London: Routledge.

Huesmann, L. Rowell, Jessica Moise-titus, Cheryl-Lynn Podolski, and Leonard D. Eron. 2003. "Longitudinal Relations Between Children's Exposure to TV Violence and Their Aggressive and Violent Behavior in Young Adulthood, 1977–1992." *Developmental Psychology* 39: 201–221.

Huff, C. Ronald. 1998. "Comparing the Criminal Behavior of Youth Gangs and At-Risk Youths." Research in Brief. October. Washington, DC: National Institute of Justice. http://www.streetgangs.com/academic/chuff_compare.pdf (accessed December 29, 2008).

Hughes, S. P., and Ann L. Schneider. 1989. "Victim-Offender Mediation: A Survey of Program Characteristics and Perceptions of Effectiveness." *Crime and Delinquency* 35: 217–233.

Huizinga, David, and Delbert S. Elliott. 1987. "Juvenile Offenders: Prevalence, Offender Incidence, and Arrest Rates by Race." *Crime and Delinquency* 33: 206–223.

Humphries, Laud. 1970. *Tearoom Trade: Impersonal Sex in Public Places.* Chicago: Aldine.

Hunt, Alan. 1990. "The Big Fear: Law Confronts Postmodernism." *McGill Law Journal* 35: 507–540.

———. 1991. "Postmodernism and Critical Criminology." In *New Directions in Critical Criminology,* edited by Brian D. MacLean and Dragan Milovanovic. Vancouver, BC: Collective Press.

Hunter, Albert J. 1985. "Private, Parochial, and Public Orders: The Problem of Crime and Incivility in Urban Communities." In *The Challenge of Social Control: Citizenship and Institution Building in Modern Society,* edited by Gerald D. Suttles and Mayer N. Zald. Norwood, NJ: Ablex.

Hunter, Ronald D., and Mark L. Dantzker. 2002. *Crime and Criminality: Causes and Consequences.* Upper Saddle River, NJ: Prentice-Hall.

Hurwitz, Stephan, and Karl O. Christiansen. 1983. *Criminology.* London: George Allen and Unwin.

Hussey, Ann C. 1997. "Incapacitation." In *Crime and the Justice System in America,* edited by Frank Schmalleger, 120–121. Westport, CT: Greenwood.

Hutchings, Barry, and Sarnoff A. Mednick. 1975. "Registered Criminality in the Adoptive and Biological Parents of Registered Male Criminal Adoptees." In *Genetic Research in Psychiatry,* edited by R. R. Fieve, D. Rosenthal, and H. Brill. Baltimore: Johns Hopkins University Press.

Hutchinson, Thomas W., David Yellen, Debra Young, and Matthew R. Kip. 1994. *Federal Sentencing Law and Practice.* 2d ed. St. Paul, MN: West.

"I'm Going to Detroit." 1988. *Time,* May 9.

Inderbitzin, L. B., C. M. Luke, and M. E. James. 1990. "Psychoanalytical Psychotherapy." In *Human Behavior: An Introduction of Medical Students,* edited by A. Stoudermire. Philadelphia: Lippincott.

Innocence Project. 2009. "About the Organization." http://www.innocenceproject.org/about/Mission-Statement.php (accessed March 20, 2009).

In re Winship. 397 U.S. 358, 90 S.Ct. 1068 (1970).

Institute for Social Research. 1994. *Monitoring the Future, 1992.* Ann Arbor, MI: ICPSR.

Ishikawa, Sharon S., and Adrian Raine. 2002. "Behavioral Genetics and Crime." In *The Neurobiology of Criminal Behavior,* edited by J. Glicksohn, 4: 81–110. Norwell, MA: Kluwer Academic Publishing.

Jackson, Elton F., Charles R. Tittle, and Mary Jean Burke. 1986. "Offense-Specific Models of the Differential Association Process." *Social Problems* 33: 335–356.

Jackson, Stevi. 1992. "The Amazing Deconstructing Woman Suggests Some Problems with Postmodern Feminism." *Trouble and Strife* 25: 25–31.

Jacobs, David. 1978. "Inequality and the Legal Order: An Ecological Test of the Conflict Model." *Social Problems* 25: 515–525.

Jacobs, Jane. 1961. *The Death and Life of Great American Cities.* New York: Random House.

Jacobs, Patricia A., M. Brunton, M. M. Melville, R. P. Brittain, and W. McClemont. 1965. "Aggressive Behavior Mental Subnormality and the XYY Male." *Nature* 208: 1351–1352.

Jacoby, Joseph E. 1994. *Classics of Criminology.* 2d ed. Prospect Heights, IL: Waveland.

Jaggar, Alison. 1983. *Feminist Politics and Human Nature.* Totowa, NJ: Rowman and Allanheld.

James, Leon, and Diane Nahl. 2001. *Road Rage and Aggressive Driving: Steering Clear of Highway Warfare.* New York: Prometheus Books.

Jankowski, Martin Sanchez. 1991. *Islands in the Street: Gangs and American Urban Society.* Berkeley and Los Angeles: University of California Press.

Jansson, Bruce. 2001. *The Reluctant Welfare State.* Stamford, CT: Brooks-Cole.

Jaquith, Susan M. 1981. "Adolescent Marijuana and Alcohol Use: An Empirical Test of Differential Association Theory." *Criminology* 19: 271–280.

Jarjoura, G. Roger. 1996. "The Conditional Effect of Social Class on the Dropout-Delinquency Relationship." *Journal of Research in Crime and Delinquency* 33: 232–255.

Jeffery, C. Ray. 1965. "Criminal Behavior and Learning Theory." *Journal of Criminal Law, Criminology, and Police Science* 56: 294–300.

———. 1971. *Crime Prevention Through Environmental Design.* Beverly Hills, CA: Sage.

———. 1977. "Criminology as an Interdisciplinary Behavioral Science." *Criminology* 16: 153–156.

———. 1993. "Genetics, Crime, and the Cancelled Conference." *Criminologist* 18, no. 1: 1, 6–8.

———. 1994. "Biological and Neuropsychiatric Approaches to Criminal Behavior." In *Varieties of Criminology: Readings from a Dynamic Discipline,* edited by Gregg Barak, 15–28. Westport, CT: Praeger.

Jensen, Gary F. 1972a. "Delinquency and Adolescent Self-Conceptions: A Study of the Personal Relevance of Infraction." *Social Problems* 20: 84–103.

———. 1972b. "Parents, Peers, and Delinquent Action: A Test of the Differential Association Perspective." *American Journal of Sociology* 78: 562–575.

———. 1980. "Labeling and Identity: Toward a Reconciliation of Divergent Findings." *Criminology* 18: 121–129.

———. 2002. "Institutional Anomie and Societal Variations in Crime: A Critical Appraisal." *International Journal of Sociology and Social Policy* 22: 45–74.

Jensen, Gary F., and David Brownfield. 1986. "Gender, Lifestyles, and Victimization: Beyond Routine Activity." *Violence and Victims* 1: 85–99.

John Jay College of Criminal Justice. 2001. "Racial Profiling Is More Than a Black and White Issue." *Law Enforcement News* 27, no. 568 (December 31). http://www.lib.jjay.cuny.edu/len/2001/12.31/facing.html (accessed March 22, 2009).

Johns, Christina. 1992. *The War on Drugs.* Westport, CT: Greenwood Press.

Johnson, Doyle P. 2008. *Contemporary Sociological Theory: An Integrated Multi-level Approach.* New York: Springer Science.

Johnson, Lee Michael, Ronald Simons, and Rand D. Conger. 2004. "Criminal Justice System Involvement and Continuity of Youth Crime: A Longitudinal Analysis." *Youth and Society* 36, no. 1: 3–29.

Johnson, M. C., and G. A. Kercher. 2007. "ADHD, Strain, and Criminal Behavior: A Test of General Strain Theory." *Deviant Behavior* 28, no. 2: 131–152.

Johnson, Richard E. 1979. *Juvenile Delinquency and Its Origins.* Cambridge: Cambridge University Press.

Johnson, Richard E., Anastasios C. Marcos, and Stephen J. Bahr. 1987. "The Role of Peers in the Complex Etiology of Adolescent Drug Use." *Criminology* 25: 323–340.

Johnson, Valerie. 1985. "Adolescent Alcohol and Marijuana Use: A Social Learning Perspective." Paper presented at the annual meeting of the Society for the Study of Social Problems, Washington, DC, August.

———. 1988. "Adolescent Alcohol and Marijuana Use: A Longitudinal Assessment of a Social Learning Perspective." *American Journal of Drug and Alcohol Abuse* 14: 419–439.

Johnstone, John W. 1978. "Social Class, Social Areas, and Delinquency." *Sociology and Social Research* 63: 49–72.

Jonassen, Christen T. 1949. "A Re-evaluation and Critique of the Logic and Some Methods of Shaw and McKay." *American Sociological Review* 14: 608–614.

Jones, T., Brian D. MacLean, and Jock Young. 1986. *The Islington Crime Survey: Crime Policing and Victimization in Inner-City London.* Aldershot, UK: Gower.

Joutsen, Matti. 1994. "Victimology and Victim Policy in Europe." *Criminologist* 19: 1–6.

Kamin, L. J. 1985. "Criminality and Adoption." *Science* 227: 982.

Kaplan, Howard B. 1975. *Self-Attitudes and Deviant Behavior.* Pacific Palisades, CA: Goodyear.

Kappeler, Victor E., and Peter B. Kraska. 1999. "Policing Modernity: Scientific and Community-Based Violence on Symbolic Playing Fields." In *Constitutive Criminology at Work: Applications to Crime and Justice,* edited by Stuart Henry and Dragan Milovanovic. Albany: State University of New York Press.

Karmen, Andrew. 1990. *Crime Victims: An Introduction to Victimology.* 2d ed. Pacific Grove, CA: Brooks/Cole.

———. [2001] 2006. *Crime Victims: An Introduction to Victimology.* 6th ed. Belmont, CA: Wadsworth.

Kasindorf, Martin. 2002. "Three Strikes Laws Fall Out of Favor." *USA Today*, February 2, A3.

Katona, D. 1999. "Challenging the Global Structure Through Self-Determination: An African Perspective." *American University International Law Review* 14: 1439–1472.

Katz, Charles M., Vincent J. Webb, and David R. Schaefer. 2001. "An Assessment of the Impact of Quality-of-Life Policing on Crime and Disorder." *Justice Quarterly* 18: 825–876.

Katz, Jack. 1988. *Seductions of Crime: Moral and Sensual Attractions of Doing Evil.* New York: Basic Books.

Katz, Janet, and William J. Chambliss. 1991. "Biology and Crime." In *Criminology: A Contemporary Handbook,* edited by Joseph F. Sheley. Belmont, CA: Wadsworth.

Katz, John. 1999. "Voices from Hellmouth." http://slashdot.org/articles/99/04/25/1438249 .shtml (accessed March 15, 2009).

Kelland, Kate. 2008. "Stop Using Laws to Spy on Public, UK Councils Told." Reuters North American News Service. http://www.blnz.com/news/2008/06/23/Stop_using_laws _public_councils_9351.html (accessed March 18, 2009).

Kelleher, Michael D., and C. L. Kellerher. 1998. *Murder Most Rare: The Female Serial Killer.* Westport, CT: Prager.

Kelling, G., and C. Coles. 1996. *Fixing Broken Windows.* New York: Free Press.

Kempa, M., R. Carrier, J. Wood, and C. Stenning. 2000. "The Evolving Concept of 'Private Policing.'" *European Journal of Criminal Policy and Research* 7, no. 1: 197–223.

Kennedy, David M. 1996. "Neighborhood Revitalization: Lessons from Savannah and Baltimore." *National Institute of Justice Journal* 231 (August): 13–17.

Kennedy, Leslie W., and David R. Forde. 1990a. "Risky Lifestyles and Dangerous Results: Routine Activities and Exposure to Crime." *Sociology and Social Research* 74: 208–211.

———. 1990b. "Routine Activities and Crime: An Analysis of Victimization in Canada." *Criminology* 28: 101–115.

Kent, Allison D. 2007. "Custody, Maintenance, and Succession: The Internalization of Women's and Children's Rights Under Customary Law in Africa." *Michigan Journal of International Law* 28, no. 2: 507–539.

Khoza, V., and P. J. Potgieter, 2005. "Deviant Driving Behavior: An Epidemiological Study." *Acta Criminologica* 18, no. 2: 56–70.

Kilcher, Jewel. 1994. *Pieces of You.* New York: Atlantic Records.

Kinsey, Richard. 1979. "Despotism and Legality." In *Capitalism and the Rule of Law: From Deviancy Theory to Marxism,* edited by Bob Fine, Richard Kinsey, John Lea, Sol Picciotto, and Jock Young. London: Hutchinson.

Klein, Dorie. [1973] 1980. "The Etiology of Female Crime: A Review of the Literature." In *Women, Crime, and Justice,* edited by Susan K. Datesman and Frank R. Scarpitti. New York: Oxford University Press.

Klinger, David. 1997. "Negotiating Order in Patrol Work: An Ecological Theory of Police Response to Crime." *Criminology* 35: 277–306.

Klockars, Carl. 1974. *The Professional Fence.* New York: Free Press.

———. 1980. "The Contemporary Crisis of Marxist Criminology." In *Radical Criminology: The Coming Crisis,* edited by James Inciardi. Beverly Hills, CA: Sage.

Knoblich, Guenther, and Roy King. 1992. "Biological Correlates of Criminal Behavior." In *Facts, Frameworks, and Forecasts: Advances in Criminological Theory,* edited by Joan McCord. Vol. 3. New Brunswick, NJ: Transaction Publishers.

Knopp, Fay Honey. 1991. "Community Solutions to Sexual Violence: Feminist/Abolitionist Perspectives." In *Criminology as Peacemaking,* edited by Harold Pepinsky and Richard Quinney. Bloomington: Indiana University Press.

Knox, Colin. 2001. "The 'Deserving' Victims of Political Violence: Punishment Attacks in Northern Ireland." *International Journal of Policy and Practice* 1, no. 2: 181–199.

Knox, George W., Jodet M. Harris et al. 1997. *The Facts About Gang Life in America Today: A National Study of over 4,000 Gang Members.* Peotone, IL: National Gang Crime Research Center. http://www.ngcrc.com/ngcrc/gfactp.pdf (accessed December 29, 2008).

Knox, George W., Edward D. Tromanhauser et al. 1995. *The Economics of Gang Life: A Task Force Report of the National Gang Crime Research Center.* Peotone, IL: National Gang Crime Research Center. http://www.ngcrc.com/ngcrc/page11.htm (accessed December 29, 2008).

Kobrin, Solomon. 1959. "The Chicago Area Project: A 25-Year Assessment." *Annals of the American Academy of Social Science* 322: 20–29.

———. 1971. "The Formal Legal Properties of the Shaw-McKay Delinquency Theory." In *Ecology, Crime, and Delinquency,* edited by Harwin L. Voss and David M. Peterson. New York: Appleton, Century, Crofts.

Kohlberg, Lawrence. 1969. "Stage and Sequence: The Cognitive-Developmental Approach to Socialization." In *Handbook of Socialization Theory and Research,* edited by D. A. Goslin. Chicago: Rand McNally.

Kolodner, Meredith. 2006. "Private Prisons Expect a Boom: Immigration Enforcement to Benefit Detention Companies." *New York Times,* July 19, C1.

Konty, Mark. 2005. "Microanomie: The Cognitive Foundations of the Relationship Between Anomie and Deviance." *Criminology* 43, no. 1: 107–132.

Kornhauser, Ruth Rosner. 1978. *Social Sources of Delinquency.* Chicago: University of Chicago Press.

———. 1984. *Social Sources of Delinquency.* 2d ed. Chicago: University of Chicago Press.

Kraidy, Ute Sartorius. 2002. "Sunny Days on Sesame Street? Multiculturalism and Resistance Postmodernism." *Journal of Communication Inquiry* 26: 9–25.

Kramer, John H., and Robin L. Lubitz. 1985. "Pennsylvania's Sentencing Reform: The Impact of Commission-Established Guidelines." *Crime and Delinquency* 31: 481–500.

Kramer, John H., Robin L. Lubitz, and Cynthia A. Kempinen. 1989. "Sentencing Guidelines: A Quantitative Comparison of Sentencing Policy in Minnesota, Pennsylvania, and Washington." *Justice Quarterly* 6: 565–587.

Kramer, Ronald C. 1982. "The Debate over the Definition of Crime: Paradigms, Value Judgements, and Criminological Work." In *Ethics, Public Policy, and Criminal Justice,* edited by Frederick Elliston and Norm Bowie, 33–58. Cambridge: Oelgeschlager, Gunn, and Hain.

———. 1984. "Corporate Criminality: The Development of an Idea." In *Corporations as Criminals,* edited by Ellen Hochstedler. Beverly Hills, CA: Sage.

———. 2000. "The Role of Poverty, Inequality, and Social Exclusion in Shaping the Problem of Youth Violence." In "School Violence," edited by William Hinkle and Stuart Henry. Special issue, *Annals of the American Academy of Political and Social Science* 567.

Kraska, P. B. 2006. "Criminal Justice Theory: Toward Legitimacy and an Infrastructure." *Justice Quarterly* 23, no. 2: 167–185.

Kretschmer, Ernest. [1921] 1925. *Physique and Character.* New York: Harcourt, Brace.

Krisberg, Barry. 1975. *Crime and Privilege: Towards a New Criminology.* Englewood Cliffs, NJ: Prentice-Hall.

Krohn, Marvin D. 1986. "The Web of Conformity: A Network Approach to the Explanation of Delinquent Behavior." *Social Problems* 33: 581–593.

————. 1991. "Control and Deterrence Theories." In *Criminology: A Contemporary Handbook,* edited by Joseph F. Sheley. Belmont, CA: Wadsworth.

Krohn, Marvin D., and James L. Massey. 1980. "Social Control and Delinquent Behavior: An Examination of the Elements of the Social Bond." *Sociological Quarterly* 21: 529–543.

Krohn, Marvin D., William Skinner, James Massey, and Ronald Akers. 1985. "Social Learning Theory and Adolescent Cigarette Smoking: A Longitudinal Study." *Social Problems* 32: 455–471.

Krueger, Robert, Pamela Schmutte, Avshalom Caspi, Terrie Moffitt, Kathleen Campbell, and Phil Silva. 1994. "Personality Traits Are Linked to Crime Among Men and Women: Evidence from a Birth Cohort." *Journal of Abnormal Psychology* 103: 328–338.

Kuznetsova, R. W. L. F. 1994. "Crime in Russia: Causes and Prevention." *Demokratizatsiya* 2, no. 3: 442–452.

LaFree, Gary, Kriss A. Drass, and Patrick O'Day. 1992. "Race and Crime in Postwar America: Determinants of African-American and White Rates, 1957–1988." *Criminology* 30: 157–188.

LaGrange, Randy L., and Helene Raskin White. 1985. "Age Differences in Delinquency: A Test of Theory." *Criminology* 23: 19–45.

LaGrange, T., and R. Silverman. 1999. "Low Self-Control and Opportunity: Testing the General Theory of Crime as an Explanation for Gender Differences in Delinquency." *Criminology* 37: 41–72.

Landsheer, J. A., Harm't Hart, and W. Kox. 1994. "Delinquent Values and Victim Damage: Exploring the Limits of Neutralization Theory." *British Journal of Criminology* 34: 44–53.

Laner, Mary Riege, and Jeanine Thompson. 1982. "Abuse and Aggression in Courting Couples." *Deviant Behavior* 3: 229–244.

Lanier, Mark M. 1993. "Explication and Measurement of the Theoretical Constructs Underlying Community Policing." Ph.D. diss., Michigan State University.

————. 1994. "Preparing for Jobs in Academia and Research" and "Experiences of Graduate School." In *Inside Jobs: A Realistic Guide to Criminal Justice Careers for College Graduates,* edited by Stuart Henry. Salem, WI: Sheffield.

————. 1996a. "An Evolutionary Typology of Women Police Officers." *Women and Criminal Justice* 8: 35–57.

————. 1996b. "Justice for Incarcerated Women with HIV in the Twenty-first Century." In *Visions for Change: Criminal Justice in the Twenty-first Century,* edited by Roslyn Muraskin and Albert R. Roberts. Englewood Cliffs, NJ: Prentice-Hall.

————. 2009. "Epidemiological Criminology: Critical HIV/AIDS Theory in a Cross-Discipline and Cross-Cultural Context." *Acta Criminologica: South African Journal of Criminology.* In press.

Lanier, Mark M., and William Davidson II. 1995. "Methodological Issues Related to Instrument Development for Community Policing Assessments." *Police Studies* 17: 21–40.

Lanier, Mark M., Ralph DiClemente, and P. F. Horan. 1991. "HIV Knowledge and Behaviors of Incarcerated Youth: A Comparison of High and Low Risk Locales." *Journal of Criminal Justice* 19: 257–262.

Lanier, Mark M., Karol Lucken, and Timothy Akers. 2010. "Further Need for Epidemiological Criminology." In *Key Correctional Issues,* edited by Roslyn Muraskin, 163–174. 2d ed. Upper Saddle River, NJ: Pearson Prentice-Hall.

Lanier, Mark, and Belinda McCarthy. 1989. "AIDS Awareness and the Impact of AIDS Education in Juvenile Corrections." *Criminal Justice and Behavior* 16: 395–411.

Lanier, Mark, and Cloud H. Miller. 1995. "Attitudes and Practices of Federal Probation Officers Toward Pre-plea/Trial Investigative Report Policy." *Crime and Delinquency* 41:
364–377.

Lanier, Mark M., and Roberto Hugh Potter, 2009. "The Current Status of Inmates Living
with HIV/AIDS." In *Visions for Change: Crime and Justice in the Twenty-first Century,*
edited by Roslyn Muraskin and Albert R. Roberts, 542–562. 5th ed. Upper Saddle
River, NJ: Pearson Prentice-Hall.

———. 2010. "The Current Status of Inmates Living with HIV/AIDS." In *Key Correctional
Issues,* edited by Roslyn Muraskin, 140–162. 2d ed. Upper Saddle River, NJ: Pearson
Prentice-Hall.

Lanier, Mark, and John P. Sloan. 1996. "Cynicism, Fear, Communication, and Knowledge of
Acquired Immunodeficiency Syndrome (AIDS) Among Juvenile Delinquents." *Crime
and Delinquency* 42: 231–243.

Larkin, Ralph W. 2007. *Comprehending Columbine.* Philadelphia: Temple University Press.

Lasley, James R. 1988. "Toward a Control Theory of White-Collar Offending." *Journal of
Quantitative Criminology* 4: 347–362.

Lasley, James R., and Jill Leslie Rosenbaum. 1988. "Routine Activities and Multiple Personal
Victimization." *Sociology and Social Research* 73: 47–50.

Latimore, T. L., C. R. Tittle, and H. G. Grasmick. 2006. "Childrearing, Self-Control, and
Crime: Additional Evidence." *Sociological Inquiry* 76, no. 3: 343–371.

Laub, John H. 2006. "Edwin H. Sutherland and the Michael-Adler Report: Searching for the
Soul of Criminology Seventy Years Later." *Criminology* 44, no. 2: 235–257.

Laub, John H., Daniel S. Nagin, and Robert J. Sampson. 1998. "Trajectories of Change in
Criminal Offending." *American Sociological Review* 63: 225–238.

Laub, John H., Robert J. Sampson, and Leana C. Allen. 2001. "Explaining Crime over the
Life Course: Toward a Theory of Age-Graded Informal Social Control." In *Explaining
Crime and Criminals,* edited by Raymond Paternoster and Ronet Bachman, 97–112.
Los Angeles: Roxbury Press.

Lauritsen, Janet L., John H. Laub, and Robert J. Sampson. 1992. "Conventional and Delinquent Activities: Implications for the Prevention of Violent Victimization Among
Adolescents." *Violence and Victims* 7: 91–108.

Lauritsen, Janet L., and Robin J. Schaum. 2004. "The Social Ecology of Violence Against
Women." *Criminology* 42, no. 2: 323–357.

Lea, John, and Jock Young. 1984. *What Is to Be Done About Law and Order?* Harmondsworth,
UK: Penguin.

Leake, Jonathan. 2003. "The Future Looks Black for Redheads." *Sunday Times,* November
16. http://www.redandproud.com/Red%20Herring%20-%20The%20Future%20Looks
%20Black%20For%20Redheads.html (accessed December 12, 2008).

LeBlanc, Marc, and Marchel Fréchette. 1989. *Male Criminal Activity from Childhood Through
Youth: Multilevel and Developmental Perspectives.* New York: Springer-Verlag.

Lee, R. W. 1999. "Transnational Organized Crime: An Overview." In *Transnational Crime in
the Americas,* edited by T. Farer, 1–38. London: Routledge.

Leiber, Michael J., Margaret Farnworth, Katherine M. Jamieson, and Mahesh K. Nalla. 1994.
"Bridging the Gender Gap in Criminology: Liberation and Gender-Specific Strain Effects on Delinquency." *Sociological Inquiry* 64: 56–68.

Leiber, Michael J., and Katherine M. Jamieson. 1995. "Race and Decision Making Within Juvenile Justice: The Importance of Context." *Journal of Quantitative Criminology* 11:
363–388.

Leiber, Michael J., and Tina Mawhorr. 1995. "Evaluating the Use of Social Skills Training and Employment with Delinquent Youth." *Journal of Criminal Justice* 23: 127–141.

Lejins, Peter P. 1987. "Thorsten Sellin: A Life Dedicated to Criminology." *Criminology* 25: 975–988.

Lemert, Edwin M. 1951. *Social Pathology.* New York: McGraw-Hill.

———. 1967. *Human Deviance, Social Problems, and Social Control.* Englewood Cliffs, NJ: Prentice-Hall.

Leonard, Eileen B. 1982. *Women, Crime, and Society: A Critique of Criminological Theory.* New York: Longman.

Levine, Murray, and David Perkins. 1987. *Principles of Community Psychology.* New York: Oxford University Press.

Levitt, Steven D., and Sudhir Alladi Venkatesh. 2000. "An Economic Analysis of a Drug-Selling Gang's Finances." *Quarterly Journal of Economics* 115: 755–789.

Liazos, Alexander. 1972. "The Poverty of the Sociology of Deviance: Nuts, Sluts, and Perverts." *Social Problems* 20: 103–120.

Lilly, J. Robert, Francis T. Cullen, and Richard A. Ball. [1989] 1995. *Criminological Theory: Context and Consequences.* Thousand Oaks, CA: Sage.

———. 2002. *Criminological Theory: Context and Consequences.* 3d ed. Thousand Oaks, CA: Sage.

Liska, Allen E., and Mitchell B. Chamlin. 1984. "Social Structure and Crime Control Among Macrosocial Units." *American Journal of Sociology* 90: 383–395.

Liska, Allen E., and Mark D. Reed. 1985. "Ties to Conventional Institutions and Delinquency: Estimating Reciprocal Effects." *American Sociological Review* 50: 547–560.

Liu, Henry C. K. 2005a. "The Business of Private Security." Pt. 3 of *World Order, Failed States, and Terrorism. Asia Times,* March 3. http://www.atimes.com.

———. 2005b. "The Failed-State Cancer." *World Order, Failed States, and Terrorism. Asia Times.* http://www.atimes.com.

Lizotte, Alan. 1985. "The Uniqueness of Rape: Reporting Assaultive Violence to the Police." *Crime and Delinquency* 32: 169–191.

Lo, C. C., and H. Zhong. 2006. "Linking Crime Rates to Relationship Factors: The Use of Gender-Specific Data." *Journal of Criminal Justice* 34, no. 3: 317–329.

Loader, Ian, and Richard Sparks. 2002. "Contemporary Landscapes of Crime, Order, and Control: Governance, Risk, and Globalization." In *The Oxford Handbook of Criminology,* edited by M. Maguire, R. Morgan, and R. Reiner, 83–111. 3d ed. Oxford: Oxford University Press.

Loeber, Rolf, and D. F. Hay. 1994. "Developmental Approaches to Aggression and Conduct Problems." In *Development Through Life: A Handbook for Clinicians,* edited by Michael L. Rutter and D. F. Hay. Oxford: Blackwell.

Loeber, Rolf, and Marc LeBlanc. 1990. "Toward a Developmental Criminology." In *Crime and Justice,* edited by Norval Morris and Michael Tonry, 23:375–473. Chicago: University of Chicago Press.

Loeber, Rolf, and Magda Stouthammer-Loeber. 1996. "The Development of Offending." *Criminal Justice and Behavior* 23: 12–24.

———. 1998. "Development of Juvenile Aggression and Violence: Some Common Misconceptions and Controversies." *American Psychologist* 53: 242–259.

Lofland, John H. 1969. *Deviance and Identity.* Englewood Cliffs, NJ: Prentice-Hall.

Lombroso, Cesare. 1876. *L'Uomo Delinquente.* Milan: Hoepli.

———. 1911. Introduction to *Criminal Man According to the Classification of Cesare Lombroso,* edited by Gina Lombroso-Ferrero. New York: Putnam.

————. [1912] 1968. *Crime: Its Causes and Remedies.* Montclair, NJ: Patterson Smith.

Lombroso, Cesare, and William Ferrero. 1900. *The Female Offender.* New York: D. Appleton.

Lombroso-Ferrero, Gina. 1994. "Criminal Man." In *Classics of Criminology,* edited by Joseph E. Jacoby. 2d ed. Prospect Heights, IL: Waveland.

Longstreet, Wilma S. 2003. "Early Postmodernism in Social Education: Revisiting 'Decision-making: The Heart of Social Studies Instruction!'" *Social Studies* 94: 11–15.

Lorber, Judith. 1996. "Beyond the Binaries: Depolarizing the Categories of Sex, Sexuality, and Gender." *Sociological Inquiry* 66: 143–159.

Losoncz, I., and G. Tyson. 2007. "Parental Shaming and Adolescent Delinquency: A Partial Test of Reintegrative Shaming Theory." *Australian and New Zealand Journal of Criminology* 40, no. 2: 161–178.

Lotke, Eric. 1993. "Sentencing Disparity Among Co-defendants: The Equalization Debate." *Federal Sentencing Reporter* (University of California Press) 6: 116–119.

Love, Barbara, and Elizabeth Shanklin. 1978. "The Answer Is Matriarchy." In *Our Right to Love,* edited by Ginny Vida. Englewood Cliffs, NJ: Prentice-Hall.

Lovibond, Sabina. 1989. "Feminism and Postmodernism." *New Left Review* 178: 5–28.

Lucken, Karol. 1998. "Contemporary Penal Trends: Modern or Postmodern?" *British Journal of Sociology* 38: 106–123.

Lydston, George F. 1904. *The Diseases of Society (the Vice and Crime Problem).* Philadelphia: J. B. Lippincott.

Lykken, D. 1995. *The Antisocial Personalities.* Hillsdale, NJ: Lawrence Erlbaum.

Lynch, Michael J. 1988. "Surplus Value, Crime, and Punishment." *Contemporary Crises* 12: 329–344.

————. 2000. "J. Phillippe on Crime: An Examination and Critique of the Explanation of Crime and Race." *Social Pathology* 6: 228–244.

Lynch, Michael J., and W. Byron Groves. 1986. *A Primer in Radical Criminology.* New York: Harrow and Heston.

Lynch, Michael, Michael Hogan, and Paul Stretesky. 1999. "A Further Look at Long Cycles and Criminal Justice Legislation." *Justice Quarterly* 18: 1101–1120.

Lynch, Michael J., and Paul B. Stretesky. 2006. "The New Radical Criminology and the Same Old Criticisms." In *The Essential Criminology Reader,* edited by Stuart Henry and Mark M. Lanier, 191–202. Boulder, CO: Westview Press.

Lynch, Michael, Paul Stretesky, and Ronald Burns. 2004. "Determinants of Environmental Law Violation Fines Against Petroleum Refineries: Race, Ethnicity, Income, and Aggregation Effects." *Society and Natural Resources* 17: 343–357.

Lynch, Michael, Paul Stretesky, and Paul Hammond. 2000. "Media Coverage of Chemical Crimes, Hillsborough County, Florida, 1987–1997." *British Journal of Criminology* 40: 111–125.

Lyng, Steve. 1990. "Edgework." *American Journal of Sociology* 95, no. 4: 876–921.

————, ed. 2003. *Edgework.* Albany: State University of New York Press.

————, ed. 2005. *Edgework: The Sociology of Risk-Taking.* New York: Routledge.

MacCoun, Robert, and Peter Router. 1992. "Are the Wages of Sin $30 an Hour? Economic Aspects of Street-Level Drug Dealing." *Crime and Delinquency* 38: 477–491.

MacDonald, Arthur. 1893. *Criminology.* Introduction by Cesare Lombroso. New York: Funk and Wagnalls.

Mack, Dorothy, and Laura Weinland. 1989. "Not Guilty by Reason of Insanity Evaluations: A Study of Defendants and Examiners." *Journal of Criminal Justice* 17: 39–45.

Mack, K. Y., M. J. Leiber, and R. A. Featherstone. 2007. "Reassessing the Family-Delinquency Association: Do Family Type, Family Processes, and Economic Factors Make a Difference?" *Journal of Criminal Justice* 35, no. 1: 51–67.

MacKinnon, Catharine. 1987. *Feminism Unmodified: Discourses on Life and Law.* Cambridge, MA: Harvard University Press.

———. 1989. *Toward a Feminist Theory of the State.* Cambridge, MA: Harvard University Press.

MacLean, Brian D. 1991. "The Origins of Left Realism." In *New Directions in Critical Criminology,* edited by Brian D. MacLean and Dragan Milovanovic. Vancouver, BC: Collective Press.

———. 1996. "Crime, Criminology, and Society: A Short but Critical Introduction." In *Crime and Society: Readings in Critical Criminology,* edited by Brian D. MacLean. Mississauga, Ontario: Copp Clark.

MacLean, Brian D., and Dragan Milovanovic, eds. 1991. *New Directions in Critical Criminology.* Vancouver, BC: Collective Press.

———, eds. 1997. *Thinking Critically About Crime.* Vancouver, BC: Collective Press.

Maedor, Thomas. 1985. *Crime and Madness.* New York: Harper and Row.

Magnusson, David, Britt Klinteberg, and Hakan Stattin. 1992. "Autonomic Activity/Reactivity, Behavior, and Crime in a Longitudinal Perspective." In *Facts, Frameworks, and Forecasts: Advances in Criminological Theory,* edited by Joan McCord. Vol. 3. New Brunswick, NJ: Transaction Publishers.

Maguire, Mike, and Trevor Bennett. 1982. *Burglary in a Dwelling.* London: Heinemann.

Maher, Lisa. 1997. *Sexed Work: Gender, Race, and Resistance in a Brooklyn Drug Market.* Oxford: Clarendon Press.

Mama, Amina. 1989. "Violence Against Black Women: Gender, Race, and State Responses." *Feminist Review* 32: 30–48.

Mander, J. 1996. "Facing the Rising Tide." In *The Case Against the Global Economy,* edited by J. Mander and E. Goldsmith, 3–19. San Francisco: Sierra Club Books.

Mankoff, Milton. 1971. "Societal Reaction and Career Deviance: A Critical Analysis." *Sociological Quarterly* 12: 204–218.

———. 1978. "On the Responsibility of Marxist Criminology: A Reply to Quinney." *Contemporary Crisis* 2: 293–301.

Mann, Coramae Richey, and Marjorie S. Zatz. 1998. *Images of Color, Images of Crime.* Los Angeles: Roxbury Press.

Mann, Coramae Richey, Marjorie S. Zatz, and Nancy Rodriguez. 2006. *Images of Color, Images of Crime: Readings.* New York: Oxford University Press.

Mannheim, Hermann. 1965. *Comparative Criminology.* Boston: Houghton Mifflin.

Manning, Peter K. 1988. *Symbolic Communications: Signifying Calls and the Police Response.* Cambridge, MA: MIT Press.

———. 1989. "On the Phenomenology of Violence." *Criminologist* 14: 1–22.

Marcos, Anastasios C., Stephen J. Bahr, and Richard E. Johnson. 1986. "Test of a Bonding/Association Theory of Adolescent Drug Use." *Social Forces* 65: 135–161.

Markle, Gerald E., and R. J. Troyer. 1979. "Smoke Gets in Your Eyes: Cigarette Smoking as Deviant Behavior." *Social Problems* 26: 611–625.

Markowitz, Fred E., Paul E. Bellair, Allen E. Liska, and Jianhong Liu. 2001. "Extending Social Disorganization Theory: Modeling Relationships Between Cohesion, Disorder, and Fear." *Criminology* 39: 293–320.

Mars, Gerald. 1982. *Cheats at Work: An Anthropology of Workplace Crime.* London: Allen and Unwin.

Martens, Willem H. J. 1997. "Psychopathy and Maturation." Master's thesis, Tilburg University.

———. 2000. "Antisocial and Psychopathic Personality Disorders: Causes, Course, and Remission—A Review Article." *International Journal of Offender Therapy and Comparative Criminology* 44: 406–430.

———. 2002. "Criminality and Moral Dysfunctions: Neurological, Biochemical, and Genetic Dimensions." *International Journal of Offender Therapy and Comparative Criminology* 46: 170–182.

Martin, Randy, Robert J. Mutchnick, and Timothy W. Austin. 1990. *Criminological Thought: Pioneers Past and Present.* New York: Macmillan.

Martinson, Robert. 1974. "What Works? Questions and Answers About Prison Reform." *Public Interest* 35: 22–54.

Maruna, Shadd. 2003. "Excuses, Excuses: What Have We Learned in 50 Years of Testing 'Neutralization Theory'?" Lecture to Cambridge University's Institute of Criminology, May 8.

Maruna, Shadd, and Heath Copes. 2004. "Excuses, Excuses: What Have We Learned from Five Decades of Neutralization Research?" In *Crime and Justice,* 1–100. Chicago: University of Chicago Press.

Maruna, Shadd, Amanda Matravers, and Anna King. 2004. "Disowning Our Shadow: A Psychoanalytic Approach to Understanding Punitive Public Attitudes." *Deviant Behavior* 25, no. 3: 277–299.

Marx, Karl. [1844] 1975. *The Economic and Philosophical Manuscripts of 1844.* New York: International Publishers.

———. [1859] 1975. "'Preface' to a Contribution to the Critique of Political Economy." In *Karl Marx: Early Writings,* edited by Lucio Colletti. Harmondsworth, UK: Penguin.

———. [1862] 1964. "Theories of Surplus Value." In *Karl Marx: Selected Writings in Sociology and Social Philosophy,* edited by Tomas B. Bottomore and Maximilien Rubel. Vol. 1. New York: McGraw-Hill.

Marx, Karl, and Friedrich Engels. [1845] 1964. *The German Ideology.* London: Lawrence and Wishart.

Mason, Gregory H. 1995. "Some Implications of Postmodernism for the Field of Peace Studies." *Peace and Change* 20: 120–132.

Mathiesen, Thomas. 1974. *The Politics of Abolition: Essays in Political Action Theory.* London: Martin Robertson.

———. 1986. "The Politics of Abolition." *Contemporary Crisis* 10: 81–94.

Matsueda, Ross L. 1992. "Reflected Appraisals, Parental Labeling, and Delinquency: Specifying a Symbolic Interactionist Theory." *American Journal of Sociology* 97: 1577–1611.

———. 2001. "Labeling Theory: Historical Roots, Implications, and Recent Developments." In *Explaining Criminals and Crime,* edited by Raymond Paternoster and Ronet Bachman, 223–241. Los Angeles: Roxbury Press.

Matsumoto, Toshihiko, and Fumi Imamura. 2007. "Association Between Childhood Attention-Deficit–Hyperactivity Symptoms and Adulthood Dissociation in Male Inmates: Preliminary Report." *Psychiatry and Clinical Neurosciences* 61: 444–446.

Matthews, Roger. 1987. "Taking Realist Criminology Seriously." *Contemporary Crisis* 11: 371–401.

Matthews, Roger, and Jock Young, eds. 1986. *Confronting Crime.* Beverly Hills, CA: Sage.

———, eds. 1992. *Issues in Realist Criminology.* Beverly Hills, CA: Sage.

Matza, David. 1964. *Delinquency and Drift.* New York: John Wiley.

———. 1969. *Becoming Deviant.* Englewood Cliffs, NJ: Prentice-Hall.

Matza, David, and Gresham Sykes. 1961. "Juvenile Delinquency and Subterranean Values." *American Sociological Review* 26: 712–719.

Mauer, M. 1997. *Intended and Unintended Consequences: State Racial Disparities in Imprisonment.* Washington, DC: Sentencing Project.

Maxfield, Michael. 1987. "Household Composition, Routine Activities, and Victimization: A Comparative Analysis." *Journal of Quantitative Criminology* 3: 301–320.

Mayhew, Henry. [1861] 1981. "A Visit to the Rookery of St. Giles and Its Neighbourhood." In *Crime and Society: Readings in History and Society,* edited by Mike Fitzgerald, Gregor McLennan, and Jennie Pawson. London: Routledge and Kegan Paul.

Mayhew, Pat, and Mike Hough. 1991. "The British Crime Survey: The First Ten Years." In *Victims and Criminal Justice,* edited by G. Kaiser, H. Kury, and H.-J. Albrecht. Freiberg, Germany: Max Planck Institute.

Mays, G. Larry. 1989. "The Impact of Federal Sentencing Guidelines on Jail and Prison Overcrowding and Early Release." In *The U.S. Sentencing Guidelines: Implications for Criminal Justice,* edited by Dean Champion. New York: Praeger.

McCarthy, Bill. 1996. "The Attitudes and Actions of Others: Tutelage and Sutherland's Theory of Differential Association." *British Journal of Criminology* 36: 135–147.

McCarthy, Bill, John Hagan, and Todd S. Woodward. 1999. "In the Company of Women: Structure and Agency in a Revised Power-Control Theory of Gender and Delinquency." *Criminology* 37, no. 4: 761–788.

McCord, William, and Joan McCord. 1964. *The Psychopath: An Essay on the Criminal Mind.* New York: Van Nostrand.

McDowall, David, and Colin Loftin. 1992. "Comparing the UCR and NCS over Time." *Criminology* 30: 125–132.

McFadden, Gerald S., Judy Clarke, and Jeffery L. Staniels. 1991. *Federal Sentencing Manual.* New York: Matthew Bender.

McGee, Zina T. 1992. "Social Class Differences in Parental and Peer Influence on Adolescent Drug Use." *Deviant Behavior* 13: 349–372.

McGrew, T. 1992. "A Global Society?" In *Modernity and Its Futures,* edited by S. Hall, D. Held, and T. McGrew, 62–102. Cambridge: Open University Press.

McKim, W. Duncan. 1900. *Heredity and Human Progress.* New York: G. P. Putnam.

McLaren, Peter. 1994. "Postmodernism and the Death of Politics: A Brazilian Reprieve." In *Politics of Liberation: Paths from Freire,* edited by Peter McLaren and C. Lankshear, 193–215. New York: Routledge.

McLaughlin, Eugene. 2001. "Deterrence." In *The Sage Dictionary of Criminology,* edited by Eugene McLaughlin and John Muncie. London: Sage.

McLean, Bethany, and Peter Elkind. 2003. *The Smartest Guys in the Room: The Amazing Rise and Scandalous Fall of Enron.* New York: Portfolio Hardcover.

Mead, George Herbert. 1934. *Mind, Self, and Society.* Edited by C. W. Morris. Chicago: University of Chicago Press.

Mednick, Sarnoff A. 1977. "A Bio-social Theory of the Learning of Law-Abiding Behavior." In *Biosocial Bases of Criminal Behavior,* edited by Sarnoff A. Mednick and Karl O. Christiansen. New York: Gardner.

———. 1985. "Crime in the Family Tree." *Psychology Today* (March): 58–61.

Mednick, Sarnoff A., and Karl O. Christiansen. 1977. *Biosocial Bases of Criminal Behavior.* New York: Gardiner.

Mednick, Sarnoff A., W. F. Gabrielli, and Barry Hutchings. 1984. "Genetic Influences in Criminal Convictions: Evidence from an Adoption Cohort." *Science* 224: 891–894.

————. 1987. "Genetic Factors in the Etiology of Criminal Behavior." In *The Causes of Crime: New Biological Approaches,* edited by Sarnoff A. Mednick, Terrie Moffitt, and Susan Stack. Cambridge: Cambridge University Press.

Mednick, Sarnoff A., and J. Volavka. 1980. "Biology and Crime." In *Crime and Justice: An Annual Review of Research,* edited by Norvil Morris and Michael Tonry. Chicago: University of Chicago Press.

Meehan, Albert J., and Michael C. Ponder. 2002. "Race and Place: The Ecology of Racial Profiling African American Motorists." *Justice Quarterly* 19: 399–430.

Meiczkowski, Thomas. 1992. "Crack Dealing on the Street: The Crew System and the Crack House." *Justice Quarterly* 9: 151–163.

Melichar, Kenneth E. 1988. "Deconstruction: Critical Theory or an Ideology of Despair?" *Humanity and Society* 12: 366–385.

Menard, Scott. 1987. "Short-Term Trends in Crime and Delinquency: A Comparison of UCR, NCS, and Self-Report Data." *Justice Quarterly* 4: 455–474.

Menard, Scott, and Herbert Covey. 1988. "UCR and NCS: Comparisons over Space and Time." *Journal of Criminal Justice* 16: 371–384.

Mendelsohn, Benjamin. 1963. "The Origin of the Doctrine of Victimology." *Excerpta Criminologica* 3: 239–244.

Menkel-Meadow, Carrie J. 2007. "Restorative Justice: What Is It and Does It Work?" *Annual Review of Law and Social Science* 3: 10.1–10.27.

Menzies, Robert, and Dorothy Chunn. 1991. "Kicking Against the Pricks: The Dilemmas of Feminist Teaching in Criminology." *Critical Criminologist* 3: 7–8, 14–15.

Merton, Robert K. 1938. "Social Structure and Anomie." *American Sociological Review* 3: 672–682.

————. [1957] 1968. *Social Theory and Social Structure.* New York: Free Press.

————. 1964. "Anomie, Anomia, and Social Interaction: Contexts of Deviant Behavior." In *Anomie and Deviant Behavior: A Discussion and Critique,* edited by Marshall B. Clinard. New York: Free Press.

————. 1995. "Opportunity Structure: The Emergence, Diffusion, and Differentiation of a Sociological Concept, 1930s–1950s." In *The Legacy of Anomie Theory: Advances in Criminological Theory,* edited by Freda Adler and William S. Laufer. New Brunswick, NJ: Transaction Publishers.

Messerschmidt, James W. 1986. *Capitalism, Patriarchy, and Crime: Toward a Socialist Feminist Criminology.* Totowa, NJ: Rowman and Littlefield.

————. 1993. *Masculinities and Crime: Critique and Reconceptualization of Theory.* Boston: Rowman and Littlefield.

————. 2004. *Flesh and Blood: Adolescent Gender Diversity and Violence.* Lanham, MD: Rowman and Littlefield.

————. 2006. "Masculinities and Theoretical Criminology." In *The Essential Criminology Reader,* edited by Stuart Henry and Mark M. Lanier, 215–220. Boulder, CO: Westview Press.

Messner, Steven. 1984. "The 'Dark Figure' and Composite Indexes of Crime: Some Empirical Explorations of Alternative Data Sources." *Journal of Criminal Justice* 12: 435–444.

Messner, Steven, and Judith R. Blau. 1987. "Routine Leisure Activities and Rates of Crime: A Macro-Level Analysis." *Social Forces* 65: 1035–1051.

Messner, Steven, Marvin D. Krohn, and Allen E. Liska, eds. 1989. *Theoretical Integration in the Study of Deviance and Crime: Problems and Prospects.* Albany: State University of New York Press.

Messner, Steven, and Richard Rosenfeld. 1994. *Crime and the American Dream.* Belmont, CA: Wadsworth.

———. 1997. "Political Restraint of the Market and Levels of Criminal Homicide: A Cross-National Application of Institutional Anomie Theory." *Social Forces* 75: 1393–1416.

———. 2001. "An Institutional-Anomie Theory of Crime." In *Explaining Criminals and Crime,* edited by Raymond Paternoster and Ronet Bachman, 151–160. Los Angeles: Roxbury Press.

———. 2006. *Crime and the American Dream.* 4th ed. Belmont, CA: Wadsworth.

Messner, Steven, and Kenneth Tardiff. 1985. "The Social Ecology of Urban Homicide: An Application of the Routine Activities Approach." *Criminology* 23: 241–267.

Meyer, Josh. 2007. "In Terrorism Fight, Diplomacy Gets Shortchanged." *Los Angeles Times,* March 18, A1.

Michael, Jerome, and Mortimer J. Adler. 1933. *Crime, Law, and Social Science.* New York: Harcourt Brace Jovanovich.

Michalowski, Raymond. 1985. *Order, Law, and Crime.* New York: Random House.

———. 1991. "'Niggers, Welfare Scum, and Homeless Assholes': The Problems of Idealism, Consciousness, and Context in Left Realism." In *New Directions in Critical Criminology,* edited by Brian D. MacLean and Dragan Milovanovic. Vancouver, BC: Collective Press.

Michalowski, Raymond, and Susan Carlson. 1999. "Unemployment, Imprisonment, and Social Structures of Accumulation: Historical Contingency in the Rusche-Kirchheimer Hypothesis." *Criminology* 37: 217–249.

Miethe, Terance D. 1982. "Public Consensus on Crime Seriousness: Normative Structure or Methodological Artifact?" *Criminology* 20: 515–526.

———. 1984. "Types of Consensus in Public Evaluations of Crime: An Illustration of Strategies for Measuring 'Consensus.'" *Journal of Criminal Law and Criminology* 75: 459–473.

———. 1987. "Charging and Plea Bargaining Practices Under Determinate Sentencing: An Investigation of the Hydraulic Displacement of Discretion." *Journal of Criminal Law and Criminology* 78: 101–122.

Miethe, Terance D., and Charles A. Moore. 1985. "Socioeconomic Disparities Under Determinate Sentencing Systems: A Comparison of Pre-guideline and Post-guideline Practices in Minnesota." *Criminology* 23: 337–363.

———. 1989. *Sentencing Guidelines: Their Effect in Minnesota.* Washington, DC: National Institute of Justice.

Miethe, Terance D., Mark C. Stafford, and J. Scott Long. 1987. "Social Differentiation in Criminal Victimization: A Test of Routine Activities/Lifestyle Theories." *American Sociological Review* 52: 184–194.

Miller, Jody. 2000. *One of the Guys: Girls, Gangs, and Gender.* New York: Oxford University Press.

———. 2003. "Feminist Criminology." In *Controversies in Critical Criminology,* edited by Martin D. Schwartz and Suzanne E. Hatty, 15–28. Cincinnati: Anderson.

———. 2008. *Getting Played: African American Girls, Urban Inequality, and Gendered Violence.* New York: New York University Press.

Miller, Joshua D., and Donald Lynam. 2001. "Structural Models of Personality and Their Relation to Antisocial Behavior: A Meta-analytical Review." *Criminology* 39: 765–787.

Miller, Lisa L. 2001. "Looking for Postmodernism in All the Wrong Places." *British Journal of Criminology* 41: 168–184.

Miller, P. G. 2005. "Scapegoating, Self-Confidence, and Risk Comparison: The Functionality of Risk Neutralisation and Lay Epidemiology by Injecting Drug Users." *International Journal of Drug Policy* 16, no. 4: 246–253.

Miller, Walter B. 1958. "Lower-Class Culture as a Generating Milieu of Gang Delinquency." *Journal of Social Issues* 14: 5–19.

———. 1962. "The Impact of a Total-Community Delinquency Control Project." *Social Problems* 10: 168–191.

Mills, C. Wright. 1940. "Situated Actions and Vocabularies of Motive." *American Sociological Review* 5: 904–913.

———. 1959. *The Sociological Imagination.* New York: Oxford University Press.

Milovanovic, Dragan. 1995. "Dueling Paradigms: Modernist Versus Postmodernist." *Humanity and Society* 19: 1–22.

———. 1997. *Chaos, Criminology, and Social Justice.* New York: Praeger.

———. 2002. *Critical Criminology at the Edge.* Westport, CT: Praeger.

———. 2003. Introduction to *Edgework,* edited by S. Lyng. Albany: State University of New York Press.

———. 2006. "Edgework: Negotiating Boundaries." In *The Essential Criminology Reader,* edited by Stuart Henry and Mark M. Lanier, 234–246. Boulder, CO: Westview Press.

Milovanovic, Dragan, and Stuart Henry. 1991. "Constitutive Penology." *Social Justice* 18, no. 3: 205–224.

———. 2001. "Constitutive Definition of Crime as Harm." In *What Is Crime? Controversies over the Nature of Crime and What to Do About It,* edited by Stuart Henry and Mark Lanier. Boulder, CO: Rowman and Littlefield.

Minor, W. William. 1980. "The Neutralization of Criminal Offense." *Criminology* 18: 103–120.

———. 1981. "Techniques of Neutralization: A Reconceptualization and Empirical Examination." *Journal of Research in Crime and Delinquency* 18: 295–318.

———. 1984. "Neutralization as a Hardening Process: Considerations in the Modeling of Change." *Social Forces* 62: 995–1019.

Mitchell, Jim, and Richard A. Dodder. 1983. "Types of Neutralization and Types of Delinquency." *Journal of Youth and Adolescence* 12: 307–318.

Moffitt, Terrie E. 1993. "Adolescent-Limited and Life-Course Persistent Antisocial Behavior: A Developmental Taxonomy." *Psychological Review* 100: 674–701.

———. 2001. "Adolescence-Limited and Life-Course Persistent Antisocial Behavior: A Developmental Taxonomy." In *Life-Course Criminology: Contemporary and Classic Readings,* edited by A. Piquero and P. Mazerolle, 91–145. Belmont, CA: Wadsworth.

Moffitt, Terrie E., Donald Lynam, and Phil Silva. 1994. "Neuropsychological Tests Predicting Male Delinquency." *Criminology* 32: 277–300.

Moffitt, Terrie E., and Phil Silva. 1988. "Self-Reported Delinquency, Neuropsychological Deficit, and History of Attention Deficit Disorder." *Journal of Abnormal Psychology* 16: 553–569.

Mokhiber, Russell. 1988. *Corporate Crime and Violence: Big Business Power and the Abuse of the Public Trust.* San Francisco: Sierra Club Books.

Monahan, John. 1992. "Mental Disorder and Violent Behavior: Perceptions and Evidence." *American Psychologist* 47: 511–521.

Monahan, John, and Henry Steadman. 1984. *Crime and Mental Disorder.* Research in Brief. Washington, DC: National Institute of Justice.

Monroe, Jacqueline. 2004. "Getting a Puff: A Social Learning Test of Adolescents Smoking." *Journal of Child and Adolescent Substance Abuse* 13, no. 3: 71–83.

Moore, Joan W. 1991. *Going Down to the Barrio: Homeboys and Homegirls in Change.* Philadelphia: Temple University Press.

Moore, Todd M., Angela Scarpa, and Adrian Raine. 2002. "A Meta-analysis of Serotonin Metabolite 5-HIAA and Antisocial Behavior." *Aggressive Behavior* 28, no. 4: 299–316.

Morash, Merry. 1982. "Juvenile Reaction to Labels: An Experiment and an Exploratory Study." *Sociology and Social Research* 67: 76–88.

Morash, Merry, and L. Rucker. 1998. "A Critical Look at the Idea of Boot Camps as a Correctional Reform." In *Crime Control and Women,* edited by S. L. Miller, 32–51. Thousand Oaks, CA: Sage.

Morgan, H. Wayne. 1981. *Drugs in America: A Social History, 1800–1980.* Syracuse, NY: Syracuse University Press.

Morgan, J., and L. Zedner. 1992. "The Victim's Charter: A New Deal for Child Victims?" *Howard Journal of Criminal Justice* 1: 294–307.

Moriarty, Laura J., and James E. Williams. 1996. "Examining the Relationship Between Routine Activities Theory and Social Disorganization: An Analysis of Property Crime Victimization." *American Journal of Criminal Justice* 12, no. 1: 43–59.

Morn, F. 1995. *Academic Politics and the History of Criminal Justice Education.* Westport, CT: Greenwood Press.

Morris, Allison. 1987. *Women, Crime, and Criminal Justice.* Oxford: Blackwell.

Morris, Terrence P. 1957. *The Criminal Area: A Study in Social Ecology.* London: Routledge and Kegan Paul.

Morrisey, Belinda. 2003. *When Women Kill: Questions of Agency and Subjectivity.* New York: Routledge.

Morrison, Wayne. 1995. *Theoretical Criminology: From Modernity to Post-modernism.* London: Routledge.

Morton, Teru L., and Linda S. Ewald. 1987. "Family-Based Interventions for Crime and Delinquency." In *Behavioral Approaches to Crime and Delinquency: A Handbook of Applications Research and Concepts,* edited by Edward K. Morris and Curtis J. Braukmann. New York: Plenum.

Motorola, 2006. *An Introduction to Biometrics.* White Paper. Basingstoke, UK: Motorola. http://www.motorola.com/staticfiles/Business/Solutions/Business%20Solutions/Biometrics/Biometrics%20Identification/_Documents/Static%20Files/INTRODUCTION_TO_BIOMETRICS_New.pdf (accessed November 18, 2008).

Moyer, Imogene L. 2001. *Criminological Theories: Traditional and Nontraditional Voices and Themes.* Thousand Oaks, CA: Sage.

Munro, Vanessa E. 2003. "On Power and Domination: Feminism and the Final Foucault." *European Journal of Political Theory* 2: 79–99.

Murphy, K., and N. Harris. 2007. "Shaming, Shame, and Recidivism: A Test of Reintegrative Shaming Theory in the White-Collar Crime Context." *British Journal of Criminology* 47, no. 6: 900–917.

Murray, C. 1997. *Does Prison Work?* London: Institute for Economic Affairs.

Muschert, Glenn W. 2007. "Research in School Shootings." *Sociology Compass* 1, no. 1: 60–80.

Muschert, Glenn W., and Dawn Carr. 2006. "Media Salience and Frame Changing Across Events: Coverage of Nine School Shootings, 1997–2001." *Journalism and Mass Communication Quarterly* 83, no. 4: 747–766.

Mustaine, E. E., R. Tewksbury, and K. M. Stengel. 2006. "Social Disorganization and the Residential Locations of Registered Sex Offenders: Is This a Collateral Consequence?" *Deviant Behavior* 27, no. 3: 329–350.

Myers, Wade, Kerrilyn Scott, Ann Burgess, and Allen Burgess. 1995. "Psychopathy, Biopsychosocial Factors, Crime Characteristics, and Classification of 25 Homicidal Youths." *Journal of the American Academy of Child Adolescent Psychiatry* 34: 1483–1489.

Naffine, Ngaire. 1987. *Female Crime: The Construction of Women in Criminology.* London: Allen and Unwin.

Nagin, Daniel S., and Kenneth Land. 1993. "Age, Criminal Careers, and Population Heterogeneity: Specification and Estimation of a Nonparametric Mixed Poisson Model." *Criminology* 31: 163–189.

Nagin, Daniel S., and Raymond Paternoster. 1993. "Enduring Individual Differences and Rational Choice Theories of Crime." *Law and Society Review* 27: 467–496.

National Advisory Commission on Criminal Justice Standards and Goals. 1971. *A National Strategy to Reduce Crime.* Washington, DC: U.S. Government Printing Office.

Naylor, R. T. 1999. *Patriots and Profiteers: On Economic Warfare, Embargo Busting, and State-Sponsored Crime.* Toronto: McClelland and Stewart.

Nee, C., and M. Taylor. 1988. "Residential Burglary in the Republic of Ireland: A Situational Perspective." *Howard Journal of Criminal Justice* 27: 105–116.

Nelken, David, ed. 1994a. *The Futures of Criminology.* London: Sage.

———. 1994b. "Whom Can You Trust? The Future of Comparative Criminology." In *The Futures of Criminology,* edited by David Nelken. London: Sage.

Nelkin, Dorothy. 1993. "The Grandiose Claims of Geneticists." *Chronicle of Higher Education* (March 3): B1–B3.

Nelkin, Dorothy, and Lawrence Tancredi. 1994. "Dangerous Diagnostics and Their Social Consequences." *Scientist* 12: 12.

Nettler, Gwynn. 1984. *Explaining Crime.* 3d ed. New York: McGraw-Hill.

Newman, Katherine S., Cybelle Fox, David J. Harding, Jal Mehta, and Wendy Roth. 2004. *Rampage: The Social Roots of School Shootings.* New York: Basic Books.

Newman, Oscar. 1972. *Defensible Space.* New York: Macmillan.

———. 1973. *Architectural Design for Crime Prevention.* Washington, DC: U.S. Department of Justice, National Institute of Law Enforcement and Justice.

———. 1996. *Creating Defensible Space.* Rockville, MD: U.S. Department of Housing and Urban Development, Office of Policy Development and Research.

Nicholson, Jane. 2000. "Reconciliations: Prevention and Recovery for School Violence." In "School Violence," edited by William Hinkle and Stuart Henry. Special issue, *Annals of the American Academy of Political and Social Science* 567.

Niehoff, Debra. 1999. *The Biology of Violence.* New York: Free Press.

Nofziger, S. 2008. "The 'Cause' of Low Self-Control: The Influence of Maternal Self-Control." *Journal of Research in Crime and Delinquency* 45, no. 2: 191–224.

Nye, Ivan F. 1958. *Family Relationships and Delinquent Behavior.* New York: John Wiley.

Observatoire Geopolitique des Drogues. 1996. *The Geopolitics of Drugs.* Boston: Northeastern University Press.

Oden, Sherri, Lawrence Schweinhart, and David Weikart, with S. Marcus and Yu Xie. 2000. *Into Adulthood: A Study of the Effects of Head Start.* Ypsilanti, MI: High/Scope Press.

O'Donoghue, Edward Geoffrey. 1923. *Bridewell Hospital: Palace, Prison, Schools, from the Earliest Times to the End of the Reign of Elizabeth.* London: Lane.

Olaussen, Leif Petter. 2004. "Why Is Crime a Social Fact?" *Nordisk Tidsskrift for Kriminalvidenskab* 91, no. 1: 24–38.

Olweus, Dan. 1987. "Testosterone and Adrenaline: Aggressive Antisocial Behavior in Normal Adolescent Males." In *The Causes of Crime: New Biological Approaches,* edited by Sarnoff A. Mednick, Terrie Moffitt, and Susan Stack. Cambridge: Cambridge University Press.

Olweus, Dan, Ake Mattsson, Daisy Schalling, and Hans Low. 1980. "Testosterone, Aggression, Physical, and Personality Dimensions in Normal Adolescent Males." *Psychosomatic Medicine* 42: 253–269.

O'Malley, Pat, and Steve Mugford. 1994. "Crime, Excitement, and Modernity." In *Varieties of Criminology,* edited by Gregg Barak. Westport, CT: Praeger.

Orcutt, James D. 1987. "Differential Association and Marijuana Use: A Closer Look at Sutherland (with a Little Help from Becker)." *Criminology* 25: 341–358.

Orlando City Council. 2006. Sec. 18A.09-02.

Orozco-Truong, Rosalie. 1996. "Empathy, Guilt, and Techniques of Neutralization: Their Role in a Conceptual Model of Delinquent Behavior." Ph.D. diss., University of Colorado.

Orru, Marco. 1987. *Anomie: History and Meanings.* Boston: Allen and Unwin.

———. 1990. "Merton's Instrumental Theory of Anomie." In *Robert K. Merton: Consensus and Controversy,* edited by J. Clark, C. Modgil, and S. Modgil. London: Falmer.

Orth, U., L. Montada, and A. Maercker. 2006. "Feelings of Revenge, Retaliation Motive, and Posttraumatic Stress Reactions in Crime Victims." *Journal of Interpersonal Violence* 21, no. 2: 229–243.

Osgood, D. Wayne, Janet K. Wilson, Patrick M. O'Malley, Jerald G. Bachman, and Lloyd D. Johnston. 1996. "Routine Activities and Individual Deviant Behavior." *American Sociological Review* 61: 635–655.

O'Shea, Timothy. 2000. "The Efficacy of Home Security Measures." *American Journal of Criminal Justice* 24, no. 2: 155–167.

Ostby, G. 2008. "Polarization, Horizontal Inequalities, and Violent Civil Conflict." *Journal of Peace Research* 45, no. 2: 143–162.

"Our Opinion: DPS Revisions Cut Profiling, Searches in Traffic Stops." 2009. *Tucson Citizen,* January 2. http://www.tucsoncitizen.com/ss/border/106626.php (accessed January 4, 2009).

Packer, Herbert L. 1968. *The Limits of Criminal Sanction.* Stanford, CA: Stanford University Press.

Palamara, Frances, Francis T. Cullen, and Joanne C. Gersten. 1986. "The Effect of Police and Mental Health Intervention on Juvenile Deviance: Specifying Contingencies in the Impact of Formal Reaction." *Journal of Health and Social Behavior* 27: 90–105.

Palen, J. J. 1981. *The Urban World.* 3d ed. New York: McGraw-Hill.

Pallone, Nathaniel J., and James J. Hennessy. 1992. *Criminal Behavior: A Process Psychology Analysis.* New Brunswick, NJ: Transaction Publishers.

Palmer, Jason. 2008. "Traders' Raging Hormones Cause Stock Market Swings." *New Scientist,* April 14. http://www.newscientist.com/article/dn13664-traders-raging-hormones-cause-stock-market-swings.html?feedId=online-news_rss20 (accessed December 27, 2008).

Paolucci, Henry. 1963. Introduction to *On Crimes and Punishments,* by Cesare Beccaria, translated by Henry Paolucci. Indianapolis: Bobbs-Merrill.

Pape, Eric. 1999. "You're Out! (The Three-Strikes Law in California)." *Los Angeles Magazine* (August).

Parikh, Rahul. 2008. "Does Bernard Madoff Have a Hormonal Imbalance?" Open Salon. http://open.salon.com/content.php?cid=65884 (accessed December 27, 2008).

Park, Robert E. 1926. "The Urban Community as a Special Pattern and a Moral Order." In *The Urban Community,* edited by Ernest W. Burgess. Chicago: University of Chicago Press.

Park, Robert E., and Ernest W. Burgess. 1920. *Introduction to the Science of Sociology.* Chicago: University of Chicago Press.

Park, Robert E., Ernest W. Burgess, and Roderick McKenzie. 1925. *The City.* Chicago: University of Chicago Press.

Parker, Robert Nash. 1998. "Alcohol, Homicide, and Cultural Context." *Homicide Studies* 2: 6–30.

Parry, Alan, and Robert E. Doan. 1994. *Story Re-visions: Narrative Therapy in the Postmodern World.* New York: Guilford.

Passas, Nikos. 1990. "Anomie and Corporate Deviance." *Contemporary Crisis* 14: 157–158.

———. 1993. "I Cheat Therefore I Exist: The BCCI Scandal in Context." In *Emerging Global Business Ethics,* edited by W. M. Hoffman, S. Kamm, R. E. Frederick, and E. Petry. New York: Quorum Books.

———. 1995. "Continuities in the Anomie Tradition." In *The Legacy of Anomie Theory. Advances in Criminological Theory,* edited by Freda Adler and William S. Laufer. Vol. 6. New Brunswick, NJ: Transaction Publishers.

———. 2000. "Global Anomie, Dysnomie, and Economic Crime: Hidden Consequences of Neoliberalism and Globalization in Russia and Around the World." *Social Justice* 27, no. 2: 16–44.

———. 2006. "Global Anomie Theory and Crime." In *The Essential Criminology Reader,* edited by Stuart Henry and Mark Lanier. Boulder, CO: Westview Press.

Passingham, R. E. 1972. "Crime and Personality: A Review of Eysenck's Theory." In *Biological Bases of Individual Behavior,* edited by V. D. Nebylitsyn and J. A. Gray. London: Academic Press.

Paternoster, Raymond. 1987. "The Deterrent Effect of the Perceived Certainty and Severity of Punishment: A Review of the Evidence and Issues." *Justice Quarterly* 4: 173–217.

———. 1989. "Decisions to Participate in and Desist from Four Types of Common Delinquency: Deterrence and Rational Choice Perspective." *Law and Society Review* 23: 7–40.

Paternoster, Raymond, and Ronet Bachman, eds. 2001. *Explaining Criminals and Crime.* Los Angeles: Roxbury Press.

Paternoster, Raymond, and Lee Ann Iovanni. 1989. "The Labeling Perspective and Delinquency: An Elaboration of the Theory and an Assessment of the Evidence." *Justice Quarterly* 6: 359–394.

Paternoster, Raymond, and Paul Mazerolle. 1994. "General Strain Theory and Delinquency: A Replication and Extension." *Journal of Research on Crime and Delinquency* 31: 235–263.

Paternoster, Raymond, Linda E. Saltzman, Gordon P. Waldo, and Theodore G. Chiricos. 1983. "Perceived Risk and Social Control: Do Sanctions Really Deter?" *Law and Society Review* 17: 457–480.

———. 1985. "Assessments of Risk and Behavioral Experience: An Exploratory Study of Change." *Criminology* 23: 417–436.

Paternoster, Raymond, and Sally Simpson. 1993. "A Rational Choice Theory of Corporate Crime." In *Routine Activity and Rational Choice: Advances in Criminological Theory,* edited by Ronald V. Clarke and Marcus Felson. New Brunswick, NJ: Transaction Publishers.

———. 1996. "Sanction Threats and Appeals to Morality: Testing a Rational Choice Model of Corporate Crime." *Law and Society Review* 30: 549–583.

Patterson, Gerald R. 1997. *Performance Models for Parenting: A Social Interactional Perspective.* New York: John Wiley and Sons.

Paulsen, Derek J., and Matt Robinson. 2008. *Crime Mapping and Spatial Aspects of Crime.* 2d ed. Boston: Allyn and Bacon.

Pavarini, M. 1994. "Is Criminology Worth Saving?" In *The Futures of Criminology,* edited by David Nelken. London: Sage.

Pavlov, Ivan P. [1906] 1967. *Lectures on Conditioned Reflexes: Twenty-five Years of Objective Study of the Higher Nervous Activity (Behavior) of Animals.* New York: International Publishers.

Pearson, Frank S., and Neil A. Weiner. 1985. "Toward an Integration of Criminological Theories." *Journal of Criminal Law and Criminology* 76: 116–150.

Peltz, Jennifer. 2008. "Some Jews Fear Madoff Case Stokes Anti-Semitism." Associated Press. http://www.google.com/hostednews/ap/article/ALeqM5jSLnvHBSvCHcE20bpw41y DZqrthAD959SJ081 (accessed December 25, 2008).

Pepinsky, Harold. 1976. *Crime and Conflict: A Study of Law and Society.* Oxford: Martin Robertson.

———. 1978. "Communist Anarchism as an Alternative to the Rule of Criminal Law." *Contemporary Crisis* 2: 315–327.

———. 1983. "Crime Causation: Political Theories." In *Encyclopedia of Crime and Justice,* edited by Sanford E. Kadish. New York: Free Press.

———. 1991a. *The Geometry of Violence and Democracy.* Bloomington: Indiana University Press.

———. 1991b. "Peacemaking in Criminology." In *New Directions in Critical Criminology,* edited by Brian D. MacLean and Dragan Milovanovic. Vancouver, BC: Collective Press.

———. 2000. "Educating for Peace." In "School Violence," edited by William Hinkle and Stuart Henry. Special issue, *Annals of the American Academy of Political and Social Science* 567.

———. 2006. "Peacemaking." In *The Essential Criminology Reader,* edited by Stuart Henry and Mark M. Lanier, 278–285. Boulder, CO: Westview Press.

Pepinsky, Harold, and Richard Quinney, eds. 1991. *Criminology as Peacemaking.* Bloomington: Indiana University Press.

Perry, Ronald W. 1980. "Social Status and the Black Violence Hypothesis." *Journal of Social Psychology* 111: 131–137.

Petee, Thomas, Gregory Kowalski, and Don Duffield. 1994. "Crime, Social Disorganization, and Social Structure: A Research Note on the Use of Interurban Ecological Models." *American Journal of Criminal Justice* 19: 117–132.

Peterson, Ruth, Lauren Krivo, and Mark Harris. 2000. "Disadvantage and Neighborhood Violent Crime: Do Local Institutions Matter?" *Journal of Research on Crime and Delinquency* 37: 31–63.

Pettiway, Leon E., Sergey Dolinsky, and Alexander Grigoryan. 1994. "The Drug and Criminal Activity Patterns of Urban Offenders: A Markov Chain Analysis." *Journal of Quantitative Criminology* 10: 79–107.

Pew Charitable Trusts. 2008. *One in 100 Behind Bars in America, 2008.* Washington, DC: Pew Center on the States. http://www.pewcenteronthestates.org/uploadedFiles/One% 20in%20100.pdf (accessed March 19, 2009).

————. 2009. *One in 31: The Long Reach of American Corrections.* Washington, DC: Pew Center on the States. http://www.pewcenteronthestates.org/uploadedFiles/PSPP_1in31_report_FINAL_WEB_2-27-09.pdf (accessed March 19, 2009).

Pfuhl, Erdwin H., and Stuart Henry. 1993. *The Deviance Process.* 3d ed. Hawthorn, NY: Aldine De Gruyter.

Phillips, Llad, and Harold L. Votey Jr. 1987. "The Influence of Police Interventions and Alternative Income Sources on the Dynamic Process of Choosing Crime as a Career." *Journal of Quantitative Criminology* 3: 251–273.

Piaget, Jean. [1923] 1969. *The Language and Thought of the Child.* New York: Meridian.

————. [1932] 1965. *The Moral Judgement of the Child.* New York: Free Press.

————. [1937] 1954. *The Construction of Reality in the Child.* New York: Basic Books.

Piliavin, Irving, Rosemary Irene Gartner, Craig Thornton, and Ross L. Matsueda. 1986. "Crime, Deterrence, and Rational Choice." *American Sociological Review* 51: 101–119.

Piquero, Alex R. 2000. "Assessing the Relationships Between Gender, Chronicity, Seriousness, and Offense Skewness in Criminal Offending." *Journal of Criminal Justice* 28: 103–115.

Piquero, Nicole Leeper, and Miriam D. Sealock. 2000. "Generalizing General Strain Theory: An Examination of an Offending Population." *Justice Quarterly* 17: 449–475.

Piquero, Nicole Leeper, S. G. Tibbetts, and M. B. Blankenship. 2005. "Examining the Role of Differential Association and the Techniques of Neutralization in Explaining Corporate Crime." *Deviant Behavior* 26, no. 2: 159–188.

Pitch, Tamar. 1985. "Critical Criminology and the Construction of Social Problems and the Question of Rape." *International Journal of the Sociology of Law* 13: 35–46.

Pizarro, J. M., and J. M. McGloin. 2006. "Explaining Gang Homicides in Newark, New Jersey: Collective Behavior or Social Disorganization?" *Journal of Criminal Justice* 34, no. 2: 195–207.

Pizzo, Stephen, and Paul Muolo. 1993. *Profiting from the Bank and S&L Crisis: How Anyone Can Find Bargains at America's Greatest Garage Sale.* New York: Harper-Collins.

Platt, Tony. 1974. "Prospects for a Radical Criminology in the United States." *Crime and Social Justice* 1: 2–10.

————. 2003. "The Frightening Agenda of the American Eugenics Movement." History News Network, July 7. http://hnn.us/articles/1551.html (accessed February 11, 2008).

Platt, Tony, and Paul Takagi. 1979. "Biosocial Criminology: A Critique." *Crime and Social Justice* 11 (Spring–Summer): 5–13.

Plummer, Ken. 1979. "Misunderstanding Labelling Perspectives." In *Deviant Interpretations,* edited by David Downes and Paul Rock. Oxford: Oxford University Press.

Pogarsky, Greg. 2002. "Identifying 'Deterrable' Offenders: Implications for Research on Deterrence." *Justice Quarterly* 19, no. 3: 431–452.

Pogrebin, Robin. 2008. "In Madoff Scandal, Jews Feel an Acute Betrayal." *New York Times,* December 23. http://www.nytimes.com/2008/12/24/us/24jews.html?hp (accessed December 28, 2008).

Polakowski, Michael. 1994. "Linking Self- and Social Control with Deviance: Illuminating the Structure Underlying a General Theory of Crime and Its Relation to Deviant Activity." *Journal of Quantitative Criminology* 10: 41–78.

Polding, Brian Earl. 1995. "Dishonesty of College Students." Ph.D. diss., University of Florida.

Police Quarterly. 2002. Special issue on racial profiling, edited by Stephen M. Cox. Vol. 5, no. 3.

Politi, A. 1998. "Russian Organised Crime and European Security." In *Illicit Trade and Organised Crime: New Threats to Economic Security?* edited by E. U. Directorate-General for External Relations, 31–57. Luxembourg: European Communities.

Polk, Kenneth. 2003. "Masculinities, Femininities, and Homicide: Competing Explanations for Male Violence." In *Controversies in Critical Criminology*, edited by Martin D. Schwartz and Suzanne E. Hatty. 133–145. Cincinnati: Anderson.

Pollak, Otto. 1950. *The Criminality of Women.* Philadelphia: University of Pennsylvania Press.

Pollock, J. M., J. L. Mullings, and B. M. Crouch. 2006. "Violent Women: Findings from the Texas Women Inmates Study." *Journal of Interpersonal Violence* 21, no. 4: 485–502.

Popper, Karl. 1959. *The Logic of Scientific Discovery.* New York: Basic Books.

Porter, S., and M. Woodworth. 2007. "'I'm Sorry I Did It . . . but He Started It': A Comparison of the Official and Self-Reported Homicide Descriptions of Psychopaths and Non-psychopaths." *Law and Human Behavior* 31, no. 1: 91–107.

Posner, Richard. 2006. "The Economics of Capital Punishment." *Economists' Voice* 3, no. 3. http://www.bepress.com/ev/v013/iss3/art3.

Potter, Gary, and Terry Cox. 1990. "A Community Paradigm of Organized Crime." *American Journal of Criminal Justice* 15: 1–23.

Pratt, Travis C., and Francis Cullen. 2000. "The Empirical Status of Gottfredson and Hirschi's General Theory of Crime: A Meta-analysis." *Criminology* 38: 931–954.

Pratt, Travis C., Michael G. Turner, and Alex R. Piquero. 2004. "Parental Socialization and Community Context: A Longitudinal Analysis of the Structural Sources of Low Self-Control." *Journal of Research in Crime and Delinquency* 41, no. 3: 219–243.

Presdee, Mike. 2000. *Cultural Criminology and the Carnival of Crime.* London: Routledge.

———. 2006. "Carnival (of Crime)." In *The Sage Dictionary of Criminology*, edited by Eugene McLaughlin and John Muncie, 32–33. 2d ed. London: Sage.

Pretorius, R. 2004. "Political Refugees as Victims of Prejudice, Discrimination, and Abuse." *Acta Criminologica* 17, no. 2: 131–142.

Puig, Claudia. 2005. "Enron: Portrait of Greed." *USA Today*, April 21. http://www.usatoday.com/life/movies/reviews/2005-04-21-enron_x.htm (accessed December 31, 2008).

Putnam, Robert D. 1995. "Bowling Alone: America's Declining Social Capital." *Journal of Democracy* 6, no. 1: 65–78.

Quinn, James. 2008. "Bernard Madoff 'Fraud': Betrayed by Their Best Friend; Bernard Madoff Wooed the Jet Set, but Few Knew How Much Was at Stake." *Daily Telegraph*, December 20. http://www.telegraph.co.uk/finance/financetopics/bernard-madoff/3853113/Bernard-Madoff-fraud-Betrayed-by-their-best-friend.html (accessed December 26, 2008).

Quinney, Richard. 1970. *The Social Reality of Crime.* Boston: Little, Brown.

———. 1974. *Critique of the Legal Order: Crime Control in a Capitalist Society.* Boston: Little, Brown.

———. 1975a. "Crime Control in a Capitalist Society." In *Critical Criminology*, edited by Ian Taylor, Paul Walton, and Jock Young. London: Routledge and Kegan Paul.

———. 1975b. *Criminology.* Boston: Little, Brown.

———. 1977. *Class, State, and Crime.* New York: David McKay.

———. 1991. "Oneness of All: The Mystical Nature of Humanism." In *New Directions in Critical Criminology*, edited by Brian D. MacLean and Dragan Milovanovic. Vancouver, BC: Collective Press.

Quinney, Richard, and John Wildeman. 1991. *The Problem of Crime: A Peace and Social Justice Perspective.* 3d ed. London: Mayfield.

Rada, R. T., D. R. Laws, and R. Kellner. 1976. "Plasma Testosterone Levels in the Rapist." *Psychosomatic Medicine* 38: 257–268.

Raeder, Myrna S. 2006. "Domestic Violence in Federal Court: Abused Women as Victims, Survivors, and Offenders." *Federal Sentencing Reporter* 19, no. 2: 91.

Rafter, Nicole Hahn. 1992. "Criminal Anthropology in the United States." *Criminology* 30: 525–545.

———. 1998. *Creating Born Criminals.* Champaign: University of Illinois Press.

———. 2006. "H. J. Eysenck in Fagin's Kitchen: The Return to Biological Theory in 20th-Century Criminology." *History of the Human Sciences* 19: 37–56.

———. 2007. "Biological Theories of Crime: A Historical Overview." University Art Museum, State University of New York at Albany. http://www.albany.edu/museum/criminal/curator/nicole.html (accessed February 11, 2008).

Raine, Adrian. 2002. "Annotation: The Role of Prefrontal Deficits, Low Autonomie Arousal, and Early Health Factors in the Development of Antisocial and Aggressive Behavior in Children." *Journal of Child Psychology and Psychiatry* 43: 417–434.

Randall, Teri. 1993. "A Novel, Unstable DNA Mutation Cracks Decades-Old Clinical Enigma." *Journal of the American Medical Association* 269: 557–558.

Rankin, Joseph H. 1980. "School Factors and Delinquency: Interaction by Age and Sex." *Sociology and Social Research* 64: 420–434.

Rankin, Joseph H., and Roger Kern. 1994. "Parental Attachments and Delinquency." *Criminology* 32: 495–515.

Rankin, Joseph H., and Edward L. Wells. 1990. "The Effect of Parental Attachments and Direct Controls of Delinquency." *Journal of Research on Crime and Delinquency* 27: 140–165.

———. 1994. "Social Control, Broken Homes, and Delinquency." In *Varieties of Criminology,* edited by Gregg Barak. Westport, CT: Praeger.

———. 2006. "Social Control Theory and Direct Parental Controls." In *The Essential Criminology Reader,* edited by Stuart Henry and Mark M. Lanier, 119–128. Boulder, CO: Westview Press.

Rappaport, J. 1977. *Community Psychology: Values, Research, and Action.* New York: Holt, Rinehart, and Winston.

Ray, Melvin C., and William R. Downs. 1986. "An Empirical Test of Labeling Theory Using Longitudinal Data." *Journal of Research in Crime and Delinquency* 23: 169–194.

Reckless, Walter C. 1940. *Criminal Behavior.* New York: McGraw-Hill.

———. [1950] 1973. *The Crime Problem.* Englewood Cliffs, NJ: Prentice-Hall.

———. 1961. "A New Theory of Delinquency and Crime." *Federal Probation* 25: 42–46.

Redl, Fritz, and Hans Toch. 1979. "The Psychoanalytic Explanation of Crime." In *Psychology of Crime and Criminal Justice,* edited by H. Toch. New York: Holt, Rinehart, and Winston.

Redl, Fritz, and David Wineman. 1951. *Children Who Hate.* New York: Free Press.

———. 1952. *Controls from Within.* New York: Free Press.

Reed-Sanders, Delores, and Richard A. Dodder. 1979. "Labeling Versus Containment Theory: An Empirical Test with Delinquency." *Free Inquiry in Creative Sociology* 7: 18–22.

Regoli, Robert, and Eric Poole. 1978. "The Commitment of Delinquents to Their Misdeeds: A Reexamination." *Journal of Criminal Justice* 6: 261–269.

Reiman, Jeffrey. [1979] 2007. *The Rich Get Richer and the Poor Get Prison.* New York: John Wiley.

Reiss, Albert J., Jr. 1951. "Delinquency as the Failure of Personal and Social Controls." *American Sociological Review* 16: 196–207.

Reiss, Albert J., Jr., and A. Lewis Rhodes. 1964. "An Empirical Test of Differential Association Theory." *Journal of Research on Crime and Delinquency* 1: 5–18.

Rengert, G., and J. Wasilchick. 1985. *Suburban Burglary: A Time and Place for Everything.* Springfield, IL: Charles C. Thomas.

Reuters. 2008. "Foundation to Close, Says Fund Manager Madoff to Blame." *San Diego Union-Tribune,* December 21, A6.

Rice, Marcia. 1990. "Challenging Orthodoxies in Feminist Theory: A Black Feminist Critique." In *Feminist Perspectives in Criminology,* edited by Loraine Gelsthorpe and Allison Morris. Milton Keynes, UK: Open University.

Riggs, David, Barbara Rothman, and Edna Foa. 1995. "A Prospective Examination of Symptoms of Posttraumatic Stress Disorder in Victims of Nonsexual Assault." *Journal of Interpersonal Violence* 10: 201–214.

Robb, G. 2006. "Women and White-Collar Crime: Debates on Gender, Fraud, and Corporate Economy in England and America, 1850–1930." *British Journal of Criminology* 46, no. 6: 1058–1072.

Robbins, Lee N., and Michael Rutter. 1990. *Straight and Devious Pathways from Childhood to Adulthood.* Cambridge: Cambridge University Press.

Robinson, David, and Stuart Henry. 1977. *Self-Help and Health: Mutual Aid for Modern Problems.* Oxford: Martin Robertson.

Robinson, Eugene. 2007. "Driving While Black or Brown." *Washington Post,* May 2.

Robinson, Laurie. 1996. "Linking Community-Based Initiatives and Community Justice: The Office of Justice Programs." *National Institute of Justice Journal* 231 (August): 4–7.

Robinson, Matthew B. 1996. "The Theoretical Development of 'CPTED': 25 Years of Responses to C. Ray Jeffery." In *Advances in Criminological Theory,* edited by William Laufer and Freda Adler. Vol. 8. http://www1.appstate.edu/dept/ps-cj/vitacpted2.html (accessed December 30, 2008).

———. 2000. "Preventing Residential Burglary." *American Journal of Criminal Justice* 24, 2: 169–179.

———. 2004. *Why Crime? An Integrated Systems Theory of Antisocial Behavior.* Upper Saddle River, NJ: Pearson Prentice-Hall.

Robison, Sophia M. 1936. *Can Delinquency Be Measured?* New York: Columbia University Press.

Rodgers, Karen, and Georgia Roberts. 1995. "Women's Non-spousal Multiple Victimization: A Test of the Routine Activities Theory." *Canadian Journal of Criminology* 37: 363–391.

Roe v. Wade. 410 U.S. 113, 93 S.Ct. 705 (1973).

Roman, C. G., ed. 2004. *Schools, Neighborhoods, and Violence: Crime within the Daily Routines of Youth.* Lanham, MD: Lexington Books.

Rose, Nikolas. 2000. "The Biology of Culpability: Pathological Identity and Crime Control in a Biological Culture." *Theoretical Criminology* 4: 5–34.

Rosen, Lawrence, Leonard Savitz, Michael Lalli, and Stanley Turner. 1991. "Early Delinquency, High School Graduation, and Adult Criminality." *Sociological Viewpoints* 7: 37–60.

Rosenau, Pauline M. 1992. *Postmodernism and the Social Sciences: Insights, Inroads, and Intrusions.* Princeton, NJ: Princeton University Press.

Rosenfeld, Richard, and Steven Messner. 1995a. "Consumption and Crime: An Institutional Inquiry." Paper presented at the annual meeting of the Academy of Criminal Justice Sciences, Boston, March.

———. 1995b. "Crime and the American Dream: An Institutional Analysis." In *The Legacy of Anomie Theory: Advances in Criminological Theory*, edited by Freda Adler and William S. Laufer. Vol. 6. New Brunswick, NJ: Transaction Publishers.

———. 2006. "The Origins, Nature, and Prospects of Institutional Anomie Theory." In *The Essential Criminology Reader*, edited by Stuart Henry and Mark M. Lanier, 164–173. Boulder, CO: Westview Press.

Roshier, Bob. 1989. *Controlling Crime: The Classical Perspective in Criminology.* Philadelphia: Open University Press.

Rottman, David B. 1996. "Community Courts: Prospects and Limits." *National Institute of Justice Journal* 231 (August): 46–51.

Rountree, Pamela Wilcox, and Kenneth C. Land. 1996. "Perceived Risk Versus Fear of Crime: Empirical Evidence of Conceptually Distinct Reactions in Survey Data." *Social Forces* 74: 1353–1376.

Rowe, David C. 1986. "Genetic and Environmental Components of Antisocial Behavior: A Study of 265 Twin Pairs." *Criminology* 24: 513–532.

Rowe, David C., and David Farrington. 1997. "The Familial Transmission of Criminal Convictions." *Criminology* 35: 177–201.

Rubin, R. T. 1987. "The Neuroendocrinology and Neurochemistry of Antisocial Behavior." In *The Causes of Crime: New Biological Approaches,* edited by Sarnoff A. Mednick, Terrie Moffitt, and Susan Stack. Cambridge: Cambridge University Press.

Rush, George E. [1994] 2000. *The Dictionary of Criminal Justice.* 5th ed. Guilford, CT: Dushkin Publishing Group.

Rushton, J. Philippe. 1990. "Race and Crime: A Reply to Roberts and Gabor." *Canadian Journal of Criminology* 32: 315–334.

———. [1995] 1999. *Race, Evolution, and Behavior: A Life History Perspective.* New Brunswick, NJ: Transaction Publishers.

Rushton, J. Philippe, and A. R. Jensen. 2005. "Wanted: More Race-Realism, Less Moralistic Fallacy." *Psychology, Public Policy, and Law* 11: 328–336.

Rushton, J. Philippe, and Glayde Whitney. 2002. "Cross-National Variation in Violent Crime Rates: Race, r-K Theory, and Income." *Population and Environment* 23: 501–511.

Russell, Katheryn K. 1998. *The Color of Crime: Racial Hoaxes, White Fear, Black Protectionism, Police Harassment, and Other Macroaggressions.* New York: New York University Press.

———. 2001. "Racing Crime: Definitions and Dilemmas." In *What Is Crime? Controversies over the Nature of Crime and What to Do About It,* edited by Stuart Henry and Mark M. Lanier, 155–164. Boulder, CO: Rowman and Littlefield.

Russell, Katheryn K., and Dragan Milovanovic. 2001. *Petit Apartheid in the U.S. Criminal Justice System: The Dark Figure of Racism.* Durham, NC: Carolina Academic Press.

Russell, Stuart. 2002. "The Continuing Relevance of Marxism to Critical Criminology." *Critical Criminology* 11, no. 2: 113–135.

Russell, Sue. 2000. "Anyone in Our Way Got Robbed." *The Independent,* August 4. http://www.independent.co.uk/news/people/profiles/anyone-in-our-way-got-robbed-696701.html (accessed March 22, 2009).

Ryan, Kevin, and Jeff Ferrell. 1986. "Knowledge, Power, and the Process of Justice." *Crime and Social Justice* 25: 178–195.

Rydenour, T. A. 2000. "Genetic Epidemiology of Antisocial Behavior." In *The Science, Treatment, and Prevention of Anti-social Behaviors,* edited by Diana H. Fishbein, 7.1–7.24. Kingston, NJ: Civic Research Institute.

Sacco, Vincent E., and Leslie W. Kennedy. 1996. *The Criminal Event: An Introduction to Criminology.* Belmont, CA: Wadsworth.

Sagarin, Edward. 1969. *Odd Man In: Societies of Deviants in America.* Chicago: Quadrangle Books.

Sagarin, Edward, and Jose Sanchez. 1988. "Ideology and Deviance: The Case of the Debate over the Biological Factor." *Deviant Behavior* 9: 87–99.

Salgado, Gamini. 1972. *Cony-Catchers and Bawdy Baskets.* Harmondsworth, UK: Penguin Books.

Samenow, Stanton E. 1984. *Inside the Criminal Mind.* New York: Times Books.

———. 2006. "Forty Years of the Yochelson/Samenow Work: A Perspective." In *The Essential Criminology Reader,* edited by Stuart Henry and Mark M. Lanier, 71–77. Boulder, CO: Westview Press.

Sampson, Robert J. 1986. "Effects of Socioeconomic Context on Official Reactions to Juvenile Delinquency." *American Sociological Review* 51: 876–885.

———. 1999. "Techniques of Research Neutralization." *Theoretical Criminology* 3, no. 4: 438–451.

———. 2006. "Social Ecology and Collective Efficacy Theory." In *The Essential Criminology Reader,* edited by Stuart Henry and Mark M. Lanier, 129–140. Boulder, CO: Westview Press.

Sampson, Robert J., and W. Byron Groves. 1989. "Community Structures and Crime: Testing Social Disorganization Theory." *American Journal of Sociology* 94: 774–802.

Sampson, Robert J., and John H. Laub. 1993. *Crime in the Making: Pathways and Turning Points Through Life.* Cambridge: Cambridge University Press.

———. 2001a. "Crime and Deviance in the Lifecourse." In *Lifecourse Criminology: Contemporary and Classic Readings,* edited by A. Piquero and P. Mazerolle, 21–42. Belmont, CA: Wadsworth.

———. 2001b. "A Lifecourse Theory of Cumulative Disadvantage and the Stability of Delinquency." In *Lifecourse Criminology: Contemporary and Classic Readings,* edited by A. Piquero and P. Mazerolle, 146–170. Belmont, CA: Wadsworth.

Sampson, Robert J., Stephen W. Raudenbush, and Felton Earls. 1997. "Neighborhoods and Violent Crime: A Multi-level Study of Collective Efficacy." *Science* 277: 918–924.

Sampson, Robert J., and William Julius Wilson. 1993. "Toward a Theory of Race, Crime, and Urban Inequality." In *Crime and Inequality,* edited by John Hagan and Ruth Peterson. Stanford, CA: Stanford University Press.

Sampson, Robert J., and John D. Wooldredge. 1987. "Linking the Micro- and Macro-Level Dimensions of Lifestyle: Routine Activity and Opportunity Models of Predatory Victimization." *Journal of Quantitative Criminology* 3: 371–393.

Sanday, Peggy. 1981. "The Socio-cultural Context of Rape: A Cross-Cultural Study." *Journal of Social Issues* 37: 5–27.

———. 2002. *Women in the Center.* Philadelphia: University of Pennsylvania Press.

———. 2003. "Matriarchal, Islamic, and Peace-Builders: The Minangkabau of Indonesia Offer an Alternative Social System." http://www.museum.upenn.edu/new/research/Exp_Rese_Disc/Asia/sanday-research.shtml.

Sanders, William B. 1983. *Criminology.* Reading, MA: Addison-Wesley.

Sandys, Marla, and Edmund F. McGarrell. 1994. "Attitudes Toward Capital Punishment Among Indiana Legislators: Diminished Support in Light of Alternative Sentencing Options." *Justice Quarterly* 11: 651–677.

Saranson, S. B. 1981. "An Asocial Psychology and a Misdirected Clinical Psychology." *American Psychologist* 36: 827–836.

Sarat, Austin. 1978. "Understanding Trial Courts: A Critique of Social Science Approaches." *Judicature* 61: 318–326.

Sarbin, T. R., and L. E. Miller. 1970. "Demonism Revisited: The XYY Chromosome Anomaly." *Issues in Criminology* 5: 195–207.

Sarre, Rick. 2003. "Restorative Justice: A Paradigm of Possibility." In *Controversies in Critical Criminology,* edited by Martin D. Schwartz and Suzanne E. Hatty, 97–108. Cincinnati: Anderson.

Sartre, Jean-Paul. 1981. *Saint Genet: Actor and Martyr.* New York: George Braziller.

Saunders, D. 1988. "Wife Abuse, Husband Abuse, or Mutual Combat? A Feminist Perspective on the Empirical Findings." In *Feminist Perspectives on Wife Abuse,* edited by K. Yllo and M. Bograd. Newbury Park, CA: Sage.

Savitz, L., S. H. Turner, and T. Dickman. 1977. "The Origins of Scientific Criminology: Franz Joseph Gall as the First Criminologist." In *Theory in Criminology,* edited by Robert F. Meier. Beverly Hills, CA: Sage.

Savolainen, Jukka. 2000. "Inequality, Welfare State, and Homicide: Further Support for the Institutional Anomie Theory." *Criminology* 38: 1021–1042.

Schafer, Stephen. 1968. *The Victim and His Criminal: A Study in Functional Responsibility.* New York: Random House.

———. 1976. *Introduction to Criminology.* Reston, VA: Reston.

———. 1977. *Victimology: The Victim and His Criminal.* Reston, VA: Reston.

Schlegel, Kip, and David Weisburd, eds. 1994. *White-Collar Crime Reconsidered.* Boston: Northeastern University Press.

Schlossman, S., G. Zellman, R. Shavelson, M. Sedlak, and J. Cobb. 1984. *Delinquency Prevention in South Chicago: A Fifty-Year Assessment of the Chicago Area Project.* Santa Monica, CA: Rand.

Schmalleger, Frank. 1999 [2002]. *Criminology Today: An Integrative Introduction.* 3d ed. Upper Saddle River, NJ: Prentice-Hall.

Schmidt, Peter, and Ann D. Witte. 1984. *An Economic Analysis of Crime and Justice: Theory, Methods, and Applications.* Orlando, FL: Academic Press.

Schneider, A., and W. McKim. 2003. "Stigmatization Among Probationers." *Journal of Offender Rehabilitation* 38, no. 1: 19–31.

Schneider, Anne L., and Laurie Ervin. 1990. "Specific Deterrence, Rational Choice, and Decision Heuristics: Applications in Juvenile Justice." *Social Science Quarterly* 71: 585–601.

Schoepfer, A., and N. L. Piquero. 2006. "Exploring White-Collar Crime and the American Dream: A Partial Test of Institutional Anomie Theory." *Journal of Criminal Justice* 34, no. 3: 227–235.

Schrager, Laura S., and James F. Short. 1978. "Toward a Sociology of Organizational Crime." *Social Problems* 25: 407–419.

Schuessler, Karl, and Donald Cressey. 1950. "Personality Characteristics of Criminals." *American Journal of Sociology* 55: 476–484.

Schulhofer, Stephen J., and Ilene H. Nagel. 1989. "Negotiating Pleas Under Federal Sentencing Guidelines: The First Fifteen Months." *American Criminal Law Review* 27: 231–288.

Schur, Edwin M. 1965. *Crimes Without Victims: Deviant Behavior and Public Policy.* Englewood Cliffs, NJ: Prentice-Hall.

———. 1973. *Radical Non-intervention: Rethinking the Delinquency Problem.* Englewood Cliffs, NJ: Prentice-Hall.

Schur, Edwin M., and Hugo Adam Bedau. 1974. *Victimless Crimes.* Englewood Cliffs, NJ: Prentice-Hall.

Schwartz, Gary. 1987. *Beyond Conformity or Rebellion: Youth and Authority.* Chicago: University of Chicago Press.

Schwartz, Martin D. 1991. "The Future of Criminology." In *New Directions in Critical Criminology,* edited by Brian D. MacLean and Dragan Milovanovic. Vancouver, BC: Collective Press.

Schwartz, Martin D., and Walter S. DeKeseredy. 1991. "Left Realist Criminology: Strengths, Weaknesses, and Feminist Critique." *Crime, Law, and Social Change* 15: 51–72.

Schwartz, Martin D., and David O. Friedrichs. 1994. "Postmodern Thought and Criminological Discontent: New Metaphors for Understanding Violence." *Criminology* 32: 221–246.

Schwartz, Martin D., and Dragan Milovanovic, eds. 1996. *Race, Gender, and Class in Criminology: The Intersection.* New York: Garland Publishing.

Schweinhart, Lawrence J. 2003. "Benefits, Costs, and Explanation of the High/Scope Perry Preschool Program." Paper presented at the meeting of the Society for Research in Child Development, Tampa, Florida. High/Scope Educational Research Foundation cited by National Literacy Trust. http://www.nationalliteracytrust.org.uk/socialinclusion/ earlyyears/highscoperesearch.html#Main (accessed January 3, 2009).

———. 2007. "Crime Prevention by the High/Scope Perry Preschool Program." *Victims and Offenders* 2, no. 2: 141–160.

Schweinhart, Lawrence J., H. V. Barnes, and D. P. Weikart. 1993. *Significant Benefits: The High/Scope Perry Preschool Study Through Age 27.* Ypsilanti, MI: High/Scope Press.

Schwendinger, Herman, and Julia Schwendinger. 1970. "Defenders of Order or Guardians of Human Rights?" *Issues in Criminology* 5: 123–157.

———. 2001. "Defenders of Order or Guardians of Human Rights?" In *What Is Crime?* edited by Stuart Henry and Mark M. Lanier, 65–100. Boulder, CO: Rowman and Littlefield.

Schwendinger, Herman, Julia R. Schwendinger, and Mike J. Lynch. 2002. "Critical Criminology in the United States: The Berkeley School and Theoretical Trajectories." In *Critical Criminology: Issues, Debates, Challenges,* edited by Kerry Carrington and Russell Hogg. Cullompton, Devon, UK and Portland, OR: Willan Publishing.

Schwendinger, Julia, and Herman Schwendinger. 1983. *Rape and Inequality.* Beverly Hills, CA: Sage.

Schwitzgebel, R. K. 1974. "The Right to Effective Treatment." *California Law Review* 62: 936–956.

Scully, Matthew. 2004. *Dominion: The Power of Man, the Suffering of Animals, and the Call to Mercy.* New York: St. Martin's.

Seis, Mark C., and Kenneth L. Elbe. 1991. "The Death Penalty for Juveniles: Bridging the Gap Between an Evolving Standard of Decency and Legislative Policy." *Justice Quarterly* 8: 465–487.

Sellers, Christine S. 1999. "Self-Control and Intimate Violence: An Examination of the Scope and Specification of the General Theory of Crime." *Criminology* 37: 375–404.

Sellers, Christine S., J. K. Cochran, and K. A. Branch. 2005. "Social Learning Theory and Partner Violence: A Research Note." *Deviant Behavior* 26, no. 4: 379–395.

Sellers, Christine S., Travis C. Pratt, Thomas L. Winfree, and Frank T. Cullen. 2000. "The Empirical Status of Social Learning Theory: A Meta-analysis." Paper presented at the American Society of Criminology conference, San Francisco.

Sellin, Thorsten. 1938. *Culture Conflict and Crime.* New York: Social Science Research Council.

Severance, Lawrence, Jane Goodman, and Elizabeth Loftus. 1992. "Inferring the Criminal Mind: Toward a Bridge Between Legal Doctrine and Psychological Understanding." *Journal of Criminal Justice* 20: 107–120.

Sharp, C., J. Aldridge, and J. Medina. 2006. *Delinquent Youth Groups and Offending Behavior: Findings from the 2004 Offending, Crime, and Justice Survey.* London: Home Office Research Development and Statistics Directorate.

Sharp, E. B. 2006. "Policing Urban America: A New Look at the Politics of Agency Size." *Social Science Quarterly* 87, no. 2: 291–307.

Shaw, Clifford R., and Henry D. McKay. 1931. *Social Factors in Juvenile Delinquency:* Report of the Causes of Crime. National Commission on Law Observance and Enforcement, Report no. 13. Washington, DC: U.S. Government Printing Office.

———. [1942] 1969. *Juvenile Delinquency and Urban Areas: A Study of Delinquents in Relation to Differential Characteristics of Local Communities in American Cities.* Chicago: University of Chicago Press.

Shea, Jennifer Susan. 2007. "Naval Deployments and Adultery: The Neutralization of Moral Commitment." Master's thesis, San Diego State University.

Shein, Marcia G., and Cloud Miller. 1995. "A Knowing, Intelligent, and Voluntary Plea: The Justice Department's Latest Oxymoron." *Champion* (National Association of Criminal Defense Lawyers) 19 (January–February): 10–15.

Sheldon, William H., Emil M. Hastl, and Eugene McDermott. 1949. *Varieties of Delinquent Youth.* New York: Harper and Brothers.

Shoemaker, Donald J. 1996. *Theories of Delinquency: An Examination of Explanations of Delinquent Behavior.* 3d ed. New York: Oxford University Press.

Shoham, S. Giora. 1979. *Salvation Through the Gutters: Deviance and Transcendence.* New York: Harper and Brothers.

Shoham, S. Giora, and Mark C. Seis. 1993. *A Primer in the Psychology of Crime.* New York: Harrow and Heston.

Short, James F., Jr. 1957. "Differential Association and Delinquency." *Social Problems* 4: 233–239.

———. 1960. "Differential Association as a Hypothesis: Problems of Empirical Testing." *Social Problems* 8: 14–25.

———. 2002. "Criminology, the Chicago School, and Sociological Theory." *Crime, Law, and Social Change* 37: 107–115.

Short, James F., Jr., and Fred L. Stodtbeck. 1965. *Group Process and Gang Delinquency.* Chicago: University of Chicago Press.

Shover, Neal, and Werner J. Einstadter. 1988. *Analyzing Corrections.* Belmont, CA: Wadsworth.

Shover, Neal, and David Honaker. 1992. "The Socially Bounded Decision Making of Persistent Property Offenders." *Howard Journal of Criminal Justice* 31: 276–293.

Shover, Neal, and John Paul Wright, eds. 2001. *Crimes of Privilege.* New York: Oxford University Press.

Siegel, Larry J. 1989. *Criminology.* Minneapolis: West.

———. 1995. *Criminology: Theories, Patterns, and Typologies.* 5th ed. Minneapolis: West.

———. 1998. *Criminology: Theories, Patterns, and Typologies.* 6th ed. Belmont, CA: West/ Wadsworth.

———. 2004. *Criminology: Theories, Patterns, and Typologies.* 8th ed. Belmont, CA: Wadsworth.

Simcha-Fagan, Ora, and Joseph E. Schwartz. 1986. "Neighborhood and Delinquency: An Assessment of Contextual Effects." *Criminology* 24: 667–704.

Simmel, Georg. [1908] 1955. *The Sociology of Conflict.* Translated by Kurt H. Wolff. *The Web of Group Affiliations.* Translated by Reinhard Bendix. Glencoe, IL: Free Press.

Simmons, Catherine A., Peter Lehmann, and Sarah W. Craun. 2008. "Women Arrested for IVP Offenses: Abuse Experiences yet Low Trauma Pathology." *Journal of Family Violence* 23, no. 8: 755–766.

Simon, David R. 2002. *Elite Deviance.* 7th ed. Boston: Allyn and Bacon.

Simon, David R., and D. Stanley Eitzen. 1982. *Elite Deviance.* Boston: Allyn and Bacon.

Simon, Jonathan. 1993. *Poor Discipline: Parole and the Social Control of the Underclass, 1890–1900.* Chicago: University of Chicago Press.

Simon, Rita. 1975. *Women and Crime.* Lexington, MA: D. C. Heath.

Simpson, Sally S. 1989. "Feminist Theory, Crime, and Justice." *Criminology* 27: 605–631.

Simpson, Sally S., and Lori Elis. 1994. "Is Gender Subordinate to Class? An Empirical Assessment of Colvin and Pauly's Structural Marxist Theory of Delinquency." *Journal of Criminal Law and Criminology* 85: 453–480.

———. 1995. "Doing Gender: Sorting Out the Caste and Crime Conundrum." *Criminology* 33: 47–81.

Simpson, Sally S., Jennifer L. Yahner, and Laura Dugan. 2008. "Understanding Women's Pathways to Jail: Analysing the Lives of Incarcerated Women." *Journal of Criminology* 41, no. 1: 84.

Sims-Blackwell, Brenda. 2000. "Perceived Sanction Threats, Sex, and Crime: A Test and Elaboration of Power-Control Theory." *Criminology* 38, no. 2: 439–488.

Sims-Blackwell, Brenda, Christine S. Sellers, and Sheila M. Schlaupitz. 2002. "A Power-Control Theory of Vulnerability to Crime and Adolescent Role Exits—Revisited." *Canadian Review of Sociology and Anthropology* 39, no. 2: 1–19.

Singer, Simon I., and Murray Levine. 1988. "Power-Control Theory, Gender, and Delinquency: A Partial Replication with Additional Evidence on the Effects of Peers." *Criminology* 26: 627–647.

Singer, Stephen D., and Christopher Hensley. 2004. "Applying Social Learning Theory to Childhood and Adolescent Firesetting: Can It Lead to Serial Murder?" *International Journal of Offender Therapy and Comparative Criminology* 48, no. 4: 461–476.

Skinner, B. F. 1953. *Science and Human Behavior.* New York: Macmillan.

———. 1971. *Beyond Freedom and Dignity.* New York: Alfred A. Knopf.

Sklair, L. 1995. *Sociology of the Global System.* 2d ed. New York and London: Prentice-Hall and Harvester Wheatsheaf.

Skogan, Wesley. 1986. "Fear of Crime and Neighborhood Change." In *Communities and Crime,* edited by Albert J. Reiss Jr. and Michael Tonry. Chicago: University of Chicago Press.

———. 1990. *Disorder and Decline: Crime and the Spiral of Decay in American Cities.* New York: Free Press.

———. 1996. "The Community's Role in Community Policing." *National Institute of Justice Journal* 231 (August): 31–34.

Skolnick, Jerome. 1995. "Sheldon L. Messinger: The Man, His Work, and the Carceral Society." In *Punishment and Social Control,* edited by Thomas Blomberg and Stanley Cohen. Hawthorne, NY: Aldine de Gruyter.

Skrapec, Candice A. 1999. "Female Serial Murder: An Evolving Criminality." In *Moving Targets,* edited by H. Birch. London: Virago.

————. 2001. "Phenomenology and Serial Murder: Asking Different Questions." *Homicide Studies* 5, no. 1: 46–63.

————. 2003. "Serial Killers, Victims of." In *Encyclopedia of Women and Crime*, edited by Nicole Hahn Rafter, 235–236. New York: Checkmark Books.

Smart, Carol. 1976. *Women, Crime, and Criminology: A Feminist Critique*. London: Routledge and Kegan Paul.

————. 1979. "The New Female Criminal: Reality or Myth?" *British Journal of Criminology* 19: 50–59.

————. 1987. "Review of Capitalism, Patriarchy, and Crime." *Contemporary Crisis* 11: 327–329.

————. 1989. *Feminism and the Power of Law*. London: Routledge.

————. 1990. "Feminist Approaches to Criminology; or, Postmodern Woman Meets Atavistic Man." In *Feminist Perspectives in Criminology*, edited by Loraine Gelsthorpe and Allison Morris. Milton Keynes, UK: Open University Press.

————. 1992. "The Women of Legal Discourse." *Social and Legal Studies: An International Journal* 1: 29–44.

Smith, Brent, and Gregory Orvis. 1993. "America's Response to Terrorism: An Empirical Analysis of Federal Intervention Strategies During the 1980s." *Justice Quarterly* 10: 661–681.

Smith, Carolyn, and Terence Thornberry. 1995. "The Relationship Between Childhood Maltreatment and Adolescent Involvement in Delinquency." *Criminology* 33: 451–481.

Smith, Lacey Baldwin. 1967. *Elizabethan World*. New York: American Heritage.

Smith, Michael R., M. Makarios, and G. P. Alpert. 2006. "Differential Suspicion: Theory Specification and Gender Effects in the Traffic Stop Context." *Justice Quarterly* 23, no. 2: 271–295.

Smith, Michael R., and Matthew Petrocelli. 2001. "Racial Profiling? A Multivariate Analysis of Police Traffic Stop Data." *Police Quarterly* 4: 4–27.

Snodgrass, Jon. 1976. "Clifford R. Shaw and Henry D. McKay: Chicago Sociologists." *British Journal of Criminology* 16: 1–19.

Solomon, B. S., C. P. Bradshaw, and J. Wright. 2008. "Youth and Parental Attitudes Toward Fighting." *Journal of Interpersonal Violence* 23, no. 4: 544–560.

Soroka, Michael P., and George J. Bryjak. 1999. *Social Problems: A World at Risk*. 2d ed. Boston: Allyn and Bacon.

South, Scott J., and Richard B. Felson. 1990. "The Racial Patterning of Rape." *Social Forces* 69: 71–93.

Spadanuta, Laura. 2008. "Cracking Down on Sex Trafficking." *Security Management* 52, no. 8: 24.

Sparks, Richard F. 1981. "Surveys of Victimization: An Optimistic Assessment." *Crime and Justice, an Annual Review of Research* 3: 1–60.

Spergel, Irving. 1964. *Racketville, Slumtown, Haulburg: An Exploratory Study of Delinquent Subcultures*. Chicago: University of Chicago Press.

Spitzer, Steven. 1975. "Towards a Marxian Theory of Deviance." *Social Problems* 22: 638–651.

Stahura, John M., and Richard C. Hollinger. 1988. "A Routine Activities Approach to Suburban Arson Rates." *Sociological Spectrum* 8: 349–369.

Stahura, John M., and John J. Sloan III. 1988. "Urban Stratification of Places, Routine Activities, and Suburban Crime Rates." *Social Forces* 66: 1102–1118.

Staples, J. Scott. 2000. "The Meaning of Violence in Our Schools: Rage Against a Broken World." In "School Violence," edited by William Hinkle and Stuart Henry. Special issue, *Annals of the American Academy of Political and Social Science* 567.

Stark, Rodney. 1987. "Deviant Places: A Theory of the Ecology of Crime." *Criminology* 25: 893–909.

Stattin, Hakan, and Ingrid Klackenberg-Larsson. 1993. "Early Language and Intelligence Development and Their Relationship to Future Criminal Behavior." *Journal of Abnormal Psychology* 102: 369–378.

Steffensmeier, Darrell. 1978. "Crime and the Contemporary Woman: An Analysis of Changing Levels of Female Property Crime, 1960–75." *Social Forces* 57: 566–584.

———. 1980. "Sex Differences in Patterns of Adult Crime, 1965–77: A Review and Assessment." *Social Forces* 58: 1080–1108.

———. 1986. *The Fence.* Lanham, MD: Rowman and Littlefield.

Stewart, F., and A. Berry. 1999. "Globalization, Liberalization, and Inequality: Expectations and Experience." In *Inequality, Globalization, and World Politics,* edited by Ngaire Woods and A. Hurrell, 150–186. Oxford: Oxford University Press.

Stiglitz, Joseph E. 2002. *Globalization and Its Discontents.* New York: W. W. Norton.

———. 2006. *Making Globalization Work.* New York: W. W. Norton.

Stitt, B. Grant, and David J. Giacopassi. 1992. "Trends in the Connectivity of Theory and Research in Criminology." *Criminologist* 17: 1, 3–6.

Stolzenberg, Lisa, and Stewart J. D'Alessio. 1994. "Sentencing and Unwarranted Disparity: An Empirical Assessment of the Long-Term Impact of Sentencing Guidelines in Minnesota." *Criminology* 32: 301–310.

Stone, Christopher. 1996. "Community Defense and the Challenge of Community Justice." *National Institute of Justice Journal* 231 (August): 41–45.

Stone, Steve. 2008. "Virginia Beach Police Seize Photos from Abercrombie Store." *Virginia Pilot,* February 3. http://hamptonroads.com/node/452689 (accessed March 19, 2009).

Strang, Heather. 2000. "The Future of Restorative Just." In *Crime and the Criminal Justice System in Australia: 2000 and Beyond,* edited by D. Chappell and P. Wilson, 22–23. Sydney: Butterworths.

Stretesky, Paul, and Michael Lynch. 1999. "Corporate Environmental Violence and Racism." *Crime, Law, and Social Change* 30: 163–184.

———. 2004. "The Relationship Between Lead and Crime." *Journal of Health and Social Behavior* 45: 214–229.

Stylianou, Stelios. 2003. "Measuring Crime Seriousness Perceptions: What Have We Learned and What Else Do We Want to Know?" *Journal of Criminal Justice* 31: 37–56.

Suchar, Charles S. 1978. *Social Deviance: Perspectives and Prospects.* New York: Holt, Rinehart, and Winston.

Sullivan, Andrew. 2000. "The He Hormone." *New York Times,* April 2.

Sundquist, James L., ed. 1969. *On Fighting Poverty.* New York: Basic Books.

Surette, Ray. 1997. *Media, Crime, and Criminal Justice.* 2d ed. Pacific Grove, CA: Brooks/Cole.

Sutherland, Edwin H. 1924. *Criminology.* Philadelphia: J. B. Lippincott.

———. 1937. *The Professional Thief: By a Professional Thief.* Chicago: University of Chicago Press.

———. [1939] 1947. *Principles of Criminology.* Philadelphia: J. B. Lippincott.

———. 1949a. *White Collar Crime.* New York: Holt, Rinehart, and Winston.

———. 1949b. "The White Collar Criminal." In *Encyclopedia of Criminology,* edited by Vernon C. Branham and Samuel B. Kutash. New York: Philosophical Library.

Sutherland, Edwin H., and Donald R. Cressey. 1966. *Principles of Criminology.* Philadelphia: J. B. Lippincott.

Sutherland, Grant R., and Robert Richards. 1994. "Dynamic Mutations." *American Scientist* 82: 157–163.

Sutherland, I., and J. P. Shepherd. 2002. "A Personality-Based Model of Adolescent Violence." *British Journal of Criminology* 42: 433–441.

Suttles, Gerald. 1972. *The Social Construction of Communities.* Chicago: University of Chicago Press.

Syed, Fariya, and Sahron Williams. 1996. *Case Studies of Female Sex Offenders in the Correctional Service of Canada.* Ottawa: Correctional Services of Canada.

Sykes, Gresham. 1974. "Critical Criminology." *Journal of Criminal Law and Criminology* 65: 206–213.

Sykes, Gresham, and David Matza. 1957. "Techniques of Neutralization: A Theory of Delinquency." *American Sociological Review* 22: 664–670.

Szasz, Thomas. 2000. "Does Insanity 'Cause' Crime?" *Ideas on Liberty* 50 (March): 31–32.

al-Talib, Nadhim I., and Christine Griffin. 1994. "Labelling Effect on Adolescents' Self-Concept." *International Journal of Offender Therapy and Comparative Criminology* 38: 47–57.

Tame, Chris R. 1995. "Freedom, Responsibility, and Justice: The Criminology of the 'New Right.'" In *The Politics of Crime Control,* edited by Kevin Stenson and David Cowell. Thousand Oaks, CA: Sage.

Tannenbaum, Frank. 1938. *Crime and the Community.* Boston: Ginn.

Tappan, Paul W. 1947. "Who Is the Criminal?" *American Sociological Review* 12: 96–102.

Tarde, Gabriel. [1890] 1903. *Gabriel Tarde's Laws of Imitation.* Translated by E. Parsons. New York: Henry Holt.

Taylor, Ian. 1981. *Law and Order: Arguments for Socialism.* London: Macmillan.

Taylor, Ian, Paul Walton, and Jock Young. 1973. *The New Criminology: For a Social Theory of Deviance.* London: Routledge and Kegan Paul.

———, eds. 1975. *Critical Criminology.* London: Routledge and Kegan Paul.

Taylor, J., and Glayde Whitney. 1999. "Crime and Racial Profiling by U.S. Police: Is There an Empirical Basis?" *Journal of Social, Political, and Economic Studies* 24: 485–510.

Taylor, Laurie. 1972. "The Significance and Interpretation of Motivational Questions: The Case of Sex Offenders." *Sociology* 6: 23–29.

Taylor, Lawrence. 1984. *Born to Crime: The Genetic Causes of Criminal Behavior.* Boulder, CO: Westview Press.

Taylor, Lawrence, and Katharina Dalton. 1983. "Premenstrual Syndrome: A New Criminal Defense?" *California Western Law Review* 19: 269–287.

Taylor, Ralph B. 1988. *Human Territorial Functioning.* Cambridge: Cambridge University Press.

Taylor, Ralph B., and Jeanette Covington. 1988. "Neighborhood Changes in Ecology and Violence." *Criminology* 26: 553–589.

Taylor, Ralph B., and Adele V. Harrell. 1996. *Physical Environment and Crime.* Washington, DC: U.S. Department of Justice, National Institute of Justice.

Telfer, Mary A., David Baker, and Gerald R. Clark. 1968. "Incidence of Gross Chromosomal Errors Among Tall Criminal American Males." *Science* 159: 1249–1250.

Thomas, Jim, and Sharon Boehlefeld. 1991. "Rethinking Abolitionism: 'What Do We Do with Henry?'—Review of de Haan, *The Politics of Redress*." *Social Justice* 18: 239–251.

Thomas, William I., and Florian Znaniecki. 1920. *The Polish Peasant in Europe and America*. Vol. 2. Boston: Gorham.

Thompkins, Douglas E. 2000. "School Violence: Gangs and a Culture of Fear." In "School Violence," edited by William Hinkle and Stuart Henry. Special issue, *Annals of the American Academy of Political and Social Science* 567.

Thompson, William E., Jim Mitchell, and Richard A. Dodder. 1984. "An Empirical Test of Hirschi's Control Theory of Delinquency." *Deviant Behavior* 5: 11–22.

Thompson, Wright. 2008. *Outrageous Injustice*. ESPN. http://sports.espn.go.com/espn/eticket/story?page=wilson (accessed March 19, 2009).

Thornberry, Terence P. 1987. "Toward an Interactional Theory of Delinquency." *Criminology* 25: 863–891.

———. 1989. "Reflections on the Advantages and Disadvantages of Theoretical Integration." In *Theoretical Integration in the Study of Deviance and Crime*, edited by Stephen F. Messner, Marvin D. Krohn, and Allen Liska. Albany: State University of New York Press.

———, ed. 1997. *Developmental Theories of Crime and Delinquency*. New Brunswick, NJ: Transaction Publishers.

Thornberry, Terence P., Melanie Moore, and R. L. Christenson. 1985. "The Effect of Dropping Out of High School on Subsequent Criminal Behavior." *Criminology* 23: 3–18.

Thornhill, Randy, and Craig Palmer. 2000. *A Natural History of Rape: Biological Bases of Sexual Coercion*. Cambridge, MA: MIT Press.

Thrasher, Frederic M. 1927. *The Gang*. Chicago: University of Chicago Press.

Thurman, Quint C., Craig St. John, and Lisa Riggs. 1984. "Neutralizations and Tax Evasion: How Effective Would a Moral Appeal Be in Improving Compliance to Tax Laws?" *Law and Policy* 6: 309–328.

Tifft, Larry L. 1979. "The Coming Redefinitions of Crime: An Anarchist Perspective." *Social Problems* 26: 392–402.

Tifft, Larry L., and Dennis Sullivan. 1980. *The Struggle to Be Human: Crime, Criminology, and Anarchism*. Sanday, Orkney, UK: Cienfuegos.

———. 2001. "A Needs-Based, Social Harm Definition of Crime." In *What Is Crime? Controversies over the Nature of Crime and What to Do About It*, edited by Stuart Henry and Mark M. Lanier, 179–206. Boulder, CO: Rowman and Littlefield.

———. 2006. "Needs-Based Anarchist Criminology." In *The Essential Criminology Reader*, edited by Stuart Henry and Mark M. Lanier, 259–277. Boulder, CO: Westview Press.

Timmer, Doug A., and Stanley D. Eitzen. 1989. *Crime in the Streets and Crime in the Suites: Perspectives on Crime and Criminal Justice*. Boston: Allyn and Bacon.

Tittle, Charles R. 1991. "Being Labeled a Criminologist." *Criminologist* (May–June): 1, 3–4.

———. 1995. *Control Balance: Toward a General Theory of Deviance*. Boulder, CO: Westview Press.

Tittle, Charles R., Wayne J. Villemez, and Douglas A. Smith. 1978. "The Myth of Social Class and Criminality: An Empirical Assessment of the Empirical Evidence." *American Sociological Review* 43: 643–656.

Toby, Jackson. 1957. "Social Disorganization and Stake in Conformity: Complementary Factors in the Predatory Behavior of Hoodlums." *Journal of Criminal Law, Criminology, and Police Science* 48: 12–17.

Tong, Rosemary. 1998. *Feminist Thought*. 2d ed. Boulder, CO: Westview Press.

Tonry, Michael. 1988. "Structuring Sentencing." In *Crime and Justice: A Review of Research*, edited by Michael Tonry and Norvil Morris. Chicago: University of Chicago Press.

———. 1995. *Malign Neglect: Race, Crime, and Punishment in America*. New York: Oxford University Press.

Tooby, J., and L. Cosmides. 1992. "The Psychological Foundations of Culture." In *The Adapted Mind: Evolutionary Psychology and the Generation of Culture*, edited by J. H. Barkow, L. Cosmides, and J. Tooby, 19–136. New York: Oxford University Press.

Topalli, V. 2005. "When Being Good Is Bad: An Expansion of Neutralization Theory." *Criminology* 43, no. 3: 797–835.

———. 2006. "The Seductive Nature of Autotelic Crime: How Neutralization Theory Serves as a Boundary Condition for Understanding Hardcore Street Offending." *Sociological Inquiry* 76, no. 4: 475–501.

Torstensson, Marie. 1990. "Female Delinquents in a Birth Cohort: Tests of Some Aspects of Control Theory." *Journal of Quantitative Criminology* 6: 101–115.

Tracy, Paul E., Marvin E. Wolfgang, and Robert M. Figlio. 1985. *Delinquency in Two Birth Cohorts: Executive Summary*. Washington, DC: U.S. Department of Justice.

———. 1990. *Delinquency Careers in Two Birth Cohorts*. New York: Plenum.

Trafficking in Persons Report. 2008. U.S. Department of State. http://www.state.gov/g/tip/rls/tiprpt.

Trahan, A., J. W. Marquart, and J. Mullings. 2005. "Fraud and the American Dream: Toward an Understanding of Fraud Victimization." *Deviant Behavior* 26, no. 6: 601–620.

Trice, Harrison M., and Paul M. Roman. 1970. "Delabeling, Relabeling, and Alcoholics Anonymous." *Social Problems* 17: 538–546.

Trojanowicz, Robert, and Bonnie Bucqueroux. 1990. *Community Policing: A Contemporary Perspective*. Cincinnati: Anderson.

Tucker, Robert. 1978. *The Marx-Engels Reader*. New York: W. W. Norton.

Tunnell, Kenneth. 1992. *Choosing Crime: The Criminal Calculus of Property Offenders*. Chicago: Nelson-Hall.

Turk, Austin T. 1964. "Prospects for Theories of Criminal Behavior." *Journal of Criminal Law, Criminology, and Police Science* 55: 454–461.

———. 1966. "Conflict and Criminality." *American Sociological Review* 31: 338–352.

———. 1969. *Criminality and the Legal Order*. Chicago: Rand McNally.

———. 1976. "Law as a Weapon in Social Conflict." *Social Problems* 23: 276–291.

———. 1980. "Analyzing Official Deviance: For Nonpartisan Conflict Analysis in Criminology." In *Radical Criminology: The Coming Crisis*, edited by James A. Inciardi. Beverly Hills, CA: Sage.

———. 1982. *Political Criminality: The Defiance and Defense of Authority*. Beverly Hills, CA: Sage.

———. 1995. "Transformation Versus Revolutionism and Reformism: Policy Implications of Conflict Theory." In *Crime and Public Policy*, edited by Hugh Barlow. Boulder, CO: Westview Press.

———. 2003. "Political Violence: Patterns and Trends." In *Crime and Justice at the Millennium: Essays by and in Honor of Marvin E. Wolfgang*, edited by Robert A. Silverman, Terence P. Thornberry, Bernard Cohen, and Barry Krisberg, 31–44. Norwell, MA: Kluwer Academic Publishers.

———. 2004. "The Sociology of Terrorism." *Annual Review of Sociology* 271–286.

————. 2006. "Criminology and Conflict Theory." In *The Essential Criminology Reader,* edited by Stuart Henry and Mark M. Lanier, 185–190. Boulder, CO: Westview Press.

Turner, Jonathan H. 1986. *The Structure of Sociological Theory.* 4th ed. Chicago: Dorsey.

Tygart, Clarence E. 1988. "Strain Theory and Public School Vandalism: Academic Tracking, School Social Status, and Students' Academic Achievement." *Youth and Society* 20: 106–118.

Umbreit, Mark. 1994. *Victim Meets Offender: The Impact of Restorative Justice and Mediation.* Monsey, NY: Criminal Justice Press.

————. 2001. "Family Group Conferencing: Implications for Crime Victims." Center for Restorative Justice and Peacemaking, University of Minnesota. http://www.ojp. usdoj.gov/ovc/publications/infores/restorative_justice/96523-family_group/ family3.html.

Umbreit, Mark S., and Robert B. Coates. 1998. *Multi-cultural Implications of Restorative Justice: Potential Pitfalls and Dangers.* Washington, DC: U.S. Department of Justice, Office for Victims of Crime.

Umbreit, Mark S., Robert B. Coates, Betty Vos, and Kathy Brown. 2002. *Victim Offender Dialogue in Crimes of Severe Violence: A Multi-site Study of Programs in Texas and Ohio.* Minneapolis: Center for Restorative Justice and Peacemaking, University of Minnesota.

Unger, Robert M. 1976. *Law in Modern Society.* New York: Free Press.

U.S. Department of Justice. 2006. *Assessment of U.S. Government Efforts to Combat Trafficking in Person in Fiscal Year 2006.* Washington, DC: Department of Justice.

————. 2008. "Project Safe Childhood: A Basic Overview." http://www.ojp.gov/cds/ internet_safety/OJP/psc/Project%20Safe%20Childhood.htm (accessed September 16, 2008).

U.S. Sentencing Commission. 1994. *Federal Sentencing Guidelines Manual.* 1994–1995 ed. St. Paul, MN: West.

Valier, Claire. 2003. "Foreigners, Crime, and Changing Mobilities." *British Journal of Criminology* 43, no. 1: 1–21.

Van Erp, Annemoon M. M., and Klaus A. Miczek. 1996. "Prefrontal Dopamine and Serotonin: Microdialysis During Aggression and Alcohol Self-Administration in Rats." *Society for Neuroscience Abstracts* 22: 161.

Vasey, M. W., D. R. Lynam, and R. T. Salekin. 2005. "Psychopathy in Children and Adolescents." *Journal of Abnormal Child Psychology* 33, no. 4: 411–503.

Vaughan, Diane. 1983. *Controlling Unlawful Organization Behavior: Social Structure and Corporate Misconduct.* Chicago: University of Chicago Press.

————. Diane. 1998. "Rational Choice, Situated Action, and the Social Control of Organizations." *Law and Society Review* 32: 23–61.

Vazsonyi, Alexander T., Lloyd E. Pickering, Marianne Junger, and Dick Hessing. 2001. "An Empirical Test of a General Theory of Crime: A Four Nation Comparative Study of Self-Control and the Prediction of Deviance." *Journal of Research in Crime and Delinquency* 38: 91–131.

Venkatesh, Sudhir. 2000. *American Project.* Cambridge, MA: Harvard University Press.

Venturelli, Peter J. 2000. "Drugs in Schools: Myths and Realities." In "School Violence," edited by William Hinkle and Stuart Henry. Special issue, *Annals of the American Academy of Political and Social Science* 567.

Vila, Bryan. 1994. "A General Paradigm for Understanding Criminal Behavior: Extending Evolutionary Ecological Theory." *Criminology* 32: 311–359.

Villarreal, A. 2004. "The Social Ecology of Rural Violence: Land Scarcity, the Organization of the Agricultural Production, and the Presence of the State." *American Journal of Sociology* 110, no. 2: 313–348.

Virkkunen, M., J. DeJong, J. Bartkko, F. K. Goodwin, and M. Linnoila. 1989. "Relationship of Psychobiological Variables to Recidivism in Violent Offenders and Impulsive Fire Setters." *Archives of General Psychiatry* 46: 600–603.

Virkkunen, M., A. Nuutila, J. DeJong, F. K. Goodwin, and M. Linnoila. 1987. "Cerebrospinal Fluid Monoamine Metabolic Levels in Male Arsonists." *Neuropsychobiology* 17: 19–23.

Virtual Center for Epidemiological Criminology. 2008. http://www.epidemiologicalcriminology.com.

Vito, G. F., Edward Latessa, and D. G. Wilson. 1988. *Introduction to Criminal Justice Research Methods.* Springfield, IL: Charles C. Thomas.

Vittori, Jodi M. 2007. "The Gang's All Here: The Globalization of Gang Activity. *Journal of Gang Research* 14, no. 3: 1–34.

Vold, George B. [1958] 1979. *Theoretical Criminology.* New York: Oxford University Press.

Vold, George B., and Thomas J. Bernard. 1986. *Theoretical Criminology.* 3d ed. New York: Oxford University Press.

Vold, George B., Thomas J. Bernard, and J. B. Snipes. [1998] 2001. *Theoretical Criminology.* 5th ed. New York: Oxford University Press.

von Hentig, Hans. 1948. *The Criminal and His Victim.* New Haven, CT: Yale University Press.

Von Hirsch, Andrew. 1976. *Doing Justice: The Choice of Punishments.* New York: Hill and Wang.

Von Hirsch, Andrew, and Nils Jareborg. 1991. "Gauging Criminal Harm: A Living Standard Analysis." *Oxford Journal of Legal Studies* 2: 1–38.

Waldo, Gordon, and Simon Dinitz. 1967. "Personality Attributes of the Criminal: An Analysis of Research Studies, 1950–1965." *Journal of Research in Crime and Delinquency* 4: 185–202.

Walker, Jeffrey T. 1994. "Human Ecology and Social Disorganization Revisit Delinquency in Little Rock." In *Varieties of Criminology: Readings from a Dynamic Discipline,* edited by Gregg Barak. Westport, CT: Praeger.

Walklate, Sandra. 1989. *Victimology: The Victim and the Criminal Justice Process.* London: Unwin Hyman.

Wallerstein, Immanual M. 1974. *The Modern World System.* New York: Academic Press.

Wallerstein, James S., and Clement E. Wyle. 1947. "Our Law-Abiding and Law-Breakers." *Probation* 25: 107–112.

Wallwork, Ernest. 1994. *Psychoanalysis and Ethics.* New Haven, CT: Yale University Press.

Walsh, Anthony. 2000. "Behavior Genetics and Anomie/Strain Theory." *Criminology* 38: 1075–1107.

Walsh, Dermot. 1980. *Break-ins: Burglary from Private Houses.* London: Constable.

Walsh, E., and T. Fahy. 2002. "Violence in Society: Contribution of Metal Illness Is Low." *British Medical Journal* 325: 507–508.

Walsh, Jennifer Edwards. 2007. *Three Strikes Laws.* Westport, CT: Greenwood.

Walters, Glenn. 1992. "A Meta-analysis of the Gene-Crime Relationship." *Criminology* 30: 595–613.

———. 1995. "The Psychological Inventory of Criminal Thinking Styles." *Criminal Justice and Behavior* 22: 307–325.

Walters, Glenn, and Thomas White. 1989. "Heredity and Crime: Bad Genes or Bad Research." *Criminology* 27: 455–486.

Ward, Tony, T. Keenan, and S. Hudson. 2000. "Understanding Cognitive, Affective, and Intimacy Deficits in Sexual Offenders: A Developmental Perspective." *Aggression and Behavior* 5: 41–62.

Ward, Tony, and Richard Siegert. 2002. "Rape and Evolutionary Psychology: A Critique of Thornhill and Palmer's Theory." *Aggression and Behavior* 7: 145–168.

Waring, Elin, David Weisburd, and Ellen Chayet. 1995. "White-Collar Crime and Anomie." In *The Legacy of Anomie Theory: Advances in Criminological Theory,* edited by Freda Adler and William S. Laufer. Vol. 6. New Brunswick, NJ: Transaction Publishers.

Warner, Barbara D. 2003. "The Role of Attenuate Culture in Social Disorganization Theory." *Criminology* 41: 73–97.

Warr, Mark, and Mark Stafford. 1991. "The Influence of Delinquent Peers: What They Think or What They Do?" *Criminology* 29: 851–866.

Watkins, K. 1997. *Globalisation and Liberalisation: Implications for Poverty, Distribution, and Inequality.* Occasional Paper 32. New York: UN Development Program.

Weber, Max. [1922] 1966. *The Theory of Social and Economic Organization.* New York: Free Press.

WebMD Live Events transcript. "Mental Illness in America." News release, JAMA/Archives, May 21, 2004. http://www.webmd.com/mental-health/news/20030507/us-lags-in-mental-illness-treatment (accessed January 9, 2009).

Websdale, Neil. 2003. "Serial Killers." In *Encyclopedia of Women and Crime,* edited by Nicole Hahn Rafter, 236. New York: Checkmark Books.

Weed, Frank J. 1995. *Certainty of Justice: Reform in the Crime Victim Movement.* Hawthorne, NY: Aldine de Gruyter.

Weinstein, Jay, Werner Einstadter, Joseph Rankin, Stuart Henry, and Peggy Wiencek. 1991. *Taylor Community Action Study: Survey and Needs Assessment.* Ypsilanti: Eastern Michigan University, Department of Sociology.

Weinsteinn, Dan, Darlene Staffelbach, and Maryka Biaggio. 2000. "Attention-Deficit Hyperactivity Disorder and Posttraumatic Stress Disorder: Differential Diagnosis in Childhood Sexual Abuse." *Clinical Psychology Review* 20: 359–378.

Weisburd, David. 1997. "Reorienting Crime Prevention Research and Policy: From the Causes of Criminality to the Context of Crime." *NIJ Research Report* (June).

Weisburg, Robert. 2005. "The Death Penalty Meets Social Science: Deterrence and Jury Behavior Under New Scrutiny." *Annual Review of Law and Social Science* 1: 151–170.

Weisel, Deborah Lamm, and Adele Harrell. 1996. "Crime Prevention Through Neighborhood Revitalization: Does Practice Reflect Theory?" *National Institute of Justice Journal* 231 (August): 18–23.

Weiss, Joesph, and J. David Hawkins. 1981. *Reports of the National Juvenile Justice Assessment Centers, Preventing Delinquency.* Washington, DC: U.S. Department of Justice.

Weiss, Joseph, and John Sederstrom. 1981. *Reports of the National Juvenile Justice Assessment Centers: The Prevention of Serious Delinquency—What to Do.* Washington, DC: U.S. Department of Justice.

Weiss, Robert. 1983. "Radical Criminology: A Recent Development." In *International Handbook of Contemporary Developments in Criminology: General Issues and the Americas,* edited by Elmer H. Johnson. Westport, CT: Greenwood.

———. 2000. Introduction to "Criminal Justice and Globalization at the New Millennium." *Social Justice* 27, no. 2: 1–15.

———. 2001. "'Repatriating' Low-Wage Work: The Political Economy of Prison Labor Reprivatization in the Postindustrial United States." *Criminology* 39, no. 2 (May): 253–292.

———. 2007. "From Cowboy Detectives to Soldiers of Fortune: Private Security Contracting and Its Contradictions on the New Frontiers of Capitalist Expansion." *Social Justice* 34, no. 3: 7–8.

Weitzer, R. 2005. "New Directions in Research on Prostitution." *Crime, Law, and Social Change: An Interdisciplinary Journal* 43, nos. 4–5: 211–235.

Wellford, Charles. 1975. "Labeling Theory and Criminology: An Assessment." *Social Problems* 22: 313–332.

Wells, Edward L., and Joseph H. Rankin. 1988. "Direct Parental Controls and Delinquency." *Criminology* 26: 263–285.

———. 1991. "Families and Delinquency: A Meta-analysis of the Impact of Broken Homes." *Social Problems* 38: 71–93.

Welsh, Brandon, and David Farrington. 2002. *Crime Prevention Effects of CCTV: A Systematic View.* Home Office Research Study 252. London: Home Office.

Welsh, Wayne N. 2000. "The Effects of School Climate on School Disorder." In "School Violence," edited by William Hinkle and Stuart Henry. Special issue, *Annals of the American Academy of Political and Social Science* 567.

Wetzell, Richard. 2000. *Inventing the Criminal: A History of German Criminology, 1880–1945.* Chapel Hill: University of North Carolina Press.

White, Helene Raskin, and Randy L. LaGrange. 1987. "An Assessment of Gender Effects in Self-Report Delinquency." *Sociological Focus* 20: 195–213.

Wiatrowski, Michael, and Kristine L. Anderson. 1987. "The Dimensionality of the Social Bond." *Journal of Quantitative Criminology* 3: 65–81.

Wieck, D. 1978. "Anarchist Justice." In *Anarchism,* edited by J. R. Pennock and J. W. Chapman. New York: New York University Press.

Wilkins, Leslie. 1965. *Social Deviance: Social Policy, Action, and Research.* London: Tavistock.

Will, George F. 2001. *Woven Figure: Conservatism and America's Fabric.* New York: Simon and Schuster.

Williams, Christopher R., and Bruce A. Arrigo. 2001. *Law, Psychology, and Justice: Chaos Theory and the New (Dis)Order.* Albany: State University of New York Press.

Williams, Frank P., III, and Marilyn D. McShane. 1988. *Criminological Theory.* Englewood Cliffs, NJ: Prentice-Hall.

Williams, Juan. 1994. "Violence, Genes, and Prejudice." *Discover* 15: 92–102.

Williams, Kirk, and Richard Hawkins. 1989. "The Meaning of Arrest for Wife Assault." *Criminology* 27: 163–181.

Williams, Terry. 1989. *The Cocaine Kids.* Reading, MA: Addison-Wesley.

———. 1992. *Crack House: Notes from the End of the Line.* Reading, MA: Addison-Wesley.

Willing, Richard. 2006. "MRI Tests Offer Glimpse at Brains Behind the Lies." *USA Today,* June 26. http://www.usatoday.com/tech/science/2006-06-26-mri-lie_x.htm (accessed February 16, 2008).

Wills, Garry. 1978. *Inventing America: Jefferson's Declaration of Independence.* Garden City, NY: Doubleday.

Wilson, Edmund O. 1975. *Sociobiology: The New Synthesis.* Cambridge, MA: Harvard University Press.

Wilson, James Q., and Richard Herrnstein. 1985. *Crime and Human Nature.* New York: Simon and Schuster.

Wilson, James Q., and George Kelling. 1982. "Broken Windows: The Police and Neighborhood Safety." *Atlantic Monthly,* March, 29–38.

Wilson, Jeremy, and Erin Dalton. 2006. "Human Trafficking in the Heartland: Variation in Law Enforcement Awareness and Response." *Journal of Contemporary Criminal Justice* 24, no. 3: 296–313.

Wilson, William Julius. 1996. *When Work Disappears: The World of the New Urban Poor.* New York: Alfred A. Knopf.

Winfree, L. Thomas, Jr. 2002. "Peacemaking and Community Harmony: Lessons (and Admonitions) from the Navajo Peacemaking Courts." In *Restorative Justice: Theoretical Foundations,* edited by Elmar G. M. Weitekamp and Hans-Jurgen Kerner. Portland, OR: Willan Publishing.

Winfree, L. Thomas, Jr., and Howard Abadinsky. 2003. *Understanding Crime: Theory and Practice.* 2d ed. Belmont, CA: Wadsworth.

Winslow, Robert W. 1998. *Crime and Society: A Global Perspective.* Dubuque: Kendall/Hunt Publishing.

Winslow, Robert W., and Sheldon X. Zhang. 2007. *Criminology: A Global Perspective.* Upper Saddle River, NJ: Prentice-Hall.

Wolfgang, Marvin E., and F. Ferracuti. 1982. *The Subculture of Violence: Toward an Integrated Theory in Criminology.* Beverly Hills, CA: Sage.

Wolfgang, Marvin E., Robert M. Figlio, and Thorsten Sellin. 1972. *Delinquency in a Birth Cohort.* Chicago: University of Chicago Press.

Wolfgang, Marvin E., Terence Thornberry, and Robert M. Figlio. 1987. *From Boy to Man, from Birth to Crime.* Chicago: University of Chicago Press.

Wong, S. K. 2005. "The Effects of Adolescent Activities on Delinquency: A Differential Involvement Approach." *Journal of Youth and Adolescence* 34, no. 4: 321–333.

Wood, Peter B., John K. Cochran, Betty Pfefferbaum, and Bruce J. Arneklev. 1995. "Sensation Seeking and Delinquent Substance Abuse: An Extension of Learning Theory." *Journal of Drug Issues* 25: 173–193.

Wood, Peter B., Walter R. Gove, and John K. Cochran. 1994. "Motivations for Violent Crime Among Incarcerated Adults: A Consideration of Reinforcement Processes." *Journal of the Oklahoma Criminal Justice Consortium* 1: 63–80.

Woodcock, George. 1963. *Anarchism: A History of Libertarian Ideas and Movements.* Harmondsworth, UK: Penguin.

———. 1977. *The Anarchist Reader.* London: Fontana.

Wright, Bradley R. E., Avshalom Caspi, Terrie E. Moffitt, and Phil Silva. 1999. "Low Self-Control, Social Bonds, and Crime: Social Causation, Social Selection, or Both?" *Criminology* 37: 479–514.

Wright, J. P., and K. M. Beaver. 2005. "Do Parents Matter in Creating Self-Control in the Children? A Genetically Informed Test of Gottfredson and Hirschi's Theory of Low Self-Control." *Criminology* 43, no. 4: 1169–1202.

Wright, J. P., and Francis T. Cullen. 2004. "Employment, Peers, and Life-Course Transitions." *Justice Quarterly* 21, no. 4: 183–205.

Wright, J. P., Francis T. Cullen, and Michael B. Blankenship. 1996. "Chained Factory Fire Exits: Media Coverage of a Corporate Crime That Killed 25 Workers." In *Corporate and Governmental Deviance,* edited by M. David Ermann and Richard J. Lundman. 5th ed. New York: Oxford University Press.

Wright, Richard A., and J. Mitchell Miller. 1998. "Taboo Until Today? The Coverage of Biological Arguments in Criminology Textbooks, 1961 to 1970 and 1987 to 1996." *Journal of Criminal Justice* 26: 1–19.

Wylie, Sarah E., ed. 1994. "Georgetown Law Journal Project. Twenty-third Annual Review of Criminal Procedure: United States Supreme Court and Courts of Appeal, 1992–1993." *Georgetown Law Journal* 82, no. 3.

Yergin, D., and J. Stanislaw. 1998. *The Commanding Heights: The Battle Between Government and the Marketplace That Is Remaking the Modern World.* New York: Simon and Schuster.

Yochelson, Samuel, and Stanton Samenow. 1976. *The Criminal Personality.* Vol. 1. New York: Jason Aronson.

———. 1977. *The Criminal Personality.* Vol. 2. New York: Jason Aronson.

Yogan, Lissa J. 2000. "School Tracking and Student Violence." In "School Violence," edited by William Hinkle and Stuart Henry. Special issue, *Annals of the American Academy of Political and Social Science* 567.

Yogan, Lissa J., and Stuart Henry. 2000. "Masculine Thinking and School Violence: Issues of Gender and Race." In *School Violence: A Practical Guide for Counselors,* edited by D. S. Sandhu and C. B. Aspey. Washington, DC: American Counseling Association.

Young, Alison. 1990. *Femininity in Dissent.* London: Routledge.

———. 1996. *Imagining Crime.* London: Sage.

Young, Jock. 1971. "The Role of Police as Amplifiers of Deviancy, Negotiators of Reality, and Translators of Fantasy." In *Images of Deviance,* edited by Stan Cohen. Harmondsworth, UK: Penguin.

———. 1979. "Left Idealism, Reformism, and Beyond." In *Capitalism and the Rule of Law,* edited by Bob Fine, Richard Kinsey, John Lea, Sol Picciotto, and Jock Young. London: Hutchinson.

———. 1981. "Thinking Seriously About Crime: Some Models of Criminology." In *Crime and Society: Readings in History and Society,* edited by Mike Fitzgerald, Gregor McLennan, and Jennie Pawson. London: Routledge and Kegan Paul.

———. 1987. "The Tasks Facing a Realist Criminology." *Contemporary Crisis* 11: 337–356.

———. 1999. *The Exclusive Society.* London: Sage.

———. 2004. "Voodoo Criminology and the Numbers Game." In *Cultural Criminology Unleashed,* edited by Jeff Ferrell, Keith Hayward, Wayne Morrison, and Mike Presdee. London: GlassHouse Press. http://www.culturalcriminology.org/papers/chap1-jock-young.pdf (accessed January 11, 2009).

Young, Jock, and Roger Matthews, eds. 1992. *Rethinking Criminology: The Realist Debate.* Newbury Park, CA: Sage.

———. 1999. *The Exclusive Society.* London: Sage.

Young, Lauren. 2008. "Why I Hate Bernie Madoff." *BusinessWeek,* December 12. http://www.businessweek.com/careers/workingparents/blog/archives/2008/12/its_2_am_and_i.html (accessed December 25, 2008).

Young, Susan, and H. Gisli Gudjonsson. 2006. "ADHD Symptomatology and Its Relationship with Emotional, Social, and Delinquency Problems." *Psychology, Crime, and Law* 12: 463–471.

———. 2008. "Growing Out of ADHD: The Relationship Between Functioning and Symptoms." *Journal of Attention Disorder* 12, no. 2: 162–169.

Young, T. R. 1995. *The Red Feather Dictionary of Critical Social Science.* Boulder, CO: Red Feather Institute.

Zaubermann, Renée R. Philip, C. Perez-Diaz, and R. Levy. 1990. *Les victimes, comportements, et Attitudes: Enquete nationale de victimisation.* Paris: CESDIP.

Zhang, Lening, S. F. Messner, and J. Liu. 2007. "A Multilevel Analysis of the Risk of Household Burglary in the City of Tianjin, China." *British Journal of Criminology* 47, no. 6: 918–937.

Zhang, Lening, John W. Welte, and William F. Wieczorek. 2002. "Underlying Common Factors of Adolescent Problem Behaviors." *Criminal Justice and Behavior* 29: 161–182.

Zietz, Dorothy. 1981. *Women Who Embezzle or Defraud: A Study of Convicted Felons.* New York: Praeger.

Zuckerman, Marvin. 1979. *Sensation-Seeking: Beyond the Optimal Level of Arousal.* Hillsdale, NJ: Lawrence Erlbaum.

———. 1989. "Personality in the Third Dimension: A Psychobiological Approach." *Personality and Individual Differences* 10: 391–418.

———. 1994. *Behavioral Expressions and Biosocial Bases of Sensation Seeking.* Cambridge: Cambridge University Press.

Index

CPSIA information can be obtained at www.ICGtesting.com
Printed in the USA
LVOW12s1237071114

412513LV00002B/9/P

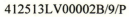

9 780813 344164